MODERN SOUTHEAST ASIA SERIES

Stephen F. Maxner, General Editor

ALSO IN THE SERIES

TRAN NGOC CHAU
WITH KEN FERMOYLE

FOREWORD BY DANIEL ELLSBERG

VIETNAM LABYRINTH

ALLIES, ENEMIES, AND WHY THE U.S. LOST THE WAR

Texas Tech University Press

This book is typeset in Minion Pro. The paper used in this book meets the minimum requirements of ANSI/NISO Z39.48-1992 (R1997). ∞

Designed by Kasey McBeath
Jacket designed by Anna Coventry-Arredondo

Library of Congress Cataloging-in-Publication Data.
Tran, Chau Ngoc, 1924–
    Vietnam labyrinth : allies, enemies, and why the U.S. lost the war / Tran Ngoc Chau with Ken
    Fermoyle ; foreword by Daniel Ellsberg.
        pages cm. — (Modern Southeast Asia series)
    Includes bibliographical references and index.
        Summary: "The memoir of Tran Ngoc Chau, one of the few Vietnamese Army officers who
    also saw service in Ho Chi Minh's National Liberation Army"—Provided by publisher.
        ISBN 978-0-89672-771-7 (hardcover : alk. paper) — ISBN 978-0-89672-777-9 (e-book) 1.
    Tran, Chau Ngoc, 1924– 2. Indochinese War, 1946–1954—Personal narratives, Vietnamese. 3.
    Vietnam War, 1961–1975—Personal narratives, Vietnamese. 4. Vietnam War, 1961–1975—United
    States. 5. Vietnam—History—Autonomy and independence movements. 6. Vietnam. Quân đội
    nhân dân—Officers—Biography. 7. Vietnam (Republic). Quân luc—Officers—Biography. I.
    Fermoyle, Ken, 1927– author. II. Title.
        DS553.5.T69 2012
        959.704'34092—dc23
        [B]   2012041960

Printed in the United States of America
12 13 14 15 16 17 18 19 20 / 9 8 7 6 5 4 3 2 1

Texas Tech University Press
Box 41037 | Lubbock, Texas 79409-1037 USA
800.832.4042 | ttup@ttu.edu | www.ttupress.org

CONTENTS

ILLUSTRATIONS, *following page 198*

Chau and his wife, Bich Nhan, after they were married in 1951

Chau and Nguyen Phuoc Dai

Chau in court

Chau with Daniel Ellsberg and Edward Lansdale

Chau and his wife with ex-president Thieu and wife in 1993

Lt. Col. Tran Ngoc Chau with Rufus Phillips and John O'Donnell

Chau and his wife surrounded by their family in 2004 on Chau's eightieth birthday

Chau and his wife in 1967 after his election to the National Assembly

John O'Donnell with his family when they met Chau in 1982

1967 photo of Chau selected by the BBC

FOREWORD

When I went to Vietnam in 1965—as a State Department member of Edward Lansdale's Senior Liaison Office in the U.S. Embassy—I met a number of people who became close friends, colleagues, and my mentors on the country's complexities. Topping that list was John Paul Vann, the subject of Neil Sheehan's masterwork, *A Bright Shining Lie: John Paul Vann and America in Vietnam*, and a major figure in the present memoir. Much of what I learned from Vann was what he himself had learned from Lieutenant Colonel Tran Ngoc Chau, whom Vann introduced to me as "the most knowledgeable Vietnamese on the subject of defeating Communist insurgency I've ever met." Chau soon made the same impression on me. Like Vann, he was to become one of my closest friends.

This book relates the remarkable story of a remarkable man—Tran Ngoc Chau—and his unparalleled involvement in more than three decades of conflict in Vietnam. Although many books about this historic period are available, *Vietnam Labyrinth* is unmatched for its narrative and for the lessons it offers about current U.S. interventions.

No one has written a memoir like this, because no one has lived a life like Tran Ngoc Chau's. Still in his teens, after seven years' training to be a Buddhist monk, Chau volunteered as an intelligence cell courier in the resistance against Vietnam's Japanese occupiers and their puppet French government during World War II. He spent four years as a Viet Minh guerrilla fighting the French effort to reconquer his homeland, rising to battalion commander and then regimental political officer.

Then, in an apparent turnaround, Chau joined the Vietnamese forces under Emperor Bao to fight against his former Viet Minh allies, at first believing claims of France's intent to grant Vietnamese independence. Chau was highly decorated for valor in this service. After the French retreat, Chau spent twelve years as a military officer in South Vietnam, and he was again highly decorated for bravery. He served under President Diem and his successors, with stints as province chief of Kien Hoa and mayor of Danang, as well as head of a U.S. CIA–supported pacification program.

Continuing his unlikely journey, Chau resigned from the military to run for election in Kien Hoa to the National Assembly, to which he was elected general secretary. He became a political thorn in the side of his former friend President Thieu (and the U.S.) by exposing Thieu's corrupt manipulations of the National Assembly.

Moreover, Chau called for negotiations with the National Liberation Front (NLF) and a coalition government to end the war with the United States.

Chau was ultimately arrested, tried, and convicted on spurious grounds—all unconstitutionally, as the Vietnamese Supreme Court found. The Court, however, did not order his release; Chau spent four-and-a-half years in prison until shortly before the Communist takeover in 1975, having been branded as a "Communist supporter" during the travesty of a trial that sent him to prison under Thieu. In another ironic turnaround, Chau found himself arrested anew by the Communist victors, and then spent two-and-a-half more years in "reeducation camps" and prisons—for *not* having been a Communist supporter.

Finally, after a lifetime of fighting for his people and governing his nation—and enduring unjust hardships that nevertheless accompanied his service—Chau's exit from Vietnam was hardly a proper sendoff: a hair-raising 1979 escape from Vietnam with his family . . . as boat people.

This man's story, reflecting so much of Vietnam's mid-twentieth-century history, is fascinating by any stretch for students of the period and for admirers of gripping biography. Yet *Vietnam Labyrinth* also suggests how Chau's life and perspective can inform U.S. foreign policy going forward. As Chau told me during our long conversations, he had left the Viet Minh and joined Emperor Bao Dai and then-president Diem "because the Communists were too harsh. They didn't respect our religion or traditions, their way of development would be too hard for us, and we needed help from the West." He thought it was possible for the government of South Vietnam—with U.S. foreign aid—to offer his people a better alternative, one that was freer and more appreciative of Vietnamese religion and traditional culture.

Chau's successful programs as province chief won over much of the population of Kien Hoa, long a hotbed of Viet Cong activity, and drew much from his experience on the side of the Communist-led Viet Minh. Chau had eventually left the Viet Minh in part because he was pressured to join the Communist Party: he found that the party's official atheism and antireligious stance conflicted with his Buddhist upbringing and commitment. Later, in another irony, his Buddhism isolated him from the opposing officer corps he joined, most of whom, under French influence, were Catholic, in a predominantly Buddhist and Confucian country.

Chau's experience in a genuinely nationalistic, revolutionary movement was virtually unique among the officer corps we supported. His work had left him with respect for many aspects of the Communist-led campaign, particularly its closeness to and concern for the rural population. Unfortunately, in these respects—and in nationalism, dedication, and lack of corruption—the Viet Minh and their heirs, the Viet Cong, were polar opposites of the GVN, the Saigon regime we supported and which Chau served. In a paper strongly influenced by Chau's views as well as their own experiences, Vann and his deputy in Hau Nghia province, Doug Ramsey, described the major GVN problem in the countryside as being that "the present leaders, bureaucrats, and province and district officials do not come from, think like, know much about, or respond to the wishes of the rural population." In all these respects—plus nationalism, discipline, competence, leadership, and honesty—they contrasted sharply with the Communist-led parallel administration in the countryside.

No U.S. president, or anyone who served him, could truly solve these problems. The Cold War anticommunism of five successive U.S. presidents and the U.S. domestic politics that came along with it drew the U.S. leaders to align almost exclusively with Vietnamese who had—with the exception of Catholic president Diem himself—collaborated with the losing French. Virtually all other field-grade officers in the ARVN, the Saigon-regime armed forces wholly financed and equipped by the United States, had fought under the French against the independence of their country from the beginning, mostly as French NCOs in the years when Chau was in the Viet Minh fighting them. Likewise, the civilian officials in Saigon and the countryside of South Vietnam, whose salaries we wholly financed, had constituted the former French colonial administration, which Diem and his successors had simply carried over.

U.S. officials, including myself and my friends, were oblivious to this devastating fact about our "allies"—whom we chose to perceive, bizarrely, as the "true patriots" and nationalists. We were oblivious that our allies' background effectively squelched any chance of their gaining legitimacy or effecting authority in the eyes of most of the population. Too, such a group had little prospect of defeating an insurgency that was truly nationalist, whatever its other defects.

Fast-forward to the U.S. involvement in Afghanistan from 2001 onward. The same cluelessness characterizes U.S. incomprehension of our lack of success with counterinsurgency tactics, along with the "allies" we have chosen to support. As Chau once remarked to me, in words that apply as well now to Afghanistan, "The U.S. is puzzled, angry, and disappointed when the leaders they have chosen for us don't command the loyalty or support of our people." U.S. officials and voters who persist in supporting our interventions abroad need urgently to learn lessons from this memoir.

The success of Chau's Viet Minh–inspired theories of how to compete with the Communists for authority and support in the countryside would have become plausible under two conditions: first, if they could have been applied nationwide by Vietnamese officials possessing the background and sensibility of Tran Ngoc Chau (an impossible requirement for the Saigon regime, which allowed scarcely a handful of "Chaus" in their rank and wouldn't promote Chau himself to general), and, second, if they had served in support of a regime that was not and did not appear to be wholly funded by and in the service of foreigners (likewise impossible in Saigon). As it was, there was virtually no chance that the GVN or its U.S. sponsors would have adopted Chau's approach, nor could they ever have effectively implemented it.

The close friends I made in Vietnam when I first arrived—all experienced in the countryside and influenced by Chau, all (except for Vann) speakers of Vietnamese—had grown to love Vietnam and its people. Like me at first, they wanted to believe—and did believe—that a U.S. presence could help the Vietnamese. That Chau had the same belief also in the first months I knew him was very reassuring to me and, I suspect, to others. The fact that such a thoughtful, brave, and patriotic Vietnamese was happy to see U.S. involvement confirmed my initial beliefs that we were there not simply to promote our own interests but to further the interests of the Vietnamese.

Eventually—partly from reading the Pentagon Papers after I left Vietnam—I came to conclude I had been wrong. Even earlier, in Vietnam, I saw that under the conditions described above I had been mistaken to believe that our presence—especially our bombing—was or ultimately could ever be good for the Vietnamese . . . or ourselves. As this memoir indicates, Chau's own views were evolving about the same time and in the same way. By opposing the GVN and U.S. policy of continuing a hopeless war indefinitely, we each, in different ways, risked paying a heavy price for acting in what we thought was the best interest of the Vietnamese people and our respective countries. Chau paid that price twice over, first under the GVN (betrayed by high-level U.S. officials who abandoned him, as well as by his former friend Thieu), and then again under the Communists. This was despite the efforts of several individual Americans to help him escape when he first faced arrest; Chau refused those offers of help because running away would allow the authorities to claim plausibly that his escape proved him guilty of collusion with the very forces with which he had been unjustly accused of associating.

At considerable risk to their careers, our mutual friends tried to spare Chau because we felt—I'm sure I'm not speaking only for myself—that we had never known a human being more faithful to his highest principles, more courageous not only physically but morally, more honest with himself and with others, more patriotic—both to his native land and later as a U.S. citizen—or more dedicated to the well-being, as Buddhists say, of all sentient beings. It has been inspiring to us, and our good fortune, to know Tran Ngoc Chau. Readers of this gripping memoir can now share that good fortune.

Daniel Ellsberg

PREFACE

In early 1943 I was a volunteer in the National Salvation Youth organization dedicated to struggle for Vietnam independence, and before the end of World War II was a junior member of the Viet Minh secret intelligence service. In late 1945 I volunteered for Ho Chi Minh's *Giai Phong Quan* (Army of Liberation) and spent almost four years resisting reimposition of French rule. During my time with the Viet Minh I served as squad, platoon, company, and battalion commander. I was a regimental political cadre on special assignment when I left the Viet Minh in 1949.

Leadership, as we learned and practiced command responsibility with the Viet Minh, consisted of spending every hour of each day with our soldiers. We shared the same kind of food (sometimes not even available), took shelter under the open sky (rarely in people's homes), marched (often barefoot) together, and received no pay. We thought ourselves fortunate to receive one or two issues of clothing a year, and had only one or two weapons for every three men. Constant training, fighting by hitting and running, long marches, and frequent change of camp comprised our methodology. Education as to national goal and individual responsibility, self-criticism, and group review was constant and the special responsibility of our political officers.

In late 1945 when the French returned to Vietnam, they still looked down on Vietnamese as the pathetic people the French had ruled as colony and protectorate. In less than a year France called back most of its former collaborators and militia to expand its territorial control. The Vietnamese resistance consisted of a national leadership composed of Ho Chi Minh and a small group of immediate staff in a remote northern location with poor communications. In some other parts of Vietnam, non-Communist patriots organized local volunteers to oppose reimposition of foreign rule. We had few weapons and insufficient ammunition, but these irregulars became accomplished guerrillas and the foundation of an army that in 1954 defeated the French in central Vietnam, and at Dien Bien Phu.

After separating from the Viet Minh, I joined the U.S.-supported South Vietnam government in 1950. I fought with a special mobile group, was promoted to major, and received the highest military medals. After Vietnam was circumstantially separated (Geneva Accords), my assignments were entirely military in nature until late 1959 when President Ngo Dinh Diem asked me to take on specific responsibilities. These were, successively, as special inspector and trainer for the Civil Guard, secretary to the National Security Council, chief of Kien Hoa province, and mayor of

Danang. Following the assassination of President Diem, in 1964 the ruling generals reassigned me to Kien Hoa province and then in 1966 made me national director of the Pacification Cadre.

When the United States decided in 1955 to ease the French out of Vietnam and assume the role of beneficent counselor, U.S. intent was honorable but ultimately proved delusional. President Diem affiliated with those who previously served the defeated French. The administration relied on secret police and security forces organized and managed by the same personnel previously selected by the French. As a result, while the new Republic of Vietnam was fortifying an archaic system, Communists seized the cloak of nationalism and grew stronger. The patriotic but self-isolated Ngo Dinh Diem failed to understand the root cause of his failure. U.S. planners thought they had the solution, maneuvering to replace Diem with more responsive generals. However, those were the same junior officers and sergeants who previously served the French.

From 1964 onward, with Vietnamese generals in charge and some facade of democracy, the United States conducted the war against North Vietnam and the Viet Cong in the South. In comparison to the first Indo-China War, opposing sides were modernized and stronger, but the core of the contest had not changed. Communists took advantage of Vietnamese cultural and political history to claim a war for national unity and independence.

Considering the late-1966 civil and military situation in terms of prospects for a military resolution of the Vietnam conflict, I decided that seeking elective office would provide the best opportunity to advocate and promote concepts for political competition. In 1967 I successfully campaigned for election as a member of the National Assembly. Three years later I was arrested, unconstitutionally tried, and placed in solitary confinement for advocating democratization of the South and political negotiation with the North. While in prison there was exceptional opportunity to have lengthy dialogues with Communist detainees (including my brother) about the United States, communism, democracy, nationalism, religion, and individual responsibility.

In July 1974, authorities released me to house arrest. I was abandoned when the North defeated the South a year later. The new Communist administration sent a team at night to arrest me. "Reeducation" and solitary confinement lasted two years. In February 1979 our family "escaped" Vietnam, and after a harrowing passage by sea, we arrived in California on the last day of October.

Although the United States claimed that it was not defeated, circumstances forced the nation to withdraw from Vietnam in 1973, leaving the most disastrous consequences for Vietnamese who had believed in U.S. steadfastness. I was one of them. We should have been as capable as the Communists if we, and American leadership, had realized that at heart this war was less about battalions and more about the political cultural feeling of the people in hamlets who were the rural backbone of the nation.

With profound respect for everyone on all sides who engaged in the 1945 through 1975 Vietnam conflict, and with sincere humility on my part, I offer this memoir as supplement to observations and thoughts previously provided by others.

Tran Ngoc Chau

ACKNOWLEDGMENTS

On completing this memoir I want to express my sincerest gratitude to the United States of America for admitting my family and me after we escaped from our native country in 1979. The United States was generous in providing us the opportunity to grow from desperate "boat people" to a well-established family of twenty-eight U.S. citizens. I have been privileged to see my children graduate from universities and become professionals in various fields in our new country.

As for individuals, my sincere and profound gratitude goes to Ken Fermoyle for his willingness to learn and comprehend the complexities of Vietnam. I found in Ken not just a friend and colleague but an intellectual brother. Our thought processes became so closely attuned that it sometimes seemed he could sense exactly what I was thinking and express my thoughts with great clarity and accuracy. Thirty-nine years after the night in 1969 when Frank Scotton offered to help me escape arrest, we finally reunited. Since then he checked my account against maps for geographic accuracy and worked with me to edit my original manuscript for publication.

When the manuscript was substantially complete, Frank Scotton, a friend for decades since our earliest meeting in Vietnam, came to visit me and offered to help by reviewing what was already written. Frank worked closely with Ken and me for almost three years, going over every sentence to assure accuracy as to description of events, locations, and personalities. Frank, beginning as a USIS field operations officer, subsequently special assistant to Ambassador Colby, and finally as a USIS assistant director, had traveled almost every corner of Vietnam and, amazingly, was familiar with most of the places where I operated beginning in 1945. Finally, it was Frank who successfully introduced my manuscript to the Texas Tech University Press. Many thanks, Frank.

For almost twenty years in Vietnam, among the many Americans I worked with, John Paul Vann is the one whom I remember above all. I am aware of his personal problems, but on the battlefield his character symbolized the best of tens of thousands of other Americans who served in Vietnam during the war: patriotic, dedicated and self-confident in their missions. John and I first met in early 1960 when I was commander of the Civil Guard and Self-Defense Forces in the Northern Delta provinces while he was advisor to the Seventh Infantry Division. Although there was no line connection between us (I was under the central command in Saigon, not under the Seventh Division), John became interested in policies and strategies that I was implementing at the time. We developed a close relationship and often rode through, or flew over, provinces to visit and observe the Civil Guard under my direction. We had long talks about the war and the Viet Cong insurgency, then in its early stages. From these talks and his action, I soon realized that Vann was a man of exceptional courage who had proved himself in combat during the Korean War. For his part, John became interested in my counterinsurgency theory and practices. He did not always fully agree with my ideas, but he respected my efforts just as I respected what he was striving to accomplish. We were close friends by the time he left Vietnam after his first tour of duty.

When he returned as a civilian with United States Operations Mission (USOM), I was province chief in Kien Hoa. John visited me regularly and took time to tour the province extensively. He observed how I was putting into practice the programs I had begun to develop earlier in the Northern Delta provinces. His seminal paper titled *Harnessing the Revolution in South Vietnam* was based in part on what he gleaned from those observations and our discussions. In late 1965 when I was appointed head of the national pacification cadres program (called the Directorate of Revolutionary Cadres by Americans and Rural Development Cadres by the Vietnamese), Vann was assigned as my advisor. He strongly supported me and we worked together closely, but we failed to convince the powers that be to put our unorthodox strategies into practice. In the end, we both lost. I resigned from the program, and Vann moved to other endeavors.

Something I learned from John Vann, above all else, was a lesson I consider basic for non-Americans who deal with Americans: "Most responsible Americans will accept ideas and concepts if you can prove them in both theory *and* action, not just in theory." I must add that senior Americans in Saigon were far, far less likely to be receptive to my ideas—which they regarded as too radical, unorthodox, or counterproductive—than those in lower echelons of American military and civilian field operators.

John also introduced me to another American who looms large in my memory, and who remains a close friend to this day: Daniel Ellsberg. Vann brought Daniel to see me during one of his visits to Kien Hoa in mid-1965. We had a long conversation about all aspects of the war, especially pacification, which was then the primary focus of the U.S. Mission in Saigon. John and Dan helped me appreciate the American people through their own personal sacrifice.

There are others to whom I also owe acknowledgment for friendship and support that they offered so generously. One is Rufe Phillips, who, while on a trip to the provinces as USOM rural affairs director, "discovered" me (this was disclosed some twenty years later) in a sense, during my first term as Kien Hoa province chief. He introduced me, and my ideas, to the American Mission, and remains a good friend to this day. Another was Sir Robert Thompson of England, who explained to me the three fundamental factors applied in defeating insurgency in Malaysia: (1) the hierarchy of command must include political, legal, and military structures, in that order; (2) all anti-insurgent measures, especially those that impact the public, *must* be conducted lawfully and within the legal structure cited in point 1; (3) all information provided to the public must be accurate, never falsified. Those three elements were practically ignored in Vietnam.

Among others who risked their lives to understand the war include Edward Lansdale and Frank Clay, Stu Methven, Keyes Beech, Tony Cistaro, Ev Bumgardner, Andre Sauvageot, Frank Scotton, Tom Donahue, John O'Reilly, and John O'Donnell.

On the Vietnamese side, first and above all, I want to present my grateful respects to the Most Venerables Thich Tri Thu and Thich Thien Minh, chairman and vice chairman of the Vietnamese Unified Buddhist Church, for acknowledging my loyalty both to the nation and the church by paying me a symbolic visit at the National Assembly before I was arrested by the Thieu government in February 1970.

Second, I am deeply grateful to Chief Justice of the Supreme Court Tran Minh Tiet, a reputable Catholic personality, for his strong defense of my case against President Thieu's persecution.

Third, I would like to express my gratitude to supporters and sympathizers during my difficult time in Vietnam, in particular to my lawyers Senators Vu Van Mau and Nguyen Phuoc Dai, attorneys Vu Van Huyen and Vo Van Quan, and National Assembly members and lawyers Tran Van Tuyen and Nguyen Khac Tan.

Finally, I must express my deepest gratitude to all the illiterate peasants who in 1945 were volunteer-soldiers in the first platoons and companies of the National Liberation Army (Giai Phong Quan), for educating me most importantly. Sharing hardship for more than four years opened the eyes of this son of the mandarin aristocracy to the miserable lives of peasants under the political and class system that existed in Vietnam for centuries. I arrived at an understanding of the motivation that turned them into combatants against oppression, just as it had their ancestors who fought valiantly, and successfully, against Chinese, Siamese, and Mongol invaders in the past. The lessons that I learned were painful when I later fought against them while serving as a soldier in the Army of the Republic of Vietnam. But that early experience also motivated and directed me toward fighting—impossibly, as it turned out—for the goal of a peaceful, democratic, non-Communist Vietnam.

Tran Ngoc Chau

1: ROOTS OF THE PAST, SEEDS OF THE FUTURE
(AUGUST 1945)

As the Imperial Seal and Royal Sword were passed from Emperor Bao Dai[1] to Tran Huy Lieu,[2] I knew I was part of a truly momentous day in Vietnamese history. This abdication by the last ruler of a traditional Vietnam dynasty and transfer of power to Tran Huy Lieu, representing the revolutionary government of Ho Chi Minh,[3] was significant, not merely symbolic. Roots from Vietnam's past were being torn out, and seeds for the future planted in their stead. It marked a turning point for the nation: the beginning of events that would affect Vietnam, and me personally, more than anyone dreamed at the time, in ways we could never have imagined.

Who could have foreseen that I would be, in turn, a Viet Minh cadre; a South Vietnamese officer and government official; mayor of Danang, and a provincial governor under both President Diem and the generals who ruled after the coup in which Diem was assassinated; secretary general of the National Assembly's House of Deputies—and then a prisoner in both South Vietnamese and Communist prisons? In the coming years I found myself just inches and seconds from death many times. I visited other countries and met people from faraway places, including American ambassadors, generals, and such well-known men as Daniel Ellsberg, William Colby, John Paul Vann, Edward Lansdale, Sir Robert Thompson, Rufe Phillips, Richard Holbrooke, Keyes Beech,[4] and many more. I would even, when arrested and imprisoned by President Thieu in 1970, be the focal point of an international cause célèbre that reached into the U.S. State Department and was reported worldwide in newspapers and magazines.

I had no inkling about any of those things on that early autumn day so long ago. The date was August 30, 1945; the place was the Citadel in Hué, where the emperor traditionally lived and worked. Such events seemed as unlikely for my future as the idea would have been just a few years earlier that our traditional leader would step aside in favor of Ho Chi Minh. Ho at that time was virtually a nonentity, known to very few Vietnamese after spending three decades in exile, mostly in Russia and France (utilizing a variety of "cover" names), studying and attempting to gain support in other countries for an independent Vietnam.[5]

Signs of excitement and change appeared everywhere in this city of mossy walls, blue water, and glossy green trees. Hundreds of thousands of men, women, and children poured into the Citadel area from all corners of the city. More people flocked in from surrounding villages. All waved the new red and yellow flag of the revolution, adding splashes of vivid color under the gray overcast skies. Milling crowds created an atmosphere that was charged with energy and anticipation.

Hué, Vietnam, and its people—indeed the entire world—had changed drastically in the last few years. Repercussions from the fall of France early in World War II were felt in Indochina. France surrendered its colonial power to Japan in 1940 and thereafter functioned as a puppet government under Japanese control. The situation, beneficial to both sides, continued until March 1945. The Japanese, threatened by an imminent invasion from Indochina, mounted a coup that overthrew the French administration. There were a few brief battles, but eventually all French not killed were captured and sent to prisons or internment camps. Japan granted Vietnam "independence" within its Greater East Asia Co-Prosperity Sphere and installed Bao Dai as ruler.[6]

Just six months later, bowing to the power of two atomic bomb blasts, Japan surrendered to the Allies—and the Vietnamese rose up to join Ho Chi Minh's fight to prevent France from taking back control of its former Indochina colony. The Japanese-supported government with Bao Dai as its figurehead had not really had time to begin functioning effectively. Meanwhile, the Viet Minh, which had spearheaded resistance against Japan, now emerged as the strongest of several nationalist factions. To many Vietnamese, Ho seemed to be the best hope to achieve eventual freedom for their country. (Being perceived as too closely associated with the Chinese compromised other potential or would-be nationalist leaders. After living in exile in China, they accompanied the Chinese troops who marched into northern Vietnam during this period. The result was that most Vietnamese viewed them suspiciously, regarding them as intruders, not true nationalists, so they were unable to muster wide support across the country.)

The dragon was awakening! On this day a new and revolutionary Vietnam began putting an end to the old, traditional Vietnam, as well as to the eras of French colonialists and Japanese imperialists. This was the setting for Bao Dai's abdication. The emperor stated with fervor and a sense of the dramatic that he would rather "be a citizen of an independent country than the king of a slave nation!" He had agreed to become Ho Chi Minh's supreme counselor. The ceremony today would make his abdication official, transmitting the mandate of heaven to the down-to-earth Ho. It attracted a crowd of thousands of my fellow countrymen who felt a sentimental attachment to the emperor. It was an emotional time for all Vietnamese, perhaps even more than most for me.

Slightly more than twenty years earlier I had been born in this city to a Confucian-Buddhist family associated with the Nguyen dynasty since the seventeenth century. My ancestor, the duke of Tien Duc, Tran Phuoc Thanh, came from Quang Nam province, where a monument erected in his memory still exists. His descendants served in the Imperial Court until the Tay Son brothers took over the country.

My grandfather, Tran Tram, the great scholar[7] and a royal cabinet minister, was gloriously eulogized at this death by Huynh Thuc Khang, himself a noted scholar.[8] This was an unusual tribute because Huynh refused to cooperate with the French-controlled government and normally showed no respect for any of the mandarins. Both my grandfather and my father, a chief judge, like most other mandarins of their fading Confucian- and Buddhist-educated generation, were strong nationalists. They never resigned themselves to French rule, but accepted the fact that it existed. They managed to use their positions to make the lives of their compatriots as bearable as possible under the colonial system.

Bao Dai was the last of the Nguyen dynasty, founded by his ancestors in 1802 when they became the sole rulers of a unified Vietnam. (He and his father Khai Dinh played only a symbolic leadership role under the French colonial system, which controlled taxation, finance, defense, and most other important matters—leaving the Vietnamese administration little to do.) He had not earned the same degree of respect and esteem that some of his predecessors enjoyed, due to his sometimes profligate ways and his collaboration with the French.

He was impressive in his abdication, however, and he was the emperor. That raised his stature, and the huge crowd cheered wildly for him.[9] Many remembered back to 1932 when Bao Dai, then just eighteen years old, hoped to institute reforms when the French relaxed their control over him slightly. Unfortunately, the young emperor, though intelligent, lacked the courage of his convictions. His enthusiasm waned, and he resumed a life of pleasure. This pleased the French, but lost Bao Dai the respect and support of Ngo Dinh Diem, a capable, honest member of the emperor's court up to that time. A fervent nationalist, Diem later was to become president of South Vietnam.

I was proud that his final act as emperor was meaningful, dignified, and patriotic. That meant a great deal to most Vietnamese. We needed the feelings of patriotism and pride in the Vietnamese nationalistic spirit that Bao Dai's words yesterday had inspired in us, for these were trying times. On that day, seeing the new revolutionary flag—red, with a yellow star—flying proudly above the Citadel strengthened my feelings of national pride. The flag was the brave symbol of our infant nation, struggling against long odds to reunite and regain its independence after some eight decades under French rule.

The Vietnamese nationalistic spirit, a term I use for lack of a better, more precise one, is something that is difficult for people from other countries to understand. Think of it as a blend of pride in one's country and its history, patriotism, and a continuing desire to throw off the yoke of alien oppressors who subjugated Vietnam over the centuries. A lack of understanding of the power of this nationalistic concept hinders most books and reports about the Vietnamese war, just as it has made things difficult for would-be conquerors of the country down through the centuries. It might best be explained by a famous poem written by the great national hero Ly Thuong Kiet, commander of the Vietnamese Army that defeated the Chinese invaders. His words motivated Vietnamese forces when they faced a Chinese army in 1076 and in other battles ever since. Well-known through the centuries, even by the most illiterate peasants, the poem served time after time as the national battle cry against foreign invaders:

> Vietnam belongs to the Vietnamese;
> That was scripted in the Divine Testament.
> Whoever refuses to heed this and comes to invade
> Will surely be exposed to defeat.

Hué is a shortened form of Thuan Hoa, the old name of the territory that included the city. An older name for it was Xuan, which meant "enriching spring" and was given to the city in 1802 by Emperor Gia Long, founder of the Nguyen dynasty. It became the royal seat in 1760, and then capital of the unified Vietnam in 1802. Hué had been my family's home for many years, so it is not surprising that I loved it and felt very much at ease there. In truth, however, it was difficult not to love Hué. The French fell under its spell during their occupation of Vietnam, as did many others over the years.

High, mossy brick walls surrounded the ancient Citadel. Tall trees inside the walls shaded narrow streets lined with imposing houses and quaint palaces that had served as offices. My grandfather had lived there. Small lakes and ponds covered with beautiful lotus flowers shone like colorful mirrors here and there around the buildings. Koi and carp swam gracefully and serenely in them as they had for many years, oblivious to the chaos and winds of change raging above their watery homes. The blue waters of several smaller rivers flowed around the Citadel's high walls and joined the larger, serene Perfume River, which divided Hué into two parts. One was the old city; the other part was the modern city established by the French during the decades of their rule, which ended in 1954.

Modern villas and colonial-style mansions hid under tall trees and behind a profusion of flowers on the southern side of the river. The French had reigned here for sixty years, giving Hué a distinct culture and character overlaid on its traditional ways. Only rich Vietnamese families and government mandarins could afford to mingle and socialize with the French. This was a city of the rich and privileged. Even after the French finally left Hué, the psychological after-effects of that wealth and privilege continued to intimidate the common class of Vietnamese.

Mountains form an almost theatrical backdrop for Hué, while the South China Sea stretches out to the horizon on the city's east. Numerous Buddhist pagodas and Confucian temples of striking traditional architecture testified to the mixed religious heritage of Vietnam. With other historic symbols of Vietnam's traditional culture, they were located throughout the old city of Hué. Catholic churches, of more modern and European architecture, clustered in the newer, largely French, section of the city. (Vietnam was approximately 85 percent Buddhist or Confucian at the time, less than 15 percent Catholic.)

These two faces of Hué symbolized the division between the new and the old. Traditions were fading. Architecture and monuments like those in the Citadel had been giving way for some time to more modern structures favored by the French— just as mandarins who followed the Confucian philosophy had been gradually replaced by French colonialists and the new class of Vietnamese mandarins they installed as administrators. Many of the old mandarins were scholars and teachers who taught as much by their deeds and example as they did from books or by the words they spoke. The modern Frenchified Vietnamese were more concerned with their careers and material things than philosophy or teaching—or ethics.

On the map, Vietnam resembles a mythic dragon, with its head staring defiantly at its gigantic neighbor to the north, China. It bears two smaller neighbors, Laos and Cambodia, on its back. Lapping at the rest of its body are the waters of a part of the Pacific Ocean that the Vietnamese still refuse to call the South China Sea (because of antagonism created by China's many attempts to conquer Vietnam in the past). Now, in this early autumn of 1945, the Vietnamese dragon was straining restlessly at its bonds, anxious to be free once more.

World War II was barely over, but our own conflict was just beginning. And we were to face many foes. Very shortly after the ceremony that made Bao Dai's abdication official, ill-trained and poorly equipped volunteers of the National Patriotic Organization (official name for the Viet Minh[10]) found themselves battling an unlikely alliance of British, French, and, yes, Japanese troops.

Not many people understand the situation of Japanese troops in Southeast Asia immediately after World War II. It's true that Japan surrendered unconditionally to the Allies. It's equally true that, in Indochina, Japanese military forces were ordered by the Allies to hold their positions, retain their arms, and maintain security. The rest of the world might have regarded Japan as a defeated enemy, but in Vietnam it appeared that nothing had changed. Soldiers retained their Rising Sun banners and their weapons, arms that were both feared and coveted by Vietnamese nationalists who hoped to establish the country's independence. Those weapons continued killing my fellow countrymen for months after the official Japanese surrender, something many Americans to this day find hard to believe.[11]

As it happened, I faced combat for the first time as a Viet Minh squad leader in an attack on a Japanese detachment of some 200 men. Such attacks during that time had two purposes: first, to free Vietnamese territory from the control of the foreign invaders, and second, to capture arms we knew would be needed in the struggle to establish an independent Vietnam.

That was still ahead of me, however. I had returned to Hué just a week earlier from the Dalat-Djiring and Nha Trang sector, which included the southern and highland areas of Annam (Central Vietnam). I had served there for the past year as a courier in a Viet Minh intelligence unit.[12] I was on leave to visit my father, who was seriously ill. He had suffered bouts of pneumonia for years; my mother was ill also. Only my youngest brother lived at home; my two elder brothers and sister (with her family) were serving in the Viet Minh.

My father was retired, and he and my mother lived a frugal life in their home on the outskirts of Hué. Father spent most of his time praying and teaching the concepts of Buddhism. When I reported to them the situation in the country, and my own current role, my father said little. He merely reminded me of the principles of loyalty to the country and filiation to the people.[13]

I had volunteered in 1944 to join my two older brothers in the Viet Minh resistance to the French and the Japanese forces that then controlled them. I was twenty at the time, a student at the lycée and a Boy Scout.[14] Earlier, as was traditional in my family, I had spent seven years as a Buddhist student.[15] In dedicated Buddhist families it is not uncommon for a son to be selected to become a bonze, or Buddhist monk. This brings great honor and joy to the family. Thus, at age nine, after my elementary education at a regular school and under a family tutor, I began training for the life of a bonze. I had an option, however; I could return to a normal secular life anytime I desired. A farewell ceremony at the family's altar marked the occasion. On my first few days at Truc Lam pagoda, I began a life of daily prayers and vegetarian meals.

I was ordained in a ceremony with others, to be on probation as a bonze—with our heads shaved for good. From then on I was under the personal tutelage of the Most Venerable Thich Giac Tien as I began my religious training and lived the life of a bonze. I enjoyed the new lifestyle and devoted myself to it enthusiastically. Thus, when I was sent a few years later to Bao Quoc pagoda (the name means "Preciousness of the Nation," implying that it was the cradle of the spiritual essence of the country), the first modern Buddhist seminary, to further my regular and religious education, I was well prepared. However, as I matured over the following five years, I realized I was not capable of continuing in the religious life. I confessed as much and was allowed to return to normal life—promising to myself to abide by the basic Buddhist rules as a good layman.

I returned to my family at age sixteen, and enrolled in a private lycée. While at the lycée, my brothers and I joined the Boy Scout Organization led by Ta Quang Buu. As early as 1942 the organization had become a hotbed of nationalistic activities, with many members joining various clandestine groups working against the French. One such group, Youth for National Salvation (*Thanh nien cuu quoc* in Vietnamese) recruited my brother and me.

When France collapsed early in World War II and Hitler established the puppet Vichy regime in Europe, the French in Vietnam realized that nationalists would try to take advantage of the situation. They funded and encouraged several youth organizations designed both to divert young Vietnamese and to exert some control over them. The move boomeranged. The nationalist spirit proved stronger than loyalty to the colonialists among French-educated Vietnamese whom the French trusted to organize and guide the groups. These leaders seized the opportunity to recruit and set up anti-French activities. We worked undercover to develop a spirit of nationalism and to prepare the youths mentally for a revolt against the French when the time arose.

I served in the clandestine Intelligence Service of the Viet Minh in the very early stages of its existence. I worked primarily as a courier[16] under Nguyen Linh, then a deputy police commissioner in the French Security Agency. He had also been recruited by the Viet Minh to serve as an undercover agent for the Resistance. His Viet Minh mission: to detect Vietnamese who infiltrated nationalist groups for the French, and to compromise those who were hard-core French loyalists. With the Japanese becoming more influential in Indochinese affairs, the French assigned Linh to Dalat, where the Japanese High Command established headquarters for all of its espionage activities. Linh's job was to monitor Japanese activities there. I followed him to Dalat in early 1944 to act in a minor role as liaison for Linh, so he could avoid being detected in suspicious circumstances by French surveillance.

When invading Indochina in 1940, the Japanese adopted a policy of ruling the conquered territory from behind the scenes. The French colonial administration served as a front for Japan, much as the puppet regime of Marshal Philippe Pétain did for Germany in Europe. By late 1944, however, American victories increased in the Pacific Theater and speculation was that Indochina would be the target of the first U.S. invasion of the Asian continent. Agents from General Charles de Gaulle's Free French forces parachuted into Vietnam, bringing weapons and orders to strike against the Japanese the moment such an invasion occurred. (De Gaulle wanted to reestablish French control over Indochina and planned this move to counterbalance favorable U.S. reaction to the determined resistance efforts of Vietnamese nationalists.)

The Japanese, concerned by growing antagonism toward them by the Vietnamese, planned as early as September 1944 to oust the French administration and grant independence to Vietnam.[17] The date for this move had been set for April 25, 1945. With the move by the Free French, Tokyo advanced the coup d'état to March 9, 1945, and moved swiftly to neutralize French colonial forces, which represented a potential threat from within if there was an invasion.

Not all the French were happy in their roles as collaborators, and many in the military very likely would have welcomed an opportunity to strike at the Japanese in support of an Allied assault. Moreover, assisting the Allies would weigh favorably in postwar efforts by France to reassert control over Indochina. It would also restore a measure of French pride and prestige, which had suffered greatly as a result of being under the thumb of the Japanese for five years. French colonialists would be pleased to regain face, knowing how important that is in Asia.

On March 9 the Japanese ordered the French governor to place his army at their disposal. He did not comply, so Japanese troops seized French garrisons. Some units surrendered (at Hanoi, for example) and were interned peacefully. Some resisted, and were slaughtered. Any semblance of French power and influence disappeared overnight. Fortunately, Linh learned about the Japanese plans on March 4 and alerted the Viet Minh. This advance notice enabled the organization to rescue many of our agents and supporters who had infiltrated the French colonial infrastructure or were in other positions that might have put them in jeopardy from the Japanese.

With the French system eliminated as even a token government and at the instigation of the Japanese, Emperor Bao Dai declared Vietnam an independent state under Japan's protection, with himself as chief of state. Bao Dai attempted to create a new Vietnamese administration in Hué to replace the ousted French, designating Tran Trong Kim as prime minister. Kim, a sincere and honest patriot, succeeded in attracting a variety of respected Vietnamese to form his cabinet. They launched an attempt to recover from the prevailing chaos and to build an independent Vietnam. This was not what the Japanese wanted, however, and though they obviously were losing the war (we had no idea that the atomic bomb would hasten its end less than six months later), they still controlled Indochina. The Japanese replaced the French governors with their own and placed the French Security Agency under their direction.

Tran Trong Kim quickly found his government as much controlled by the Japanese as the previous Vietnamese government had been by the French. Other factors also complicated his efforts. For one thing, recovering from the administrative breakdown caused by the sudden ouster of the French proved almost impossible. In addition, Allied bombing caused a communications breakdown, crop failures and famine created havoc in Tonkin and Annam, and the Japanese imposed direct military rule over Cochinchina.

But the rising tide of nationalistic sentiment was beyond the control of the Japanese, Tran Trong Kim, or circumstances. Young people, intellectuals, and the masses were ripe for revolt. By the time the Japanese surrendered, Viet Minh cadres had emerged as their leaders. In particular, the former Boy Scouts of Ta Quang Buu, members of Phan Anh's Frontline Youth, and the Avant-Guard Youth of Dr. Pham Ngoc Thach provided the Viet Minh with tens of thousands of active cadres. Most served in the military. Not all nationalist groups joined Ho Chi Minh and the Viet Minh initially, but they were overwhelmed by the forces that rallied to Ho, and most formed ranks with the Viet Minh for the sake of national unity.

Ho Chi Minh and the Viet Minh refused to support the Bao Dai regime and continued their policy of harassment and resistance against the Japanese. They hoped that this would weigh in their favor after the war ended. On April 27, 1945, Ho met for the first time with Major Archimides Patti, the American OSS officer (Office of Strategic Services, forerunner of the CIA) whose team infiltrated into North Vietnam from China. His mission was to gather intelligence on Japanese strength, positions held, and logistics capabilities, as well as to establish liaison with Vietnamese resistance groups. I'm sure he was also ordered to assess the caliber of the resistance fighters and how much support they could offer in the event of an Allied invasion.

Major Patti was impressed with Viet Minh efforts, especially the intelligence network that the organization had established. He welcomed the hard intelligence that our network developed on the Japanese. The Americans found it to be accurate and reliable. In turn, the major and his men provided a limited amount of radio equipment and small arms.

Major Patti also filed favorable reports with his headquarters on the capabilities of the Viet Minh and the results of the resistance movement that its nationalistic members had waged over the previous five years. Despite this, and the major's personal sympathy for the Vietnamese cause, the OSS team was ordered to end its mission and leave Vietnam in October 1945. The American brass at that time had no desire for U.S. military representatives to become embroiled in any way with the fighting that had begun between the Vietnamese and the French, often aided by the Japanese.

2: A JOURNEY OF AWAKENING (1945)

A few weeks after Bao Dai abdicated his position as emperor, passing over the symbols of chief of state to Ho Chi Minh's representative, I set out on a memorable four-day journey. It brought me a new understanding of, and appreciation for, the Vietnamese people. As I explained earlier, I was born into a family of mandarins who had a long history of honorable service in varied provincial and imperial court positions. We lived comfortably, if not ostentatiously.

In retrospect, I realize I had been somewhat spoiled and insulated during my early years from many ugly realities that most Vietnamese faced during that time. The seven years I spent studying in the Buddhist monastery altered that to some extent. The life had been demanding, with none of the comforts I enjoyed before, but it was still out of the mainstream of Vietnamese life in many respects. I underwent privations, but voluntarily, knowing that I could return to my normal life.

Even my experiences during the prior few years working in intelligence for the Viet Minh changed my perspective to only a limited extent. For the most part I socialized with the same classes of people I had known all my life. My contact with peasants and working-class Vietnamese was restricted. As was true for many others in my situation, I understood little about the difficulties and hardships that these countrymen of mine faced every day of their lives. Nor did I appreciate the intrinsic value of these rural compatriots, and the vital role they played in helping shape Vietnam's destiny.

Like many others of the privileged classes who enjoyed the benefits of an education and comfortable living, I suppose I had looked down on the illiterate farmers and others who made up the bulk of Vietnam's population (about 25 million at that time). I admit these things with some shame—a sense of regret and guilt that began to surface on the four-day train ride from Hué to Trai Mat, south of Dalat. During that time I looked at people from all walks of life, in particular the farmers, through new eyes. I began to understand the great gap that existed between the privileged Vietnamese and the French colonialists, who were determined to reestablish their rule, and the underprivileged in this country. We saw many reminders of that as our train took us southward.

For me, that trip was a journey of awakening.

A patriotic fervor swept the country during the days following the emperor's dramatic abdication. High schools were closed, as teachers and students left to join the swelling army of Viet Minh recruits. The new soldiers scurried around buying

themselves uniforms and trying to purchase weapons, usually from Japanese soldiers. (Many Japanese were willing to sell, finding more security in cash than guns
that they knew would soon have to be surrendered to Allied troops anyway.)

Tens of thousands of these volunteers filled the streets, all willing to fight to establish Vietnam as an independent nation once more. Most had little or no training;
very few of those who managed to obtain firearms even knew how to load, aim, and
fire them. About half had only machetes as personal weapons. The men who led
them frequently had no more military training or skills than the novice troops
themselves.

When I boarded the train at the Central Station in Hué I saw many of my friends
and school classmates. Nearly all of them were from well-to-do families and spoke
French fluently. I don't know how significant the journey proved to be for them or
how many shared the awakening I experienced during the four days to follow. As we
rode the overloaded train through the countryside we received an enthusiastic welcome at each of the many stations where we stopped. Whether it was day or night, in
the mountains, amid rice fields, or by the seaside, people gathered to greet us, to
acclaim the volunteers who were being sent to help in the battles for the South.
People even lined up, row upon row, along the railroad tracks, to wave and cheer us
on as we rolled past them.

At each station young children gathered, chanting patriotic and traditional
Vietnamese songs. I remember that one song popular at the time went like this:

> It's time for the valiant army to launch forward,
> The country was resounding with the cry of war.
> Forward we all go on a glorious march,
> Fighting bravely for final victory.[1]

Old men and women considered the volunteers their "adopted children," and vied
with each other to embrace the new soldiers. Emotional tears mixed with cheerful
laughter from those of us on the train as well as from the people who came to show
us their support for the cause of Vietnamese independence. It was an impressive
expression of the nationalism and deep desire for our country's freedom that bound
us together in a new brotherhood, whether we were city dwellers or farmers.

The people along the way brought food and other refreshments, offering it free to
any of us who wanted to partake. Most of those welcoming us were peasants or men
and women who eked out difficult existences in low-paying jobs. Many could ill afford the generosity they showed in sharing their food and drink with us. We knew
that most were living on short rations voluntarily, to help relieve the serious famine
caused by Japanese policies, implemented by their French lackeys in the puppet government. Before the Japanese conquered Indochina, Vietnam had exported large

quantities of rice. The Japanese, however, were more interested in industrial crops: jute, peanuts, and especially cotton, to use in making gunpowder. At their bidding the French forced more and more rice-growing acreage to be used for nonfood crops.

Add to this the fact that the Japanese confiscated large amounts of rice for their troops, and the result was growing shortages of the country's main food staple. The problem really became severe by the summer of 1945. Dikes along the Red River in the North had not been maintained well during the years of Japanese occupation and gave way in several areas during the rainy season. Some of the area's best rice-growing areas flooded, wiping out a significant quantity of the normal harvest. Since the North produced only slightly more rice than it consumed in the best of times (most of the surplus exported had come from the South), a terrible famine developed. More than two million people, out of the total population of twenty-five million, starved to death.

In the South and Central sections of the country, the Viet Minh called for everyone to set aside each day a portion of the rice they would normally eat to help their desperate northern countrymen. Most people responded, and the move had an additional benefit. It helped all Vietnamese feel common bonds: anger toward the French and Japanese, sympathy from those who shared their rice, and gratitude from those who received it.

How could these illiterate men and women, young and old, living in the obscurity of their rural villages, feel so strongly about driving out the French and regaining independence for Vietnam? Why did they care so much for national independence, and what were their expectations from it? This was one of the first widespread outpourings of the national spirit I experienced, and to this day it remains one of the most impressive examples that I witnessed personally. If these people, living under miserable conditions in rural and city areas, could care so much, how could we not do likewise?

We felt guilty, remembering that we had often looked down on the peasants in the past like so many of the educated Vietnamese did. We realized that, without the uprising, we would have lived as our fathers lived, accepting the de facto rule of the French. With self-satisfaction we would have enjoyed the privileges that they accorded to us, ignoring the miserable living conditions suffered by most Vietnamese, in cities as well as in rural areas. The awakening had begun! Now the peasants rallied to the cause of Vietnamese independence once more, spurred on at least in part by another emperor, Bao Dai, and his declaration that he would rather be a free citizen than a slave emperor. He had his flaws and had made mistakes, but he set an example for millions of other Vietnamese when he made that statement and abdicated in favor of Ho Chi Minh.

The French obviously were determined to reestablish their prewar control over Vietnam and the rest of Indochina. For the moment, however, they were unable to take aggressive military action because they lacked sufficient troops and transportation; they also lacked weapons and other equipment. This soon changed as the Allies, especially England, came to their aid.

Our nationalist forces, enthusiastic as they were, faced problems that prevented them from taking immediate advantage of the French weaknesses. We had even fewer weapons than the French.[2] Also, the Vietnamese volunteers were poorly trained. Some had fought as guerrillas in the resistance, and a few had prewar military training under the French.

Had I known what was to happen soon after my arrival in Cau Dat, I would have volunteered for the army immediately and quit the clandestine intelligence organization. Instead, still aflame with enthusiasm and patriotic zeal, I reported immediately to Nguyen Linh, chief of my intelligence unit.

He first inquired about my father's health, then asked eagerly about the events at Hué and what I had encountered during my trip. I launched into an excited account of the scene at the Citadel, when Bao Dai handed over symbols of the Mandate of Heaven to Ho Chi Minh's representative. Then I gave him a detailed report on the tumultuous receptions we received everywhere on the trip south. Linh exulted over the positive reaction of our people, from all areas and all classes, to the prospect of driving out the French and winning independence for a united Vietnam once again. He hung on my every word as I described how they cheered for the volunteers on the train, how they chanted patriotic anthems all along the way, and how they lined up to share with us food and drink from their own meager supplies. We talked far into the night.

Finally, exhausted, I went to my room for some much-needed sleep. I wanted to be well rested so I could resume my duties as quickly as possible. Little did I realize that soon I would lose all enthusiasm for the intelligence organization and work that had been the focus of my life for three years—and that I would soon make a decision that would change my life dramatically.

We enjoyed comfortable quarters in Cau Dat, a little town some fifteen kilometers from the center of Dalat. Situated at an elevation of about 1,500 meters, Dalat was another resort built by the French as a cool oasis in which they could escape the heat and humidity of lowland summers. Many French officials and prosperous businesspeople had second homes there, beautiful villas set among silk trees (mimosa), pines, and other evergreens. It was an exclusive area; aside from the workers who served the French, only the most elite Vietnamese were seen there usually. Businesses were run by Chinese, rich Vietnamese, and some French.

Usually a quiet backwater, Cau Dat was filled with crowds when I arrived. Refugees from Dalat and Vietnamese volunteers, many of them new volunteers like those who had ridden the train south with me, swelled the normal population. As had happened in other provinces a few days after the Japanese surrendered to the Allies in August, people in the area responded to urgings of the Viet Minh cadres and took over the administration. By the end of August, the entire country, north to south, was under the de facto leadership of Ho Chi Minh. Bao Dai recognized this reality when he abdicated and accepted the title of Ho's supreme counselor.

A few weeks earlier the Japanese had launched an all-out attack to drive the Vietnamese administration and its ragtag troops out of Dalat.[3] Actually, the Vietnamese government, such as it was in those confused, disorganized days, had no real military forces at the time other than local volunteers who formed a paramilitary organization of sorts.

Not much effort was required to clear the Vietnamese from the city, and now the Japanese were in full control of Dalat. That was why Cau Dat was crowded with government officials, civilian refugees, and a motley collection of army and paramilitary troops. The new provincial command had issued an order that Dalat itself was in a state of military blockade, and that no supplies or other assistance would be allowed to enter the city. The plan was to starve the Japanese and French inside the city into submission. The blockade was effective, causing a serious shortage of food inside Dalat.

Tea plantations and small factories, which processed a variety of exotic teas, surrounded the Cau Dat area. The French, who had built and lived in large colonial-style villas, owned nearly all of these operations. The Vietnamese who served them as workers and servants lived in slums bordering the tea plantations. However, since the Japanese conquest of Indochina, the French had deserted their homes and moved into Dalat. Our intelligence unit was quartered in three of the villas the French had left behind.[4]

I awoke from my sleep feeling refreshed and ready for a bright, new day. It was a somber morning, however—cold and cloudy—which somewhat dampened my spirits. As I looked out of the villa it seemed the crowds were especially large and animated. The city seemed too small for the thousands milling in its streets, and there was tension in their excitement. The gray, forbidding skies seemed curiously appropriate for the ominous air of agitation that the people generated. I shivered slightly, and hurried to find out what was happening.

Bits of muttered conversations drifted to my ears. "An execution . . . ," I thought I heard someone say. And from another quarter came something about "three spies." Unlikely, I told myself, but they would know at headquarters. I made my way there as rapidly as possible. I learned quickly that indeed there was to be a public execution of three people, two men and a woman, that afternoon at the railroad station.

That was grim news—made even more shocking when I learned that Hong, the young woman accused and condemned, was an acquaintance. I had met her through Huong Giang, a girl of my age who was a good friend at the time.

The men were accused of collaborating with the French. Hong's crime was that she had been caught trying to sneak into Dalat with food for her mother, who was a governess for a French family that lived in the heart of the city. I knew everyone involved: the young woman, her mother, and the French family. The latter included a professor from the lycée, his wife, and their three teenage children. All were charming and friendly people. The professor and his wife were definitely not overbearing colonialists. In fact, they had developed great affection for our country. I remembered them saying that they would like to see an independent Vietnam, independent of direct French rule, though perhaps still allied to their mother country. They hardly seemed like dangerous enemies of the people.

I immediately went to see Nguyen Binh, a local cadre, since he was a member of the committee that had sentenced the trio to death, and inquired about the situation. I tried to save the young woman, arguing vehemently that her life should be spared. After all, I said to Binh, what crime had she committed other than trying to get food to her hungry mother?

My arguments were in vain. "The decision has been made," Binh said, "and it cannot be reversed. The revolution demands harsh measures." Apparently the committee felt that there was too much confusion at the time and that it was necessary to begin enforcing discipline if the objective of national independence was to be attained. That was my understanding of the situation, at any rate; I was of very junior rank at the time and had no authority, of course, so it was not felt that I needed any further explanation. During our discussion Binh stressed one point as though it was a lesson I must learn: "The revolution is brutal in character because brutality is necessary to meet the challenge of our enemies, the French and their associates and lackeys." That was my introduction to the concept of "revolutionary brutality."

The day remained cold and cloudy, almost as though the weather reflected the mood of the events. By afternoon, several hundred people had gathered around the railroad station at the invitation of the provincial committee. When I arrived, the three condemned persons were standing, tied and blindfolded, awaiting their fate. As I looked at the young woman who was about to die I could feel myself trembling inside, almost as if I were she. Suddenly the image of her mother, who was blockaded in the city and could not be there, appeared in my mind. I imagined the anguish she must be feeling, for I was sure she knew what was happening; news passed readily and rapidly between Dalat and Cau Dat despite the blockade. I realized tears were running down my cheeks. It became too difficult for me to look at the condemned anymore. I sat down, losing myself in that human mass and ignoring the voices around me. All became quiet in an instant; then a lone voice read the sentences.

A short, sharp burst of rifle fire shattered the silence that followed—and it was all over. Three lives were wiped out in a split second. The crowd dispersed quietly, but I remained seated there, oblivious to everything, long after everyone else was gone. My brain was numb. Finally the cold penetrated my consciousness and I returned to my quarters. I was still dazed, shocked, and sickened by the execution. I couldn't sleep, and I vomited all night long.

As a Buddhist, killing was unthinkable to me—but as a fighter for national independence, killing was unavoidable. I was ready to face killing and death on the battlefield. But deaths like those I witnessed that sad day were inconceivable to me. They could not be justified according to my beliefs. I felt that, except on the battlefield or when facing imminent danger, taking someone's life was inexcusable, especially so abruptly and with no real trial. I couldn't bear the image of that young woman being executed so callously and after such a simplistic "judicial" procedure.

What made my shock even worse was the realization that my own intelligence unit had played a major role in capturing and accusing the three people who had been shot as spies. Would future actions of mine have similar results? I found it difficult to face that possibility, and I realized that performing my assignments in the future might be difficult. Would I be able to turn in reports on anyone when I knew those reports might have tragic results, whether I felt the results were justified or not?

Then I made a decision: I would rather serve in our combat units. The duty might be more hazardous, but I would be fighting openly against foes who were also armed and prepared to kill. I could no longer serve with good conscience in the clandestine intelligence service. I would rather kill or be killed than be implicated in executions over which I had no control.

The decision cleared my mind, but just then I suffered my first malaria attack. It kept me in bed for two weeks, suffering from depression as much as the malaria. Nguyen Linh came to see me while I lay in bed tossing with fever. I told him I wanted to transfer to a combat unit, without adding any explanation. He accepted my decision without question—but for the wrong reason. He suspected I had loved the young woman, and asked me if that had been the case. "No," I told him bluntly. "It was the process leading to the condemnation and execution of the three accused spies that disturbed me. I did not think the killings were justified." I explained my doubts that I could continue to serve effectively in the organization that had been instrumental in that process. At first Linh tried to dissuade me, but he finally realized how strongly I felt. He agreed to let me go and gave me a letter of recommendation.

Two days later I presented his letter at a military training center for cadres in Trai Ham. I filled out papers with information about my date and place of birth, my parents, and so on. The training center provided food, housing, and classrooms in two large villas, vacated by the French, that overlooked the Dran valley. Beyond that, we had to be self-sufficient. The commandant was Pham Thai, a northerner about thirty years old. Four instructors assisted him. We were scheduled for one month of training, but it was cut to fifteen days so we could be sent to take part in an upcoming action against 200 to 300 Japanese troops holed up in the former Phan Rang provincial headquarters compound near Thap Cham. More of the training time was devoted to political lectures than to military subjects. Many of the lectures stressed the need to replace suffocating French colonialism with Vietnamese independence. Others stressed how to live with and among the people, how to live together within the unit, and how to improve physically, intellectually, and in our new profession as soldiers.

We learned about our weapons and how to use them, though none of us fired more than ten shots. I realized very quickly that most of our military training would consist of on-the-job experience, and that our leaders would be learning tactics and similar skills right along with us. After fifteen days we assembled and moved out to the Thap Cham area for our baptism in battle. I was appointed leader of a squad in the newly formed platoon.

As we were gathering ourselves for a war of liberation, the forces that would be arrayed against us were readying themselves also. Ho Chi Minh made his second attempt to win U.S. support for an independent Vietnam, sending a request for help to President Harry S. Truman. Perhaps President Truman felt like his predecessor, Franklin D. Roosevelt. On January 1, 1945, just three months before his death, FDR made this remark to Edward R. Stettinius, his secretary of state: "I still do not want to get mixed up in any Indochina decision. . . . Action at this time is premature."[5]

At the conference of Allied leaders in Potsdam one month before Japan surrendered, plans had been made to disarm Japanese troops in Vietnam. The country was to be split at the sixteenth parallel, with Chinese Nationalists disarming Japanese in the North and the British taking responsibility for the South. Implementation of the plan began in September 1945—and it brought disaster in both halves of our divided country.

"The British commander, General Gracey, was miscast. A colonial officer with limited political experience but a genuine affection for his Indian troops, he held the paternalistic view that 'natives' should not defy Europeans. Officially, his was not to reason why. Lord Louis Mountbatten, the Allied commander for Southeast Asia, told him bluntly to avoid Vietnam's internal problems and merely handle the Japanese. But Gracey, guided by his prejudices, violated instructions. Despite Ho's assertion of

Vietnam's independence in Hanoi on September 2, he said publicly even before leaving India for Saigon several weeks later that "civil and military control by the French is only a question of weeks."[6] In the absence of French troops immediately, however, the British postponed disarming Japanese units and used them against what they considered the "rebel regime." Lord Mountbatten (Louis of Battenberg) reported on October 2, 1945, that the only way he could avoid using British/Indian forces was "to continue using the Japanese for maintaining law and order and this means I cannot begin to disarm them for another three months."[7]

A young American OSS lieutenant colonel, Albert Peter Dewey, though pro-French himself, disapproved of Gracey's Francophile bias and was ordered out of the country by the British—under suspicion of collaborating with the Viet Minh. Dewey, with background as an author and foreign correspondent, wrote a prophetic note before leaving: "Cochinchina is burning, the French and British are finished here, and we [the United States] ought to clear out of Southeast Asia."[8] He was killed in an ambush on his way to the airport, the first of nearly 60,000 Americans killed in Vietnam. The French and Viet Minh blamed each other for his death.

Meanwhile, Ho Chi Minh held firm command in the North, but floods that burst Red River dikes in the summer of 1945 had aggravated food shortages created by the Japanese. The first of the Chinese Nationalist troops, designated by the Potsdam plan to disarm Japanese units in North Vietnam, arrived in Hanoi in September 1945. Eventually 200,000 of them, under General Lu Han, swarmed into the North.

"They resembled a horde of human locusts. Hungry, tattered, and even barefoot, many racked with scurvy and other diseases, their ranks included poor peasant boys and ragged soldiers dragging along their wives and children. They had plundered villages during their march down from China. . . . Once in Hanoi they continued to pillage promiscuously. They barged into private homes and public buildings, stealing light bulbs and unscrewing doorknobs, and they pushed through markets, filching fruit and vegetables, even biting into bars of soap they mistook for food."[9]

I knew a little about these events at the time and learned more details in the following months and years. My attention during those weeks was concentrated on my own small part in the revolution, uprising, War of Independence—call it what you will.

3: FIRST COMBAT: AN INAUSPICIOUS BEGINNING (1946)

The day of reckoning arrived. The first shot I fired at an enemy in combat was aimed at a Japanese soldier. Did I hit him? I still wonder. My weapon on that November morning late in 1945 was a French *mousqueton,* one of the six firearms allotted to our squad of fourteen men. We also had another French mousqueton, two Japanese rifles, a German Mauser, and a British Sten. We received about fifty rounds of ammunition per rifle for this attack on the Japanese in a former provincial government headquarters not far from Thap Cham. Those without firearms carried machetes.

The compound included the provincial governor's mansion, the treasury building, a school, and a hospital. Vietnamese volunteers had been blockading it for several weeks, repeatedly asking the 200 Japanese occupying it to abandon their position and give up their arms. (This was three months after the Japanese had officially surrendered to the Allies.) They were willing to compromise, but rejected the terms proposed. Though the blockade was effective, the Japanese seemingly had adequate supplies, and their plight was not desperate enough for them to agree to the Vietnamese demands.

We spent two days preparing for a decisive battle to oust the Japanese from their refuge. The commander and his political commissar first worked out a detailed plan and went over it carefully with all company commanders and platoon leaders. Tra, my platoon leader, in turn took me and the other squad leaders during the day to where we could see our attack positions, how we were to advance, and our objective. The Japanese by now were accustomed to seeing us move around and had driven off our previous sorties with ease. They paid little attention as we scouted the positions; at least we drew no fire.

The plan called for my platoon to launch a diversionary attack as soon as the sun set; the rest of the task force would lay down a preliminary volley of fire to keep the enemies' heads down. We hoped the Japanese would concentrate on our platoon long enough for our main attack to get well under way. My platoon's real objective, a small building behind a mass of well-laid barbed wire on a corner of the compound, would be attacked only after another company had taken the big building next to it.

Our machine guns and 60 mm mortars (the nearest thing to artillery we had) opened up promptly at sunset and poured heavy fire into the compound. Strangely, the Japanese did not shoot back, not even a single round. But we did hear shouting and movement. This odd response created some confusion and a bit of anxiety. The three squads in my platoon began the planned diversion on schedule, alternately advancing and providing cover fire for each other. As we approached a thick hedge of hibiscus on the perimeter of the compound, a series of explosions burst from the bushes. Two of our men went down, seriously injured by booby traps laid for us. Grenades had been connected to trip wires and secured in the thick hibiscus foliage. We set them off when we tripped the wires concealed in the path of our advance.

Suddenly shooting started again on the other side of the compound; we could hear shouting, amplified by megaphones, and the sound of horns. The Japanese apparently began firing back, but at a very slow rate. Mines exploded; one building caught fire, lighting up the entire area. A team in the squad next to mine opened a breach in the wire, causing the enemy to begin firing at us in earnest. I spotted the location of one Japanese soldier. I was sure it was a live enemy, not a dummy, because I saw the muzzle flash of his rifle when he fired. I aligned my sights on him and pulled the trigger. In my excitement I forgot the little training I'd had and neglected to clamp the butt of the mousqueton firmly against my shoulder. I soon learned why that was so important.

The short-barreled mousqueton, a French carbine, had vicious recoil; my 140 pounds were no match for it. The rifle went flying one way and I went flying another, landing on my *derriere,* to use the polite French term. Or flat on my butt—in the more colorful terminology of the American friends I was to make later. I thought at first that I had been shot but quickly realized I was only the victim of my own weapon, an inglorious beginning to a military career. Happily, it was not typical, and later events proved that I was a good soldier. All of us who took part in that fight and survived learned lessons that were valuable in future firefights.

As it happened, my personal experience set the tone for the entire operation. In the end we had won a victory, but the canny, experienced Japanese troops pulled several surprises that made it a hollow one. The enemy kept up a barrage of small-arms fire long enough to stall our advance completely. We shot back only sporadically, conserving our slender supply of ammunition. The Japanese fire slackened, but grenades and mines kept exploding. We suffered heavy losses, and those assigned to medical evacuation duties were busy with our wounded. One platoon succeeded in breaking through the barbed wire near the compound's main building but was unable to move out quickly because they became entangled in many rows of loose barbed wire hidden behind the outer perimeter. The platoon was wiped out almost entirely.

The shooting continued for an hour that seemed much more than sixty minutes. Then we were ordered to stay in position and to shoot only if the Japanese fired on us. No more shots came from inside the compound. After the din of the previous fighting, it seemed almost unbelievably quiet. Explosions and sudden flare-ups in one of the burning buildings punctuated the silence periodically. During this lull, my platoon leader was gravely wounded trying to break through the barbed wire and was evacuated. His deputy was killed at the wire a short time later. The company commander asked me to take over as platoon leader. As my first duty I checked on all the men in the platoon's three squads. It took me an hour to locate everyone and to learn that we had fifteen casualties: six killed, nine wounded and evacuated. Only twenty-eight men remained in the platoon, including five who were wounded but stayed with us.

The Japanese set fire to the ammunition dump and a few buildings to cover their withdrawal, then escaped from the back of the complex in the darkness and confusion. They moved through a gap in the perimeter of our lines to the undefended riverbank to rejoin the main Japanese force in Dalat. We had been attacking empty buildings for much of the night. Most of the "shots" we heard during that time had been firecrackers, and the soldiers we fired at during that time had indeed been dummies. The latter had been dressed in authentic uniforms and ingeniously rigged so they could be moved, making them very lifelike.

Our headquarters command decided not to pursue the Japanese. Instead, we began clearing up damage from the battle. A big victory celebration gathered momentum as people came in from the surrounding countryside to honor our feat. They brought food in plenty, rejoicing that their entire area from the provincial headquarters to Thap Cham, a span of more than ten kilometers, was now liberated. Never mind that the Japanese fooled us in so many ways, that we had suffered unnecessary casualties, or that the enemy had slipped through our lines and escaped. To the people, all the volunteers were heroes. They brought us fruits, hogs, chickens, a goat; I was more exhausted by receiving congratulations and gifts than by my new duties as platoon leader.

For two days we stayed in the compound school, taking over quarters recently used by the Japanese. With the company commander and his political commissar, we reviewed the performance of the company in action. Then each platoon, squad, team, and individual was reviewed. This kind of assessment was standard practice among the Viet Minh, and I feel it was an important element in developing the organization's military capabilities.

These reviews or critiquing sessions were more extensive than most military debriefings. They began at the operational command level; in this case, that included all company commanders, and their political commissars and deputies. Company-level reviews came next, with all platoon cadres participating. Finally, all members of each platoon held their own reviews. These postoperation reviews allowed everyone to learn by pooling their experiences, assessing the personal behavior of each individual under fire, and studying the impact of the operation on people in the vicinity, as well as on the enemy.

Then orders came for us to reinforce troops facing a combined force of French and Japanese in the Dalat area. The Japanese we fought were part of the main force stationed in Dalat. They were reluctant to attack us after their country's surrender. Then the British arrived and ordered the Japanese not only to hold their positions but to expand their control over the surrounding territory and to secure it for the French. Consequently, the Japanese force in Dalat had moved units into positions well beyond the city limits.

On the way to the Thap Cham depot to catch the train, we met more volunteers. They were arriving by the hundreds to join forces in the South against the French, the British, and the Japanese. In theory, the British were there to disarm the Japanese but instead were allowing the French to use them almost as mercenaries in some cases. In Saigon, the British also rearmed French soldiers recently released from Japanese captivity, and provided support for them to fight against the Vietnamese. When General Phillipe Leclerc arrived from Vung Tau[1] with fresh troops, he used Japanese units to open his offensive.

One almost had to feel sorry for the Japanese who were deployed as shock troops by the French on several occasions. Any pity was quickly lost when one remembered the two million Vietnamese who died of starvation in the North as a result of the famine that Japanese policies created. Generally speaking, however, the Japanese remained in defensive positions, within their garrison limits, probably for three reasons. They lacked motivation to fight against us. Perhaps they also felt guilt at the damage and two million deaths they had already caused in our country. In addition, the British or Chinese (who were there, after all, to disarm their former foes) were reluctant to involve them in more active operations.

Thap Cham was the railway hub for trains running to and from Dalat, to the South and the North. Volunteers for the Army of Liberation filled its large railroad station from October to December of 1945. The highly motivated but poorly armed, ill-equipped, ill-trained, and unpaid force mobilized to fight for Vietnam's independence. The Dragon was starting to unsheath its claws! Patriotic and revolutionary songs filled the air. One of the most popular, roughly translated from Vietnamese, went like this:

> Vietnam has been suffering for years
> Under poverty and cruelty imposed by imperialists[2]
> Let's exterminate the imperialists and their lackeys
> So we can build up the democratic republic system,
> With that, we would regain our food, clothing, and liberty.

The young volunteers represented all classes and all walks of life, from sunburned farmers to pale office and industrial workers from the cities. Despite their military inexperience, their discipline was strict, for it came from a self-discipline imposed by a sense of honor and respect for their country and its people. The need for this kind of self-discipline was impressed on us in lectures from the time we volunteered.

There was an incredible rapport between the volunteers and the rest of the population. Older men and women embraced us as their sons just as they had on my train journey south from Hué not too many weeks earlier. Many of the volunteers were from the privileged class of Vietnamese, men who traditionally looked down on or paid little attention to the poor and illiterate. Many began the same sort of transformation I experienced on my own recent journey of awakening. Traveling, training, fighting, and living with volunteers from the poorer classes made them realize that these men were individuals, too, men who might not be wealthy or highly educated but who brought their own form of riches and wisdom to the struggle for independence. All in all, the popular mood of nationalism unified us more than I could ever remember. The revolution against French colonial rule was a great and noble cause that created new bonds between Vietnamese of all classes.

It was probably there in Thap Cham, near the crowded train station, that I first thought about the men who had created such a radical climate of change. In my mind I was paying homage to all Vietnamese leaders of the time. Many I had long been familiar with: Bao Dai, Huynh Thuc Khang, Bui Bang Doan, and Nguyen Tuong Tam. Others I had learned about more recently: Ho Chi Minh, Vu Hong Khanh, and Nguyen Hai Than. What political labels they bore—Communist, Nationalist, or anything else—meant little to me.

And of them all, four meant most in my mind. First was Bao Dai, so impressive when he abdicated in favor of Ho Chi Minh. The others were Ta Quang Buu, my Boy Scout leader, and Huynh Thuc Khang and Bui Bang Doan, all of whom chose to support the Viet Minh. In the South, people were impressed when such esteemed and reputable men as Drs. Pham Ngoc Thach and Pham Van Bach rallied to Ho. I did not know them personally, but I respected them greatly. I did know that, while our struggles and sacrifices as volunteers were just beginning, some of these men had been fighting and suffering many years in their quest for Vietnamese independence.

We left Thap Cham and headed for Dran,[3] a small valley town at the junction of two important highways: one that ran northwest from Thap Cham to Dalat, another which crossed that road and ran southwest to the Finom junction with the Saigon-Dalat highway. Dran had a 4,500-foot-high mountain as a backdrop on the Dalat side and a cliff that dropped off abruptly to the Phan Rang plain on its southwest perimeter. Its normal population was about 10,000. It had been a center for French plantation owners, but, as in Cau Dat, the French had long since fled to Dalat. Their villas, warehouses, and outbuildings now housed Vietnamese refugees who flocked in from Dalat and the surrounding area. Most of the men joined the revolutionary forces.

My platoon was assigned to defend a small pass that crossed the Dran-Finom road. This pass ran northeast to the Dalat area and was a possible route the enemy could use to flank our lines facing Dalat, or even to mount an attack from the side or rear against area headquarters in Dran itself. Another of our units was strung along the Saigon-Dalat road at the Finom junction to guard against an attack from that quarter. To our west was the range of high mountains that encompassed and extended beyond Dalat. To our east, the road to Phan Rang debouched onto flat rice fields that extended toward an immense forest, a vast hunting preserve for the emperor and high French officials. The preserve had long been the home for many wild elephants, tigers, deer, and water buffalo.

Guarding the pass was easy duty. We were far from the front lines, and the Japanese were content merely to maintain a defensive posture. They showed no signs of aggression after extending their lines to their current positions. We needed only to send out patrols at night, then relax during the day. Our peaceful routine was shattered one cold morning as my platoon returned from an uneventful night patrol. Shooting and the sound of heavy transport vehicles and armored cars seemed to come from everywhere, diffused by fog that covered the valley. Since our forces had no such vehicles, we knew that an enemy convoy was approaching our position. It happened so quickly that we were cut off from all communications with our command post. (This wasn't difficult because our "communications" were limited to messengers on foot or bicycle.) Our company commander ordered all platoons to take cover and stay hidden until he could find out what was happening.

It didn't take long to learn that the Japanese had attacked on foot, while a French mobile force cleared the road network and occupied main towns along the highways. Our lines at Cau Dat and Finom had been overrun; the French had bypassed our position en route to Dran, and my company now was behind the French lines. We stayed hidden in the forest all day, short on rations and wondering what was happening. Late in the evening the company commander sent me with a squad from my platoon to reconnoiter along the road to Dran. We set off, moving cautiously and taking cover when the French shot off flares to light up the road.

As we approached Dran we met hundreds of soldiers and civilians all mixed together and hiding in the forest. They informed us that French troops and tanks had taken Dran, Finom, and the towns between Dalat and Dran. They controlled all the roads in the Dran-Finom-Dalat network. Our troops, followed by thousands of civilians, were regrouping in various locations in the jungle. I kept my unit moving forward, on the alert all the time, until we made contact with the new temporary command post just after sunrise.

I received orders to return to our company and tell the commander to proceed through the jungle to the vicinity of Krong Pha, the railway station south of Dran on the Tour Cham–Dalat line and wait there for new orders. My patrol traveled the fifteen or so kilometers back to our company as rapidly as possible; I posted men every two or three miles along the way to guide the company through the night along the first leg of its move to the new rallying point. We encountered hundreds of civilians, old men, women, and children hiding under the pine trees and trembling from cold, hunger, and fear. We could do nothing for them, having virtually no food even for ourselves. It was heartbreaking, and something we were to see all too often in the future.

We completed our march without incident and regrouped with other units in the jungle about thirty kilometers from Krong Pha, which was occupied by the enemy. The French, fortunately, seemed satisfied with the results of their lightning offensive; they were content to occupy the towns and made no attempts to venture into the hills and forests. Orders came from command headquarters that our company was to push on toward the coastal region of Phan Rang. We set out again and soon began meeting other friendly units withdrawing from Finom and Entrerays. They carried several wounded with them; the dead had been left behind.

Our progress became slower and slower as the narrow trail running downhill along the course of a river grew steeper. Heavy civilian traffic using the same trail also slowed us frequently. We were getting exhausted, particularly those of us who had made the thirty-kilometer reconnaissance earlier. None of us had eaten anything for thirty hours. At sunset, we decided to halt and prepared to spend the night on a high cliff overhanging the river far below. It was so cold that we risked lighting a fire for warmth. Then we saw other fires springing up for miles up and down the trail from our position. By midnight, troops and refugees were awakened by the welcome arrival of civilian volunteers from villages and towns, mostly now under French occupation. They brought lots of cooked rice and dried fish for us. Simple as it was, that food tasted better to me than many seven-course feasts I had enjoyed in the past. What made us all appreciate it more was that we knew the risks those simple, brave, patriotic country people had taken to bring it to us. There was always the danger of meeting French patrols. Just making their way over the steep trails in the dark was perilous, something few of us would have cared to attempt. Almost as welcome as food was news that the new arrivals also brought.

We learned that the French offensive was made by troops fresh from France and French territories overseas. Commanded by the famous General Jacques Philippe Leclerc, they landed on the beach at Vung Tau and drove north in armored columns. Our lack of even the most basic communications other than messengers kept us from learning they were on the way. Of course, we had no weapons capable of engaging armored vehicles, but we might have at least slowed their advance with improvised mines and Molotov cocktails if we had been forewarned. And our casualties certainly would have been fewer.

The French columns continued driving north on the Saigon-Dalat route, punching through our meager lines at the Finom junction and continuing on to Dalat. From there, they launched an attack back down the Dalat–Thap Cham highway, after the Japanese opened fire from their defensive positions to pin down the Vietnamese troops holding Entrerays. Moving rapidly down the road with their light tanks and other vehicles, French forces took and occupied all the towns as far down as Dran. Most civilians in the occupied towns chose to evacuate and left with our troops.

So now we knew: We no longer faced just the Japanese and a relatively small number of lightly armed French colonial troops who had been released from Japanese internment camps only a few months earlier. New, well-equipped French troops under a famous general, and apparently with the backing of the Allies, had entered the arena. Our war of liberation suddenly looked much more difficult.

The next morning we continued our march toward the plain, still following the river. We walked from one mountain to another and spent another night by the river. The food supply was better organized now. As we passed through a control point we were given hot tea, cooked rice, and more dried fish. The troops shared rations with the refugees, giving priority to the aged and children. The third day of our march found us descending the last mountain grade to the Krongpha plain. It was so vast and covered with elephant grass far higher than our heads that we knew we could get lost very quickly. Our faithful guides, the river and trail that followed its course, seemed to get lost here, swallowed up in that swampy morass of vegetation. It was probably the first time in history that so many people had wandered into the area.

Perhaps our company commander felt I needed more exercise because he selected me and my platoon once again for reconnoitering duty. We were to search out a path that would take us across the trackless plain toward the coast. We decided the best plan was to retrace our steps back to the first plateau above the plain and get our bearings. It took us more than an hour of hard climbing to reach a spot where we had a good view out over the elephant grass below. There was a small mountain standing alone out on the plain. It was between us and the coast, so we decided we could use it as a marker. When we reached it we could again climb high enough to reorient ourselves and pick out the way to go. We clambered back down the steep trail and set out across the plain toward the small mountain.

Trees were scarce, but frequent enough so a scout could climb one periodically to see if we were still heading in the right direction. Our progress was slow, but steady. We were concerned about meeting some of the wild animals we knew were plentiful in the area: tigers, elephants, and boa constrictors. I think the giant snakes scared us most. Fortunately, we figured, most of the wildlife would leave us alone unless we aggravated them. We were almost right, as we learned that night.

For us, it became the "night of the tigers." Just before sunset we reached a clump of trees and decided to spend the night there. To be safe, we climbed the trees, three to five of us in each one, and tied ourselves to branches. We were all exhausted and looked forward to a good sleep. A few hours later, however, savage roars reverberating through the night woke us abruptly. Tigers surrounded our trees! We could see their silhouettes and glaring eyes as they prowled the clearing below us. One sat directly under the tree I shared with several comrades. His eyes shone in the moonlight, and we could smell his foul breath when he stood on his hind legs and swatted at the tree just below our perches. I called to the others not to shoot unless they were in extreme danger of attack. We could not spare any ammunition.

Suddenly the tigers left, probably because we made so much noise. Now the cold became a threat, and hunger was our worst enemy. We had not noticed either so much before, while our attention was focused on the tigers. It was a relief when the sun broke through a fog that seemed to rise out of the plain just before daybreak. We slid down from our roosts in the trees, first checking the area carefully to make sure no more wild beasts lurked nearby. We ate the last of our rice and continued our march through the tall grass. We learned why elephants had such thick hides; they needed them to survive the grass. Its knifelike edges inflicted cuts on all of us.

At noon, we struggled out of the grass into a clearing at the edge of a large stream. We rested for a half-hour, then set off downriver through flat jungle dotted with trees five to ten feet high. To our relief the going was easier now. Just as the sun was setting we met three local men, the first we had seen during our trek. None spoke our language, but we communicated with hand signs and drawings made in the sand with a stick. They let us know that thousands of soldiers and civilians had already passed through on their way from the Dalat area toward the coast. We offered them a blanket, asking in return that they give us some food and directions so we could join the others who had gone this way earlier.

They led us to their village, about an hour away. It was hidden under the dense foliage of tall trees. The villagers gave us corn, potatoes, and salt. We slept a few hours, and then two young men from the tribe led us through the jungle by torchlight. We began to meet other groups of all types: men, women, children, and troops. Soon we reached the assembly point where all units from our command were gathered.

From Ton That Thien, a former Boy Scout leader,[4] we learned that my company had arrived a day earlier. After sending my platoon ahead to reconnoiter the terrain, several other units came down the trail with knowledgeable guides to lead them. The company joined them, leaving behind a three-man team to let my platoon know what happened when we returned, and to leave after five days if we did not show up. Our rallying point, called Tra Kor, was deep in the jungle, surrounded by several villages inhabited by tribespeople.

It was relief to rejoin the company and see familiar faces again, although some were missing. Several had been killed or wounded and left behind after our recent actions, so we were down to just ninety men. We spent three days reorganizing and recouping our strength. Inhabitants came from all over the area, even as far as the coast some thirty kilometers away, bringing in food and other basic supplies.

Our situation was becoming very precarious. We had more people than we could care for and feed. We had to depend on the local population for food, and supplies were already running low. The French probably could not penetrate the jungle to this sector, but they knew where we were. A small Morane reconnaissance airplane flew over us and dropped leaflets occasionally. The leaflets urged people to return to their homes, and promised that there would be no reprisals against them.

Hard decisions had to be made, and when they were, the course of our young war of liberation changed dramatically.

4: PREPARING FOR LONG-TERM GUERRILLA WARFARE (1946)

The French offensive continued all through the spring of 1946. Mobile armored columns transported troops quickly up and down the road network. All major towns along the national highways and railway lines were taken and occupied, except in Inter-zone V from south of Danang through Phu Yen. Such resistance as our forces were able to put up was no match for the experienced, well-equipped soldiers France was now putting into the field. Our poorly armed volunteer army obviously could not be successful against them in conventional warfare.

The High Command realized that some volunteers would have to return home with the civilians. We simply did not have enough available supplies, arms, or ammunition for everyone. Our leaders did not want it to seem like they were rejecting anyone, however. That would cause serious loss of face. Besides, volunteers would be needed again in the future. If alienated now, would they respond as enthusiastically if they were called to fight again? The orders that came through for us to reduce our units to smaller sizes made it clear that everyone who left would be doing his duty just as much as those who remained. They would be placing "the interests of the country above their personal pride and dignity," the High Command pointed out. Those who stayed in the field faced difficult days and would have to be in excellent physical condition to survive and fight effectively. Those who returned to their homes would have to lend their support—and be prepared to return as soldiers when they were needed. Many went home reluctantly because they were not in shape to withstand the rigors of a tough jungle campaign.

All cadres had assembled the day before that dramatic decision was announced. Our leaders briefed us on national and local conditions. They informed us that the central government, headquartered in Hanoi and under Ho Chi Minh's leadership, now controlled nearly all regional and local resistance organizations. In the South our control ended in Phu Yen province, about 150 kilometers north of our present location, and roughly midway between Hué and Saigon.

The Chinese were moving into Hanoi and other major cities north of the sixteenth parallel, ostensibly to fulfill their mandate of disarming the Japanese in the North. There were about 200,000 Chinese—mostly new recruits who had been hungry for years and were literally starving. The Chinese also brought with them Vietnamese allies who were rivals of Ho and the Viet Minh. China intended to support these nationalists against the Viet Minh in their struggle for power. While the French were negotiating with the Chinese and Ho Chi Minh to take over the task of disarming Japanese soldiers in the North, the Chinese-supported nationalists became very aggressive. There were bloody encounters almost daily between them and Viet Minh adherents in the streets of Hanoi and in towns along the China-Vietnam border.

In the South, with the British helping (and the Japanese also, at times), General Leclerc and his recently arrived French troops captured the main cities and lines of communication, and were pushing toward the highlands. The Japanese were finally disarmed and repatriated by early 1946. Our Vietnamese forces had been forced to withdraw into the countryside and jungles. Practically speaking, we were capable of only small guerrilla actions: harassment, ambushes, and destruction of portions of main road and rail lines. (Acts of terrorism against the French and their Vietnamese collaborators also occurred frequently in French-controlled cities.) We had to reorganize and plan our tactics accordingly.

Reducing the size of our units came first. In my company, for example, twelve of the ninety men remaining finally volunteered to "make the sacrifice" and go home. A new company was formed, with two platoons instead of three. The platoon I led was reinforced and expanded to fifty-six men. My new company commander was Le Quang Nam, twenty-four years old, a former Boy Scout and elementary school teacher. The company political commissar was Ho Dac Tong, about the same age and a former clerk.

Headquarters instructed us to operate as independent companies; we would seldom be regrouped for combat at the battalion or higher level. A battalion commander and his counterpart political commissar would coordinate our efforts. They would also set up local guerrilla organizations. Units such as ours that made up the Viet Minh "Regular Army" were augmented by these auxiliary paramilitary organizations. They included provincial militia or Territorials, and local Self-Defense Forces made up of people from individual hamlets or small groups of neighboring villages.

The territorial units consisted of inhabitants who continued their normal civilian lives but who volunteered to serve in the struggle against the French and their collaborators in many ways: propaganda and conversion of the enemy to the revolutionary cause, gathering intelligence, placing mines and booby traps, setting small ambushes, harassing enemy positions, and even kidnapping and assassination.

The Self-Defense Forces included all cooperating local villagers—men, women, and children of all ages. Booby traps, mines, and hidden rifles were their usual weapons. Many of the men who left when we streamlined the regular units became active in the Territorial militia or local self-defense units when they returned to their homes. These units were independent, but they often backed up our operations and were our best source of intelligence.

The battalion commander and political commissar had many and varied duties. In addition to coordinating the activities of the regular forces, they were responsible for recruiting and organizing the local Self-Defense and Territorial units. They also had to contend with serious logistics problems: arranging for networks to provide food and other supplies for the regular troops, and setting up communication links in their own area and to organizations in other parts of the country.[1]

Overall, political commissars faced a more difficult task than the battalion commanders. The same was true at the company level.[2] In addition to duties already outlined, they also handled community relations, education (emphasized greatly, as we will see), propaganda, and a variety of other tasks. Most scholars, historians, and journalists who have written about Vietnam and the thirty years of war between 1945 and 1975 either have not realized the importance of the programs for which political commissars were responsible or have not stressed them enough in their writings. Since I saw how the commissars worked from the beginning, and later served as a battalion political officer myself, I may have a better perspective on their activities and importance. To my mind, their educational and community relations efforts were critical and may have had longer-lasting effects than anything else they did.

Policy demanded that volunteers who were illiterate must learn to read and write simple sentences within three months of joining a regular unit. Political commissars were responsible for organizing instruction, with those of us who had been fortunate enough to get good educations teaching others who had been less fortunate. They also organized the self-critique sessions that were an important part of our training and education, although the commissars did not run the meetings.

Many subjects were covered in these weekly sessions, which were led each time by a different person (selected at the beginning of each meeting) and attended by everyone, officers included. We discussed our work and operations since the last meeting; military life, our relations with each other and people in the surrounding communities, the need for self-discipline, and what we had learned during the previous week. Our commissars conducted political indoctrination meetings for the local populace as well as soldiers under their command. Their community relations work demanded high priority, since we were so dependent on local support.

We literally lived with the people, being billeted regularly in small groups with families in our areas of operation. When we left after staying with a family even one night, one member of the group was assigned to check and make sure that everything was left just as we had found it. By being as little a burden as possible we made sure we would be welcome there—and in other local homes—in the future. The importance of treating local people properly was emphasized in all of our self-discipline training.

The French occupied the cities of Phan Thiet, Phan Rang, Cam Ranh, Nha Trang, and a few other towns along Route 1, the main national road that paralleled the coast along the southern belly of the dragon between Saigon and Cap Varella. The French were unable to venture far on either side of that route outside the cities, however. To consolidate their control they had begun calling on former Vietnamese officials to rejoin them so they could set up a new puppet Vietnamese administration. They also recalled noncommissioned officers (there had been no Vietnamese commissioned officers) who had served with the French military before 1945. Those Vietnamese who joined them were organized for the most part in auxiliary units that manned fortified posts along the main routes.

Despite these measures, our revolutionary forces completely controlled the countryside, jungles, and mountains. Although many Vietnamese joined the French—or rejoined them, in the case of former collaborators—the overwhelming majority of the population supported our fight for independence. This fight went on openly in the country, secretly in the French-controlled cities. We received all of our supplies and intelligence from deep inside areas supposedly under the rule of France. Groups of people from those French-controlled areas often visited us. Our military intelligence personnel infiltrated such locations regularly, disguised as normal civilians. They often talked to French soldiers, usually in restaurants and bars. Many bar girls and prostitutes worked for our cause.

My company was assigned to operate in the area along the thirty-five- to forty-five-kilometer stretch of Route 1 from Thap Cham to Cam Ranh, about 225 kilometers east and slightly north of Saigon. We enjoyed few military successes during the early days of our assignment. We spent much of our time working, training, getting organized, and learning about the enemy and terrain in our operations area. For two months we worked closely with local guerrilla units—protecting the area's inhabitants, cutting trenches in the highway to delay traffic, and harassing fortified posts set up by the French but manned by Vietnamese. We did very well against these outposts but not so well against the better-armed French troops, including many combat veterans of World War II. Finally, however, we scored our first real victory over French troops.

The day started in routine fashion with a French armored patrol making its usual morning run to open the road between Thap Cham and Cam Ranh. Patrols had been making this same run daily for months without incident, except that they regularly had to stop at many places because of dummy mines placed in the road (we did not yet have enough real mines to use for this purpose) and trenches cut across its width. Often they rousted out local inhabitants to fill the cuts.

On this day, however, the patrol was stopped a few miles before reaching Cam Ranh by trenches in the road at the same place they encountered gaps the day before.

This time, however, the trench was larger and deeper. There were no peasants in sight to make repairs. Nor was there a mound of dirt nearby that could be used to fill in the trench; we had carried it away with the help of local Self-Defense Forces. After trying for more than an hour to get past the gap in the road, the patrol bypassed it, taking a detour toward Cam Ranh. Two or three miles away, the vehicles turned off on a trail that led to a village at the edge of the forest. The patrol's leaders probably hoped to find people they could conscript into a road repair crew.

I was surprised when I realized that the French were driving into the trap our company had been preparing for weeks. They were running their four armored vehicles into the ambush set down the trail, not even taking the precaution of deploying scouts in the rice fields on either side of the road. As rehearsed I let them move past the positions where my platoon lay hidden. The first vehicle ran into the well-camouflaged trench that lay in wait like a giant tiger trap. Hidden troops from the other platoon in my company opened fire simultaneously. The action was over in less than five minutes. The surprise was so complete that the French barely got off a few shots from the heavy machine guns mounted in the armored cars before our men cut them down.

I watched all this from my position less than a quarter-mile away where my platoon still lay hidden and silent, prepared to stop enemy reinforcements that might come at any time. Two French soldiers ran past us without their weapons. They were lucky; we were waiting for bigger game and let them escape. But the French in the garrison twenty-five kilometers away seemed to be unaware of the firefight that had just occurred. At least there was no sign of them yet.

Not until the rest of the company had "cleaned" the battlefield and withdrawn into the jungle did a Morane fly into sight. My platoon had been ordered to rejoin the company, and the last man from the unit had just gotten into the edge of the forest when the light plane appeared above the area. It spotted the ambush site and began circling to examine the situation. The company, well dispersed under trees, remained absolutely still and silent so as not to reveal our position. As the Morane moved away from our position, I slowly raised a pair of binoculars I had captured previously from the Japanese and looked over the scene. The four armored cars were still burning, and there were several bodies in sight. Three or four appeared to be severely injured, but still alive.

A relief column suddenly appeared on the road from Thap Cham, consisting of several transport trucks loaded with soldiers, plus armored cars to protect them. A second Morane flew above them. As the convoy approached the spot where the trail to the ambush site branched off from the road, the vehicles stopped and more than one hundred soldiers jumped out of the trucks. Then the convoy and soldiers on foot began moving cautiously down the trail; it took them more than an hour to go a distance that might normally be covered in about fifteen minutes. They rescued the wounded, recovered the dead—about thirty as far as we could tell—and began to withdraw as the sun was setting.

Then two fighter planes (British Spitfires, we learned later) flashed overhead. They dropped bombs on the neighboring villages and strafed the entire area for about fifteen minutes. As they flew back to their base, four more Spitfires roared overhead to drop more bombs and continue the strafing runs. Houses in the villages burned until well into the night, and two men from my platoon were hit during the strafing, one fatally.

It was ironic that my platoon, although not part of the actual firefight, suffered the only casualties. The dead man, Thao, was just seventeen years old and freshly out of school. He used to play the harmonica so well that all of us fell silent to listen whenever he drew it from his pocket or pack. I embraced him one last time; as I looked into his pale but serene face I couldn't help crying silently for a long moment. We buried him that night under a big tree and marked his grave with stones we found nearby.

Now it was the third day after that successful ambush, and we relaxed high above Cam Ranh Bay and the surrounding valley. As was our custom, we reviewed the action in great detail, trying to learn as much as we could from what had occurred. We tried to determine what improvements we might have made in our ambush plan so that we would do even better next time. One thing disturbed us: we could not be sure who had wounded three of our men from the platoon that launched the assault. Had they been hit by French bullets, or by friendly fire? We were uncertain, but we resolved to improve our fire control and discipline in the future, especially since this was not the first time we suspected that our own men had been hit by bullets from their fellow soldiers. Our policy of rehearsing actions over and over again before implementation was proving to be effective in all ways but this one, so further work was necessary.

On the plus side, the company captured a dozen British Sten submachine guns and two Bren machine guns. We were unable to remove the heavy machine guns mounted on the armored cars quickly enough to salvage them, so we destroyed them.

After three months of fighting in ambushes, harassment, and attacks on small posts manned by Vietnamese affiliated with the French, the company was reasonably well supplied with weapons. We now had about sixty rifles, ten submachine guns, two Bren guns, and one 60 mm mortar. About half the men were still armed only with machetes, however; they acted as ammunition bearers. Our big problem was the supply of ammunition and grenades. We couldn't carry enough with us, so we arranged to "lend" quantities to the Territorials in various areas. They supplied us when we needed the materiel, and used it in their own guerrilla activities as necessary. This fit in with the pattern of cooperation and division of duties previously described between army units, Territorials, and the People's Self-Defense Forces.

The Self-Defense Forces were the eyes and ears of the resistance. Since the organization included everyone—men, women, and children of all ages—living in areas controlled by the Resistance, those eyes and ears were everywhere. They kept widespread and constant surveillance over their areas, and gave the alert if enemy units approached. When an alert was signaled, everyone went immediately to hiding places prepared in advance: tunnels, remote forest retreats, and caves.

Then the Territorials activated mines and booby traps, and harassed the invaders with sniper fire, ambushes, and even attacks. In some cases when actions could be planned ahead to take advantage of special circumstances, our company (and regular army units in other areas) joined them. Sometimes we were able to inflict serious damage on the enemy in such actions.

French reaction after these ambushes and attacks was merciless. They burned houses and killed or captured any Vietnamese unlucky enough to be found. Women and young girls routinely were raped; many suffered group rape and died or were traumatized for the rest of their lives. Some were killed as they tried to escape the horror.

Actually the enemy forces were only partially French, most often the officers or noncommissioned officers. Many Foreign Legionnaires were deserters from the German Army. French colonies such as Morocco, Algeria, and Tunisia supplied many other recruits. Each month the French forces became better organized and better equipped; by this time they had artillery, tanks, and air and naval support. Many of their individual weapons were French-made, but there were also British and American heavy machine guns, mortars, artillery, and aircraft. We frequently saw British Spitfires and Mosquitoes and German Junkers in the skies above us.

It was less than six months since I joined the Liberation Army, but already more than thirty men in my company had been killed and several others severely wounded. New volunteers filled the ranks; all of them came from the Territorial forces, so they already had some basic training and experience. Now I was to leave the company and join a cadre group bound for the South Central Command Headquarters in Quang Ngai province, three hundred kilometers north of our present position. I would take special training with a new mobile regiment being formed to conduct larger, wide-ranging actions against the enemy. Lai Hung, my assistant platoon leader, was promoted to replace me.

Two days earlier, after my new orders had come through, the company had given me an emotional farewell party while we were still relaxing on the hillside above Cam Ranh Bay. It was both a sad and happy occasion: sad because only twenty of the forty-two men in my platoon were veterans of the original unit, happy because we had survived more than twenty actions against the enemy. We all reflected on the blood, suffering, and emotions we had experienced in just six months, including the loss—dead or wounded seriously—of twenty-two of our comrades. Everyone wished me well in my new assignment, knowing that just reaching headquarters in Quang Ngai province would mean a hard, dangerous trek.

The French controlled the road network in that area for approximately the first 100 kilometers of the distance to command headquarters. From Cam Ranh to the border between Khanh Hoa (Nha Trang) and Phu Yen provinces they had built many fortified posts, manned by their Vietnamese auxiliaries. French garrisons supported these outposts with mobile patrols, day and night, and artillery. Light observation planes flew the area during most of the daylight hours. All this activity made it very hazardous to be on or near the roads.

I joined the group of thirty men selected from various battalions operating in different parts of the South. When they entered our area, I reported to the leader, Ha Thanh Toai, a man of about twenty-five with an accent that identified him as a native of Quang Ngai. Toai was a Railway Systems employee before joining the Army of Liberation; he had rapidly been promoted to company commander at a regiment base in Phan Thiet, about one hundred kilometers north of Saigon.

We began our march just before sunset. Two guides from the local Territorial unit led the way, and an armed squad from the provincial Territorials brought up the rear. People from the local Self-Defense Force helped guide us in their areas and supplied our food. During our trip we were passed from one group of Territorials to another as we moved into different areas of operation. The same was true of help supplied by the Self-Defense Forces; people from each locality assisted and supplied us as we passed through their villages and hamlets.

Everything went smoothly as we wound our way along jungle trails that first evening and through the night that followed. By sunrise the next morning, although we were still in a dense forest, the guides told us we were approaching a large open field. We stopped, ate some rice and dried fish, then stretched our raincoats out on the ground and lay down on them to rest. Everything was quiet and we slept, taking turns to stand guard in pairs to keep watch for enemy patrols or dangerous wild animals. Many of the latter lurked in the area, including several varieties of large snakes.

We were all awake again by three o'clock in the afternoon. After a simple meal, more rice and dried fish, the group leader called a meeting to review our march so far and our itinerary and schedule for the days ahead. Such items as individual physical and emotional health and individual and collective discipline were discussed. To conclude, several of us had to deliver a brief autobiography: family background, military history since joining the Army of Liberation, actions against the enemy his unit had been involved in, and any other items of interest. One or two of us would relate his story each day; thus, everyone would have a turn before the end of our march.

One young man who told of his past that day was Mang, a twenty-two-year-old unmarried farmer from the far north. He had been landless and worked on a French rubber plantation in the South before volunteering. Mang was typical of the landless farmers who had to work for landowners, generation after generation, just to make enough to exist. The French demanded that all Vietnamese adults pay an annual tax, whether they earned any money during the year or not. They also had to work without pay for the community a certain number of days each year. Like tens of thousands who were unable to pay the "personal tax," Mang signed up to go south and work on French plantations. Recruiters for French planters were strongly supported by local Vietnamese administrators (under French supervision). The agricultural recruits received enough money to pay personal taxes for themselves and their families. However, once in the plantations, a thousand miles from home, they had to work under the harshest conditions for wages so low that local inhabitants refused to take such jobs. (Farmers in the South were better off than those in the North.) It isn't surprising that Mang and thousands of others in the same situation were among the first to volunteer for the Liberation Army. The big French rubber plantations, like Michelin north of Saigon, were incubators for the Viet Minh and then the next-generation Viet Cong.

Other benefits came from these meetings and relating our autobiographies to each other. We learned a lot about ourselves, individually and as a group; we also learned a lot about what had been happening in the war over the past six months. These things all contributed to our ongoing education about our revolution, our country, and our grasp of military matters.

Soon it was time to continue our march. We fell in behind the guides, following their footsteps along the narrow forest trails. We continued through the darkness all night and by daybreak reached the location where new guides and an armed squad from a different Territorial unit were scheduled to meet us. They weren't there, which caused us great concern. The guides and squad who had accompanied us this far were not authorized to take us any farther. They would be going into a new, unfamiliar area, and there was a chance that they would unknowingly lead us all into danger. Uncertain about what to do, we finally decided to stay where we were and hope our new guides would show up eventually. We arranged a guard duty schedule; those who were not on watch went to sleep. Our guides were restless, however, and decided to reconnoiter the area, taking half the armed squad with them, to see if they could find a trace of our missing "welcoming party." They would also make sure our location was secure and that there were no enemy patrols in the vicinity.

I was on guard duty, rather bored and still a bit sleepy, when gunfire erupted from the jungle. Everyone was wide awake in seconds. The firing was relatively close, but we could see nothing through the dense forest foliage. The shooting continued, obviously heading our way. Two men from the armed squad who had gone out with the guides suddenly burst into sight and ran toward us. They waved for us to turn and run also. Instead, we posted the remaining six men of the armed squad in a defensive combat formation and waited for the worst to happen. We all agreed that if the enemy did pursue, they would have to follow the same trail as our men because the forest was so dense they could not penetrate it otherwise.

The two men ran into our midst, winded and peering fearfully down their back trail. They had been ambushed by a French patrol when they reached the edge of the forest. The two guides and two other members of the armed squad were either dead or captured. The pair who escaped were certain the French were in close pursuit. Still we saw no sign of the enemy patrol. In a quick conference we all agreed with the group leader that we were not adequately armed to fight a French patrol. Instead, we must try to save ourselves and survive to become cadres for the new unit as our orders commanded. We moved off the trail and hid in deep cover, reasonably sure by now that the French could not find us because of the difficult terrain.

Airplanes began circling overhead, probably light observation planes. Then came the throatier roar of powerful Spitfires, boring in for bombing and strafing runs; aircraft probably were used because we were too far from the French positions for artillery to be effective. The Spitfire pilots kept up their sorties for hours, periodically leaving to refuel and rearm their aircraft, but without much success. Many of their bombs fell as far as two or three miles away from our hiding places. None of us was hurt. The bombing and strafing finally ended, but we remained hidden until nearly sunset. Then we spotted another group of Vietnamese, also guided by Territorials, approaching on the same trail we had used. Another man and I were appointed to greet the new arrivals while the rest of our band remained undercover, just in case. We quickly learned that the newcomers were on their way to Quang Ngai for new assignments, just as we were. The group consisted of some twenty-five men and ten women; they had been on the trail for a week since leaving the Phan Rang headquarters in the Ba Rau jungle.

"Chau, Tran Ngoc Chau!" a voice called out suddenly. I glanced around in confusion at hearing my name in this remote forest. I was even more confused for just a moment when I realized that the caller was a girl. Then I recognized her: it was Huong Giang, a young woman of nineteen whom I had met more than a year ago in Dalat. She was a graduate of the Convent of Birds (Couvent des Oiseaux) and daughter of a hotel owner in that lovely resort city. This convent, founded by French missionaries, was reserved exclusively for the daughters of wealthy French and

Vietnamese businessmen or high-placed government dignitaries. The last empress, Bao Dai's wife, had been a resident student at this convent.

Huong Giang was a beautiful girl, with her long black hair undulating as smoothly as the water flowing between the two banks of the Perfume River at Hué, where her family also resided. When I first met her I was especially attracted by her lovely dark eyes, so deep and penetrating that they seemed to look into my soul. They certainly reached my heart. Through her I had met the young girl, Hong, who was responsible for me being where I was at that time. Hong was the young woman who had been shot as a spy in Cau Dat, and whose death made me decide to leave the intelligence service and volunteer for combat.

Our two groups gathered that night around a well-concealed fire near a stream and discussed our situation. Should we go forward, stay where we were, or send someone back to ask for further instructions? First, we decided that the guides should not venture another forward reconnaissance. Then we decided to join forces, with the two leaders sharing the command. The leader of the second group would become political commissar due to his seniority. Early the next morning we posted two three-man teams near the trail in case more of our people showed up. The rest of us marched up the stream to hide signs of our passage. We waded through shallow water for about a mile, then stopped and took cover again. Late in the day, a group of local Territorials, led by one of our two former guides who had been missing since the ambush, met our two teams, who led them to our new campsite.

We were now able to reconstruct what had caused the ambush of our two guides and their patrol. The night before we were to meet our new escorts, a French unit had moved into the area. They knew the trail was used frequently by Vietnamese to bypass their controlled areas, but the French forces rarely attempted interceptions. On those occasions when they did, Territorials punished them with mines, booby traps, sniping, and ambushes, causing heavy casualties. This time, however, the French had infiltrated successfully, bypassing our Vietnamese surveillance. They captured the waiting guides, but our armed squad was far enough behind so that its members were able to withdraw silently. The French had remained in position, however, waiting for another group to stumble into their ambush.

Fortunately, the two guides and patrol members who had been with us went ahead and triggered the French trap, so the rest of us escaped. Even now, however, a large group of French and their auxiliary forces were occupying the area. We expected them to mount a reconnaissance into the jungle and launch an attack if they located us. We sent the surviving guide and what remained of his squad back to report our situation to headquarters. Meanwhile, we would remain hidden in our new campsite, knowing we were safe because the French couldn't trace our passage through the stream. We remained there two days without any communications.

Although a tense time, I personally found it very pleasant because it gave Huong Giang and I time to talk about what had happened to us since we had last seen each other. I learned that she had volunteered to serve with the Red Cross when the War of Independence began the previous August. She had taken abbreviated nurse's training and had served at the regional command headquarters, caring for wounded. She had been encouraged to return home but refused, as did several of her girlfriends. Later she had been selected to join the group going to Quang Ngai for assignment. Two of her girlfriends had also been sent on the same mission; I had met them briefly in the past but did not know them well.

In fact, teenaged Vietnamese boys and girls of our class did not have much opportunity to become acquainted in normal times. They went to separate schools, and dating in the American sense was virtually unknown. A young boy and girl might meet in the presence of their families, but usually only after a promise of engagement had been made and accepted by both families. Young people who had secret dates were rejected by their families and scorned by others. It was a very straitlaced, almost puritanical society. One of my brothers and my two sisters saw their spouses for the first time on their wedding days. All wedding arrangements were made by the two families concerned.

There were some occasions when a boy and girl might see each other briefly, at family parties and other social events, but always in the presence of others, never alone. In Dalat, my first meetings with Huong Giang had been in a library; we met there on occasion by arranging to arrive "accidentally" at the same time. We did not pay obvious attention to each other, however, talking only a little and always very quietly. We often spoke about books; once she asked if I had read *Paul and Virginie*, and another time she asked if I liked *Graziella*. (In fact, I had read both several years earlier; the two French romances were considered "musts" for boys and girls between fifteen and seventeen at that time.) Another time I found her to be fascinated with Victor Hugo's *Les Misérables*.

Her reading gave me clues to her character. She not only had a young girl's normal delight in romantic literature but she showed a concern for society by her interest in Hugo's work. This was further demonstrated by her decision to volunteer for service. Our tenuous relationship had been interrupted when I left Hué, but her penetrating eyes and beautiful hair had often been in my memory. Now we met again, and the revolution had changed our lives dramatically, as we both realized. We could talk freely and openly about any subject.

The character of everyone was challenged, from the nobles and aristocrats down through the bourgeois to "les misérables," the peasants and urban poor who made up the vast majority of Vietnam's people. It became obvious that noble birth or position did not guarantee nobleness of soul, and vice versa. Many wealthy, highborn

Vietnamese joined in the fight, and peasants often proved to be intelligent, capable leaders. Patriotism and the desire to change an unjust, inhumane society became the powerful hidden source of energy, vitality, and compassion that propelled the whole nation. The rich and the poor, the privileged and the exploited, the intellectuals and the illiterate all embraced the revolution, thirsting for national and individual dignity and freedom. The vast majority knew nothing about communism or socialism; few even knew the names of Marx or Lenin, much less were familiar with their writings.

None of us, virtually all from classes regarded as reactionary according to Communist ideology, ever wondered about Ho Chi Minh's Communist affiliations or what communism would mean to our country in the future. For now, we considered those who expressed sympathy with our cause as friends, those who sided with the French as enemies. People were interested only in the fact that Ho Chi Minh had proved capable of raising the entire nation against all outsiders who were trying to force Vietnam back into its pre–World War II state of oppression.

There were those who collaborated with the French, of course; some believed sincerely that the French were unbeatable and fighting them would only bring unnecessary harm to the country. They felt that World War II had changed world politics drastically and France would have to improve conditions for its colonies. Most Vietnamese allied with the French, however, were mean, selfish opportunists, pretending to oppose Communism to further their own interests. Basically, there were only two choices at the time. Ho Chi Minh with Bao Dai and other prominent Vietnamese nationalists represented one side; the French invaders and their toadies were on the other side.

After spending two days holed up in our concealed campsite waiting for orders from the High Command, we received word that we could no longer use the route originally planned for us. The French not only remained in the area but were also building a strong garrison to expand their control over the whole sector. A new group of Territorials arrived with two tribal guides from the highlands to help us find a new and safer route. They led us upstream first, with all of us wading through the shallow water again so we would leave no sign for the enemy.

The soaking completed the destruction of the shoes I had been wearing for many months, and I was forced to walk barefoot. (As it happened, it would be a full two years before I was able to wear shoes again.) It was painful, and became more painful each time I had the malaria attacks that had been regular events for months. When malaria first hit me, at Cau Dat, I was unable to move or eat for several days. A large dose of quinine cured it, or so I thought. Then, four months prior to this point, the attacks began occurring every week. Others had the same problem, and we soon exhausted our meager supply of quinine. By now I was so used to the acute malaria attacks that I could predict the day and hour when they would hit me. About twenty of us in the group suffered the twin problems of malaria and walking barefoot through the cold water of the stream.

Huong Giang nursed all of us who had malaria, but openly showed her special concern for me. The group was tolerant of our obvious attachment to each other, since we had been friends earlier in civilian life and because our relationship, although more than simple friendship, remained strictly platonic.

We now resumed our daily unit discussions, and new members of the group had opportunities to introduce themselves. Instruction in reading and writing began again; we often used the ground as our blackboard to write out words and illustrate various points. We even recited poems and chanted songs. I was given the title of "poet" because of my recitations of works ranging from Vietnamese poets Xuan Dieu, Huy Can, and Quach Tan to such Frenchmen as Victor Hugo and Paul Verlaine. It was a painful journal physically, but mentally energizing. Nobody in the group ever complained, even when we had to reduce our food rations severely because our supply was very low. We were always climbing, moving always upward into the highlands.

Five days after we began our detour on the new route we were high in the mountains in the vicinity of Cam Ranh Bay. It was almost as though we were on a cliff immediately above the sea. The stretch of flat land between the foot of the mountain and the ocean was so narrow when viewed from this altitude that it seemed almost to disappear. We had left the big stream the day before and had spent the previous night in the first hamlet of highlanders that we had encountered. The village consisted of about ten homes built of logs and covered with a roof of thatched grass. It was warm now, though chilly during the night. We enjoyed a fire after a big meal of chicken and a little drink of liquor that the Montagnards made from corn and stored in large earthen jars. It was the first time these primitive but charming people had met "lowlanders," as they referred to us. They were very self-sufficient, happy with their life in which nature supplied all of their simple needs.

Their manner was natural and innocent. Men and women both wore skirts of a sort, but the women did not feel it necessary to cover their upper bodies. None of the villagers took notice, but the women in our group felt somewhat embarrassed. I did, too. I remembered what our religious teachings recorded: that Buddha said it was the insanity of the mind, the conscience, and the soul inside a person that pictured the objects outside. These primitive people surely had purity and innocence inside them so they felt natural and at ease with their seminudity, while more civilized people, as we considered ourselves, might not have the same inner purity.

We spent another day relaxing and enjoying the villagers' hospitality. After days on short rations it was a pleasure to have abundant meals again. The rest gave everyone in the group a chance to recuperate from the trip up the rugged mountain streambed. When we set out on our journey again, we changed our schedule. Now we marched during the day and rested at night. We lit big campfires to warm us and to keep wild animals and snakes at bay. My feet were less painful now, as calluses formed and thickened. Our individual packs were lighter because we gave some of our clothes to our Highland hosts, who accepted the clothes with excitement, but probably more as items of curiosity than anything they needed for comfort.

The wild trail we followed was difficult, whether we were climbing another steep grade or descending toward the plain we reached after crossing the mountainous barrier separating Pham Rang and Khanh Hoa provinces. We had to follow this route to avoid the French, who controlled the main road linking the two provinces and the narrow plain that extended along the coast between the sea and the mountain range. We used ropes to help each other and as insurance against anyone falling down the precipitous slopes.

We had trekked for twelve days when we finally reached the edge of the plain in Khanh Hoa province on the other side of the mountain range. It was noon when we arrived. Rice fields stretched out before us, level and green, in sharp contrast to the mountains we had just left. We saw farmers and their water buffalo working in the paddies, while others went about their chores on dikes that separated the fields.

Guides from the lowlands replaced the Montagnards who had led us through the highlands. We were now in contact with the local Territorial forces, who told us that the French had yet to venture into this area. They recommended that we not travel during daylight, however, because there were aerial patrols by light reconnaissance planes. We would be easy to spot in the open terrain. We crossed the open fields that night, reaching another forest long before sunrise. We rested for the remainder of the night and set out again the next morning. We were now in a thick forest with tall trees towering above us as protection from discovery by airplane patrols. The trails showed traces of frequent use by buffalo, used to haul timber in the area. We covered more miles in that one day than we had in the last four or five days we spent coming down the mountain.

The next day, however, we learned that the French had attacked in force at a location called the Stream of Cam Xe, destroying a transit center there and driving our people to flee in all directions. Once more we had to halt and wait for clarification of the situation, and perhaps another change in our routing. The French soon withdrew, suffering losses to snipers and booby traps. Order was reestablished, and we set off once more. Two days later we found ourselves near Route 21, which linked Nha Trang to the Highlands via Ninh Hoa.

Open fields stretched for miles. The area was well patrolled and guarded day and night. It would be impossible for a group as large as ours to cross the highway without a good chance of being spotted out in the open, even at night. We broke up into small teams of no more than five, planning to cross the road and open area surrounding it at intervals during darkness, while the Territorials provided diversions by faking attacks on several guard posts two or three miles from our points of passage. The plan worked perfectly. The French rushed to the positions where the Territorials feinted attacks, leaving behind only limited forces that stayed well undercover in the posts near us. We were somewhat threatened by flares and artillery fire, but made the crossing without any casualties. We regrouped long before sunrise far on the other side of the patrolled highway.

We spent the next day resting and took up our march again at nightfall, passing through an entire sleeping village in the dark. The night was quiet, but we heard occasional artillery fire from far behind us, in the area where we had crossed the highway the previous night.

Since the beginning of the revolution, all dogs in country villages near French positions had been sacrificed so that guerrillas could operate without drawing attention. People gathered almost every night to cut trenches and place obstacles in roads, usually with grenades or mines hidden in them, to halt vehicle traffic. The French had to reopen the routes daily, exposing themselves to casualties from booby traps and snipers hidden along the roadsides.

It took us ten days to finally cross a plain (interspersed with small woods or forests where we could hide) about 110 kilometers wide. By then we had reached the foot of another mountain range, one that separated the provinces of Khanh Hoa and Phu Yen. The only highway and railway passing through tunnels in the mountains and the narrow pass near Cap Varella were in the firm grasp of the French. But we were too excited at the prospect of reaching the "Free Zone" on the other side of this range of mountains to be concerned for the moment about how we would cross our newest obstacle.

5: TREK TO THE "FREE Z" (1946)

We didn't realize the difficulty of the task that still faced us as we regrouped on the other side of Route 21. Nor did our guides give us any time to think about what lay behind or ahead of us. They pushed us to move rapidly, wanting to get as far away from the highway as possible before sunrise. The trek was painful. We had spent a great deal of energy over the past three days, and we had to carry an extra burden. A man and a woman in the group came down with such bad cases of influenza that they could not keep up with us; we had to take turns carrying them. Much to our relief we reached a village as the sun was clearing the horizon, and we were still well covered by a heavy fog. The villagers fed us a hot meal, tea and chicken, which tasted like a banquet after days on short rations. We then split up into teams of three to five and were billeted in houses scattered through the village.

For now we were safely out of sight, with friendly villagers to keep watch for us. So we slept the whole day, awakening in the evening to enjoy another big meal. We discussed the events of the past few days, covering the performance of each individual and of the group as a whole. The hospitable villagers gave us enough food for the next day, and we set out once again on our march. With the highway and French patrols far behind, plus a dense fog for cover, we felt more secure than we had in days.

We followed the same schedule for three more nights and four days: marching along narrow trails all night and holing up in villages during the day. Then we arrived at the jumping-off point for our climb. I'm sure the others in the group were as awed as I was by the menacing face of the mountain as it stretched up, almost straight up, it seemed to me, toward the clouds.

By contrast, our resting place was a natural Eden, next to a large stream with water cascading melodically down stair-steps of stones, and hidden under a canopy of tall trees. Flowers, shrubs, and ferns surrounded us. The site was a regular stop-over point for groups en route to and from the Free Zone. Members of a Territorial unit and volunteers from the local population who lived about twenty-five kilometers away took turns coming here to supply food whenever they were notified that groups like ours were due. Rice and salt were cached there; there was plenty of dried beef, and fishermen from the coast supplied dried fish.

We were in the midst of what formerly was a huge French farm, or ranch, with thousands of acres of rich land and stocks of cattle, buffalo, sheep, and fowl. The farm supplied food to cities along Highway 1, sending stock and produce to market via the railway that paralleled the highway from Saigon to Hanoi. Just one track, used by carts and trucks, linked the farm to the nearest railway station, about fifty kilometers away.

A year earlier, in March 1945, after the Japanese coup, the French owner abandoned the farm and disappeared from the scene. Local people destroyed all buildings on the property on orders from the revolutionary provincial headquarters. This was part of the national resistance policy of destroying anything that might be useful to the French in their efforts to force Vietnam back into subservient colonial status.

All of the animals had been running loose ever since, so there were thousands of domestic cows, buffalo, sheep, and chickens dispersed in the area, breeding and furnishing food for the resistance. Hunting them, or any of the wild game animals that thrived there, with firearms was strictly forbidden. There was no spare ammunition to waste, and shots would alert French reconnaissance units if they managed to infiltrate the area. It was not very difficult to catch enough of the formerly tame stock, using traps and snares, even bows and arrows, to feed the local cadres and troops in transit through this sector.

The French did make several sorties from their nearest garrisons at Van Gia and Tu Bong. Both were near the coast on Highway 1, about thirty kilometers away. They succeeded on one earlier raid in reaching the area where we were now staying because the Territorial forces were taken by surprise and had to disappear into the dense forest at the foot of the mountain. Since then, the local units worked hard to prepare for enemy raids. They studied the terrain and set mines and booby traps at key points along the main track and lesser trails that might be used to enter the heart of the huge farm in surprise attacks. They selected positions for snipers and ambushes. Even the best resting places along the way were planted with explosive surprises for invaders. The Territorials rehearsed time after time how they would react to attacks. First, they would oppose the enemy if possible. Second, against strong forces they would retreat and evacuate civilians; third, they would set out ambushes in the path of enemy advance and withdrawal routes. As a result, French units suffered serious harassment during later raids, and had nothing to show for their trouble in the way of prisoners, resistance members killed, or captured arms. They found the price too high to try very often.

In Hanoi, now capital of the newly formed Democratic Republic of Vietnam, the French and Ho Chi Minh signed the March 6 Accord, which recognized Vietnam as a free state. In return, the accord authorized the French to move into the North to replace the Chinese forces who first arrived to disarm Japanese troops. The hurriedly formed Chinese "army" included only a small percentage of regular army soldiers; the rest were hungry Chinese, poorly armed and undisciplined, who were recruited into the army mainly to ease China's severe postwar problems. Every day dozens died in the streets, simply because they ate too much too fast after years of starvation during their war against the Japanese. Vietnamese nationalists led by Nguyen Hai Than who returned from China with the ragtag troops thus suffered a bad image problem as a result of their association with the Chinese. The same thing happened in varying degrees to other Vietnamese nationalist leaders supported by China.

As a result, more people rallied to Ho Chi Minh and the Viet Minh, despite claims by some nationalist leaders that Ho was "selling out the country" to France while he was negotiating the accord. During the same period France made a deal with Kuomintang China (the National People's Party). It returned the Guangzhouwan area (now known as Zhanjiang), transferring title to the Yunnan Railroad, and relinquished extraterritorial rights in Shanghai and other cities, in return for agreement that French units would replace Chinese troops in North Vietnam. With the Chinese withdrawal and French arrival, opposition nationalist leaders and their followers faded away in the North, leaving Ho Chi Minh in firm control.

In the South, the situation was more confused. The British, while performing their official duty of disarming Japanese troops south of the sixteenth parallel, rearmed the French. Later, with new troops arriving from France and other French colonies, Britain returned authority over South Vietnam to the French generals. French troops had gradually extended their territory in recent months, expanding their control to the edges of the mountain highlands; the resistance still controlled the countryside. Guerrilla activity continued, by various combinations of the Army of Liberation and Territorial and People's Self-Defense forces acting alone or in coordinated actions.

Huong Giang and I were able to enjoy a few moments alone. She had changed physically: from the graceful, romantic girl I had first known two years earlier to a thoughtful, athletic woman in her early twenties. The hardships of war and the inspiration of the revolution transformed her and other women in her group, as it had done for millions of other Vietnamese. Huong Giang's penetrating eyes still had the same effect on me, however, disturbing not only my heart and sentiments, but also my head and reasoning. The more I fell in love with her, the more closely I felt our love was intertwined with the mutual love we shared for our country and its people. By now there was no question about the depth of our feelings for each other, but neither of us dared to express them in words. We seldom even looked at each other directly for more than an instant. We were both unsophisticated. I had completed seven years of Buddhist religious education not many years earlier, and Huong Giang had been educated in a Catholic convent school. Neither of us had experience in dealing with the opposite sex on a personal level.

Also, we were both so dedicated to the struggle for independence that we felt this was no time for romantic attachments. We had pledged ourselves to our country and belonged to it so completely that there was no room for personal involvement. In a sense, we were betrothed to our cause; giving in to our feelings for each other would dishonor that betrothal. I know that my longing to hold Huong Giang in my arms made me feel very guilty and unworthy, as though I was betraying a trust. Yet often I caught her eyes watching me so intently and innocently that my heart was afire and my head reeled.

At times she was reflective and talked about how many of us had lived in a "golden cage":

"But how about the futures of our country and men like the ones we have been helping learn to read and write? We both know that neither you or I nor any other individual could do anything to regain our country's independence or change the human conditions of its people. They would continue in the darkness of ignorance as servants or workers for people of our class. And their children would continue on the same path, serving to enrich our children and make their lives comfortable. If all of us work together, however, we *can* change things! Our fathers and ancestors, whether by active cooperation or passive acceptance, enabled the French to impose a colonial system that produced both inhumane treatment for the masses and riches for the privileged people like you and me. Are we going to follow their paths or should we pay their debts and rid Vietnam and its people of its oppressors? By fighting to free our country of the enemy we can free ourselves from the enemy's mold: Western comfort, 'civilized' rhetoric, and unconscionable selfishness."

Suddenly I realized that Huong Giang was crying, softly and with great sadness. I was deeply moved myself, with my religious beliefs adding weight to the words of this slim young girl, who was far wiser than her age would suggest. For years to come I remembered Huong Giang as she was on that day and how her silhouette was reflected on the water of the stream beside us.

Another group came up from the South to join us on the final leg of our journey to command headquarters in the Free Zone of Quang Ngai province. We set out early in the morning with local guides in the lead, followed by three three-man teams whose job was to plant stakes and ropes to help the rest of the group make the climb. The trail was very steep and narrow. We quickly learned that our knees did indeed touch our mouths as we climbed! By noon we were high on the mountainside; the sun must have been high overhead but we couldn't see it; the vegetation was too dense. The trail snaked along a narrow ledge beside waterfalls that plunged down the streambed. We were all hot and sweating, despite the fresh, cool air and shade. The women climbed slowly but made steady progress.

One man fell, taking with him a second man who tried to stop his fall. They managed to grab some trees before they went too far and were only bruised and shaken.

It took them an hour to regain the spot from where they had fallen, however, even though we let ropes down and took turns helping them.

We spent two more days and nights following the same routine, finally reaching the top of the mountain at noon on the third day of climbing. The cliffs that had hung over us gave way to a broad, flat mesa with trees growing so tall and thick overhead that no small trees or shrubs grew under them. There were teak and other valuable timber trees, but the area was so remote they had never been harvested.

The guides seemed to lose their way for a long hour, but eventually came back and led us to a comfortable campsite. It was sheer luxury to rest on level ground and enjoy the warmth of a campfire again. The next morning we walked out of the woods and into the bright sunlight, which dazzled us at first, after our days in the dim jungle. We stood on an immense plain atop the high mountains in the narrow waist that linked the south central highland to the shores of the South China Sea. Trees became scarce, and there were patches of cultivated ground. From here we could see greenery that seemed to stretch to infinity across jungles, forests, hills, and mountains of all shapes and altitudes in every direction. Far to the east, the green blanket sloped smoothly down until it appeared to dip into the blue sea. We were all invigorated by the splendor of the scenery and the clear mountain air mixed with the tang of salty breezes blowing in from the coast. A new team of guides from Phu Yen province met us that night and led us to a Montagnard village for our overnight stop.

It had taken almost four days to traverse the mountains in Khanh Hoa province. Now we were in Phu Yen province at the southern limit of the Free Zone. This side of the mountain was more hospitable than the Khanh Hoa side, sloping gently down with Montagnard villages spaced eight to fifteen kilometers apart. We spent another night in one of these villages, then arrived at a Vietnamese community. I've never forgotten its name: Lien Hiep My, which means approximately "the Federation of America" when translated into English.

Now we were back in typical Vietnamese lowlands, with rice fields seeming to stretch out to the horizon and farmers silhouetted against the hazy skies. Standing alone in that plain of rice was a hill, a small mountain really, that rose abruptly out of the flat land. Local people called it Nhat Son (the One Mountain). We stayed in a nearby hamlet, warmly received by the villagers, who offered us flowers, food, and tea. A cow was roasted for the occasion, and a party followed our meal, with songs, classical theater, and speeches.

We were honored as heroes of the Resistance and vowed to continue our struggle against the colonialists and their puppets. We were told that the final victory would free all of us from colonialism, illiteracy, and oppression. Everyone would be equal; the people would share resources exploited by the French for years. We now had a de facto Vietnamese government, even if it was not internationally recognized, created in the interests of the people. The people would have a voice as to who governed them in the future.

Speakers stressed that those who had worked under the French and their puppets, by choice or force, would be welcomed back to the cause of our motherland without prejudice. As if to prove the rhetoric, the village committee chairman introduced a committee member who formerly was a village official under the French system. Nearly all of the other committee members were farmers, however, except for one teacher and several small landowners.

The next day we passed quickly through rice fields to a path running along a canal leading to Tuy Hoa City. The French had built the canal as a waterway to transport such products as lumber, rice, and sugar from outlying areas to the Tuy Hoa railway station. That night was the first we had spent in a city since beginning our march about three weeks earlier. But little was left of Tuy Hoa as it had been when it was provincial capital of Phu Yen. There was no electricity, and buildings had been reduced to rubble as part of the "Destroy to Resist" policy. Only a few small houses were still habitable, and trenches had been dug everywhere to protect residents from French air raids and naval bombardment, which leveled almost everything that the local population had not previously destroyed.

Our route toward Quang Ngai, capital of Quang Ngai province, took us along Route 1, the north-south national highway that parallels the coast. We spent fifteen days and nights covering the about 500 kilometers, marching fourteen to sixteen hours each day. En route we saw the same scenes repeated: buildings and bridges destroyed, railways and highways cut by deep trenches every half-mile or so. Individual- and group-slit trenches dug by the people for protection against French incursions dotted the landscape, and the people were all organized, with Territorial units ready for action at a moment's notice.

Whenever we stopped in a village for the night, or passed one during the evening before stopping, we saw crowds of residents gathered for political lectures and informational talks. A tremendous sense of unity and patriotism was evident everywhere.

Our march was relatively uneventful, especially when compared to our previous adventures and hardships. French reconnaissance planes surprised us several times, calling in warplanes to strafe and bomb. We got dirty from diving for cover but suffered no casualties. Ours was a tired but exultant group upon finally reaching our destination after a long and arduous trek.

Quang Ngai—unlike Tuy Hoa and Qui Nhon, two provincial capitals we had passed through—was deep inland, not on the coast. So it was immune to naval bombardment, and too far to be reached by planes from the French base at Nha Trang—

thus safe from air raids. Most of its buildings remained intact, and people from a wide area of the surrounding countryside filled its streets. The city was headquarters for the Regional Administration and Military Command of South Central Vietnam, which covered the vast territory, including all the coastal and highland provinces. This territory's northern boundary lay near Danang to the north. The southern boundary was just north of Bien Hoa province, next to Saigon.

Quang Ngai was also the assembly area for all units moving down from the North or up from the South. Residents had long been known for their heavy regional accent. Now, however, you could also hear people speaking with the diplomatic nuances of Hanoi, the new national capital; the poetic accent of Hué, the old capital; and the popular accent of the far South. There was a daily train running to some outlying localities, and even a few cars and trucks in the streets. Quang Ngai had become a cosmopolitan city in its own small way.

Our quarters occupied a compound that formerly had housed the French Civil Guard, a colonial military force of Vietnamese troops commanded by French officers and noncommissioned officers.[1] A high brick wall with just one entrance encircled the compound, which was guarded day and night. All but one or two of the buildings housed us while we trained to become part of a new and different kind of regiment. ("Antirevolutionaries" were confined in the remaining buildings.) The name of the new regiment was Trung Doan Doc Lap, which has a dual meaning in Vietnamese: "independence" and "independent." Both meanings applied to the unit. It was to be a strike force in the War of Independence, and it was to operate independently from any other unit, directly under the Southern Central Vietnam High Command. Trung Doan Doc Lap was made up of men assembled from different units spread out over the entire military region. We underwent intensive training split into two phases: political and military.

Our commander in chief was General Nguyen Son, a strong, sturdily built man of about forty-five or fifty, who was famous for his oratory, his strict discipline, and his ability to launch surprise attacks against the French. He had fled Vietnam as a young student during the 1920s to escape arrest for his anti-French activities. He then joined the Chinese Communists and shortly became an officer in the Red Army. After he survived the Commune of Canton and the Long March, a division commander by that time, Mao Tse-tung named him a Chinese national hero. Son returned to Vietnam in 1942 and offered his services to Ho Chi Minh, who appointed him commander of the central Highland and South Central Vietnam.

Such detailed stories about many of our leaders were uncommon. We actually knew very little about the men in the command hierarchy and were ready to accept any accounts that made them seem worthy of admiration. We needed modern Vietnamese leaders to look up to, since there had been none so far in the twentieth century to match such legends of our past as the Trung sisters, Le Loi and Tran Hung Dao, who repulsed the forces of Kubla Khan in the thirteenth century. As a result, Ho Chi Minh assumed almost godlike stature in the eyes of the people, and charismatic leaders like Nguyen Son were accorded only slightly less reverence.

Whatever his background, Nguyen Son had earned respect; his oratorical skills were especially formidable. He could always be heard clearly, even at a distance, without need for any kind of amplifying system. His themes were always simple, but moving. He constantly reminded us of the evils of French rule, blaming colonialism for everything evil in Vietnam. For more than eighty years the French had exploited the natural resources of the country for their own benefit. They had limited education for our people so that they could maintain control more easily, and they had killed or imprisoned Vietnamese nationalists, even those moderates who wanted only limited freedom and consideration for the people.

Nguyen Son accused the French of monopolizing the production of wines and strong spirits, which they used to encourage intoxication among poor Vietnamese as a further means of control. Only a small group of mandarins and civil servants, plus some merchants and small landowners, prospered, and they had to pay very heavy taxes. All Vietnamese had to pay an annual personal tax, as mentioned earlier, regardless of their income, even those whose income was almost nonexistent. Nguyen Son constantly reminded us of these injustices, speaking with such power and eloquence that his audiences were deeply moved. I often saw people crying openly while listening to him. He won over the masses wherever and whenever he spoke.

Our training began with three weeks of indoctrination on political relations and what might be termed "community relations." Extensive lectures, followed by group discussions, covered such subjects as relationships between the troops, cadres, and the people, stressing correct behavior by and toward individuals, groups, and the public at large. All males were lectured on the correct way to behave toward women, for example. It seems that the War for Independence had increased social contacts between men and women, and many of the prewar barriers had been reduced. Many of the young women in the country came into contact with men from cities for the first time and often were impressed by their greater sophistication. The result was that the High Command received complaints concerning seduction of daughters and wives in the area. Personally, I don't know how anyone in our organization found the time for such extracurricular activity, considering how little free time we had. We spent all but one-half day per week undergoing training. Perhaps troops and cadres outside the compound had more spare time.

The indoctrination lectures and discussions ended with a series of exercises on how to conduct individual and group critiquing sessions. The importance of such critiques was stressed as vital to the success of the Resistance. Session leaders explained how group and self-critiques would help us develop a sense of responsive-ness and personal responsibility toward each other and society as a whole. This would help create a good relationship between our military forces and the civilian population, which was vital in the kind of war we had to fight against the much more powerful French.[2] "You must be as fish in the water," our lecturers said, "with the people being the water in which you swim."

Nothing was private in critiquing sessions. "There will be no such thing as a private life," we were told. "Every individual must commit himself or herself totally to the war, body and soul, and all of our actions must be considered in light of that commitment. When you eat you must think of your many countrymen who do not have as much to eat, because of the French and those who collaborate with them. Use such thoughts to remind yourself of the need to drive the French out of our country, and to reinforce your determination to do so successfully. Always consider the people and their interests!"

Those were the messages that were drilled into us constantly. We felt good about everything, however, because we were all absorbed in the love that occupied everyone: fighting for our independence.[3] One lecturer made a point that hit home with special emphasis for me personally. "Even when you fall in love you must be sure your personal love does not go against the interests of the people." That re-minded me of Huong Giang. I did not see her often. She lived in a different area some five miles away, for women only. She also was in training and had little free time.

The last time we parted we promised to keep in touch, but anticipated we might not see each other for a long time. We knew we were in love, but neither of us dared to talk about it openly. Not only were we shy, we both felt that our individual desires and plans were less important than the cause to which we were pledged. Shortly before the Doc Lap Regiment left on its first mission, we got a day off. I set out im-mediately to see Huong Giang. I had visited her once before, and she had come to see me on those Sunday afternoons when she had no classes scheduled. I had to wait half the day before her training session ended. I was tense already, knowing that we would go into combat soon; the wait only increased the intensity of my feelings, es-pecially those for the girl I was so anxious to see. I had decided to clear my mind, to talk about what lay between us, and to come to an understanding.

As soon as we were alone I explained that my unit would be leaving soon, that I had come to say good-bye. "It is certain now that we will not see each other for a long time; it is very possible that we may never meet again. I want to make sure that you understand what could happen to me. I may come back or I may not. I want you to know that I want you to be happy with or without me."

I didn't have to elaborate; Huong Giang knew the dangers I would face as well as

I did. And in the kind of war we were waging, she had no guarantee of safety either. She kept those penetrating eyes fixed on mine for a very long time without saying a word. I realized that we were both crying silently, and I was seeing her through my tears as though she were a blurry image in a mirror. Then she spoke, quickly and vehemently, and perhaps with a touch of the same embarrassment I was feeling: "How can we be so ridiculous? We both knew this day was coming, and yet now that it is here we are behaving like children. What did we expect; what do we want? Can we give up everything we have vowed to accomplish for our country and its people? Dare we be so selfish?"

She was stating what I knew was right. I had felt so noble just a second ago saying that I wanted her to be happy, with or without me. Paradoxically, however, I felt a bit hurt and disappointed that she was agreeing with me. It hit me then how much I had come to love her since our meeting on the trail north, and how confused my love often was: pure and chaste at times, fiercely physical at other times. But that was due to Huong Giang herself. Her eyes and hair and innocent demeanor reflected her virginal purity; her shapely body, made even lovelier by the physical efforts we had undergone, and her smiling, enticing lips created sensual visions in my head, and appeared many times in my dreams.

It was fully dark now, and we stood up to say good-bye. Suddenly, as if a dam had burst under extreme pressure, I took her in my arms and kissed her silently. There was no resistance. She put her arms around me and returned my kiss, her hair enveloping my face. Without quite knowing how it happened we were lying on the ground, caressing each other. Then, as we were nearing the moment when we might consummate our passion, she stopped me and stood up.

"No, we can't be irresponsible. What will happen to us next, to you and to me? Are we going to give up our plans and our honor? I can't. I don't blame you, Chau, but you better leave."

I cooled down in a second, avoided looking at her, and said, "I am sorry, but I am so confused."

Then without saying anything more I left, and she was by herself. I stopped at a distance and looked back, just in time to see her silhouette disappear inside her quarters just a few hundred meters away. I carried that silhouette and other memories of Huong Giang with me for a long time. I would see her once more before leaving Quang Ngai with the regiment, and then again two years later, but in some ways I have always remembered that night as though it were our final parting.

6: REGIMENT DOC LAP'S FIRST BATTLE TURNS INTO DISASTER (1946)

We began our military training after the political indoctrination ended, but even simulated combat exercises included political factors. The role of the political commissar was accentuated during this period, and instructors never allowed us to forget the importance of maintaining good relations with the civilian populace.

For example, we were reminded that whenever a unit moved from one location to another, we must clean the area where we had lived, inside and out, and thank all members of the house and village that had extended us their hospitality. The political commissar was charged with seeing that we attended to these duties, as well as to paying for all expenses and for any damage that had been done. Meanwhile, a team would be making arrangements for us in the area where we were to relocate. The team would find us housing with local inhabitants, see to our food supply and hygienic needs, and even arrange for entertainment and the inevitable training and critique sessions.

Our instructors were a mixed bag of Japanese, Austrians, Germans, and Vietnamese. Many Japanese deserted and joined the Viet Minh after Japan surrendered. Most notable of these was Ho Chi Tam; legend had it that his Vietnamese name had been given to him by Ho Chi Minh, who regarded him as an adopted son. Tam reportedly had been a colonel with an important position on the general staff of the Japanese Imperial Army. He later married a Vietnamese woman, with Ho's blessing. The Austrians and Germans were said to be former German Army officers who escaped capture and joined the French Foreign Legion. They had been sent to Vietnam with the first Leclerc contingent. When they realized the nature of the war, they deserted and joined Ho Chi Minh. One German also enjoyed the same "adopted son" status with our leader as Ho Chi Tam; he was given the Vietnamese name of Ho Chi Long.

My brother, Tran Ngoc Hien, was in charge of "turning" enemy soldiers (encouraging them to desert the French and join us) as part of his counterintelligence work. He was now a high-ranking cadre, deputy head of the Intelligence Department. Hien had surprisingly good success. I had heard that more and more deserters were coming over to our side, including Tunisians, Moroccans, Algerians, and Senegalese, who made up the bulk of the French Expeditionary Forces in Vietnam. Many were eager to fight against the French, who had also established colonial rule in their countries. Some of these men from French colonies had joined the military because there were no other jobs for them in their own countries.

Despite concern voiced for "the people," Viet Minh leaders did not treat one particular segment of the populace kindly. These were the so-called antirevolutionary suspects imprisoned in a large building near our company barracks. None of us was much concerned at the time, because we felt our leaders knew best and that the people detained there were collaborators or others who were against the War of Independence. We paid little attention to the truck that came every night and stopped in front of the detention barracks for a short time with its motor running. We heard doors opening and people shouting and protesting, then the truck drove off. I'm not sure whether I consciously connected those nightly happenings with the sounds of shots that followed about an hour later from several miles in the distance. If I did, I was like the other cadres and trainees, too wrapped up in our own work and plans to be concerned.

Some years later I realized that many of the antirevolutionaries executed during that period, and others, were also nationalists, just as much as I was. Their "crimes" were being from different groups, organizations that represented potential future threats to the political ambitions of Ho Chi Minh and the very few Communists in the Viet Minh at that time.[1] During that period, however, our attention was focused on our demanding training schedule, to the exclusion of virtually everything else. I seldom had time even to think of Huong Giang, except at night when she sometimes crept into my dreams and fantasies.

Our critiquing sessions during the indoctrination portion of our training included review and analysis of battle reports sent in by commanders of units in the field since the War of Independence began. These reviews gave us valuable insights into what had happened during actual field operations. Since most of us had had only six months or less of military experience, such analyses were especially useful. They provided sound theoretical training.

Instructors based our tactical training on real combat experiences provided by the units involved. Each session began with a detailed account of an entire operation, from its inception at the command level. What was its purpose, politically as well as militarily? How was the operation planned and conducted? Did actual events disclose flaws in the planning or leadership? How well or poorly had the units and individuals involved conducted themselves during the action? What impact did the battle have on the enemy and on the people in the vicinity? Again, this latter point was more evidence of how we must concern ourselves about the fate of the civilian populace. Our instructors impressed on us that we must learn and understand the reasons for any gains or losses resulting from each operation we studied.

Our field training became progressively more rigorous. It included many night operations. All officer trainees were organized into combat units and sent, with our instructors, on long marches through the countryside. We carried our weapons, normal combat gear, and supplies for fifteen days. During that time we slept by day and operated at night. We had difficulty adjusting to this schedule at first, but soon became accustomed to it. We were ready for sleep as soon as the sun rose. When dusk fell we were on the move again. We studied tactics and then put them into practice, deploying units on training maneuvers. We spoke with civilians, learning the practical side of building goodwill on one hand, and how to gather intelligence in the field on the other.[2] We continued our discussions of training material provided to us. We practiced camouflage techniques to make ourselves invisible to detection by enemy ground or air reconnaissance. Trainees took turns acting as unit commanders and staff officers, while the instructors served as coordinators and critics.

Shortly after our return to headquarters at Quang Ngai, the entire regiment assembled on the compound parade ground for presentation to Nguyen Son. It was an impressive sight, although there were still not quite enough weapons to arm everyone. (We were told to make capturing additional weapons from the French and their collaborators one of our highest priorities during our first combat operations.) Otherwise we were a fully self-sufficient regiment, with our own kitchen and medical facilities.

More sophisticated armies would consider that, as a mobile unit, we suffered one serious deficiency: we did not have a single motorized vehicle available to us, not even a small Jeep. This was not as big a drawback as it might seem, however. We would be traveling much of the time in terrain where cars and trucks would be of little use. Most road networks, including main highways and good secondary routes everywhere we would operate, were either in the hands of the French or subject to their aerial observation. As true foot soldiers we would move over little-used paths and trails.

Nguyen Son arrived to review us as the sun reached its apex. Everything suddenly became so silent that it seemed the few thousand people assembled could hear nothing but the beating of their own hearts. The general walked through our ranks, followed by Vi Dan, the regimental commander, and four or five other cadres. (We did not use the term "officers" then.) Then he mounted a platform and started a speech during which he proved again that he was indeed a master orator.

I had heard essentially the same theme at least twenty-five or thirty times during my nine months of army service, from far in the South up here to Quang Ngai, and from a variety of cadres and lecturers. Still, Son held me spellbound, as he did the rest of his audience—not so much because of what he said but because of his intensity. No doubt the legends, or myths, that surrounded him also contributed to my fascination.

We got the next day off, but were told to be back by midnight. The entire regiment was restricted to quarters during the following two days as new assignments were announced. I was appointed commander of the Third Company, Twenty-Seventh Battalion. My battalion commander was Nguyen Cam, and Phan Tram was political commissar. All the cadres assembled for a detailed briefing. We were given some background on the situation in the Quang Ngai area and details on our first operation.

Quang Ngai had been a nationalist hotbed since long before the War for Independence began. The French and Japanese had attempted to wipe out the resistance several times. They had also paid a great deal of money to Vietnamese in the province who denounced their fellow countrymen as resistance members or sympathizers. As a result, thousands were arrested, tortured, and imprisoned or killed.

When the uprising occurred in August 1945, resistance members began a bloody revenge. Thousands of villagers suspected of being French collaborators were killed. In many cases entire families were massacred, from young children to old men and women. Their bodies often were burned in their own homes or thrown into deep wells. Other thousands who supported the Viet Minh cause, but were thought to be too moderate in their views, were also killed. Slowly Ho Chi Minh's cadres succeeded in gaining control of the situation, but not before much harm had been done. Relatives of those who had been murdered demanded revenge on those who killed their kinfolk. I saw thousands of women and children dressed in white (the traditional color of mourning in Southeast Asia) demonstrating in the city. This particular Quang Ngai pathology was developing into a dangerous cycle in which all Vietnamese involved were the losers.

This background explained one reason for Doc Lap's first operation. The regiment's mission actually was a show of force, carefully designed to convince the people that we must all be united in the fight for our country's independence. Our new regiment, composed of men of all regions, religions, and social classes, was a symbol of the total unity we must achieve. Good behavior of the men therefore was critical, our leaders explained. We must remember and practice all we had learned about dealing with the civilian populace. The series of maneuvers would also demonstrate that our army must be getting stronger if it could field a well-trained, well-armed unit such as the Doc Lap regiment.

We moved swiftly the first two days, passing through two villages known to be unsympathetic to the revolutionary government and its leaders, heading east toward Thu Xa, on the coast. We camped in the open and set up a theater for the regiment's well-organized and trained theatrical group to perform songs and dances. People came from miles around to attend, providing an audience for provincial political figures to address during intermission. They discussed the political problems that had plagued the province and stressed the necessity of presenting a united front against the French in the present struggle.

"We must forget our differences, which only weaken us and make things easier for the French, and cooperate in the struggle for independence," was the theme. Most of the audience seemed to respond favorably, and many took part in the question-and-answer session that followed. Men from the regiment were invited into many of the nearby houses and given tea and food.

We halted our march at Thu Xa for a full day of rest. My company was billeted in the palatial compound of one Nguyen Than, well known as a traitor who had collaborated with the French for many years. He helped put down uprisings by his countrymen against the colonial rulers on several occasions. France appointed him as a local "ruler," ostensibly to "assist" the emperor. In reality, he monitored and supervised the puppet Vietnamese administration. Among his material rewards was a large landholding on which he built the compound and mansion that we now occupied. His holdings were confiscated when the War for Independence began and were almost abandoned, but they remained as a grandiose landmark.

We continued our maneuvers along the coast for another week, then returned to our Quang Ngai quarters. The next day, we received orders that initiated a combat mission on the largest scale any of us had ever experienced. All cadres from company level and above assembled for briefing on the operation. Our targets, several days' march from Quang Ngai, would be French positions in the mountains near An Khe in western Binh Dinh province, where the French had recently expanded their control. The entire Doc Lap Regiment, reinforced by cadres from a training center and some Territorial units, would launch simultaneous night attacks on fifteen mountain strongholds.

One purpose of the mission was to establish that the Vietnamese indeed were united and fighting for their country's independence. The French, after expanding their occupation to all of the mountainous highlands of Central Vietnam, now had an elaborate plan to separate this area from the rest of the country. Our military offensive would be another show of force to demonstrate to France and the world that the Highlands area was an integral part of Vietnam. This would bolster the position of the Vietnamese delegation currently negotiating with the French in Fountainbleu. We were undertaking a military operation that had political objectives, but many of us would die.

We spent the next few days studying and rehearsing the operation in the compound, at the battalion level for some units and the company level for others. Then each platoon, squad, and team spent time learning and practicing their roles in the mission. My company's objective was an artillery position consisting of two cannons protected by a platoon of infantry and well entrenched in a fortified position atop a hill. A sabotage team was attached to the company; their tasks would be to breach the enemy defenses for our assault, and then to destroy the artillery pieces. We rehearsed by mounting practice attacks on a hill a few miles outside Quang Ngai. We simulated the enemy position as best we could. Two Japanese trained the sabotage team, but they were refused permission by the High Command to join us in the real mission.

Huong Giang was not with the medical unit. She visited me shortly before we left Quang Ngai and told me of her decision to serve in the Women's Association. She said that she had volunteered for the more active job because it would give her more opportunity to travel around the territory and to work closely with women cadres at all levels. That meeting was less dramatic than our previous one. I said again that we might not be able to see each other for a long time, if ever, since I faced the uncertain future of a soldier. I told her that it would be best if we made no commitments to each other, feeling very honorable and unselfish as I did so.

I admit that I was quite taken aback when Huong Giang immediately agreed with me. "I was going to say the same thing!" she said. I realized then that what I had said was not necessarily what I felt, or knew in my mind was correct. It ought to have felt right to convince myself that I wanted no ties or commitments, so I could be stronger and freer to concentrate on my military duties. In my heart, however, I yearned to have some understanding between us, some tie to her that I could re-member in the difficult days ahead. As if she could read my mind, Huong Giang went on to say,

"Isn't it beautiful, the love between two people who are attracted to each other? I've thought about that because of our knowing each other for so long. But I came to the conclusion that if we stay close to each other, we would eventually be overcome by our natural desires. And under the circumstances, that might interfere with the other love that inspires us both, and can never end for us: the love of our motherland and its people, the people who might never learn to read and write, who are born to be slaves to the French unless they are fortunate enough to be born in the classes of our fathers and us. If we forgot that love because of our personal desires, it would eventually kill the love that now lies between us. We have only one life to live and I want to live mine in a way that I won't one day regret. I'm sure you feel the same, so don't say anything now to agree or disagree with me. We must part feeling free and uncommitted; you go your way and I will go mine, but I'm sure we will follow similar paths, with both of us heading in the same direction."

What more could I say? Nothing! So we had reached an understanding, and talked about other things for the rest of the afternoon. We were not allowed any visi-tors after that, so that was the last time I saw Huong Giang until two years later.

Soon, for the second time in less than a year, I rode a train south along the coastal route, but starting from the half-destroyed station at Quang Ngai instead of Hué.

There were other major differences, too. The landscape had changed; buildings we passed last August now lay in ruins, in compliance with the "Destroy to Resist" national strategy. Roads, railways, and bridges were torn up or blocked. Slit trenches and individual foxholes had been dug nearby as havens during artillery barrages and air raids. The People's Self Defense and Territorial Forces were responsible for destroying anything that could be of use to the French, and for expanding, improving, and maintaining the protective trenches and foxholes and the obstacles on roads and highways. They also trained civilians how to take cover during air attacks.

Such attacks, although frequent in Phu Yen province near the French air base in Nha Trang, were rare in Quang Ngai and Binh Dinh provinces. This portion of the railroad therefore had been repaired well enough to carry trains. Thus, we were temporarily enjoying the rare luxury of traveling on something other than our own feet. The entire regiment and its equipment rode the overloaded train.

Troops rode on the roofs as well as inside the cars. The train moved slowly, bumping over the hastily repaired railway tracks. Unlike last year, there were no huge crowds bearing refreshments waiting to meet us along the way. Troop movements were too common now. We were still given food and tea at some stations, however.

When the train finally arrived in Binh Dinh province, we set off on an eight-kilometer march to the provincial Citadel. Similar to the Citadel at Hué but much smaller, it had been used for housing and working quarters for provincial officials. It was notable as the site from which one of Vietnam's most popular and respected heroes had emerged: Emperor Quang Trung, mentioned earlier, one of three peasant brothers who led the Tay Son revolt against the infamous regent of the southern territory of Vietnam, Truong Phuc Loan, in the late 1770s.

We spent the night and all the next day at that historic site, resting and preparing for the task ahead. We moved out just before sunset, following Route 19 toward the Highlands. It was a difficult march because the road was deeply trenched about every half-mile. Struggling through the cuts carrying our heavy loads of supplies and equipment cost us time and energy. The road was uphill all the way, winding between hills and steep mountain scarps. Only occasionally did we pass narrow rice fields or small, isolated hamlets.

We arrived at Phu Phong, the first town on the route, before dawn. Located on a big river near a destroyed bridge, it was producing uniforms for the Ve Quoc Quan (Army of National Defense), the new official name for what had been called the Giai Phong Quan (Army of Liberation).

As the sun set and fog rolled into the town, we began crossing the river. We couldn't use the ruined bridge and the current was powerful, so it was a chore to get everyone across in the few small sampans available. It took an hour just to get my company to the other bank. We then set out to cover the twenty-five kilometers to our assigned destination deep in the jungle. The company was now completely isolated, out of touch with and independent of other units, who were all headed for their own jump-off points for the attack.

We arrived at midnight. At noon the next day I took the platoon leaders, the leader of the sabotage team, and nine three-man teams (three from each platoon), plus the Territorial Forces guides assigned to my company, on a reconnaissance of the trail toward the French artillery position. There was no enemy activity on the ground or in the air. It took us two hours to push through the dense vegetation and get to a place where we could survey the enemy position: a small fortified post. It was about half the size of a soccer field and sat atop a low hill, with an adjoining blockhouse. We watched for a while, then returned to the company area, leaving the three-man teams along the trail so that they could guide their respective platoons into position for the attack.

We ate before nightfall, then marched in a column to our assigned places, taking the trail we had reconnoitered earlier. We were in position three hours before the attack was to start. All unnecessary equipment was left behind, guarded by three men, in the area where we were to regroup after the battle. Ammunition was distributed: 30 rounds per rifle, 100 for each of our seven submachine guns, 300 each for the three machine guns, and 40 rounds apiece for our two grenade launchers. I decided not to use the 60 mm mortar because of its slow rate of fire and the extra burden that carrying it, plus ammunition, placed on our men.

I made a final check of all platoon leaders to ensure that we were all prepared for the attack. Man, the company political commissar, reminded everyone of the political importance of our mission: to remind France and the world that this area was part of Vietnam and should not be partitioned off as a separate state.

We reviewed the battle scenario one last time. By now everyone in the company knew what his role was. We still had two hours to wait. The night grew cold and the ground fog thickened. There was no noise except a low murmuring of the wind blowing through the trees. The image of Huong Giang appeared in my mind: energetic and beautiful, imposing and desirable. I wondered if I would ever see her again.

At the stroke of 1 a.m., the time agreed upon for the simultaneous attacks, the first Bangalore torpedo exploded in the enemy barbed wire. More blasts followed quickly, and shots began ringing out from our advance unit. Several men used megaphones to shout at the outpost and create more confusion. Man led the first platoon through the breach and was inside the small barrack before the French began to recover from their surprise. The second platoon rushed into the compound and headed for the cannon. Grenade bursts and rifle shots echoed throughout the compound.

Suddenly enemy fire exploded from a camouflaged blockhouse on the far side of the compound, catching the second platoon in it. This was a shock, because we had no hint of any enemy there. I ordered the third platoon to open fire and feint an attack on the blockhouse, while sending a squad to flank it and approach from the rear. It took some minutes for the flanking squad to get into position, but they finally hurled grenades into the blockhouse; enemy fire from within stopped. By now, the company occupied the entire compound, but some shooting was still coming from near the artillery emplacement. Then a series of explosions from that location signaled the destruction of the two cannons.

Man, the political commissar, was in charge of the assault and mop-up phases of the battle. I was responsible for the overall mission, and for arranging a safe withdrawal. According to plan, the first platoon began to withdraw, followed by elements of the second platoon. Except for the unexpected resistance from the blockhouse, the mission was going quite successfully up to this point.

Then we got our second shock. Artillery fire from some other French stronghold began to rain down on us, inflicting immediate casualties. Our dead and wounded were sprawled around the compound, mixed in with enemy casualties. I made a quick check of the bodies and found that my deputy, Thanh, was seriously wounded. He refused evacuation, urging us to withdraw immediately before more men could be hit by artillery fire. I was unable to find Man, and thought he was making sure the cannons were out of commission. Artillery fire continued to pour in from the hidden source, causing more damage and disorder. I ordered the remainder of the company to leave the compound. We would take the wounded and all the weapons we could carry, but would have to leave the dead behind. It was not worth the potential cost in more dead and injured to try taking them with us.

We set fire to the outpost, again according to plan, but that proved to be a mistake. It hindered our withdrawal more than it helped, as the flickering light made it even more difficult to pick our way through the dense vegetation.

We finally made it back to our staging area shortly before sunrise. We had long since left the artillery fire behind, and it had eventually stopped. As soon as it grew light, however, an enemy observation plane appeared overhead, circling the area. We knew that there was no way the French could pursue us on the ground, but an artillery and air attack was imminent. So we decided to disperse in small groups, hiding in the surrounding jungle. We spent the rest of the day resting, tending to the wounded, counting casualties, and reviewing the fight. Man had been killed in the artillery position along with three others from the first platoon. The second platoon suffered eleven killed, four wounded; Thanh was evacuated with the other wounded, over his protests.

We had counted approximately ten enemy dead and twelve wounded. Another dozen or so escaped through a back gate into the jungle. Only a few of the outpost defenders had been French; the rest were Montagnards and some Vietnamese. We had captured two men, a Vietnamese and a Montagnard from the Rhade tribe in the Highlands. After brief questioning and a political lecture, I decided to take them with us for further interrogation. Due to our casualties and the heavy artillery fire that prevented a more orderly withdrawal, we did not get away with as many weapons as hoped. We did capture two machine guns, eight submachine guns, a 60 mm mortar, and several Colt and P38 pistols, but many more had been left behind in the burning barracks.

Since we had no radio there was no quick way to find out how other elements of the regiment had fared. I dispatched a messenger to try contacting battalion or regimental headquarters. As expected, French artillery and airplanes fired into the jungle and areas near Route 19 all day. We encountered no enemy patrols on the ground, and the shells and strafing were not close enough to be a threat. We ate dried fish and rice and waited for the return of our messenger. He arrived late in the afternoon with a team of guides, one of them a Bahnar, from the local Territorial unit. He brought orders that we should stay under cover until dark, and then follow the guides to a prearranged meeting place.

The next morning we reached the banks of a large river, far from the road and deep in the jungle. We were now completely out of enemy reach; not even their airplanes could spot us in the dense forest. After resting a few hours I took the company across the river in two- or three-man groups. Observers posted high in the trees could warn us of any enemy activity while it was still far, far away.

We completed the crossing, and by midnight we had reached our destination. We saw no evidence of any human activity. Unfortunately, there was no sign of any food either. We were all very hungry by this time, and we had eaten the last of our rations earlier in the day.

One of our wounded died on the trail, and we now had time to bury him. It was Khanh, who had begged us to abandon him back at the outpost, saying he would die anyhow and didn't want to be a burden that might cause the company to lose more men. He was just nineteen, single, and a volunteer from Binh Dinh. I kept his little diary, as well as information about the other dead and seriously wounded men. Man, our political commissar, normally handled these duties, but he was also dead. We held a brief ceremony for Khanh and buried him where we had stopped. I said a brief eulogy for him and the other dead we had left behind in the blazing French outpost.

The day passed and still there was no sign of anyone else from the regiment. I decided to send a platoon leader with one of the guides to locate a village, see what they could learn, and get food for the men. The pair returned early the next morning with a bag of rice and a pig—but very confusing information. It had taken them three hours to reach the nearest village they could find. It was about a half-hour walk from Route 19. That village, and others along the highway, had been heavily bombarded in retaliation for our attack. The nearest town had been under almost continuous artillery fire ever since. The town and villages had been severely damaged, and there were many civilian casualties. The news was very disturbing.

The villagers reported that friendly troops were still regrouping in different locations in the nearby jungles, and that there were many dead and wounded among them. It seemed clear that the series of concerted raids on the French positions had been very costly in all respects. We were now into our second day, seemingly no closer to making contact with other units than we had been the day before. Explosions from artillery fire, bombing, and strafing continued to reverberate, seemingly at random, through the jungle. I decided to take the company back to the coast where it might be easier to hook up with battalion or regimental headquarters. Not for the first or last time, I cursed the lack of some form of radio communications.

By nightfall we were back in the vicinity of Phu Phong, the small town near the ruined bridge where we had been attacked from the air just a few days earlier. It was out of enemy artillery range, but had suffered three or four air raids during the past two days, more reprisals by the French. I made arrangements with the town committee to get provisions and worked out a plan to get back to the Citadel at Binh Dinh. I left guides and a platoon leader in town in case more information filtered in, and moved the rest of the company out of town before sunrise. We would wait until evening and then head for Binh Dinh. By noon, however, the men I had left in Phu Phong caught up with us, bringing with them our battalion political commissar, Cam. We were all happy and relieved when we saw him, but the news he brought was not comforting.

Our major attack had not been a success. Of the twelve French strongholds targeted along Route 19 in the An Khe Pass area, only four or five had fallen, and the regiment suffered very heavy losses. In our battalion alone, almost an entire company, the Second, was nearly wiped out. It had included most of the cadres from the training center unit in Quang Ngai, and three-fourths of them had been lost. This was a blow, since these were among our most experienced men. Someone at the command level had made a serious mistake by concentrating these cadres in a single outfit.

The French also had reacted swiftly and successfully to the attacks on most of their positions. Our effort seemed to have been one of the more successful ones, since we had succeeded in our objective: putting the two cannons out of commission and overrunning the fortification.

After passing along his news, Cam ordered us to remain in place and await further instructions. Before leaving, he recommended that we take time now to review our recent operations and draw what lessons we could from them. He also warned us that we would not get any more food for at least another day.

7: THE FIRST VICTORY: A LESSON IN STRENGTH (1947)

Some of the company criticized me during our review of the attack on the artillery outpost for not bringing out the dead with us. They argued that men we had taken for dead might only have been seriously wounded. Others said that was doubtful, pointing out that the sudden, unexpected barrage of artillery shells left little time for anything but a split-second decision.

Everyone agreed, however, that the biggest problem was lack of information about the blockhouse. Most of the men we lost were hit by fire from that position, yet nothing had been said about it in our briefing for the mission. There were three possibilities for this: original intelligence reports were incomplete, headquarters was careless in relaying the information to us, or the blockhouse had been added too recently to be included in our briefing. Then we missed it on our reconnaissance patrol because it was on the far side of the compound where it could not be seen from our surveillance position. And it was so well camouflaged that nobody saw it during the initial attack. At that, the blockhouse had been dealt with effectively. The third platoon succeeded in diverting the heavy fire from that point, and the flanking squad had destroyed it with commendable speed.

There were other general criticisms about the operation, but there were no complaints about any individual's bravery or performance under fire. And there was praise for many, plus no little pride in the company's overall performance. Above all, morale was high.

When the battalion finally reassembled, almost half of its original men were gone: killed, wounded, and missing. When the second battalion arrived a day after, it also was down to nearly half strength. Orders then came for both units, or what remained of them: they should be reorganized into one full battalion and move to Phu Yen province. The new unit would become part of the Fifth Military Region Command there.

Four days passed. We got little rest because of the many meetings necessary to reorganize personnel, weapons, and equipment. We reviewed individual and unit condition and combat readiness, and we held critiques and self-criticism sessions on our performance and experiences in the recent battle. It was a relief when the provincial theater group arrived to put on a beautiful performance recalling the Tay Son revolt of almost two centuries earlier. A young woman representing the provincial council delivered an emotional speech at intermission. She expressed the gratitude and compliments of all the people in the province to the troops for their heroic actions against the enemy.

She did not resemble Huong Giang physically, but she spoke with the same passionate tone, projecting the same fierce, but romantic, idealism. Her theme was the usual one: the French colonialists and their policies were the roots of all evils in Vietnam, and getting rid of them was the sine qua non to begin a renaissance in our country, a repetition of the independence achieved by the Tay Son brothers. She concluded by saying that with the Tay Son spirit and experience to guide us, we could do even better today for every class of society. The peasants would be freed from the perpetual slavery to illiteracy and a crushing feudal system, and the bourgeois freed from the guilt of their cooperation with the oppressors.

The battalion left for its new location and assignment the next day. Our mission would be to implement a new policy of "static defense," a course the High Command decided to follow after the unsuccessful attempt at a coordinated major offensive that had cost us so many casualties—civilian as well as military. It took us ten long days to march the 300 kilometers across jungles, mountains, rice fields, and the coastal plain from Binh Dinh province to our post along the Ca Lui River in Phu Yen province. We were now attached to Regiment Seventy-nine and assigned to hold a line of defensive outposts facing the French front lines across the river, which marked the border between the Delta and Highland areas. Our mission was interdiction: to deny the French access to the Free Zone from the territory they occupied in the Highlands of Banmethuot province. A valley eight to fifteen kilometers wide, bounded on both sides by dense forests and high mountains, was the only route they could use to get to the Free Zone.

No Vietnamese lived along this part of the border between Banmethuot in the Highlands and the coastal province of Phu Yen. Vietnamese congregated in the provincial capital, Tuy Hoa, and smaller towns and hamlets that were along the coast, or in district centers—somewhat like county seats in the United States. Montagnards, mostly of the Jarai tribe, lived in the outlying areas. They, and the Rhade, were the most "Vietnamized" of the dozen or so Highlands tribes. ("Montagnard" is a French term meaning an inhabitant of the mountains or, more simply, a Highlander.)

There were about 700 to 800 Jarai living in family settlements and small communities. Usually an entire family of twenty to thirty people lived together in a "long house," with separate quarters for married couples and their children, and for single men and women. The Jarai were seminomads, living in one place for three or four years, then moving to a new location when the land lost its fertility. Women were heads of families in the Jarai's matriarchal society. When they married, their husbands came to live with them in the wives' homes.

Vietnamese looked down on the Montagnards for centuries, calling them *moi*, which means "barbarians." They took advantage of the Montagnards' isolation from civilization and innocence, largely in small business operations, selling to them at very high prices, and buying what tribal people had to sell at very low prices. It was easy for the Montagnards eventually to understand how they were being exploited.

When the French took over, with their missionaries helping, they took steps that seemed to make them protectors of the Montagnards: providing material assistance, spiritual guidance, and other services. The fact that they proved more powerful than the Vietnamese impressed the mountain people also. Power was something they recognized and respected. In fact, however, the French were simply more sophisticated in their exploitation of the Montagnards. They expropriated their most fertile lands and turned them into plantations on which the Montagnards labored for very low wages. The French made it look as though they were doing good deeds because they created jobs for the Highland tribes. The truth was that the tribesmen now worked on land they formerly owned.

So the Montagnards generally liked the French better than the Vietnamese. Many were recruited to serve in French auxiliary military units, especially in fortified positions. These outposts were scattered throughout the Highlands at critical route junctions. One such outpost occupied the opposite bank of the Ca Lui River, just ten kilometers from our base near the Jarai village of Buon Mathieng. The French stronghold included an artillery battery, used primarily to provide cover for patrols that occasionally fanned out from the outpost.

The garrison consisted of about two-thirds Montagnards and one-third French troops. When they ventured out of their fortified position on patrols, usually to the few Montagnard settlements along the river, they suffered casualties from snipers and booby traps we set on trails they used. Meanwhile, we had greater freedom of movement. Most of the few hundred Montagnards in the region had been won over to our cause and were friendly to us. We also had a number of Montagnard cadres by this time, mostly from the Rhade tribe. They had gone through basic, but intensive, political indoctrination by cadres from the North. These instructors were themselves ethnic minorities who had earlier joined the Viet Minh. The Rhade cadres were helpful in securing support for us among the local people. They helped dispel the idea that the French were benevolent protectors of the Highlands people.

Routine patrols and ambushes produced few contacts with the enemy during the monsoon season. Our troops spent time studying: conventional subjects such as reading and writing; political indoctrination; and the basic strategy of "Protracted Resistance Will Surely Win" developed by Truong Chinh, a member of the Vietnamese leadership. At one point a delegation of high officials made the long trek from Hanoi to visit us, covering almost half of the 1,000-kilometer distance on foot. With them was one of the country's most respected poets, Xuan Dieu. Unfortunately,

I was unable to see them because my company stood guard during their stay, as protection against a possible raid.

The French launched a major attack. We could hear the roar of heavy trucks and tanks mingling with the sound of continuing cannon fire. A French unit began setting up a portable bridge to span the river so that their tanks could cross to our side. My company, the first line of defense, opened up with the heaviest weapons we had: one 60mm mortar and several grenade launchers. In just minutes a withering hail of heavy machine gun and mortar fire pinned us down. My company suffered casualties from this direct enemy fire. The continuing artillery barrage killed or wounded men in the companies behind us.

We used up all of our mortar and grenade launcher rounds in less than an hour. Ammunition for our other weapons was also running short. Some enemy units had already crossed the river and were waiting for tanks to join them. Orders came down from battalion HQ for us to withdraw. We left our positions in the trenches, carrying with us three men who had been killed and five more wounded. Suddenly, the artillery fire stopped, but now we could hear the sound of tanks and had to assume that they might pursue us. I took the company into the forest, which offered our best hope of eluding the French units. The ground was slippery and the mud hampered our movement, but it would do the same for the enemy behind us.

Then a torrential rain struck. Water poured down, inundating the entire valley. We could not move any farther, but the French were also stuck. Their tanks, most still on the far side of the river as nearly as we could tell, mired down. Their artillery fire ceased, probably because it was just as likely that shells would strike their own troops. It was still mid-morning, but the sky seemed to press to treetop level and we could see only a few feet around us. The rain continued for several hours without pause. I sent a platoon to flank the enemy troops and harass them at the river crossing.

The French succeeded in establishing a bridgehead on our side of the Ca Lui, but only one light tank crossed successfully. The river, swollen by the downpour, became a raging torrent. It swept away some enemy equipment, increasing their difficulties. Soon the French and their Montagnard auxiliaries were in disarray. They shouted at each other and fired wildly into the jungle. They dared not try to advance any farther.

Our flanking platoon dispersed into three-man teams, sniping at enemy troops working on the river and changing positions immediately after firing. We were better at fighting in these conditions than they were. We didn't know whether we were causing many losses, but when the rain slowed and the sky began to clear in late afternoon, it was apparent that the French had aborted their operation without pursuing us beyond their small bridgehead. We learned later that the attacking force was estimated at more than battalion strength. It had come down from the Banmethuot about 100 kilometers away.

Shortly after that battle, the battalion received orders to withdraw to the Dong Cam area in the interior of Phu Yen province. We were to be integrated into the 80-83 Inter-Regiment. Our operational area now would cover Khanh Hoa and Phu Yen provinces, but our tactics would change completely. The High Command apparently realized that we didn't have the strength, experience, or armament to fight the well-armed French using conventional tactics. The attack on fortified positions at An Khe and attempt at defending a line at the Ca Lui River proved that.

Our new mission did not require us to defend any particular point. We would move between Khanh Hoa and Phu Yen provinces. We would fight the hit-and-run war for which we were best suited. Instead of head-to-head battles, we would use harassing tactics and ambushes to chip away at the enemy's strength instead of trying to overwhelm him in pitched battles. This strategy made sense to me, and soon proved its effectiveness when we set up an ambush to surprise a French convoy.

It was spring 1947, about eighteen months after I first volunteered for combat duty. My company and I were part of a combined 450-man task force of the Viet Minh Fifth Military Interzone lying in wait for a French convoy.[1] The task force included three infantry companies, one heavy-duty weapons company, and three demolition teams. The location was ninety-five kilometers inland from the city of Nha Trang. It was on Route 21, which linked the coastal province of Khanh Hoa to the highlands of Banmethuot. We had planted mines in the road, then concealed ourselves along both sides of the road. We knew from intelligence reports that a convoy would make a routine trip that day from the French logistics base at Nha Trang to the city of Banmethuot deep in the jungles of the Highland. Only today the journey would not be so routine.

We started preparing for this ambush three weeks earlier. The task force commander, a medical student just eighteen months earlier and with no more than three months of military training since, brought all company commanders and political commissars to the area. The area selected was a climbing, serpentine section of road where the convoy would slow down, bunching the vehicles closer together than they might be on a more open stretch.

We examined it carefully, looking for the best ambush site, studying the possibilities for concealment, deciding where to plant mines, and considering how best to position our men. Back at our base, we set up a similar landscape and rehearsed the planned ambush for a week. Then, like the other company commanders, I took my platoon and squad leaders to the ambush site. While we were on the scene and could examine the terrain closely, we discussed the plan of attack. We covered in detail the positions their units would occupy and their missions. Then we returned to our base for more rehearsals and critiques.

Now we faced the real thing. I felt we were well prepared. The only thing lacking was an adequate supply of arms. Only ninety men in my company of 120 had weapons: French and Japanese mousquetons, German Mausers, and a submachine gun. Two light machine guns, a British Bren, and a 60 mm mortar completed our arsenal. The other thirty men carried machetes, first aid necessities, and other gear. They would retrieve captured equipment and be in charge of prisoners. For the entire operation we received thirty rounds of ammunition per rifle and 300 each for the machine guns. The situation was the same in each of the other four companies.

The sound of a light airplane engine in the distance alerted us. As expected, a Morane observation plane flew ahead of the convoy, checking the road to make sure the route ahead was clear. That was why we had taken such pains to conceal ourselves carefully. This was the critical moment. If the plane did not spot us, we anticipated that our ambush would be successful. Flying low, it followed the twists and turns in the road until it was directly overhead. I pressed my body hard against the earth, trying to make myself as small as possible, knowing that every other man in the task force was doing the same. Then the plane flew past us, and we could hear the engines of an armored platoon, leading the procession as it had been doing uneventfully for nearly a year.

We knew that the convoy of some forty heavy trucks would follow the armored platoon, and that another armored platoon would bring up the rear. Our intelligence operatives had been watching this convoy operation for some time. Their reports indicated that the French never varied their routine. That was bad for them, good for us. We planned to introduce some dramatic variations into that routine.

The company's political commisar and I, the only ones in position to observe the convoy, watched as the leading armored car neared the spot where we had placed our mines. Our company and two others were assigned to assault the convoy exactly twenty counts after the mine exploded, so I tensed as the vehicle moved closer and closer.

The roadway erupted suddenly. Multiple explosions staggered the armored car. Automatic weapons and mortar fire followed so quickly and furiously that we couldn't distinguish between friendly and enemy fire. Actually, the convoy was so surprised that there was not a great deal of defensive fire. Some of the startled French soldiers jumped out of the trucks without their weapons and ran. Some escaped only because our companies quickly began checking on casualties and preparing to retreat. (For us, at all unit levels, a safe, orderly retreat was considered as crucial as a successful attack.) Our systematic assault and nearly three-to-one manpower advantage decimated the entire convoy in less than thirty minutes.

As rehearsed, unarmed bearers carried away the captured weapons and ammunition.[2] Some of them no doubt would use those same weapons in our next engagement. The rest of us helped clear our portion of the battleground. We counted thirty-two enemy bodies in our company area. Two armored cars and fifteen trucks were destroyed, but we captured only twenty-five weapons. The company had ten casualties: five killed (one hit by a truck that went out of control when it hit a mine) and five wounded.

Overall, the task force killed nearly 100 of the enemy and destroyed some twenty trucks and Jeeps, plus four armored cars. We captured more ammunition than eighty unarmed bearers and the rest of us could carry away. Captured weapons included sorely needed French rifles and submachine guns, six machine guns, and some mortars and heavy machine guns. As we gathered the enemy bodies by the roadside we noticed that they were a mixed force: Moroccan colonial troopers, French Foreign Legionnaires, and French regulars. Before we left we posted a big sign that bore this warning for the French: "We are a nation of 25 million people determined to defend our land and drive you into the sea. Stop letting yourselves be killed merely to further the interests of the colonialists."

We disappeared from the ambush site an hour before a flight of Spitfire fighters came looking for the missing convoy.

We spent the night in a well-protected cave hollowed out of Hon Heo Mountain near the seaside. Caverns honeycombed the mountain, all connected by small passages and underground streams. It could, and sometimes did, hold an entire regiment of more than 2,000 men. The French had tried unsuccessfully many times to blockade the entire area. We stored enough food, medical supplies, and other necessities there to withstand a siege. Our strategy when the French attempted a blockade was for the regular troops to stay holed up in the caves, which were virtually impregnable to invasion, while Territorial units outside harassed the encircling French forces with snipers and ambushes. As a result, the enemy always found such a blockade costly, both in the immediate area and in other locations where forces were reduced to concentrate troops for the siege.

Early the next day a group of us went out to see how the French had coped with the mess we left for them. They had cleaned up the battle site quickly, removing their dead and wounded as well as any abandoned equipment. They had also burned several nearby civilian houses. We found that our sign was still there, but the French had added their response.

"It is true that you are a nation of 25 million people, but you are underfed, sick with malaria, and ill-equipped, while we are a professional army, healthy and with enough equipment, technology, and experience to grind you into pieces. You may cause us some harm, but we will ultimately get you under our control and discipline. Be wise; stop getting yourselves killed foolishly."

The exchange of signs obviously changed no minds on either side, and we took the French reply lightly at first. During our review session the next day, however, we discussed the theme of the French message and agreed that it made good sense from the enemy point of view. Our army in fact was no match for the French militarily. We needed help from the people to conduct a protracted war that would eventually wear down the French and their will to continue. Those of us carrying rifles might be temporary heroes but we were replaceable, while the common people would always be there and ultimately would be the deciding factor.[3]

The French message drove home that point to all of us. It helped us realize why our political indoctrination and its emphasis on maintaining good relations with civilians was so necessary. It also underscored the fact that we faced several enemies, including disease, ignorance, and passivity. We had to put as much effort into conquering them as we did fighting opposing military forces.

With respect to military aspects of the operation, the ambush proved conclusively that such hit-and-run tactics were far better suited to our capabilities than concerted attacks or trying to defend static positions.

A group from the city of Nha Trang visited us on the third night after the battle. The French had occupied the town for almost a year now. It served as a headquarters and supply base for the entire region, which included the central Highlands provinces and the surrounding coastal provinces of Khanh Hoa, Phan Rang, and Phan Thiet. Although the French controlled Nha Trang completely, most of the Nha Trang people supported us solidly, if covertly. The group that visited us brought with them necessities and luxuries: food, medicine, toothpaste, soap, and magazines of all kinds (most of them French, ironically enough). Representatives of women's and youth organizations as well as other groups in the "occupied areas" (the term used for sectors controlled by the French) congratulated us warmly. The visitors put on a party for us, with a show, songs, and speeches. They spent the night, and we gave them a grand tour of the wonders of the caverns.

We returned to Phu Yen and rejoined the battalion operating in that sector. The area was not as free of French activity as it had been the previous year. A series of enemy outposts now ran along the foot of the chain of mountains that stretched across the southern part of the province from Cap Varella to our location at the time, Nui Hiem.

By this time we were fighting a seesaw war in which each side had certain advantages but neither could establish a decisive edge. The French could gather their forces for major operations into our Free Zone, just as we could mount offensives into their pacified areas. Fortified outposts manned mostly by Vietnamese units protected the French pacified territory—big cities and villages and towns near highways or railroads. The French armed, uniformed, and paid these auxiliaries, who were roughly the enemy's equivalent of our Territorial forces, to protect town officials who collaborated with them.

Most people in those areas were passive on the surface, apparently cooperating with the French, while working secretly with those of us actively fighting for independence. As a result, the French could never completely prevent supplies from reaching us. In this contested area the French harassed the farmers regularly with day and night artillery fire into fields and villages. They also set up ambushes and sent out patrols to capture livestock and rice and to burn villagers' homes. Women also were popular targets of the raids; rape was common.[4] Our Regular Army units, with help from Territorials and the People's Self-Defense Forces, fought to stop the French and their Vietnamese auxiliaries from venturing too far from their bases. Our operations gradually made their forays so costly that they seldom left their fortified posts.

The French then changed tactics, stepping up their indiscriminate artillery fire and aerial attacks on areas they couldn't reach easily in raids by small units. They would gather units from different places every two to three weeks and mount large-scale operations, supported by tanks, artillery, aircraft, and naval batteries, into areas normally under our control.

We had long since prepared for such eventualities. Elements of the Self-Defense Forces gave the alert and reacted swiftly whenever such an offensive was about to occur. Their units assembled, most civilians hid in prepared locations, and children and very old people remained in their homes. Guerrilla teams and Territorial units were deployed to snipe, activate booby traps, and harass the enemy whenever and wherever possible. Meanwhile, Regular Army units counterattacked or set ambushes on a larger scale. We couldn't stop these ambitious enemy offensives completely, but our combined efforts made them very costly in terms of casualties and equipment losses. The same scenario kept recurring month after month.

We were following the simple tactics popularized by Mao Tse-tung: "The enemy advances, we retreat; the enemy halts, we harass; the enemy tires, we attack; the enemy retreats, we pursue."

The French continued their established strategy, setting up headquarters and supply bases in big cities, with air or naval bases nearby. They used these facilities and elite mobile forces to support the fortified outposts in their spheres of authority. Their objective was to maintain tight control so their puppet Vietnamese government could solidify its regime and the Viet Minh could be annihilated.

Resistance efforts continued, however, and even increased. Sabotage and ambushes were common. The French and their auxiliary units suffered casualties almost daily as they went through the now-routine task of opening roads each morning, clearing them of obstacles, and filling in gaps created during the night.

Fortified outposts became targets of Viet Minh attacks, harassment, and propaganda.

The French and their Vietnamese allies retaliated with more and more pressure on civilians—in particular, those in rural areas near military and paramilitary outposts. Most of these farmers, being politically oriented since the Revolution began, engaged in clandestine cooperation with the Resistance. Others were forced to cooperate for fear of reprisals. In either case, they could be accused of being "Communist sympathizers." Many were jailed and tortured or killed; if women, they were raped. Burning of homes, even entire hamlets, and confiscation of food and livestock escalated.

Such brutality only increased the support we received from the people. Even those who worked for the French began to cooperate and atoned for their collaboration by providing intelligence and supplies of all kinds, using friends and relatives as go-betweens.

So the situation in the two provinces was a stalemate. As elsewhere, the French controlled the area by day, with the people for the most part feigning passive acceptance of their rule. The nights continued to belong to us, as did the hearts and minds of most of the population.

The struggle took its toll; in one year my company lost more than half its strength to deaths and injuries. The best of the survivors were selected as cadres for newly formed units or replacements for losses in other companies.

Then I was promoted out of the company, replacing our battalion political commissar, who was transferred to another regiment. This meant more responsibilities in a job I wasn't sure I could do well. It also signaled the beginning of a period during which I went through severe emotional and intellectual stress. I had seen a variety of men perform duties as political commissars over the past few years; some were weak and others were strong. In general, however, they were models of men dedicated to a cause they believed in with almost religious fervor. Everyone in their units looked up to the best of them.

Most often the political commissar was a unit's top man, setting a high standard for others to emulate. He looked after the welfare of all the men in his command: their physical condition, intellectual growth, professional advancement, their morale, and even their psychological and moral complexities. He usually was the point man under fire; and those were only the military facets of the political commissar's job. His duties vis-à-vis the civilian populations were at least as important. It was critical that he develop and maintain a good relationship between his unit and the people in the area in which it operated. This was key to Mao's fish-in-water concept, which was so vital to our long-term success in the fight against colonial rule.

We could not survive without support from the people—which meant a relationship that went beyond the normal bounds of military discipline and justice. The relationship first needed to be founded on the political commissar's personal conviction of the necessity of winning, of maintaining civilian goodwill and support to win our war, and of bringing about a social revolution. It was equally vital that the political commissar be able to impart that conviction to everyone in his unit.

In slightly more than five years I had gone from the contemplative life of a Buddhist monastery to the brutal reality of war. For about half that time I plunged into military training and political education that were almost diametrically opposed in concept and philosophy to everything I had learned in my earlier life. At times I felt the confusion and strain of being both an active killer and pacifist Buddhist. Was it right or wrong? At such times I looked at the men around me who fought so bravely and realized that they had been pacifists, too. One day I saw that Bon, my liaison man who had killed at least twelve of the enemy, was horrified at the sight of a friend cutting a chicken's throat. But the war and my position as a combat unit commander left little time for meditation. Like others, I faced the kill-or-be-killed realities of war. I had been able to accept the need to fight, to change from a philosophy that emphasized peace and gentleness to a militant one in which killing and dying were commonplace. I strove to give myself fully to the cause of my country.

My latent internal struggle intensified with my promotion. Instead of just accepting war and the precepts of the Viet Minh as necessities to win the struggle, I felt I must now fully commit myself in every way. It was like converting to a new religion—an aggressive, dynamic, and often cruel one that differed totally from my Buddhist beliefs. I suffered great mental torture as a result. On one hand, the struggle for social justice, compassion, and liberation of the individual was compatible with Buddhism. On that basis I had been able to rationalize my involvement in the war so far. On the other hand, the obsessive hatred of the enemy and the cultivated brutality toward the enemy, other individuals, and an entire social class was contradictory to my personal beliefs.

I often remembered that people of all classes revered my grandfather, the late great scholar and Imperial Minister Tran Tram, and my father, a former mandarin and one of the last of the traditional judges. And there were many other mandarins, intellectuals, and landowners who were just as compassionate and patriotic as my father and grandfather. Was it necessary now for us to hate and revile such men? Could a movement based on such hatreds, and the savage cruelty that often resulted, create the more perfect society it envisioned?

Despite my doubts and mental anguish, the new assignment left little time for personal philosophizing. I became fully absorbed in the fighting and training (in which critiques and self-criticism sessions continued to play large roles) within the battalion, plus the added duties of strengthening our relationship with local inhabitants.

Normal activities continued, with both sides mounting attacks, ambushes, and harassing maneuvers. The civilian population paid the highest price, but savagery by the French and their Vietnamese collaborators often backfired. Increasing numbers of men abandoned their homes, often after their families were killed and brutalized and their homes burned, to join our fighting forces.

French atrocities also helped us establish an excellent intelligence network, with agents recruited from Vietnamese who on the surface cooperated with the French. Another excellent source of information was the string of bordellos the French had set up at every battalion-level base for the "entertainment" of their personnel.[5] Most of the women who joined these "clubs" did so because it was the only way they could make a living during those difficult times. Some women were captured by the French, raped, and then turned over for a life of prostitution in areas so isolated and far from their homes that they had no chance to escape. These women often learned valuable information and relayed it to us.

My brother, Tran Ngoc Hien, was deputy chief of intelligence and counterintelligence for the entire South Central Vietnam area at the time and was responsible for these operations. The effort paid off frequently, enabling us to prevent the French from surprising us with large-scale attacks. One such occasion occurred when the battalion was warned that the French were planning a major offensive in our area. This word came both from regimental HQ and via messengers from the provincial Territorial forces.

I reviewed our unit dispositions briefly with the battalion commander and then took my usual liaison team to join the first company. That company was assigned to ambush the enemy on their return from the operation. The company commander met me at the entrance to the forest where the company was located. The entire company was already prepared for action, he informed me.

We both moved to an observation post that overlooked the entire plain below. It was still dark but already we could hear motors roaring from the only vehicular pass that led from the coast, about twenty-five kilometers away, to our location. Unlike the last three big enemy operations, the French this time seemed to be moving through the Cap Varella Pass before sunrise, which meant they did not have the advantage of aerial cover. The sound grew closer, and we could see vehicle lights flaring through the night. Soon we could make out groups of twenty to twenty-five trucks, each with light tanks protecting them, stopped at intervals along the road.

It became obvious that the attack force included at least three or four battalions, with tank and artillery support. All units were now forming up on various lines of departure, probably waiting for daylight to move. Explosions suddenly burst through the darkness, followed by the rat-a-tat of small arms fire. Our Self-Defense and Territorial forces were setting off hidden mines and grenade booby traps and sniping. Enemy tanks and artillery began firing haphazardly. This continued until daybreak. As the rising sun burned off the heavy fog, two Morane observation planes appeared on the horizon.

We could see most enemy troop movements from our observation post. A light tank company and elements of an infantry company moved quickly through rice fields, probably trying to set up a blocking position behind a group of villages on the far side of the plain. Three infantry battalions next began advancing from their respective lines of departure, converging on a line that separated the plain from the mountains. They leapfrogged from hamlet to hamlet under the watchful eye of the Moranes. There was a constant din of fire from rifles, automatic weapons, mortars, and artillery.

Platoons from our battalion fought back doggedly from positions along the enemy route. Territorial units also contributed to the defense—sniping and setting traps. French progress gradually slowed. They began evacuating wounded late in the day.

Meanwhile, our units increased their pressure all across the plain and along the road where the trucks and artillery were located. As the sun began to set, we realized that the French were not going to leave the hamlets, which they had always done in previous operations. They had never dared to keep great numbers in the contested area as they were doing now. Flaming houses lit up the night as the French burned whatever they could set afire to protect against snipers hiding close to their positions. Artillery poured in covering fire. The situation stayed the same for most of the night. At about 3 a.m., shooting suddenly blossomed from all around the French artillery and command post.

Our regiment earlier sent in nearby units to reinforce us, and these new troops had launched a counterattack. After an hour of fierce fighting, the French position was overrun and shooting stopped. It was time now for the company I was with to fulfill its mission by ambushing the enemy withdrawal. Anticipating that survivors would escape toward a nearby outpost, I decided to prepare a suitable reception before they could reach that haven. We reached the outpost in less than an hour and set up our ambush almost on its doorstep. Those inside the compound had withdrawn deep within its perimeter. Apparently they were daunted by the intensity of the battle so close to them and made no effort to engage us.

As expected, enemy survivors from the artillery and command post soon came running down the road toward the supposed safety of the outpost. My companion, the company commander, ordered his unit to open fire. Shooting intensified as troops inside the outpost joined the fray. An artillery shell exploded suddenly nearby and blew me high into the air. My entire body felt the shock, and I drifted into unconsciousness. When I came to I smelled blood and tasted it in my mouth; sharp pains stabbed me in my left arm and leg and in my abdomen where I had been hit by shell fragments. Thus the battle ended abruptly for me.

8: CHANGE OF HEART (1948)

A small, almost bald mountain stuck out as the most noticeable landmark visible from the headquarters of Regiment 83, my new assignment. I arrived here in mid-1948 after leaving the hospital and spending a month on convalescent leave. Nui Chop Chai (or Fish Net Mountain, because it looked like a fish net as it sank into the sea) rose out of a flat plain. This area produced great quantities of betel for sale in and beyond Phu Yen province. Thick bamboo hedges encircled small hamlets scattered like islands in a sea of rice fields. Most houses were built of bamboo and clay, covered with elephant grass; each had its own betel garden.

Regiment 83 HQ sat at the foot of Fish Net Mountain, about two kilometers from Tuy Hoa. Capital of Phu Yen province, Tuy Hoa was on the northern bank of the Da Rang River at the junction of Highway 1, the north-south railroad line, and Route 7, which led to the Highlands. Until shortly after the revolution began in August 1945, Tuy Hoa had been a busy market town with tens of thousands of inhabitants. Trains stopped daily at the nearby station to unload goods from the North and load local products. At such times it had looked like a vast open fair.

Now it was virtually a wasteland of demolished brick buildings with temporary shelters scattered haphazardly among the ruins. Hundreds of wild monkeys inhabited the city's highest point, a small hill almost in its center. The French bombarded the city frequently, by air from the Nha Trang air base less than 160 kilometers to the south and from warships operating from the Cam Ranh Bay naval base. Most buildings were in ruins, and the majority of the people were gone. Members of the Resistance "destruction department," headed by my brother-in-law Le Van Kinh, leveled any buildings left standing by the French. This was part of the "destroy to resist" policy.

During one bombardment the headquarters of the Twenty-seventh Dai Doan (Army Corps) of Cao Van Khanh was caught off guard, and my brother, Tran Ngoc Hien, then deputy chief of the intelligence agency of South Central Vietnam, was almost completely buried in a foxhole for hours.

Hien remained in the intelligence agency after I volunteered for combat in 1945. He moved quickly up the ranks, becoming head of intelligence and counterintelligence for the entire Central Highland and South Central Vietnam region. He was now a powerful and almost mythical figure as a result of his exploits. He might be seen talking to a Vietnamese mistress of a French officer in a French-controlled city one day, then be back at Military Zone headquarters 100 kilometers away the next day. He succeeded in convincing many to desert the French and join our forces. He compromised Vietnamese who worked with the French by fabricating evidence that they secretly worked for the Resistance. This turned the French against some of their most loyal lackeys, who might be executed as a result.

Regiment 83 chose this site because the surrounding area offered natural obstacles to enemy incursions. Bare, sandy terrain and open rice fields made surprise attacks difficult and would slow any enemy advances. Trenches were dug everywhere to provide protection during air attacks or shelling by naval cannon. It was also high enough to serve as a perfect observation post in case of large-scale enemy raids. Headquarters personnel, several hundred in all, lived with local inhabitants. Billeting five to ten men per household was customary in our army.

As was also customary, the regiment had two staffs. One was a conventional military organization responsible for operations, intelligence, and logistics. The other was a department of political affairs, which handled propaganda, indoctrination, public relations, troop morale and entertainment, and selection and promotion of cadres (NCOs and officers). Although the regimental command (commander, deputy commander, and political commissar) all had authority over and access to both staffs, the regimental commander worked chiefly with the military chief of staff, while the political commissar worked mostly with the chief of the political department.

The concept was the same as I've described it at lower levels. The political commissar's responsibility was to provide the inspiration, will, and motivation for the troops to fight. The political staff helped him perform those tasks. The commander handled military matters: going after the enemy, fighting the battles, and preparing his troops to fight even better next time. The deputy commander had to be ready to take over either job should it be necessary. Thus he was a member of the unit command and took part in making decisions. Although the political and military staffs were separate, their working relationships were tightly entwined due to the mutual understanding and joint responsibility of the unit command.

I was assigned to the political department as head of the office of propaganda and instruction (training). My duty was to prepare material for use in lectures and indoctrination aimed at building morale among the troops, strengthening their determination to fight, and encouraging them to improve their individual and collective behavior. As always, we stressed maintaining a good relationship with the people. These materials were prepared according to the political commissar's instructions, documents received from high levels, and information culled from battlefield and unit reports.

In my new job I began to learn more about the close connections between Marxist-Leninist doctrine, our Vietnamese leaders' beliefs, and the impact of those doctrines and beliefs on the men and cadres in the combat units. For example, among the many precepts credited to Marx and Lenin were two that still stick in my mind (expressed in my own words as I remember them):

1. Every potential of the people must be mobilized for the war. The entire nation must be converted into a revolutionary front.
2. Every individual must contribute to that effort.

One of Ho Chi Minh's primary doctrines, which he expressed in the early stages of the Resistance, sprang from such principles:

> A military army can come into existence only after an army of propagandists succeeds in mobilizing the populace—so a political army must come first. This [organization of the political army] has to be done immediately, followed by rapid expansion. Under the present situation that requires a struggle against the Japanese and the French, these questions should be asked: who should fight and would volunteer to fight? Thus we must be sure the people fully understand the cause politically before they take up weapons to fight.

Ho's point was that the cadres making up the "political army" had three major tasks:

1. To understand that political awareness was paramount in pursuing the war.
2. To instill that political awareness in the people while mobilizing them for the war.
3. To motivate the people to such an extent that they would support the fight all the way from their homes and hamlets to the front lines.

General Vo Nguyen Giap went further, saying, "Without a revolutionary people, without strong political support from the people, those farmers and workers who formed the regular army and were led by the [Communist] Party, no growth would be possible for the People's Armed Forces."

For more than three years I lived under and was indoctrinated in these principles. But during that time I was fully absorbed in the daily life of a military cadre, either preparing to fight or actually in battle. I had no time to think about anything other than maintaining the condition of my men—physically and psychologically—and their morale. The basics of fighting and surviving occupied almost every waking moment, and even disturbed my sleep at times.

Now, in my new position and in an environment that was relatively peaceful and secure, I had time to contemplate, to consider such things as doctrine and philosophy, and how they related to reality. It was strange, and I sometimes felt as though I was afloat in an alien world. I had shared life in crucial situations during the past three years with hundreds of others from all walks of life: peasants, workers, bourgeois, and those from wealthy families. We worked, trained, and fought as equals, loving and respecting each other without any sense of separation that I could see or feel. More than a few times some of us had died trying to protect our comrades, without any thought of whether they had come from privileged or underprivileged backgrounds.

I recognized, as did many others of my class, that social conditions created by the French and the feudal system that had preceded them for centuries needed to be changed—and that to effect the necessary changes our country must first win its independence.

Many of us from all classes had in fact joined together and were cooperating successfully in the struggle for independence. Why then was there such repeated emphasis on the dominant role of the peasants and workers? And why was there constant repetition of the need to hate the bourgeois, the mandarins, and other classes? Certainly many of them deserved such castigation, but others did not. It seemed to me that we needed everybody, regardless of background, who was willing to fight for a new and independent Vietnam. There had been too much discrimination against broad categories of people in our past; we had to develop a sense of individual worth and respect.

Yet as I read more and more about the "proletarian dictatorship," the idea of one vengeful social class dominating and repressing all other social classes haunted me. This was at odds with my Buddhist religious belief in the equal value of men and other living things. Buddhism converts by virtue of compassion and setting good personal examples, not by hatred or rancor. The fundamental teaching of Buddhism is to "do good and behave well."

It was confusing to realize that our leaders—President Ho, General Giap, and their entourages—all came from the very classes we were now being indoctrinated to hate. I asked myself this question: *If they are all well-intentioned leaders committed to changes that improve social justice for the underprivileged and oppressed, should they not promote equality and leadership opportunities for everyone, regardless of their social backgrounds?*

I hope I'm not giving the impression that I favored my own class, or any class, because the idea of such discrimination nauseated me then (and still does). The previous few years had taught me much about the worth of individuals; the deeds and sacrifices of illiterate peasants and workers inspired me. But would they be any better than the French or feudal lords if they became privileged leaders of the proletarian dictatorship? It seemed to me that the peasants were now being deceived by a new set of alien missionaries who preached Marxist doctrine instead of Christianity.

Very vaguely, I suspected that there might be a group of unhappy mandarins and bourgeois among the current leaders who intended to use the proletarian class to preserve their leadership and protect them against others of their class who might challenge them later. I quickly rejected the thought, amazed that such an idea could enter my head. How could I doubt the sincerity of our leaders? Had they not abandoned their comforts and privileges and risked their lives to awaken the nation and lead it in the fight for independence? Surely they deserved my respect! Still, the idea flashed through in my mind. I realized that I had changed—and learned—a lot while studying and working to be an advocate for the cause of the Revolution and the social class struggle.

My immediate superior was Ho Ba, head of the political department. Ba and I had much in common. About the same age, we were both the sons of mandarins and both had two brothers who had joined the fight for independence. He set a good example for everyone around him in his daily life as well as his work. We enjoyed each other's company and discussed such varied subjects as our work, politics, love, poetry, and humor.

His superior was Nguyen Duong, regimental political commissar. He talked and acted very much like a man dedicated to his cause. I admired him, "probably because you don't know him well!" said some of my friends, who had much less respect for Duong. To many of us, the fact that Duong had abandoned a comfortable position in the French administration and parted with his beautiful fiancée to join the Resistance made him worthy of our respect.

Not all commanders at this level and above were exemplary leaders. Tran Cong Khanh, former commander of our military region, was known as a vicious old man who seemed to be trying to make up for more than a decade he spent in French prisons by running after young women. Khanh had been a political prisoner for his clandestine activities against the French; he was released during the uprising in August 1945. Senior inmates while in jail had converted almost all former political prisoners like Khanh to communism. After being liberated they were rewarded with responsible positions in the army or Ho Chi Minh's administration. So far, however, few had been successful in the area with which I was familiar: the lower half of Central Vietnam, and the entire Highlands. The revolutionaries of Tran Cong Khanh's era gradually and quietly disappeared into anonymity, giving way to a new generation of leaders.

New military commanders of regions, regiments, and battalions replaced the older men. All were in their twenties and came from mandarin and well-to-do families. All were educated and knew as much about French literature as they did about Vietnamese literature. With their families they had prospered under the French administration, and had little previous understanding of how the peasants and others had suffered under that same regime.

This was just part of the drastic change that occurred in the three years since the Revolution began. The central government and President Ho Chi Minh had abandoned the cities as the French grew stronger and forced them into the jungles. As a result, much authority had to be delegated to the regional administration, military zone, and interzone commanders. The country was divided into three de facto zones of influence:

1. The Free Zone, under Vietnamese control, included the provinces of Thanh Hoa, Nghe An, and Ha Tinh in the North, plus Quang Ngai, Binh Dinh, and Phu Yen in Central Vietnam.

2. The French Occupied Zone consisted of most of the cities and towns of the other forty or so provinces. The contested area included sectors, which neither side controlled completely, but from which both sides took turns in launching attacks on each other.

3. Our Fifth Interzone, the southern half of the Free Zone, was bordered on the north by the city of Danang, in the south by Khanh Hoa province, and on the west by the Highlands. To the east, the French Navy firmly controlled the South China Sea. We were able to attack, ambush, and harass the French and their Vietnamese auxiliary units even in the heart of their occupied zone. All three of our forces—Regular Army, Territorials, and People's Self-Defense units—took part in such operations, in varying capacities and as conditions warranted. Our army avoided direct, unplanned contact with the enemy, however, choosing its targets carefully.

Despite difficult wartime conditions, our forces had made gigantic strides. Young veterans and replacements from Territorial units strengthened our companies. We now had captured enough French weapons and ammunition to arm the troops adequately. Medical and pharmaceutical supplies flowed in from French-occupied areas. And for the first time we began to receive pay: thirty piasters per month (about two to three dollars). We also got two uniforms manufactured in Nam Dinh in the North and Phu Phong in Central Vietnam, plus one hat, one pair of shoes, and one pair of rubber sandals per year. Everyone also received blankets, and nylon sheets (used as raincoats) were also distributed to everyone. Underwear, towels, and toilet accessories were also issued. Finally, logistics were under control and morale was high.

The French ventured into the Free Zone occasionally, using naval vessels with infantry units aboard. They commandeered Vietnamese fishing boats. The soldiers transferred to the captured boats, landed on the coast, and rushed inland to link up with paratroops and armored units. During these assaults, the French destroyed houses and crops, slaughtered animals, captured "suspects," and often raped many unfortunate women. In return, they suffered considerable losses from mines, booby traps, and ambushes, usually set by local Territorial and Self-Defense units.

The recently formed Regiment 83 included personnel and elements from Regiment 79 and the ill-fated Doc Lap Regiment. With Regiment 80, it was now a component of Lien Trung Doan (Inter-Regiment) 80-83. This combined unit's primary mission was to protect the southwest border of the Free Zone against French incursions. Units of Regiment 83 took turns harassing the French. They ambushed mobile units and attacked French static positions along the French defense perimeter, which ran from Cap Varella to the Highlands.

My office developed training and indoctrination materials that addressed five key points:

1. Establish a firm conviction among the men that national independence can and must be regained from the French colonialists to attain social justice for all, and that Ho Chi Minh's leadership was a necessary ingredient for final victory. Efforts to improve social welfare and justice and reduce illiteracy must be carried out during the war and continued thereafter in every corner of Vietnam, in the Highlands as well as lowland areas.

2. Help people realize that the war would be a protracted one and that everyone—men and women, young and old, rich and poor, educated and illiterate—must be involved. We stressed, however, that farmers and workers would be the deciding factor in the outcome of the war as well as the social revolution.

3. Drive home the idea that all three elements of the armed forces had critical roles in the actual fighting. The People's Self-Defense Force, the Territorials, and the Regular Army must complement and support each others' activities, with the Self-Defense Force serving as the backbone for the other two. The importance of the relationship between the three elements, and the relationship between the military and the people, continued to be stressed in all indoctrination sessions. We reminded our troops constantly that these relationships were essential for ultimate victory.

4. Convince the troops that colonial and capitalistic regimes everywhere began to decline after World War II. Stress that power all over the world was passing into the hands of people struggling for independence and a social revolution—with the Soviet Union leading the way.

5. Educate the troops at every level, from privates to generals, using critiques and self-criticism sessions. This method, derived from Leninist doctrine, was designed to help every individual improve his personal conduct, to make the individual responsive to the collective group, and to foster group responsibility for the betterment of every individual. The goal was to make every person a "perfect individual giving himself completely to the cause of the Revolution." Another important pur-

pose of the sessions was to review and learn lessons from combat experience, and to apply that knowledge in relations with the people and in other situations.

One evening in late 1948, Ho Ba looked more serious than usual as the dim, flickering light of a coconut oil lamp played over his features. He asked if we could have a private, personal conversation, and then he took me into his confidence. Nguyen Duong, regimental political commissar, was very impressed with my work and my conduct, Ba told me.

"He thinks you are an excellent cadre and a good example for the troops, and he wants to know if you are willing to join the Communist Party. The party will make you an even better man and cadre to serve the country and the people with much greater efficiency," he said.

His words took me completely by surprise. I had never received such a proposal before, nor had I thought about joining the party. After a long moment, I asked Ba, "Are you a member?"

"Of course I am," he replied swiftly.

This time I couldn't hide my amazement. "How long ago?" He said he had become a full member several months earlier, after being a provisional member[1] for six months.

I told him that I hadn't really given the idea any thought before and needed time to think about it, as well as to learn more about the party. But it was another hour and a half before we finished our conversation.

During the long and sometimes heated discussion, Ba confessed that he was now convinced that, in the long run, only workers and farmers—the oppressed and underprivileged—would endure in the struggle for independence and social revolution. He told me that he realized now how wrong the people of the middle class were in believing that the United States and other Western Bloc nations would support us in the fight against French colonialism. To back up his belief, he brought up the race discrimination question: "They are all white and all capitalists who will back each other against yellow and black people, regardless of nationalities."

I pointed out that the Chinese and Japanese had a long history of colonialism and oppression among their fellow Asiatics—and that the Russians were more white than yellow.

Ba was not impressed with my opinion and reminded me that Ho Chi Minh had begun his crusade for independence by first seeking support from French progressives, and then from the United States and other Western nations. He turned to Russia only after the other nations spurned his efforts.

"Even then," he said, "Ho cooperated with the Americans, not the Soviet Union, during World War II. In the first two years of resistance against the French [1945–47] he repeatedly implored the United States to intervene with the French to grant Vietnam a status similar to that of the Philippines. Remember that this was after Emperor Bao Dai had solemnly abdicated in favor of Ho Chi Minh; therefore Ho was representing the entire nation, not just a splinter group of revolutionaries. Now, with France enjoying the tacit support of America and England, the Vietnamese must welcome support from anyone who will help—and so far Russia is the only country to provide any assistance."

When I asked Ba how much he knew about communism, his reply ran along party lines rather than covering basic ideology. He repeated what I had been hearing in political lectures and indoctrination sessions for several years: "The oppressed, the workers and the farmers, make up the vast majority of the population, and they have a right to freedom from French colonialism and the feudal system. They need leadership to convince them of the rightness and need for a social revolution so that they will contribute actively to the war effort."

Ba then expressed despair and embarrassment over the present position of his father, a high official in the current French-supported administration. Ba's father, Ho Ngan, a mandarin who had served earlier administrations in various capacities, was governor of Quang Nam, the largest and most populous province in what we called the Fifth Military Inter-Region. He came out of retirement to take the post. In his earlier days he was a provincial governor under the French protectorate system, known and well liked as a mandarin of integrity. He and many other mandarins at the time felt that little could be done to overcome the French, so they served the people as best they could under the prevailing conditions. The French did not interfere with mandarins like Ngan as long as their interests—security, collecting taxes, and reaping economic benefits—were met.

Ba, however, regarded his father and the few other remaining compassionate mandarins like him who tried to make life more bearable for the people as obstacles to the revolution. "It is easier to arouse the people to fight for the revolution in areas where French-appointed officials deal harshly with the people," he said.

Ba told me that despite his familial respect for his father, Ba could not forgive his association with the French under the current circumstances—especially since Ba and his two brothers had been with Ho Chi Minh since the beginning. Ba believed that mandarins were too deeply rooted in the ancient feudal system to accept change; they would serve the French against their own people to perpetuate the system and retain their rank and privileges.

His father's position hurt Ba deeply, but he said he was committed to compensating for his father's "crime" and his own debt to his country by fighting for Vietnamese independence. He explained that he had long since decided between his father and the old system on one side, and the people and the Revolution on the other. He was firmly for the Revolution.

That night as I thought about Ba's invitation to join the party, I realized I really knew little about communism—but what I did know caused me to have some misgivings about embracing it completely without careful consideration. I certainly wasn't anti-Communist—I wasn't knowledgeable enough for that—and I admired almost all of the professed Communists I had met. They were the best of us for the most part, dedicated men and women who were brave in battle and totally committed to the struggle for Vietnamese independence. However, some of the Communist philosophy and practices that I had been exposed to did not sit well with me. During the following months, Ba made a determined effort to convert me, pressing on me documents and arguments that supported his belief in communism.

We changed the location of regimental and regional headquarters frequently to confuse enemy intelligence, so I was able to move around and to observe things on a much wider scale than during my years with combat units. Life also was much easier and safer at this level; air attacks and naval bombardment were the main hazards.

The French did launch one large-scale attack on Tuy Hoa and the surrounding area about that time, probably in an effort to wipe out our headquarters. They mounted a two-pronged offensive by about 3,000 men. One group came by road from Nha Trang through Varella Pass. A combined amphibious force, with infantry supported by paratroopers, came by way of the South China Sea. They were well covered by air support and shelling from warships lying offshore. We learned of their intentions from our intelligence units several days before the attack and were well prepared. Civilians evacuated. Mines and booby traps were set, a series of ambushes was arranged, and the regimental staff was well protected.

Both Territorial and Regular Army units were ordered to avoid direct confrontation because the French force was so large. This was in line with our policy of "nothing in the garden and empty houses." At the end of three days the regiment had suffered no casualties, but the provincial Territorial forces' casualties include five killed, seven wounded, and three captured. Our civilians fared less well. Many houses were burned, and about thirty men and women were discovered and captured. Some of the men were tortured and killed. The women, as young as ten and as old as seventy, were brutally raped. French casualties included twenty dead and many wounded.

As was routine after an enemy attack of that nature, my Propaganda and Training Office busied itself analyzing reports and preparing information for the troops and civilians in the area. We coordinated our activities with those of the provincial administration and Territorial command. The propaganda repeatedly emphasized enemy brutality and atrocities against civilians. We reviewed the enemy actions and our counteractions for use in newly developed combat training materials. We also drew on experiences during the attack to improve means of protecting civilian lives and property; these methods were then taught and practiced.

Producing all this material required many meetings and discussions with civilians and cadres involved in each different area of interest. And everything had to be done immediately, to be ready for new actions, which could come at any time. I worked sixteen- to eighteen-hour days, and many others did the same. I rarely saw Nguyen Duong or Ho Ba take time to sleep. Many times Ba and I suddenly realized the sun was rising after we had spent a long night discussing the various problems that faced us. It seemed we were always fighting deadlines of one kind or another. The work also required a great deal of travel around the province, contacting different units and levels of command.

My travels allowed me to visit my sister and her family occasionally. They were on the move a lot, too, because of her husband's job. Le Van Kinh, a public works engineer, was educated by and worked for the French administration before joining the Resistance in 1945. He was from a wealthy landowner family in the northern province of Thanh Hoa and married my sister in the 1930s when my father was one of the district chief justices in that area. The marriage was arranged, in the traditional fashion that consolidated the feudal system, to establish family connections. He had never met my sister before the wedding.

Thanks to his training in modern technology, the French administration employed Kinh as head of the departments of public works in various provinces as well as in a French concession territory in South China. In his last position with the French he was in charge of public works in Phu Yen province. While the old and less desirable city of Tuy Hoa was the capital of Phu Yen, headquarters for the French Residency, where the French governor lived, was in the newer, resortlike Song Cau. The Residency controlled construction, taxation, and production of alcohol, among other lucrative activities. It also supervised the Vietnamese provincial administration, where Kinh had worked.

The surroundings were alluring, with beautiful villas on view everywhere and government buildings set on the beaches under gently waving coconut trees. Kinh earned one and a half times the salary of the Vietnamese provincial governor, and he had a servant, chauffeur and car, and one of the lovely villas as his family residence. I spent a summer vacation there with his family before the Revolution. The small community of French and Vietnamese working for the French formed the elite of provincial high society (although the humblest French were regarded as superior to the highest Vietnamese).

Despite all these privileges and advantages, Kinh and his family enthusiastically joined Ho Chi Minh (whom they had never heard of previously) and the Resistance. From supervising construction for the French, he became head of a Vietnamese "destruction department," implementing our "destroy to resist" policy. One of his first tasks was to demolish his own villa and everything else in Song Cau that could be used by the French if they returned there. He and the family, which included five children, moved with provincial headquarters from one village to another to elude the French. In each village, the family lived with local people. The children went to their respective schools, which frequently had to move to new locations.

Many other Vietnamese from the upper ranks of the country's society felt as Bo Da and Le Van Kinh did: that they owed a debt to their country because they and their families before them had served the French. One was Kinh's good friend, Dr. Pham Nhu Phien, an outgoing, jubilant man who also had worked for the French and lived in Song Cau. In his serious moments, Phien told me that he and others like him were repaying that debt—while people of my generation, who had no history of collaboration and thus no debt to repay, were simply giving of themselves for the betterment of the country and its people. He called young men like me "chiefs," implying that we were a new generation of leaders.

The central hospital for our military area was in An Thuong, a small village near the foothills of a mountain chain that separated the French-occupied Highlands from Binh Dinh province in the Free Zone. In early 1949 I made the 100-mile trip to the central hospital from Regiment 83 headquarters in Phu Yen province partly on foot, partly on a stretcher. Malaria and old wounds had combined to incapacitate me.

An Thuong consisted of fewer than 100 houses; a dozen hospital buildings made of straw, bamboo, and clay; plus a few more substantial brick homes, all surrounded by coconut trees. A wide, clear river flowed nearby, on its way to Bong Son located about ten kilometers away on Highway 1 near the coast.

Three months prior an infection had developed in my arm, due to a shrapnel fragment still lodged there from the wound I received in the battle at Nhi Hiem. This aggravated my chronic malaria. I'd had recurring attacks almost weekly since early 1945 but was able to live with it. The weekly malaria attacks became a daily crisis and, with my infected, painfully swollen arm, made it impossible for me to do my work.

I spent a month in bed at headquarters, cared for by the regimental medical staff. Then I was transferred to An Thuong with a group of casualties being evacuated to the hospital there. A surgeon removed the shrapnel that had been in my arm for more than a year, but the daily malaria attacks continued. There were also other complications. My doctor, a woman named Nguyen Thi Hoang, said my liver and pancreas were badly damaged, and I needed medicine the hospital did not have. Fortunately, my brother Tran Ngoc Hien, head of intelligence in the Free Zone, was able to get French medicine through his connections in the French-occupied cities. It was ironic: he was my savior in this instance but would be my downfall less than two decades later.

I spent my recovery period savoring a peaceful life that contrasted sharply with the combat, hardships, and turmoil of the four previous years. As my strength returned, I used to walk along the river to Bong Son, a bustling town so crowded with civilians and troops that it had become known as the unofficial capital of the South Central area. Shops and restaurants lined Highway 1 for most of the several kilometers between Bong Son and Tam Quan, another coastal town. The crowds dispersed to shelters when enemy airplanes raided two or three times a week, then resumed their normal activities when the planes left.

After two months, I felt well enough to ask that I be returned to the regiment. I was surprised when orders came through for me to report, not to my former post, but to the Office of Cadres at Military Zone Headquarters, which had recently moved back to the Quang Ngai area. A new policy had been established for all cadres, Tran Luong, head of the office, had told me when I reported to him. It was based on the concept that the cadres (officers) play the determining role in the continuity and success of the entire war. Thus, all army and government cadres must be educated to understand fully three vital points:

1. The relationship between the people, the three branches of the armed forces, and the government is the foundation of the people's war.
2. The people must always be treated with respect because they represent the base of the revolution's human, material, and motivational resources.
3. Since the majority of the population was rural, peasants must be given a primary role, but workers from urban areas would have slightly more important leadership roles because they were more aggressive and innovative.

Luong added that cadres from other social classes were also offered the same opportunities for leadership—but they must first adopt the new concept and denounce the exploiters and oppressors of their own classes. He then asked me to take time to recuperate fully, and to use the time to learn more about the Communist Party and the war. Voluminous documents were available through the department and would be at my disposal. Luong explained that, like the other cadres undergoing this recuperation/study regime, I would receive double rations to help my body mend completely, and I would have plenty of free time for study. What it amounted to was more of the indoctrination we had been exposed to almost constantly for the past four years, only this time it was to be self-administered, broader, and perhaps on a higher level.[2]

By now my mind was in turmoil. I still believed fervently in independence for my country, but was Ho's way the only way to achieve it? Or was it even the best way? I knew of other developments in the country. Emperor Bao Dai had recently reached an agreement with the French granting independence to Vietnam. Bao Dai and French President Vincent Auriol signed the pact officially at the Champs Elysées in Paris. Many of us believed that this resulted from a compromise reached between Ho Chi Minh and Bao Dai, then Ho's supreme advisor, before Bao Dai left the country in 1946.

Then one day in mid-1949 I received orders that changed things considerably. I was to be assigned as Dac Phai Vien (special representative observer) to the northern front in the Quang Nam–Danang area. My reports would not only provide information to the Inter-Zone Headquarters in Quang Ngai but would provide a test of my willingness to change my mind concerning party membership. Without acknowledging the necessary leadership role of the party I would never be allowed promotion to greater responsibility. Tran Luong wished me well, saying that he felt I would prove myself as able as I had in the past. More important to my mind, however, was that he gave me a two-week leave before I had to report for my new assignment.

I set out immediately to visit Huong Giang.

I knew where she was because I had received her first and only letter while in the hospital. A friend of hers was now a nurse working at the An Thuong hospital and had written to tell her I was a patient there. In the letter to me, Huong Giang had included her address where she worked, and the address of an aunt where she expected to spend time on leave soon.

It took me days on foot to cover the distance to Tam Ky, where she was currently stationed. You can imagine my disappointment when I learned that Huong Giang had left for her aunt's home just a few days earlier. I set out on another two-day march through isolated villages separated by jungle, forest, and rice fields. Most of the time, the roads were empty except for me. Although the area was remote, beyond the reach of French raids by land or air, I saw the familiar pattern of trenches, foxholes, and obstacles along the paths and trails. Banners and posters related to war and the Revolution displayed prominently in every village were other reminders of the violence elsewhere.

Huong Giang just stared at me without a word for a long while when I arrived at her aunt's house. I could hardly talk myself. Finally her aunt broke the awkward silence by inviting me into her home, a large house that stood amid a fragrant grove of cinnamon trees. The whole district, stretching all the way to the surrounding mountains, was named Que Son (Mountains of Cinnamon) because so many of the prized trees flourished there.

The aunt gave me a room and some clothes left by one of Huong Giang's cousins. Exhausted by my long trek, I went to bed and slept soundly that night after enjoying the unaccustomed luxury of a shower and an excellent meal. The following days were happy and serene, more exciting in some ways than my past combat experiences—because Huong Giang was almost constantly at my side. Her aunt obviously was well aware of the deep feelings between us and made no attempt to be a stern chaperone; rather she let us wander around the garden and talk without interference.

And we had much to talk about. I covered my activities over the past three years, and she told me proudly that she had joined the Communist Party two years earlier. She was happy that she could now give herself to the causes she believed in so deeply: independence for our country and liberation of the oppressed. Obviously she had embraced communism, as it had been taught to her, with every fiber of her being. She then asked me if I had been given the opportunity to join the party. I explained that I had, and told her about my experiences over the past few months. I added that I didn't feel comfortable with the idea yet and wanted more time to think about it, just as I had told Ba in Tuy Hoa several weeks before leaving for the central hospital.

"I didn't expect you to come here, and you shouldn't have done it!" she suddenly blurted out. I was taken aback by her vehemence at first, but then understood what she meant. She was torn between her pleasure at us being together again and her concern that it might affect our commitment to independence and freedom for our country. She was undergoing the same internal struggle between her personal desires and causes she believed were more important that had marked our previous two meetings. "I am greatly tempted also, just as I am sure you are. It would be wonderful to marry and settle here, but it is too late now. We have both changed so drastically from what we once were that we couldn't return to a 'normal' life and consider only our own selfish desires. We have invested too much to change our society and the future of our country; we have changed too much within ourselves."

A few days later Huong Giang bluntly told me that we were both being foolish. "I am instrumental in your weakness, and I can't continue like that. I've decided we can't stay here together and consider only ourselves, over everything else we believe in and have sacrificed for." She said she would report for her trip north, and asked me to go with her the next day to provincial headquarters—then to leave her there. "Neither of us knows what will happen to us in the future, any more than we did in our past meetings, so it's better if we don't make any pledges. We must just keep on with our other passion, the never-ending one: our country and its people."

During the two days' journey to headquarters at Tam Ky, we gradually grew more distant from each other. It was as if we were preparing ourselves for the parting we soon would face. We talked about the people we had met and places we had been since our last meeting three years earlier. We said nothing about ideology or love, but she wondered, "The war will not last forever. Will you wait for me until then?" Then just as quickly and without giving me time to reply, she continued quietly, as if speaking to herself: "Just let time supply the answer."

When I left her at Tam Ky, each of us walked off hastily in opposite directions as if we were afraid that our sentimental feelings would overflow and collide with the harshness of the real world.

I immediately headed north to report to my new commander, Dam Quang Trung. He was a rarity among our leadership: a Highlander from the Thai minority group. He was one of Giap's original forty-man army back in the early 1940s. On my way I stopped to visit a friend, a commander in the Territorials. He informed me that the revolutionary court for the area was to sit in judgment that very night. The defendant was Ho Ngan, father of Ho Ba, my department chief at Regiment 83 three months earlier. Ho Ngan had served as governor of Quang Nam province in the French-installed government. He was captured in Hoi An, provincial capital, and spirited away in an operation set up by my brother Tran Ngoc Hien.

I decided to attend the trial, and it turned out to be a memorable night. The setting was not a wood-paneled courtroom, but an open field lit by several kerosene lamps. About 200 people gathered to watch the proceedings. The judge was Pham Phu Tiet, a respected provincial governor under the French colonial system before the Revolution. Tiet joined the Army of Liberation at the beginning and so far had sent many collaborators to Resistance jails. Tonight he had to decide the fate of an old friend and colleague, someone he had known for almost half a century. Tiet and Ngan were related by marriage, and Tiet knew that three of Ngan's sons were serving brilliantly against the French in the War of Resistance. One of them of course was Ho Ba, head of the political department of Regiment 83 and a dedicated member of the Communist Party.

Ho Ngan, unbound and without shackles, was brought in by two unarmed guards and ordered to sit in a chair facing Pham Phu Tiet. Judge and accused stared silently at each other long moments before the court session began. After the preliminary formalities, the prosecutor stated his case. In brief, it went something like this:

Ho Ngan was born in Quang Nam some sixty years earlier, had served in the colonial Vietnamese administration for more than twenty-five years, and had retired as a provincial governor long before the revolution began in 1945. In 1948 his former colleague, Tran Van Ly, reactivated him to serve as governor of Quang Nam province. Tran Van Ly, chairman of a provisional executive committee under French control, advocated the return of Bao Dai as chief of state of a Vietnam with new status as a republic within the French system. The prosecutor concluded that Ho Ngan had collaborated with the French in their scheme to reconquer the country and should be punished accordingly. There was no mention of any other crimes, his past record of honorable service, or the fact that three of his sons (none were present) were serving in the patriotic army.

When Judge Tiet asked if the defendant had any statement to make, Ngan stood up and said, "Both you and I, Judge, are working toward the same goal for our country: to recover national independence. But we are working in different ways." He added that in the present situation someone had to serve in the post he had accepted and he thought he could better serve his province than someone else who might put personal gain or advancement over the best interests of the people. "But I understand the duties of this court and will accept whatever decision it sees fit to make." Ngan was sentenced to twenty years of detention.

The trial and its implications affected me profoundly. I knew the reputations of both Pham Phu Tiet and Ho Ngan and that the latter had long been regarded as a man of high integrity. There was no doubt in my mind that neither had ever used their positions purely for personal gain. Was Ho Ngan really a criminal, a traitor who deserved such a harsh sentence? If he had been a bad man who exploited the people for his own gain, I could agree that he deserved the sentence meted out. As it was, I could not agree that it was warranted. Nor could I agree with Ngan's statement that both sides were fighting for the same thing: independence for Vietnam. I had come to understand that Ho Chi Minh wanted more than that; he wanted a *Communist* Vietnam. What's more, I realized that he and the other Communist leaders were already working to squash any possible postwar opposition to his plans, and had been doing that for some time.

I returned to the home of my friend, the Territorials commander, only to learn more depressing news: a French bomb had killed a close personal friend, Le Dinh Luan. He was the son of Dr. Le Dinh Tham, current president of the Revolutionary Administration in South Central Vietnam. Luan's brother-in-law was Nguyen The Lam (alias Nguyen Ken), commander of the Sixth Military Region. Luan, who might have used his family connections to secure a nice, safe position, did just the opposite. He always sought assignments with combat units, and was a battalion cadre when he died.

Oddly enough, I never thought much about dying, and it never was a matter of concern during my years of fighting. I looked upon death as a natural thing that could happen at any time; we Buddhists called it "release." Now, however, I wondered if I would die one of these days like Luan, and like so many others around me. So much vitality was gone. Were bodies piled on bodies the only way to achieve independence? Had blood been spilled in vain for fiascos like the one Nguyen Son initiated in the mass attacks on a fortified position near An Khe?

Or was there another way, as Ho Ngan had suggested at his trial? Did the agreement Bao Dai had reached with the French have validity or merit? Was Ho Chi Minh's way the only way Vietnam could be free, or was it just the only way Vietnam could be free to adopt communism? And if that happened, would the country really be free—or would it just exchange one form of oppression for another? I was in a state of profound ideological confusion and mental depression. I was far lower in my mind than I had ever been, even when enduring the most extreme hardships with the army in the field.

I had been content and fulfilled during the entire time I was with combat units in the field and later with the never-ending work at the regimental level. I had looked at everyone around me as my brothers and sisters, but I no longer had that sentiment. My feelings of misery, confusion, and some disillusionment were so strong that I felt I could not continue.

I would rather change course.

9: CHANGING UNIFORMS: AMID A PERIOD OF SOUL-SEARCHING (1950)

Separating from the life and cause I had embraced for nearly half a decade was difficult: I had made up my mind but it wasn't easy. I was leaving a great deal behind: the people I had learned to love; comrades-in-arms I had both taught and learned from, and had faced death with more than once; men I respected, like Ho Ba, Nguyen Duong, and Tran Luong. Unfortunately I could not share their philosophies—now that I understood them. I felt strongly about the impact my action would have on friends I had known for years. They would consider me a traitor, a deserter. Was I being honest with myself? I did some thorough soul-searching. Was I merely hiding cowardice under the noble cover of ideological conflict? Was my decision to leave the Viet Minh influenced by the fact that not joining the Communist Party would block me from further promotion? Did the harsh living conditions affect my thinking? Did Huong Giang's attitude exasperate me?

I considered these points over and over until I finally resolved them in my own mind. When I joined the Resistance five years earlier, my enthusiasm and devotion sprang from a fervor to free the country from the exploitation and subjugation of the French and feudal Vietnamese. My goal, which at the time I thought the Viet Minh shared, was to free poor and underprivileged Vietnamese from the discriminatory treatment, inhuman exploitation, and social injustice imposed on them by French colonialists and their Vietnamese puppets. In the following years, however, I learned that Viet Minh leaders felt that those goals could only be achieved by building a "dictatorship of the proletariat," which would use "revolutionary brutality" to suppress and annihilate such other classes as mandarins, landowners, bourgeois, intellectuals, and capitalists, unless they bowed to the new order. And although, on the surface, the Viet Minh called for the unity of all classes and religions, I gradually learned that the political cadres had begun to condemn religions, calling them poisons that served to help keep people enslaved to the French colonial and Vietnamese feudal systems. I learned more and more about these "new truths" through the documents Ho Ba gave me to read in his efforts to enroll me in the party.

Finally I determined that it was not cowardice, blocked ambition, harsh conditions, or Huong Giang's attitude that caused my decision. My faith in the new ideology and my conviction in what I was doing had crumbled. Conviction had motivated me for the first four years. The weakening of that conviction began in 1949, and soon coalesced with my physical, mental, and psychological frustration. My commitment to the Viet Minh and what it represented no longer seemed valid, or even worthy. In my mind and conscience I knew I *had* to leave.

I must admit, however, that I was not just disenchanted with the Communist ideology. The prospect of living the life of an exemplary Communist, like Ba, scared me. I had not been able to accept the life of a Buddhist priest, so how could I become a dedicated Communist, giving myself body and soul to the party? Then I realized there were major differences. Although I hadn't made it as a Buddhist priest, I still retained my faith in the religion and tried to be a good Buddhist layman. I didn't feel that way about communism. The more I thought about it, the more I realized my devotion to Buddhism distanced me from Communist ideology.

Another element had also entered the picture. Since late 1948 I had followed closely the news about Bao Dai and his efforts to create a new Vietnam. I hoped, like many of my friends, that a possible "entente" could be negotiated between Bao Dai and Ho Chi Minh. Then, in March 1949, when Bao Dai and French President Vincent Auriol signed the Élysée Accords granting independence to Vietnam, I realized this was a momentous event. Until that time, France, and presumably the world, treated Bao Dai as merely the equivalent of a high commissioner (formerly called the governor general). Now he was recognized and treated as a true head of state. I concluded that there might now be an alternative for Vietnamese independence, a different solution than the harsh class struggle that the Communists proposed. And despite his personal flaws, I still felt the traditional loyalty of my family to the Nguyen dynasty that Bao Dai represented.

With my decision firmly made, I considered practicalities; it would be no simple matter to return to my home and family in Hué. I would have to make my way from where I was in Tam Ky to Hoi An, capital of Quang Nam province. That was the nearest city—about sixty kilometers northeast—outside Viet Minh territory. From there I could get to Hué.

Viet Minh forces controlled the most direct route, Highway 1, so I decided to bypass the highway. I set out toward the coast, among groups of villagers going to and returning from marketplaces. A day's march on narrow trails through sandy dunes and rice paddies brought me to a point halfway between Highway 1 and the ocean. Clusters of hamlets nestled among the dunes and paddies, surrounded by bamboo and connected by footpaths. The area was inaccessible to vehicles. For centuries, at least three-fourths of all Vietnamese had lived in similar hamlets dispersed throughout the country.

At that time, news of war and revolution filtered into such backwaters via government sources and Viet Minh cadres on leave or recuperating from injuries or illness. Although the war had been raging for almost five years, people in these dispersed hamlets near the coast seemed to lead a peaceful life—despite great changes in their environment. Every hamlet entrance was plastered with information bulletins, signs, and revolutionary slogans. Foxholes, trenches, and bamboo walls were scattered around the homes, and members of the People's Self-Defense Force patrolled everywhere.

I spent the night in the big brick home of the father of a friend who was in Regiment 83 with me. The man, a widower for years, shared the home with his daughter and her husband. He showed me inflammatory material placed all around the house, ready to set ablaze, in case French troops came to occupy the area. He still owned some land and regularly received rice quotas from his tenants—part of which he contributed to the "budget of resistance" to feed Viet Minh troops in the field. He also took part in village activities to promote the "new life" campaign.

I explained to my friend's father that I was to report to a new assignment on the northern front, but was still recuperating from my recent illness. "I still feel weak, and I don't think I'm fit enough for a long overland march," I told him.

"I understand, my son," he said sympathetically. "I will make arrangements for you to take passage on a small courier boat that travels up and down the river." He was referring to the intercoastal waterway parallel to the coast from Tam Ky all the way to Hoi An. I embarked that evening on a small wooden craft thatched over with coconut leaves. A two-man crew propelled it with oars and poles. As compensation for carrying messages and cadres along the waterway, they were also allowed to carry passengers for a fee.

Aboard with me were eight other passengers, two men and six women. We sat wedged tightly together in the small cabin. We traveled all night, moving slowly along the stream, which averaged about fifty meters wide and no more than a few meters deep. As the other passengers drifted off to sleep, I watched for hours as the boat slipped peacefully past rows of straw and wood houses on the bank. Silhouettes of people moved about in the dim light of oil lamps.

The small town of Cho Duoc lay at the junction of two rivers. One flowed down from the mountain highlands; the other (which we had traveled) linked Viet Minh territory and the area controlled by French and Vietnamese forces. Cho Duoc was, by unspoken agreement, a sort of neutral zone, a hive of intelligence activities by both sides. Ranks of boats crowded the riverbank, while shops and restaurants lined the shore. The French left it alone and allowed merchandise of all kinds, including pharmaceutical products, to flow in from the cities they controlled. This allowed their agents to mix with real merchants as cover for intelligence activities. It also gave them a showplace in the Viet Minh zone where they could display all the "good things of life" available in sectors under French military control, but now officially part of the independent Vietnam with Emperor Bao Dai as head of state.

Viet Minh cadres, soldiers, and ordinary people crowded the streets of Cho

Duoc, all there to shop and relax. It served as a sort of rest and recuperation center where people could escape the realities of war going on just a short distance away. I went to a coffee shop, ordered noodle soup and a cup of coffee, and began talking to two men who were already waiting for their meals. Both were Territorial cadres on routine surveillance duty with their men. Specifically, the unit manned checkpoints and provided patrols and backup for the police.

My new acquaintances took me to meet their commander. After checking my papers, he discussed possible infiltration routes and methods that enemy forces or agents might use to get in and out of the area. The information helped me plan an itinerary for the next day that would get me to the Thu Bon River. On the other side was Hoi An and the perimeter of Vietnam that was controlled by French military and their Vietnam allies—what the Viet Minh called the Occupied Zone. The Thu Bon River began as a small stream in the border region near southern Laos. It expanded to about one kilometer wide, and its depth increased markedly, in this area near the coast. Viet Minh and French security forces were very active on their opposing banks of the stream.

On the morning of my crossing I put on my khaki uniform and a fatigue cap that bore the emblem of a field-grade Viet Minh officer and hired a small sampan to take me to the other side. The middle-aged women who operated the sampan looked at me for a long moment, as though she was about to question me. Perhaps the uniform and pistol I wore at my side confused her. Then she seemed almost to shrug—as if thinking *it's none of my business*—and moved her boat into position so I could board it.

I knew I was navigating on a tightrope, with death waiting if I faltered. Once I was on the water, either side might capture me, Viet Minh or French. In either case it could be fatal, but I knew I had a better chance to survive with the French. Just a few months earlier I witnessed the execution of a platoon leader who was caught leaving Viet Minh territory with the intention of deserting. That incident occurred in Phu Yen province, but the same penalty would apply here.

The prospect of being caught, condemned, and executed as a traitor had been a heavy burden on my heart since I decided I could not become a Communist and continue with the Viet Minh. My mind was made up, however, and I would not back down now. I felt that I would be a greater traitor if I turned my back on my religious and philosophical roots than I would be by continuing to fight for the Viet Minh and their Communist ideology. Besides, I felt no guilt or sense of betrayal. I hoped, in fact, that I might open a better way for many of my former comrades-in-arms—most of whom were not Communists—to fulfill their nationalistic beliefs and to achieve their dreams of true independence.

As these thoughts occupied my mind, the small sampan glided smoothly over the water. It was a peaceful early morning, and other sampans moved along the Viet Minh bank. A few motorboats crisscrossed the river to and from the French side. My boat didn't seem to attract any attention from either side. As we approached the French-controlled riverbank, I picked a moment when the woman operator of the sampan was not watching and slipped my pistol into the water. I did not want to be captured with the weapon or have to surrender it officially. I wanted to feel, and be looked upon, like a nationalist Vietnamese who had fought for his country's liberty, then lost his conviction because of the way the Viet Minh were pursuing that goal.

It was still early in the morning when I disembarked and proceeded to the Vietnamese provincial headquarters, a few hundred meters away. When I arrived at the entrance, the sight of my uniform and insignia caused turmoil. Several guards gathered as I approached, but they calmed down as they realized I was unarmed. I shouted, "I am a Viet Minh officer and I want to talk to your officer." Confusion reigned for five to ten minutes, then a uniformed officer came out and asked, "What do you want?"

"I am a Viet Minh officer and son of former justice Tran Dao Te," I replied. "I have just quit the Viet Minh and want an audience with the provincial governor."

The officer asked me to repeat my statement and wrote it on a piece of paper, then requested that I take a seat and wait. He reappeared in a few minutes and asked me to accompany him. I entered a large room to find several officials waiting. We shook hands, and they introduced themselves in turn. In the absence of the provincial governor, Secretary General Tong Quynh (who would become governor of the province himself just a year later) was the first to welcome me. Then Cabinet Chief Trong Ngoc Diep (who would become provincial governor of Dinh Tuong, south of Saigon, in the early 1960s) did the same.

I explained bluntly that I had decided to quit the Viet Minh because I felt that Emperor Bao Dai and the Vietnamese allied with him could achieve national independence without abolishing my family's traditional roots and religious beliefs. I made it clear that I chose to return to the Vietnamese government but not to the French. I made it clear that I would rather kill myself than be turned over to the French by the Vietnamese.

Both Quynh and Diep said they knew my father by reputation and assured me that I would be under Vietnamese national jurisdiction. There would be no question of giving me over to the French. I then asked if I could stay temporarily with an old friend of my father who lived nearby. They agreed that I was free to do so. Father's friend was an elderly man who lived with his wife and a daughter in a big house near the city's center. Some thirty years earlier he had met my father, who was chief of Que Son district at the time. They had remained friends ever since. The family owned land, including a vast cinnamon plantation in Que Son, but had moved to

Hoi An in 1945 when the revolution began. They greeted me effusively, and the old man showered me with affection. I spent the rest of the day talking with him and his wife, and he showed me several letters he had received from my father during the past few years.

The next morning, as I was eating breakfast, two Vietnamese men came and asked to see me. I had met one of them at provincial headquarters the previous day. He introduced his companion as deputy chief of the Federal Sureté (comparable to the U.S. Federal Bureau of Investigation). They told me that the chief of the Sureté, who was a Frenchman, invited me to visit him at a time convenient to me. I was surprised at the "invitation" and told the men that I must consult with Vietnamese authorities before I could comply with the request. I then went to talk to Truong Ngoc Diep, chief of Cabinet, about the matter. He reassured me and explained the situation.

Although France had ceremoniously granted Vietnamese independence to Emperor Bao Dai in the March Accords, the French still controlled much of the administration—security and the military, in particular. The Federal Sureté handled all political activities and military matters related to the war against the Viet Minh. Vietnamese people in those fields of operation were directly under French command. The newly created "independent Vietnam" was divided into three (soon to be four) regions: North, Center, and South, with the "Crown Territory" (which would cover the Central Highlands) to be added in the near future. A Vietnamese governor administered each region, with a French commissioner responsible for military command and territorial security. The Vietnamese who had worked in the French colonial security system, and had not joined the Viet Minh, were integrated with the French Federal Sureté and placed under French chiefs, and they received their salaries from France. Several of those Vietnamese received promotions to much higher positions than they held previously. On the military side, Vietnamese who served in French regular or territorial forces and the Vietnamese militia under the colonial system were treated similarly. They were integrated into French regular forces or Vietnamese territorial units and placed under French command. Former Vietnamese NCOs and junior-grade officers became officers and field-grade officers, respectively.

Here in Hoi An, the Vietnamese governor ran everything in Quang Nam province, except that the French Federal Sureté could arrest and detain those suspected of pro–Viet Minh activities. The Vietnamese military commander of the province, a former NCO recently promoted to lieutenant, was actually administrative officer, for all practical purposes. His companies were assigned separately and placed under the French territorial command.

The French chief, a man in his forties and a veteran of nearly twenty years in the organization, greeted me warmly at the Sureté compound. He spoke Vietnamese perhaps better than his native language. He ushered me into his large office, where we talked, in Vietnamese, for almost two hours. I learned he had been fully informed about my background, even going back generations in my family. He asked specifically about my activities during the five years with the Viet Minh, other cadres I had worked with, and my relationship with my brother, Tran Ngoc Hien, who had recently been promoted and now commanded all Viet Minh intelligence and counter-intelligence agencies in South Central Vietnam and the Highlands. He was credited with capturing the former provincial governor, Ho Ngan, from this city several months ago, as mentioned earlier.

I provided some information, but short of any details that might help the French in action against my former comrades. He did not insist on more, knowing I would refuse.

Three days later, I was "invited" to the French military command headquarters in Danang. My "hosts" installed me in a room in the most luxurious hotel in town. Each day a French lieutenant escorted me to headquarters for debriefing. French forces were ambushed in the Deo Hai Van (Cloudy Pass) between Danang and Hué during the past year and had suffered heavy losses. My questioners wanted to know more about units, commanders and resources involved in that action, as well as in other operations. They were especially interested in Dam Quang Trung, Viet Minh commander of the Danang–Quang Nam Front. Trung had led many successful operations on this front.

I explained that I might know less about the man than they did—beyond the story that he had been one of the forty volunteers recruited by Vo Nguyen Giap to form the first Vietnam platoon for guerrilla actions against the Japanese. When they realized that I had not even reported to my new commander and knew little about this area, they ended the debriefing and flew me to Nha Trang for more questioning.

Nha Trang served the same purpose in southwestern Central Vietnam that Danang did in north-central Vietnam. Like Danang it was a big city and major seaport that the French used as a command center and logistical support base for troops operating in provinces along the coast and far up into the Highlands. It also was home for French naval and air bases. Stretches of coast and most of the mountainous Highlands between Nha Trang and Danang, much of it jungle, had remained firmly under Viet Minh control since the revolution began.

A Captain Papou interrogated me in Nha Trang. He was about thirty, well educated, and courteous, much different from the usual type of colonial officers—who typically were much older in that rank, and ruder when dealing with most Vietnamese. In meetings that followed, he showed me maps and aerial photos and asked questions about numerous military operations he felt I should have been familiar with, considering the positions I had held over the years. The interrogation went on for several days. Captain Papou was unfailingly pleasant and courteous, probably using his mild manner to encourage me to talk freely and openly, in hopes he could draw forth the maximum amount of information. I responded by giving him a great deal of information, but all of it was obsolete.

One day he took me on a flight in a light reconnaissance airplane to pinpoint locations where battalions, regiments, and military zone headquarters had been based. He seemed amazed when I cooperated by doing so with great precision. The captain probably never realized that I did so because those Viet Minh units never stayed in one place very long, and they used so many different locations that the French could never find the right one at any given time.

He halted the interrogation for two days at one point, and I was allowed to roam around the city and nearby beach. There were many shops and stores, well stocked with goods of all kinds. Men and women of all ages looked happy and content.

Suddenly my memory flashed back a couple of years to the time when a group of similar people slipped out of Nha Trang to visit my unit in the caverns of Hon Heo after one of our successful ambushes against a French convoy. I remembered their radiant expressions and the way they cheered our efforts against the French on that earlier occasion. The merchandise I saw in Nha Trang's shops that day also resembled the gifts we received under the lights of torches in the caves, amid dancing, songs, and applause from our guests.

The last night before my return to Danang I had another reminder of that night in the caverns. A French officer in the Foreign Legion invited me to dinner in a restaurant at the beach.

On the way back to the hotel he stopped and led me into a bar. As we sat down in the dim interior, a young hostess came over, wrapped her arms around the officer, and sat next to him. She soon sensed my presence and turned toward me with a glance that soon became a glare. I looked more closely at her, and then stared in amazement. She was one of the young girls who had been in our group of visitors from Nha Trang! On that earlier night I sat in the front row and watched her and the rest of the group perform dances and songs as they paid tribute to the troops after the victorious battle on Route 21. Instinctively I tried to avoid being recognized. I was confused, asking myself whether she was a genuine hostess or one of the numerous women spying for my brother Hien in the heart of the French-controlled city.

Back in my room later I tossed and turned for hours, unable to sleep. Memories the woman had awakened about that night in the Hon Heo mountain cave tormented me. I felt guilty for having accepted the admiration and love of the visiting civilians from Nha Trang two years earlier. I strove to overcome the feelings of being a deserter, and reviewed the reasons I should not feel like a traitor.

As the aircraft taking me back to Danang flew over Highway 1 the next morning, I could see and revive memories of the routes I had used, the locations where I had been based, and the battlefields where I had fought in my four years with the Independence (Doc Lap) Regiment and Regiments 79 and 83. Images of men I knew who had been killed or wounded ran through my mind. Pictures of Huong Giang, both glamorous and defiant as she was at times, came unbidden to my mind—and stabbed deep into my heart; I knew she was now lost to me forever. I then realized that my sentiments remained attached to all those people who made that part of my life so vivid and meaningful, but my confrontation with Communist ideology had intervened and caused me to realize that ideology conflicted with my most ingrained and cherished beliefs.

An opportunity to visit my parents soon dispelled such thoughts, or at least pushed them to the back of my mind.

My mother and father showed little outward expression upon seeing me, although I felt sure they must be deeply moved. In the five years since the revolution began, our large, once close-knit family had been divided and separated. Two of my sisters and their families had followed the Viet Minh. They had lived in the Viet Minh Fifth Military Interzone ever since. My brother Hien and I had been operating in the same interzone, but we seldom saw each other. Two of my older brothers joined the Viet Minh in the early 1940s. One, Tran Van Chuong, left Hanoi for the jungle with the Ho Chi Minh government after the successful French offensive in 1946. The other, Tran Chau Khang, had returned to Hanoi and had a successful business there. Another married sister lived with her husband and children in Danang.

Because of the constant fighting in the vicinity my parents had abandoned their property on the outskirts of the city and moved into the Citadel area of Hué. Only my youngest brother, Tran Huong Que, a college student, lived with them now. Both mother and father looked much older than their ages. My father was still in good health, but my mother was not. Neither questioned me much at first, inquiring only about the living conditions for my sister Hong Lien and her family, and how my brother Hien and some of their old friends were doing. One evening a few days later, after the ritual prayer, my father turned to me and asked, "Son, would you mind telling me the reason you returned?"

"I lost my original conviction, Father, and without it I felt weak, lost, and desperate," I answered. "I found I could not fully accept the Communist philosophy, so I decided to leave the Viet Minh. I became a different person after I lost my conviction, and became more concerned about preserving my life than when I was deeply committed to the Viet Minh cause."

Despite my explanation I suddenly felt both guilty and ashamed again, as if I had committed an act of cowardice and disloyalty to friends and people I had lived with for so many years. But even in that moment, although I retained my affection for Ho Ba and the few other Communist cadres I had known, I had no remorse or guilt for my actions in regard to them. I felt I had been loyal and acted honorably in respect to them personally, but had only disagreed with them ideologically.

My father didn't say anything for a short time, perhaps sensing that my mind was wandering along its own disturbing paths. As I focused on him again, he ended our conversation on a comforting note. "Son, I believe and trust in you. It would not be suitable nor am I capable of telling you what to do. I just remind you that under no circumstances should you neglect to review your thoughts and actions daily, so you won't stray from the family heritage and the guidance of our religion."

My mother sat quietly as usual, without interrupting, during our talk. I could see that she was saddened by the fact that she might never again see some of her children and grandchildren, who had been the focus of her entire life.

A few days after I returned, the governor of Central Vietnam, Phan Van Giao, sent for me. Giao had been a close friend of my elder brother, a linguist who joined Ho Chi Minh years earlier and served as an official translator in Vietnamese, English, and French for the Viet Minh Politburo and Central Committee. Giao also knew the reputations of my father and grandfather.

Giao spent two hours talking with me that day. He showed great interest in my story and asked numerous questions about the living conditions and psychological status of the troops, officers, and people in the areas where I had lived during the past five years. He then asked me to devise a plan to rally people who were still fighting on the other side to the new Vietnam. During our conversation, only his secretary, a lovely young Frenchwoman, interrupted us occasionally to serve coffee and cookies. Before I left, Giao gave me an envelope and asked me to accept it as a gift from a brother to help me resettle. He also asked me to return and discuss with him any ideas I developed that might bring back some of those in the Resistance who might be having second thoughts about the Viet Minh and communism, as I had.

The following day I got a call asking that I present myself to the Second Bureau (J2) of the General Staff of the French Central Vietnam Command. My reception there was cool. The French major who received me was in his forties; his insignia identified him as an officer of the colonial infantry. He asked me to write a complete history of my life and activities from my school days to the present, including all contacts and meetings I had had since I left the Viet Minh. This was a hard blow to my feelings and expectations. I began to realize that rallying to the new Vietnam under Bao Dai had cost me a great deal of pride and dignity. During the years I fought against the French I looked down on them. They were intruders, oppressors, in my country. Now that I had returned to what I expected would be an independent, non-Communist Vietnam, the French obviously regarded me with disdain and suspicion.

I asked the major to let me do the writing at home and to give me a few days to complete it. I then arranged another meeting with Governor Giao and told him what had happened. He explained calmly that the procedure was normal. "The French for now are in charge of the war and security so they must do the job properly. We have little leverage on our side to attain full independence," he said. "Instead, how much independence the emperor can get and how fast we can gain it depends to a great degree on how Ho Chi Minh's forces fare against the French."

He looked me in the eye, smiled, and commented maliciously, "We are all Vietnamese, on both sides, and we complement each other. Both sides want national independence. The French used us and in a sense we have used Ho Chi Minh and the threat he represents to regain the degree of independence we now have. Just be patient and have faith in the emperor."

Then Giao picked up the telephone and asked to speak to a certain colonel on the French General Staff. I stepped out for a few minutes to let him have a private conversation. When I returned he told me that the matter was settled but suggested that, as a face-saving gesture for the French major, I should write a few pages as my "history" and present it to the officer on the following day. I did so, and the major didn't say much this time, but did demand that I report to his office once a week and inform him about my activities and contacts.

At a later meeting he took me to meet the colonel to whom Governor Giao had talked on the telephone. This officer was much more cordial than the major; in fact, he offered me a new opportunity. "If you agree, I will send you to Vietnamese officer training school for a few months to learn about modern tactics and weaponry. Then you could be commissioned as an officer in our newly created Vietnamese army."

"I appreciate your generous offer," I temporized politely, "but I would like to have time to consider the idea."

For several weeks I had been observing the new faces and structure of the independent Vietnam under the emperor. Bao Dai held the title of chief of state and served as prime minister. His deputy and minister of defense was a Vietnamese-born French general, Nguyen Van Xuan, who was educated in France and had served in the French Army for his entire military career. He spoke very little Vietnamese. Most other cabinet ministers were known for their scholarly or professional achievements, or had served under French and French-supported Vietnamese administrations. Either they never had any connection with Ho Chi Minh, or had joined the Viet Minh briefly in the revolutionary fervor of 1945 but had left after a few months.

The central government had only limited authority. It worked with the French

Commissioner General's Office (formerly the French Governor General's Office under the colonial system) to set up procedures and formalities for a changeover of
whatever duties France agreed to transfer to our government. As a result the real
Vietnamese authority lay in the hands of the regional governors, who had performed
only a restricted role as administrators for civilian affairs under the Japanese, who
excluded them from military and security matters. Almost all civil servants in 1949
and 1950 were holdovers from the French-Vietnam colonial government system.

The military school that the French colonel suggested I attend had been established in 1947, long before the French even considered granting the country independent status under Bao Dai. Located on the outskirts of Hué in the former
Customs and Registration[1] (Douanes et Regies) facilities, it had produced sixty-
some second lieutenants in its brief existence. Most graduating lieutenants were assigned to lead Vietnamese territorial platoons manning the multitude of fortified
blockhouses and other posts protecting areas within French-controlled territory.
These were sectors that the French called "pacified territories," while the Viet Minh
term for them was "temporarily occupied areas." Such fortified posts were under the
direct operational command of the French military, which provided them with
weapons, ammunition, and other combat equipment.

Nguyen Van Thieu was among those graduated from that first officer-training
course. He later became a major general and the last U.S.-supported president of
South Vietnam.[2] Other graduates included Nguyen Huu Co, later a major general,
deputy prime minister, and minister of defense; and Dang Van Quang, who also
made major general and was one of Thieu's most important counselors. Similar
schools in Cochinchina (the South) and Tonkin (the North) produced officers of
similar caliber during the same period. Best known of them was Nguyen Khanh,
later a general and U.S.-supported chief of state for a short time between Presidents
Diem and Thieu.

When the French colonel suggested I attend the school, the second course was in
its third or fourth month. The idea repelled me, however. Everybody knew the
school was created solely to produce Vietnamese officers for regional units used by
the French to make up for their lack of Regular Army forces, and that almost all
trainees were recruited from among NCOs and interpreters who had been serving
France since the Revolution began in 1945. During even the short time I spent traveling between and staying in Hoi An, Danang, Nha Trang, and Hué, I saw how
people despised such officers and their Vietnamese troops. Nearly everyone looked
down on them as mercenaries selling their blood for the French and acting against
their own country.

People had reason to feel that way; they knew the best of their countrymen, especially the youth, had joined the Viet Minh and continued to fight the French. They

also knew that the term "independence" was barely mentioned on this side, and people considered that Bao Dai had been installed more as a figurehead to cover up the real authority still held by the French than as head of a truly independent Vietnam. As I wandered around visiting friends and relatives, I realized that only a few of those who had joined the resistance in 1945 had returned, although "return-ees" who had been civil servants or in the military were offered financial incentives: full back pay from the time of the Japanese coup, even covering any period they had been with the Viet Minh.

I found that very few people bothered to hide their sympathy and admiration for those on the other side, whom they referred to affectionately as "the Resistance." The term "Communists" was seldom heard, used mainly in official French and Viet-namese media and occasionally in Catholic circles. The public had been told that Ho Chi Minh and his lieutenants were Communist agents and that under commu-nism there would be "no family, no religion, no Motherland." Almost no one seemed to comprehend what that meant. What they did know was that Ho and the Viet Minh had fought consistently against the French, and against both the Japanese and French during World War II. They also knew that many well-known and respected Vietnamese—from the emperor Bao Dai, who abdicated in favor of Ho Chi Minh in August 1945; to scholars, young boys and girls, aristocrats, bourgeois, poor peas-ants, and workers—had joined Ho's forces. The elite had Viet Minh adherents they could identify with, as did those of various religions.[3] Even at the present time, after Bao Dai was again recognized as leader of a newly independent Vietnam, the real power still was in the hands of the French. Most Vietnamese knew that granting in-dependence and installing Bao Dai as head of state were only French tricks to de-ceive them.

When I returned to meet with Governor Giao, I was very blunt when we dis-cussed a plan to rally members of the Resistance to the new Vietnam. "It is my opin-ion that, under current circumstances, we would be likely to attract only the least desirable elements from the Viet Minh," I said. "And that would only consolidate the other side.

"If, in late 1948, I had not been transferred to the regimental staff to work in the political department with Nguyen Duong and Ho Ba, and if they had not tried to enroll me in the Communist Party, I might not have left. It was only then that I had the opportunity—indeed the obligation—to study in depth the final objectives of the 'war for independence.' Because of that I soon realized that, although I was whole-heartedly for independence, social justice, and freedom, I could never support class struggle or denial of religious beliefs, which are key points in the Communist ideol-ogy. Not many of the cadres, especially those who spend most of their time on the battlefield, have an opportunity to study and fully understand these points."

Before any plan to attract defectors from the Viet Minh could work, I told him, the Bao Dai government must be truly independent, with all the powers the French still retained. Vietnamese who served in the military and civil services must be equal in spirit and dedication to those on the other side.

Gaio nodded agreement. "The more successful Ho Chi Minh is, the more concessions Bao Dai can wring from the French," he added. He ended the discussion with this observation: "As of now the Vietnamese loyal to Bao Dai are in two categories: opportunistic profiteers and nationalistic idealists—and idealism usually is short-lived when it confronts materialism!" With that parting shot, Gaio asked me to contact Captain Nguyen Ngoc Le, commanding officer of the regional force,[4] to make arrangements for my "normalization" so that the French Sureté and Second Bureau[5] would cease harassing me. And that situation did have to be resolved, I realized, before I could make any decision as to my future.

Captain Le welcomed me warmly and talked to me as if I were his young brother. In his forties and a sincere man, Le served in the French colonial military corps as an NCO. He had recently been promoted to captain and transferred to the newly formed regional force. His command theoretically covered all Vietnamese units in Central Vietnam. Realistically, however, the force, composed mostly of Vietnamese who had also served in the French colonial military, was spread across all provinces in the region. It was divided into platoon- and company-size units, all under direct French command. Thus, Le and his staff—who had also been career noncoms in French auxiliary units—performed only administrative duties and supplemented French activities in dealing with those suspected of being Viet Minh agents. A first lieutenant (there were only two in the entire force at the time) was the second senior officer; all other officers on Le's staff were second lieutenants.

Rapid developments during the following months affected me deeply.

By early 1950 the United States, Great Britain, and Thailand had recognized Vietnam as an independent nation. The war was intensifying. A new government of relatively respected Vietnamese had been formed (Nguyen Van Xuan, the Vietnamese-born French general had resigned), and France had ceded more authority to Bao Dai and his Vietnamese administration. One concession was an agreement that territorial and auxiliary units attached to the French Corps were to be reorganized and integrated into a Vietnamese army. Officers and NCOs of those units retained their status in this new national service and wore Vietnamese Army uniforms. Suddenly I was uncomfortable, clad in my quasi-uniform and being a subordinate of all those officers for whom I had little respect. I had no desire to serve in an army that was merely an extension of the French forces, but now that we were to have our own military service my feelings were confused.

I went to see Governor Giao. A few weeks earlier he had been promoted to major general, the first Vietnamese army general and the only one at that time. He was to take charge of organizing the new Vietnamese national army, which was nonexistent at the time. The territorial and auxiliary units had always been under French command. Giao told me the government planned to draft all young Vietnamese men under age thirty-five into the army. He explained also that the first Vietnamese Military School of Inter-Arms (patterned after the French Military School of Inter-Arms at St. Cyr and West Point in the United States) was being formed. He suggested that I would be wise to attend that school for nine months. Upon graduation he would send me to France for higher training, and then he would appoint me to his staff where my experience and training could be best employed.

I spent many days and nights agonizing over what decision I should make. Then I realized, and was amazed at, my moral dishonesty. I had quit the Viet Minh because I wanted independence for my country but not with its traditional society and roots totally destroyed, which was the Communists' goal. I wanted to preserve the value of our culture and my religion, to see peace and social justice for everyone, but without unnecessary class struggle. Yet now I hesitated about getting involved in the fight to achieve those ends—simply to preserve my pride and satisfy my haughty attitude. I was both confused and ashamed. I decided to talk to my father. That wise, elderly man listened to me silently as I poured out my conflicted thoughts. When I finished he sat silently for a long time. Then he offered this advice:

"You seem to be in a state of inner conflict. First, you must resolve that by making peace within yourself. Sleep well tonight. Wake up early tomorrow, bathe, put on clean clothes, have a cup of tea, and go to the altar.[6] Turn on the light, but keep it dim. Burn three sticks of incense, pay your respects to your grandfather and to Buddha, then pray and meditate. With the moral integrity of your grandfather and the spiritual power of Buddha guiding you, you will come to the right decision."

I followed my father's instructions to the letter, and realized that since my return to the new semi-independent Vietnam I had acted selfishly and arrogantly. I had strayed from the humble spirit of my grandfather and from the teachings and principles of Buddhism. As a result, I was in danger of losing my compassion for the country and its people. I now felt I owed everybody an apology. Reinvigorated, I was ready to work toward a new and better Vietnam in any and every way possible.

10: I BECOME AN OFFICER IN THE SOUTH VIETNAMESE ARMY (1951)

ow ironic, I thought to myself as I awoke early one morning early in 1951. Here I was, a devout Buddhist, a man once in training to wear the saffron robe and carry the begging bowl of a bonze, a Buddhist priest. As a youth, I thought my life would be devoted to meditation and prayer, yet I had just spent nearly four-and-a-half years fighting in a revolutionary army.

Now, attending the military academy, I was committed to a career as a professional officer. Waves of doubt swept through me, but I recalled the words of encouragement from my father and the soul-searching they inspired. I had made my decision and could not look back. I must do everything I could to make my country free and independent, especially now when Vietnam was at a critical point in its history.

It was more than a year since I decided to join the Vietnamese Army, created after French President Vincent Auriol officially recognized Vietnam as an independent state within the French union.[1] I volunteered to be a member of the first class at the academy, then known as the School of Military Inter-Arms. It was patterned after the French military academy at St. Cyr. The school's entire staff—administration, service staff, and instructors—were French,[2] and French was the teaching language.[3] We even ate French food, being allowed only two Vietnamese meals each week.

Initial recruiting for the academy's first class was somewhat discouraging. Only a few hundred young Vietnamese men volunteered, and fewer than 100 were accepted.[4] Of the thirteen candidates selected from the Central Vietnam area, only three of us were civilian candidates. The remaining ten were already in military service, as noncommissioned officers (NCOs) in Vietnamese Regional Guard units, or as interpreters or NCOs in the French Army. Some candidates from the South came from paramilitary groups formed by religious sects (Cao Dai, Hoa Hao, and Binh Xuyen). The number of cadets who first began training was so small that authorities initiated an accelerated recruiting program that brought in about fifty additional cadets to join us. All these were civilian candidates with no military background. They also were younger, generally between nineteen and twenty-two years old, and they were not required to take the three- to four-month preparatory military training that those of us in the original group underwent before entering the School of Military Inter-Arms.

Our academy occupied a former Japanese base in the beautiful city of Dalat.

French colonialists, as mentioned earlier, created Dalat as a resort in the mountains of Central Vietnam some sixty years earlier. After the Japanese withdrew and the French returned, the facility was used to train about a dozen Vietnamese holding French citizenship to serve as officers in the Republican Guard of the Autonomous State of Cochinchina (in the southern part of Vietnam).[5] Among them were several who later became generals and held important positions in South Vietnam: Nguyen Khanh, who became chief of state in 1964, and Tran Thien Khiem, a prime minister under President Thieu.

My first few days as a cadet disturbed me deeply. I was not used to French military discipline. Discipline in the Viet Minh had been even harsher in some ways, but then we had worked and lived under harsh conditions that demanded a strict regime. It also seemed more democratic because of the self-criticism sessions, plus constant reviews of our conduct and operations. Now we followed a strict code of military regulations that governed almost all of our behavior, even in minor respects.

As cadets, our French officers and instructors ordered us how to dress, when and how to eat (using knives and forks instead of our traditional chopsticks), and how to arrange our quarters. They woke us up in the middle of cold nights to dress in combat uniforms and run around the area conducting various field exercises. This approach seemed rather superfluous to me, especially when I recalled the years I had commanded a platoon, then a company, and finally a battalion of Viet Minh troops in attacks against the Japanese and French. I admit to being somewhat resentful because I now had to take orders from a French lieutenant who had never seen a day of combat. That was not easy for me.

I also compared my Viet Minh training with what we experienced at Dalat. Political education, human behavior, and community relations constituted more than half of the six or seven months of that Viet Minh training—from basic to company and battalion level. (Community relations included working to erase illiteracy, helping people rebuild homes, and working on community improvement projects.) Instructors stressed guerrilla tactics and Ho Chi Minh's "swim among the fishes" concept in the actual military phases of our training.

At Dalat, instructors ignored such subjects. They concentrated on pure military subjects: topography, weaponry, battlefield communications, use of artillery, air and naval support—subjects covered either in rudimentary fashion or not at all by Viet Minh instructors. Thinking back years later, I realize that the combination of Viet Minh and French instruction gave me a broad education in both guerrilla and conventional warfare. The political and social phases of Viet Minh education provided insight into the ills of our society, ills that I felt must be corrected if Vietnam was to become a truly independent, cohesive nation.

Shortly after graduation, with my new first lieutenant bars still bright and shiny, I took some leave time to visit my parents in Hué. I wanted to get their approval to marry eighteen-year-old Bich Nhan, daughter of Mr. Ho Tanh, who was a respected district chief in Quang Tri province during the early 1940s when my father was a provincial chief justice.

I had met Bich Nhan the first time a few weeks after I returned to Hué following my departure from the Viet Minh. She looked very much like Huong Giang, which both attracted and disturbed me. We spent time together, but quite strictly chaperoned, as was traditional at that time. We found we enjoyed each other's company. Both her mother and mine approved of the relationship and made it obvious that they hoped to see us marry. My mother, who was very ill at the time, told me she would like to know that I was married to a fine woman like Bich Nhan before she died. "My future is still too unsettled for me to consider marriage at this time," I told her, "but I agree that Bich Nhan will make a wonderful wife, and I will ask her to marry me when the time is appropriate." I said much the same thing to Bich Nhan, and she agreed to marry me when I was in a position to take a wife and start a family.

After our wedding we returned to Dalat where I was assigned as an instructor. We arranged to share a villa in the married officers' quarters on the academy grounds with another newly married couple: Nguyen Van Thieu and his wife. Thieu graduated from the Hué School for Vietnamese Officers in 1948 and went to the Applied Infantry School in France (similar to the U.S. training program at Fort Benning). When he returned to Vietnam, he served as a company commander in the Delta. He was assigned to the academy at Dalat shortly after my appointment.

Thieu was just one year older than I, but appeared much more mature and sophisticated. He had spent the past five years in the cities of Vietnam and France, while I was living in jungles with Viet Minh soldiers, peasants, and tribesmen of the Highlands. Despite our differences, we quickly became fast friends, as did our wives. In fact, the four of us were almost like brothers and sisters. Our friendship continued for nearly twenty years. Then, in the late 1960s, our differences over what was best for South Vietnam became irreconcilable. It is difficult even today to believe that such a close friend could accuse me of being a Communist or Communist sympathizer, as Thieu did out of political expediency. We shared our thoughts and discussed our philosophies too many times over the years for him to believe that of me. He knew that I was—first, last, and always—a nationalist, and that the Communist philosophy was repugnant to me.

Even while we enjoyed the comforts and prestige of being instructors at the academy, conflicting emotions fought within me. As I looked at the cadets we were preparing for combat, I felt guilty. I would be enjoying this safe, pleasant post while most of them soon might be fighting, perhaps even dying, for the freedom of South Vietnam. I knew that I was performing an important, necessary duty, but that did not quiet the guilt. I never mentioned this to Thieu, knowing that he already had seen at least some combat against the Viet Minh while stationed in the Delta.

Then I had a strong disagreement with one of the French officers. The altercation became physical, and I knocked him down after he grabbed me by my uniform. The assistant commandant summoned me to his office the next day. The academy commandant, a colonel, was present, and he reviewed the military rules and regulations (which we had learned previously, of course). He asked me to agree to a punishment of fifteen days confinement and to make a public apology before the corps of cadets.

I refused categorically. The next day I submitted my resignation from the academy and a request for transfer to the airborne branch. The commandant then called me to his office and asked me to reconsider my decision. I took a week's leave of absence. I then sent my wife back to Hué to live with her parents and flew to Saigon to join the First Vietnam Airborne Battalion. At the time, it was one of only two airborne battalions in the newly created Vietnamese Army.

Enlisted men and NCOs were mostly Vietnamese transferred from French Colonial units, but battalion and company officers were French. There were two Vietnamese platoon commanders; the rest were French.

While I was in the second phase of training to get my jump certification, Major Tran Van Minh, chief of staff for the Ministry of Defense, called me to his office. He told me I was being reassigned permanently to Military Region II in Hué. A week later I reported for duty there and was received by Lieutenant Colonel Nguyen Ngoc Le, commandant of the region and province governor. Le, a former NCO in the French Indigenous Guard, was the officer who had "normalized" me two years earlier. He had been promoted to major, and only recently made lieutenant colonel.

Lieutenant Colonel Le appointed me his personal aide-de-camp, to act primarily as a liaison officer with the French High Command. It was essentially a desk job. Again, I found myself in a curious position: I left one comfortable assignment for another one that was no less disturbing to me in terms of inner guilt. Lieutenant Colonel Le treated me well. I soon realized that affection for, and caring about, people was just one of his admirable traits. I respected him greatly as a result. I did not feel the same about some of the other officers in the organization, whose dedication and efficiency left much to be desired.

Furthermore, the many families of those who joined the Resistance with me in the 1940s and who were still with Ho Chi Minh were cool to me at best, disdainful at worst. The company and affection of my wife at home were not quite enough to let me act naturally in public. I finally decided to seek yet another transfer, this time to

Hoi An in Quang Nam province. I had no connections outside the military, so I first contacted Major Vo Van Thanh, commander of the Indigenous Guard there. Thanh was Lieutenant Colonel Le's protégé and subordinate in the Indigenous Guard, so I knew that the colonel would honor any request from Thanh. I explained to Thanh that I wanted to join his regiment and asked him to request my reassignment. He did so, and Lieutenant Colonel Le approved my transfer.

I received a fifteen-day leave before reporting to Major Thanh for duty. I spent most of the time with my wife, then pregnant in her sixth month. I also visited my father, relatives, and friends living in and around Hué. The area surrounding the city was relatively calm during daylight hours but totally insecure at night. Viet Minh agents were everywhere—and nowhere. People either sympathized with them or were fearful of them. French and Vietnamese security forces were almost incapable of detecting these very active Viet Minh agents, who committed acts of sabotage, assassination, and kidnapping almost daily in and around the city. Pro–Viet Minh leaflets appeared everywhere, particularly at schools. Most students and teachers made so-called camping trips outside the city. Everyone knew such trips were just a pretext so they could meet with the Viet Minh.

Although officers who had graduated from Dalat received greater respect and consideration than other Vietnamese officers, people in general still showed little sympathy toward the Vietnamese military. Many considered us mere tools of the French colonial forces. My father told me that he had difficulty explaining why my brothers and I differed so openly that we joined opposing sides.

At least when I arrived in the provincial city of Hoi An, I was almost anonymous, just another officer; I felt less conspicuous in my contact with the people around me. Still, word soon got around that I had been a Viet Minh intelligence officer. People, including fellow officers, were cool toward me. I realized later that the cause was local Viet Minh propaganda that identified me as a former battalion cadre who had deserted their ranks.

The situation in this area had not changed much since late 1949. The Viet Minh still controlled the three coastal provinces of Phu Yen, Binh Dinh, and Quang Ngai, and this southern part of Quang Nam province.[6] The rest of coastal Quang Nam and the city of Danang, called the Autonomous Sector of Tourane, was under the command of a French colonel and staff. The sector was divided into three subsectors, each commanded by French senior officers.

The Vietnamese regiment and its commander, Major Thanh, manned a series of fortified blockhouses built along the main roads. Similar posts protected village headquarters in the "pacified" half of the province. Regiment HQ served mainly as an administrative unit. All of its companies were dispersed throughout the province and came directly under the command of the French subsector commanders.

Major Thanh commanded the regiment headquarters and just two companies assigned to protect the provincial capital. A company of French Foreign Legion stationed on the outskirts of the city shared protection duties. Major Thanh and the French captain commanding the French Foreign Legion company both came directly, but independently, under the command of the French lieutenant colonel commanding the subsector of southern Quang Nam. This arrangement shows how, in 1952, after more than two years of "independence," the French still strictly controlled the Vietnamese Army and government.

In such an organization, my role as regimental intelligence officer had little to do with intelligence gathering or analysis. We played only an auxiliary role as provider of information to French intelligence. I visited platoon and company posts (blockhouses) regularly. Each post sent out a patrol, normally of platoon size (forty men), to cover an area of approximately one-and-a-half kilometers around its base during the day. The men rarely ventured out at night. If they did, they covered less than half the distance patrolled during daylight hours. As a result, I gathered little useful information on my visits.

After a few weeks in Hoi An, I felt it was not yet appropriate for my wife and my newly born daughter to join me. I was plotting ways to get out of the boring intelligence officer job. It interested nobody and served no purpose.

The occasion soon occurred. At the time, the French Command had only one mobile group for their entire First Military Region, which covered all of Central Vietnam. The mobile group was entirely French, but the French now wanted to incorporate two Vietnamese battalions into it. Those would be the Thirtieth Battalion, with Vietnamese personnel transferred from French colonial infantry units, and the Twenty-seventh Battalion Infantry. The Twenty-seventh Battalion was newly formed, consisting of recruits from the well-known Catholic Bui Chu-Phat Diem area in the North. Its entire personnel—enlisted men, NCOs, and officers—had served there in local self-defense forces. All were recognized as hard-core anti-Communists. They transferred to Hué as a unit and were integrated into the Vietnamese Army.

But there was a problem: their officers were experienced in combat but not in the technology and language needed to work and communicate within the framework of a mobile group. That required graduates from Dalat to volunteer for service in the battalion. I promptly volunteered to be a company commander. The battalion base was located some twenty-five kilometers from Hué, so I could see my wife and child a few days a month and visit my father occasionally.

A most impressive sight greeted me when I reported for duty with the Twenty-seventh Battalion at Kilometer 17, as the Groupe Mobile (abbreviated to GM by French and Vietnamese) base camp was known. It was an early Sunday morning in 1952, and the entire battalion, 700 strong, stood rank on rank for a ceremony as its

Catholic chaplain read a prayer.[7] I soon learned that this was a Sunday morning tradition for this mostly Catholic battalion when it was not on duty.

I soon realized also that I was the only company commander who was a non-Catholic and a Buddhist. Only four of the twenty-some Dalat academy graduates who volunteered to serve as officers in the new battalion were non-Catholics. Because of my seniority, I was placed in command of the 150-man Third Company, with two young officers[8] and two senior NCOs as platoon leaders. Enthusiastic about my new command, I began to familiarize myself with the men in it, one by one. I was the only non-Catholic in the 150-man company. Upon reflection, that was understandable, because all the enlisted men came from, and had served in, the Catholic dioceses of Bui Chu and Phat Diem in the North.[9] This did not cause any difficulties for me among the men in my company. We soon learned to respect each other and work together as a team. I did, however, feel ill at ease with some of my fellow officers in the battalion because of our differing traditions and backgrounds.

One thing hinted of discrimination. All other companies occupied the 17 Kilometer base camp, which had comfortable quarters and was well fortified. My company, however, was stationed in a temple several kilometers away in a less secure position with few amenities.

The French High Command replaced the battalion's original French officers with Dalat graduates to ensure adequate coordination and communication between the Vietnamese units within the elite Groupe Mobile and supporting French elements (armor, artillery, air). All officers graduated from the Dalat Academy spoke French and were schooled in French military tactics. My battalion commanding officer, Major Nguyen The Nhu, had been promoted rapidly from the rank of master sergeant in the Indigenous Guard. He commanded a provincial guard unit under the French in the first few years after the French retook control of Vietnam in 1946. The unit nominally was a regiment, but actually it was an administrative unit for a provincial force under French command. It was broken down into squads, platoons, and companies posted primarily along communication lines to safeguard bridges, village and district headquarters, and other administrative installations.

The major was about thirty-five years old and an amiable man. In the years we spent together I found him to be very intelligent, capable of learning new military techniques quickly. His battalion executive officer and first company commandant helped him considerably. Both were among his closest confidants, and each had received training from the French in 1948.

At first, we argued, sometimes heatedly. He objected to one of the practices I began after each operation when I first took over the company. As soon as I made sure all weapons were disarmed and cleaned, I gathered the entire company together for a form of debriefing or critique session. I encouraged each individual to review his role in the operation and to explain if, and how, he could have improved his performance. Next, each squad, then platoon, reviewed their performances. I set an example by critiquing my own actions, taking responsibility for any shortcomings and inviting comments and suggestions from the men and noncoms who might help us in the next operation. Later, when the major learned what I was doing, he called me to his office. "The critiques you have after each operation are not standard military practice. They did not teach you that at the academy in Dalat, did they?"

I admitted they had not.

"I have heard complaints that they resemble some of the enemy's practices too closely and may tend to undermine the authority of officers. I want you to discontinue them immediately." I didn't agree but could only concur. Major Nhu also disapproved of my use of artillery and air support, feeling that I did not take full advantage of the firepower available. I felt that many officers called in artillery and air support when it could provide only minimum help at best. The enemy was too fluid and could disperse so rapidly that artillery fire, bombing, and strafing usually were wasteful and ineffective. Moreover, artillery fire sometimes fell short and was a greater threat to my company than the enemy.

Gradually, however, as Major Nhu and I worked together and shared time under fire in combat, we developed a mutual respect and esteem for each other.[10]

I had arrived while the new battalion was in full preparation for its first mission since formation. The battalion would be attached to the French Centre Groupe Mobile, a unique organization in that it was fully self-sufficient and operated wherever needed in the entire Second Military Region. That region covered the entire southern portion of Central Vietnam, east from Laos to the South China Sea, and from Quang Binh province in the North to the Viet Minh–controlled territory south of Quang Nam–Danang. The GM, as it was commonly known, had its own artillery unit, armor, staff engineers, air support liaison, and motor transport, mostly GMC trucks and Jeeps. We were prepared to move far and fast in pursuit of the enemy.

In the two months allotted to prepare for our new assignment, we received new weapons, uniforms, and other equipment, including U.S. M1 Garand rifles to replace the French MAS 36 weapons that other Vietnamese units still used. During this period, our battalion was responsible for securing the northern perimeter of Hué. This task included coordinating and supervising some thirty Civil Guard posts. Almost every night we had to intervene to help some of the posts attacked by Viet Minh units.

In fact, this city, the imperial capital of Vietnam until 1945, was "secured" by some 100 posts of this type, typically blockhouses, each manned by a squad, platoon, or company of Vietnamese regional forces. All these units came under the command of district French or Vietnamese officers. Several districts were then placed under the command of French subsector commanders. They, in turn, reported to a French colonel commanding the entire sector, which covered the province of Thua Thien and the city of Hué.

Each post commander's mission was to provide security for village headquarters and other administrative installations; lines of communication, particularly bridges and major roads; and government personnel and civilians living in and around the posts. The sector commander and subsectors' commanders had mobile or reserve units up to battalion or multibattalion size, artillery, armored units, and air support to intervene on calls for help by post and district commanders. This was the military organization in Thua Thien province and Hué at the time, and the situation was very similar in other provinces as well.

The preparation period finally ended, and we joined the Groupe Mobile officially and permanently. We were no longer responsible for supporting territorial units securing the area. We still kept the 17 Kilometer camp as our battalion base, primarily for regrouping after extended operations and for logistical purposes.

With another battalion, the Thirtieth, commanded by Major Le Van Nghiem (lieutenant general in later years), we were the only two Vietnamese battalions in the entire French Groupe Mobile. The two other battalions were the Twenty-seventh Algerian Infantry and a Foreign Legion battalion. The staff, engineers, artillery, and armor were all French. A French colonel commanded the Groupe Mobile. He was under direct command of the French general who commanded the entire territory of Central Vietnam. The Vietnamese commander and his staff nominally in charge of the military region command actually played the role of administration and inspectorate of Vietnamese troops scattered around the region. In essence, they were virtually under the French command. Although the command and staff of our battalion was now Vietnamese, we still had a French liaison team. (Neither the French nor Vietnamese used the term "advisors" at this time. That description came into use later with the Americans.[11]) This team was composed of the French major and two captains who were battalion and company commanders before they passed the command to us. The French team was very sensitive to the status of the new Vietnamese unit. They treated us as equal comrades in arms, and we all worked well together.

Our battalion and the entire GM were now totally mobile, with all supporting elements such as artillery, engineering, motor transport, and air support liaison officer fully available. Boats were provided for amphibious operations.

During the next few months we moved continuously back and forth across the vast First Military Region that covered the four provinces of Quang Binh, Quang Tri, Thua Thien–Hué, and Quang Nam–Danang. The entire region was considered "pacified" by the French High Command. A Vietnamese administration was in place, and the area was under the military control of French and Vietnamese troops, under French command. Thousands of small garrisons of squad, platoon, and company size were deployed along roads and at almost every bridge, administrative office, and installation to safeguard against Viet Minh attacks, which could come at any moment.

The usual mission of our Groupe Mobile was to launch attacks on large Viet Minh units as soon as possible after they were detected. We also intervened to rescue friendly units under Viet Minh attack. Our other duties included protecting convoys sent to resupply isolated garrisons under siege, and to protect engineers while they constructed new fortified garrisons, repaired damaged blockhouses, or performed similar functions.

For almost a year we conducted all the above missions. We encountered little resistance from large Viet Minh units. They did not mass their forces to confront us directly, knowing we had superior resources for an all-out battle. Instead, they continued ambushes and hit-and-run operations I was familiar with, striking quickly and dispersing before we arrived on the scene. This led to frequent fruitless pursuit on our part. Skirmishes with local guerrilla forces were common, however, and we often suffered casualties from snipers, land mines, and booby traps. The enemy suffered, too, at about the same degree as we did; but it was almost impossible for us to distinguish the guerrillas from civilians. In keeping with Ho Chi Minh's "swim with the fish" strategy, they all dressed the same.

To accomplish our mission we were on the move almost constantly, sleeping on the bare ground most of the time. Then, unexpectedly, a big showdown occurred in early 1953.

After three weeks of unsuccessfully searching for a Viet Minh force that launched a bloody ambush and destroyed a big convoy of our forces in the far south of Quang Nam province, we returned to our base, exhausted. The entire battalion, except my company, regrouped in the secure and comfortable 17 Kilometer camp. My company, as usual, was separated from the rest of the battalion in our temple billet. We were also ordered to provide extra security to a local company guarding a strategic bridge. As a rule, after a long operation of a month or more in the field, we were allowed from five days to a week R&R (rest and recuperation).[12] Each company could allow half of its strength to go on leave at a time. Accordingly, I signed leave papers for my deputy, two platoon leaders, and some sixty men to go on leave. Those of us who remained had our first hot meal in a month. Then we lay down on the cement floor of the temple for a good sleep, the first time in many days. I was exhausted after a full day jouncing over bad roads in a Jeep. I fell asleep immediately.

When the duty officer shook me awake at about 3:00 a.m., I heard the sounds of heavy artillery booming through the night. The duty officer gave me the microphone and told me Captain Bui Bach, the battalion deputy commander, was on the line. (The battalion commandant, Major Nguyen The Nhu, and half of the battalion, some 300 men, had just gone on leave a few hours earlier.) Bach asked me about how many men I still had available in the company. Some seventy altogether, I told him.

He explained that an ARVN company guarding a site at Duc Trong where the military engineers were building a garrison, some fifteen kilometers away, was under heavy attack by a superior force. The half-strength Groupe Mobile, augmented by several local units, was ordered to go to the rescue. Captain Bach told me to get my company ready to board the first four GMC trucks behind the tank company that would spearhead the operation. Artillery and machine-gun fire boomed and chattered in the distance. A light airplane circled over the besieged area, dropping flares.

I assembled the men and drew them up in ranks at the roadside. It was more than a hour later when the tank company rumbled into view at the head of the convoy, but there were no empty GMCs for my company. All trucks were filled with battalion troops from the 17 Kilometer camp.

I conferred hastily with Captain Bach, who explained that there had been a mix-up. "Three empty trucks will be along soon," he told me. "Load your men and follow us as quickly as possible." I was upset at the time, not knowing that the delay would literally be a lifesaver. The empty trucks appeared some fifteen minutes later, shortly after 4:00 a.m. We clambered aboard and set out to catch up with the convoy. Low ground fog obscured the rice paddies lining the road we traveled. We covered several miles, then suddenly the firing ahead increased in volume and explosions flashed through the darkness. Almost simultaneously, gunfire erupted from the rice paddies on both sides of the road, punching holes in metal and striking some of the men. It was instant bedlam.

I ordered the men out of the trucks.

"Take cover and return fire, but only if you have a definite enemy target!" I yelled as I quickly assessed the situation. The ambush area was a lethal trap. Rifle fire poured in from our left, where it appeared that an assault team was preparing to charge and try to overrun us. To our right were several machine gunners trying to pin us down for the assault team's attack. I knew we were sitting ducks, and eventually would be dead ducks, if we stayed where we were. I recalled that there was a cemetery just 400 or 500 meters ahead at a bend in the road and near a river. It was filled with several hundred elaborate crypts and tombstones that would give us cover and allow us to set up a defensive perimeter. I got word to the men to move up the road to the cemetery. We took off in classic leapfrog fashion, with one group moving away from the ambush scene while the rest of us kept up a covering fire. Then we moved forward through the first group, while it covered us. When we reached the cemetery, I immediately set up a perimeter. Seven wounded men didn't make it all the way with us, so I sent a team back to collect them and move them into cover in the crypts.[13] We now had a tenable defensive position, with the crypts serving almost as small, individual fortresses and the tombstones providing additional cover. The river at our back protected against an attack from that direction.

Still our situation was dire. We had a limited supply of ammunition and no rations. We lost our communications early in the ambush when Captain Bach was killed and the battalion command center, my only point of radio contact, was destroyed. So I could not call in artillery or air support, and this was a spot where either or both would have been welcome. The plane dropping flares had disappeared earlier. Now an observation aircraft was on station. Soon it began calling in artillery strikes. Many scored hits on the enemy, but several shells hit the cemetery. Thirteen of my men died from that friendly fire. Although the cost was great, the shelling did discourage the Viet Minh from making an all-out attack on us. They probably figured I was in communication with the artillery battery and could call on it for support if they tried a frontal assault. In fact, they drew back to positions further from us, but they kept up a steady fire.

Then the voice of an enemy officer using a megaphone echoed through the graying dawn.

"You are fully surrounded, so you might as well surrender now as later. We have only to wait until you run out of ammunition to overrun you."

Realizing that he was right and that our foes were not attempting to attack our position, I ordered the men not to fire until they had a clear and definite target.

"Save your ammo to fend off an enemy charge," I told those around me, and sent runners to relay the message around our defense perimeter.

Just then we saw a disorganized group of some twenty men from one of the other battalions fleeing from the main ambush site. I grabbed my megaphone and called out to them. "Rally to us here in the cemetery. We are Third Company, Twenty-seventh Battalion, holed up in the cemetery. Join us! We have a good defensive position."

Bullets glanced off a tombstone inches above my head. I ducked instinctively, then repeated the message over and over. The dazed survivors, fleeing in panic, were only too glad to hear a friendly voice and quickly raced toward us. Three were hit before they made it.

This group, a mixture of Algerians and Legionnaires, quickly took cover among the crypts and tombstones. My company was now down to about thirty-five men still capable of fighting, so I was as happy to welcome them as they were to find relative safety, especially since they all had their weapons and ammunition. They did not have a radio, however.

The Viet Minh attacked us many times during the rest of that day. With our increased numbers and firepower, we held them at bay. We were helped by the fact that an observation plane remained in the area most of the time. Our foes did not want to be on open ground, with no cover, long enough for the artillery to zero in on them. Finally, the Viet Minh began to withdraw. They had already scored a big victory and had no desire to confront the reinforcements that would come in strength eventually.

Still, we dared not move from our position. We didn't know at the time that the main body of the enemy had retreated. We did sense that some troops were withdrawing but I was concerned that might only have been a feint to draw us into the open where we would be more vulnerable. In addition, groups of guerrillas stayed behind, keeping up sporadic fire.[14] They would melt away and mingle with the local population when a relief column appeared, but meanwhile they were still a threat. So we stayed in place, isolated through the night and into the next day. Time seemed to crawl as we watched and waited for relief. We had no food, so we were hungry as well as tired.

It was two or three in the afternoon before the relief column arrived. Later, back at base camp, we learned more details of the ambush. The Viet Minh attacked Duc Trong with the express purpose of drawing a reinforcement convoy into a trap. They had a large body of camouflaged troops lining both sides of the road along the approach to Duc Trong. The predawn light and heavy fog made them almost invisible. They waited until the whole column was in the ambush area before opening fire. Land mines exploded, mortar rounds arced into the column, heavy machine guns chattered, and rifles cracked. Almost half the Groupe Mobile was destroyed in minutes. Total casualties included 200 killed in action, fifty missing in action, and thirty severely wounded.

My company ran into a secondary ambush, set up to trap reinforcements or cut down survivors from the main ambush who tried to escape back up the road. We were fortunate in that this group was smaller and more lightly armed than the main force closer to Duc Trong. That, and the fact that we were able to get to the cemetery, were all that saved us. We learned later that it was Viet Minh Regiment 95 accompanied by local guerrillas that set the ambush. Regiment 95, a battle-hardened regular Communist infantry unit, had infiltrated into our territory and created havoc far out of proportion to its size. The Ninety-fifth Regiment regularly ambushed or shelled convoys along Route 1, the main north-south artery, especially on the stretch of road between Hué and Quang Tri. Losses had been heavy, to the extent that French soldiers called it *la rue sans joie* (street without joy).

When we arrived back at 17 Kilometer camp, we had little time to rest and regroup. Preparations were already under way to assemble a powerful force to encircle, trap and destroy Regiment 95. The effort was named Operation Camargue, and it involved a simultaneous landing of troops along the sandy central Annam coast, plus two coordinated thrusts by armored units to prevent escape by the Communists. It was the biggest military unit yet assembled to force a fight with a major Viet Minh unit. Drawing from North, South, and Central sectors, it included elements of ten infantry regiments, two airborne battalions, most of three armored regiments, one squadron of armored launches, an armored train, thirty-six transport aircraft, six reconnaissance aircraft, twenty-three bombers, twenty-two fighter-bombers, and about twelve navy ships (three of them landing ship tanks).

Despite this overwhelming force, we spent fifteen days in a vain attempt to locate and engage the Viet Minh in a pitched battle before returning to base. Part of the problem was difficult terrain, for which our vehicles, amphibious craft, and tanks were not well suited. The enemy was simply too mobile for us to pin down.[15]

Some time later, both the French and the Vietnamese honored me with medals for my role in the Duc Trong affair. I received France's highest military honor, the Croix de Guerre, and the Vietnamese equivalent, Anh Dung Boi Tinh.

11: SURVIVING AN ONSLAUGHT (1953 AND 1954)

Perhaps as a result of my leadership of the Third Company of the Twenty-seventh Battalion during the fighting at Duc Trong, I was selected for advanced staff study at the Center for Military Studies in Hanoi. As we flew over the Red River Delta toward Hanoi in a lumbering C-47 aircraft in early 1953, my mind wandered back over the importance of this ancient city in Vietnamese history. The flat, fertile rice fields of the Delta made the whole area an important agricultural center. Access via the Red River to the port of Haiphong some 130 kilometers to the east guaranteed it would be a hub of commerce. Hanoi and the Delta were also important strategically and politically. A chain of mountains and forests stretched from the South China Sea on the northeast to the far northwest, separating China (just 145 kilometers away) and Laos from Vietnam. The Hanoi area had often been occupied by China, but also had witnessed at least three major victories by Vietnamese over the Chinese.

Hanoi was the country's capital for more than a thousand years, until the early eighteenth century when Hué became the capital. Ho Chi Minh restored it as the capital of the Democratic Republic of Vietnam for a short period, from August 1945, when Emperor Bao Dai abdicated in his favor, to December 1946, when the French attacked and regained control of the city. It then became the actual headquarters of the French High Command in Vietnam, although Saigon officially was the seat of both the French military command and civilian high commissioner.

We landed and rode across the Long Bien Bridge and through narrow, bustling Hanoi streets to the Center of Military Studies, a group of buildings formerly occupied by the French governor and his staff. We were divided into two groups: battalion commanders and staff officers. I was in the group for battalion commanders, and my friend Lu Lan was in the staff officer contingent. The campus was beautiful, and the curriculum offered for each group was practical and well prepared. It included many field trips and case studies, as well as lectures. All instructors were French, and all lectures and discussions were in French. (Most instructors were veterans of combat in Vietnam, and all lecturers had commanded troops or held staff positions in field units.) Despite this, there was little or no discrimination practiced. We Vietnamese were treated as officers and equals.

The case studies were especially valuable, because they covered actual combat engagements with the enemy, including all maps and documents available to help us study the operations in detail. The instructors went over them carefully, pointing out both good and bad points of troops and officers. Where our forces initiated operations, we learned why they were mounted and what outcome resulted. We studied strategies used by the Viet Minh closely in each case, endeavoring to learn all we could to help us during actual battle conditions in the future.

I knew that the Red River Delta and Hanoi had seen a great deal of activity during the past year. After more than five years, French control over the area was still tenuous. They kept roads and bridges open, protected government and military installations, and manned small fortifications among the villages of the countryside. This approach worked during the daytime, but as so often in many, if not most, areas of Vietnam during the war years, the nights belonged to the resistance. Except for patrols and ambushes, the French and their allied military units stayed in their fortified compounds from dark to dawn. And still, they suffered serious losses. The Viet Minh, as usual, followed a strategy of never attacking large units head-on. Instead, they mounted ambushes, which could occur anywhere. Road convoys, river patrols, and small, remote blockhouses were favorite targets. They would assemble a large complement of soldiers or auxiliary guerrillas, then literally overwhelm the much smaller French forces. Sniping was common, too, as were hit-and-run mortar attacks like the one we underwent during our training.

The French made a major command change in 1953. Lieutenant General Henri Navarre took over the French forces in Indochina on May 28 from General Raoul Salan. Salan had been deputy to General Jean de Lattre de Tassigny until illness forced de Lattre to return to France in 1951. (He died in January 1952 and was promoted to Marshal of France posthumously.) General de Lattre's period of command was marked by some success but more failure. He instituted a system of blockhouses and fortresses to pacify the area. (His son, Lieutenant Bernard de Lattre de Tassigny, was killed, ironically enough, defending one such fortress at Ninh-Binh. The death of his only child broke de Lattre's heart.)

Our training course lasted four months. When it ended, I returned to Hué on leave to spend a week with my family. Then I reported to my next assignment as deputy commandant of the Forty-fourth Battalion at Hoi An, about 160 kilometers south of Hué.[1] One of my first steps there was to survey the base and make plans to strengthen weak points of the battalion compound, which occupied part of the city of Hoi An. On the other side of the compound was a large river. Not far away was a company of French Foreign Legionnaires. There was also an artillery unit about ten kilometers distant, part of a large French military base.

Four companies of about 150 men each made up the Forty-fourth Battalion. Three companies routinely manned defense posts in and outside the compound. The fourth company was a mobile or reserve unit that conducted intelligence patrols, went after small Viet Cong groups operating in the area, and reinforced the other three companies as needed. The Viet Cong was an antigovernment insurgent group that began forming in the South after the Geneva Accord and Vietnam was split into two states, North and South. "Viet Minh" was the term used to describe the army that Ho Chi Minh began forming in 1944 to fight for Vietnam's independence. It was officially known as the "Army of the Liberator" in 1945 and several other designations theraafter.

The situation here was typical. By day we controlled the area; no Viet Minh were to be seen. At night, they prowled the area with impunity in units of varying sizes. We sent out patrols and set up ambushes in an attempt to protect the city and surrounding area, with only limited success.

The battalion commandant, Major Dang Van Son, a former French Army non-com, was a pleasant, capable man. Unlike some of the officers in my previous posting, he gave me wide latitude in battalion operations and the authority needed to implement them. I set up a system of night patrols, and later began constructing additional perimeter defenses. We built fences and strung literally miles of barbed wire. After a week of this I was physically exhausted.

Just then, we had a visitor: Captain Pham Anh, an intelligence officer from Military Security at the Second Military Region. He was billeted with me while at the base, sleeping in the living room of my small house. I was so tired that first night that I spent little time in conversation with him, but went to bed and fell into a deep, sound sleep.

Suddenly, Captain Anh shook me awake. "Chau, there is heavy incoming fire in the compound! We are being attacked with mortars and bazooka rockets!" I was bare chested, wearing only a pair of pants. I grabbed my web belt with pistol holster and the artillery communication plan (including coordinates for calling in fire) that I always kept at my bedside. Anh followed as I rushed outside, heading for the command post in one of two bunkers dug into the compound only five meters apart. I could see troops everywhere, but many looked unfamiliar. I later realized that they were the initial wave of Viet Minh shock troops that had already breached our perimeter defenses. Fortunately, they were withholding fire until getting the signal for a concerted attack. We got to the command post just as that signal came, and everything exploded. Mortar shells and rockets rained in from outside the base, and the Viet Minh inside the perimeter swept the area with small arms fire. As soon as they controlled the battle, they began to load captured weapons and supplies into our own battalion trucks as they ransacked the base.

I used a radio to call the nearby Foreign Legion post, only to learn that it, too, was under heavy fire. We could expect no help from that quarter. As a last resort, I asked to be patched through to the artillery post about ten kilometers away. I was able to contact a French captain and requested that he direct artillery fire on to our base.

"Are you sure?" he asked incredulously. "You and your men might all be killed!"

"There is no other way. The enemy is in full control of the base and will kill us all anyway. Even if taken prisoner, we will probably be killed eventually. And the Viet Minh have ransacked the camp, loading all sorts of weapons and supplies into our own trucks, materiel which will be used against us later. No, artillery is our only hope." I gave him the proper coordinates and urged: "Please commence firing immediately!"

He still argued with me, so I finally demanded that he relay my request, as deputy commandant of the battalion, to the sector commander. The commander was close by, aware of the attack on us, and quickly directed the artillery unit to commence firing. First came a sighting round, which I confirmed was on target. A steady barrage of shells followed. The Viet Minh were completely surprised and disoriented. Officers began ordering their troops to withdraw.

"Leave everything but what you can carry and get out of here! Follow the withdrawal plan," I heard them shouting. The order was repeated over and over. They abandoned the trucks full of looted supplies and fled hastily.

Now I could sit up and observe the action more clearly. As the Viet Minh retreated, I directed the artillery and kept them under fire for about half an hour. They used two escape routes, both of which were targeted by coordinates in the artillery plan, so the barrages were accurate and effective. Many Viet Minh were killed or wounded as a result. Many of their wounded were left behind in their haste to escape the deadly artillery fire. They came back while it was still dark to collect casualties, but somehow overlooked two wounded men. We found them later. One turned out to be a severely wounded company commander, who furnished valuable information about the attack. He died of his wounds a short time later.

Shortly after dawn, we saw a small observation airplane, a Morane-Saulnier Criquet, circling overhead and established radio contact with it. We soon were able to communicate with Military Sector HQ and sent a report to the sector commander, a French lieutenant colonel. HQ told us that what was called an "intervention force" would arrive "at any time."

In actuality, it was three hours before the relief column reached us. It only had to cover about six or seven miles but did so very cautiously, fearing an ambush. It was a common Viet Minh practice to attack a strongpoint, then trap the relief column in a deadly ambush. (I related how that happened at Duc Trong in the previous chapter.) Another delaying factor was that the colonel commanding the sector from Danang wanted to join the intervention force. So they had to wait for him to arrive in a heavily armed convoy.

A final count revealed that about 150 of our men had survived, roughly one company, a quarter of our normal complement. I was heartened to find that many of these survivors had been taken prisoner and only escaped because the Viet Minh became so disorganized by the surprise artillery barrage. This group even included my superior—the battalion commander—and his family, who were captured by the enemy early in the engagement. They had been taken about three kilometers from the compound when the artillery fire commenced and eluded their captors in the ensuing confusion. I was overjoyed at this turn of events and that Major Dang Van Son and his family were unharmed. He joined me in directing clean-up operations.

By the time the intervention force arrived, about ten in the morning, I had the men formed up in ranks, in full uniform and with their weapons, to greet it with a snappy salute. The force was a formidable one, more than a battalion strong. It included tanks, trucks, and armored cars. The French colonel surveyed the scene, then leaped from his vehicle and approached me, smiling broadly. He shook my hand heartily and addressed me by name. "We've never met before but I have heard good things about you from your previous assignment here as an intelligence officer." We talked for a while, and I gave him as full a report as I could at the moment about the attack of the previous night.

Finally, he congratulated me again and pinned a medal to my uniform jacket. "This is the highest honor I can bestow as sector commander [roughly equivalent to a division commander in the U.S. Army] but we plan to propose you for an even higher decoration based on your actions here."[2]

With so many of our men killed or wounded, our base was a sad place for days and days after the attack. Wives came to learn the fate of their husbands, often to find they were now widows. Whole families mourned lost relatives. The sight and groans of the wounded were horrible reminders of the carnage the enemy had left behind. It was an agonizing time because there was little we could do to relieve the pain for any of those widows, families, or wounded men.

That is why I reacted so strongly late one afternoon when a Jeep drove into the compound as Major Son and I, both exhausted after a long, hard day, sat down to our first meal in many hours. Two nicely dressed women stepped out of the vehicle, smiling. One was the major's wife; the other was my wife.

I was infuriated.

"How could you come here like that?" I demanded. "Don't you realize that people are suffering here? It is not the place for people all made up and dressed as though going to a party. It is an insult to the women and children who are grieving for their husbands, fathers, or brothers. Please leave, right now!"

The major stood there, not saying a word during my tirade.[3]

My wife was crying as she got back into the Jeep. The provincial chief arranged for the ladies to stay with his family for the night. Next morning he came to see me and urged me to come see my wife.

"I can't do it," I replied. "There are too many widows and children here who will never see or be able to talk to their loved ones again. I feel I would dishonor them if I ignored their pain to enjoy a visit with my wife at this time. Please ask her to return to Hué."

Perhaps that wasn't fair to her—and in retrospect I do regret that I caused her pain by not being more tactful in explaining why I felt as I did. She had gone to a good deal of trouble to make the trip from Hué after hearing about the Viet Minh attack. It was the way I felt, however, and I would probably do the same again, given similar heart-wrenching circumstances.[4]

A week later I was promoted to captain and given the National Order medal, the highest honor the country offered. It was given only to those who had earned five Army-level citations for bravery in action. At that time I had received seven such citations.

The incident with my wife perhaps illustrates my state of mind at the time. Another incident that happened about a month later explains the morale of many Vietnamese soldiers then.

It occurred some weeks after the attack on our base and involved the Forty-third Battalion, located around twelve kilometers from our Hoi An base. The battalion received orders to move to a new location in the Highlands. The men mutinied; they refused to move. Majors Tran Thien Khiem and Nguyen The Nhu flew in from Hué to Hoi An to investigate and to implement the relocation. Khiem[5] was chief of staff at the Military Region, and Nhu commanded the Twenty-seventh Battalion at the time. I met them when they arrived and took them to visit the Forty-third Battalion base and its commanding officer, Captain Nguyen Van Em. I went along with them, not in any official capacity, but merely as a courtesy to my senior officers. We drove in my Jeep, with an escort vehicle (a French version of the Jeep) for extra protection. When we arrived, Major Khiem discussed the problem with Captain Em.

"I can do nothing, and I have tried," the commander said. "The men will not obey the order. They say they will not move from this location. They have their families here and complain that there will be no place for their families if we move to the Highlands. That is the main problem."

This upset me greatly. I was very aggressive at the time, and although I had no official standing in the matter, I couldn't contain my feelings. "Are you not the commander of this battalion?" I shouted at him. "It is your responsibility to lead them, to see that the battalion relocates as ordered!"

Then I realized that I was overstepping my bounds, that this situation was none of my business. So I backed off. I murmured an apology for my outburst and told the two majors that I had to leave for Danang.

After spending a few hours in Danang, I headed back to Hoi An. A French captain waved us down at a checkpoint just a few miles later. "Are you Captain Chau?" he asked. I said that I was, and he explained that he had been ordered not to let me go back to Hoi An because my life was in danger.

"Why?" I demanded.

"Some soldiers in the Forty-Third Battalion have revolted and are searching for you. They have threatened to kill you," he told me. I learned later that a group of noncoms and enlisted men heard about my outburst to their commander. They were angered by my vehemence in urging that the relocation order be followed. Unfortunately, they took their anger out on another officer that they mistook for me. Knowing that I was a captain, they seized the first strange captain they found, Phung Ngoc Trung, a finance officer visiting the battalion to do an audit. They beat him severely before finding he was the wrong person.

I was anxious to get back to my own battalion in case problems developed there. I asked to see the subsector deputy commander and explained my concern to him. "The battalion is not in a good state of mind, and I should be there. If you stop me from returning to Hoi An tonight and something happens, you will be responsible." At that, he backed down and agreed to let me proceed.

The Forty-third Battalion eventually moved to its new location between the jungle and the coast. The men were reprimanded but not punished. The French were occupied with Dien Bien Phu and, later, negotiations leading to the Geneva Accords. Dealing with a mutinous Vietnamese battalion obviously ranked low on their list of priorities.

Shortly after surviving the ambush by the Forty-third Battalion malcontents, I was suddenly promoted to major. The notification came in a telegram from the French sector command and was a surprise because I had been a captain for less than three months. The order also gave me a new assignment: commander of the Twenty-seventh Battalion. The circumstances of this new order were odd, however. I was puzzled by such a sudden promotion, so I flew to Hué and visited Major Tran Thien Khiem, who, as explained earlier, was chief of staff at Military Region HQ.

"I don't understand about my promotion to major. How did it happen? Is this just a mistake?" I asked him.

"What promotion?" Khiem replied. "I don't know about any promotion for you." Here he was, chief of staff for the region, and an old friend, and he knew nothing about me being promoted to major. "Show me the telegram," he said. I took the document from my briefcase and handed it to him. He looked it over and nodded. "It's official, certainly, signed by the sector commandant." Khiem shook his head in puzzlement, and then called in his chief of section 1, personnel. That officer also knew nothing about my promotion. Khiem finally called Sector HQ.

"Oh yes, Tran Ngoc Chau's promotion to major was made by the Vietnamese

General Headquarters in Saigon on the order of the French general commanding in Central Vietnam. There simply has been a delay in sending you a copy of the order," the sector personnel officer told Khiem.

This was not an uncommon occurrence and illustrates how the French often treated the Vietnamese military command: as merely an administrative or auxiliary operation. Such incidents were belittling and did not help morale among our officer ranks. On the other hand, the French had shed much of their earlier reluctance to place Vietnamese officers in more important assignments than was true in earlier days. My assignment as Twenty-ninth Battalion commander was an example of this. I first reported to the French colonel commanding the Tourane Sector, and then to the battalion, based near Danang.

The Twenty-ninth Battalion's task was an important one: defending the northern part of the Danang subsector, northern Danang province, and part of Thua Thien province. Its tactical operation area was bordered on the north by Hué, with Laos to the west, the China Sea on the east, and the Center subsector to the south. As battalion commander, I also was in charge of the subsector. In addition to the Twenty-ninth Battalion, there were several hundred men in small units guarding Route 1 checkpoints and blockhouses, plus two Groupe Mobile companies. Commanders of these two companies, both experienced French captains, reported to me. I was the first Vietnamese officer to hold this post in a sector.[6]

Then came announcement of the cease-fire! This created great confusion among both the French and AVN forces. Suddenly the future loomed unclear for us, and it was difficult to join in the general jubilation as people across the country celebrated. Many of the men joined their families in their festivities, but I was not among them. I had doubts about how the Viet Minh would honor the cease-fire. Would they take advantage of this cessation of hostilities to attack and destroy us? Would they continue guerrilla operations to catch us napping during the euphoria of thinking the war was over? These possibilities concerned me day and night as I exhorted my troops on the need to keep our guard up, not to be lulled into a false sense of security. I worked incessantly to prevent that from happening.

Soon the Geneva Accords were signed, so there was a peace agreement confirmed by all parties. Almost immediately I received a new assignment from the AVN Command of the Second Military Region, confirmed by the French sector command. I took command of the Eighth Battalion with orders to join the Twenty-First Groupe Mobile. Our mission was to reoccupy the Viet Minh Free Zone south of Quang Nam. Prior to the accords, this region consisted of coastal provinces where the French had never been able to establish a presence.

The Eighth Battalion was based in Quang Tri for years. Its tasks included static defense in the region: guarding bridges, performing logistic and administrative installations, and manning highway checkpoints. They had settled in; many had their families with them. To say they were reluctant to leave for a remote area unfamiliar to them is an understatement. They also complained about their former commander. At first they simply refused to go. "Why should we move to a faraway place we know nothing about, leaving our families behind, where people may be hostile to us? We have suffered and served for years; now that there is peace, we don't want to do it anymore. We will give up our weapons and equipment and become civilians again!"

I spent hours explaining why the move was important, that we needed to secure the territory that had been ceded to the South by the Geneva Accords. I stressed that they could have frequent visits from their families and maintain a regular correspondence with them. I appealed to their patriotism, their love of their country and dreams of creating a truly independent state. It was one of the more difficult non-combat tasks I faced in my military career. Eventually I won the men over and they agreed, however reluctantly, to follow orders and relocate.

Lieutenant Colonel Le Van Nghiem,[7] commander of the Groupe Mobile, led the move. Three regular battalions, including mine, together with armored, engineer, and artillery companies, made up the GM.

The Viet Minh indeed complied with the letter of the Geneva Accords, withdrawing to the North all Regular Army troops from the region, but they left behind a network of "underground cadres." These cadres not only observed our activities but they monitored and even directed the actions of the populace. They fomented fear, distrust, and antagonism toward us among the people. It soon was evident that the fears of my battalion about receiving hostile treatment in the area were well founded. Several serious incidents occurred even as the GM slowly made its way to its new posting.

One problem was that the people refused to supply water and shelter for our troops.

At one point, a large mob of civilians, undoubtedly organized and led by undercover enemy cadres, surrounded an entire battalion. After a great deal of shouting and arguing on both sides, the mob forced the troops to give up their weapons. Fortunately, no one on either side was killed or seriously injured. An even worse situation developed in the Tam Ky area. Again, there was a confrontation between a large crowd of civilians and GM troops. Provocation escalated and shooting eventually broke out. A dozen or more people were killed.

We progressed very slowly; it took a month to get to a point not far past Tam Ky. Meanwhile, I spent a great deal of my time discussing the situation with my battalion, stressing the need for us to move with caution and not to react against the provocation and enmity of the local people. "We will only make matters worse if we lose our tempers and take action against these people," I told them time after time.

"Remember, they are our countrymen, and we want to win them over to our side. We can't do that by being aggressors ourselves. I know it is difficult to accept their scorn and hostility, but not to do so will only cause us bigger problems in the future."

After a month, we were only about eighty kilometers from our starting point. Then I received notice from the Second Military Region HQ informing me that I should turn the battalion over to my deputy commander, Captain Nguyen Thanh Sang,[8] and report to Hué immediately for a new assignment. At the HQ in Hué, I had long discussions with some of my friends in the AVN. It quickly became apparent that with the defeat at Dien Bien Phu, and enforcement of the Geneva agreement, the French had silently abdicated their authority and were pulling out of the country. We Vietnamese were now in charge of our own destiny and would have to manage on our own.

There was no indication that the United States, still smarting from the stalemate and losses sustained in Korea, would offer anything more than limited support. We did not expect, or even visualize, the extent to which Americans would later become involved. That was still almost a decade away. There was, however, already enough American influence to create political problems. A major conflict developed between the newly appointed premier, Ngo Dinh Diem, supported by the United States, and chief of staff of the Vietnamese Armed Forces, General Nguyen Van Hinh, favored by the French.

Against the backdrop of serious political infighting, I was appointed, by Colonel Truong Van Xuong, military region commander, to be commandant of the Regional Military NCO School in Hué. This unit was roughly of battalion size, with an armored company attached. It would become an intervention force in case of an attempted coup against Premier Diem in Saigon. It was a difficult situation for me. I had little interest in politics at the time, and absolutely no political aspirations for myself. My efforts were directed solely and absolutely toward being the best professional military officer I could be. I rebuffed approaches from Diem's followers and neither knew nor cared much about General Hinh's political intentions.

I could not ignore the fact that I had ties to the general, however. He knew me personally when I was a cadet, and later an instructor, at the Dalat military academy. Hinh was a French Air Force lieutenant colonel at the time, on detached duty to serve as Emperor Bao Dai's chief of Military Cabinet. Major Khiem, Nguyen Van Thieu, and other old friends, most from the South, were firmly in Hinh's camp. I made no political decision but was inclined to favor Hinh because of these ties. The situation resolved itself without serious incident or requiring me to take action for either side. General Hinh decided to return to France with his French wife and leave Diem as leader of the country. Major Khiem and I went to Saigon as representatives of the Second Military Region to take part in a formal farewell ceremony for the general.

Upon our return to Hué, there was a call for all of Hinh's followers to visit Ngo Dinh Can, the brother and personal representative of Premier Diem in Hué and the Central Region. I refused to go, expecting this to result in my discharge from the military.

Instead, Khiem interceded with the General Staff in Saigon and arranged for my transfer to Dalat, where I took over as commandant of cadets at the military academy, replacing a French major and becoming the first Vietnamese officer to hold that post since creation of the academy in 1950.

12: WITH AMERICANS: A LEARNING AND ADJUSTMENT EXPERIENCE (1955–1958)

Dalat looked much the same when I returned in October 1954. There was one major change, however, both in the town and at the academy. As elsewhere in Vietnam, the French were conspicuously absent. After decades of enjoying Dalat as their favorite resort, French military officers and civilians had virtually abandoned the city. Some 100 wealthy Vietnamese and Chinese families, who had prospered substantially due to their connections with the French regime, now occupied the elegant villas, chalets, and mansions, most built during early colonial times.

The few French who remained included a group of ten liaison officers. Led by a lieutenant colonel and joined by a like number of U.S. officers, they were part of a mixed advisory unit formed to help in the transition of the academy from French control to management by the Vietnamese military. The reluctant marriage of convenience between the two sets of advisory officers was difficult. No question but that France as a whole felt a severe loss of pride as a result of its defeat by "a bunch of rag-tag peasants," as some described it. This was especially true of the French military officer corps. A feeling of failure, guilt, and shame for the defeat was inevitable.

The Americans, on the other hand, tried diligently to avoid projecting a "you blew it" attitude, to conceal their innate cockiness, the near-arrogance that came from confidence in the capabilities of their own military forces. After all, was not the United States the mightiest power the world had ever seen? It did help that the American lieutenant colonel in charge spoke fluent French and was able to communicate easily and directly with the French team.

Both advisory groups were determinedly correct with each other, but there was a definite undercurrent of unease. It dissipated somewhat over time but never disappeared totally. It did not help matters that circumstances surrounding the academy during this time of drastic change guaranteed that there would be a certain amount of confusion. In a face-saving measure to lessen the embarrassment of being forced out of Vietnam, a French officer served as chief in each advisory position at the academy, with an American officer assigned as his deputy.

Caught in the middle of this charged atmosphere, we Vietnamese tried our best to make the transition as smooth as possible, but that was not an easy task. The roles of the three groups involved—French, American, and Vietnamese—sometimes were difficult to define. The plan was for South Vietnam to administer and manage the academy, with the French and American officers "advising" on how the training of

Vietnamese officers should be implemented. In practice, West Point gradually became the model for our officer training program; by 1960 the similarity was extremely close.

One practical problem was that France and the United States had two quite different military cultures. Their organization, training methods, arsenals of weapons, and sometimes even their basic strategies differed in varying degrees. Another amorphous difficulty was that the Vietnamese military was always subordinate to the French in the past. The French were the stars; we were the supporting cast. Understandably, many of my fellow officers felt some tenuousness in assuming their new roles.

I was determined to avoid such misgivings in my new assignment as commanding officer of the entire Cadet Corps. I regarded this not only as a job and a challenge but as a major opportunity, if not a sacred trust, to contribute to the future of my beloved country. Once again, as with the Twenty-Seventh Battalion, I was taking over a post previously held only by French officers.[1] This meant that I was the first commandant of cadets to address the Cadet Corps in Vietnamese. Ever since the academy's founding in 1949, French was always used for training and communicating with the French officers in charge of the school. This was a significant change and one that helped instill an extra portion of national pride among both the academy staff and the officers-to-be.

I thought the war was finally over, that Ho Chi Minh would reconcile with South Vietnam after the French departed at the end of 1956. I expected the United States to become our peacetime ally, sort of a benevolent Big Brother supporting a fragile, but independent, new nation. Had I known how misplaced this buoyant optimism was, I probably would have experienced utter despair.

Lieutenant Colonel Nguyen Van Chuan, an old friend from Hué, had taken over command of the academy from a French colonel only a few months earlier. He greeted me warmly, and we chatted about the old days in Hué. We exchanged thoughts on the academy's future in general, now that it was in Vietnamese hands and, in particular, we could make improvements in the curriculum to produce a better-trained, more effective professional corps of military officers.

The next few months proved to be an exciting time for me. More and more Americans arrived, and I began to work closely with them. Perhaps for that reason, in June 1955 I received orders to report to Saigon, where I was told I was to be part of a group of twenty-five Vietnamese officers being sent to Fort Benning, Georgia, for advanced infantry training. I was surprised because at the time I did not speak much English. I was also elated; this would be a wonderful opportunity to learn more about the United States and its people. It would also help me toward my goal of increasing my knowledge and effectiveness as a career military officer.

We left Vietnam in August 1955, flying via Guam, Hawaii, and San Francisco, where we were taken in transit to Fort Mason.[2] The next day, a military bus (not Yellow Cabs) delivered us to the Oakland train station. Our three-day, cross-country journey to Columbus, Georgia, was a revelation. The United States seemed so immense and so varied. We watched in awe from the train's scenic dome as we rolled over mountains and across deserts, past farmland and huge factories, through sleepy small towns and busy large cities. It was all so different from our homeland. Even the large, comfortable train was a sharp contrast to our slow, narrow-gauge Vietnamese variety.

We arrived at Fort Benning to a warm reception by staff and instructors, and soon settled in to a life of unaccustomed military luxury. Maids cleaned our quarters and made the beds every day. We enjoyed color TV and refrigerators in each building.

All was not a life of ease, however. The training was demanding, comprehensive, and thorough. It included classroom studies as well as sessions in the field. We each received a daunting pile of training material—all, fortunately, printed in both English and Vietnamese. Instructors lectured in English, and Vietnamese translators repeated the lessons in our native language. I found it interesting that the Vietnamese staff of translators and interpreters was larger than our group of officer-students.

Most of the subjects—ranging from battalion- to division-level maneuvers with artillery, armored cavalry, airborne, and other support elements—were new to us. There was special emphasis on effective use of support groups, particularly artillery, to provide fire cover during every phase of an engagement. Technical subjects mainly covered use of support units: how to provide hot food or clean clothes for troops in the field. Instructors introduced us to the Pentomic Division[3] with its tactical nuclear capabilities. Map exercises helped teach us how to coordinate troop movement with nuclear artillery cover. (Fortunately we never resorted to using nuclear weapons.)

The months passed swiftly, and in September 1956 we began our journey home. During a stopover of several days in Hawaii, I sat on the white sands of Waikiki Beach, enjoying an excellent view of Diamond Head and the mountains in the distance. The weather and scenery in Hawaii were close to that of Vietnam, making me feel somehow closer to my wife and family. I longed to see them again and was happy to know that I would soon be with them in Dalat.

I also looked forward to returning to my duties at the academy. My ten months at Fort Benning had been fruitful ones, adding a great deal to my military knowledge. I now had greater insight into battalion and division tactics as well as the Pentomic division concept and organization. U.S. Army capabilities in supporting its troops, even in such matters as feeding and clothing them, impressed me. The firepower that the U.S. Army possessed was truly formidable, far beyond anything I had ever experienced. The image of rolling fire created by infantrymen with awesome weapons, supplemented by artillery and air strikes, lingered in my memory.

One day at Waikiki, my mind wandered back to my early days as a young volunteer in the National Army of Liberation. I chuckled to myself at the "training" I received at that time: a thirty-day politico-military course, with as much or more emphasis on the "political" as on the rudimentary military part of the program. After that, I was sent into the field as a squad leader, in charge of fourteen men, none of whom had more than three days' training. As for firepower, we had only six rifles between us: two French, one German, one British, and two Japanese. . . . And we were the best-equipped squad in our platoon.[4] Later, as a company commander with the Liberation Army in 1946, I attended an "advanced" training course in Quang Ngai, another mixture of political indoctrination and military tactics. The most sensational weapons shown to us at that time were an 81 mm mortar and a Jeep, both captured from the French in an ambush.

When I arrived back in Saigon, full of high expectations for the future, I found a city that was familiar in many ways but very much changed in others. It felt strange not to see French military personnel on the streets and in cafés or shops. Even French civilians were rarely seen, I soon discovered. Instead, Americans in military uniforms and civilian clothes were now a common sight in the crowded heart of the city. The new U.S. military headquarters located between Saigon and Cholon[5] was fully operational.

Saigon appeared more colorful, faster paced, and noisier than I remembered it being just a year before. Perhaps it was the influence of the growing number of Americans, I reflected. Foreign influences in the city were still more French than American, but that was changing. There were more U.S. military and civilian personnel present. I also noted that American products were now available, displayed by vendors, and increasingly popular with Vietnamese residents. Then a thought occurred that made me chuckle and say to myself, *Saigon now seems very faintly like a Vietnamese version of some of the towns I visited near Fort Benning!* Little did I realize then how much truer that would be in the future as the American buildup in our country accelerated.

I spent a few days in Saigon, enough to be even more aware of how the city had changed in my absence, and then I returned to Dalat. It was sheer joy to be reunited with my wife and three children after such a long absence. The two girls enjoyed the Catholic school where they attended third and fourth grades, respectively—thriving on the education they received from the Vietnamese nuns in everything from academic basics to proper manners. Three months earlier, my father-in-law, Ho Tanh, had joined them. He had been removed from his position as director of finances in Central Vietnam when he refused to cooperate with the governor for Central Vietnam,[6] Nguyen Don Duyen, protégé of Prime Minister Ngo Dinh Diem. Our reunion was joyous, but brief, because I reported for duty the next day.

I had noted a difference in Dalat as well when I returned in the fall of 1955 after a three-year absence. Coming back this time, after less than a year away, even more changes were evident. Some of the change was subtle, some more obvious. Exodus of the French was nearly complete. All military personnel had long since departed, and very few French civilians remained. Those still there (mainly proprietors of private businesses or teachers at the French schools) kept a low profile. Most were in the process of selling their properties before relocating to France—their homeland, but ironically a place many of them had never even visited.

Vietnamese in the city were now accustomed to having Americans in their midst. The newcomers from the United States often occupied villas vacated by the French or, in some cases, new and better ones. Still, not many Vietnamese spoke English, and Americans hardly knew even a few words of Vietnamese. Communication between the two groups was limited.

The American advisors studied current operations, curriculum development, performance of Vietnamese counterparts and instructors, and instruction methods at the school. This had to be done largely through interpreters.

Lieutenant Colonel Ho Van To replaced my old friend and colleague, Lieutenant Colonel Nguyen Van Thieu, as the new commandant shortly after my return. At the end of hostilities in July 1955, To and I were both in the Groupe Mobile 21; he was a captain then, a staff officer, and I was a major commanding the Eighth Battalion. Now our situations were reversed, and he was my superior. To had an excellent background, however. He had been regarded as one of the best Vietnamese NCOs in the French Garde Indigene (Civil Guard auxiliary force), and was selected to be trained as an officer in the first unified officers school created by the French Expeditionary Forces in Hué. After six months of training, To graduated first in his class. He spoke fluent French but no English, as was the case with most other officers at the time.[7] Colonel To appointed me director of instruction. My advisor was Major Butterfield, a West Pointer. He was a nice guy, courteous and friendly.

I concentrated on transforming the present French St. Cyr–inspired academy program into a four-year program more like that of West Point. I formed a small committee of officers and civilian instructors to look into the military academy systems used by the French at St. Cyr, the Americans at West Point, the British at Sandhurst, and military education in Taiwan. Our goal was to extract the best features of those programs for our academy. I also felt it was vital to include general education courses (as was done at West Point) and material on Vietnam's history and culture. I told the committee that I wanted to blend several elements into the new four-year program:

1. The French method of making decisions.
2. Recognition that guerrilla warfare was what South Vietnamese officers were more likely to face than battles between massed forces opposing each other.
3. The Vietnamese cultural heritage.
4. Recognition that North Vietnam was the obvious potential foe of the future. Ho and General Giap knew—and had proved very effectively— the value of hit-and-run tactics by guerillas who could "swim with the fish" by blending into the populace after their raids and ambushes. Young officers must be trained to recognize these threats, as well as more conventional ones. The technology of Sandhurst and West Point also needed to be adapted to such circumstances.
5. Providing young cadets with a broad education in addition to the training in military skills. Helping them learn and understand the proud history of their country and the many ways that communism ran counter to that heritage would inspire them to be effective officers and leaders. I knew from personal experience how successful the Communists were at indoctrinating their military to fight wholeheart-edly and unstintingly for their cause. We needed to counteract that by instilling a sense of nationalistic pride and purpose in our own military, especially the officer corps. The academy at Dalat up to this point had never included anything in the curriculum that explained why they should fight communism. This kind of motivation and a broader range of nonmilitary courses were, I felt, necessary in any new officer training program.

The last two points were critical, in my mind.

I also wanted all instructors and teachers at the school to be replaced with battle-proven, decorated, and highly educated officers. Those selected would first be sent to appropriate institutions for training. I recalled how I had admired and respected several of my superior officers in the Viet Minh for their knowledge, devotion to duty, personal honor, and proven bravery in combat. They became my role models, and I wanted our military academy to turn out officers with similar qualities, men who would be role models for those with whom they served. I felt strongly that the Viet Minh model of emphasizing patriotic motivation and promoting high standards by personal example would be critical to developing our own effective officers.

While addressing the project, we also had to work feverishly on translating all documents from French into Vietnamese and prepare instructors to switch to the "new" teaching language: Vietnamese.

Meanwhile, other developments swirled around me, some that I became aware of only after they surfaced. One that I did know about and tried to resolve arose from Major Butterfield. As I've mentioned, he was a nice guy, never arrogant or dictatorial with me, but he simply did not understand why I was so concerned with creating a whole new curriculum and modus operandi for the Dalat academy. He favored a different approach, modeled along the lines of his alma mater, West Point, as put into place by the United States in the Philippines. This would mean our cadets would have traditional military training, though without much of the broader educational courses offered at West Point, Sandhurst, St. Cyr, or even the Taiwan Military Academy. The emphasis would be on conventional warfare between opposing armies, as in World War II and Korea, with little emphasis on the kind of guerrilla war that had been fought in Vietnam, and presumably could be again.

"We have a perfectly good program there [the Philippines], one that has proved successful in combating the Communist insurgency. Why not just use that as the model for this academy? They have good teachers. Why don't we just invite them here to supplement your own instructors and set up our own program of instruction? I'm sure you have good ideas, but you're complicating things and we don't have time to implement them."

I tried my best to explain why I felt a program tailored to the special circumstance of Vietnam was preferable, but my limited English made it difficult and left both of us frustrated. And Major Butterfield was not the only one who did not understand. I went to Superintendent To to explain my proposals and to register my objections to Major Butterfield's approach. I hoped the colonel would accept my reasoning and support my proposals. At first I was heartened because he listened intently to what I had to say. Finally, however, I was disappointed.

"The Americans plan to spend millions to modernize and expand the academy, and their West Point is regarded as the best in the world. So why don't you just listen to them and go along with what they recommend?"

This attitude prevailed throughout our Vietnam military. I found a similar attitude when talking with officers from the General Staff, infantry units, and provincial forces. It stemmed from the unconscious arrogance and superiority complex of Americans and the inferiority complex on the part of Vietnamese after more than eighty years of subjugation under the French. It was a kind of "Father knows best" attitude; predictably, it proved disastrous in the long run.

The people who knew Ho Chi Minh's tactics best were Vietnamese who had fought with or against him or, in a few cases like mine, had done both. Sadly, the

Americans seemed uninterested in what we knew from bitter experience, and we were not confident or vocal enough to make ourselves heard. Thus, the mistakes of history would repeat themselves, as they always do, and the American military would pay a hefty price for its overconfidence. Unfortunately, my beloved homeland would pay an even greater price.

Meanwhile, more sinister, and ultimately more detrimental to me personally, were actions by the "commissar" of the local Can Lao[8] party, Major Ly Trong Song, executive officer for the academy. The Can Lao was organized by President Diem's brother, Ngo Dinh Nhu, as one of thirteen security groups he established while in charge of security in his brother's administration. The Can Lao was a clandestine society (although everyone knew about it) with secret initiation rituals, but Nhu arranged to have it financed by the government. Author and journalist Neil Sheehan aptly described its purpose: "to covertly penetrate, and so better manipulate, the officer corps of the armed forces, the civil bureaucracy, and business and intellectual circles."[9] At the time, I was not interested in political matters one way or another, the Can Lao included, until my encounter with Lieutenant Colonel Huynh Cong Tinh, the Can Lao local commissar and military subsector commander. He wanted to recruit me into the party. I rejected the overture.

In later years, in several positions that required me to deal with Can Lao members, I came to understand that Mr. Nhu's purpose for creating the Can Lao was ostensibly high-minded. He wanted to use it to implement a form of democracy, first at the roots—the villages and the rural peasantry. Although I refused to join, I was excited by the concept. I also realized over the years, however, that his idealistic concept was subverted at lower levels by the very people who were supposed to implement it. For the most part, these people used Can Lao and their positions to gain power and wealth for themselves.

Major Song wielded a great deal of power in his post as the top Can Lao representative at the academy. I learned that the hard way when suddenly an order came from Saigon HQ relieving me of my post as director of instruction in Dalat and transferring me to the Fourth Infantry Division in Bien Hoa.[10]

I was stunned. What had prompted this unexpected transfer right at a critical stage in my task, as director of instruction, to help accomplish a complete transformation of the academy? Colonel To seemed pleased with my efforts. Major Butterfield and I had different visions of the school's future, but he also respected the efforts I was making. I was certain our differences could be worked out amicably as we were able to communicate better. I was equally certain that he had not instigated the transfer; he was an honorable man, and I was positive he would not have made such a move without telling me first.

I went to Colonel To for some answers.

"What caused this transfer so suddenly?" I asked him. "I thought you were satisfied with my work here. You said you were. You know I've been working day and night on translation of the required material and to direct an overhaul of the curriculum. You even recommended me for promotion and gave me a copy of the report you sent to HQ stating my qualifications and the excellent performance of my duties under your command. Have you changed your mind?"

Colonel To looked at me apologetically and made a helpless gesture. "I have been very satisfied with your work and I did not request your transfer. The order came from the General Staff and the Ministry of Defense. I had nothing to do with it." Then he shook his head and grimaced, as if to say, "I can do nothing about it." He was plainly embarrassed at this point.

"Fine," I said. "I will report to the Fourth Division as ordered. But once there, I will lodge a formal complaint about the transfer because I feel it is unjust and unwarranted, especially since you, as my commanding officer, did not request it." Then I left his office, still bewildered at this cataclysmic turn of events in my life. The situation also must have bothered Colonel To a great deal. The day before I was to leave for Bien Hoa, he called me into his office. He asked me to close the door and told me this was a very private conversation.

"I know you are a man of honor and will not reveal what I am about to tell you. If you do, I will have to deny we ever had this conversation or I would be ruined."

I agreed that I would respect his wishes and remain silent about anything we discussed. Only then Colonel To explained that Major Song, as leader of the Can Lao faction at the academy, had a direct channel to higher levels, including presumably, the Ministry of Defense. He had used his influence to get me relieved of my post in Dalat.

I was surprised. I had little interaction with Song; he didn't attend staff meetings at which I was present and appeared to have little interest in what I was doing. Why did he want to get rid of me?

Colonel To said that Song claimed I was too close to the U.S. officers, especially Major Butterfield; that I had become too "Americanized"; and that such orientation would be reflected in the program I recommended for the academy. This was a bitter pill to swallow, since it was absolutely contrary to the efforts that I was really making to develop a new curriculum. As Colonel To and I talked further, it became clear that Song's antipathy stemmed largely from the fact that I was the only officer of my rank who spoke some English. (Song himself spoke no English at that time.) Limited as my command of the language was, that apparently was enough to make him suspicious of me. My ten months of training at Fort Benning probably reinforced his feelings. In addition, of course, I was a Buddhist from a mandarin family and a former

Viet Minh combatant, while he was a Catholic and the son of a former NCO in the French Colonial Army. We could hardly have been more different.

I duly reported to the Fourth Infantry Division at Bien Hoa, about twenty-four kilometers from Saigon, where I soon learned that the long arm of the Can Lao also reached to field units.

Lieutenant Colonel Ngo Dzu was commanding officer of the division. I had served with him in the Second Military Region, and we became friends at that time. He appointed me acting chief-of-staff and sent a request to the General Staff to make the appointment permanent. The General Staff agreed and passed the request on the Ministry of Defense, as was required for positions of that level. A few months later the Minister of Defense himself, Tran Trung Dung, nephew-in-law of President Diem, sent an official letter to the division denying my appointment, saying that "Major Chau does not have the qualifications to serve as Divisional Chief-of-Staff."

Instead, Major Le Van Nhut, a former NCO in the French Army, was assigned to the job. He had only minimal education, little advanced military training, and had never commanded a unit in combat, but he was a Catholic from the North. Prior to this event I had not taken much notice of the background of people in the military— whether they were Buddhist, Catholic, or some other religion, and whether they came from the North, Central, or southern areas. Now I realized that these things made a great difference under the current administration.

Colonel Ngo Dzu was somewhat embarrassed by this turn of events. "This is not fair, but what can I do? My hands are tied," he said to me.

I understood perfectly well. I was disappointed naturally. I told him I would do to the best of my ability whatever job he assigned me. The colonel relaxed visibly at my calm acceptance of the situation and appointed me deputy chief of staff. My major duties in that post were to take charge of operations and training.

Actually, this was an important post at the time. The division was the first chosen to make the change from the old French-Vietnamese mode to a modern American-Vietnamese unit. We reorganized the division completely, installing new staff procedures, training methods, and combat strategies. Everyone in the division got new American-style uniforms, and we were completely reequipped. Garand M1 rifles became the standard weapon for the troops, a big improvement over the French M-36 rifles that they replaced. We spent most of our time in various types of training, including large-scale maneuvers, during which we used the engineers, artillery, and other components now integrated into the division. The work was hard, constant, and grinding as we went through this massive transition period.

My experience at Fort Benning now stood me in good stead. I had learned there to think of combat on a different scale than we did under the French. The use of artillery and air support was more important, and would be more available in our reorganized army. Most of the officers who had been through the Fort Benning training with me were also now attached to the Seventh Division. A group of U.S. Army officers served as advisors during this period. They were stationed at their own post, several miles from the main Bien Hoa camp, where they enjoyed comfortable quarters in a "Little America" enclave that included a PX, sports facilities, and other amenities.[11]

Then one day several months later, in early 1957, Lieutenant Colonel Dang Van Son came to visit the division. Colonel Son was my battalion commander at Hoi An when the enemy invaded our compound and I was forced to call in artillery fire directly on our own encampment. He and his family had been captured but escaped in the enemy's confusion during the artillery barrage. We had become very good friends after that, and he showed his respect for my ability by giving me a great deal of authority for the rest of the time I was his deputy. Colonel Son had since been promoted to deputy to General Nguyen Ngoc Le,[12] commandant of the huge Quang Trung Training Center. To my surprise, he told me he was a member of the Can Lao party.[13] He explained the workings of Can Lao and how its members had arranged my transfer to Bien Hoa, and later denied my appointment as Fourth Division chief of staff.

He was very upset about the situation. "You should be chief of staff here, not a deputy. If not here, then you should be assigned to that position someplace else. But you should not have to remain here as deputy chief of staff!" he said vehemently.

I shrugged as if to say "what's done is done." I thanked him most sincerely for taking the time to visit and for his thoughtfulness in bringing treats for my children. I went on with my work after he left and gave his comments no more thought. My work went on without incident for several months.

Just a few months later, however, I received a real surprise: orders from the Minister of Defense appointing me chief of staff for the Quang Trung Training Center. And yes, this was the same minister who denied my chief of staff appointment at the Seventh Division. (Lieutenant Colonel Son apparently had been able to upgrade my qualifications significantly in the minds of the higher-ups in the Defense Ministry.) So my family and I soon moved once more.

The French established the training center originally, but on a much smaller scale. Now, with American assistance, it was a huge operation, accommodating some 10,000 trainees and staff. A strong U.S. military team worked with the Vietnamese staff to organize and implement the operation. General Le, base commander, greeted me warmly when I arrived at Quang Trung. He made sure I was introduced to key members of the staff and was briefed on the training center's mission and operations.

The first emphasis was on training—or retraining, really—about 2,000 NCOs to adapt to the new organization, strategies, and equipment of the Americanized Army of the Republic of Vietnam (ARVN). The Quang Trung base also was the basic training site for all army recruits and draftees. Every week one group of the latter completed their training and a new group began the basic training cycle. So the training center was a constant beehive of activity, requiring heavy logistical support. Just feeding the many people there was a major task, let along providing housing, equipment, clothing, laundry, and similar necessary services.

As chief of staff of this operation, I faced a formidable job, dealing with all phases of training center operations except the actual training. On my level, reporting directly to the commandant, there was a major in charge of finances and a lieutenant colonel who served as training director (but in reality the U.S. team ran the training program). The U.S. team consisted of about twenty men, four or five officers and the rest experienced NCOs. They set up the training schedule, went into the field on training missions with the troops, and supervised all phases of the operation. This organization held true for all three generals I worked with during my time at Quang Trung: Nguyen Ngoc Le, Ho Van To, and Mai Huu Xuan.

General Le was transferred two or three months after I arrived at Quang Trung. My old friend Ho Van To, now promoted to general, came from the academy at Dalat to replace him. General To left Quang Trung under something of a cloud as the result of a rebellion among the trainees about five or six months after I took up my position there. Two things caused it: bad food and general discontent fueled by secondhand Viet Minh propaganda. It occurred this way.

The training center program provided opportunity for relatives and friends to visit trainees on weekends. These visits were festive affairs, combining elements of huge family reunions, open-air markets, and American-style county fairs. Families enjoyed each others' company, ate, and exchanged the latest news, which always included large doses of latent Viet Minh propaganda. Their relatives were always quick to pass on to trainees the latest antigovernment stories and disinformation spread by the remnant Viet Minh in their home villages. The cumulative effect finally reached a critical mass, and the camp erupted. I suspect a few of the more charismatic leaders among the trainees sparked things, and soon all of the training center trainees picked up sticks of firewood as impromptu weapons and defied staff members who tried to defuse the situation.

I hurried to headquarters as soon as I learned what was happening. Major Le Thien Giao joined me there. We called General To's quarters and home but were unable to locate him. I then called HQ in Saigon to apprise them of the situation. By now, the troops had marched out of the camp en masse and were headed to Saigon to air their grievances. "You stay here and handle communications," I told Major

Giao. "I will take a vehicle and head off the trainees before they go any farther. Maybe I can negotiate and get them to return before any serious harm is done." I was concerned about a confrontation between the trainees and forces that Saigon was assembling to stop their march.

"No, no," he protested. "You must remain in charge here and stay in contact with HQ and any field commanders who have been alerted. I will go after the mutineers and see what I can do with them."

The major proved to be an extremely effective negotiator. He jumped into a vehicle and, accompanied by just two troopers, set out after the trainees. When he got to the head of their column, he left his vehicle and started a dialogue with the group's leaders. He listened to their complaints sympathetically, agreeing that they should have a hearing. He also promised that they could return to the training center immediately, but if they did not, they might suffer serious consequences. At length, the mutineers agreed to return, and things gradually returned to normal.

I congratulated Major Giao on his efforts and thanked him personally for defusing what could have been a disaster. Throughout the entire series of events, the two of us were left in charge because we never were able to locate General To. Not long after, he left the center, and later General Xuan replaced him.

Things changed with General Xuan's arrival. Whereas his predecessors both knew me and left to me details of running the center, except for training and finance, Xuan and I had no previous contact. Moreover, he came from an entirely different, nonmilitary background: the French Sureté, where he was a high-ranking officer, an inspector. He was a French citizen and the administration had seconded him to the army as a colonel for political reasons.[14] He was wary of and cool toward me. He questioned me constantly about matters involving the base. Later, when we became friends, he told me that he felt uneasy, even a little threatened in his role as commandant, because I obviously had many times more military experience than he did.

Two more incidents during my first six or eight months at Quang Trung come to mind.

One involved a slogan that was printed in large letters high on the walls of each barracks: "Down with Ho Chi Minh, Long Live President Diem." When a high-ranking officer entered one of the barracks, the noncom in charge was supposed to salute and lead the trainees in shouting out the slogan. The trainees usually complied, but I heard that they sometimes reversed the slogan, shouting "Down with President Diem, Long Live Ho Chi Minh." This was an indication of the festering residual Viet Minh influence among the recruits, an influence that helped cause the camp rebellion.

Another problem a short time later related to poor food and the trainee mutiny. When I returned home from my office one day, my wife said, "A man came by to see you today and left this basket and a note for you." I opened the envelope. Inside was a business card and 50,000 piasters. My salary at the time was 20,000 piasters per month, so this sum was significant. I didn't recognize the name on the card immediately, but when I inquired from my assistant I learned that he represented the company that supplied meat and fish for the training center. My assistant also informed me that, as chairman of the purchasing committee, I had to sign for all food and things like soap received at the center every day. Previously, my assistant had simply given me the papers, already signed by the other four or five committee members, acknowledging receipt of the items. Perhaps he assumed that my role as chairman of the committee had been explained to me. Actually, it had not, and I was so busy with other matters that I paid little attention to this area and regarded signing the documents as a mere formality. Now, however, I realized it was something I could no longer overlook.

I immediately went to General Xuan and told him about the man leaving the money and gift basket for me. He listened carefully, and then told me to leave the money and to keep the candy and fruit for my children. He said he would return the money to the man who left it for me and warn him not to repeat such action in the future. I did not keep the fruit and candy, but donated it to the infirmary for soldiers to enjoy. I also gave the entire supply purchasing procedure some thought and set out to learn more details of how it worked. I began making regular visits—at least once a week and sometimes more often—to the receiving area where contractors delivered supplies. I found contracts that specified the standards to be met by vendors who furnished the training center with rice, soap, fish, and various other food products.

I wrote a letter to the Ministry of Agriculture's equivalent of the U.S. Food and Drug Administration asking that a team be sent to the center equipped to test samples of supplies we received. I explained that I wanted to ensure that each item met vendor contract requirements. Before results of the tests came back, General Xuan called me into his office.

"Why did you do this without letting me know in advance?" he demanded.

"I didn't feel it was necessary," I replied. "I was just going by the book; such testing is supposed to be part of SOP [standard operating procedure]." The general acknowledged that with a nod and said no more.

When the test results arrived, they revealed that products delivered to us were indeed significantly below standard, usually by 25 percent or more. The meat supplied, for example, had more fat than meat. On further investigation, I uncovered systematic shorting of quantities delivered. That is, if we were supposed to get fifty cases of an item, we might actually receive only forty-five. Suppliers were making huge profits and had been doing so for a long time. I realized that there had to have been bribery of and collusion by training center officials, possibly up to the highest level. Since General Xuan had been at the training center such a short time, however, I did not believe that he was part of the scheme. At any rate, I went to him, armed with all the facts I had assembled, including the test results and vendor contracts. I explained in detail what I had learned. Again, he listened carefully, then said he would consider the matter and get back to me with a decision as to what measures we would take to remedy the situation. He took a whole week before he summoned me to his office with his decision.

"We will issue stern warnings to all vendors involved and cancel the contract of the worst offender," he told me, adding that we would levy fines based on the amounts of each vendor's contract and gaps in quality and quantity of the goods they delivered. The vendor whose contract was canceled was the meat supplier.

After that incident, General Xuan's attitude toward me changed substantially. He placed more trust in me and seldom questioned my decisions. On a personal level, he became much more cordial, often inviting me into his office for informal chats about training center operations, and even personal confidences. On several occasions he invited our family to visit him at his home, an extensive and impressive plantation. The valuable property was given to him by the French colonial administration before leaving Vietnam, as a reward for his faithful service in the Sureté.

13: MY FIRST LESSON OF INSURGENCY— FROM A WOMAN (1959–1961)

Some time after the vendor episode was resolved, General Xuan was appointed head of a team of officers being sent to Israel to study the kibbutz program operating so successfully there at the time. The object was to see what elements of the program, if any, could be adapted to our country. When he returned about two weeks later, he gave me a stack of documents, brochures, reports, and other items he had accumulated during the trips. "I want you to study this material and prepare a report for me to present to the president and chairman of the Joint Chiefs of Staff." As it turned out, this demanding, but straightforward, assignment ultimately would change my life dramatically.

I first read all the material thoroughly and requested that the U.S. embassy supply even more data from a U.S. State Department expert on Israel and its kibbutz program. I then worked about four days, mostly at night after routine duty hours, to prepare a rough first draft of the report. It was lengthy and interspersed with many questions. General Xuan and I went over it carefully, and he answered my questions. I reworked the report and we met again.

"It is too long," he objected. "If we present such a thick report, someone may or may not read it, but it probably will not get to the president. I want you to find some way to condense it, to make it easier to assimilate." I gave the matter a lot of thought, and then reduced the twenty-one pages of the second draft to just seven pages, but with references to sections of the earlier material. Then, thinking that might even be too long for a quick reading, I prepared a three-page version. Again, I referenced sections of the seven-page version.

So now I had a report in three parts. Part 1 was an abridged, annotated overview of the gist of the material. Part 2 was an expanded version of Part 1 that provided more detail, as well as references to even more detail in Part 3, which was the original twenty-one-page version. General Xuan was very pleased with this approach, and made only a few changes in it. Glad to have that assignment completed, I forgot completely about the report while coping with day-to-day operations of the base— until two or three months later, when General Xuan invited me to dinner at the villa assigned to him on the main training center campus.

The general was in high spirits during our pleasant two-hour dinner, the result of a long meeting he had earlier with President Diem. He had attended meetings with the president before but always with groups, never alone, face-to-face, and never one that lasted an entire afternoon, as this one had. It turned out that President Diem had indeed read the report and was very impressed with it. He had requested that Xuan meet with him to discuss it in more detail.

"Toward the end of our meeting," the general told me, "President Diem remarked that the report must have taken a great deal of time and intelligence to prepare. He asked me if I had done the report myself or had an aide do it. I told him that all the material and instructions came from me, but that the actual writing and preparation of the report was by my chief of staff, Major Tran Ngoc Chau. I wanted you to get credit for the fine work you did."

I enjoyed the dinner and thought it was good of General Xuan not to claim all credit for the report, which many superior officers would have done. But it meant little to me. What effect would the mention of me to President Diem have on my life? Would he even remember the name of a mere major? Not likely, I reflected, especially since General Xuan told me that the president made no notes during that portion of their meeting. I dismissed the event as being of little importance to me. Imagine my surprise when, about ten days later, a letter came from the president's office requesting that I meet with him. I was excited and elated at this unexpected turn of events. So was General Xuan, who by this time had assumed a sort of "older brother" status with me.

"I am very, very happy to have you recognized by the president. You deserve it. I might lose you here, but you deserve to move up," he told me. I duly presented myself for the meeting, in my best full-dress uniform. An aide-de-camp ushered me into President Diem's office,[1] then left the two of us alone. I saluted, removed my cap, and stood at attention.

He greeted me pleasantly but said nothing about the report I had written or any other business matter. Instead, he started talking about my grandfather and my family. He seemed to know every detail of my grandfather's career and his writings, and commented on them at great length, for at least an hour. The president actually knew more than I did about my grandfather, who died when I was fourteen. He also discussed my father, but only briefly.

"Your grandfather was a great man," the president finally concluded, "an eminent philosopher, judge, and minister in the Royal Cabinet, as well as a great humanitarian."

Then he told me I should leave and go back to work. During all this time he never asked me a single question or said anything remotely related to military or political matters. As a result, I was almost dazed when I left him. Why did he call me in for this meeting? Where did he learn all that he knew about my family, especially my grandfather? It was very puzzling.

After I returned to camp, General Xuan asked about the meeting. When I explained what had happened, he looked at me rather strangely. "That is odd," he said.

"You mean to say that the president called you in for a meeting and talked about your grandfather for over an hour? He didn't say anything about your work, the report you prepared, or any other business?"

"I've told you exactly what happened," I replied, slightly peeved. "Do you think I am not being truthful? Why should I make up such a story?"

Later, I realized why he didn't believe me. As a former member of the French Sureté, he had a suspicious mind and was accustomed to intrigue. He may well have thought that I received special instructions from the president to report on his activities. At any rate, General Xuan was thereafter quite distant with me.

Less than a month after my strange, one-sided meeting with the president, in late 1959 I had a new assignment. President Diem ordered my transfer from the Regular Army to the Civil Guard and Self-Defense Corps (commonly referred to simply as the Civil Guard). I was one of four field-grade officers, three majors and a lieutenant colonel, appointed as inspectors in the Civil Guard. We each had different tasks. I was appointed inspector for psychological and social affairs. Another major was named inspector for training, and so on. We reported to the inspector general, a lieutenant colonel, who in turn reported directly to the president.

This corps was somewhat similar to the National Guard in the United States but very different in important respects. It was not part of the regular military but was under the control of the presidency; the head of the Civil Guard Directorate reported directly to President Diem. Civil Guard soldiers served full-time, but in their own home areas. Their primary duty was to protect people in local villages, cities, and provinces. These local units came under direct control of province chiefs, not the Regular Army establishment.

President Diem himself assigned me my first task in this new position. He told me to visit all forty of the country's provinces to observe and evaluate these local forces. He then wanted me to prepare a comprehensive report on my findings, both on the Civil Guard's effectiveness from a military standpoint and how its troops interacted with the civilian population. This was the first time since I left the Viet Minh in late 1949 that I had a chance to see and understand what was going on in the smaller communities of the country, the most remote areas where the peasants lived. During the intervening ten years I had been occupied with purely military matters. Now I toured the countryside for nearly four months with no fanfare or ceremony. Just two soldiers, a driver and bodyguard, accompanied me in a military vehicle, a four-wheel-drive Land Rover. I slept and ate in the villages.

So I was able to take a close, personal look at what was happening in small villages and farming hamlets. In all, I visited twenty provinces, which I selected as representative of their areas, based on such criteria as size and density of population, religions practiced, social status and characteristics, and history of their involvement in the anti-French war.

What I found was disheartening.

First, Civil Guard troops were poorly paid, poorly armed, and poorly trained. They had no political training or indoctrination, which left them unmotivated and unable to foster good relations with people in the areas where they were posted. The poor pay made things worse. Civil Guard soldiers commonly preyed on the peasants, demanding tribute that the peasants could ill afford or stealing from them.

Second, the lack of decent equipment, including weapons, and adequate military training made Civil Guard units mostly ineffective for accomplishing their mission of protecting local residents. There was some variance from province to province, but even the best units were barely adequate.

Third, I learned quickly that almost all provincial and local government officials and employees—including those in intelligence, security, and police organizations, as well as the military—were holdovers from the French regime.

This disturbed me greatly. South Vietnam was undergoing profound changes, struggling to reinvent itself as a free and democratic nation after nearly a century of colonial rule by France. The new Republic of Vietnam had been created with Ngo Dinh Diem as president and the Americans providing personnel and impressive financial aid to help in the major shift from colony to sovereign country.

In the countryside, however, nothing had changed. Lives of the peasants went on as usual, and they appeared indifferent to, even not aware of, the transformation being attempted. Small wonder! The same people were in charge. Differences in the daily routine of government seemed imperceptible. Extreme poverty was still the norm. Land reform was nonexistent, not even a wishful dream for most of the people—if they even knew what "land reform" meant. Corruption and bribery were still the norm. Landowners, especially in the Mekong Delta, continued to collect their 25 to 50 percent of tenant farmers' crops.[2] Formal education was almost nonexistent. (Many of the peasants could not read or write, though this did not mean they were ignorant. They learned from an oral tradition of songs, stories, and communal theater.)[3]

Moreover, there were no apparent attempts to change the situation. Province and community leaders were content with the status quo, especially since many of them worried that changes might reduce or eliminate the power and prestige they enjoyed. Little was done at the top levels of government to motivate these leaders with a sense of national purpose. Without training, motivation, and indoctrination themselves, how could local leaders be expected to rally their constituents to believe in and support the national government?

And where was the leadership for change at the national level? President Diem himself was surrounded by bureaucrats who previously worked for the French colonial authority. Minister of the Interior Bui Van Luong, the national police chief, many other top security officials, and most of the military leadership had served in the French governing apparatus during the decade-long "French War," some even before that. The French were gone, but their policies and attitudes, particularly toward the peasantry, lived on. The oppression, duplicity, and corruption of the past remained firmly in place. The coming of the Americans did not affect this, which suited the Communists just fine. For years they had described Vietnamese government officials as lackeys of the French. Now they just switched to calling them "lackeys of the Americans."

Attitudes of those in power at all levels also remained the same in another important respect: anyone who supported Ho Chi Minh's forces in the fight against French colonialism was suspected of being a Communist sympathizer. I ran across examples of this constantly during my twenty-province tour.

One case stands out in my mind. It occurred early in my tour when we stopped for refreshment about midday at a tiny outdoor café. It was in one of the first communities where I planned to conduct a survey and interviews. The village was only about forty kilometers from Saigon, but far more remote in atmosphere than that distance would indicate. An attractive young woman served tea to my driver, my bodyguard, and me. Oddly for that time, she appeared to be running the small establishment by herself. That made me curious, so I asked about her later when talking to the village police chief.

"She's a spy, a Viet Cong supporter!" he said.

Surprised, I asked how he knew that.

"Her father was known to have killed several French soldiers and Vietnamese who worked with the French during the war. He was later killed himself."

"Did she ever act suspiciously or do anything wrong?" I asked.

"Not that we know of or can prove, but it's difficult to tell. We have our suspicions, however, and we watch her activities because of her father and because she doesn't attend public meetings in the village."

So the woman was considered an enemy and more or less ostracized by the villagers (no wonder she didn't attend public meetings) simply because she was related to someone who had fought the French. I found such guilt by association also extended to relatives of people who moved north after the 1954 Geneva Agreement.[4] This attitude was common among local officials everywhere I went on my tour. Compounding the problem was the fact that the "informants" (only the other side had "spies") supplying information about the Viet Cong were the same people, the same families, who did the same work for the French. Some may have had relatives

killed or wounded by the Viet Minh; for them, it was payback time. Their "information" often was tainted by their prejudices, desire for revenge, or in some cases, simply to get out of repaying loans.

It was unfortunate that patriotic nationalists were made pariahs in their own
home areas, because, properly treated and motivated, the same people could have
been a strong base of support for the national government. Instead, they became
prime fodder for the underground propaganda activities of the residual Viet Minh.[5]
As a former Viet Minh soldier, I found this especially disturbing. How many were
there who, like me, were not Communists but had fought to free Vietnam from
French rule and now were regarded as spies or worse?

All in all, what I saw were the seeds for the second Vietnam War, and they were
rooted in the same place where the first war sprouted against the French: the rural
countryside. I didn't recognize that at the time, of course, though I did realize that
many serious problems needed to be faced if South Vietnam was to endure as a free,
independent nation.

Looking back, President Diem obviously missed a great opportunity to ensure
that future for our country. He should have done away with the government structure that was so much a legacy of the French. Replacing abusive officials and policies
with others that improved the lot of the rural population could have rallied peasants
to support the national government instead of regarding it as the enemy. He should
have implemented a policy of reconciliation with former Viet Minh soldiers and
supporters. Instead, his police and security forces persecuted them and drove them
into the arms of the Communists. President Diem and his Vietnamese and American
advisors clearly had little respect for the peasants and did not understand their importance. Those mistakes cost us all dearly in the coming years.

Still another problem struck me. Americans ignored the Civil Guard. All their
advisors and military aid went to the Regular Army, despite the fact that the army
saw no action at this time. Whatever fighting there was occurred between the Civil
Guard and antigovernment guerrilla units. These were mostly small skirmishes, but
Civil Guard troops were too poorly equipped and trained to be really effective even
in such small-scale actions. Vietnamese and American military leaders would have
been better advised to focus some attention on the Civil Guard, which was really the
front line of defense during this period.

After completing my tour, I prepared my report. I pulled no punches—explaining the problems I encountered, the reasons for them, and suggestions on how they
might be corrected. I had some concerns about this because I suspected that most of
Diem's advisors told him things he wanted to hear, not necessarily factual information. I could not do that.

The officer who was my superior, as inspector general, reinforced that feeling after he read the report. "I think there are many things bad about your report, things you should not report to the president."

"Everything in it is the truth," I replied, "and I do not feel I can change that. I was ordered to report on the status of the Civil Guard, and it is my duty to relate what I learned as fully and accurately as possible. That is what I have done."

The colonel was silent for a moment. Then he said, "I am the inspector general, but as you say, you were assigned a specific task by the president. It is not my prerogative to interfere with your performance of your duty as you see it. Therefore, I will submit it to the president. However, if the president asks you, would you tell him that I did not read it?"

"Why?" I asked. "I don't understand."

"Because I don't agree with many of the things you say, but I can't stop you from making the report. I will submit it without any comments or recommendation."

"Fine," I told him, "as long as you submit it."

As it turned out, neither of us needed to worry. About three weeks after my discussion with the inspector general, President Diem called me to his office. It was obvious that he had read my report, and seemed to consider its implications very thoughtfully. He asked many questions—mainly details about how I determined the facts and arrived at my conclusions. We discussed various aspects of the report at length. Finally, he directed me to prepare a refresher course for provincial Civil Guard commanders and their deputies. The goal of the program was to correct, by education and motivation, many of the problems I cited in my report.

"You will be director of the program, with Major Thanh as your deputy," he told me.

I worked with Major Nguyen Viet Thanh, who had been training inspector up to that point, to develop the most effective means of implementing the program. I drew heavily on my experience with the Viet Minh during the 1940s, but kept that fact to myself. We stressed political aspects, not military tactics or strategies. Instead of lectures, we emphasized self-critique discussions patterned after those the Viet Minh used so successfully. I kept the president's rather innocuous term—Refresher Course for Provincial Commanders and Deputy Commanders of the Civil Guard— as the formal name for the program.

The interactive self-critique sessions proved far more effective than a series of lectures would have been. Although it was an old technique, the approach was novel for those who attended the training course. The commanders and their deputies participated enthusiastically in the training sessions, so much so that I often felt like I learned more than the students.

Major Thanh, a very intelligent man,[6] was amazed. He was much younger than I was at the time, so he had never fought against the French or Viet Minh and had no knowledge of Viet Minh indoctrination tactics. Thus, he learned even more than I because my past experiences and more recent tour through the provinces made me aware of many, but far from all, of the things that came out during the training classes. Many problems surfaced, some unique but most were common to all provinces. Various solutions and the tools needed to implement them were discussed. In some cases, commanders or their deputies suggested strategies that had worked for them.

In every session, however, I stressed the importance of three factors that were crucial to future effectiveness of the Civil Guard:

1. Motivating both troops and civilians
2. Developing accurate intelligence sources
3. Refining military strategies

I did this as subtly as possible, by guiding discussion and presenting some of the points I wanted to make as possible answers to problems raised during training sessions.

For example, most of the Civil Guard leaders complained that the people did not cooperate with them or did not trust the Guard to protect them. "Why is that so, and how can you best change their attitudes?" I asked them in reply. That usually led to rather frank discussions of problems within the Civil Guard itself. These leaders admitted that low pay and poor training resulted in low morale among the troops and abuses committed against civilians they were supposed to protect.

This gave me an opening to emphasize the importance of motivation, which I felt, or rather knew, to be the key factor in turning things around. It was easy to implant the idea of using interactive, self-critique sessions for this purpose, given the enthusiasm of the commanders for the course they were taking. The idea almost suggested itself in most cases.

I reminded them that the objective of the Civil Guard was to protect the people. "To do this, you must earn the trust of the citizenry by convincing them that you, the Civil Guard, are on their side and that you have only good motives, better than the Viet Cong, who only use them to further the Communist cause. You can only do this if your troops respect the people and treat them properly. You can't expect the people to trust you if your men act worse than the Viet Cong, stealing food or extorting money, mistreating women, treating civilians as the enemy. Such abuses are exploited by the Viet Cong and are among the most important causes of all your problems," I exhorted them.

We all agreed that low pay was a major difficulty, but I could offer no simple solution for it. It was a function of the national government and could only be corrected at that level.

I focused on things they could accomplish, encouraging them to share ideas about how they could implement training and indoctrination programs for their men, offering suggestions designed to promote active participation by course attendees. I pointed out that such programs would cost almost nothing but could be very effective in raising morale. I wanted to cheer when one province commander commented, "That's true, and if the men take more pride in their unit and the job they are doing, they will do better. They will feel more like they are accomplishing something important."

That was the attitude I hoped to foster.

The second item of importance—gathering useful, accurate intelligence—required establishing a new mind-set in Civil Guard leaders. A few leading questions confirmed what I already knew: they still relied on the same informants used during the French regime. In other words, anyone who fought against the French or supported the Viet Minh was suspect—never mind that they were staunch nationalists, not Communists, and could now be valuable allies. I pointed out the need for confirming intelligence on the Viet Cong (as the government now had begun to refer to Communist elements) or Viet Minh from any source to ensure that it was not bogus or motivated by fear, hatred, personal gain, or revenge. Since the police and security forces still relied largely on informants from the French legacy, this might require Civil Guard leaders to work at requiring these other agencies to improve their information gathering as well as to develop their own intelligence sources.

The third factor, improving purely military operations, proved easier to address. Many of the commanders and their deputies contributed useful ideas. I found little need to interject my own thoughts, except to suggest that the Civil Guard study enemy tactics to learn how best to combat them. I pointed out that since the Viet Cong struck mostly at night, more night patrols and ambushes should be mounted. Commanders and their deputies agreed, but brought up some of the logistical and other problems involved. Some said that lack of training might blunt the effectiveness of such actions. There was general agreement on most of the military matters we covered.

When the training program ended, the Civil Guard leaders generally agreed on two other subjects.

First, all agreed enthusiastically that they had learned a great deal from the Refresher Course, most of it from themselves. Their input and shared information provided more "education" than they received from us, even if all of them did not recognize that fact.

Second, they were not sure how, or even if, they could implement any of the improvements and reforms discussed during the course. One province commander put it this way:

"What can we do when we go back to our posts? You have helped open our eyes to many ways we could do better but you are only instructors, not our commanders. Once we go back to our own areas we are under the command of the provincial chiefs, and they have not been exposed to the same information that we have. Thus, it might be impossible to make them understand the reason, the need, to change the way we operate. They might very well insist we go on as we always have: ignoring the relationship between Civil Guard troops and civilians, trusting the same informants as in the past, and using the same, safer military tactics."

He made an excellent point and, again, one for which I had no ready answer. That was exactly what I said to the president when I reported to him.

"Civil Guard leaders responded enthusiastically to the Refresher Course," I told him. "The province commanders and their deputies all agreed that it was very helpful and that they learned a great deal from it. They also agreed that it might be difficult to implement the improvements and reforms we covered, given that they are under the command of provincial governors, who may or may not want to make the necessary changes." I also confessed to him that I probably learned more from the Civil Guard leaders' input than they learned from me, that the success of the course was due more to the frank discussions and sharing of ideas than from instruction that Major Thanh and I provided.

President Diem listened thoughtfully. "Let me think it over," he said at last. Then he astonished me by adding, "Meanwhile, you have a new job, one in which you will put into practice the reforms you have told me about and what you have learned from the Refresher Course."

And on the spot he appointed me commander of the Civil Guard and Self-Defense Forces for the seven eastern Mekong Delta provinces: Long An, My Tho, Kien Tuong, Kien Phong, Vinh Long, Vinh Binh, and Kien Hoa. These already were centers of great unrest and Viet Cong strongholds.

My first chore when I arrived at the Mekong area was to organize the forces there, something that had never been done. There was no system whatsoever; each unit seemed to go its own way, operating in haphazard fashion. As part of the reorganization, I instituted a training program for all Civil Guard and Self-Defense Forces. It was similar to the Refresher Course we conducted for provincial commanders and deputies, but on a much larger scale.

I set up a rotation system so that each unit went through the training as a unit, including everyone from officers and noncoms to private soldiers. Again, this was something I learned from my Viet Minh days. The interactive discussion and self-critique sessions worked better when the trainees knew and were comfortable with each other. Their shared experiences made it easier to identify problems they could relate to, both as individuals and as a group. Their familiarity with others in the unit made them more open and willing to engage in meaningful discussion than would have been true if we had brought individuals from different units together randomly.

To give the training a hands-on, practical side, I arranged with the province chiefs to take over the whole area around the training center. The villages and village committees were placed under my control. In return, we provided security for the entire area, relieving the province chief of that responsibility. This allowed us to supplement discussions and lectures with real-world exercises. Both the Civil Guard units and villagers benefited from the resulting interaction.

This was an opportunity that I threw myself into wholeheartedly, because it seemed to offer promise for correcting some of the problems facing our fledgling nation.

It became even more interesting because I first started working in the field with Americans during this period. Although no U.S. advisors were assigned to Civil Guard and Self-Defense units, only to the Regular Army, my Civil Guard headquarters and those of the Vietnamese Seventh Division were both in My Tho. I commanded the Civil Guard and a Regular Army colonel commanded the Seventh Division, with U.S. Army Lieutenant Colonel Frank Clay assigned as Seventh Division advisor.

Colonel Clay[7] had no official connection to my own command, but he called on me and I was glad to give him a tour of our headquarters and training center. I explained in detail what we were attempting to achieve and how we were going about it, more so I gathered than was true at the Seventh Division. He was interested and soon was a regular visitor. We became good friends, enjoying wide-ranging discussions about social, military, and political matters in Vietnam. One day he brought with him a group of American generals, including General Lionel Charles McGarr and General Charles J. Timmes, and Robert Thompson (later Sir Robert Thompson), a British pacification expert who had gained fame for helping suppress the Communist insurgency in Malaysia.[8] He had come to Saigon as head of the British Advisory Mission to Vietnam.[9]

I took the group on a tour of our facilities, explaining our operations in some detail. When they inquired about the Viet Cong, I described the VC infrastructure, how they interacted with the peasantry, and the guerrilla tactics they used. I emphasized how they "swam with the fishes," or were indistinguishable from the local population during the day. I explained something of their indoctrination methods, how they were able to win support of the peasants, and how they exploited South Vietnam government and military missteps. The entire group was very interested, and Colonel Clay pronounced the visit a great success. Soon after, he arranged for me to go to Saigon to speak with staff on some of the same subjects: organizing and

retraining the Civil Guard and Self-Defense Forces, our training methods, and the
Viet Cong.

Soon President Diem called me to Saigon and, once more abruptly, gave me a
new assignment:

"You have done a fine job in your current assignment with the Civil Guard. Now
you can leave it for others to carry on because I want you to come here and work in
the National Security Council. But first I want you to go to Malaysia to tour the
country and study their counterinsurgency methods. Determine how their pacification programs work and what we can learn from them. Learn all you can about the
way they combat insurgents, because whatever they are doing seems to be effective.
When you return, we will explore what, if anything, we can adapt for use here in
South Vietnam. You can also begin your duties with the National Security Council
at that time."

A few days later I said good-bye to my family and flew to Malaysia, where I was
to spend nearly two months. That time turned out to be both enjoyable and
eye-opening.

Most important, I learned about the great differences between Malaysia and
South Vietnam, and how those differences affected my country's efforts against the
Communists in general and the Viet Cong in particular. These differences broke
down into three major areas:

1. Organization of the Malaysian government infrastructure
2. Law and how it was implemented
3. Propaganda and the paramount importance of supplying honest
   information

First, Malaysia was a very well-organized federation of eleven separate states, which
had gained its independence only recently, in 1957. (The federation was now an autonomous member of the British Commonwealth of Nations.) Each state had its
own head of state. These eleven potentates elected a national king from their own
ranks to preside over the entire federation for a term of five years. So there was a
well-defined chain of command and responsibility.

Counterinsurgency and pacification programs were separate from the other facets of government, however, and were still under British direction. Robert Thompson
bore the title of secretary general of the Defense Committee and was in charge of
these operations, with the king and chiefs of the eleven states playing no role in
them. At the state level, a prime minister appointed by the king oversaw local counterinsurgency efforts, with the state police chief as his deputy. The prime minister
had ties to religious leaders. Significantly, the military played only a supporting role.
Units were assigned missions in specific areas and for limited times. A representative

from the police accompanied the troops on every counterinsurgency mission. Essentially, then, containing the insurgents and promoting pacification fell under the direction of political leadership, not the military.

This helped explain how law was regarded and implemented in Malaysia. True, we had a constitution in South Vietnam, but it often was honored more in the breach than in actuality. Province chiefs, appointed by the president, usually ruled their domains as virtual fiefdoms, with little regard for legal niceties. Not so in the Malaysian federation. Leaders there followed the rule of law very strictly. People were not jailed or punished arbitrarily, without due process. Efforts were made to ensure that laws were applied equitably and equally to all citizens. Even those accused of terrorism or guerrilla activity received a defense and their day in court. This was far different from cases I witnessed in Vietnam where a "suspected Communist sympathizer" was sentenced to five years' imprisonment without benefit of defense counsel, because no lawyer dared represent him for fear of angering the province chief. The Malaysian philosophy was: "We are lawful people, a lawful government. We beat the enemy because we respect the law and they do not. They either have no law or do not conform to our national laws, and we do so in all our activities."

Finally, I was impressed by the attitude toward propaganda and communication of information. The British attitude was that any information made public should be true. "If the truth might be harmful to you, then it's best to say nothing at all, but never lie and never distort the truth" seemed to be their slogan.

This represented a totally different attitude from that of the Vietnamese government officials and the Americans in South Vietnam. From the mid-1950s into the 1970s, they routinely distorted, even falsified, information released to the public.[10] As the buildup of U.S. forces grew, military officers began holding daily briefings at 5 p.m. Reporters soon learned that the briefing information differed, often greatly, from what they found when they ventured out into the field to investigate for themselves. Thus was born the great distrust of "official news" by such veteran correspondents as Keyes Beech, Stanley Karnow, Mal Browne, and Homer Bigart, and shared by Neil Sheehan, David Halberstam, Peter Arnett, and the other Young Turks of the media who followed them.

I concentrated on these factors in preparing my report for President Diem when I returned to Saigon. From earlier experience I knew he favored brief reports, but he would explore in greater depth points that caught his interest.

That is exactly what happened. Our first meeting lasted almost a full day. The president was so interested in my report that he almost forgot to eat lunch. He customarily ate a frugal meal, much like those fed to hospital patients, brought in on a cart by an aide. This day, President Diem was so engrossed in questioning me about what I had observed and drawing out my conclusions that he left the food untouched until it was completely cold. About 4 p.m., he brought the session to an end. "I am tired now," he said. "We will stop for today, but you must come back tomorrow and we will continue our talk."

We spent the better part of the second day discussing the counterinsurgency measures being used in Malaysia and what we could learn from them. Finally, he reached for the phone and called his brother Nhu (Ngo Dinh Nhu), who was his chief counselor and headed the secret police. Nhu was widely, and rightly, regarded as the second most powerful man in the country.

"I have just finished two days of meetings with Major Chau, who just returned from his tour of Malaysia where he studied the counterinsurgency methods being used there. I found his report extremely interesting. I think it would be helpful for you to meet with him and hear what he has to say."

The meeting occurred about four days later. Nhu appeared serious and attentive during the entire time I spent with him. Unlike his brother, however, he didn't ask any questions. Finally, after more than two hours, I concluded my report.

"You raise many interesting points, Major Chau," Nhu commented. "We may have things to learn from Malaysia, but you must remember that our two countries are very different. We have our own situation and problems here in Vietnam, and Malaysia has its problems and ways of solving them. Those methods will not necessarily apply in this country."

Nhu then opened a book on his desk and indicated that our meeting was over. I never discussed my report with him again.

14: IN KIEN HOA PROVINCE, THE VC "CRADLE OF REVOLUTION" (1962)

Iworked to the best of my ability for the president in my assignment on the National Security Council, but it was frustrating to be witness to a bureaucracy consistently at odds with the realities of the countryside. One day after Counselor Nhu and I arrived back from a trip to the provinces in early 1962, a phone call from Gia Long Palace summoned me to a meeting with President Diem. I walked into the president's office-bedroom, with no inkling that this was a pivotal day for me, that this meeting would change my life unalterably. I recall the setting even today. President Diem sat in a large chair at the foot of his bed, as he always did for these meetings, with a table placed in front of him. Bui Van Luong, minister of the interior, sat at the president's left. I sat facing Minister Luong across the table on the president's right. (Nobody ever sat facing President Diem.)

With little preamble, President Diem announced, "I want you to go to Kien Hoa province and take over as the new provincial governor.[1] You should leave as soon as possible." Astonished, I objected immediately.

"With all due respect, President, I cannot accept such an assignment. I'm a military man, a soldier with no knowledge of civilian administration![2] How can you even consider me for such a job? I would much prefer to return to the army."

Minister Luong gasped, shocked by my audacity in opposing President Diem like this. The president went on calmly, however, as though I had not spoken.

"You are a good man, and you come from a family that has a long, honorable record of service to our country. You have proved that you are also a capable man in a series of increasingly important positions in recent years. I am confident you will do well in this one."

I started to object again, but the minister interjected this time, almost gently, as if to head off any further objections from me.

"It has been decided, Chau; the president has made up his mind and I agree. You will have a capable staff, and I will be available to assist you at all times." (Ironically, I never met with him again after that day and seldom even had contact with him.)

So, like it or not, I soon traveled to Ben Tre,[3] provincial capital, to assume my duties as governor. I was not a total stranger to the province, having spent time there on my current and previous assignments. So I knew something of the province's makeup and history.[4]

As I left the ferryboat landing on the Kien Hoa side, I recalled vividly an incident from a visit a few years earlier. I had come across a morbid spectacle: the bodies of seventeen people laid out in a row with four or five World War II rifles lying beside them. They ranged in age from two boys of about twelve to two men in their sixties. Two were women. Appalled, I had asked who they were.

"They were all Viet Cong," was the answer. "Twelve were active VC guerrillas who participated in raids and ambushes. The other five were VC supporters who spied on us and spread enemy propaganda."

The sight of these dead men and women affected me deeply. Utter sadness, almost despair, swept through me. I had seen many dead bodies over the years, but these seemed different somehow. They looked just like the people crowding around the street where they lay, and were even dressed in the same fashion. Why had they been so alienated, so hateful toward the government, that they felt compelled to join the enemy? We, in the government I represented, were trying to protect them, were we not? How had we failed them? I knew many of the reasons, of course, and have catalogued them in previous pages. I felt terribly frustrated, yet even more driven to change the conditions that led to such tragedies.

The conflict in our struggling young nation took on new meaning for me on that Kien Hoa street. The sight of those corpses caused a sea change in my thinking. Their images haunted me and were a factor in most of my future decisions and efforts.

The incident drove home to me the fact that the enemies we faced today were not faceless, anonymous combatants, but they were *us*: our neighbors, even our relatives. During the previous fifteen years as a soldier, I faced many enemies: Japanese, French, and Viet Minh. I saw hundreds of dead bodies in combat during those years. I always grieved, hurt personally, and felt compassion for the dead and their surviving relatives. My consolation was always the realization that death was one of the brutal facts of war.

This was different. It was the first time I had seen the bodies of people from local peasant families who were somehow motivated to fight against the government that was trying to build a new nation which would offer them a better life.

Yes, I felt compassion but I was also angry. And I felt confused. None of the friends and relatives of the dead cried, as rural Vietnamese normally do in such circumstances. One woman, about thirty, glared at me so intensely that I literally felt her hatred as a tangible force.

Why did these people, farmers living in relatively peaceful villages, choose to join insurgents who roamed from village to village, killing their fellow Vietnamese, collecting "taxes," and promoting an alien philosophy, communism? Why did they forsake their peaceful lives to take such risks? Another question also plagued me. How could they remain for the most part undetected, even protected, by villagers in areas controlled by the South Vietnamese government?

I stayed in the village for three days on that occasion, talking to people and try-ing to find answers to my questions. I learned that the dead were indeed connected with the Viet Cong, or National Liberation Front (NLF). It was common for the South Vietnam government and military officials and the Americans to refer to all insurgents generically as "Communists" at the time. I did not think this was true. I felt certain that the people lying dead in that street, like most rural Vietnamese, knew little or nothing about communism. Most of the Viet Cong and their support-ers were more dedicated to Ho Chi Minh than to Marxism or abstract Communist ideals. To the peasantry, Bac ("Uncle") Ho was a mythic figure, the hero who fought the Japanese and defeated the French. Peasants regarded the cadre left behind in the South by the Communists after the Indochina War as Ho's personal representatives. As such, villagers honored, protected, and listened to them.

This contrasted sharply with the peasants' negative attitude toward local repre-sentatives of the Diem government. I understood this completely. After all, these government functionaries were for the most part the same people who oppressed them during the French colonial period and the 1945–54 War against the French.

Previously part of Cochinchina, a colony under the French, Kien Hoa consisted of three extensive islands lying between the two branches of the Mekong, close to the sea at the mouth of the Delta. It lay along the Vietnamese coast of the South China Sea, some 85 kilometers (km) south of Saigon. It was about 50 kilometers across at its widest point and about 120 kilometers long (about 1,500 square miles, roughly 70 percent the size of Delaware's land area).

When I took over as province chief, Kien Hoa's population was about 600,000 people, almost half of whom were Catholic. Buddhists and some of the Cau Dai sect made up the rest of the population. Kien Hoa was divided into nine districts at the time, each with its own district chief, who dealt mainly with police, security, and military matters. The minister of the interior appointed these district officials, usu-ally on the recommendation of the province chief. They worked out of small offices and compounds, and most did not have a great deal of direct power over the villages in their districts. They acted more as overseers, coordinators, advisors, and com-manders of the Civil Guard and Self-Defense Forces.

The province was very fertile, benefiting from rich soil deposited by periodic flooding of the river. It was famous for its coconut plantations, which accounted for about half the land under agriculture. Rice paddies and sugar cane fields occupied most of the remaining farmland. It was also famous—or infamous, depending on your viewpoint—as a hotbed of antigovernment activity. It earned the sobriquet "Cradle of the Insurgency" because underground resistance to the Saigon regime began there even before the official formation and announcement in December

1960 of the National Liberation Front, as the Communists called their new public face to the world.

I knew that I was going into an extremely difficult situation. I was determined to turn that around by applying the things I had learned over the past twenty years. My main goals would be to pacify the rural population by gaining their confidence and support. I reasoned that this would eliminate support for the Viet Cong, and ultimately cause the insurgency to wither and die. I approached the task with one simple, but fundamental, fact in mind: the conflict with the insurgents was primarily political, not military. It would be won or lost by winning the minds and hearts of the people, not by counting dead bodies of the enemy.

My reasoning ran like this: Kill a VC and you eliminate a single enemy. But how many more do you create? That dead person has a family and friends—people who almost invariably will be driven into the enemy camp or further into it. If they were neutral, they may become willing, even enthusiastic, VC supporters; some will seek revenge by joining in VC ambushes and terrorist activities. Conversely, win one enemy over to the government side and a similar ripple effect takes place, but in the opposite direction.

When I arrived, estimates were that only about 80,000 of Kien Hoa's people supported the government—or at least were considered to be under government control.[5] Adding to my problems, I was replacing a popular governor, Pham Ngoc Thao, a highly respected lieutenant colonel who had been there just nine months. The province chief before Thao lasted for only three months.

I faced yet another hurdle: the innate resentment of southerners toward Central Vietnamese. Southerners viewed those of us from the central provinces, especially those from the Hué area, as aloof, arrogant, and imbued with a sense of the right to leadership. Perhaps I did inherit some of these characteristics, but I attempted to play them down in my relations with the people of Kien Hoa (although, of necessity, I had to assume a leadership role). How successful was I?[6] Elizabeth Pond put it this way in *The Chau Trial*: "He [Chau] would never win over some Southerners . . . but he did gain the profound respect of those who worked under him and of the province's population at large. In an attempt to minimize the differences he consciously adopted a Southern accent and word usage in Kien Hoa."

I began by getting acquainted with my staff. Each province chief had two deputies, one for general administration and one for military matters. The administrative deputy oversaw the provincial civilian staff made up of the heads of various departments: security, administration, economic affairs, finance, and personnel. There was also a chief of cabinet, who functioned somewhat like a military chief of staff and had almost as much authority as the deputy province chiefs.

The province chief also headed a Provincial Security Council, which controlled all security matters involving the Viet Cong. A province chief was the final judge in all such cases, and could impose sentences of up to twenty years for anyone found guilty of belonging to or supporting the VC.

There was also a provincial chief justice, who was in charge of the civil and criminal justice system. He sat on the Provincial Security Council and acted as a legal advisor to the province chief for insurgency-related cases. We inherited this system from the French, and it had not changed to any degree by 1962, except that province chiefs were now Vietnamese, not French. In fact, my civilian administrative deputy was a veteran professional administrator who had been trained by the French and had held the same post for about fifteen years.

One of my most important assets was my personal secretary, Lieutenant Le Chu Thien.[7] He had been with me since the Fourth Division days in Bien Hoa. He was invaluable; he knew my ways and was very organized. In those precomputer days, he served as my human PC, keeping track of all my files, correspondence, and schedule.

In addition to the Vietnamese staff, we had two teams of American advisors, each independent of the other, working with us. One was a military group headed by a major at first, then by a lieutenant colonel. The other was a civilian team from the U.S. Operation Mission (USOM) Office of Rural Affairs. U.S. Army officers in the first group concerned themselves with strictly military affairs: air and artillery support, advising on tactics and strategy in the area, and coordinating with Saigon military headquarters, both Vietnamese and American. They worked only with Regular Army units. The Civil Guard and Self-Defense Forces came directly under the control of the province chief.

As my first official action, I spent a day in the operations center with the military deputy and staff. They briefed me on current military and security matters, including known details of the Viet Cong "shadow government" in the area, as well as current estimates of Viet Cong strength and activities. The story was a familiar one. We, the government side, controlled the province—roads, villages, hamlets, all populated areas—in the daytime. At night, however, when our military forces, from army troops to village self-defense militias, retreated into their fortified positions for the most part, the Viet Cong took over. We mounted patrols of squad and platoon size and set some ambushes, but they were not very effective. In truth, as was often the case, the VC owned the night. And, I reflected, that was not likely to change, no matter how we improved our military forces and strategies. We needed more than military might to at least contain, if not defeat, the Viet Cong.

Next, I scheduled a meeting with all department heads. I told them frankly that I was a soldier with plenty of experience in military administration but virtually no civilian administrative experience. To help me get acquainted with their operations, I asked each of them to prepare a one-page report outlining the mission of his department, progress in accomplishing it, and what I could do as province chief to help. I also asked them how often they went out into the province to check on how their efforts were progressing. With some hesitation, but not embarrassment, they gave me to understand that such trips occurred very, very rarely. "It's a matter of security," said one. "Too dangerous," agreed another. And heads nodded in accord all around the table.

The following day I visited each department head individually to collect his one-page report and discuss it with him. In most cases, things appeared very satisfactory on paper, and in the charts and graphs displayed prominently on the walls in some of the offices. I knew, however, that I had to go out into the real world of Kien Hoa's hamlets to learn the truth. So, ignoring the fears and advice of my department heads, I soon began personal tours by Jeep of the province. I visited as many villages and hamlets as possible during the following weeks, keeping things as simple as possible. A driver and bodyguard accompanied me in a Jeep. A second escort Jeep with three Civil Guard soldiers provided added protection. These trips were not without incident. Snipers fired on us with depressing regularity. We frequently encountered land mines and booby traps. On one occasion the escort Jeep ran over a mine; the ensuing explosion killed all three Civil Guard soldiers.

I learned quickly that there were discrepancies, often substantial, between what the various departments reported and what the countryside realities were. I found truly deplorable conditions in the province hospital and several orphanages. All these facilities were overcrowded, with patients and orphans often sleeping on the floor, packed together almost like sardines in a can. Sanitation was virtually nonexistent. There were no screens on the windows, for example. Medicines were scarce in the hospital, as were X-ray machines and other medical equipment.

The Catholic nuns who ran the hospital and orphanages could not be blamed. They were dedicated women who did the best they could with what they had. They simply did not have funds to improve matters. In one hospital I saw the corpse of a man being carried out of a room.

"Who is he and what happened to him?" I inquired.

"He is a local farmer and was killed by artillery shrapnel," I was told.

"Where is his coffin?" I asked.

"We have no coffins available and no money to buy any," came the rueful reply. "We can only wrap him in a cloth shroud and bury him in an unmarked grave." I resolved to do something about that situation as quickly as possible.

As soon as I returned to headquarters in Ben Tre, I summoned my chief administrative assistant and told him of my experience.

"It's sad," he replied, "but there are no funds available to provide coffins for the dead."

"But we do have money available in various other accounts, do we not?" I asked.

"Yes, but it is all earmarked for other purposes."

"Well, I don't care how you do it, but I want you to find the money for coffins somewhere. Just attend to it, please."

He appeared ready to argue further, but seeing my expression, he just nodded briefly and left my office. His body language left no doubt that he disapproved of my disregard for long-established budgetary protocol.

President Diem's chief of staff called me soon after that, about ten days after I arrived in Kien Hoa.

"The president wants to meet with you tomorrow, Chau. I will send a plane to pick you up in the morning."

President Diem surprised me by opening the meeting on a very informal and personal note.

"Has your family joined you in Kien Hoa yet?"

"No," I replied. "I've been busy acquainting myself with the province staff, military and administrative briefings, visiting district facilities and villages, among other thing. Also my wife had matters to settle before moving."

"I think they should join you right away. Kien Hoa women are known for their beauty, attractive enough to tempt even the most virtuous of men," President Diem said in an almost jocular way. He then continued in a more serious, concerned tone. "You hold a position of great responsibility now. It would be bad for you, both personally and professionally, to be distracted from your duties in any way. I am relying on you to perform your job capably, as I know you can, to vindicate my judgment in appointing you as governor of one of the most troubled provinces in the country."

He spoke to me as an uncle might to a favorite nephew, or even a father to a son. I felt both honored and humble at this show of concern.

"I will arrange for the move immediately," I said.

The president then got to the real business of the meeting.

"Have you formed any opinions of your predecessor, of his performance in Kien Hoa?"

"No," I answered quite honestly. "I know Colonel Thao, of course, and he seems to have been popular during his six-month tenure as province chief. Beyond that, I've been too occupied with trying to familiarize myself with as many aspects of the province as possible to concern myself with how Colonel Thao did his job."

The president nodded in understanding, then spoke again, seeming to choose his words carefully.

"During the next few weeks I want you to learn what you can, so that you are able to give me an informed impression of Colonel Thao's operations in the province. You should not be too overt about it or make it appear as though you are conducting an investigation. I will expect a report on your findings no more than six weeks from today."

A bit puzzled, I asked if there were any specific area on which I should focus. No, said the president, he did not want me to concentrate on anything special, just for me to learn what I could and to include my overall assessments and impressions in the report.

We discussed a few minor bits of business, and the meeting ended. I left the palace, buoyed by thoughts of the early, informal part of the meeting, a bit perplexed by his request for a report on Colonel Thao.

On the way back to Ben Tre, I mentally reviewed what I knew about the man. Pham Ngoc Thao was the ninth child in a family of southern Catholics. Like me, he caught the nationalistic spirit in 1945 and joined the Viet Minh resistance. At this point he changed his name from Thuan to Thao (with the "hoi" tone marker in Vietnamese, it could mean either to honor or to debate, depending on what other word appeared in combination). He moved up through the cadre ranks to serve as both commander and political commissar of the Tay Do Regiment, which acquitted itself well against the French colonialist troops. His brother, Gaston, also joined the Viet Minh in 1945, but stayed in the North after the defeat of the French at Dien Bien Phu. Gaston eventually was appointed North Vietnam's ambassador to East Germany.

Thao, however, cast his lot with the South. After the defeat of the French, Bishop Ngo Dinh Thuc introduced Thao to his brothers, Diem and Ngo Dinh Nhu. The Catholic connection clearly worked in his favor, and Nhu recruited Thao to South Vietnam's intelligence service, working closely with Tran Kim Tuyen. He went on to become an influential officer in the South Vietnamese government with easy access to U.S. commanders, with whom he quickly became a favorite. After his recall from Kien Hoa to Saigon, he served as a special adviser to the president.

He cut a dashing figure, with a very correct military bearing, his mystique enhanced by the glass eye he wore as result of a combat wound suffered while with the Viet Minh. Thao was very intelligent, a dedicated nationalist who exuded charm and authority. Even his opponents were often, at least temporarily, swept up in his schemes. Clandestine politics was, for him, a game of skill—and one in which he excelled. Our paths never crossed during the Viet Minh period, but I had come to know and respect him over the intervening years.

I know now that because of his past links to the Viet Minh, and because his brother Gaston was a high official in the North, he was closely watched by the secret police.[8] President Diem's request to me indicated that perhaps he did not fully trust

Thao—with good reason, since Thao eventually participated in preliminary planning for the coup that overthrew Diem and resulted in the assassination of the president and his brother, Nhu.

I felt that Thao was loyal to South Vietnam if not to its flawed current leadership, despite the prominent position and influence he enjoyed. The corruption that extended from Saigon through most of the provinces dismayed and disgusted both of us. We agreed that adhering to the French system and maintaining most of the same Vietnamese bureaucrats who served under the French in the government infrastructure was wrong. We agreed strongly that that the struggle against the Viet Cong insurgency was as much, if not more, a political battle than a military one. Our background in the Viet Minh persuaded us of this, and convinced us also that the enemy was doing a far better job in this combat arena that we were doing. It was evident from our conversations, however, that we differed significantly on how to remedy the situation.

Where I believed in working within the system to promote change, Thao apparently felt more drastic measures were necessary. With hindsight, I think his participation in the coup against Diem was one step in an effort he hoped would topple the regime and ultimately replace it with younger, more progressive leaders who would set the country on a course better calculated to "win the hearts and minds of the people," to quote that much-abused slogan.

During the next few weeks I sounded out various people in the province about Colonel Thao, doing it as casually and unofficially as possible. The result was almost universally positive; on the whole, he was very well liked. A few Catholic priests subtly questioned his loyalty to the South and possible ties to the North. Since other priests expressed favorable opinions about the colonel, I felt the doubters' concerns stemmed from Thao's service with the Viet Minh and his brother's high place in the Communist ranks. Since my situation was similar, I tended to discount their assessments.[9]

One lieutenant colonel from the upper Delta area called to congratulate me on my new assignment, then launched into a diatribe against Colonel Thao. "The man is a Communist, an agent for the North!" he insisted over and over again. I put his reaction down to jealousy; he had been a government favorite with substantial influence in Saigon—until Thao came along and overshadowed him to a large degree.

I did have one serious disagreement with Colonel Thao's policies. He brought in many outsiders from other areas to serve as district, village, and police officials. I felt this was both unnecessary and a serious mistake. I told the president just that when I reported to him some two weeks before the six-week deadline he had set for me. "That is not unusual," President Diem replied. "Many province chiefs find it helpful,

if not necessary, to bring in men from other provinces because of a shortage of qualified local personnel."

"That is not the case in Kien Hoa," I stated, and continued, "The province has a
lot of resources, including men qualified for the positions Colonel Thao filled with
outsiders. His policy in that regard has created problems that otherwise would not
exist. For one thing, the people of Kien Hoa resent this influx of outsiders. In many
cases this resentment is justified by the overly harsh treatment Colonel Thao's appointees have inflicted on people in their jurisdictions. Often this occurs as part of
efforts to control the VC, but too frequently it is overdone.

"A major part of the problem is that the outsiders are not familiar with their areas
and the people in them. This lack of knowledge about local customs and personalities has created a general feeling of resentment and hostility in most areas of Kien
Hoa. I've sensed it during my travels from one end of the province to the other.

"As a result, I propose to replace most of these outside officials as soon as possible. I will retain only those I feel are qualified, are working well with the local populace, and agree to comply fully with my policies. I will begin with the district chiefs.
I plan to recruit their replacements from within the province, calling upon village
elders and local religious leaders for advice in making my selections."

The president considered my statement for a moment, seeming not to be fully
convinced by my arguments. In the end, however, he agreed. He even said he wanted
the offending district chiefs punished. I learned later that some were even jailed.

While working on the president's request for a report on Colonel Thao, I began
implementing programs and policies that were—to me, at least—far more important. They would be key to my goal of winning converts to the government side instead of running up an impressive body count of enemy dead. Chief among these
was a Census Grievance (CG) program, something I had experimented with successfully in my earlier post as commander of the Civil Guard and Self-Defense
Forces for the seven eastern Mekong Delta provinces.

I developed this program because the South Vietnamese intelligence system was
almost a joke. Networks and informants were holdovers from the French era, with
almost all the same personnel, biases, and flaws. The enemy had long since identified
virtually all agents and informants and treated them in three ways. Many they simply insulated from any useful intelligence and used them as conduits to feed misinformation to their handlers. Others they recruited as double agents—moles who
provided information about South Vietnamese and U.S. government and military
activities.

Some, especially those who were most effective and therefore most dangerous,
were eliminated, by assassination or other means. A diabolical twist the Communists

used in some of the latter cases was to discredit agents and informants to the point where our own side did their work for them.

I knew the details of one such case. It involved a man—we'll call him "Van"—who began working with the French in the mid-1940s. His information consistently proved to be accurate, so the French came to rely on Van as a reliable source of intelligence. The Communists made a run at him, trying to recruit him as a double agent. Van refused. Unbeknownst to him, however, they photographed those meetings, showing him with known Communist agents. One of those photographs was delivered to the French by an enemy double agent. This aroused suspicions about Van, which the Communists fanned with damaging misinformation funneled through sources they controlled. Ultimately, the French decided Van was an enemy agent and executed him. So a good man died at the hands of "friends" because enemy intelligence was superior to French intelligence operations.

Twenty years later, the Thai Khac Chuyen case—in which an intelligence operative for the U.S. Special Forces (Detachment B-57) was convincingly portrayed as a Communist "double agent," ruthlessly interrogated, and "terminated with extreme prejudice"—may have been a reiteration of the same game. The shame of these affairs is that we will never know the truth of the matter.

Consequently, I wanted to institute my own, very different approach to intelligence gathering in Kien Hoa. I planned to do it by implementing what I called a Census Grievance (CG) program, using a concept I had worked up during the interim between my service with the Civil Guard and Self-Defense Forces in the Upper Delta and my recent appointment as governor of Kien Hoa. I would organize pacification teams. Each one would be composed of five specialized sections: Census Grievance, social development, open arms, security, and counterterror. Because the Census Grievance approach was absolutely fundamental to the operation of the other four sections, I referred to these teams overall as "Census Grievance teams." In the beginning these teams were small in size, but eventually as our program expanded into contested areas, the teams grew in size to sometimes almost sixty cadres.

I trained the first small team myself, most recruited from the Civil Guard and Self-Defense Forces. We screened their backgrounds carefully. I interviewed each member of the census grievance section and leaders of the other four sections personally. I was especially careful about selecting candidates for the core of the group: the three to five men who would conduct the CG interviews, both those selected for the original CG section and for all the subsequent teams we formed.[10] They were critical to the success of the program. They interviewed every member of the village or hamlet in which they were operating every day, without exceptions.

Two sections within each team ranked right behind the CG interviewers in importance: the social development and open arms sections.

Members of the social development section worked with the villagers to improve living conditions generally: helping to build small bridges and dig wells, setting up schools and medical clinics in areas where they were lacking, and organizing projects to improve the raising of chickens, pigs, and even fish.

The open arms section was also called the "Returning Team." Its function was to counteract Viet Cong indoctrination, and persuade VC supporters and active members that it was in their interest to join the government side. We did indeed greet returning VC with open arms, helping them to get settled back in their villages and find jobs, and even providing financial aid. Families of the returnees also received monetary rewards. I further saw to it that the men who returned were not drafted into the army. I had to fight very hard to win that concession. The draft was universal, and the returning VC men were prime targets for the draft. I knew the prospect of having to serve in the military would be what we in the United States now call a deal breaker.

My approach ran counter to the situation that prevailed in other provinces—and previously in Kien Hoa where known and suspected Viet Cong were given no quarter. Body count was the measure of counterterrorist success, with no effort being made to combat VC indoctrination or win back VC cadres. Families of suspected VC members suffered, too, even when suspicions were unfounded and based on faulty, even malicious, intelligence.

Then there was a security or protection section of six to twelve armed men who provided protection for the CG (pacification) team. Since the team worked with up to ten villages at a time, the security section alone was not enough to provide protection for the entire area. In such cases, a detachment of Civil Guard troops was assigned to provide extra security against VC activities, including raids on villages, kidnapping and assassinations, extorting money or food from villagers ("tax collections"), and propaganda or indoctrination sessions.

Finally, each CG team included a counterterrorist section. This was, more or less, my weapon of last resort. With intelligence garnered by the CG interview cadres, we were able to build a rather clear picture of the Viet Cong influence in a given area. We were able to determine those families and individuals who supported the VC because of fear and coercion and, on the other end of the scale, the most dedicated, recalcitrant, hard-core VC who directed and participated in the most virulent activities. The latter cases were screened thoroughly and information confirmed at the province level. Only then was a counterterrorist unit called upon to arrest or kidnap a VC cadre. Only in the most grievous cases of VC terrorists, when an arrest or kidnapping was not feasible, was the ultimate sanction invoked: assassination.[11]

Villagers understandably greeted the Census Grievance process with great suspicion at first. As in my earlier experimental effort in the Upper Delta provinces when I commanded the Civil Guard, CG team interviewers asked just three questions.

1. Did anything significant or unusual happen in the area during the past twenty-four hours? (This could involve either VC or local government activities.)
2. Do you know who was involved?
3. What can the government do to help or protect you and to improve your living conditions?

Many people were reluctant, or afraid, to answer even these simple queries. They still had to spend the minimum of five minutes with the CG cadre. Gradually, however, as they began to see that we were not trying to entrap or do them harm because of their testimony, they became more responsive.

One factor that contributed greatly to acceptance of the CG procedure was that people soon began to see that we were serious about stopping abuses not only by the Viet Cong but by government officials and the military as well. Some villagers might report—often defiantly, as if daring us to do something about it—that a village chief was molesting their women or that Civil Guard units were stealing their crops or livestock. When accusations like this surfaced, I made sure they were investigated. If they proved true, the offenders were punished. Some lost their jobs; others went to prison, depending on the degree of their offense.

I remember two incidents very well. One involved a family that raised fish in a pond on their small farm. The other was a rape case.

The case of the stolen fish actually predated my appointment as Kien Hoa's governor. It seems that the fish-raising family's farm was close to a fortified Civil Guard outpost.

Periodically, the Civil Guard unit here reported a night raid on the post by Viet Cong.

Coincidentally, these raids occurred most often at times when fish in the pond had matured and were ready to be eaten. Even more coincidentally, the ready-to-eat fish disappeared during each reported attack.

The family became convinced that the Viet Cong attacks were faked so Civil Guard troops could steal the fish and blame it on the Viet Cong. They made this accusation during census grievance interviews. We investigated and found that the family was correct in its suspicions. Civil Guard members involved in stealing the fish were disciplined, and the family was reimbursed for its losses.

Many other instances like this contributed to the success of the census grievance program. The open-arms teams helped immensely, too. As people in the countryside saw that we were sincere in our efforts to peacefully win back VC supporters and active members, many more of them rallied to the government side and convinced family members to leave the Viet Cong ranks.

The success of the program also had its consequent risk. Members of the census grievance teams became prime targets for assassination by the Viet Cong. As I stated earlier, we often had to beef up security for the groups by detaching Civil Guard units of varying sizes to provide added protection for them.

Small wonder that the Viet Cong struck back. As our intelligence grew in volume and accuracy, Viet Cong members no longer found it easy to blend into the general populace during the day and commit terrorist acts by night. Our counterterrorist actions against hard-core VC cadres hampered them further. We soon learned that hundreds of Viet Cong left the province entirely to escape imprisonment or worse. Toward the end of my first year as province chief, no fewer than 1,000 active Viet Cong guerrillas fled from Kien Hoa to other provinces because they no longer felt secure.[12] The census grievance process made them vulnerable to discovery, and they came to fear being captured or killed by the CG counterterrorist units. The Viet Cong ranks dwindled further as lukewarm members left because of our open-arms policies.

I had been in my post as governor of Kien Hoa just a few months when visitors began to show up—American visitors. (Other than President Diem, no South Vietnamese government or military officials showed any interest in my programs— not enough interest, at least, to come and learn about them firsthand.) My first significant contact with a U.S. Army officer in the Mekong Delta area had been while I was assigned to head the Civil Guard and Self-Defense Forces in the seven Upper Delta provinces. As I outlined in the previous chapter, Lieutenant Colonel Frank Clay, senior advisor to the Vietnamese Seventh Division, became interested in my work. He, in turn, brought others to see me, including Generals McGarr and Timmes and Sir Robert Thompson.

This time, however, one of the first to visit me was General Edward Lansdale, the famous "Cold Warrior" credited with playing a major role in helping President Magsaysay defeat the Communist-led Huk insurgency in the Philippines. Because of his background in intelligence work (he served with the OSS during World War II) and psychological warfare, he seemed to grasp the intent of my policies and their goals quickly and accurately. I'm not sure how much his influence had to do with the support that the Americans offered later, but I suspected it was considerable.[13] Among the items I did request—and received—from the Americans was radio equipment. As I told them, I felt a radio station that I could use to communicate with Kien Hoa's populace would be more valuable than a division of troops. That proved to be the case.

Using the radio, I reported regularly to the people on the concrete, beneficial results of the census grievance program. When I announced that a well had been dug in this village, a bridge had been dug in that hamlet, or an oppressive police chief had been fired and punished, the peasants could check the facts for themselves and learn I was telling the truth. This was a huge step in getting them to trust and support the government side.

Actually, the radio station was just an extension of a practice I had adopted earlier: public "open door" sessions during which people could come to meet me face-to-face and make their complaints to me personally. At first, I set aside one day each week for this purpose. Initially, few people came to see and talk to me. Such a policy was unprecedented, and they feared some sort of reprisal if they aired their grievances in such a public fashion. Gradually, however, they came to trust me, to see that I was sincere in my desire to improve their lot. People began to appear at provincial headquarters in increasing numbers. Soon I had to extend the meetings to two days per week. Sometimes I had to suspend this practice due to other duties, but we always resumed as soon as possible. Things were improving in Kien Hoa, but not so in other provinces.

15: AT THE HEART OF THE BUDDHIST CRISIS (1963)

The Buddhist crisis developed in early 1963 after an ill-advised move by the Diem government. The administration ordered enforcement of an old law stating that only national flags could be flown in public. In theory, the order meant that flags of Catholics, Buddhists, and other organizations could no longer be displayed to celebrate significant days or festive seasons, as had been customary in Vietnam for many years. In fact, the order came exactly at the time of year when Buddhists traditionally raised their flag[1] to celebrate the birthday of Buddha. Thus, Buddhists saw the move as more persecution, another in a continuing series of discriminatory acts and policies against their community and religion.

As a Buddhist myself, I was outraged by this arbitrary and offensive move. As a political supporter of the government, I reckoned it would do tremendous damage to our efforts to win over the people; the timing meant it targeted a religion practiced by more than 85 percent of the Vietnamese people. I felt that this was a major political mistake by President Diem, himself a Catholic from a prominent Catholic family and with a heavily Catholic administration.[2] Moreover, enforcement would be just weeks after Catholics had been allowed to display Vatican flags.

An aide brought a cable containing the order to my residence just as I was preparing to take a bath. I immediately called the president's office and arranged a meeting with President Diem. Early the next morning a small plane arrived to take me to Saigon. "Mr. President," I began when we met, "this ban against flags cannot and should not be enforced."

President Diem then began to explain the reasoning behind the order. "There has been widespread abuse of flying flags in this country by all religions, not only the Buddhists. We want to bring it under control in general and not just target the Buddhist community."

"Mr. President, unfortunately the timing makes it appear otherwise. We have already entered the celebratory season for Buddha's birthday, and Buddhist flags are already being flown over temples and residences everywhere. No other religion will be affected immediately, so most Buddhists will regard it as a specific affront to them. I don't know about other provinces, but enforcing this order will make it extremely difficult, if not impossible, for me to govern in Kien Hoa. I have enough to deal with there without coping with a situation that the government, which I represent, has created."

"You cannot carry out the order in a different way, one that will not create problems among the people?" the president asked.

"No, Mr. President. I implore you to reconsider the order. Please do not make me enforce it in my province. It will hurt the province, it will hurt the people, and it will hamper me immeasurably," I replied.

Finally, after a long silence during which he toyed with a cigarette in a hand that trembled slightly, the president spoke again.

"Well, every time you have a problem you should discuss it with me. This time seems different, however. You have spoken with such seriousness and sincerity that I can feel it very deeply. So I will leave you free to do whatever you can about the flags."

Thus, he didn't say yes and he didn't say no.

I went back to the province and met with Buddhist religious leaders. To begin with, I asked them if it would be possible to restrict use of the flag to temples. They all said that it would not, because it was already being displayed in other public areas and at private homes all over the province. Removing the flag from all these places would create havoc. Finally, they agreed to fly both the Buddhist and national flags at temple entrances, but only Buddhist flags within the compounds. I decided that was the best I could accomplish, which was what the president had said I should do in his final words. So I told my staff to pass down the word that the national flag should be flown next to the Buddhist flag at entrances to pagodas, but there should be no interference with individuals who chose to display only the Buddhist flag.

Elsewhere, however, Buddhists' frustration and resentment grew. Buddhist demonstrations against the government became commonplace. The situation came to a head in Hué when officials refused to let the Venerable Thich Tri Quang, my onetime monastery classmate and leader of the central area Buddhists, deliver his annual message over the Hué radio station.[3] Thousands of Buddhists gathered near the station to demonstrate in protest. Facing them were police and government soldiers, some in armored troop carriers. Reports of what exactly happened were contradictory and confusing, with each side blaming the other for what followed. The outcome, however, was not in question. The government forces broke up the demonstration by firing into the crowd, killing nine people. (In Kien Hoa I was isolated from much of this antigovernment activity by Buddhists, but little did I know that I would soon be thrust into the thick of it).

Tragically, fiery suicides by Buddhist monks became common. They doused their bodies with gasoline and set themselves on fire. These acts first occurred in Hué but quickly spread through Central Vietnam and down to Saigon and the Delta provinces.

The sight of these flaming human torches flashed on television screens in

America and around the world, creating widespread antagonism towards President Diem's regime. This was unfortunate, partly because I do not think President Diem held any particular malice toward Buddhism or its followers. (A conversation we had less than a month later tended to confirm this.) He was a devout Catholic and favored Catholic Vietnamese, but this did not automatically make him a virulent opponent of other religions. Actually Catholic Archbishop Ngo Dinh Thuc and Counselor Nhu, the president's brothers, were the architects of the Diem administration's oppressive policies toward Buddhists. Nhu and others of Diem's inner circle viewed Buddhists and members of other religious sects as possible threats to the regime's continued political power. Archbishop Thuc was openly hostile to Buddhism and its believers. The president often displayed great political naïveté, but he was also a very intelligent man. It is difficult to believe he would establish policies that alienated some 80 to 85 percent of the country's population without being convinced of the necessity by someone with great influence on his decisions.

It was common knowledge at the time that the Americans wished fervently that the president would rein in Nhu's powers and stop relying on him as his chief, often his sole and always his most influential, advisor. Many Vietnamese, myself included, felt the same way, but many others owed their positions of power and privilege to Nhu's influence, so they supported him totally. Nhu's power and influence seemingly were enhanced further because of his close relationship with his older brother, Archbishop Ngo Dinh Thuc, himself a very important figure. Diem's reliance on his family for support and guidance gave these two men important voices in policy-making during their brother's regime. I believe their influence was responsible to a great extent for some of the policies and actions that eventually doomed the Diem government.

Diem himself must have understood by this time that Nhu was a liability in many respects. In a conversation I had with the president some weeks later, he indicated that he had given some consideration to sending his brother and Madame Nhu abroad to distance them from his administration and quiet the critics. The pretext would be a face-saving political appointment, perhaps as an ambassador or South Vietnam's representative to an international body. In the end, Diem's reliance on his brothers and absolute trust in their loyalty to him made it impossible for him to do so.

Shortly after our conversation about the Buddhist flag situation, the president surprised me with another sudden new assignment. He called to say he wanted me to play an important part in solving the Buddhist crisis. "I originally planned to send you to Hué," he said, "but I feared some sort of conflict might arise between you and my brothers."[4] This made me think that the president had come to realize that the Buddhist policies advocated by his brothers were wrongheaded and responsible for the current crisis.

President Diem then explained that he had decided to send me to Danang, the second-largest city in South Vietnam, about ninety-five kilometers south of Hué, to be mayor of the city and governor of the Quang Nam province–Danang city area. "In your new assignment you will be accountable *only* to me," he emphasized. Obviously he wanted to forestall any objections I had about accepting the new assignment because of potential hindrances due to bureaucratic frustrations or political considerations. I wanted more clarification than this, however, about exactly how much freedom I would have to make on-the-spot decisions. More important, I *needed* to know how he expected me to treat the Buddhists. I posed this question to him: "I understand that my new assignment is to help solve the Buddhist crisis, but I must first ask you to tell me exactly what your attitude and policies are toward Buddhism and the Buddhist community that has been revolting against you and your administration?"

The president seemed to ignore my question for a minute or two. Instead, he appeared to be looking inward, playing idly with the cigarette in his fingers. Then he turned to me suddenly and spoke. "Whatever steps you take to help solve the crisis should be along the lines of your own attitude toward Buddhism and the Buddhists."

I understood this to mean that he had confidence in me, as a Buddhist, to do the right thing, to treat fairly the Buddhists and others involved. I also understood that he was giving me complete authority to do what I felt was right, and not feel that I was bound by previous government policies or directives. The president also told me that he considered the matter urgent, that he wanted me to leave for Danang early the next morning and to take over as mayor as soon as possible after arriving in the city. He said he would expedite preparation of the necessary orders and documents.

We then discussed the matter of my replacement as province chief in Kien Hoa. The logical candidates were two of my three deputies, Majors Cao Minh Quan, deputy for pacification matters, and Le Huu Duc, military deputy. (I felt either of them could continue our efforts in the province better than the civilian administration deputy.) It was a hard decision because both were good men. I finally decided on Major Duc and the president concurred. I returned to Kien Hoa and spent the whole night with the deputies, working out details of the transition of province leadership to Major Duc. The situation had developed so suddenly that we were dealing with unfinished business right to the time of my departure.

Early the next morning, as promised, the president's plane arrived in Ben Tre to take me to Danang. First, however, we flew to Hué, where the government delegate for Central Vietnam, Mr. Ho Dac Khuong, joined me on the plane. Once aboard, he opened an envelope containing sealed orders from the president. Until that moment he did not know that his task was to escort me to Danang and assist in my takeover as mayor of the city. The envelope also contained the president's order appointing me to replace the current mayor of Danang.

We arrived in Danang at about 2:00 p.m. Mr. Khuong called Mayor Ha Thuc Luyen and arranged a meeting in his office. Mr. Khuong introduced me, and then handed over the document naming me as the new mayor of Danang. Mayor Luyen went into near-shock as he read the order. His face turned white, his limbs trembled, and he appeared close to a collapse for a time. I felt great empathy for him. He was among the most senior officials in the government and was a longtime supporter of our Catholic president, although Luyen himself was a Buddhist. In fact, he had accompanied Diem when he returned from exile in 1954. It was no wonder Luyen was so affected by this sudden and surprising turn of events.

I would like to have explained to him that my new assignment had been every bit as surprising to me as it was to him, that I had neither sought nor desired the job into which I had been thrust. I kept silent, however, feeling anything I tried to say could make matters worse and more embarrassing. Both Mayor Luyen and Mr. Khuong were quiet, too. The silence lasted for about five minutes, as all three of us remained lost in our own thoughts. Then Mr. Khuong spoke:

"Well, what can we do? We have the presidential order mandating the change and we must comply with it. I am simply here as an official observer to witness the passing of mayoral duties over to Lt. Colonel Chau. According to President Diem's decree, that must be done immediately so that Mayor Luyen can board the president's plane and fly back to Saigon, as ordered."

When Luyen read that part of the order, his distress was obvious. My heart went out to the man once again as I saw tears in his eyes. I could only imagine the humiliation he must be feeling, not only at being so abruptly removed from his position but also being forced to immediately leave the city where he had lived with his family. My first thought was that it was cruel of President Diem to uproot him in this fashion.

Only later, about two or three weeks after I took over as mayor, did I realize that the president had valid reasons for his order. He feared that Luyen had made so many compromises, was involved in too many controversial policies and with too many diametrically opposed factions, that his continued presence in Danang would only make my job harder. He was right, too. I quickly found that the situation was chaotic and difficult enough without having the former mayor in residence to serve as a focal point for opposition to policies and solutions that I would propose. He certainly would have been an object of sympathy and a source of resentment against me by a significant segment of the populace.

After some discussion of details for the changeover, Mr. Khuong and Mayor Luyen left for the airport. I called in the mayor's deputy, Nguyen Quoc Dan, who happened to be my wife's uncle and fellow Buddhist. He briefed me on the current situation, which was not good in any respect. I knew that was the case beforehand, of course, but hearing details of some of the problems in the city made me realize how bad things really were and what a difficult task I faced. Two other senior city officials joined us and provided more information.

Next, I spent time with Mayor Luyen's personal secretary. He was a Catholic, well connected with the Catholic hierarchy and lay leaders. He was also a very fair, intelligent, and honorable man, so much so that I kept him on as my personal secretary during my tenure as mayor of Danang. He filled me in on prevailing Catholic attitudes and the general tenor of relations between the various factions in the city.

After all these discussions I had a reasonably clear picture of the current situation. Danang was a tinderbox, divided into bitterly opposed factions and ready to explode. I had already seen evidence of this earlier on the drive from the airport to the mayor's office. Scattered throughout the city were small groups of Buddhist priests, surrounded by larger groups of Buddhist laymen. They were contained in perimeters of concertina wire and guarded by soldiers carrying rifles with fixed bayonets, partly for their own protection but mostly to prevent them from mounting more Buddhist demonstrations to inflame the city.

Following my meetings with the city officials, I arranged to meet with the Buddhist Venerable Thich Minh Chieu, who was the leader of the local Buddhists. At first he refused to come to my office and demanded I go to him. I sent my deputy to explain that I could not do that, any more than I would go to meet with a Catholic leader. To do so would show weakness or favoritism, something I simply could not afford on my first day in office. My deputy must have been most persuasive because Venerable Chieu finally agreed to visit me in the mayoral office. After a long discussion I told him that I had come to Danang only after assuring myself that the president had no intention of suppressing the Buddhists. I had come to make the government work, to resolve the differences between Catholics and Buddhists, pro-government factions and dissenters—in short, to calm the situation in the best manner possible.

"This will require all sides to compromise," I told him. "I cannot expect to perform miracles and make everyone perfectly happy. All I can do is work toward a solution that is at least reasonably acceptable to all, one that restores order in the city and allows people to go about their lives and their work normally. Thus, I ask you not to disobey the orders of the central Buddhist hierarchy."

I knew that there was a division of sorts between the elders of the Buddhist hierarchy and the younger priests, who were more militant and more into the political aspects of the situation. I hoped I could persuade Venerable Chieu to follow the lead of the more moderate elders. He raised many, many objections, and we ended our discussion without reaching any agreement. A compromise was still a long way off.

By this time it was after 1 a.m. I had now gone about forty-three hours with only a few hours of sleep and could hardly remember my last meal. I was hungry but almost too exhausted to think about food. However, when I opened the office door, I found the personal aide to the mayor standing there.

"You must be hungry, Mr. Mayor. You haven't eaten since you arrived early yesterday afternoon. There is food prepared if you would like to eat something." Then he led me to a large dining room where six servants, two chefs, and the waiters, in white uniforms, were waiting. They had prepared all sorts of food and were ready to serve them.

"How many will be eating?" I asked.

"Only you," the aide replied.

"How come then that there is so much food and so many people to serve just one person?"

They explained that since it was my first day there, they were hesitant to ask what I might want, so they prepared this large variety of dishes for my choice. They had also laid out fine china and silverware, all with initials in French. This was far different from the more austere way I was accustomed to in Kien Hoa. I said nothing, but simply ate what I wanted and thanked the staff for their thoughtfulness. Next morning, however, I discussed the matter with the personal secretary. He explained that such elaborate dining rituals were standard protocol, holdovers from the French era.[5]

I also sent an emissary to the Venerable Thich Mat Hien with a message explaining my difficulties with the local Buddhist leader and asking for any help he could provide. I added that if an acceptable compromise could not be reached, I would feel it necessary to resign as mayor, assuming the president did not replace me first.

Next, I called in the military deputy, Colonel Dam Quang Yeu, who was in charge of troops garrisoned in the city: he coordinated with the local police and reported to the mayor. I asked him to take me on a tour of the city. Once again I was struck by the number of wire-enclosed enclaves in many public areas filled with Buddhist priests and laymen. Other Buddhists came in droves ostensibly to bring them food and water. It had been like this since nine Buddhists were killed in the Hué demonstration less than a week earlier. The tour of the city reinforced what I learned from my previous briefings. The colonel and I discussed some of the key elements necessary to keep things under control in the city. I told him that I would work very hard with all factions during the next few days to cool things down, to find acceptable compromises that would get the city back on a more normal footing.

The colonel agreed that relatives of soldiers serving in the army made up the most virulently anti-Buddhist groups in the city. Most were Catholics who had come down from the North after the Geneva Accords partition. I told him that his first priority should be keeping the two groups separated, to prevent a clash that might ignite the city.

Then I began a round of meetings with leaders of the community, attempting to assess their concerns, placate their fears, and find solutions to the problems that faced us all. This was all preliminary groundwork, not immediately productive but necessary to test the waters, as it were.

Meanwhile, Venerable Thich Mat Hien came down from Hué. I went to the city's main pagoda to meet with him and local Buddhist leaders. My old mentor wasted little time in stating his opinion. "You must remember," he said, "Mr. Chau is a staunch and loyal member of the Buddhist family. I am certain he is trying to do his best for all concerned, including Buddhists. I recommend to you that you strive to reach an accommodation with him. If you do not, he may resign as mayor or be replaced." Having said that, he left the meeting to return to Hué. His words hung in the air, however, their unspoken implication clear to all: if I left, my replacement might be far less tolerant of them and their followers than I would be. We continued our meeting in a subtly changed atmosphere.

The Buddhists' principal demand was that the troops be withdrawn and that the priests and laymen no longer be penned up inside the barbed-wire perimeters. My request was that the Buddhists disperse and confine their protests and demonstrations to their pagoda compounds. In short, I wanted to restore order, to end demonstrations in public streets and squares that disrupted life in the city, and to reduce potential confrontations between Buddhists and anti-Buddhists.

We finally reached an agreement. I would withdraw the troops at 11 p.m. and have the barbed-wire enclosures torn down. In return the Buddhists would do as I requested, but would retain the right to use loudspeakers to air their complaints against the government to areas surrounding their compounds.

I returned to my office and summoned Colonel Lam Van Phat, the commander of the Second Division. When I explained the agreement to him, he protested vociferously. He flatly refused to obey my order to withdraw his troops back to their quarters, saying it was too dangerous. He fully expected me to yield since I was a lieutenant colonel and he was a colonel. "The city would erupt!" he said, pounding my desk. "We would have rioting on a grand scale."

We argued for a time. Finally my patience ran out.

"I suggest you consult with your staff and superiors about the chain of command. I think you will find that, as mayor and governor of the Quang Nam province–Danang city area, I outrank you in this matter. You must obey my order for the first seventy-two hours in an emergency situation. You can appeal it to Saigon, but you must comply unless and until it is countermanded at a higher level."[6]

The colonel stormed out of my office. Not too much later, he called me and said, with obvious reluctance, that he had been advised that I was right. He said he would withdraw the troops but needed extra time to do it, asking if I would extend the deadline two hours, from 11 p.m. to 1 a.m. I agreed.[7]

I called the president on my special access line to tell him what had happened. I also wanted to let him know that either the colonel or I would have to go; it was obvious now that we could not work together. The president was silent as I went through a detailed account of the entire situation, from my round of meetings to the agreement reached and Colonel Phat's reaction. When I wound down, the silence continued. After waiting about five minutes I decided the line was dead and hung up. Exhausted, physically and emotionally, I put my head down on my desk and fell asleep at nearly 2 a.m.

Shortly after I awoke in the morning, my aide announced that Lieutenant Colonel Truong Van Chuong was waiting to see me. I knew the colonel, having served under him at one time. I wondered why he was visiting me but told my aide to send him in.

I was completely surprised when he introduced himself as the new commander of the Second Division, replacing his recalcitrant predecessor. I realized that the president had lost no time in acting on my complaint about Colonel Phat resisting my direct order the previous day. Understandably, this show of support heartened me considerably.

Lieutenant Colonel Chuong confirmed what my aides had said earlier: the withdrawal of troops and dispersal of Buddhists from their barbed-wire enclaves had taken place with no unduly disruptive incidents. He also assured me that the division stood ready to support me in any way it could, and my orders would be carried out with all due dispatch. The city returned to near-normal and things went smoothly, especially in comparison to the situation I found on my arrival.

Then, a week later, my aide rushed into my office, holding a document and greatly agitated. "You must look at this order immediately, Mr. Mayor," he said, with an urgency he seldom displayed.

I scanned the paper quickly and was appalled. It was an order from the High Command for the army to raid Buddhist temples and compounds and to arrest almost all Buddhist priests. Army units then took their captives to the local prison on an island in the river and turned them over to the local police for detention. They left only one or two clerics as caretakers at each pagoda. This was a disaster. I could not believe that President Diem could have even considered such a move. It would only inflame the already volatile situation.[8] As devastated as I was, both personally and from a political standpoint, I realized there was nothing I could do. This was now an army matter, completely out of my hands, except for one thing.

Among the Buddhists arrested was the most senior cleric for the sector, an elderly man. I was concerned about his well-being in the island jail where the detainees were being held. Since the jail was a Danang police facility, it fell under my jurisdiction. So I drove to the island and had the priest released to me, arranging that he be held under my custody at the city headquarters where my office was located. I installed him in one of the guest rooms there. I apologized for the raids and arrests, explaining to him that those orders came from Saigon and I was powerless to do anything about them. "You are still technically under arrest and confined to your room but you will be more comfortable here than in the jail," I told him.

There was great consternation and outrage among the Buddhist community, of course. Determined to do whatever damage control was possible, minimal as it might be, I contacted Buddhist lay leaders and arranged a meeting with them.

It was a stormy session. No matter how much I explained that I had nothing to do with the raids and arrests, I was the most visible and highest-ranking representative of the government in the area. The assembled Buddhists quite naturally took much of their frustration and anger out on me. I tried to remain calm and placate them as much as I possible. Finally, they wound down somewhat and agreed on one thing: they wanted to mount a protest demonstration, a huge one in the form of a march through the city's streets, and demanded that I allow them to have it.

I was pleased that we finally arrived at something that could be negotiated. I agreed that they could have their protest march, but with conditions.

First, we would have to agree on a route, and the protestors would have to follow the assigned route with no deviations.

Second, I would provide security along the route of the march, to control traffic and to prevent disturbances that would disrupt the demonstration.

Third, they must agree to maintain order among their followers, to ensure that they would not take provocative actions that might create riots and inflame the city.

We settled on a route and agreed on the second and third points.

The day of the demonstration dawned clear and bright. Things went relatively smoothly until the marchers neared their destination, the city's main Buddhist temple. There was an incident when some of the marchers passed the large Catholic cathedral that sat proudly on one of the city's major thoroughfares. One group of demonstrators hurled stones at the church. With hindsight, I realized later I should have made sure the march route bypassed such a tempting target. No great damage was done, however, and the incident could have been smoothed over with an apology and compensation for what damage did occur. This is not to say that the incident was insignificant and did not incense the Catholics. (One priest in particular castigated me severely for allowing the demonstration to be staged at all, as I will recount later.)

A much more serious situation erupted as the demonstrators approached the end of their march at the city's main Buddhist pagoda. Two Jeeps appeared on the boulevard, now crowded with marchers. They were headed in the opposite direction, returning to division headquarters from a routine mission. Each vehicle contained an officer and three soldiers. Through an oversight, they had not been notified about the demonstration and provided with an alternate route for returning to headquarters.

As the lead vehicle neared the crowd, its driver somehow lost control and the Jeep ran into a cluster of marchers. I was not on the scene, and reports were conflicting about how and why the accident occurred. Fortunately, nobody was killed or critically injured, but the orderly crowd suddenly became a raging mob.

People swarmed over the Jeeps, hauling the officers and men into the street and beating them severely. (The captain was hospitalized later with serious injuries.) They seized all the weapons, stripped the captain of his hat and uniform insignia, then overturned one of the vehicles and set it afire. They dragged all the soldiers into the pagoda compound, treating them as captives.

When my aide burst into my office and told me what had happened, I was alarmed and upset. I sped immediately to the pagoda. The Buddhists greeted me excitedly, almost falling over themselves to tell me about the accident and almost boastfully displaying their reaction to it. They seemed to think I would be pleased. I soon disabused them of that notion.

"You overreacted!" I told the Buddhist leaders. "Certainly the accident was a bad thing, but it was an *accident*, not a deliberate attempt to harm any of you by the soldiers. They were merely returning from a routine operation and knew nothing of the demonstration. I suspect that the sudden sight of a mass of people in his path unnerved the driver and contributed to his loss of control of the vehicle. Whatever the cause, however, it was not your place to retaliate with violence. First, that is not the Buddhist way. Second, you should have trusted the authorities, me in particular, to investigate and see that justice was done.

"You *really* overstepped your bounds when you treated the captain as you did and then dragged him and his men in here like hostages or prisoners of war. You must release them and return the weapons and other items you seized to army division headquarters at once, with an apology."

There was a storm of protest. Voices came from all sides, defending their actions. Some ranted that running the Jeep into the crowd may have been deliberate, not an accident. Many repeated all their past antigovernment diatribes. Some castigated me for not providing better protection for the demonstration.

Things gradually calmed down, and I discussed the situation with the group's leaders, one monk, and several laymen. After much argument, they finally agreed to return the weapons, captain's hat and insignia, and other gear to the division, but flatly refused to issue a formal apology.

When I returned to the city headquarters building, I found another unwelcome encounter awaiting me. My aide hurried up to me in the mayoral office anteroom and in hushed tones informed me that Father An, in his sixties and the second-highest-ranking Catholic priest in the area, was in my office. "He is very angry and has been waiting to see you for quite some time," the aide warned.

I walked into the office and greeted the priest politely. He paid no attention, but launched immediately into an angry tirade. "Are you deliberately trying to start a riot, to see the city go up in flames? Allowing this huge demonstration was insanity, and what your Buddhists did to the cathedral was an outrage! Pelting such a sacred edifice with stones and who knows what else was unforgivable. It was an insult to the bishop, all of the city's clergy, and every Catholic in the area." That was just for starters. Father An went on in that vein, growing almost apoplectic in his anger. Finally I interrupted his harangue:

"Father, I agree that what happened at the cathedral was most unfortunate, and I will see that reparations are made for any damage. I have already spoken to the Buddhist leaders. They, too, regret the incident. However, it is over and done. We cannot change that. As for the demonstration, it is my considered opinion that forbidding it would have had more serious consequences than actually occurred.

"What we need now are no recriminations but efforts by all sides to return life in the city to as near normal as possible. I trust that you and your colleagues want that also, and will cooperate in making it possible. This city is split almost evenly, about 50 percent Catholic and 50 percent Buddhist and smaller non-Catholic sects. If we do not control the situation and they clash, we could have hundreds, even thousands, of casualties. To prevent that, all of us most work together: religious leaders, city officials, and the army."

"I will take care of the Catholics, and you should take care of the Buddhists," the priest said, still in an arrogant, preemptory tone.

"Thank you very much, Father An," I replied. "If you want to take that responsibility, fine. However, I must remind you that, as mayor, I am the personal representative of the president of the Republic. As such, I am responsible for *all* citizens of Danang: Catholics, Buddhists, and nonreligious citizens. If you want to help with the Catholics, and by extension help the entire city, please go back to your church and do everything you can to cool tempers and keep things calm."

The priest ignored my words, beginning another harangue the minute I paused.

He was repeating himself now, and the more he talked, the more abusive, if not downright insulting, he got.

Finally I had enough. "Father An, I have listened to you for some time now, and would continue to listen as long as you like if I did not have to contend with other very serious matters. You can castigate as much as you like and register all of your complaints in as many different forms as you desire, and I promise to listen to them. But not now. I will turn on a tape recorder and you can continue at will. Meanwhile, I must excuse myself." With that, I punched the "Record" button on the tape recorder on my desk and took my leave.[9]

I made the rounds of the city during the next twenty-four hours, making occasional stops to discuss the situation and cool tempers wherever and whenever possible. I visited Colonel Chuong and Colonel Dang Van Quang (First Military Region chief of staff) for briefings on how the military was faring. Fortunately, there were no incidents of clashes between soldiers and civilians.

I went to the compound where families and dependents of the soldiers stationed in and around the city lived. Almost all Catholic, they were preparing as if for a battle: building barricades in the streets, and arming themselves with stones, clubs, and machetes. I tried to calm them, telling their leaders several things.

"First, I am a Buddhist, as you are well aware, but this area is my ancestral home and I want no harm to come to it or its inhabitants. Second, I was specifically appointed by President Diem, a devout Catholic. Do you think he would have sent me here if he thought I would favor Buddhists over Catholics and not be fair to everyone?

"Finally, you can pick up the phone and call Catholic priests and lay leaders in Kien Hoa, where I was governor before coming to Danang as mayor. Ask them about my service there and how I dealt with the population in general and Catholics in particular.

"Please consider these points before you misjudge me and arbitrarily decide that I am playing favorites in this very difficult time."

This seemed to give them pause, even appease them to some extent. Passions subsided gradually on all sides, and relative calm returned to the city. You could still feel tension in the air, but it grew markedly less as time passed.

Things went smoothly for the next few days. Then Lieutenant Colonel Chuong came to my office. He was obviously agitated about something.

"I have some disturbing news that you should know about, but I would be in serious trouble if anyone knew I passed it on to you. We are old friends, however, and I know I can trust you not to reveal the source. A group of generals is meeting clandestinely here in Danang," Chuong explained, "and I strongly suspect that they are planning a coup against President Diem. One of them is General Khanh [military commander of the Second Military Region, headquartered in Pleiku], we have been very close, and he told me about the meeting himself."

"You don't have to worry about telling me to keep it secret," I assured him. "I will tell no one, but this sounds serious and I will look into it."

I waited for a few days, making regular rounds of the city and talking to people at all levels. Conditions stabilized, and the situation seemed to be under control. I decided to fly to Saigon to learn more about the rumors of a coup.

Chau and his wife, Bich Nhan, after they were married in 1951. She is an amazing woman who had to cope with many problems over the years, including supporting and keeping the family together during Chau's seven years of imprisonment, arranging for their escape as "boat people," and working on an electronic assembly line during the family's early years in America.

Chau and Nguyen Phuoc Dai, one of his lawyers during the trial. She was a senator and vice president of the Senate who had been a well-known lawyer in France before returning to practice law in Saigon.

Chau in court, remonstrating with Judge Lieutenant Colonel Thieu Khac Huynh during trial.

Chau (right) with Daniel Ellsberg (center) and Edward Lansdale at the airport in Saigon in the mid-1960s.

Chau and wife with ex-president Thieu and wife in 1993 when Thieu visited Chau in his Woodland Hills, California, home. "The past is past, let us forget it," Chau said to the former friend who had turned against him for political expediency.

Lieutenant Colonel Tran Ngoc Chau, as governor of Kien Hoa province, with Rural Affairs Director Rufus Phillips (center) and USAID Representative John O'Donnell during their visit to check progress in province during 1964.

Chau and his wife surrounded by their family in 2004 on Chau's eightieth birthday.

Chau and his wife in 1967 after his election to the National Assembly where he was secretary general of the House of Deputies.

John O'Donnell, Chau's U.S. counterpart in Kien Hoa, with his family in 1986.

1967 photo of Chau selected by the BBC, which flew Chau to Britain in 1991 for a documentary on the war in Vietnam. The BBC selected this photo because in it Chau appeared "so young and so thoughtful." Chau's role in Vietnam was a major part of the documentary.

16: DEATH OF THE REPUBLIC—
FOR A BETTER WAY? (1963)

L ittle did I think as I rode to the airport the morning of November 1, 1963, that I would fly into the midst of a bloody coup. Something unexpected occurred at the airport. While I waiting to board the plane for Saigon, I met Colonel Do Cao Tri, an old friend from Dalat and now commanding officer of the First Division stationed in Hué. It surprised me to see him there because he had nothing to do with my geographic area. I wore civilian clothes (as always during my time in Danang), but I saluted him and we shook hands. Then he asked where I was going.

"I'm flying to Saigon," I replied.

"For what?" he asked rather sharply.

"I'm going for one of my routine meetings with the president," I replied. "I make the trip almost every week to brief him on the situation here in Danang." The colonel nodded briefly and we parted with perfunctory good-byes. *Why is he questioning me like this?* I wondered. I was not under his jurisdiction and what I did was none of his business. But hints of the coup made me wary. Was that behind the colonel's interest in my activities?

I puzzled over his appearance in Danang, and his questioning me, during the two-hour flight to Saigon. Later, I realized that he was trying to learn if I might have gotten wind of the coup. My close relationship with President Diem was well known, and it would have been logical for the coup's plotters to suspect I was going to Saigon to warn, or support, the president.

Rumors of coups had circulated for months now, in the military, government offices, the media, and among the public. I heard that the foreign press even joked about "the coup of the month" in their Saigon gathering places. So it was not easy to take seriously the threat of one right now.

When I got out of the airplane at the Saigon airport, usually a bustling beehive of activity, it was almost deserted. There were no people on hand to greet the incoming passengers, no porters asking if we wanted help with our luggage. It felt strange, ominous even, and the atmosphere got worse as I left the airport. I heard gunfire from the direction of the General Staff headquarters, about one-half mile away.

I found a taxi driver, but he was afraid of getting caught in the middle of a firefight. His abandoned cab stood nearby. "This is nonsense," I told him. "If the fighting continues it will surely spread to this area so near the airport—and then you will be in serious danger. So why don't you drive me to my home? We can take a secure route, avoiding the General Staff area where the fighting seems concentrated, then you can go on to a safer place than this."

He hesitated, but finally agreed, and so I gave him directions to the home of my good friend, Lieutenant Colonel Chuong, about three miles from the airport. Along the way we saw crowds of people scurrying for safe places to hide from the gunfire in the distance.

The house was empty save for Colonel Chuong's house servant, who recognized me and invited me to enter. I turned on the radio immediately and learned that there was indeed a coup under way. It was then two o'clock in the afternoon, and the eighteen or twenty hours that followed were among the most horrific and frightening of my life. I feared not so much for myself, though as a confidant and supporter of the president I might be in some danger, but for President Diem's safety as well as for the stability and direction of our country should he be deposed.

The radio station appeared to be controlled by the generals leading the coup. It broadcast martial music almost incessantly, interrupted at intervals by reports that the entire military establishment had mounted a coup against the regime of President Diem. Appeals for people to remain calm followed these announcements. It was obvious, of course, that all military forces had not joined the coup. Otherwise, why would there be fierce fighting, as indicated by the continuing sound of gunfire and explosions?

I turned down the volume on the radio slightly and telephoned General Tran Thien Khiem, second-highest-ranking officer on the Joint Chiefs of Staff and a friend since 1952. "Is this coup the real thing?" I asked him.[1]

"Indeed it is, Chau." However, we had joked about coups, rumors of coups, and failed coup plots so often in the past that Khiem thought I might not take him seriously. He passed the phone to General Nguyen Ngoc Le, once commandant of the training center where I had served as chief of staff, to confirm his statement.

"This is a real revolution, Chau. The army is rising up against Diem and his family, and I want you to be part of the revolution. If you agree, talk to General Khiem and we can send an escort to bring you here to General Staff headquarters." Then he gave the phone back to Khiem.

Khiem asked if I wanted an escort, adding that he would arrange for security to protect me. "Just let me know," he told me. I thanked him but declined his offer for the moment.

"Just let me think about it for now. I will get in touch with you again later."

Meanwhile, the radio began broadcasting messages of support for the coup from the provinces and from various military commands. If you believed these messages, it seemed that the revolt had widespread approval. Again, however, the sounds of a battle raging in the city indicated that there was a significant military force opposing the coup.

After an hour of listening to the broadcasts, I tried calling the president's office in the palace. All was confusion there, but I finally managed to get his chief of staff on the line.

"What is the situation there? I am in Saigon now; is there anything that I can do? Can I talk to the president?"

"No, the president is not available to anyone, no exceptions. And I can't give you any advice except to listen to the radio. Since you are alone I don't think there is anything you can do right now."

The line suddenly went dead. I tried calling back several times without success. Later I learned that a major fight was going on between the Presidential Guard and coup forces even as we spoke. As the rebels seemed to be gaining the upper hand, the president's aides spirited him and his family, including Counselor Nhu, to Cholon about five or six kilometers away. Cholon is the Chinese section of Saigon, on the right bank of the Saigon River. Diem took refuge there in the home of a reputable Chinese businessman.

I spent the rest of the day and night listening to the radio. It became ever more obvious that coup leaders controlled the radio station and allowed no real news to be broadcast. There were only messages of approval for the uprising and requests for all government and military units, as well as the general public, to support it. It appeared that the group of dissident generals leading the coup called themselves the Revolutionary Military Committee. Their titular leader was General Duong Van Minh, or "Big Minh." I suspected even then that General Minh was just a figurehead. He was selected because he was popular in most circles (and possibly so he would be the chief scapegoat in case the coup failed). The real leader and driving force of the group was General Tran Van Don, recruiter, plotter, and coordinator of the coup from start to finish.

I felt totally helpless. Without troops to back me up, I could do nothing to help President Diem. I didn't even have a weapon to use to protect myself, let alone the president!

I still thought that perhaps the revolt was not going as well, or did not have the backing that the captive radio station would have us believe, until about four or five o'clock in the afternoon, when I heard the voice of General Huynh Van Cao, broadcasting his support for the Revolutionary Military Committee. When I heard that, I was astounded, and I lost heart as well. If anyone should have been loyal to Diem, it was General Cao. I knew him well, from the time I was a major in Hué and he was a captain. Since then he had enjoyed many privileges and rapid promotions, all courtesy of President Diem. The president had made Cao his chief of staff after earlier promoting him quickly to lieutenant colonel, full colonel, and then general, commanding the Seventh Division. He currently was commandant of the Fourth Military Region. His reputation as a military leader was somewhat spotty, however.[2]

I recalled that at my last meeting with the president, about ten days before the coup, he had quizzed me about defense of Saigon. "I know you are friendly with all the senior military officers, so you know General Ton That Dinh. What do you think of him? Can we rely on him to defend the capital?"

I responded as sincerely as possible. "I've known General Dinh well since we were both platoon leaders. He is a good guy, but I can't pass judgment on his professional capabilities because I never served with him or under him. There is one thing I must say, however, since you ask me specifically. My impression is that he is not an entirely stable person, in that he can vacillate from one side or opinion to another quite readily. My feeling is that he can easily be swayed, but I could be wrong."

"Then who among the generals do you think could be trusted to be in charge of the security here?"

"Why don't you transfer General Dinh to replace General Cao as commander of the Fourth Military Region and bring Cao here to head the defense forces? I feel we can rely more on Cao than Dinh in a difficult situation because he is a more stable person and he certainly owes great loyalty to you," I replied.

"Well, you know that here in Saigon it is very difficult to rely on any of them, but we probably should have Dinh here because I feel he could control the other generals better than Cao."

That was the end of the discussion.

Now I was listening to the voice of the very person whom I had suggested as best to protect the president broadcasting that he supported the coup against his long-time benefactor. I couldn't believe my ears. I was also chagrined at the thought of what could have happened if President Diem had listened to me. Cao might have led the fight against the leader he was supposed to protect. It seemed that never had my judgment been more wrong.

It was ironic, too, as I learned later, that among the coup leaders and Americans supporters were the very same men who had been instrumental in helping President Diem achieve power. Lucien Conein was one of Lansdale's chief assistants during the 1955 battles that put Diem in power, and now he was the CIA liaison to the coup plotters who were overthrowing President Diem on this November 1. Two important supporters in the 1955 fighting, Generals Mai Huu Xuan and Duong Van Minh, were now also key leaders of the 1963 coup group.

I listened to the radio through the evening and most of the night, getting very little sleep. In the morning I began to learn about the real situation for the first time since I landed at the Saigon airport.

The coup started between one and two o'clock, not long before I arrived at the airport. Action began when rebel military units attacked the Special Forces camp and headquarters complex next to the General Staff headquarters. That was the shooting I had first heard at the airport. Colonel Le Quang Tung, commander of the Special Forces, and his deputy were both killed right away by the conspirators for refusing to join in the plot. They accused the generals of treachery and called out that they should remember who had given them their stars. Leaderless, the Special Forces units fought on for some twenty-four hours before finally surrendering.

Meanwhile, troops moved from outside the city to encircle the Presidential Palace. They were led by Colonel Nguyen Van Thieu, then commander of the Fifth Division. In later years, Thieu told me that he earlier received an order to turn over command of the division to Colonel Do Van Dien. Colonel Dien, however, went to the General Staff and told them he was ill and would not be able to take over the Fifth Division as ordered for another week or two. The General Staff decided that the changeover in command would be delayed until November 3 or 4, just a few days after the coup took place. This left Thieu, a converted Catholic,[3] in command of the Fifth Division and therefore a leading figure in the revolt almost by happenstance.[4]

The fighting was severe around the palace, with the Presidential Guard mounting a strong defense against the attackers. Both sides suffered heavy casualties. As night fell, however, the rebels got the upper hand and the Presidential Guard surrendered. By this time, however, the president and his party had escaped to Cholon.

About 9 a.m., the radio station announced that the palace had been captured and both President Diem and Counselor Nhu had committed suicide. I was now totally disheartened, and very skeptical of the suicide report. I felt that President Diem was too good a Catholic to commit the sin of taking his own life, for one thing. For another, I suspected that the rebel generals, especially Big Minh, wanted Diem out of the way permanently to ensure he could not possibly return to power.[5]

Despair set in. I knew that Diem had flaws, but I had become convinced that he was still a viable choice to lead South Vietnam. He was a true nationalist and resisted U.S. efforts to turn his administration into a puppet regime totally under control of the Americans, the obvious reason being that they had plotted with the generals to overthrow him. Diem himself was honest and incorruptible—traits not shared by many other government and military officials. His major flaws were that he was too insulated from the ordinary people of the country, especially the peasantry, and that he relied too heavily on officials and the infrastructure he inherited from the French. I believed his administration's treatment of Buddhists was primarily the work of his brothers, Counselor Nhu and Archbishop Ngo Dinh Thuc, especially the latter.[6]

My own experience with President Diem proved that, given the right information, he was open to change and reform. His conversation with me just weeks earlier about sending Nhu abroad suggested that he had contemplated major changes in the administration. His instructions when he appointed me mayor of Danang indicated he had come to realize that the government's anti-Buddhist policies were wrong. He seemed finally to recognize this and be willing to take measures to change the situation, to soften the pro-Catholic, anti-Buddhist bias of his administration. It was too late for such speculation now, of course. The coup had succeeded, and President Diem was dead.

Finally, I called General Khiem.

"Now that the coup is successful and the fighting is over, why don't you send a car and escort to take me to the General Staff, and then send me back to my city? I am still officially mayor of Danang, and my place is there until the generals decide what to do with me."

General Khiem sent two Jeeps and met me as I alighted from the vehicle at General Staff headquarters. He looked exhausted and completely dispirited, not at all like a leading figure in a successful coup. "They killed the president!" he whispered in a soft, sad voice as he drew near me. That's all he said. Then he turned, and I followed him to his office.

"What do you want to do?" he asked. I repeated my request to return to Danang. He protested that the air space was closed temporarily and no flights were permitted in the area. I held firm.

"Until the generals decide my fate, I remain the mayor of Danang and that is where I want to go."

Eventually Khiem shrugged and called Colonel Nguyen Cao Ky, the flamboyant commander of the air base then (and later a rival of Thieu for the presidency). Ky argued that he could not violate the "no-fly zone" rule and military aircraft were patrolling the skies to enforce it, but Khiem cut him off.

"That's your concern. I am telling you that I want a light plane to fly Colonel Chau to Danang right now, and you *will* take care of it."

I met a captain at the airfield. He explained that they had been able to contact all but one of the fighter planes patrolling the no-fly zone. He said that it could be risky because the one air patrol plane they had not warned of our flight might shoot us down.

"You know more about that than I do, but if we delay we will not be able to make it to Danang today in this airplane. Besides, if I get shot down, you get shot down, too." And we took off, making the flight without incident.

A car met me at the Danang airport, and I went immediately to my office to meet with my staff. Everything seemed to be under control, with no disturbances of any consequence reported.

It seemed that every radio in the city was turned on, however. Each blared out martial music interrupted frequently by pronouncements from the military leaders in Saigon and exhortations for everyone to remain calm and to support the coup. People listened intently but got no real direction or news from them, so almost everyone seemed confused, uncertain about what to do—for the moment, at least. I spent the entire night in the office, catching up on paperwork and keeping in touch with my aides in the field by telephone.

About nine o'clock the next morning, my military deputy, Lieutenant Colonel Dam Quang Yeu, came to my office and announced that the situation had suddenly turned explosive. The festering, pent-up hate against the Diem regime and its supporters was about to erupt in major demonstrations, he explained. "And some of the anger is directed at you, because you represent the Diem government in the minds of the people. You could very well be in danger."

The colonel explained further that the largest demonstration was developing at a local high school, where several thousand citizens and students, most of them Buddhist, were already gathered and more were arriving.

"Very well," I said. "Let's go there."

"No, no, no," cried the colonel. "That is crazy! We would be killed."

"I'm going," I told him. "Will you come with me? I will drive the Jeep myself and go unarmed." He argued vehemently that it was too dangerous. When I got behind the wheel of the vehicle and he saw I was determined to go, alone if necessary, he relented and climbed in beside me.

People filled the schoolyard to the bursting point. My arrival obviously took them by surprise. I paid no attention, driving right up to the speakers' platform. That brought a hostile reaction from the crowd, but the leader of the demonstration, a Buddhist layman, motioned for the crowd to be quiet and took the microphone.

"Please be calm!" he pleaded. "The mayor comes without an escort and unarmed. Let him talk."

As I walked across the platform to the microphone I saw banners condemning the superintendent of schools, Ngo Van Chuong, as a member of the Can Lao society. The signs accused him of recruiting teachers to the Can Lao and discriminating against Buddhists, and even suggested that he be hung. I also heard vehement protests from some quarters. "Don't let him talk. We don't want to listen to him."

Others in the crowd shouted them down, however. "Let him speak. Why not? He's alone and can't do any harm here. Let's hear what he has to say."

Things gradually quieted as I began speaking. "You surely have reason to hold this demonstration, to do whatever you want to express your feelings at this crucial time. You have cause to act against President Diem's government, and against Mr. Chuong. I must say, however, that Mr. Chuong was under my authority. I don't know what he did or didn't do, but as mayor of the city I must take responsibility for his actions just as any commander in the field is responsible for the actions of his subordinates. So please, place the blame on me. Remember, too, that the government you hated has fallen and the generals are now in command. What do you want to do now? Punish those who were in charge? Just let me know your desires, and I will convey them to the Revolutionary Military Committee in Saigon." I spoke for a few minutes more, mainly driving home the message that harming people they had a grievance with was neither necessary nor part of the Buddhist tradition.

"As for myself, I know both Buddhists and Catholics have criticized my actions at times, often bitterly. I have tried to act fairly to all sides during my time as mayor here in Danang, which is what President Diem told me he wanted when he appointed me mayor. Perhaps in your eyes I failed in that endeavor; that is for you to decide." I left then, and nobody in the crowd raised a hand against me or attempted to stop the vehicle.[7]

When we got back to the office, the colonel and I discussed the situation, and he assured me that he and his men would be extra vigilant to prevent unruly demonstrations or mob violence.

Miraculously enough, relative calm prevailed throughout the city during the following days. I'm not sure why and I can't attempt to take credit for it, but we experienced no serious disturbances in Danang over the next few weeks, unlike the rest of the country.

Our island of calm contrasted sharply with the demonstrations, riots, and general chaos that prevailed in almost every other city and province. People died and beatings were common as various factions clashed. Province chiefs were relieved of office, even arrested and jailed in the very provinces they formerly ruled. People's Committees sprang up as ad hoc replacements for the formal government infrastructure.

About four days after the incident at the high school, Nguyen Quoc Dan, my deputy mayor, came into my office and closed the door behind him. "Mr. Mayor,"[8] he began, "you were appointed by President Diem and were a loyal member of his government; therefore, you did not support the coup. At this point, however, Danang is the only city in the country that has not sent a message of support to the Military Council. If this continues it will appear that all of us oppose the new regime. That cannot be. All of us on your staff understand your position in the current situation and we respect it. We must make our voice heard, or all of us in this city may suffer unpleasant consequences.

"So we request that either you send a send a message of support to Saigon or we will do it without your approval. We would also like your order to remove President Diem's pictures from this building and other sites in the city. We will give you twenty-four hours to make your decision."

207207207207207207207720720720720720720720720772072072077207207207207720720720772072072077

"I won't take twenty-four hours to make my decision," I told him. "I will give it to you in an hour."

I mulled things over. I was torn by my loyalty to President Diem and feelings that he might have been the best choice for my country in the long run, against the practicalities of current events. The coup was a fait accompli; nothing I could do or say would change that. Still, I hesitated to give my personal approval to a bloody revolt that had ended in the assassination of an honorable man, no matter how misguided some of his policies had been. Finally I drafted a carefully worded statement to go to the Military Council.

It stated simply that I recognized that the country now had a new government and, "as a holdover from the previous regime, I hereby submit my resignation so the new administration can appoint a mayor of its choice. In the meantime, before my resignation as mayor is accepted, I will carry out whatever orders you [the high military council] issue."

As for President Diem's photographs, I told my staff that it was up to each department head as to whether the pictures were removed or remained in place. "For myself," I added, "I could not turn my back on the man I respected, even after his death. It would not be honorable and would beneath my dignity. So I will keep the photograph on the wall in my own office."

Shakeups occurred across the country; some government officials and military officers lost their jobs and were disgraced, or worse. Others, those who joined in the coup, received their rewards. Colonel Do Cao Tri, the officer who questioned me at the airport on the day of the coup, now wore a general's stars and commanded the military region. Lieutenant Colonel Chuong, the Second Division Commander, was now Colonel Chuong.

Newly appointed Corps Commander General Tri called me a few days after the coup, on November 4 or 5. "As an old friend I must warn you that your behavior has been unacceptable to the Military Council. You know that I am your friend, but I will be able to do nothing if Saigon decides to take action against you. And you know well that General Minh has an explosive temper and can be very brutal. Say just one wrong word and you could be killed."

"Thank you for the warning," I replied. "The fact that I am still alive is a miracle. I can't worry about dying. I do care about my life and my family, but only if I can live with the dignity of a man and an officer. So thank you for your friendship, but don't commit yourself to protect me. I trust you won't do anything against me, but I don't expect you to do anything to help, especially anything that might put *you* in jeopardy."

Nothing happened for several days; then I received an order from the Military Council directing me to arrange a big demonstration for a visit from General Ton

That Dinh, representing the High Military Council, to the city. This was simple, what we now call a "no-brainer." All we had to do was put out the word, and masses of people assembled to welcome him. Most were Buddhists; Catholics kept a low profile at this point, knowing they no longer had a government that generally favored them over non-Catholics. This was just as well because a clash between the factions could easily have turned the welcoming demonstration into a disaster, with riots breaking out across the city. I had the Danang police and local military units on high alert to stop any outbreaks immediately, before they could get out of hand. I also visited the Catholic bishop to discuss the situation with him, pointing out that it was in everybody's best interest to keep things calm. He seemed to understand how delicate things were at the moment. I don't know for certain, but I strongly suspect he put out the word to keep calm and do nothing to disrupt the welcoming festivities. At any rate, things went off without a hitch.

I went to the airport to meet General Dinh's plane. As I approached him he spoke in French: "It's over, Chau. Finished! No more Can Lao." I had to smile to myself at this because Dinh had been a member of Can Lao while I never was. "No more Can Lao," he continued, still in French, "no more Diem. We are now responsible for conducting the war. You agree with me?"

I didn't answer directly, just smiled and saluted him. We shook hands, and I led him to my vehicle.

In truth, I was grateful to the general. We had been good friends since serving as platoon leaders at the beginning of the war against the French in 1945. He and General Khiem had been my protectors since the coup. If not for them, I might have been imprisoned, even killed, for remaining loyal to President Diem and not joining the coup when offered the opportunity. General Minh especially was very angry with me. Fortunately for me, Dinh and Khiem actually held more power in the Military Council, though General Big Minh was its figurehead leader; they were able to shield me from his wrath. General Le, my former commanding officer at Quang Trung Training Center where I was his chief of staff, also argued on my behalf. The other three generals were neutral. So I survived.

Huge crowds assembled all along the route to the mayoral office, applauding and waving banners and signs welcoming General Dinh. When we arrived at my office, the general went out on a balcony overlooking a large square. Dinh spoke for an hour, interrupted frequently by thunderous cheers from the crowd below. His speech ended, the crowd began to leave, and we sat down to enjoy some refreshments.

Suddenly, after the crowd dispersed completely, a group of some forty protesters drove up to the building entrance in four GMC military trucks. They were members of a small Vietnamese Nationalist party, the VNQDD, demanding to see General Dinh. We agreed to receive a small group, just four or five, of their representatives.

When they entered, their leader, Cao Xuan Huy (who later served with me and supported me in the National Assembly), began a harangue against me.

"The mayor should be removed from office and punished!" he declared, citing a list of grievances against me. He then went on to indict the superintendent of education and about twenty other city officials.

Dinh answered him quietly. "I will report your grievances to the Military Council when I return to Saigon, and we will consider your petition. For now, you should take no action on your own. If trouble breaks out in the city after I leave, I will consider you and your group as the agitators."

When they left, I told Dinh I had already submitted my resignation, explaining that I felt the new regime needed to appoint someone else as mayor. General Dinh exploded. "You're crazy! Why did you take such a step without discussing it with General Khiem and me? We need you here. You didn't do anything wrong so far. We have heard no complaints against you before this group that was just here, and how many are they? A hundred, two hundred maybe; certainly only a tiny percentage of the city's population."

"This protest has nothing to do with it," I told Dinh. "I think it would be bad for me to stay here, a provocation of sorts that might inflame people who harbor a lot of hate for the Diem government. No, I think it best if you just take me back to Saigon and have someone replace me. It would be better for the city, for the new government, and even for me. It's not that I'm afraid for myself, but it might be too difficult to do a good job if I stay in Danang."

Dinh finally accepted my arguments and asked if I had anyone in mind to take over as mayor. I didn't, but told him that Colonel Chuong might suggest someone. He got the colonel on the phone immediately, and they agreed on a candidate. "Now I think it's best if you leave with me right away. Make arrangements for your family to go back to Saigon later. I plan to visit other cities as a representative of the Military Council, to speak to the people as I did today. There will be various official ceremonies and demonstrations like those here, and I want you by my side for them. That will make it apparent that you do not oppose the new regime without you having to make any formal statement."

I told him that this made me uncomfortable. I had not joined the coup because I was loyal to President Diem, and I had been greatly disturbed by his assassination. "The new government is now a fact and I have no desire to oppose it. I don't want to appear as a turncoat, however, someone who shifts with the wind to save his own hide. That seems shameful to me."

"Listen to me, Chau. I am now General Ton That Dinh, representing the High Military Council. This is an order; you *will* go with me!"

"Okay," I said, and we left a few hours later.

At first I tried to hang back, not to be seen at his side in public appearances. In Dalat, our first stop, I stayed in the airplane while local dignitaries welcomed him. When Dinh noticed I was not in his party, he called for me. I had to accompany him to the stadium and stay near him throughout his visit. It was the same at all other stops before we returned to Saigon. "Okay, now you're free. Get settled and bring your family here. If anything comes up, call me or General Khiem," Dinh said as we parted.

Dinh called me to his office the next day. He was now minister of security, an extremely high-level position. His organization included the former Ministry of the Interior and much more. "Chau, I want you to be my special envoy to visit the provinces, see what reforms need to be done immediately, and to take whatever actions you feel are necessary. Check with me when you need my authority to implement them and keep me posted on your activities."

"Thank you very much; this is a big, big honor. But I must tell you frankly that my mind is in a state of confusion right now. So much has happened in so short a time that I can't think straight. I'm worried about my family, for one thing. I must find a place for us to live and get my wife and children safely to Saigon. So let me have a few days to get organized."

"Alright, you have five days, then report back to me," Dinh said.

I left his office feeling more conflicted than ever. I regarded Dinh highly and valued his friendship a great deal, but I worried about working directly for him. We were both strong-willed men, and our perspectives on the war, government policies, and the like did not always agree. There was the inevitable possibility that, working closely together, we would clash one day. I knew that Dinh could be quite mercurial, and that a major disagreement between us could rupture the bond of friendship we had enjoyed for so many years. Did I want to risk that?

In addition, I was spent, mentally, physically, and emotionally. The stress of crisis after crisis over the past year, capped by the coup and Diem's assassination, had left me drained. I felt I had no resources left to draw on and needed some period of relative calm to recharge my batteries, as the saying goes. I mulled all this over in my mind while getting my family moved from Danang and settled in Saigon. Then I went to see another old friend, Colonel Duong Ngoc Lam, national commander of the Civil Guard.[9] I asked if he had a place for me in his organization.

"I'm not sure where I could place you because all suitable positions are filled. But I will ask that you be assigned to me, and we will work something out."

Then I went to see General Dinh, who was now head of the Military Council (somewhat akin to being chairman of the U.S. Joint Chiefs of Staff, but with much more power). For all practical purposes, he was now commander of the country.

I explained, diplomatically, my reservations about taking the job he had offered me. "I don't think I would be very effective in that position," I told him. "Would the province chiefs representing the new government feel comfortable or cooperative with me, knowing my past affiliation with the Diem government? Would they regard me as a true and proper representative of the government that you now head? These are the questions I ask myself, and the answers, I'm afraid, are mostly negative. I am honored by the offer, but I think it would be better for all concerned if I took on a less visible position."

"Where do you want to go?"

"I did talk briefly with Colonel Lam, and he said he might have a place for me," I replied. "I am familiar with the Civil Guard, as you know, and would feel comfortable there."

The general told me to go home and relax, that he would arrange for me to be assigned to Colonel Lam. Next morning I received orders to report to Civil Guard headquarters. Once there, I learned that Lam had already reassigned his chief of staff as a regional commander and that I was his new chief of staff. If I thought that this would be a restful, relaxing assignment, I soon learned differently.

My first days on the job went by in routine fashion. Then Colonel Lam called me into his office and told me he expected to get another assignment very soon. "When that happens, you will replace me as national commander of the Civil Guard," he explained. This unexpected announcement surprised me and, frankly, left me a bit skeptical. I wasn't sure that could happen without General Minh's approval—something I didn't think would be easily forthcoming. However, I thanked Lam, said I would be honored, and went back to work without much additional thought on the matter.

One evening not long after that, shortly after I arrived home from work and was preparing to bathe, Colonel Lam's principal aide came to our house. "I have an urgent message from the colonel," he told me a bit breathlessly. "I must take you to his office where I am to give you a sealed document."

"What is in it?" I asked.

"I have no idea. Colonel Lam said he would call you with additional instructions after we get to his office."

The sealed orders contained a list of people I was ordered to take into temporary custody. When Colonel Lam called, I realized that another coup (this time an almost bloodless one[10]) was taking place and that I was involved, if only peripherally. After the coup, Lam became mayor of Saigon while retaining his post as national commander of the Civil Guard. I would remain as his chief of staff, but Lam also appointed me as his special assistant for civic affairs. He explained that he couldn't give me an existing job and title at that point, much as he would like to do so.

"All suitable positions are already filled," he explained, "and I don't want to disturb things right now." He continued, "You can be more valuable to me in other ways, anyhow. I've never been a civil administrator before, and I'm not sure just how everything functions here. You've had experience as mayor of Danang so you're more familiar with a city's operations. I want you, as my special assistant, to look into the activities of the various departments, get to know their personnel and their duties, and identify where there might be problem areas. I especially want to know where we need to improve security, if any current officials need to be replaced, and what departments need to be strengthened or reorganized.

"Don't make it appear that you are conducting an investigation. Both of us should make it known that you are simply acting as my eyes and ears, helping me to learn what I need to know if I am to be an effective mayor, not an easy task in a city as large and complex as Saigon[11] is today."

He set me up with an office, a secretary, and a car and driver. I quickly began making the rounds of city departments. I found many things to be as grim as I expected from my previous experience, especially in Kien Hoa and Danang. The police and other security forces were satisfied that their intelligence networks provided adequate information on antigovernment activities. I knew this was misplaced confidence because most such sources were not very reliable at best. At worst, they were channels used by the North and the NLF to funnel disinformation to our side. This made the capital of our country extremely vulnerable to all sorts of enemy spying and more dangerous activities.

I explained this to Lam, now promoted to general, and proposed that I switch my operation to one of coordinating and improving security efforts. Lam agreed, and I began organizing the project.

I barely started before an American CIA friend, Stu Methven, came to see me. "We heard you're working on improving security measures in the Saigon area," he said.[12] "We want to help in any way we can."

I outlined what I had in mind and what implementing the project might require. Methven said he would see what could be done to help and that he would get back to me soon.

Sure enough, he was back just three days later, with unexpected news. "Jorgenson[13] is very interested but right now he is more concerned with security in the provinces than here in Saigon. You'll be hearing from him," Methven told me.

I never did hear from him—not directly, at least. What I did get was a new set of marching orders, sending me back to Kien Hoa as province chief. The orders came directly from General Khanh, the new military ruler. When I asked Lam about it, he said he didn't want to lose me and had already discussed the orders with Khanh, to no avail. In current parlance, it was a done deal.

I had mixed feelings about the transfer. I liked my current job well enough, but I was still emotionally drained from all the recent turmoil. I was no longer comfortable in this new "coup-driven" army, with all its intrigues and politics. Returning to Kien Hoa, where I felt my efforts were worthwhile, seemed attractive in many ways. I could contribute and would be relatively free of the military's political machinations. We, my family and I, enjoyed life there and had made many friends in the province.

On the other hand, I felt uncomfortable going back as province chief for the Military Council after having served there as President Diem's man. Would people regard me as a turncoat, willing to serve any master? Would they think I had tried to curry favor with the new regime just to get my old job back? Had the situation in the province changed so that I would not be welcomed back? Finally, would circumstances be so different that I could no longer function effectively to govern the province?

These thoughts were all somewhat irrelevant. My orders were clear, and very soon I was on my way back to Kien Hoa.[14]

17: RETURN TO KIEN HOA, MEET WITH MY COMMUNIST BROTHER (1964–1965)

My return to Kien Hoa was happy and sad, joyous and disheartening: happy and joyous because the people welcomed me so warmly, and sad and disheartening because conditions had deteriorated considerably in little less than a year.

I say that I received a warm welcome on my return, but there was one notable exception.

At the time, Kien Hoa was in the Third Military Region, now commanded by General Lam Van Phat, none other than the former colonel of the Second Division at Danang. He was relieved of his command after our heated disagreement about withdrawing troops from the city and allowing Buddhist clergy and lay activists to leave the barbed-wire enclosures in which they had been confined. After being relieved from command of the Second Division, he was transferred to the General Staff, but had no specific duties. In fact, he helped lay the groundwork for and was one of the leaders of the November 1963 coup. After the coup, he was promoted to general and given command of the Third Military Region, which he commanded from offices in Saigon.

I knew I must make a courtesy call on him but feared the meeting would be less than pleasant. I phoned his Saigon office anyway and spoke to his aide. We arranged an appointment for the next day. I arrived at the set time, only to find the general alone in his office, not an aide or secretary in sight. This was highly unusual, but I shrugged, knocked at his door, and entered his office, documents in hand. "Give me your papers," he growled, without a greeting or asking me to sit. He glanced at them briefly, then telephoned General Nguyen Khanh,[1] a military academy classmate of Phat and now head of the Military Council.

"Such an appointment!" Phat almost shouted. "You should have consulted me. I am military commander of this region and you should have asked my opinion before appointing a province chief in this jurisdiction. No one asked me anything about it, and now I am confronted by Chau with orders covering his appointment. This is inconceivable."

The two argued for several minutes, then General Phat slammed down the phone. Next, he called General Khiem,[2] reciting his same indignation and objections to my appointment. Evidently he got no joy from that conversation because he finally hung up, glared, and threw my orders across his desk to me.

"Take your papers and go to your province. I don't care."

I walked out, not feeling angry at him so much as wondering how I could work with him, given the rancor he obviously bore for me. It could be an impossible situation. How I would be received by people in the province also concerned me. Would the Buddhist leaders be turned against me because I supported President Diem and not the coup? Would the Catholics still trust me after some of my policies and actions in Danang, which they might consider anti-Catholic and pro-Buddhist? Did the failures of the province chiefs who followed me damage the confidence in and authority of anyone sent to govern the province?

In any event, my fears proved groundless.

A day after my confrontation with General Phat, I informed province headquarters when I would arrive[3] and drove to My Tho province to catch a ferry to Kien Hoa. As I neared the ferry landing, I saw the province chief's car, an escort, and my former aide, Lieutenant Le Chi Thien, waiting to greet me. Lieutenant Thien and I discussed the current situation in the province during the hour-long ferry ride. At one point he chuckled and told me what to expect when we arrived.

"The province chief you are replacing asked us to keep your return quiet; he didn't want the changeover to be a big public event. Somehow word of your return spread rapidly, however, and it seems everybody in the province capital knows you are coming back. And they are very happy about it. You know that there have been four different province chiefs since you left."[4]

As we approached the ferry dock I saw that security was heavy, with many soldiers patrolling the area. I asked Lieutenant Thien about it.

"Things are not the same as when you were here. There is more unrest and Viet Cong activity now, so security is tighter than it used to be."

As we drove from the ferry port to Ben Tre, people lined the road at regular intervals. Lieutenant Thien said that proved his earlier point.

"People have learned of your return and are coming out to welcome you."

It took about an hour to drive from the ferry landing on the Kien Hoa side to the province capital. Again, I noticed that security was heavy along the route. Small crowds also gathered along the way to wave and shout greetings as we passed. Many people also were on hand to welcome me when we arrived in Ben Tre. These sincere, spontaneous signs of esteem by the people helped dismiss my feelings of anxiety and embarrassment at coming back to the province.

We completed the official changeover ceremony quickly and with no fanfare, as requested by Colonel Nguyen Van Dam, the man serving as province chief up to my arrival. This coincided with my own wishes. Only department heads and members of the provincial council attended. Incredibly enough, as Lieutenant Thien had mentioned on the ferry, Colonel Dam was the fourth province chief to hold that post since I left just a year earlier. The major who took my place originally lasted only three or four months; two lieutenant colonels and Colonel Dam followed him. This rapid turnover of province chiefs indicated that there were indeed serious problems to be faced. It also helped account for the overall low morale among officials and many residents in the province.

Surveying the security situation occupied the next three or four days. Results were discouraging. Whereas Viet Cong influence and depredations were mostly well in check and on the wane when I left, they had recovered significantly and Viet Cong now controlled large areas of the province. The Civil Guard, which provided most protection for the territory, was reduced to manning defensive positions for the most part. Villages and hamlets that had been freed from Viet Cong domination, with most local insurgents either won back to the government side or forced to flee the area, were once again under Viet Cong control. Almost half of the Strategic Hamlets we established earlier[5] had been virtually destroyed by the Viet Cong, who harassed them unmercifully.

Perhaps the most heartbreaking thing for me personally was the discovery that my Census Grievance program was in shambles. It still existed to some extent on paper, but it was dead for all practical purposes.

Next I talked to the American provincial advisor, who confirmed what I learned in my staff briefings and personal survey: the province was in a bad way. He registered complaints of his own, too. One example helped explain one reason that conditions had gone downhill so rapidly in the province. "Your predecessor held big parties every weekend," he told me indignantly. "He even had one of his staff officers bring in dancing girls from Saigon to entertain!"

I was a little surprised to hear an American complain about such a matter because most of them were known to enjoy a good party. On the other hand, it showed the dedication most Americans who toiled in the field—as opposed to those who spent their time in Saigon offices—felt toward their work.

Despite all the problems, I was happy to be back doing meaningful fieldwork. I was encouraged by the evident pleasure many people, from members of the Provincial Council to Catholic, Buddhist, and Cao Dai leaders, expressed at having me back. It was a boost to my personal ego, I admit, but it also indicated that I could expect earnest cooperation in efforts to restore the province to the more stable, less dangerous state that we had achieved before.

Top priority on my agenda was to rebuild the moribund Census Grievance program, since that was the basis for all of my pacification efforts. I drew immediate encouragement from the many core CG personnel from my first tour as province chief who flocked back to join me when they learned of my return to Kien Hoa. This cheered me immensely because I didn't have to begin completely from scratch to restart the program and retrain an entire new cadre for it.

One big problem was that neither the Vietnamese government officials nor the

American military understood my admittedly unorthodox pacification efforts, if they were aware of them at all. As a result, we were often at cross-purposes.

We had a new provincial U.S. military advisor, Major Andrew Simko, and he had no conception of what I was trying to do, nor that it had been proved effective in my first tour of duty. He kept asking me why I did not mount more military operations, urging me to set up more day and night operations. He wanted more patrols and ambushes, and more reports to document those kinds of activities.

"No," I told him. "That is not my way of doing things. Please just allow me to do my job as I conceive it. To achieve my objectives it is not necessary to kill the enemy. In most cases this just creates more problems and promotes VC recruiting, especially if we make mistakes and kill innocent people—as happens too frequently. I believe that it is necessary to protect the people from both the Viet Cong *and* from corrupt elements in the government. We must weed out officials who prey on the people in one way or another. Only by protecting the people from corrupt local officials can we get the general populace to have confidence and trust in us. Villagers have been under pressure from both sides for years. Killing Viet Cong alone is not the solution. Dealing with corruption at district and village levels is just as important as curbing Viet Cong raids and demands on the people.

"I don't believe you win hearts and minds of people by killing their friends and relatives. Ask me why and how I implement my program for pacification, but do not push me to launch more ambushes or other military actions. That is not my way. I believe that military action should be a last resort, used only when necessary to protect hamlets and villages and my Census Grievance cadre. If the Viet Cong don't threaten them, I'm happy to leave them alone."

"But I got instructions from MACV [Military Assistance Command Vietnam][6] to file detailed daily reports on the number of military operations, such as patrols and ambushes, how they were conducted, how many Viet Cong were killed or captured, how many weapons were captured or confiscated," the major explained in frustration. "MACV wants numbers, and if it doesn't get them, it will conclude that you are doing nothing toward pacifying the province. I know you're very active, but it won't seem that way to my superiors in Saigon if I don't file these daily reports. And I can't explain what you are doing in terms they will understand, especially since I'm not sure I fully understand it myself."

"Okay," I said finally, "let's make a deal." I called in my military deputy and told him to work with Major Simko so that the necessary reports could be sent to MACV.

"So you can file any kind of report you want, to satisfy your superiors' request," I said. "Meanwhile, you come with me and see what's going on out in the field and learn firsthand about what I'm trying to do. I can learn from you and you can learn to understand my methods of pacifying the province, especially the Census Grievance program. Once you understand, perhaps you can find ways to help us."

Major Simko began accompanying me on many of my trips through the province.[7] We grew friendlier and often talked for hours at a time. He gradually developed an appreciation for my methods, and eventually Major Simko became an enthusiastic supporter.[8]

Four particularly significant events occurred during my second tour of duty in Kien Hoa province.

A matter that I dismissed as insignificant at the time may have been related to two of these events. I only realized that after the fact. It occurred not long after my return to Kien Hoa. I received an envelope marked "personal" in my daily mail. Inside was an illustration torn from a propaganda leaflet of an American soldier with his foot on the neck of a Vietnamese lying prone on the ground. No note or message was included. I tossed it away and thought no more about it, until later, as I explain below.

First, there was a serious attempt to assassinate me, which failed only by happenstance.

Second was my first meeting since 1948 with my brother, Hien.

Third was my initial meeting with Daniel Ellsberg, when John Paul Vann brought him to visit me in Ben Tre.

Fourth was a military operation that went seriously wrong.

The assassination attempt took place on a busy day for me and failed only because of something I drank several hours earlier. The occasion was a benefit to raise funds for widows and orphans of soldiers killed in the war. It featured a famous troupe of performers from Saigon and was held at a theater in the provincial capital, not far from provincial headquarters and my residence. Announcements for the benefit appeared many weeks in advance and reported that I would attend in my official role as province chief. Thus, the Viet Cong plotters had ample time to prepare and all the information they needed to plan my death in detail.

As it happened, the father-in-law of my old friend Nguyen Van Thieu died shortly before the benefit, and I went to My Tho to pay my respects to the family in the morning, several hours before the performance was to begin. My wife and children were to be ready for me to pick them up and go on to the theater on my way back from the funeral. As I arrived at provincial headquarters on my way home, the head of the province council stopped me. "Won't you stop to say a few words, and perhaps join us in a traditional toast at our welcoming and thank-you celebration for those involved in putting on today's benefit performance?" he asked.

I agreed and went with him to make a short, impromptu speech thanking everyone who helped arrange or participate in the benefit. I stressed that funds would aid people who needed, and deserved, any help we could provide. Someone handed me a drink so I could join in the celebratory toast that followed. I almost never drank and was reluctant to do so on such a busy day. But I raised my glass with the others and downed the drink. (Ironically, unlike many who have lost their lives to liquor, I owe my life to that single drink.)

On the short walk from the province headquarters building to my residence, I suddenly became violently ill and vomited profusely. I half-staggered the rest of the way home, to find my wife, children, and civilian deputy waiting impatiently for me. "I'm very sick," I said, "and I can't go to the performance in this condition." I explained what had happened and urged my wife to take the children and go to the theater without me. She refused, saying she wanted to stay and take care of me, that she would keep the children at home, too. So my civilian deputy left for the benefit alone while my wife and children tried to make me comfortable.

An explosion soon shocked us all. It came from the theater, we soon learned. A bomb had exploded directly under the chair I would have occupied had I not been taken ill. Tragically, it claimed other victims. One was the mother of my military deputy, who had been placed in the seat of honor in my place.

The meeting with my brother Hien, which eventually led to trouble for both of us, occurred after my oldest brother Khang came from Saigon to visit me in Kien Hoa. "Your brother Hien wants to see you," he told me. My first reaction was that perhaps Hien wanted to defect from his position as an intelligence officer for the North. If that was the case, I wanted to help him in any way I could. On the other hand, I began to think about the picture I received in the mail, and the assassination attempt, in a new light. Was it possible that the picture of the GI and the prone Vietnamese was a subtle warning to me? And was Hien's request for a meeting in any way tied to the failed effort to kill me? I hated to think that was a possibility, but it did cross my mind. I made a mental note to bring it up if I did see Hien.

"Okay, here is my card," I said. "Give it to Hien. Tell him he can come here at any time, show it to the guard, and he will be directed to my residence."

Hien showed up a week or ten days later. Fortunately, I came home earlier than usual so I was in my residence when he arrived. When the guard on duty told me I had a visitor and showed me the card I had given Khang, I told him to bring the man to me. When Hien entered the room there was a long silence as we studied each other intently. It had been sixteen years since we last met, and each of us struggled to control his emotions. Finally I broke the silence.

"It's good to see you, Hien. What can I do for you?"

"I'm here for a few days on my way to Paris and wanted to come and see you," he replied.

I sensed that more than just personal reasons were involved, and Hien's next words confirmed that.

"I also have a personal letter for you from Senior Cadre Tran Luong.[9] You remember him, I assume?"

I certainly did remember the man. He was head of cadres, an extremely powerful position in the Viet Minh, when the Communists tried to recruit me to the party in 1949. He was now a member of the Politburo and even more powerful in the hierarchy of the North. "Thank you, I appreciate it. I still hold Mr. Luong in great esteem because he treated me well and seemed to understand my reservations about joining the party all those years ago."

Hien took out the letter and held it out to me.

"No, I cannot accept it, as a matter of principle. I meet with you today as brother to brother, not as two representatives of opposing sides. I am a provincial governor, however, and if I accept the letter, I must report it and I do not want to do that."

Hien nodded slightly, as if he understood and accepted my reasoning, then began to talk:

"I come here on a mission. The Central Command selected me because I am your brother, but I did not suggest it. The decision to approach you was made by the highest authorities in Hanoi. The decision was not taken lightly, and such an approach is very rare, not made to many people. I know you are a true nationalist, Chau, and I don't understand how you can ally yourself with the Americans and their corrupt, elitist puppet government. The American imperialists are no better than the French. They treat your so-called Republic as a colony, just as France did."

"There is little point in arguing, Hien. You have your views and I have mine. Perhaps we can discuss them at length later, but first please tell me exactly what your mission is, and why you have come to me at this particular time."

My brother looked at me for a moment, then nodded his head slowly and said that the Central Committee in Hanoi wanted me to arrange a meeting for him with Ambassador Lodge.

"The ambassador will certainly not agree to a meeting with someone he considers an underling!" I protested.

"Don't concern yourself about that," Hien replied. "I will have suitable credentials that will satisfy the ambassador and his staff about my status and qualifications to meet with him."

We discussed the matter at some length, and I finally agreed to consider his request. "I make no promises, Hien, but I will explore the possibilities."

Then Hien resumed his efforts to convince me that I should cast my lot with the North and not remain, as he phrased it, "a lackey of the Americans."

This reminded me of my earlier thoughts about the picture in the mail and the assassination attempt. I described both incidents to Hien. "Is it possible, my brother, that you come to me trying to recruit me to your cause only after the effort to kill me failed?"

"Please do not think that!" Hien protested. "I had no knowledge of it before this. You must understand that such an operation would be planned and mounted locally. I would know nothing about it since it would be outside the scope of my operations. However, I will make sure that no such future attempts are made on your life."

"That is not necessary," I told him. "I don't expect that kind of protection because I am your brother. I just wanted to be sure that it was not something that involved you. I expect to take my chances with my foes just as everyone else does."

After Hien left, I thought hard about what I should do. I thought I should report Hien's visit to my superiors in Saigon, but that might have dangerous consequences for both of us. Finally, I decided to confide in John Vann,[10] who I considered a trusted friend and reliable source of information on developments beyond Kien Hoa. I could confidentially discuss with him how best to handle the situation. I would wait for a few days, however, to allow time for Hien to leave the area for his trip to Paris.[11] I let two days go by, then met with Vann. I told him in detail about my brother's visit. He agreed to relay Hien's request for a meeting to the ambassador. He thought it best, for my own protection, to report the incident to the CIA, but agreed I should not mention it to government officials because of the probability of high-level Communist penetration.

Both the embassy and the CIA Saigon Station encouraged me, through Vann, to maintain contact with Hien. They agreed that he might prove to be a useful back channel for communication, even exploratory negotiation, with Hanoi. In fact, the ambassador first told Vann that he would agree to a meeting with Hien. A short time later, however, he expressed second thoughts. He called Vann and said that he did not think such a meeting was appropriate at the moment. He did leave the door open for a possible meeting in the future.

Little did I know then what consequences Hien's visit would later have: both of us would wind up in South Vietnam prisons.[12]

Vann came to visit me regularly in Kien Hoa. One day in the fall of 1965 I invited him to attend a minor ceremony at the provincial capital.[13] He showed up with a slender, intense young man in his mid-thirties. John had brought many people to meet me since we first met, but this one struck me immediately as someone special.[14] His name was Daniel Ellsberg, and we remain friends to this day. Vann, Ellsberg, and I had dinner that night and talked at length. As the evening developed I found myself thinking of my new friend as an "intellectual hawk," in contrast to

Vann, whom I considered a "military hawk." He spoke of the United States' capabilities and how they could help solve the problems in Vietnam.

"There is no point in discussing how exactly we got involved so deeply in this war," Ellsberg said at one point. "It happened and there is nothing we can do to change that. What we need to do is concentrate on the situation as it exists now, the internal problems and those involving the enemy. We *can* do something to help in those areas, and we will. I personally am here to learn about those problems and how best to use America's capabilities to overcome them." Ellsberg went out the next day to tour some of the province's pacified areas and to get a firsthand look at how the Census Grievance program worked. I did not go with him but designated several of my most reliable and knowledgeable staff officers to brief him on our projects and their progress.

"I learned a lot and I am impressed," Ellsberg told me after returning from his long day in the field. "This has been a very interesting visit. Vann did good by introducing us. I have found out more useful information than anywhere else since I arrived in Vietnam." We discussed his tour for a time. I felt that he had grasped very quickly what I was trying to do and how I was going about it. This set him apart from many of my other American visitors, who took much longer to understand my concepts and methods—if indeed they ever did. He seemed to agree with the idea that pacification could only be accomplished by using techniques that truly won the hearts and minds of the Vietnamese people and not merely by military might.[15]

The disastrous military ambush came about in this way.

In province after province, both government and military officers typically considered certain districts to be "pacified" because little overt Viet Cong activity occurred in them. In most such cases the powers-that-be were wrong. The Viet Cong left certain areas free of incidents because they used them as communication corridors and routes to move troops and supplies. Through intelligence gathered by my Census Grievance teams and other sources I determined in the summer of 1965 that an apparently peaceful district in the north-central part of the province was being used in this fashion. To disrupt the Viet Cong operations I began conducting ambushes and other harassing operations in the area by small hit-and-run units.

Apparently these tactics were effective, because after a short time our intelligence indicated that the Viet Cong planned to retaliate. We received a series of reports about a significant enemy force buildup in the area. Strength of the assembling forces was hard to pin down, but it appeared that it was at least about battalion strength. It seemed the Viet Cong planned to set an ambush to crush any provincial units that dared move into the area.

The military units at my disposal—Civil Guard and militia—were too limited to face such a force. So I contacted Colonel Nguyen Bao Tri, who commanded the

Seventh Division, and explained what we had learned, emphasizing that we did not know the exact strength of the enemy, but that it was a formidable one. He already had one company in Kien Hoa, and sent additional troops to make a full battalion to face the enemy.

The operation began early in the morning, not long after daybreak. The troops moved out cautiously, with scouts in front and to the flanks. They encountered no signs of the enemy. It was very hot and the terrain was not hospitable, a thick, dense forest of palm trees and underbrush that made movement difficult and often restricted range of vision to as little as three or four meters. Tired, hungry, and thirsty, the battalion stopped to rest and eat after some six or seven hours in the field. When the troops moved out again they were much less cautious, having encountered no resistance so far. This was a terrible, costly mistake because they walked into a carefully planned enemy ambush.

The VC were masters of concealment, and the area they selected for their killing ground could hardly have been more favorable for the trap they set. They waited until the entire ARVN battalion moved into the ambush site, then opened up with deadly fire. The ARVN battalion took heavy casualties immediately. Another battalion was sent in to carry on the fight. The battle went on through the rest of that day and night, with both sides suffering heavy losses. More than one hundred of our men were killed, and at least that many were wounded. Finally, early the following morning the Viet Cong disengaged and retreated, taking most of their dead and wounded with them.

General Khiem flew in from Saigon, greatly disturbed by the large number of casualties. Colonel Tri blamed the disaster on "faulty intelligence provided by the province." I merely told General Khiem what I had relayed to the division: that the Viet Cong had assembled a large force, which I suspected was of at least battalion strength, for an operation in the area. I had suggested that the division should commit a strong enough force to combat the enemy successfully. I pointed out that there was no way I could pinpoint the enemy's exact location in advance, just the general area where we suspected the Viet Cong troops to be. I made no reference to the manner in which the operation had been conducted.[16] I was sickened by the loss of so many of our soldiers and felt there was enough blame to spread around to everyone concerned.

Not long after that tragic event, something else occurred that would change my life in drastic fashion once more. In retrospect, I suspect that events were set into motion much earlier, but I did not realize it at the time. What happened requires some background explanation.

Rufus (Rufe) Phillips was a protégé of Colonel Ed Lansdale and had first come to Vietnam in August 1954 as part of Lansdale's Saigon Military Mission. He stayed until 1956. He returned in 1962 as director of rural affairs for the U.S. Operation Mission (USOM) in Saigon. He had also spent time in Laos during his 1950s tour, so he had significant experience in Southeast Asia. I met Rufe not long after his return to Vietnam in 1962. He heard from various sources of my efforts in Kien Hoa. He came to the province, taking the time to tour the area with me and to learn about my pacification philosophy and projects, especially the Census Grievance program. He quickly offered to support me in any way he could. Our working relationship aside, we became good friends on a personal level.[17]

The help Rufe could offer was not inconsequential. In addition to his current position at USOM's Rural Affairs, he had friends in high places of the South Vietnam military and government. One measure of his support for my efforts is described in a passage from *Prelude To Tragedy: Vietnam 1960–1965*.[18]

John O'Donnell, one of the eight contributors to *Prelude*, went to Vietnam in 1962[19] to serve as a provincial representative ("Prov Rep" in the vernacular of U.S. officials at the time) in the USOM Rural Affairs program. He wrote the following in his chapter of *Prelude to Tragedy*:

> After a few weeks of working directly with Rufe on the development of the Provincial Rehabilitation Plans, he called me into his office and told me that he wanted to assign me as the USOM provincial representative for the seven provinces in the upper Mekong Delta area south of Saigon. He wanted me to pay special attention to the program in Kien Hoa Province where he thought Lt. Col. Tran Ngoc Chau had some excellent ideas for combating the Viet Cong. When I asked him what he wanted me to do, he said, "You go out there and work with province chiefs and MAAG[20] sector advisors to get the Strategic Hamlet Program going, and then come back and tell us what we should do to support you.

As new personnel joined the Rural Affairs group, O'Donnell passed the responsibility for the other Upper Delta provinces on to new Prov Reps and was assigned specifically to work with me in Kien Hoa. He proved to be a valuable ally, as did other MAAG and CIA representatives who took the time to learn and understand what I was doing in the province.

At one point when Lansdale came to visit, after returning in 1965 for another assignment in Vietnam, he said something in the course of our usual long discussion about developments and problems in the country that I paid little attention to at the time. "You're doing a fine job here, Chau, but Kien Hoa is only one province. We must do something effective in all the provinces if we are to succeed in turning back the Viet Cong in the long run. Reforms must be implemented countrywide, with programs that provide economic benefits to the people while we indoctrinate them against VC propaganda. We both know that this is a political struggle as much or more than it is a military one, and that military measures alone will not win the overall battle."

I mention these things as background, to help explain what I deduced only after the fact.

One day in the late fall of 1965, General Nguyen Duc Thang visited me in the province. This was surprising because he was now a "super minister" in the Saigon government. His ministry was in charge of all programs related to pacification, which were many and varied.

After exchanging the usual pleasantries, General Thang surprised me even more. "Your efforts here in Kien Hoa have attracted attention in higher circles," he began. "You are doing excellent work, and this has not been overlooked. General Ky and I plan to inaugurate a new national pacification cadre program, and we agree that you are the right person to take charge of the project."

This almost floored me. First, my "efforts" in Kien Hoa had been largely ignored by Saigon since the coup and President Diem's assassination. I doubted that any of the generals running the government had any true idea of what I was doing. In fact, I had been chided at times about not following "proper procedure."

Second, I doubted very much that Ky had voluntarily and on his own decided I was "the man for the job." We had little contact and no personal relationship over the years. I never made a secret of the fact that I did not regard him highly as a candidate for high office in the South Vietnam government, certainly not as president. He may have known that I was province chief of Kien Hoa, but I felt he knew little more than that about my current activities.

Looking back much later, I remembered what General Lansdale had said about expanding a program such as mine to all provinces. I suspected that Lansdale and the Rufe Phillips disciples at USOM Rural Affairs—perhaps with an assist from John Paul Vann, Ev Bumgardner, and some of the CIA people who knew me and my program—were instrumental in arranging my new assignment. Back then, however, there was little time to dwell on the reasons for national leaders choosing me to head the national pacification cadre program. I needed to decide how best to leave my projects in Kien Hoa in good shape and in good hands. I also had to uproot my long-suffering wife and children, yet again, and arrange for their move to Saigon.

18: DIRECTOR OF PACIFICATION CADRES (1966)

As I rode through the streets of Saigon on the last day of 1965, I realized how dramatically the city had changed since the austere days of the Diem regime. Bars and nightclubs had been closed by presidential order during that time, subduing the traditionally vivacious and bustling atmosphere of the city. Now it was more of a boisterous, exciting beehive than it had ever been, a frenetic mixture of military and civilian activity that mirrored the confusion of the time. Signs of the war surrounding the city, and even invading it on occasion, were evident everywhere, coexisting with the peaceful, everyday life of the people.

I had been here on business several times since the Diem coup but only for short visits of a few hours each. I had also been helicoptered in from Kien Hoa three times to undergo emergency treatment for my chronic asthma, each time confined to the hospital during my stay. Thus, I had had little time or inclination to pay much attention to my surroundings. Now, after my release from all duties as governor of Kien Hoa province, I had a few days to reacquaint myself with the city, to see and understand the changes it had undergone in the past two years.

Near the airport were the huge compounds that were headquarters for the Vietnamese General Staff and U.S. Military Command. The Vietnamese had inherited their installation from the French, with tall, impressive brick buildings surrounded by well-cut lawns and tree-shaded streets. The U.S. Military Assistance Command–Vietnam had moved from its previous location on Pasteur Street, building its own headquarters on a vast field next to the airbase, just a few hundred yards from the Vietnamese headquarters. Because of its immense size and shape, and the dominance of its occupants, the media and public called it "Pentagon East." U.S. personnel in the country now totaled almost 200,000, compared to the 16,500 troops and 3,563 civilians who had been stationed in the country at the time of the coup two years earlier. Chase Manhattan and Bank of America had opened branches in Saigon to serve American personnel. About three kilometers from Tan Son Nhut and just a few blocks from the American embassy, the Saigon River was crowded with military and contracted merchant ships delivering cargo for what was now a major combat zone.

Saigon's civilian population, previously about 2 million, had almost doubled due to people who had flocked to the city from demolished villages and war-torn rural areas. Many peasant girls had been transformed into bar girls and hostesses in the nightclubs and bars that dotted the city like an infectious rash. Patrons came not only from the large American colony but also from among the many Vietnamese and Chinese who prospered by catering to Americans and dealing in the flourishing black market for U.S. military and PX goods. There were accounts of corrupt Vietnamese government and military officials making fortunes from graft, theft, and bribery.

Saigon was becoming accustomed at the time to the presence of more and more American troops, sightseeing or going about their duties during the day and crowding into the various types of pleasure palaces that welcomed them at night. Joining them were Australians, New Zealanders, Filipinos, Koreans, Thais, and others who had been "invited" by the United States to join in the fight against the Vietnamese Communists. As the war escalated, President Johnson tried to get more countries involved to soften the growing opposition to the war in the United States and around the world.

Rock music blended with traditional Vietnamese melodies against a backdrop of automatic weapon and artillery fire from the perimeter of the city. The rattle of small arms and explosions of bombs from frequent sabotage and terrorist acts against U.S. installations within the city itself added to the din. None of this prevented the burgeoning of the busy life, day and night, on the streets and in the stores of Saigon and Cholon, the Chinatown district. Goods and merchandise, much of it still bearing PX marks, were displayed in shop windows and sidewalk stalls. Luxury items from Europe were plentiful also. People flooded restaurants, hotels, and cabarets far into the night. Several large hotels, including the Rex, were leased by the U.S. military for officers' and NCO clubs. The aroma of barbecued ribs and hamburgers became as common in some areas as that of cha gio (egg rolls)[1] and pho (beef soup with noodles and spicy vegetables).

Yet for all the superficial prosperity and gaiety, there was an underlying sadness, fear of hidden dangers, and misery and poverty among many of those who had fled their homes to seek refuge and food in the city. Crippled, scarred, and wounded civilians and soldiers, Vietnamese and American, were constant reminders of the war being fought just outside the city and often within its boundaries.

I was here to take over the newly created position of national director of the Pacification Cadre Program. Americans had first used the term "revolutionary development cadres" but then had to change it to "rural construction cadres" (Can bo Xay dung Nong Thon) to correspond with the title of the supervising super-ministry headed by General Thang. In Kien Hoa when I started my program for pacification, I named it "Civilian Affairs" (Dan su vu). The fact that so many different names were applied to the cadres involved in the various pacification programs over the years indicated how confused the French, Vietnamese, and Americans had been about the concept of "pacification." There had been little consistency with respect to the objectives, means, and origination of the various programs supposedly designed to achieve pacification.

With the war expanding and more and more American and Allied troops pouring in, the search for enemy forces widened to cover more territory, whether in open rice fields or thick jungle. When pinpointed, Communist troops were hit by ground fire, artillery shelling, and air strikes. Many villages were destroyed during such action, with the inhabitants fleeing their burned-out homes to take shelter in government-controlled areas. "Revolutionary cadres" were expected to do many things to win the people over so they would support the Saigon government.

That was the situation when I took charge of the pacification cadres. They were expected to play the primary role in fighting "the other war" of pacification, a struggle to win over the people, as opposed to the military war. Under my direction, the cadres would be trained and equipped to operate in hamlets and villages secured by military and paramilitary forces. Their aim: to "win the hearts and minds of the people," to deprive the Communist "fish" of the friendly waters they needed to swim in successfully and unnoticed. Although the prime minister made the decision, the CIA (and the amorphous Lansdale-Vann-Bumgardner team) actually worked behind the scenes to get me nominated for the job because of the experimental program I had established in Kien Hoa province (with CIA help) and operated successfully for several years. I hoped that the success of that program could be repeated, if not duplicated, on a national level. I looked forward to the task, feeling it could be a vital one in the war against the Communists. At the same time I knew that implementing the program on a vastly larger scale would present new challenges. I had no idea how monumental those difficulties would become. Little did I realize that it wasn't just the enemy that was capable of sabotage. I had no inkling of the political infighting and backstabbing that would complicate my new job.

All that was ahead of me, however, as I set off for my meeting with Gordon Jorgenson. It was held at his residence, a villa like many others in its upper-class neighborhood, but protected by discreet security measures. It was no match for the majestic mansion that housed the American military commander, General William Westmoreland. This was misleading, however, since the office Jorgenson held gave him as much covert and behind-the-scenes power as Westmoreland enjoyed openly.

Gordon Jorgenson's official title was special assistant to the U.S. ambassador and member of the U.S. Mission Council. He actually was chief of the CIA Saigon Station, an extremely powerful position in that time and place. Like previous chiefs of station, he purposely kept out of the public eye, so he was little known outside the circles of American and Vietnamese insiders. CIA involvement in Vietnam predated U.S. military involvement, having begun in 1954. Other members of the U.S. Mission were General Westmoreland, political and economic counselors, and the directors of the United States Information Service (USIS)[2] and the U.S. Agency for International Development (USAID). Actually, however, the CIA provided most of the intelligence not just on the enemy but on everything else, from America's Vietnamese allies to the U.S. Mission in Saigon and even the White House (via CIA headquarters in Langley, Virginia). This gave the organization great influence over decision-making with respect to the Vietnam War, in Saigon and in Washington. Saigon Station also created and covertly conducted the "conditions" or operations to implement U.S. policies.

General Westmoreland, as the top military man, controlled the giant, visible, and lethal U.S. war machine; he was the on-scene commander who implemented U.S. policy and dealt with the visible enemy. Jorgenson exercised a more subtle role, but one that was no less important, because he influenced policy. The CIA waged its own hidden war, which helped create conditions that required and influenced subsequent actions. CIA reports to Washington also had great influence on U.S. decisions regarding Vietnam.

If the CIA had understood the nature of the insurgency in the South in the early 1960s and succeeded in helping Diem counter it with appropriate policies, the war would never have escalated to the scale it reached in 1965. The bulk of the population then, 85 percent, lived in rural hamlets and villages. If more projects like my Census Grievance program and the few others that showed promise had been implemented, the insurgency would never have become so widespread and potent.

North Vietnam would have had a dilemma. Without the Viet Cong creating both military and political problems for the South, Ho Chi Minh's forces would have had little choice but to fight a conventional war to achieve victory. That would have been suicidal, since that was precisely the kind of war that the United States and the U.S.-equipped and -trained ARVN were prepared for—and could have won handily. Also, had the United States decided not to overthrow Diem, American troops would not have had to venture deeply into a kind of war they did not know or understand.[3]

Direct CIA activities began right after the 1954 Geneva Agreements were signed, partitioning the North and South. A succession of CIA men played major roles in creating the South Vietnamese government and to a large extent helped determine its composition and direction. Colonel Edward Lansdale, already a legend for his exploits in the Philippines (and hoping to duplicate that success in Vietnam), arrived in 1954. He helped the exodus to the South of a million Vietnamese, mostly Catholic, during late 1954 and early 1955. A number of these refugees were then selected for training as agents. Beginning in 1957 they were infiltrated back into the North to stimulate a kind of insurgency, which failed to materialize. Most of these operations were planned and implemented by William Colby. Nguyen Cao Ky, a Vietnamese

Air Force officer who later in 1965 became prime minister of Vietnam, piloted some of the missions. Both Lansdale and Colby worked for the CIA.

The large group of refugees, allied with the Catholic minority already in the South, had formed the backbone of the Ngo Dinh Diem regime (and the core support group for the regime that replaced Diem). In 1954–55, when Diem almost fell into disgrace and out of favor with the U.S. ambassador and the White House, Lansdale intervened. His machinations saved Diem and helped establish the Diem period of Vietnamese history. In the following years Diem successfully dethroned Bao Dai as head of state, promulgated the first South Vietnamese Republic, and got himself elected the first president of that republic. U.S. support kept President Diem in power until 1963, and although he attempted to resist over-Americanization of his country and the war, there is no doubt that he knew he owed a great deal to the United States in general and the CIA in particular.

The CIA also played a major role when Diem's policies, and the activities of his brother, Ngo Dinh Nhu, Diem's chief political advisor and head of the secret police, turned U.S. officials against him. Colonel Lucien Conein served as middleman for then-newly appointed U.S. ambassador Henry Cabot Lodge and a cabal of Vietnamese who were previously lieutenants and NCOs in the French military. They had been rapidly promoted to general officer grade because of the growth of the Vietnamese Army, Diem's generosity, and their supposed loyalty to him, rather than for their real merit.

Most CIA operations were self-described successes. This helped its leaders and agents retain their powerful position in Vietnam. The only notable exception (in official Washington) had been the attempts to create a clandestine war of sabotage and propaganda in North Vietnamese territory. Ironically, while the CIA failed in attempts to induce insurgency in the North, despite having a pool of 1 million refugees to draw from for their activities, the North was successful in leading an insurgency in the South. The North had drawn refugees to its side, too: 100,000 of them who fled from the South to the North after the 1954 partition. The Communists were successful in infiltrating many of them back to the South. Their first efforts were to propagandize the people and to carry out small acts of terrorism and sabotage (1957–60). Their activity escalated into armed insurgency and guerrilla warfare (1961–63), and finally into full-scale war during 1964–65. The difference in terms of success was probably because agents moving to the South from the North found more supporters and a less resistant populace than did those the CIA sent to Communist territory in the North.

My career since 1955 had put me in positions that allowed me to observe and be involved in various American military and CIA operations. After my selection for the first group of Vietnamese officers to participate in an advanced infantry training

course at Fort Benning, as related earlier, I served successively as director of instruction at the Dalat Military Academy, deputy chief of staff for training and operations
of the first Vietnamese division to be reorganized and trained along American lines
and equipped with U.S. arms, and chief of staff of a major training center that trained
Vietnamese NCOs and troops in American tactics. During the last six years in particular I had been in direct contact with the insurgency at the grass roots, and had
been involved in the wider war in a variety of positions: a regional commander of
regional and popular forces, rapporter to the National Security Council, and mayor
and provincial governor. These varied positions had given me a deep insight into the
overall picture of the war.

Thus, I saw how the Vietnamese Army was transformed from groups of battalions and disparate units into a well-trained and well-equipped military organization
modeled after the U.S. military. This Americanization of the army, as well as similar
impressive transformations in the air force, navy, and marines, had made the
Vietnamese military potentially the decisive power in the hands of its generals. Only
the United States, which financed this military power, could influence it, as demonstrated by the Diem coup and the current situation.

Unfortunately, as the generals kept deploying infantry, airborne and marine regiments and divisions, modern tank and artillery units, and various aircraft in pursuit
of the enemy in jungles and hills, the real war was left to the ill-armed and ill-
equipped platoon and company leaders of the irregular forces. The real war was born
and matured in the rural hamlets, and was still being waged there.

The conversation at that meeting in Gordon Jorgenson's villa ranged from a brief
review of the general situation to a discussion of various specific aspects of the war.
We both agreed that conventional combat operations against the enemy were not
going well, and that the Rolling Thunder bombardment of the North served more to
boost morale of South Vietnamese troops and officials than to discourage the North
Vietnamese. But we were both optimistic that, with the increase in U.S. military intervention and expansion, and strengthening of Vietnamese military and paramilitary forces, we would be able to stop the enemy and regain the initiative.

This meant we must prepare to work more closely with the military to "pacify"
contested areas and those villages and hamlets that were removed from Communist
control. To achieve that objective, the CIA needed to coordinate its activities with
other U.S. agencies. The CIA would also take charge of supporting the Vietnamese
government in developing and implementing the centerpiece of an overall pacification plan. Its goal was "to win the hearts and minds of the people." That phrase has
since been mocked and discredited, but it represented my sincere goal at the time.
Jorgenson and others in the CIA felt the same way, to an extent. They agreed on the
need to clear hamlets within our "pacified" territory of all potential enemies and

turn them into strongholds that supported the South Vietnamese government and deny access to them by North Vietnamese infiltrators or Viet Cong.

Although Jorgenson and I apparently agreed on everything that day, in the course of time I learned that he and his men only shared with me the organizational and technical facets of the concept. We never got to the cardinal point I considered so essential: devotion to the nationalistic image and resulting motivation of the cadres. Without that motivation, the cadres I was to produce would be more or less similar to the various cadre groups that the French earlier, and Diem later, had employed for the same purpose. And they could be no more successful at generating support from the populace. Such a nationalistic motivation could only be successful if the program appeared to be run by Vietnamese; the CIA would have to operate remotely, covertly, and sensitively, so that the project would be seen and felt to be a totally Vietnamese program, without foreign influences.

At that first two-hour luncheon meeting, Jorgenson seemed more intent on assuring me of his total support than on listening to my conceptual presentation. He contended that General Nguyen Duc Thang, who would be my new boss, was an excellent choice to head all cabinet ministries involved in that effort. I reserved my judgment to an extent, knowing that although Thang was dedicated and honest and had been an excellent soldier, his career had been strictly military until appointment as a super-minister[4] by former military academy classmate, current prime minister General Nguyen Cao Ky. (Ky had also promoted Thang to major general.)

In ending the conversation, the CIA chief said he was confident I would work well with his assistant, Tom Donahue, in the project. "I will be available any time you want to talk to me and will offer any help you feel you need," he added.

My private assessment of Jorgenson was that he was more of an administrator than a man accustomed to thinking creatively. This was in contrast to William Colby, who had been chief of Saigon Station several years earlier and had since moved back to a higher position at the CIA's Langley, Virginia, headquarters. Colby and I had had many long conversations during his visits to Kien Hoa while I was governor there. I felt Colby had a much better insight than Jorgenson into Vietnam in general, and the pacification process in particular. I also realized that Jorgenson did not fully understand the motivational aspect, and that I must make allowances for his relative unfamiliarity with the situation we faced. I couldn't expect him to understand the problems or potential solutions as well as Colby or Lansdale. Colby had been thoughtful, yet aggressive and willing to consider new ideas. Jorgenson appeared to be cautious, tending more to conservative expediencies that would not rock any boats rather than to open-mindedness.

I soon had proof that Jorgenson did not understand or appreciate some of the basic facts of life that should apply in our pacification efforts. After lunch, Jorgenson had one of his assistants take me to a compound only a few blocks from his villa. It included several large buildings, all painted white, air-conditioned, and beautifully furnished, but it was obviously part of a foreign complex. "Mr. Jorgenson thought you might find these buildings would make suitable headquarters for your new department," the aide told me.

I was stunned. The idea of setting up headquarters for the pacification program in the midst of what was patently a CIA compound would guarantee the failure before we even started. A key point of the plan had to be a perception on the part of the peasants, workers, and others whom we wanted to convert into solid supporters of the Republic of Vietnam that this was indeed a Vietnamese program. The less it appeared Americans had to do with it, especially the CIA, the more effective our pacification efforts would be. Jorgenson obviously did not grasp that point.

Another point about the meeting disappointed me: Jorgenson hadn't mentioned the report I had made to Tom Donahue about my Communist brother, Tran Ngoc Hien, visiting me several months earlier in Kien Hoa province. I had hoped we could discuss it, and that I could explain my thoughts about Hien to him in more detail.

My next important meeting was with General Thang. It was short, but I was able to explain about the problem inherent in using the CIA buildings as headquarters. He instructed me to take over the compound that had housed headquarters of the former deputy prime minister for pacification, Nguyen Ton Hoan, set up my offices, and begin to work with the CIA. I was to report our progress to him regularly.

Thang, a man in his late thirties and, at about six feet, very tall for a Vietnamese, was energetic and hard working. He was a Catholic from the North, an asset for career advancement under Diem and the post-Diem anti-Communist regimes, but Thang had not earned his promotions by favoritism alone. He had been drafted from college into the army in 1951 and fought brilliantly during the war in an artillery unit. I first met him in 1954; I was a major commanding the Eighth Infantry Battalion, and Thang was a lieutenant commanding an artillery battery in the same Twenty-first Mobile Group. When the war ended and the artillery unit was reorganized into a group, Thang was promoted to captain and made its commanding officer. He stood out in an army where most unit commanders became accustomed to a high lifestyle. Thang lived a simple life, eating the same food as the troops and walking with them on long marches, carrying a heavier load than any of them, while his Jeep followed behind the column. I had lost track of him until his recent promotion to general and appointment to the ministerial position. A month earlier he had flown down to Kien Hoa and told me that Prime Minister Ky had assigned me to his ministry to take charge of the newly created Directorate of Pacification Cadres.

I understood that Thang was in a difficult position. First, though he owed his advancement and position to Ky, he certainly did not favor Ky's flamboyant lifestyle.

Thang himself was religious and not on the take, in contrast to many officers and officials. He was neither a drinker nor a womanizer. He was also in the middle of a struggle for power and American favor between Prime Minister Nguyen Cao Ky and Nguyen Van Thieu, then figurehead chief of state.

Maintaining any sort of neutral position between them was difficult at best, and my appointment only complicated things. Thang knew very well that I was a friend of Thieu and still enjoyed an excellent, continuing relationship with him. Thang also knew that I had been imposed on him by the Americans to head the most crucial part of the entire pacification program. He also remembered that I had once out-ranked him, and now had considerably more experience in the military, government, and administration than he had. Considering all these factors, it was little wonder that Thang was reserved in his dealings with me.

At the huge compound that had been vacant since the departure of Dr. Nguyen Ton Hoan, I found no directives or instructions that I could use. The reason was simple. Dr. Hoan had exiled himself in the United States for almost twenty years, before General Nguyen Khanh invited him to return and assigned him as his deputy prime minister for pacification. (Hoan's was not the only "fantasy appointment" Khanh made; he also named General Do Mau, a former NCO in the French colonial military, who had never attended college, as a deputy prime minister for educational and cultural affairs.) All this was shortly after General Khanh had toppled the military junta that had brought down Diem. When Khanh's short-lived government fell, Hoan's job was gone.

It took me a few days to get the compound organized, and to assign specific duties to the group of senior civil servants and military officers under my jurisdiction. Then I began working with Tom Donahue to set up plans for forming and operating the cadres. I also began probing to see how much actual authority the CIA and Thang would give me.

It was obvious from the start that I would have more than adequate material support, thanks to the CIA and its resources. For example, a control center with modern audiovisual equipment was set up in a few weeks with everything brought in directly from Taiwan and Japan, bypassing Vietnamese channels. I could fly privately in Air America planes and helicopters, even when travel requests were made on short notice. General Thang also complied with my requests for a group of experts to help prepare the directives and documents needed for the pacification efforts.

But I considered all of these things, helpful though they were, as secondary to my main objectives. It was much more important that both the CIA and Thang understand, and agree to, the basics of the program. In Thang's case, it was also vital that he communicate these basics to provincial governors and district chiefs and see that they were carried out effectively. The basics were as follows:

1. A sense of nationalistic conviction and motivation on the part of everyone involved

2. An orderly sequence and coordination of activities between civilian, military, and intelligence

In my working sessions with Tom Donahue and his CIA assistants, we spent long hours discussing the organization of the cadres. It soon became clear that the CIA and I differed on the size of the cadre groups. I wanted eighty-man teams, forty of the men designated to work on population census and grievance procedures, while the other forty would be organized along the lines of previous PAT (People's Action Team) units as they had been developed during 1964 in Quang Ngai.[5] The CIA wanted fifty-man teams, with forty cadres allocated for PAT duties and only ten assigned to what I considered the primary duties of the teams: census taking, implementing a grievance procedure similar to the one I had established in Kien Hoa, and other similar efforts aimed at true pacification, not merely paramilitary activities to discover and eliminate Viet Cong agents, cadres, and supporters.

It was clear from their insistence on the smaller teams that the CIA officials with whom I was dealing considered PAT operations as the primary goal of the pacification cadre teams, with other activities of minor or secondary importance. They obviously did not fully understand the reasons that my pilot program in Kien Hoa had been successful.

19: AN AMERICAN OR VIETNAMESE PROGRAM? (1966)

I fought strenuously to change the thinking of CIA representatives involved in the pacification cadre program. I tried my best to convince them that the census and grievance elements needed to play the leading role in each pacification cadre team and that this could not be done successfully with just fifty men. I explained again how the census and grievance elements would work together to canvass all the members of every family in every hamlet to be pacified. They would come to know the religious and political affiliations of every family, their economic status and living conditions, as well as specific matters than concerned each family. This approach would have two benefits.

First, it would provide information on local Viet Cong supporters and their activities. Second, collecting grievances from people on the conduct of local government and military personnel would provide a truer picture of what goes on in hamlets than ever before available. All earlier intelligence-gathering efforts had relied solely on the police and military security. No attempt had been made to involve the local populace, especially peasants, in any way until I set up the grievance program in Kien Hoa. My previous five years of experience in various local governments had convinced me that the old method, using personnel and techniques inherited directly from the old French, had long since proved to be corrupt and counterproductive.

This colonial and postcolonial legacy led to the assumption that everyone with any sort of ties to the Viet Minh during the fight against the French and their Vietnamese puppets were automatically suspected of being Viet Cong or Viet Cong sympathizers. As a result, village populations were divided into three groups. One group included all of those affiliated with the government: political officials, civil servants, the police and intelligence agents, and military personnel. The vast majority of these were holdovers from earlier French and French-Vietnamese regimes. Viet Cong and their sympathizers made the second group. Those in neither camp made up Vietnam's "silent majority." In most villages the first group controlled the local government, collected taxes, and passed judgment on what villagers were Viet Cong or Viet Cong sympathizers. Those who really were Viet Cong made their own demands on the villagers, harassed local officials and Vietnamese and U.S. troops in the area, or joined other enemy units in larger military operations. Those in the middle adopted a two-faced attitude in order to maximize chances of survival.

During the 1940s and 1950s, most of the people not affiliated with the government had either joined the Viet Minh in the fight against the French and its puppet Vietnamese or had supported the Viet Minh to varying degrees, so government, police, security, and military officials regarded this silent majority with suspicion. Most peasants, the very people whose hearts and minds we wanted to win, were thus the objects of discrimination and oppression. Too often, as I've mentioned earlier, officials also had personal axes to grind, accusing people of Viet Cong activities to get revenge or for other personal reasons. Recognizing these truths and acting on them should have been the key to winning the hidden "silent war," a new and radical solution to winning politically as opposed to simply conducting the usual war of guns and soldiers.

I had learned in Kien Hoa and elsewhere that 95 percent of those who had supported the Viet Minh against the French were nationalists, not Communists. In fact, they knew little or nothing about communism. I had made it a point in Kien Hoa to make the police, security, administrative officials, and the military observe and understand the consequences of automatically assuming that all former Viet Minh supporters were enthusiastic Viet Cong supporters. Our goal should be to reconcile the silent majority of the people with those who had served directly or indirectly under the French in the previous war, and rally all factions to the new South Vietnam cause.

Although no one else had understood this simple concept and put it to work before, I had achieved remarkable successes in Kien Hoa province.[1] I believed that what happened in Kien Hoa could be expanded nationwide. This would cause the Viet Cong to lose their rural bases and resources, undermining Vo Nguyen Giap's "people's war" and the "fish and water" strategy. Thus, the first two phases of the "revolutionary war" would not be possible and we could win the war at the village level. That was the rudimentary concept fully described in my book *From War to Peace: Restoration of the Village*, written and published in Vietnamese in 1967.

Although the Saigon generals ignored my success in Kien Hoa, the CIA, John Vann, and General Lansdale took notice and helped install me as the first national director of pacification cadres. Suddenly I understood that the CIA's alterations, if adopted, would destroy the very factors that made the Kien Hoa program successful. In accepting the new position I was enthusiastic about producing the kind of cadres who would be morally motivated and technically equipped to achieve our objectives in the villages. Now, Donahue apparently agreed with me in general terms, but remained firm in demanding that the PAT team have the major role in the cadre pacification teams, with the other elements reduced in size from my original plan, and playing a secondary role in the pacification program.

General Thang at first supported me fully, but he called a few days later and asked me to compromise with Donahue. "The CIA has the money, and that's the way they want it," he told me in effect. Extensive discussions finally produced a compromise agreement for fifty-nine-man cadre teams. I learned much later that this compromise was based on the CIA's reluctant acceptance a year earlier of changes to the PAT format initiated in Binh Dinh province, where Nguyen Be ignored the CIA sizing.

After that decision was made, I had a long talk with Vann, telling him all about the problem.[2]

"Will the fifty-nine-man team do the job you had envisioned for eighty cadres?" Vann asked.

"When I proposed eighty cadres, I had in mind making each group self-sufficient, able to protect itself while performing specific pacification duties, and capable of training the villagers against Viet Cong infiltration and attack," I told him. "Now, with just fifty-nine men, I will have to drop the latter objective: self-protection training for the villagers, which I still consider an inherent part of the pacification effort."

"But surely the local district chiefs and provincial governors can handle that, can't they?"

"Yes, they can," I replied, "but I wanted our cadres to do it because they would be trained in and motivated by revolutionary new concepts and techniques, as we have discussed. As a result, I feel they would be better equipped than anyone else to do the job successfully. To me, it's not so much a matter of the size of the groups as it is a matter of understanding the basic concepts and of placing proper importance on various facets of the pacification program. If the program is handled correctly we can revolutionize Vietnamese society, starting at the bottom in areas marked for pacification. We must reconcile differences between officials and the people in those areas, set up free local elections, and organize the villages so that they can provide their own security against Viet Cong depredations. The populace will then feel that the government is working for them, and thus is worthy of support because the traditional corruption and oppression by officials, police, and troops would be greatly reduced if not stopped completely. Then the economic facts of life would become increasingly important, and people would realize that with security, responsible local government, and national assistance, their villages can develop economically."

"What will happen now that the decision has been made to reduce the size of teams to fifty-nine cadres and stress the PAT portion of the program?" Vann asked.

"Things will be much the same as when the French and Diem attempted pacification programs," I told him glumly. "Only with technical improvements and plentiful resources available." Then I brightened up and added, "But we are better off today than we were yesterday, and I am determined to keep fighting so that we can implement the proper concepts as part of pacification efforts in the field."

"I don't see how the kind of revolution we envisioned can succeed without the guys at the top understanding and supporting it. But be patient; I'll do my best to sell the idea to Americans powerful enough to get things done," Vann concluded. At the time, he, with Ev Bumgardner and Frank Scotton, had written up ideas similar to mine in a paper titled "Harnessing the Revolution," which John had submitted through the U.S. hierarchy and circulated widely.

It was becoming apparent, however, that Jorgenson and Donahue were much more concerned with mass-producing cadres to perform field operations that were vastly different from what I felt were vital and fundamental to a true pacification program. They wanted more emphasis on the paramilitary and repressive aspects of the program than on attempts to "win hearts and minds." They planned to subordinate census and grievance procedures, propaganda, indoctrination, intelligence, and "psy-war" (psychological warfare) efforts to the singling out and eliminating of "subversive" or "antigovernment" elements. I knew this would be self-defeating.

I then requested that John Vann be assigned as my American counterpart in the pacification program. With him in that capacity and serving as manager of the AID portion of pacification, he could be a buffer and provide temporary cover for Tom Donahue and the CIA. When he moved into that slot and began working with me, I asked him to make an effort to have the CIA transfer overt control of the program to AID. Donahue could run things from behind the scenes, but having Vann and AID in apparent control would increase public confidence in our efforts.

I made this suggestion with good intent and sincerity, thinking that Vann was in better position to put the point across to the CIA in view of my somewhat strained relationship with the organization after our disagreement over the size and roles of cadre groups. Neither Vann nor I anticipated what the consequences would be.

I discussed the matter with John Vann and asked for his help. On my recommendation and request, Vann, who had been assigned as USAID project manager, also became my senior advisor, because now I was fighting openly for the CIA to move to the background. Vann was enthusiastic, not because he wanted the position for his own sake, but because he shared my view that the CIA would be more effective if it operated the program from behind the scenes. Vann went on to try selling the idea to various members of the American hierarchy in Saigon. Just who was involved I'm not sure, but the results were very frustrating and landed us both in trouble.

Friction slowly increased but remained in the background until shortly after I moved to Vung Tau. I went to take charge of the training center that had been built there two years earlier, and to reorganize it to accommodate revised training for the new pacification program trainees. Until then, the center had been set up to train a variety of people for CIA programs in a number of provinces (as previously discussed). Best known and most effective in terms of doing the jobs they were assigned had been the People's Action Teams (PAT) and Counterterrorist Teams (CT). The

PATs originally developed in Quang Ngai in early 1964 based on district chiefs working with USIS officer Frank Scotton and province advisor Bob Kelly. The first units were locally organized, trained, and operated. Their mission had been to move around the countryside, conducting ambushes, spending time with villagers, and helping improve their living conditions by providing very basic medical care and immediate simple civic action. Subsequently, in the late summer of 1964, the project was assumed by the CIA, "regularized," and expanded to other provinces.[3] In Binh Dinh, Major Nguyen Be audaciously (with the help of Bob Kelly) took the newly introduced program away from the CIA advisors and "localized" the concept to pursue real pacification goals.

The CTs kidnapped and eliminated Viet Cong agents operating in and around hamlets and villages. Effectiveness over time varied from province to province, and for most rural citizens the conduct and impact of CT activity were indistinguishable from that of the Viet Cong.

Despite their usefulness, the PATs and CTs in most provinces were only improved versions of several similar programs the French and Vietnamese had tried earlier. They lacked the key ingredients: nationalistic image and inspiration, plus the local training required to implement the reforms I have outlined on previous pages. As the CIA expanded application of PATs, reliance on the colonial-based police, security, and government systems for intelligence, which placed so much of the local populace in suspect status, became an unfavorable characteristic.

Vung Tau was a relatively peaceful resort city on the beach some 120 kilometers northwest of Saigon. The training center had sufficient barracks and training facilities to accommodate 3,000 men at a time. Actual results achieved by the cadres trained here were controversial.

Although the CIA financed, equipped, and trained the cadres, their recruitment and the way they were employed was the responsibility of provincial governors and district chiefs. As a result those officials wanted the teams to seem efficient and have effective records. They usually approved of the teams' operations because local police, security, and military officials routinely concurred with team reports. District chiefs also had a tendency to make the PATs look good for the CIA by padding their scores, if you will. That is, they credited killings of Viet Cong elements actually done by popular and regional paramilitary units to the PATs to earn higher marks, and more support, from the CIA.

Little control over local officials from above resulted in many abuses. I frequently uncovered problems of this nature while I was governor at Kien Hoa. Those mentioned above, if not typical, at least were not uncommon. There were many similar instances in which people were denounced, arrested, or killed because of jealousy, revenge, or opportunities for profit on the part of local officials. Executions carried out on such flimsy grounds were not unusual. People who had the ear of PAT or CT members could resolve feuds or rid themselves of personal enemies, even business competitors, by reporting that they were VC guerrillas or active supporters.

This was not just criminal injustice, but it was obviously also counterproductive in terms of winning the hearts and minds of the people. First, we had absolutely no chance of winning the heart or mind of somebody who had been killed. Second, such unjust and unnecessary executions were perhaps the most effective recruiting tools the enemy could have desired.

I estimated that, as a rule of thumb, every such killing created at least five new hard-core National Liberation Front supporters, often more. Surviving relatives and friends of the victim who may not have been firmly committed to either side usually became active foes of the Saigon government and the United States.

My solutions to this problem in the Kien Hoa program were twofold. First, after intelligence work identified the loyalties of everyone in the pacification area, every effort was made to convert VC sympathizers (and even those who engaged in guerrilla activities) by helping to solve their personal and family problems, usually created by local authorities and troops. If these efforts did not succeed, we tried compromising the individuals in various ways so that they would either have to work with us, or at a minimum they would be less effective for the other side. Only then were more drastic methods considered, such as imprisonment, kidnapping, or assassination, and these extreme measures could not be taken independently.

Previously in Kien Hoa I had integrated the antiterrorist teams into the overall pacification group, but in such a way that their actions were directed and supervised by another independent unit within the group: the Census Grievance team. This team had to make its own investigation of the facts, checking information from several sources, before it could authorize kidnapping or elimination of those who proved to be implacable enemies. I planned to emphasize these same techniques as part of the training program for the new pacification cadre teams.

The Vung Tau Training Center was soon expanded to accommodate about 5,000 trainees. It consisted of three camps set about six kilometers from each other, each camp controlled by an officer who reported to Captain Le Xuan Mai. He was an ARVN Signal Corps officer who had been working with CIA since the late 1950s.[4] Some sixty civilians under contract handled meal preparation, supplies, camp sanitation, and other logistical details.

I was impressed at first by the austere, businesslike atmosphere at the center. All cadres and trainees wore black pajamas and went about their routines efficiently. But the group of political instructors, who provided training materials and indoctrinated the trainees, interested me most. They were introduced as the center's "think-tankers," yet few of them had ever experienced the difficult life of the peasants who were literally in the middle, suffering from abuses by both sides: the South and the Viet Cong. Several of the instructors were just draft dodgers and most were city boys, hired because they had college educations or agreed with Captain Mai's political philosophy. I spent some time listening to their lectures and reading their training documents. After a few weeks of this, I was shocked at my findings: the CIA's much-vaunted training center was training cadres to be both anti-Communist and antigovernment at the same time.

Trainees were indoctrinated to reject the Viet Cong, true, but their training material and lessons also emphasized antigovernment doctrine. It turned out that Captain Mai was a member of the southern branch of one of the original parties dedicated to a free and independent Vietnam. The intensely nationalistic and anti-Ky political sect's aims were to create a third force in the country to fight some of the ills prevalent at the time in Vietnam: corruption at most levels of government, over-dependence on American aid, and lack of concern for the common people at the top in Saigon. Under Captain Mai, "a Southern branch of the Dai Viet (one of the original nationalist parties in Vietnam) had secretly used the RD Center to organize its own partisan cadres, complete with three-man cells and clandestine midnight training."[5] They were being motivated to reject both the Viet Cong and current government policies, and to work for a better Vietnam.

I couldn't help but sympathize with many of the party's teachings; they paralleled my own feelings in many ways.[6] "As Chau found out more about this [Dai Viet] party," Pond writes, "he faced a dilemma. He heartily approved of the third-force aims of the party, which in its intense nationalism was anti-foreign, anti-American, anti-corruption and anti-Ky. Chau despised Ky, the flamboyant Air Force vice marshal who had taken over as Prime Minister in 1965 and whose temperament was so different from Chau's own."

I was uncertain about the real position of the CIA in regard to the covert activity. Were CIA officials truly unaware of the way their program was being used? Or were they secretly backing Mai and his followers, despite the official U.S. policy of support for Prime Minister Ky's government? As Pond put it, "On the American side, the backing or ignorance of the CIA in the clandestine Dai Viet activity was never clear. Either way, such activity was certainly contrary to the declared U.S. policy at that time. He [Chau] decided the U.S. could not tolerate the undercover activity at the Training Center, whether in defiance of or egged on by CIA officials."

I'm still not sure of the answer. Either situation was possible. The former American representative to the center had been there only in the daytime. Other CIA employees at the camp spoke no Vietnamese, and neither Jorgenson nor anyone else from U.S. agencies had ever bothered to monitor classes or have training materials translated. Although ostensibly a Vietnamese facility, all of the signage was in English.

As much as I disapproved of some of the current government's policies and sympathized with the Dai Viet, I felt it was not right for either Ky or the CIA to use American and Vietnamese resources to favor one political party over another. I refused to be involved in such manipulations. On the other hand, perhaps the CIA was totally ignorant of what was going on, and I owed a certain amount of loyalty both to that organization and the Saigon government. I did not feel I could ignore what was going on at the Center, and must either do something about it or resign my position. Pond wrote, "Chau had been hired by the Saigon government, however, and felt he could not condone such blatantly anti-government activity. Either he would have to say nothing and resign, or else he would have to blow the thing wide open. After much soul-searching, he finally chose the latter course, stirring up as he did so bitter enmity toward himself among many of the Vietnamese operatives of the Dai Viet."

I first brought up the matter with Tom Donahue, who didn't seem very concerned. In fact, he supported Captain Mai. This made me wonder even more about the CIA's involvement; perhaps Mai had been working with them. I then went to John Paul Vann and told him what I had learned. He grew very upset and excited. He went straight to the office of Ambassador William Porter (as revealed years later in Neil Sheehan's *A Bright Shining Lie*) and talked to Richard Holbrooke, Porter's assistant who "found Vann's story too fantastic to credit." He agreed to investigate, however. Vann came back and advised me to sit tight and wait for developments.

Holbrooke and Frank Wisner II, another Porter assistant, checked out my story. (I noticed translators from Saigon working in the center, checking the training materials.) When they learned it was indeed true, they arranged an appointment for Vann with Porter. Meanwhile, Daniel Ellsberg, working with Lansdale's team, which had been acting as liaison between the embassy and Thang's ministry, also looked into the matter. The reports from Vann and Ellsberg impressed Ambassador Porter, but Jorgensen would not accept the loss of face that would be involved in admitting that he had been deceived. He had enough clout as chief of the Saigon CIA Station to get his way.[7] It took from March to June of 1966 before Major Mai was transferred.

I finally came to the conclusion that the training center curriculum had to be changed drastically to create an ambience and environment needed to install the necessary nationalistic identity and patriotic spirit in the cadres. I felt that a new framework was required to motivate the trainees to work toward eradication of all enemy psychological and guerrilla warfare tactics, as well as to stamp out local government corruption and abuse of power. On my recommendation, General Thang appointed Lieutenant Colonel Le Van Thinh to replace Captain Mai. While the changeover was being processed I continued to work in Saigon.

A few days later, on a Sunday, I was notified that the 3,000 trainees at Vung Tau had revolted and were holding Colonel Thinh as a hostage until Captain Mai was reinstalled as camp commander. I flew to Vung Tau and made a quick tour of the camps, talking to some of the trainees who had refused to join the revolt. The situation was serious. Most of the trainees inside the camps had been issued weapons and live ammunition. (This was unusual, since only those trainees on security guard and patrol were authorized to keep their weapons after each training session.) They held Colonel Thinh under guard in one of the camps and asked him to sign a statement relinquishing his position, but he had refused.

I contacted Donahue's assistant, "Ace" Ellis, and asked for assistance. He refused to "interfere," saying that the training center had been transferred to the Vietnamese and it was up to the Vietnamese to solve the problem.[8] (That was ironic, considering the efforts Jorgenson had made to ensure that the CIA maintained control over the program.) I flew back to Saigon, reported to Thang on the situation, and suggested that he take up the matter with the CIA. I was astonished the next day when he gave me a memo over General Ky's signature authorizing me to "retake" the training center. A battalion of paratroopers and the mayor of Vung Tau, with the forces at his disposal, were placed under my command for the operation. Further, the Third Military Region, which included Vung Tau, was to provide additional support. When I landed in the Vung Tau stadium a few hours later, the paratroop battalion was already there.

I spent the night checking out the situation thoroughly, talking to people on the scene and carefully considering the intentions of Prime Minister Ky, General Thang, and the CIA in the whole affair.

I sensed that I had lost CIA support. Jorgenson had said to me at one point, "I thought you were our friend!" And I was; I proposed and planned what I did for the Pacification Cadre Program because I thought it was best for all of us, that it was the most effective way to make the project work. I was concerned with doing the job properly, not with backstabbing the CIA or helping Vann build an empire, as Jorgenson seemed to think. I had concentrated so much on the task at hand that it was like I had been wearing blinkers that blinded me to the political ramifications of what I did and said.

As for General Thang and Prime Minister Ky, they would never do anything that benefited me. They were suspicious of my long friendship with Thieu, and Ky knew I disapproved strongly of his lifestyle and his policies. General Thang also seemed to want to cut me down because the two of us differed so greatly, with him being a Catholic from the North while I was a Central Buddhist. He might also have felt uncomfortable to have a man under his command who at one time during the war had outranked him, and who was much more experienced than he was in his own field.

It seemed that I was being set up as the scapegoat in this situation. If I ordered an attack on the rebellious trainees in the center, inevitably there would be bloodshed and casualties. Ky, Thang, and the CIA could say piously that they had put the matter entirely in my hands and I was responsible for what happened. I decided I would not play into their hands and use force; my mind rebelled at the idea of firing on the trainees anyhow. They had come here to learn and work toward building a better Vietnam. Shooting at them because they were misguided would be no solution and would make it doubly difficult to conduct the pacification program effectively.

The next morning I stepped into an open Jeep with my driver, both of us un-armed, and rode to the center headquarters. The gate was firmly closed, with armed men guarding it. I identified myself (though they probably knew who I was) and asked to be admitted so I could talk to Captain Mai. The CIA men who used to be on prominent display in the office at the entrance to the main building were conspicu-ously absent. I sat waiting in the Jeep nearly thirty minutes until Lieutenant Nguyen Xuan Phac, deputy to Captain Mai, came out and led me to the office where Mai was sitting. He didn't answer my greeting, merely waved me to a seat. I quietly sat down, ignoring his provocative attitude.

I looked him straight in the eye, waiting for him to say something, but he sat there silently, evidently waiting for me to speak first. "Captain Mai," I began, "by now you must be aware that I have the authority and capability to either isolate and blockade the whole complex, or to call on the government forces available to me to bring you down. I chose not to do either because I don't want anyone to suffer injury or humiliation. Instead, I came here, alone and voluntarily, to talk with you personally.

"Considering that from the beginning until recently, the training center was un-der the direct control of the CIA, I am in no position to comment about your perfor-mance of your duties. You and the people who work with you cannot be discriminated against or considered badly because you worked for the CIA. The Agency is just another branch of the U.S. establishment. As for moral and intellectual integrity, there is no difference between Vietnamese who work with the CIA, AID, USIS, or MACV. The Vietnamese government requests help from, and works with, those or-ganizations. I have been working with all of them for years. All of us, from the top to the bottom of our government, owe our present existence to their help.

"But times have changed. The training center has been transferred to the Vietnamese government. I must change its image, and let it be known that there is a change. It must no longer be thought of as a CIA institution, staffed by Vietnamese who are subservient to the Americans who actually run it and think they are doing so to promote the Vietnamese cause and ideology. The Americans named our organization the 'Revolutionary Development Cadres.' And that's exactly what all of us want and need it to be, if we are to end this war, which otherwise will last forever. But such a revolution cannot be successful if it is tarnished by having the wrong image.

"Look at the Communists. They gave themselves to that alien Marxist-Leninist ideology, but they have been careful to present a Vietnamese character among themselves and to the Vietnamese masses. Thus, the majority of the Vietnamese—the peasantry, the poor, and the less-than-middle-class—do not think of the Viet Cong and North Vietnamese Communists as representing an alien ideology that would destroy their traditions, religions, and culture.

"Those are the people we must win back. To do that, we must compete with the other side by presenting a nationalistic Vietnamese image externally, stemming from a nationalistic motivation inside our program. We cannot do that if we are perceived simply as hired hands of the Americans, doing their bidding in a program they think is best for us. We must appear to the populace to be dedicated Vietnamese working in their best interests and for the betterment of our country. We must inspire the cadres we will recruit and train with that attitude.

"The CIA image doesn't bother you, me, or others who know the Americans and have worked with them. We know they have no colonial aspirations and would like nothing better than to see a strong, free, independent, and non-Communist Vietnam. The people we must win over, the targets for our pacification program, don't know that, however. They are suspicious of Americans, as they tend to be of all foreigners, and of any Vietnamese who work closely with or for the U.S. Therefore, I say again, we must shed the image of being CIA hirelings.

"You are being replaced not because you do not fit the purpose of the program but because you do not fit the new image. You have been too closely associated with the CIA in the minds of too many people. I will leave you to think about this and to decide what you must do for the good of your country. Now may I depart?"

Before he showed me out, Mai explained that the whole thing was the result of a misunderstanding and the emotional reaction by the trainees to his leaving the center. He said he would talk to them later. The next day Colonel Thinh was released, and the training center returned to normal. As for Mai, he received a surprising promotion to major and was reassigned to the Vietnamese Army.

So the tense situation was defused without bloodshed, much to my relief. I was pleased that I could go back to Saigon and report to General Thang that the crisis had been resolved satisfactorily, without any need to use the military and police put at my disposal. I wondered if the result was as satisfactory for General Thang and Prime Minister Ky, who might have been happier if I had mishandled things; then they would have an excuse to replace me with someone of their own choice. I decided not to discuss the situation with my CIA counterpart for fear of embarrassing him, but it was certain that friction was increasing in that quarter, too. I needed to distance myself from the daily operation of the Vung Tau training center. Fortunately, just at this time Major Nguyen Be, who had been running a complete pacification operation in Binh Dinh province, was available for reassignment, and with my approval he was appointed as the new training center commander.[9]

Knowing that the training center was now under responsible command, I was able to turn my attention to other aspects of the national program. I conducted field inspections of the program in several provinces. I was concerned that pacification teams on returning to their home provinces were being employed more as an occupation presence in the countryside, displacing Viet Cong simply by taking up space, than conducting the political aspects of what they were being taught.

In the First Military Region, specifically in the northern three provinces, there was an additional and serious complication. During March and April 1966, a simmering dispute between the central government and the First Military Region commander, General Nguyen Chanh Thi,[10] boiled over. General Thi had begun to appoint some civilians as province chiefs. He had good relations with Buddhist leaders. Removing him from command and placing him under home detention provoked outbreaks of protest led by Buddhists and other local political leaders. Prime Minister Ky and General Thieu were circumstantially forced to pledge elections for a constituent assembly that would draw up a new constitution. Even after the "struggle" movement was suppressed in Danang, Hué, and Quang Tri, the Armed Forces Council was not able to withdraw the pledge for elections, significantly because the emergence of an elected government was finally supported by American policy.

Frustrated by my disagreement with the manner of applying our pacification teams, I began to think that my ideas and contribution might best be advanced through election to the proposed constituent assembly. I submitted a request for retirement so that I could stand for election, but my request was denied. And so, still frustrated, I assumed a reduced role as inspector for pacification in my old home area, the First Military Region.

The Constituent Assembly of 117 members was elected in September 1966. Even as I undertook field inspections that winter, I resolved to follow the deliberations closely so that I could understand and explain to others the constitutional form of government that the assembly would propose.

20: OBSERVATIONS ON THE WAR AND PACIFICATION (1967)

My responsibility for inspecting pacification in I Corps required frequent travel to Central Vietnam. Most of Saigon would still be sleeping as I headed to the airport. The exception was along the three kilometers of Cong Ly Boulevard that linked the center of the capital to the huge MACV complex and Vietnamese military headquarters—both adjacent to Tan Son Nhut airport—and the small Air America terminal. Hundreds of staff officers, logistical personnel, government officials, and civilian advisors boarded aircraft at Tan Son Nhut every day, because that had become the primary means of transportation, even to destinations as close as a one-hour drive. Planes and helicopters were not only faster than vehicles, but also safer. Although surrounding areas were shown as "pacified" or "controlled areas" on maps, this was deceptive.

It was not large enemy forces that usually caused problems for road movement. The task of harassing and blocking traffic by setting mines, sniping, and conducting small-scale ambushes was allocated to local fighters who lived among or very close to the peasants. Indeed, they were usually indistinguishable from them because they were peasants themselves. People who were friendly toward the government, and who lived in and around villages and hamlets, were reluctant to interfere with the local Viet Cong or even report their activities for fear of assassination or reprisals. Thus, overland travel was always risky for individuals and small groups.

Besides, airplanes and helicopters were now plentiful. In 1963, before the Vietnamese generals seized power, the United States used obsolescent helicopters, like the H-21, assigned primarily to shuttle Vietnamese troops into battle. In general, they were slow, unreliable, and especially (as was learned at Ap Bac) vulnerable to ground fire. Now more than 2,000 newer models, particularly the UH-1D, were available for liaison as well as assault and support missions.

In 1966 alone, U.S. Air Force planes based within South Vietnam, combined with others from aircraft carriers off shore, flew more than 128,000 sorties, delivering some 128,000 tons of bombs. This was an enormous increase from the 55,000 sorties and 33,000 tons of ordnance expended on targets during 1965. The intensification of aerial onslaught certainly helped keep the Communist forces at bay, at least for the short term, but the war was far from a turning point.

Despite having most of its supply depots, strategic installations, and primary lines of communication heavily damaged or destroyed, North Vietnam refused to signal that it would negotiate on American terms. Ho Chi Minh and General Vo

Nguyen Giap continued to send more units and replacements to the South, increasing the scope of operations against Vietnamese, American, and other Allied troops. The concept of bombing our foe to the point of tractability seemed remote and unrealistic.

In fact, reliance on a war from the air was counterproductive in some respects.

First, the relative primitiveness of the North Vietnam military and industrial components meant that it was far less vulnerable to strategic bombing than the Axis powers had been during World War II. The Vietnamese Communists relied much less on vehicles and railroads to move troops and supplies. The famed Ho Chi Minh Trail was not yet a sophisticated system of hard surface roads, or gleaming parallel rails, that could be destroyed by rolling air strikes. Supplies moved along a web of paths within which the line of advance could be shifted. Bicycles, not trucks, and with men and even women as the motive power, were the rule. As a result, Americans deployed costly aircraft and precious highly trained air crews to attack relatively minor targets. No huge military bases, airfields, supply dumps, or irreplaceable industrial complexes presented lucrative targets. The rally cry set by Ho Chi Minh was *"Khong co gi quy hon tu do, doc lap"* (Nothing is more precious than freedom and independence). In other words, anything else lost would be replaceable. It began to seem that the Vietnamese in the end would be capable of paying any price, bearing any burden.

Second, certain traits of World War II aerial warfare were not exercised, to the credit of the United States. Carpet bombing by incendiaries or other munitions, as was applied to German and Japanese cities, was not adopted by the U.S. government during the Vietnam War. When significant damage occurred in urban areas, it was generally due to proximity of the area to a legitimate target, like a bridge or antiaircraft site. Furthermore, the Red River dike system (something like the Mississippi River dike system) was specifically ruled out of bounds as a target throughout the war. When there was inadvertent urban or dike damage, the government in the North immediately took every opportunity to charge our side with committing a war crime.

Third, although the damage done by our air raids was not crippling for the Northern war effort, it was devastating for many Vietnamese families in the South as well as in the North. Having their hamlets wiped out and family members killed by air strikes, often as a result of faulty intelligence, inclined some South Vietnamese toward the enemy.

One could examine the geography of our war while flying from Saigon to Danang. A few kilometers from Bien Hoa, the huge U.S. military complex at Long Binh came into view. Construction of this facility transformed the landscape, vastly expanding the small Tan Mai base originally built by the French. After Americans took over, many amenities were added: BOQ (Bachelor Officer Quarters), a shimmering swimming pool, and tennis courts. Tall trees shaded an area where senior officers lived in air-conditioned comfort. But in spite of the appearance as a resort-like oasis in the midst of war, danger lurked. The complex was first raided by the Viet Cong in 1959, and always represented a potential target.[1] The complex was ringed by fences and guard posts that belied an otherwise peaceful rear-area appearance.

Flying over the narrow coastal strip between the Highlands and the sea, we could observe striking contrasts created by the war. Cities, large towns, and highways offered an attractive, animated image of traditional homes and official buildings blended with new construction. But from our altitude one could easily see hideous bomb craters and defoliated tracts of land. In some areas, B-52s had obviously paid more than one visit. Bombs pockmarked several square kilometers, and there were overlapping craters.

I knew this area well from those years when I fought with the Viet Minh. I thought of that zone from the resort city of Dalat through Phan Rang, and even all the way to Danang, as my personal homeland. I viewed terrible changes to the landscape. The French had not had the firepower capability to alter the very fields and mountains as did the Americans. France's air force, ground, and naval artillery were primitive by new American standards. Artillery and aerial bombardment had chewed chunks from mountains and shredded the greenery of forest and jungle. More disturbing were the large patches where trees and shrubs had been stripped of their foliage by chemical defoliants such as Agent Orange.

But the enemy today was also much stronger than the Viet Minh had been. By the spring of 1967, enemy order of battle was estimated to be 280,000, including North Vietnam and NLF regular units, regional forces, and guerrillas. Arrayed against them were about 400,000 Americans and more than 750,000 Vietnamese and other allied troops. The Viet Cong had no navy or air force, although both were being developed in the North, and air defenses were rapidly improving. Mechanized transport, tanks, artillery, and the overall firepower of the North Vietnam Army and the Viet Cong combined were inferior, but improving; and the combined combat capabilities of both sides intensified the war and impact on the countryside and its people.

The scars of war were not the only observable changes. Picturesque sandy beaches and rural fields had been transformed into huge port facilities and airfields, all connected by improved highways more extensive than previously seen in our country. The American presence not only applied destructive power but also produced remarkable feats of construction up and down the coast. Cam Ranh Bay, long recognized as one of the world's finest natural harbors, was previously underpopulated and hardly used. No more. It was becoming the largest military seaport in

Southeast Asia, with ten unloading berths for deep-draft vessels. Two runways capable of handling the largest aircraft ran across the Cam Ranh peninsula. The Nha Trang, Qui Nhon, and Danang facilities were expanded as major air, naval, and logistical bases. Even more spectacular was the construction of totally new major airfields at Tuy Hoa and Phu Cat.

Whenever I returned to Danang it was not as stranger, having been mayor there during the first Buddhist crisis, both before and after President Diem's assassination. But now American soldiers and marines, sometimes in combat dress and gear, strolled on the streets. American merchandise was on every street, sometimes at a lower price than within the PX. I learned many of the items were "thrown away" as trash by PX employees collaborating with American black marketers. Vietnamese accomplices quickly collected the goods. American largesse was fostering a culture of crooks.

At night GIs crowded into bars and dance clubs, and many found companions among the bar-girls who had been innocent peasant girls not too long before. About one million refugees from areas savaged by the war had moved into the city or to adjacent refugee camps. All were competing to earn a living by providing services of some sort to U.S. troops. Many of the shrewdest, including the prettier women, were earning more than they had before, but it was a demeaning existence. Frequently they supported entire extended families from their earnings.

A cousin, Tran Van Hoa, lived here. He was a high school teacher when the August Revolution exploded in 1945. He left his wife and three children to join the Viet Minh in the jungle, returning home after less than a year and going back to being a teacher. Like other civil servants, teachers, and military who had served under the French administration, Hoa received a hefty sum—an amount equal to what his salary would have been during the period of his "absence"—when he returned. This opportunity was only for those who left the Viet Minh without having committed "criminal activities," and the policy was only applied for a year or two. My cousin used his money to purchase a small house, where he and his wife had been raising their children ever since.

During the several months that I was mayor in Danang, I observed my cousin's lifestyle, that of a typical Vietnamese teacher and devoted Buddhist. Like most other elementary school teachers, he not only gave lessons in the classroom but also taught through personal example. He was a model of frugality in his daily life, and he enjoyed harmonious relationships with family and friends. He and his family attended a Buddhist temple every Sunday and on days of special observance. In many conversations he told me that he respected the men of North Vietnam for their combat heroism, willingness to make material and physical sacrifice, and contribution to national independence.

However, he categorically rejected communism.

With respect to South Vietnam, he loved the professed ideals of social liberty and political democracy. In practice, though, he had seen President Diem using a democratic facade to build an authoritarian regime administered by his family and cronies. After the coup of 1963, my cousin came to understand that the Americans, and the Vietnamese generals whom they supported, were insensitive to the needs of Southern and Central Vietnamese. This lack of sensitivity and consideration provoked bitterness throughout South Vietnam.

"They are arrogant and debase our culture and traditions. Corruption flourishes, and so all their talk about freedom and democracy is just that, *talk*," Hoa would say indignantly. "Not even the French and their Vietnamese subordinates behaved so badly, and so openly, toward us. The actions of the Americans and their Vietnamese generals provide justification for the NLF's and North Vietnam's core propaganda theme: that they are fighting to save the South from American neo-colonialists and their Vietnamese puppets."

His modest salary and some extra income that his wife earned, doing tailoring and seamstress work, enabled them to maintain a decent life until the massive influx of Americans came to Danang. The family's living standard plummeted. The buying power of his civil service salary dropped abruptly due to the surge of money and commodities that accompanied the mushrooming U.S. presence. I spent a day with him, and he showed me around the city.

"The population has nearly tripled since you were mayor," he explained, "with refugees streaming in from destroyed and abandoned hamlets even thirty or forty kilometers from here. Some of them came from hamlets that were supposedly 'pacified' and protected by U.S. Marines," he said scornfully. "They seek better security than they could obtain even in such pacified areas—where Viet Cong, and sometimes even our local officials and 'friendly' troops often make life difficult for them. It seems that the claims of 'pacification and protection' are better sounding than in actual performance. Virtually the entire city is now economically dependent on the Americans," he told me with some bitterness, explaining that newcomers from the insecure countryside earned their living from the new American service economy. "They are taxi and pedicab drivers, waiters in restaurants and bars, clerks in stores catering to foreigners. Some are sidewalk vendors, usually peddling black-market goods. Hundreds of others are employed on American bases and other installations."

Despite the animated, bustling environment of the overpopulated but generally prosperous city in wartime, I learned from my cousin and others about the simmering animosity that a considerable portion of Vietnamese civilians, and even military, felt toward the Saigon government and the United States. The hostility dated most recently to the spring of 1966 when the Buddhist majority in Central Vietnam, and even sympathizers in Saigon, conducted demonstrations against the generals holding power in Saigon. The great majority of people, wanted the American-supported generals, especially Nguyen Cao Ky and even my friend Nguyen Van Thieu, to prepare for general elections and establishment of civilian authority. Two army divisions, the First and the Second, as well as provincial forces in three northern provinces, joined the protest movement. The mayor of Danang openly supported those opposed to Saigon. The USIS Office and U.S. Consulate in Hué were seriously damaged.

The situation culminated when Prime Minister Ky, in mid-May, moved five battalions of Vietnamese Marines (utilizing U.S. air transport) to Danang and crushed the protest movement in that critical city. About 100 protestors, soldiers, and civilians were killed, and another 100 wounded. This was in significant contrast to the first Buddhist crisis that occurred under President Diem. The scope of the Buddhist-led popular demonstration against the generals in 1963 far exceeded that which was instrumental in bringing about the American-supported coup against President Diem later that year.

Colonel Nguyen Ngoc Loan, military academy classmate of the prime minister, took charge of both the civilian police and military security forces; the hard core of protest leadership was soon arrested and jailed without the formality of charges. An unknown, but substantial number, of "suspects" were also detained. The mayor of Danang and a dozen or so generals, colonels, and other officers involved in the protest movement were disciplined: some placed on trial and others summarily dismissed from service. General Nguyen Chanh Thi, whose dismissal had been the spark initiating the movement, was exiled to the United States.

Repressive operations terminated open revolt, but fanned smoldering animosity against the military regime and the supportive American presence to greater intensity. About thirty Buddhists burned themselves to death in protest. Most of the population in Danang, Hué, and even other towns and provinces were now so bitter that they were receptive to Viet Cong propaganda. Buddhists and other non-Catholic community leaders countrywide petitioned for the government to step down. Venerable Thich Tri Quang, another Buddhist leader who was instrumental in the 1963 protests against the Diem administration, sent letters to U.S. President Lyndon Johnson outlining the problem and requesting intervention. All was in vain. The Buddhist leadership had not accurately assessed the situation. Quite simply, the United States needed to keep the corrupt, ineffective generals in power in Saigon.

Most politically and militarily knowledgeable Vietnamese were by now convinced that the United States had supported the coup against President Diem because Americans could not control him, and could not rely on him to fight the insurgency as the United States felt it should be fought. At that time the Americans had economic leverage and advisors, but no maneuver units of their own in the field. Now there were almost 400,000 American troops in Vietnam, and the U.S. leadership needed cooperation of the Vietnamese generals while Americans conducted the war in their own way, the American way. There was no realistic possibility that President Johnson and his advisors would condone forcing Prime Minister Ky and Chief of State Thieu from office to have them replaced by a civilian government that might prove as balky as President Diem's. The huge military and economic commitment made by the Americans was inducement for avoiding risk associated with change.

Besides, some Americans believed that Ky and Thieu were handling matters satisfactorily, for the most part. In my opinion, Americans discounted the significance of this second Buddhist uprising, entirely missing its importance. The attitude appeared to be that the brutal manner in which Buddhists were suppressed just compensated for the way Catholics had been treated after the fall of the Diem government. Buddhists and other non-Catholics seemed to have the upper hand then, and the Catholic minority had complained long and loud to foreign friends. The case that they made was persuasive for some Americans for a couple of reasons.

First, although in the overall minority, Catholics made up a large percentage of the relatively wealthy and well-educated upper class, thanks to the decades of favor enjoyed during the French colonial period. As a result, they were more closely involved, and better able to communicate, with Americans.

Second, the United States in general regarded Catholic Vietnamese as the core anti-Communists in Vietnam. The Catholic community had been the backbone behind anti-Communist Vietnamese leaders from the beginning. This supposition was shared by hard-line personalities at home in the United States and the average American in Vietnam who tended to see the Catholics as lonely representatives of Western civilization. So many Americans would therefore regard struggle against a Catholic-supported government as Communist-inspired. They would be immediately suspicious of Vietnamese who initiated or took part in such movements.

What American officials, civilian and military alike, completely failed to realize was that ignoring the basis for the protests, while supporting suppression, did more harm to the long-term war effort than the actual protests. Whether I realized this at the time, it was during this period that I began to feel the war could not be won as long as it was conducted so incongruently with Vietnamese realities. I was certainly aware we could not win with the current Saigon regime, but I was hopeful that leadership could be changed and thus produce enlightened policy.

Continued discussion with my cousin while a guest in his home was illuminating. He was uncomplaining about his own state in life. He and his wife had raised four children, one of them a Vietnamese marine lieutenant who was one of those ordered to put down the citizens' uprising. Now my cousin was troubled, bitter, even verging on rebellious: "My son came to see me after his unit took part in the suppression operation. He was shaken and confused. What could I tell him? As a Buddhist, I was very upset over President Diem discriminating against Buddhists; but also because I am a Buddhist, I was just as disturbed over Diem's murder. He deserved to be overthrown, but not murdered inhumanely by generals acting on, as everybody knows, American instruction. Such treatment is contrary to the best of Vietnamese culture and tradition. I don't think that he should have been murdered, and I blame the Americans as much as the Vietnamese generals. I feel ashamed of the Buddhist involvement in bringing about such a barbaric end."

It was obvious that the way events had evolved since the bloody 1963 coup, and the present overwhelming presence of Americans in his city, greatly disturbed him. "I have lived in this city for almost all of my fifty years. Thirty years of my life was under French colonialism, which all Vietnamese agree was pretty bad. Yet I have never seen anything, or imagined anything, so devastating to our country, people, and culture as I have witnessed since American troops landed on our shores a few short years ago."

I received a very different assessment of the situation from a Catholic friend named Le Van An, a deeply religious man closely connected to the archdiocese of Danang. He served for a long time as personal secretary to the mayor of Danang who preceded me. He had probably expected me to replace him when I took over office, knowing that I was Buddhist. However, I had seen that An was well-informed and competent, and so I retained him in the same position. We became close friends. During my first mayoral term in Danang he was my trusted confidant. Now, almost three years later, he was still a civil servant, although in a different capacity, and he was well informed concerning city affairs.

Normally a quiet man, An was excited and emotional when we met again after such a long time. After a warm greeting, his words spilled forth as he responded to my query about how he viewed the current situation. "Sir, I must tell you that like other members of the Catholic community, I was deeply disturbed and hurt when President Diem was murdered. Since then we have been living in humiliation, even fear, because of the way that we are discriminated against by the government and Buddhists."

"I can't argue with you, An," I replied, "because I know there is some truth in what you say."

"I know that you are a Buddhist," he answered, "but I also know you to be a fair man. And you are as devoted in your way to your faith as I am to mine. I must tell you, however, that we Catholics were not sorry to see the Buddhist movement 'nerve center' uprooted here and in Hué."

"Your opinion is understandable," I said, "although I am concerned about the excessive force employed."

"Yes, well, I suspect that there would have been bloodshed no matter what happened. The friction between Buddhists and Catholics has been increasing all the time. I am afraid that the tension and ill feeling would have led to more bloody communal battles like the one in late 1964 at Thanh Bo near the coast."

"How did that happen, An?"

"We Catholics believe that the Buddhists started the trouble with at least the tacit consent, if not outright urging, of the local military commander. They seemed sure of protection from his forces."

"Has that kind of situation persisted?"

"Certainly the discrimination continues, despite the arrival of the American troops in Danang. We had hoped that arrival of foreigners would ease our situation, but circumstances have not changed greatly. Recent events have made us more optimistic, and with Americans more involved in combat, we are hopeful that the war will be won."

"How is daily life for you and your family?"

"My wife has a small business selling Vietnamese handicrafts to Americans. Sometimes she takes items in trade from the Americans and then resells to Vietnamese. We're doing well materially, and are able to afford some things that we never could have before. But we would willingly trade all those benefits for peace and relief from the discrimination that we have suffered these past years."

I looked at the situation in Quang Tri as a special case because it was a major battlefield zone and had a large number of relocated persons due to the impact of war on hamlets. This was one of the provinces where pacification was most challenged. Dong Ha was the frontline logistics and air base that provided support for troops guarding against infiltration and attack by the North Vietnamese across the Demilitarized Zone (DMZ) and the Laotian border. It was just thirty to fifty kilometers from those lines.

The Laotian border ran north to south, roughly parallel to the coast, along the western edge of South Vietnamese territory. Mountains and hills covered with dense vegetation and tall trees concealed the border and overlooked the narrow, open strip of plains and rice paddies between the hill country and the coast. By early 1957, after President Diem, backed by the United States, refused to hold elections for unification, the North Vietnamese began to open the route south that became the famous Ho Chi Minh Trail. It ran roughly parallel to the Laotian border but actually within the almost uninhabited jungles and mountains of Laos itself. Since that time, the trail had been developed into the Communists' main line of communication between the North and South. Its location made things doubly difficult for our side. If South Vietnamese and U.S. troops respected the border of Laos, it was impossible to interdict movement along the trail. At the same time, the terrain and natural cover hid Communist troop and supply units using the route. These factors led to the "Secret War" in which troops, especially U.S. Special Forces and the local units they trained and led, fought on the ground and U.S. warplanes dropped 200 million tons of bombs along the Ho Chi Minh Trail or in areas held by the Pathet Lao.[2]

The DMZ, set up by the 1954 Geneva Peace Agreement as a neutral area between the opposing forces, ran along the seventeenth parallel and the Ben Hai River from the Laotian border on the west to the South China Sea at its eastern point. As a result of that provisional line, Quang Tri province, where Dong Ha was located, lost approximately one-third of its territory located in and north of the zone. The rest of the province consisted mostly of low, bare hills and rice paddies in the narrow coastal plain.

The river that ran from Dong Ha to the coast was also kept open for small boats, providing another supply and communications route to that strategic base. Further west, almost on the Lao border, a U.S. Special Forces camp had long operated about ten kilometers west of an expanding marine base at Khe Sanh. So, at this point in spring 1967, U.S. forces were well along with development of western Quang Tri into a fortress zone intended to fend off attacks by enemy units operating from Laos, while expediting their own special operations against movement along the Ho Chi Minh Trail.

The thousands of Vietnamese evacuated from ruined villages near the DMZ were relocated in "new life hamlets" where they were protected by South Vietnamese Territorial and paramilitary Self-Defense units, which were, in turn, backed up by the U.S. Marines and Special Forces. The Vietnamese First Division was also nearby. I was in this area with the district chief to assess performance of pacification cadre teams. I knew that many of them had gone through the Vung Tau Training Center while I was still director. I wondered if they had applied their training to good use. I also wanted to see what was being done in terms of nonmilitary help for local peasants. I mentioned this to the district chief.

In addition to the military-oriented construction and road building, numerous "Rural Development" projects had been completed or were under way, he explained proudly. "Oh, many wondrous things indeed," he told me. "You must see the new health stations [clinics], schools, and village offices that have been provided." He told me that small bridges and side roads were being built, over and above work on the main highways. "And there are new thatched homes for the villagers, with protective fences to help keep them safe," he added.

I found that much indeed had been done to improve the lot of the people who had been relocated. Rice and other foods had been provided. In some respects the farmers and their families, who traditionally had lived off the land and crops or livestock they raised themselves, had never had it so good. They were introduced to food and commodities they and their ancestors had never known. Everything from candy and new kinds of soaps to Coca-Cola, beer, and even *Playboy* magazines were now familiar to the rural Vietnamese and to the hundreds of primitive Montagnards who had been evacuated from the jungles of Laos and resettled in this area. *But is this really progress?* I asked myself wryly.

Talking with people, I realized that most of the evacuees felt resettlement was a mixed blessing. They missed their ancestral homes and the traditional life they had enjoyed, but they were getting more help, from the Americans and the Saigon government, than ever before. Probably most important, they enjoyed more safety and security than most had known for some years. "The war seems to stop at the perimeter of the military defenses," the district chief told me in his briefing. "Since the American troops arrived and began operations in and around the plateau, our Vietnamese units have encountered little enemy activity, and there have been few casualties, military or civilian." He explained further that the campaign to uncover suspected Communist infiltrators and arrest or "eliminate" them was still being waged.

I held a series of talks with individual cadres to probe deeper into implementation of the pacification program. I wanted to hear about their personal experiences and to get suggestions.

They all agreed that they could not say much that contradicted official reports, except that little of what they had learned at the training center was put to use. I was expecting this, but it still disturbed me. I learned that the technique of collecting information from village residents relative to the conduct of government officials and troops was being ignored.

"When we tried to do such things, the district chief told us not to," one cadre told me dejectedly.

"What methods are being used to detect Viet Cong suspects and infiltrators?" I asked, fearing that I knew the answer all too well.

"Nothing has changed!" he burst out. "It is the same now as before! The police and military continue with heavy hands. Village officials sometimes use their positions to point suspicion at their personal enemies, regardless of whether they are Viet Cong or Communist sympathizers. Many innocent people have suffered as a result, and that makes it harder for us to convince others that our efforts are worthwhile."

I walked through a group of hamlets near the U.S. Marines' camp. Some of the hamlets had been there for years; others were built to house evacuees. I tried to match what I had been told with what I could see. Layout of the new hamlets was standardized. Each had an office, which served as pacification headquarters and was well equipped with maps and charts of its local area. Location of each house was clearly marked and the names of its occupants listed. Residents were organized into categories according to their age, sex, type of work, and religious affiliation. Each hamlet was run by an elected committee, under the strict direction of the district chief, a nonelected official who was always a military officer and received his orders from another nonelected official, the province chief.

Pacification cadres performed a variety of tasks: providing basic health services, teaching the rudiments of literacy, planting fruit trees, digging wells, raising pigs and chickens, and so on. Moreover, they trained local villagers to take over those jobs eventually. Most villagers looked healthy and well cared for, thanks to combined Vietnamese and American efforts. The local people rarely ventured far from their settlements, so they seldom encountered the enemy physically. The Communist presence was pervasive, however. Enemy propaganda leaflets were common. Grenades and mines brought down from the North turned up regularly even in the heart of the pacified area.

I talked to a Viet Cong prisoner captured just a few days earlier and learned he was a member of an armed propaganda team that was operating in the district. He was caught while trying to contact a relative who lived in one of the resettlement hamlets. The relative was also arrested, although there was no evidence that he supported the Viet Cong, or was even aware that his relative was in the area. No matter; he was subject to the "no-law" laws, and might be tortured, imprisoned, or even executed.

Ordinarily my father rarely talked about politics. For years he immersed himself in his own spiritual world, devoting himself to prayer, meditation, and teaching. He all but ignored the turbulence of war that surrounded him. But on one visit almost immediately after we exchanged proper greetings and I had paid my respects to Lord Buddha and our ancestors, my father launched into a political discussion, beginning with a surprising revelation.

"You know that I had little respect for Diem and his family, Chau. But I feel a sense of guilt for his murder. I blame it on the Buddhist leaders," he told me. "And as a Buddhist myself I must share the blame for their act, which was contrary to the teachings of our religion."

"Do you really feel that such an attitude is justified?" I asked him, thinking that he was being unfair to himself in taking on a personal share of guilt for an action over which he had no control.

"Yes, I do, and as a result I have separated myself from the Buddhist Church and refuse to meet with or recognize those leaders I regard as responsible for Diem's death."

I was shocked, because I knew how much Father's religion meant to him, and I knew he was wrong about Buddhist involvement in Diem's murder. I realized I would have to convince him of that to repair his unnecessary estrangement from Buddhism.

Next he asked me a series of questions. "Who are these generals who are in charge now in Saigon, and where did they come from? What are their backgrounds?"

Because he had remained aloof from the political machinations in our country for so long, he knew virtually nothing about the men who were now our "leaders." And from their actions, he found them so lacking morally and spiritually that his rigid standards would not allow him to consider them true leaders in the traditional sense. According to his lights they were opportunistic upstarts who had climbed into power on the back of a murdered man, and they maintained their rule at the cost of the lives of many more dead among their countrymen.

"Why have the Americans, who sided with the Buddhists in bringing down Diem's oppressive regime, become even more tyrannical than Diem ever was?" (This was my father's assessment of the current situation, and painful as it would have been to Americans, it was also the view of most Vietnamese in Central Vietnam at that time.) "Why did they [the Americans] direct the generals to use extreme force against civilians and military personnel?" he asked next. "I understand that hundreds of the dissidents were killed."

Suddenly Father looked at me intensely, with an expression of mingled sorrow and great concern. "Son, I am worried for you. I know you are different from those callous opportunists who have somehow become generals and our rulers in Saigon. You left the other side because you felt it was the right thing for you to do, and surely you will not rejoin the Communists. I am at a loss as what to recommend to you, but I want you to weigh your situation carefully; consider the difference between sharing privileges with those generals and complying with your conscience. Is it possible for you to seek a way out of this distressing situation, to avoid collaboration with these callous people who have so little regard for their fellow countrymen?"

His sadness and distress were obvious; I let him compose himself for a few minutes before I asked his permission to explain the situation to him as I understood it. He said he would listen.

"I am certain that the United States has no plans to replace the French and conquer Vietnam. The Americans' desire is to preserve South Vietnam as a non-Communist state, admittedly for their own self-interest. But we Vietnamese will also benefit if we can preserve our people from Communist control, which would destroy our most treasured traditions and culture.

"Most Americans are well-meaning; their problem more often is not understanding the realities in our country. Nor do they have a great deal of patience; as a rule, they want quick and clear results. As they assessed things, President Diem had failed to rally the people and win the war. He was also recalcitrant about complying with their wishes, not wanting Vietnam to become totally Americanized. The U.S. decision was to take over direction of the war and commit American troops to reinforce the Vietnamese Army. Because they felt that Vietnamese civilians were unable to assert their own leadership, U.S. policymakers chose to rely on the generals. They believed military leaders would assure them the stability and commitment in government they needed to conduct the war successfully."

In regard to the 1963 coup and murder of Diem, I explained that the Americans had never consulted with any Buddhist leader in their effort to overthrow the president. "Instead, they worked it out with a group of generals who would welcome any power that could provide them with more opportunity for higher positions and material gains. They are the same opportunists who dealt with the French when Ho Chi Minh was still weak, and with Ngo Dinh Diem when Bao Dai became weak and the French departed. Then it was Diem's turn to be betrayed.

"The Buddhist leadership did not participate in the coup or the murder that followed, but it is true that the Americans seized on the Buddhist crisis in 1963 to change the direction of the war to their liking."

With respect to the Buddhist suppression almost a year earlier, I explained to my father that the United States now thought of itself as the major bulwark against Communism in Southeast Asia, even more than the French did in their time. "The Americans, and many Vietnamese who have lost their roots and adopted foreign customs and ideas for their own gain, have a difficult time understanding the Buddhist attitude toward Communism and other forms of dictatorship. The idea of winning others over by persuasion and presenting an exemplary example does not seem practical or realistic to them. As I said, they tend to be impatient and want fast results. Since they don't understand, they suspect the Buddhist leaders of temporizing, of being what they call 'soft on Communism,' if not actively pro-Communist.

"They also realized that Catholics suffered setbacks after Diem's regime was overthrown; they lost power and influence. I believe the Americans felt they had to remedy that situation, especially since they perceive Catholics as being the strongest anti-Communist bloc in Vietnam. Thus, they wanted to reestablish an order in which Catholics regained more control.

"There are some Americans who do understand the situation in our country, who have taken the time to learn about us. I hope, in time, they can get across their message to the U.S. leadership."

Father listened attentively and nodded approval for me to continue.

"After the coup, Ky managed to unseat two of his commanders in succession and won appointment as commander of the Vietnamese Air Force," I continued, as Father listened closely. "There was a very personal rivalry between Ky and General Nguyen Chanh Thi. Both were members of the military Young Turks involved in the series of coups before and after Diem's overthrow. Both attempt to project a bold, reckless air and favor bold, dramatic moves. Thi began his military career with French military; after his mother was murdered by the Viet Minh he joined the airborne. Under Diem he rose to a full colonel commanding the Vietnamese paratroops. He was known for his willingness to jump into battle with his men. He failed in a 1960 coup against Diem, escaped, and later was exiled to Cambodia," I told my father.

I went on to explain the intricacies of the various coups attempted during the early 1960s, and that Thi returned only after Diem was ousted. "Each coup resulted in a new set-off of Vietnamese officers being promoted to generals, and Thi rapidly became a three-star general commanding I Corps and First Military Region, which encompass South Vietnam's most northern provinces, the stronghold of the Buddhists, as you know, Father.

"Finally, after the last coup, the group of generals known as the Young Turks proposed that Nguyen Van Thieu be named 'chairman of the National Leadership Committee' and Nguyen Chanh Thi be appointed 'chairman of the Executive Council.' Thi rejected the offer and supported Ky for the position. Returning to his northern command, Thi courted and won the sympathy and support of both the Buddhists and Vietnamese troops in the area.

"His relations with Ky became strained, and he has run his command quite independently, defying the prime minister on several occasions.

"So the position of executive chairman came to Ky only after Thi refused it, which Ky felt diminished him. The influence and esteem Thi enjoyed in I Corps also rankled, and Thi's defiance wounded Ky further. Then last year when the Buddhists demanded that both Thieu and Ky return to the military and relinquish their government positions to civilians who would set up constitutional elections, Ky suspected Thi of supporting the Buddhists. General Thi was also very critical of corruption on the part of other general officers, and he began to appoint civilian province chiefs as one way of breaking the chain of military corruption that reached down to the countryside.

"Ky dismissed Thi. Buddhists and troops in Thi's region demonstrated against a series of generals Ky tried to appoint in Thi's place. Soon, what started as peaceful demonstrations turned into armed rebellion, with two army divisions and territorial forces joining the protests. Bloody repression followed.

"The Communists must be grateful to Ky, Lodge, and others who supported the extreme force used because, as you told me earlier, animosity toward the government and the United States now runs high among the troops and people in the region. And it will persist.

"Thus, in this whole affair, the Americans proved too naive in trusting Ky's motives, and so they were deluded and abused by him at the same time."

In conclusion, I told Father that I believed that the time of colonialism was over and that true nationalism would prevail eventually. "I am concerned, however, that the way the United States is fighting the war, and the caliber of the leaders it supports, will strengthen the enemy cause. Excessive bombing and ill-conceived 'pacification' efforts have killed and injured many people who could have been won over firmly to our side. Their friends and relatives, plus many who have been driven from their ancestral homes, become more and more receptive to Communist propaganda. The actions of the Saigon generals, more concerned with their power and prestige than with the country, generates more support for the Communists and undermines the desire and motivation or our own troops to fight," I said to Father.

"I tell you again, my son Chau, that communism or any kind of ideology alien to the traditional and religious Vietnamese culture will never last for a long time!" he insisted. "It might win in the short term but cannot prevail in the long run."

We broke off our conversation shortly and went to bed. It was the first night in some years I had spent in the family home. The next morning I told my father that the demonstrations of 1966 had succeeded to the extent of forcing the Saigon generals to accept general elections for a constituent assembly. The constituent assembly was formed in September (1966), and now a constitution would be prepared requiring elections for a National Assembly, president, and vice president.

I added that I had begun to seriously consider running for the National Assembly, and hoped to be one of the new leaders who might help bring about that rebirth and recovery. "I'm convinced that is the best way for me out of my present 'distressing situation,' as you put it so well in our conversation last night."

As we walked to the gate where my Jeep was waiting, Father informed me that my Communist brother Tran Ngoc Hien had visited him recently. "He visited many others in the area, too. As we discussed last night, there is much dissatisfaction in these parts today. I suspect Hien's presence has something to do with the Communists' efforts to take full advantage of that." He paused to reflect for a moment. "I don't feel that either you or Hien are bad or wrong because of the sides you have chosen. I know both of you want what is best for Vietnam and its people, though you disagree totally on how to achieve it. It would be wonderful if the two of you somehow could get the leaders on both sides together to combine their efforts and ideologies, to mix the best of Western democracy with a social revolution for a new and reunified Vietnam.

"If only that could happen, our country could serve as a model of peace and harmony that might inspire mankind and nations all over the world." He sighed a bit, as though realizing the monumental difficulties that stood in the way of reaching such a goal.

21: PACIFICATION OR MILITARY OCCUPATION (1967)

During all my travels I received briefings from province chiefs and other officials. I visited the new life hamlets and talked with cadre teams. The same statistics were cited and the same rosy picture painted wherever I went: increasing numbers of hamlets were being pacified, and clinics, bridges, wells, roads, and other facilities were being built. People were being registered by categories (age, type of work, religion, organizations, etc.) in the People's Self-Defense Forces in their villages. And most important, the briefings always claimed increasing numbers of "returnees" (Viet Cong deserters) and enemies killed or captured.

The numbers and statistics were translated into impressive charts, diagrams, and maps that were included in optimistic reports that went all the way up the hierarchy to Saigon, to "Pentagon East" (as the U.S. Military Command headquarters was known), and probably on to Washington. They were part of the "proof" that the war and pacification program were being waged successfully, that light finally could be seen at the end of the tunnel. Such reports, while not necessarily untrue or completely distorted, were all too familiar to me. I had been seeing similar such reports and hearing similar briefings for years, back to the days when the French were still heading the war effort. They didn't help France win, nor would they make the joint South Vietnamese–American effort a success.

So, I always did my own research to complement routine reports and statistics, focusing on what I considered the vital essence of pacification efforts. These were questions I asked: Who really were the people who lived in new life hamlets? How did they feel about the government officials, troops, and Americans with whom they had daily contact? What did the people think the government and the United States should, or should not, do for villagers like themselves?

Did people in the hamlet have relatives joining or cooperating with the Viet Cong? If so, why? And what must the government do to win back the disaffected? Equally important, I wanted information to come through, or at least to be confirmed by, sources I considered reliable.

That did not include the police and intelligence services. In the main, they were legacies of the French, with preconceived notions and prejudices left over from the French regime. They tended to turn up "information" slanted the way they felt superiors wanted it. They regarded everyone who had supported the Viet Minh cause as potentially pro-Communist, discounting the sheer nationalistic appeal the Viet Minh originally held for many Vietnamese patriots. Also, too many of them were corrupt enough to denounce innocent villagers for revenge, to protect their positions, or for personal gain.

In turn, police and intelligence operatives were regarded with suspicion by the local populace. Villagers lied to them, or hid their true feelings and activities from such operatives. This made it impossible to assess the real value of information from these sources.

I had hoped information that I regarded as essential might come from a new generation of pacification cadres motivated by human compassion and desire to build a better nation, the kind of cadres I thought I had been asked to develop in my role as national director of pacification. Inquiries I made during my numerous visits throughout the country were tremendously disheartening in that respect. Individual cadres in many cases had assimilated the spirit and intent of pacification as I had attempted to develop it, but their efforts were thwarted by officials from the village level to the highest posts in Saigon. Concepts I cherished the most—and had proved in practice—were entirely ignored, even ridiculed in some quarters. The type of pacification program I had developed in Kien Hoa and had hoped to implement nationwide never materialized.

The reason was obvious: General Thang, super-minister for pacification, never understood that the program needed a special kind of motivation and purpose to be successful. Thang, the other generals, and most province chiefs viewed the program only in concrete, material terms: how much additional American support it could garner by providing more arms, personnel, food, and commodities to shelter, feed, and clothe people displaced from war zones. Things that were important to them were how much construction (schools, clinics, roads, etc.) had been completed and how many people had been relocated. Those categories could easily be quantified and included in fancy reports prepared for the High Command, which could pass them along to the Americans as "evidence" of how well things were going.

Thang and the others like him were not intentionally dishonest, in my opinion (though there were some cynical, utterly selfish Vietnamese who cared nothing about pacification projects except as a facade to appease U.S. officials). Their concept of pacification was simple: add more weapons, more men, more commodities, and more troops in and around hamlets and villages, which then would then be "pacified."

I saw one showcase example of that sort of materialistic concept during a visit to a series of new life hamlets either built or consolidated under the pacification plan. Pacification cadres were almost nonexistent, but the hamlets were organized and the residents were taken care of very well, largely by U.S. Marines stationed in the area. The marines not only protected the hamlets but also were involved in much of the building and other projects normally carried out by cadres. The marines were generous and well behaved, and inhabitants were doing well under their care and protection. But there was no political component and no long-term benefit.

A major problem was that much of the rural population viewed the program as more American than Vietnamese. I had hoped to have the Americans, particularly the CIA, keep a lower profile, as related earlier. This was not done and, with the inflow of so much goods and equipment that was obviously American, it was not difficult to understand why the people in pacified hamlets may have felt they were living in American villages.

Considering the overall situation, for almost four years now, the war had been growing in numbers and intensity, but real success was still as elusive as ever. Neither more bombs and armament, advanced technology, nor more troops and new generals had achieved victory.

Second, the idea of pacification—winning the hearts and minds of the people—turned out to be merely a French cliché, polished up and given an American look. About 1 million peasants were now listed as being relocated in pacified new life hamlets (with a few million more estimated as having simply abandoned their rural home to live, unregistered, in the cities). Vietnamese and Americans alike trotted out the fancy statistics and reports detailing this "progress" in the war and saying optimistically that they indicated the "prospect of victory." They buttressed their arguments by citing the enemy's tremendous losses, ignoring the fact that the losses were quickly and constantly refilled by local recruits and new personnel infiltrated from the North.

Third, while the Vietnamese and U.S. experts claimed they were winning the hearts and minds of the peasants in rural areas, the insensitivity and ill-conceived policies of the men at the top, Saigon generals and American officials alike, were turning many of the people in the cities, and even some in the Vietnamese Army, against them. Our entire country was being devastated by fire, iron, and chemicals. People and soldiers continued to die for causes (freedom, justice, social and economic equity) that they heard a lot about, but had never enjoyed. Many of those who weren't killed or wounded lived in suffering and misery.

Fourth, only an elite group of opportunists profited from the war, creating prosperous (if often illegal) businesses and career opportunities out of it.

I thought about the numerous orphans, widows, and disabled people who were among the casualties of this terrible war. I asked myself what would happen to my children and the generations following them if the war dragged on, or if neither side should win under the present circumstances. I foresaw that more of the same would follow if the war continued on course: more destruction, more killing, more repression.

Should the war end in victory for the United States and South Vietnam, both

North and South Vietnam would be in terrible shape: parts of cities in ruins, the countryside devastated, and millions dead or disabled. Thousands of the allies now fighting on our side—American, Filipinos, Koreans, and others—would have to remain indefinitely, providing security from guerrillas who would never quit, and helping with reconstruction.

If the Communists won, thousands of Vietnamese in the South might be purged in a bloodbath of epic proportions. Other hundreds of thousands would be "detained" for long periods, treated as the Chinese Communists had done with the Chinese Nationalists after the 1949 Communist victory. I expected the "revolutionary brutality" policy I had witnessed back in 1945 against big and small landowners would be applied on an even larger scale.

A Communist victory would also mean that future generations would lose their Vietnamese identity. Buddha, Confucius, and Jesus Christ would be replaced by Marx, Lenin, and Ho Chi Minh. Nor would there be any guarantee that a proletarian dictatorship would be less oppressive and corrupt than the present dictatorship of Ky and Thieu.

Such thoughts chilled me.

I was unable to fall asleep that night, so I got up and sat on the floor to meditate about the outcome of the war and the consequent effect on my family, my children, and myself. I would not and could not simply quit. I renewed my decision to fight harder and harder to help improve the situation, but on a new front: in an elected National Assembly. I would work with others there to build a true democratic society to provide a viable alternative to Communist doctrine.

For many years now, the United States had repeated its message to the Vietnamese, its own people, and the world: the war against the Communists was being fought to defend democracy and freedom. After more than a decade, however, South Vietnam was still waiting to enjoy its first taste of freedom or democracy. Some elite individuals and groups attained varying degrees of freedom and opportunity because of the protection and favoritism their ties to ruling regimes earned them. They formed a privileged category apart from those less fortunate. Even the privileged few, in common with everyone else in South Vietnam, lacked the protection of genuine constitutional law and a legitimately elected government. The reason was simple: our previous constitution, National Assembly, and elections had been farcical, a cosmetic cover for those in power and the privileged classes. The great majority of the people paid dearly as a result. It was no wonder that our leaders, from Diem to the military juntas, failed to attract and motivate the people, or even their troops, in the fight against the Communists.

I made this solemn promise to myself that night: If elected to the National Assembly I would work with others to make democracy and freedom a reality for all the people, to provide good government that would be responsive to the needs of the Vietnamese people, and to enact effective, constitutional means to elect different leaders if the ones in office failed in their duties. I would join with other assembly members whose aim was to motivate the people to support a government that actually offered the freedom and justice we had been promised.

It was clear to me now that, under Diem, the Vietnamese leadership had been responsive only to Diem himself. Diem based his leadership on a Confucian concept that when men of high morality govern, their moral qualities are reflected by the actions of their government. Honestly convinced that he knew what was best for the country, Diem isolated himself from the common people and lost any rapport with them that might have attracted their support.

Moreover, the Saigon generals who had seized power from Diem were so interested in conforming to the wishes of the U.S. military and diplomatic officials, so interested in accumulating wealth, that the Americans had become our de facto leaders.

Ky and most high-ranking Vietnamese generals lacked a strong background in Vietnamese culture and traditional moral training; they had little education outside the military sphere. They fought with the French against their own countrymen during the 1940s when most Vietnamese were supporting national independence. They adopted foreign ways so thoroughly that they had little understanding of their own people, especially of the feelings that motivated those Vietnamese who despised and battled against them. Finally, they had inferiority complexes vis-à-vis their American tutors and counterparts. They were well aware that they had risen quickly from NCOs in service to the French to general officer ranks more because of fortunate circumstances than true ability or military professionalism.

There were dedicated high-ranking Vietnamese officers who preferred to maintain dignity and self-respect, rather than to fawn over the Americans. These were not the ones with whom the proconsul generals and ambassadors from the United States wanted to deal. They preferred the Vietnamese officers who might complain and argue about minor points, but in the main let the United States run things the way it saw fit. That was why the Americans supported Ky over Thieu for such a long period; Ky was more amenable to their wishes and fawned over them more than Thieu.

Henry Kissinger disclosed in his book *White House Years* that just one week before the 1973 Paris Peace Settlement was signed, "We still did not have the agreement of that doughty little man in Saigon, President Thieu. Nixon was determined to prevail. 'Brutality is nothing,' he said to me. 'You've never seen it if this son-of-a-bitch doesn't go along, believe me.'"[1] Alexander Haig delivered a scorching letter from Nixon to Thieu on January 16. Seven days later, on January 23, the agreement was officially signed by Kissinger, representing the United States, and Le Duc Tho, representing North Vietnam.

The net result of all this mismanagement, confusion, and political machination was that the war and popular discontent in the cities and villages had steadily, and predictably, escalated. To me and many others with similar grassroots knowledge, the way to win the war was simple and apparent. It must first be won at the hamlet level; that was fundamental, an absolute necessity. To do that, local government officials and soldiers operating in the area must first win the confidence and sympathy of the people in the hamlets.

Once this basic requirement of winning over the villagers was satisfied, the Viet Cong fish in the South would find precious little water in which they could swim and grow. The Communists who infiltrated from the North would be isolated from the people, bare and exposed to quick detection.

I met Americans who learned and understood this basic need: John Paul Vann, Daniel Ellsberg, Frank Scotton, Everet Bumgardner, Andre (Jean) Sauvageot, and Tony Cistaro, among others. The problem was that they did not have the highest-level support from their own government. They were regarded as the best of the field operators, as "field mechanics," but the U.S. government could not bring itself to place these men in charge, despite their superior ability. Furthermore, confounding senior officials, sometimes they even expressed lively differences of opinion among themselves.

Vann, for example, firmly believed that the Americans could lead the Vietnamese to accomplish what was necessary. Ellsberg had a similar opinion at first, but eventually did not agree; he felt that only the Vietnamese themselves could do it. But before they could succeed, they must truly understand the concept of a responsive government. Such terms as "social justice," "revolutionary development," and "winning the hearts and minds of the people" had been spouted freely by generals and politicians alike, but they were merely buzzwords. They became stale clichés without meaning because no serious, sincere, and realistic efforts were made to give them substance, to translate them into reality. The people knew that, despite the talk, their lot was no better; in fact, the quality of their life for the most part had deteriorated as the tempo of war increased (except for the elite, black marketers and other opportunists who profited from the situation).

Everet Bumgardner, Frank Scotton, Phil Werbiski, and Andre Sauvageot kept working in a variety of guises to produce special operating teams that were imbued with almost revolutionary motivational training. They appeared to consider the "big unit" war almost irrelevant if they could just generate enough local popular demand in the countryside for change to responsive government. Their vision was close to my own.

High-level leaders, Vietnamese and American, were so removed from the common people that they had no idea how to create and carry out effective programs that had a real chance of changing things. Former president Diem had relied on his Catholic and Confucianist beliefs, but his provincial governors, district chiefs, and generals did not have the same training and background, so they were never able to follow through on his ideas. Instead, they took the path of least resistance, being seduced by the material comforts and opportunities that became available to them as a result of the influx of American aid. Many, if not most, of our leaders were sincere, honest, and patriotic, but they had been educated to think of the war in French and American professional military terms: to win, throw in more soldiers, more ammunition, more bombs, and more napalm.

They failed to understand that the Communists did not have to compete on that kind of military level. Certainly they fought, usually on their own terms and choice of battleground, but they also waged a subtler, underground war in which soldiers and arms alone were of minimal value.

I realized that after twenty-three years of learning about such things by experiencing them personally, and after spending the previous three and a half years struggling to convince Vietnamese and American leaders about where the problems lay, I had failed miserably. I was now pinning my hopes on a new way to fight, hoping that an elected National Assembly would provide an effective arena in which I could battle. I requested early retirement so I could run for the National Assembly; the election was scheduled for September 1967.[2] Then I went home to prepare my plans for the future.

John Vann telephoned and asked if he could come to see me one night. We talked for an hour, then ate and continued our discussion until early in the morning. I didn't go over old ground, covering things we had covered many times in the past, but concentrated on my decision to retire and run in the coming election. We argued, because he disagreed with my feeling that I could be more useful in the eventual National Assembly than in the government or the army. He said that he would support me in any role I chose should I change my mind and remain in the government. Finally, when he realized that my decision was firm, he suggested that he would be happy if I would work for him as a consultant after I retired.[3] He was so passionately sincere in his offer that I made a pretense of taking it seriously, though it seemed somewhat comical to me. After all, I was leaving the army and government because I hoped to help create a new Vietnamese-oriented government that would be freer of American influence. How could I be interested in working for a strictly American operation? I did, however, appreciate his concern and the respect for my ideas and abilities that the offer indicated.

John and I went to Binh Duong province to observe the condition of refugees from the war zone. We landed on the red-hued earth of Phu Loi, fifteen kilometers from the provincial capital. Some 8,000 people, mostly women, children, and elderly men, had been evacuated from their villages in what was considered "enemy" territory. The villages then were destroyed to prevent them from being useful to our foes. The displaced villagers were living with the pigs, chickens, and ducks they brought with them in hundreds of nylon-roofed tents and dozens of thatched huts. The immense complex was surrounded by barbed-wire fences and divided into sectors. (Coincidentally, the refugee camp was located near the Phu Loi Detention Center for Viet Cong.)

Camp residents sweltered under the hot sun during the day and shivered from the cold at night. Some young men and women fled the camp to join the Viet Cong; many were captured and detained by American forces, then turned over to Vietnamese authorities.

Vann, as head of U.S. Civil Operations and deputy to the U.S. general commanding U.S. forces in the Third Military Region, was in charge of taking care of the refugees and "evacuees."

The work of providing shelter, food, medical care, and screening of Viet Cong suspects was done by Vietnamese agencies, assisted and supervised by American advisors.

Tents were erected, wells dug, and toilets provided. Vietnamese doctors conducted physical examinations, doling out shots and medicine. Rice was plentiful, provided by USAID (the United States Agency for International Development). Loudspeakers scattered throughout the complex blared a constant stream of Vietnamese patriotic songs, interspersed with anti-Communist, pro-government, and pro-American slogans. But the people seemed apathetic and strangely remote. Children cried because of the heat and discomfort of unfamiliar surroundings. Women were busy caring for their children or sitting quietly in corners staring apprehensively at the sky. A few old men lay here and there on flattened cardboard cartons. The shortage of young men was noticeable; the few who had been rounded up during the evacuation operation were detained.

While Vann toured the area conferring with his men, I walked around and talked with a variety of officers, pacification cadres, and camp residents. I asked the latter about the circumstances that brought them there. Most replied that they had no warning about the operation until American heliborne troops landed, followed by units of a Vietnamese battalion sent in mostly to do interpreting and police duties. Americans had interrogated Viet Cong suspects while Vietnamese questioned the rest of the populace.

None of the evacuees were happy with their situation. Although they all cautiously took care to mask their discontent for fear of reprisals, their conversation revealed many complaints. The children missed their familiar schools and familiar places to play; most were missing fathers and brothers who had fled, or had been captured and detained by American troops. (The father of one lad was killed while rushing home on his bicycle from a nearby village.) The women I talked to were bitter about having their homes burned out or destroyed by soldiers, and not knowing the whereabouts or fate of their husbands. One old man refused to answer my questions; he just stared at me silently, but his look of hatred and loathing spoke volumes.

When Vann joined me, he kept complaining, as he had since I first met him in 1962, that Americans were passive, and the Vietnamese were insensitive to the sufferings of the Vietnamese peasants. They were more interested in pouring in bombs and ammunition than they were in protecting the people.

The area from which these people had been evacuated covered a loop of the Saigon River and was only about thirty kilometers from the Cambodian border. About forty kilometers north of Saigon and twenty kilometers from Binh Duong, provincial capital, the area was covered with dense forests and jungles. For twenty years, the sector was a favorite hiding place for those fighting the French in previous wars, and later for the Viet Cong and North Vietnam infiltrators. One end of the area was called the Iron Triangle; the other end was divided into Combat Zones C and D.

A seemingly peaceful and prosperous village that I had visited in 1957 and 1960 sat isolated at the point where the river flowed out of the forest and began its course through flat, fertile rice paddies. The village, known as Ben Suc, was a shipping point for timber; logs cut deep in the forest were hauled here on ox carts, tied together in rafts and floated to mills downriver. About 400 rice farmers, mango and grape growers, and wood cutters lived in and around the village. They had been under the South Vietnamese administration since 1954, after the French war. A garrison of a territorial platoon and a few dozen militiamen provided security, but the area had remained peaceful for years, even when war had raged all around it.

A rumor persisted that both sides were interested in keeping Ben Suc that way: the South Vietnamese, so they could collect a large amount of taxes (and "gratuities" for local officials); the Viet Cong, so they could collect their own taxes, continue to use the village as a shipping point for supplies, and to gather intelligence.

That changed in mid-1964 when the Viet Cong attacked, destroying the South Vietnamese garrison and killing the village chief. The South Vietnamese later launched several attacks in efforts to retake the village but were repulsed each time with heavy losses. Since then Ben Suc had been regarded as a Viet Cong stronghold, a center for storage and transit of food, medical supplies, and materiel, and a hub for intelligence networks. Artillery shelling and air attacks by South Vietnam and U.S. forces caused casualties among people and livestock alike, but failed to dislodge residents. They pockmarked the area with trenches and foxholes, even digging shelters in their homes, and went about their lives. Abundant water from the river, timber from the nearby forests, and fertile soil for rice paddies provided them good incomes, despite the hardships. Their numbers had swelled to 6,000 by 1967 due to an influx of people from neighboring villages that had been hit even harder by the war.

I learned from former villagers how, on January 8, 1967, the relatively prosperous Ben Suc had ceased to exist as the result of an American operation called Cedar Falls. A thunderous orchestration of bombs and artillery shells exploding, small arms fire, and airplanes zooming overhead at low altitude awoke the villagers early that morning. Instinctively they dove for the safety of foxholes and trenches dug under their beds and around their houses. The cacophony grew louder and closer; then the thatched roofs started flying apart as dozens of helicopters dropped down to land in the middle of the village.

The villagers weren't sure what was happening or what they should do. Nothing like this had happened during the French war years. The people had no idea how much more powerful than the French the Americans were in terms of firepower and mobility, and how they used these capabilities to fight the current war.

American GIs, accompanied by some Vietnamese to act as interpreters, swarmed out of helicopters as they landed and spread out through the village, searching for Viet Cong. (This at least was familiar, a scene played out fifteen years earlier by the French, except they came in by parachute or walking behind armored cars, and without the accompaniment of bombs and artillery shells.) The village was completely surrounded; the few possible escape routes to the jungle were sealed off, and the jungle was being heavily bombed and shelled. At times the ground trembled in a manmade earthquake caused by the impact of hundreds of tons of bombs released by B-52 bombers flying high overhead.

But in and around the village no enemies were captured, just a few young men whose presence in this "enemy" territory was enough cause for them to be detained for further investigation. This could mean they would be tortured until they "confessed," die of exhaustion, or kept imprisoned indefinitely as a result of a summary provincial security trial. (Defendants were not represented by lawyers at such trials.) Another twelve unarmed men believed to be Viet Cong were killed when found hiding or while fleeing.

Vietnamese military commanders and the province chief were kept in the dark until after the operation was launched. The U.S. Command wanted to prevent leaks and suspected that the Vietnamese military and civilian government channels were heavily infiltrated by Viet Cong agents; most previous operations had obviously been blown by such leaks, with Viet Cong clearing out of the areas, sometimes just minutes before troops reached the raids' objectives. But the surprise attack on Ben

Suc, although a well-kept secret, proved to be almost as futile. The same was true for other similar operations carried out for nearly two months in the Iron Triangle and War Zones C and D. Few actual enemy soldiers were captured, and the Viet Cong later returned to the area.

The American generals were ecstatic, however, claiming that they had killed many Viet Cong, while destroying the enemy's bases and capturing food and weapons caches. On that basis they demanded more bombs, shells, napalm, and troops to fight the war in the way they believed to be so successful. For the two months of operations in the area, reports listed 3,748 enemy bodies counted, 6,000 bunkers destroyed, and Ben Suc and several other villages in the area razed. American forces reported the capture of hundreds of tons of provisions (primarily rice and dried fish), millions of enemy documents, and thousands of weapons, including grenades, rockets, and ammunition.

The pacification cadres, who worked among the refugees and got direct information from former inhabitants of the operational area, shed a different light on the official reports. They told me that few weapons had been captured in direct encounters with the enemy; most had been found in tunnels or other hidden caches. Most of the bodies counted were unarmed villagers taking refuge from the assault in foxholes, trenches, and tunnels; there was no proof that they were active enemy soldiers, or even Viet Cong supporters.

Vann and I left the refugee camp to visit the site Ben Suc had once occupied. We soon saw for ourselves the devastation created by combined use of ground and air power, bolstered by defoliating chemicals. The sector was a showcase for the lethal and destructive power of U.S. forces. Tall trees on both sides of the few paths that crisscrossed the area were flattened. Four or five hamlets along the edge of the forest had been demolished, with all buildings burned and leveled. Green fields were pockmarked with bomb craters filled with muddy water. Spotted through the forest were a multitude of small ponds carved out by B-52 bombs that had scythed down trees in mile-long stretches; they could be seen easily because trees that remained standing had lost most of their leaves to defoliants such as Agent Orange.

Even rice plants in the paddies were defoliated. American forces must have been ordered to make the whole area uninhabitable to deny the enemy any assistance from local people or use of the sector for troop transit. I wondered if this was the U.S. answer to the Communist strategy of "fish and water."

We landed at the helipad next to Vann's residence before nightfall. His cook had prepared a meal and we ate silently, each of us thinking about what we had seen that day. Vann finally broke the silence as we moved to the living room. We had a long discussion through the evening. He could see that I was not impressed with what we saw that day.

"Oh yes, in a sense I am impressed. How could we, in the past, keep complimenting ourselves about our military victories and pacification progress, while fortified enemy bases have been located for years only about thirty-five kilometers northwest of the capital?" I asked. "And then, when we do make a move, it requires the equivalent of more than three American and Vietnamese divisions to secure the area."

"But we will do it one area at a time and keep expanding, joining the areas together as oil drops spread and join on a sheet of paper. Thus, we can move the troops from one pacified spot to occupy another spot, pacify that one and then move on again." argued Vann.

"The French tried that and failed!" I retorted. "Tell me where there is any 'pacified' place in the country that does not have a military unit to protect it, unless it is close to or inside a perimeter of military positions," I challenged.

Vann continued to debate but with less enthusiasm, telling me that after the successful Ben Suc and Iron Triangle operations, most American generals he had talked to agreed that the war now was on the right track. One of them, General DePuy, commander of the U.S. First Infantry Division, which played a major role in the operation, summed up the prevailing opinion: "With so many of the enemy eliminated, so many of his bases destroyed, and being so isolated from food, weapons, and the local populace he relied on for support and cover, victory should come soon."

I ended the long conversation that night with a recommendation and comment prompted by my memory of a remark my cousin in Danang had made to me a few weeks earlier.

"Don't forget to remind the generals that to achieve pacification they should make an effort to win the hearts and minds of the people. They should find that easier now; many people who were too far away to reach before, in Viet Cong–controlled areas, are now either in our pacified cities, new life hamlets, or right there behind the barbed wire in our refugee camps."

I was thinking that it might be difficult to win the hearts and minds of those villagers who were forced to leave their rice paddies, gardens, and timberlands behind to accommodate to a new lifestyle. How could they not resent having to exist in this new fenced-in environment, living in makeshift shelters amid Americans and the very Vietnamese whom the Viet Cong had been telling them for years were nothing but "replacements for the French colonialists and their puppets"? Those villagers had watched U.S. and South Vietnamese troops destroy their homes and villages, and had seen them arrest or kill some of their male friends and relatives, regardless if they were Viet Cong. They had been forced to come to the refugee camp I had visited with Vann, and others like it throughout the country, to live on the generosity of their "hosts."

22: TAKING A POLITICAL PATH (1967)

As I rode in the Jeep back to Saigon late that night, I was reminded of a dramatically different side of the war, but one no less tragic in its way. On a stretch of several miles of the road that linked the Bien Hoa airbase to the Saigon highway, I passed at least a hundred small, primitively built nightclubs and bars with their names spelled out in glowing, garish neon: "Paradise on Earth," "Hollywood Tonite," "In Love with You," "Make Love and Fight War."

There was little activity around them now because of the curfew (which usually began at 5 p.m.). When I passed this way during the daytime I knew I would see young women and even girls barely into their teens, heavily made up and seeming near-nude in revealing costumes, running after and embracing GIs in full combat uniforms. Most of the women and girls came from the refugee camps and had been innocent country girls only a short time earlier. Many were helping to support their families. In a way, they were casualties of the war just as much as those injured in battle.

In accordance with the new constitution I would be allowed to run for the National Assembly while serving as an officer. General Thang, who had not acceded to my request months earlier, now had to release me.[1] I discussed the situation with my wife and asked her to arrange for her mother and father to take care of the children. Fortunately, we had income from a rental property so this would not be an economic burden for her parents.

She was disappointed with my decision and showed some anxiety about the changes it would make in our family life, but in the end she was supportive as ever. Since our marriage eighteen years earlier Nhan had been an exemplary wife and mother, managing our household and raising the children on my salary, though admittedly her family helped us at times. During those years, she had seen most of my classmates get fast, easy promotions to more secure and prosperous positions than offered on the path I had taken. A few were now generals, and their wives wore diamonds while their children went to the best French schools.

What I admired in Nhan was her calm acceptance of the life I had chosen. Though at times she may have felt embarrassed wearing her more modest apparel on occasions when other ladies displayed their jewels and finery, she never complained, was jealous, or showed any interest in having me attain more material success. Nhan knew, of course, that I would have progressed further and had better-paying, more prestigious jobs at times had I been content not to make waves. She never tried to dissuade me from following the course my conscience dictated.

"Are there any other reasons that influenced you to make this drastic decision?" she asked, still probing to understand my thinking fully, perhaps so she could better reconcile her own feelings about the matter.

"Yes. For a long time after I quit the Viet Minh and joined South Vietnam, I just wanted to be a good nationalist and a career military officer, leaving political considerations to people in government whom I considered superior to me in such matters. When President Diem called on me to work in his government, I felt I owed him both respect and gratitude for selecting me, though I knew his esteem for my family was at least partially responsible for my appointment.

"With time and the opportunity to work directly with him for almost three years, I came to know him well, and to admire and respect him even more. I took him as my model of a nationalist, patriot, and religious person. I tried to do my best in my various positions without thinking much beyond the present. After his death I worked much harder, trying to help both the American and Vietnamese leaders to win this war, believing they had good aims and intentions, but did not have the same background knowledge and experience that I did.

"I realize now that my efforts have been fruitless. If I stay in the army or government, I still will be a subordinate, even if I should have stars pinned on my shoulders. I would only be able to obey orders, and not to argue or put forth different ideas. For unlike Diem, who had confidence in himself, our current opportunistic Vietnamese generals in power are insecure men. They fear that paying heed to advice from people of equal or superior knowledge might make it appear that they are not capable of or qualified for their positions.

"Everything I try to do for others and for our country," I said in conclusion, "will also benefit our children in the long run." My wife was born and raised to understand the meaning of what I said, but she must have wondered and been concerned about the uncertainty of what I planned to do and hoped to accomplish.

I spent a few more days arranging family affairs, then began work on my new mission. I looked on it with revitalized hope and energy. I was enthusiastic at the prospect of being an elected official, free and independent from all influences, except to represent the best interests of the people who elected me to office. I hoped to use the National Assembly to make my voice heard, so I could express the lessons I had learned from the people over the prior twenty-three years. I ached to improve the situation of all my countrymen who had been bearing crushing burdens of war for so long, to rally enough force to build a viable South Vietnam.

At that time, even while the war intensified on the ground in the South and in the air over the North, Saigon and other cities in the South offered a remarkably peaceful appearance, despite the extreme turmoil of the preceding two years. Executive Chairman Nguyen Cao Ky and his police chief Nguyen Ngoc Loan had succeeded in cleaning up the chaos of demonstrations and had silenced all opposition to the generals in power.

Leaders of the Committee for Defense of Peace, Dr. Pham Van Huyen and Professor Ton That Duong Ky, had been expelled to the North. Other prominent peace advocates, including the well-known lawyer Nguyen Long, chairman of the Movement for Self-Determination, were arrested and jailed. Several leaders who opposed Ky and Thieu had been assassinated. The Venerable Thich Thien Minh, the Buddhist leader, had survived an assassination attempt, but National Assemblyman Tran Van Van was not so fortunate.

The police had invaded and searched the central Buddhist church, forcing the Buddhist leaders to interrupt their fast of opposition. Some twenty Buddhist priests and nuns had immolated themselves in protest against the generals. Buddhist leader Thich Tri Quang, who had written to President Johnson several times asking for his help in changing government policies, was placed under house arrest in a Saigon hospital.[2] All other religious leaders, except for the Catholics, asked for replacement of the generals with an interim civilian government that would set up free elections. This only resulted in harsher crackdowns on the opposition.

Finally, responding to the demands for general elections by both the Vietnamese opposition and American critics, Ky had set up elections for a Constitutional Assembly. The process of drafting a constitution began in October 1966, but people were skeptical. Many felt Ky would maneuver to delay completion of the constitution and arranging national elections until he could be sure of victory in a presidential race. Although the generals had no interest in setting up elections, the Americans did, to have at least a façade of the democracy and freedom they claimed the war was being fought to preserve.

President Johnson finally made it clear that there should be no further delays during his March 20, 1967, meeting with Ky in Guam. "My birthday is in late August," he said to Ky. "The greatest birthday present you could give me is a national election."[3] Results were prompt. The Vietnamese Constitution was promulgated on April 1, 1967, and presidential and senatorial elections were scheduled for the following September, with election of House members of the National Assembly to take place the following month.

As the elections neared, Thieu and Ky struggled mightily over which one would hold first place on the presidential ticket. Thieu's situation seemed desperate, if not hopeless, at first. Ky had the support of all military region commanders, police, intelligence service and military security chiefs, and province chiefs (governors). Most had been promoted and appointed by Ky. Ky also was assured of U.S. support. He was complimented by Ambassador Lodge the previous year for his determined crushing of the Buddhists in the spring of 1966. In fact, the clique of Vietnamese generals in power had sent General Thang to visit Thieu while he was still in the hospital recovering from an appendicitis operation. Thang's mission: to tell Thieu that they, the generals, had decided to back Ky, and to ask Thieu to withdraw his candidacy. This never became common knowledge, but Thieu himself told about the incident later, while I was still his confidant. He was extremely indignant about the incident.

General Westmoreland himself later came to Thieu's home and made a similar request. He promised Thieu that, in return for dropping out of the presidential contest, the United States would support Thieu for the position of supreme commander of all Vietnamese military forces.

Daniel Ellsberg was working on an analysis of potential presidential candidates about that time, and I visited him to share my assessment. I rejected Generals Duong Van Minh (Big Minh) and Nguyen Cao Ky out of hand as unsuitable. I favored civilian candidate Tran Van Huong, former mayor of Saigon, and was neutral about Thieu. I explained my thinking to Ellsberg.

I knew Minh when he was military advisor (commandant of the field force, without troops or operations) to President Diem. I was then rapporteur of the National Security Council. I told Ellsberg about one time when President Diem asked Minh for his ideas on how to control the DMZ and the Ho Chi Minh Trail. Minh's reply was taken almost word for word from a document that U.S. military advisors had previously submitted to the president; I had read it earlier and made notes on it for the president, so we both knew that Minh's report didn't represent original thinking. I was not surprised, as I never thought highly of Minh's intelligence. I also did not consider him morally suitable for the presidency after the way he maneuvered in the coup and the cowardly murder of President Diem.

As for Ky, elevation to his present post had been a moral affront to the great majority of Vietnamese, and a disaster in terms of American and Vietnamese efforts to win the hearts and minds of the people.

I knew little about Huong except that he had resigned as mayor of Saigon under Diem and had openly joined a group of Saigon notables in 1960 to ask the president for reforms.

I told Ellsberg I did not feel I could give an impartial assessment of Thieu because of my long personal relationship with him. I also told Daniel that I felt the Americans would prefer a general rather than a civilian as president of South Vietnam, so for all practical purposes the choice would be between Ky and Thieu.

I spent the next few days in Saigon, contacting friends and politicians to get a clearer picture of the country's situation as reflected in the minds of people in and outside of government. Most of my former classmates and many of my former cadet students from the military academy at Dalat had long since become senior officers. Many held influential positions in the army, air force, or administration, and some were now generals. Nearly all of them felt very confident of America's determination and capability to win the war. Some doubted that complete victory was possible but believed firmly that the United States would never abandon South Vietnam. When I talked to officers of lower ranks and pacification cadres, however, the story was different. These were men who had spent the previous three years on the battlefields or in direct contact with the rural population. They expressed their desperate hope that the war and its devastation would end as soon as possible, but were convinced that the killing would never end.

In my travels I learned that my brother Hien had been visiting and contacting a lot of people in Saigon. I was concerned for his safety, as well as my own and that of the people he had contacted, because I was certain Hien had been followed closely after I told Vann and Donahue about his first visit to me in 1965. At that time I believed Hien when he told me he only visited Saigon once in a while. Now I was fairly sure he had lied, and that he came to the city regularly. I sent word to my older brother Khang, asking him to tell Hien to come see me as soon as possible. A few days later Hien arrived at my home. He seemed to have had no difficulty finding it, and he arrived at a time when I was there. Since I normally ran a tight but irregular schedule, because I was on the move a lot and spent a great deal of time in Kien Hoa preparing for the National Assembly race, he probably had someone keeping track of my movements.

I let him sit down for a few minutes, then got bluntly to the point.

"I think you are being unfair to me, Hien, by telling me lies. You have been seeing a lot of people, and thus compromising them. Your activities and your routes of travel must have been discovered by the police and CIA, at least in the recent past. You know I've had to notify the CIA that you have visited me, just to protect myself. I don't want to bear the responsibility for your arrest or death."

"Thank you for your concern," Hien replied, "but I am very well protected by the people around here, and wherever I am. Don't you remember while you were in the Fifth Military Interzone [during the French war in the 1940s] how our cadres and troops were always covered by the people? In those days you and I had coffee at times right in the heart of French-controlled cities," he added mockingly.

"But this is a different time," I reminded him. "This war is different. You and I are different, and the people are different. You cannot enjoy the same popular support; you have lost the identity of Vietnamese fighters for independence that you enjoyed at that time," I answered forcefully. I went on to tell him what our father had told me about his visit to Hué, and that our uncle Dr. Nguyen Dinh Cat told me about Hien, having lived in his home for several days not long ago. I said that a few other relatives and some of Hien's classmates mentioned his frequent visits.

My brother assured me he did not stay long in any one place, and when he came to Saigon he got in and out fast.

"You might be too confident for your own good," I retorted. "I think you're being more closely monitored than you suspect, and if something happens to you I don't want you or anyone else to think I had anything to do with it." Then I changed the subject, feeling I had made my feelings clear enough.

"I have decided to run for the National Assembly," I told him, explaining that I wanted more freedom to operate than the army or government permitted me.

"Why do that?" Hien demanded. "The National Assembly will be just a tool for demagoguery, another form of political deception that will serve the Americans and strengthen the South Vietnamese repressive system. Once you quit the government and join that body, you will no longer be in a position to do any of the useful things you expect to accomplish."

I replied that I had already held some important government positions and had tried my best to change things for the better, but I had failed. "Now that there is a new system, imperfect though it might be, as a member of the legislature, and thus free of the executive, I will be able to make my voice heard directly by the people. And they will be the ones to pass judgment on me and my ideas, determining whether I rise or fall back."

When he finally realized he could not change my mind about running for a seat in the House of Deputies, Hien asked if I needed help from the Front (NLF) in my race.

"Why should I?" I asked.

"Because the Front controls most of the population in Kien Hoa province," he replied.

I was furious at his assessment, feeling sure that I enjoyed the support of a majority of Kien Hoa's people. "I don't need help from the Front because I'm sure I can win there. If I accept help from the Front my position would be tainted and I would be compromised!" Then, to avoid appearing totally ungrateful and hurting Hien unnecessarily, I added that the one thing I would appreciate is if the Front would not harass people or disrupt the elections on voting day.

Hien in his turn asked what my position would be, as a deputy, with regard to resolving the war.

"I am still anti-Communist, but I am also realistic. I will try to compromise my ideological concerns with my compassionate sentiments for the people in the best way I can, without violating my basic principles."

As I showed Hien out, I sensed he was hiding some embarrassment and concern.

That night I worried, too. I kept thinking that Hien could intentionally have not been discovered, and I considered whether the CIA might be "protecting" him temporarily to learn more about his activities and connections. I felt that if he were arrested, it would be his own responsibility, not mine; I tried to warn him. I felt I was in the clear should that happen because I had informed Vann. Vann had reassured me that Ambassador Lodge wanted me to maintain contact with my brother (another reason I believed that Hien might be under CIA surveillance). Beyond that, whatever the CIA knew about my relationship with Hien, they must by that point have been convinced of my integrity and consistent loyalty to the South Vietnamese cause.

Later, just before dawn, I became increasingly nervous, feeling uneasiness about Hien's reminders of the time of the resistance against the French in the 1940s. At the time, the people in the cities and areas controlled by the French and their Vietnamese subordinates had been considered pacified, yet they provided cover and abundant covert support for the Viet Minh. I was startled at the idea that the same situation might now exist in Saigon and elsewhere. If so, the situation could be even worse than it had been before in terms of "the enemy within," because of the millions of registered and unregistered refugees who moved to "secure pacified areas."

I talked to Vann about my anxieties and concerns soon after that. He listened attentively and took notes. About a week later he came to my home and proposed that he arrange for me to talk to Ambassador Ellsworth Bunker about my concerns.[4] I agreed, but doubted that the haughty, cool, and distant "proconsul ambassador" (as he was called in Saigon's intellectual circles), who was used to giving orders to Vietnamese presidents and generals, would humble himself to listen to an unassigned lieutenant colonel.

A few days later Vann called before my usual 5 a.m. arising to say he would come to my home at noon for an appointment that would occupy the rest of the day. I was surprised when he arrived and told me that Ambassador Bunker did want to talk to me.

The meeting was conducted discreetly in Deputy Ambassador Porter's residence. In addition to Ambassadors Bunker and Porter, those present were George Jacobson, Bunker's chief of staff, and Lieutenant General Weyand (later the general commandant of all U.S. forces in Vietnam), who was commandant of the U.S. Second Field Force and senior advisor to the Vietnamese commander of the Third Military Region (which included Saigon and surrounding provinces). There were two other civilians, but I can't recall their names.

I was the only speaker for almost three hours, talking without notes and reiterating the summary observations I previously shared with Vann.

I tried not to offend the American officials, but emphasized that villages and cities that supposedly were pacified and under our control were by no means actually secure. I reminded them that millions of the people now living in those areas were discontented and resentful. Many were bitter about being uprooted from their traditional homes. Among the many unregistered refugees, and perhaps even among those who were registered, there undoubtedly were large numbers of Viet Cong agents and supporters. There were also demoralized elements in our military, enlisted men as well as junior officers.

To cope with the situation, I recommended that pacification efforts be focused on populated centers, with regional (provincial) forces assigned to provide mobile patrols around the perimeters of hamlets, villages, and government-controlled towns. I suggested that ARVN be organized into mobile brigades and stationed in places where they would be available to come to the aid of regional units when necessary. Some American and Allied troops should be positioned to blockade the Ho Chi Minh Trail and the DMZ, while deploying others in strategic locations to react when ARVN encountered sizable enemy units.

Even in areas considered to be under government control, conduct of government officials and troops should be monitored and investigation of suspected Viet Cong and enemy agents should be maintained consistently. I strongly recommended using the Census Grievance approach detailed earlier in the book to reduce civilian unrest, obtain useful intelligence, and generally help in the pacification process.

My theme throughout was that we, Americans and South Vietnamese alike, must avoid overconfidence just because areas seemed calm and free of enemy influence. Look to the threat from within as well as to the enemy without, I said in essence. We have more enemies than we think, ready and waiting to attack us in the heart of areas we consider firmly under our control.

General Weyand was the only one who stopped me a few times to ask questions. Apparently he took notice of my warnings and recommendations. Ambassador Bunker simply sat there, virtually motionless with his eyes fixed on me, listening imperturbably for nearly three hours. There was no indication of his reaction. The others present also sat quietly and without comment, but they all showed intense interest in my comments.

I left that meeting with renewed appreciation for John Vann's willingness to make special arrangements on my behalf. I believed I had done my best to alert top U.S. officials to problems in populated areas that we liked to consider under government control. In good conscience now, I could turn toward the coming elections.

There were a dozen slates of presidential and vice-presidential candidates, and another dozen senatorial tickets (each listing ten would-be senators). American Deputy Ambassador Porter had made it clear that the United States wanted only one military president / vice president ticket, so there that would no fragmenting of votes and potential power struggles after the fact. The Vietnamese Armed Forces Council convened and reversed their decision to support Ky for the top job. He would now run for vice president, with Thieu heading the ticket as presidential candidate.

Among the other tickets of candidates, only that headed by Truong Dinh Du, a lawyer, was regarded as a serious threat to the Thieu-Ky slate. Du advocated a peaceful settlement with the Viet Cong, directly in opposition to the Thieu-Ky position.

The dozen senatorial tickets were composed of various combinations of individuals, mostly based on religious affiliations. Most of the ten-person tickets consisted of Catholic candidates; only one was made up of Buddhists. The Buddhist Church was generally boycotting the 1967 elections on the premise that they would not be impartial while the generals were in power and in charge of the balloting.

I traveled through several provinces, calling on friends and sympathizers among the army, administration, pacification cadres, and other organizations to promote support for the Thieu-Ky ticket and for General Huynh Van Cao's senatorial slate. Cao had offered me a place on his ticket but I refused. I had already made up my mind to be an independent legislator, representing the people of Kien Hoa province and without being obligated to anyone. I soon realized that Thieu and Ky didn't need my support. The province chiefs, all appointed by them, would take care of the elections, and there would be few observers who would dare challenge their authority. The exceptions would be in a few provinces where members of the Buddhist, Cao Dai, and Hoa Hao congregations, or the Dai Viet and Quoc Dan Dang political parties, were influential. (The Catholic Church in a sense had opted to support Thieu and Ky a year earlier when it did not join other religious leaders in the petition requesting that Thieu and Ky turn power over to a temporary civilian government to run the elections.)

The nationwide senatorial race had no clear-cut leaders, and the Senate contest was more politically sensitive. Virtually all candidates sang the same tune: win the war, negotiate with the North from a strong position, and reject the National Liberation Front. I had promised to support Cao's ticket. He had brought together a well-balanced combination of intellectuals and professionals, most with Buddhist or Confucian affiliations, though Cao himself was an ardent Catholic. Other tickets led by Catholics were better financed and organized, however; most featured well-known Catholics formerly associated with Diem's government. Thus, a great deal of effort was needed to assure Cao's success.

I was at the Huong My district headquarters on the night the elections closed and ballot tabulations were completed. Huong My was part of Kien Hoa province, located on an island in the Mekong River. The district chief there, an army captain, asked me a curious question.

"Sir, would you tell me who Mr. Truong Dinh Du is?"

"Certainly," I told him. "Mr. Du is a reputable, well-known attorney in Saigon and ran on a platform of recognizing the NLF and negotiating a peaceful end to the war. Why do you ask?"

"Nobody in this district knew who Mr. Du was before the elections, but it turned out he was far ahead of all other candidates in the presidential voting. It created a situation that I just managed to circumvent for the generals."

"Why and how did you do that? Why didn't you just send in the results as they were recorded?"

"We [meaning all district chiefs] were told several times by the province chiefs to make sure that the generals were elected, and I did my best to comply with those instructions," he told me.

"How did observers for the other candidates react to your arrangement?"

"I don't know whether or not Mr. Du and the other candidates paid them, but I did. And besides, they need my protection."

As a result of such "arrangements," Thieu and Ky won with 1.6 million votes. Du ran second with 800,000. Nine other candidates garnered from fewer than 100,000 to 500,000 votes. The governor of Binh Dinh province told me later that he too had to reverse election results to give Thieu and Ky a lead over Du.[5] In Saigon, where the government in power was more closely watched by the foreign press and outside observers, the Thieu-Ky ticket ran far behind the Du-Chieu and Huong-Truyen tickets.

I felt guilty supporting candidates who had won by cheating, even though I had no part in rigging the results. I was pragmatic enough to admit the results were fore-ordained anyhow. The Constitution and general elections had been allowed for le-gitimizing the American effort in the war and to counter petitions made earlier to remove the generals from power. The American preference was obviously to retain Thieu and Ky at the head of a military-oriented government that would conduct the war as U.S. policy directed.

I recalled a conversation I had with General Lansdale in mid-1966 when I in-formed him I intended to run for a seat in the Constituent Assembly. "What will be your purpose? Do you merely want to write a document?" he asked me. "Remember that you had an elected president [Diem] for nine years and you didn't solve those problems."

"True, and now we must learn from that lesson. Diem made the mistake of trying to govern the country by following a Confucianist philosophy, though he was Catholic. The difficulty was that only he himself and a few others believed in and followed the philosophy. Most of his officials in intermediate roles—provincial gov-ernors, district and village chiefs, and military officers—had not been raised and educated with the same moral and ethical principles as Diem. And since Diem kept himself relatively isolated, it was easy for those Diem relied on to carry out his policies to preselect election winners, even before they were announced as candidates. Provincial governors, who had been appointed by Diem's underlings, were told to make sure that the chosen ones would be 'elected.' So there was no truly representative government under Diem."

"But you know very well that under the actual circumstances, laws and rhetoric served less than a bayonet, although I agree with you that a truly representative system of government is vital to ending the war victoriously," Lansdale stated. He then advised me that I would be more effective staying in the government than by leaving it.

Lansdale told me two stories in 1967 about the perceptions of two famous Americans, Ambassador Lodge and former vice president Nixon. When Lansdale stressed to them how important it was that our upcoming elections in South Vietnam should be free and fair, Lansdale quoted Lodge as saying, "Remember that 'electoral irregularities' occur even in the United States." Later, when Nixon visited Saigon as a vice president of Pepsi-Cola, and Lansdale discussed the need for honest elections with him, Nixon's reply according to Lansdale was this: "The elections must be honest, as long as our men win!"

The day after the presidential elections, I went to congratulate Thieu at his home. His wife was more excited about the victory than Thieu himself, and I knew why. Although Thieu had won the top spot as president and Ky theoretically was under him as vice president, Ky still held the balance of power. The new vice president had appointed all the men who held key positions in the provinces, and in the cabinet, army, and police. This would diminish Thieu's authority and complicate his administration. By way of encouragement, I reminded Thieu that he now held the highest position in the land. "Use it to end the war and you will be revered as a national hero. I pledge to help you in every way I can. If I am elected to the House of Deputies, as I hope to be, I will do my best to get others to work with us."

As I left the compound where Thieu's residence was located, I stopped to congratulate Huynh Van Cao. He had led his ticket of ten candidates to victory in the Senate race. Of the six winning tickets (ten candidates each for the sixty Senate seats), four had Catholic backing, one was Buddhist-supported, and the other was Caodaist.

General elections for the House of Deputies (or Lower House) of the National Assembly were held six weeks after the presidential and senatorial elections. Deputies were to be elected for four-year terms on a provincewide basis. I spent most of that time campaigning in Kien Hoa, crisscrossing the province and contacting people I knew during the three years of my two periods as governor. It was two years since my last term as province chief, so I had to renew acquaintances and reestablish myself with Kien Hoa residents as a good candidate to support. This was critical, because the province was allocated only two deputies, yet there were nineteen candidates for those positions. Eighteen of the candidates had either been born in Kien Hoa, were married to someone who had been born there, or had lived long and honorably in the province.

My biggest asset was total support, either tacit or openly, from all of Kien Hoa's religious leaders. Even though I was a Buddhist, the Catholic priests and nuns, always well organized and communicative, supported my candidacy in their sermons and speeches in the villages. I made only two promises to these leaders. First, their voices would be heard and their complaints would be investigated thoroughly. Second, I would work toward an ending of the war that would satisfy the honor and dignity of both sides.

Three days before the elections, at night, Major Bui Tan Buu, a fervent Catholic and chief of Binh Dai district, stole into the home of one of his relatives, where I was staying. He asked me to withdraw from the elections, not from personal choice but for a very different reason. Buu explained that the current provincial governor, Lieutenant Colonel Huynh Van Du, had held a meeting with all nine of the district chiefs and ordered them to make "arrangements" so that Chairman Nguyen Van Hao and Nguyen Van Hieu of the Provincial Council would be assured election as the two Kien Hoa deputies. Buu said that circumstances compelled him to follow the governor's orders, and he felt the other district chiefs would do the same. He didn't want me to continue running because he felt I would certainly fail, and be dishonored.

Early the next morning I called Vann and asked him for the use of a helicopter for a day. To protect myself from any charges of violating the election regulations, I asked that the chopper meet me in My Tho, outside Kien Hoa provincial limits. I drove to My Tho and then flew to Can Tho to talk with General Nguyen Van Manh, commander of the Fourth Military Region, which included Kien Hoa. I felt he had a hand in planning the election's outcome. I went straight to the point: "You cannot do this to me, take me out of the race even before the elections open!"

He stared at me with surprise. After we discussed the situation briefly, I realized that he really didn't know anything about the plot to rig the election. I told him the whole story, and he paused to think for a while. Finally he said, "Listen and believe me: I was kept in the dark about these things. The only instructions I have received so far with regard to the House of Deputies elections have been that I should not get involved. I was told that Ky's personal assistant, Nguyen Thien Nhon, was to be in charge." As the general showed me out of his office he asked me not to disclose that I had discussed the elections with him, or that he had told me about the involvement of Ky and Nhon.

I flew back in the helicopter. As we neared My Tho, the engine suddenly got very noisy, then stopped. The young pilot tried for a smooth emergency landing. We set down in a rice paddy full of water flowing in from the Mekong River at high tide. Several helicopters from the U.S. base at Dong Tam quickly came to our rescue, plucking us up amid the roar of rotors flailing and Viet Cong rifle fire. We were lucky that we landed about a hundred meters beyond the range of accurate Viet Cong fire and maybe a dozen feet from the strong Mekong current.

I finally got back to my car and drove two hours to Saigon and Thieu's residence. As I arrived, I saw Huynh Van Cao standing on the porch. I stopped to tell him the whole story. "Can you do anything about it?" I asked him.

"You better talk to Thieu," he replied.

I went inside. After Thieu and I greeted each other with our customary handshakes, I repeated the story for him and asked him to intervene. "I only want to ensure that Kien Hoa does indeed have free elections. I'm not requesting your support or that you do anything to boost my candidacy. If the elections aren't rigged in advance, I'll be happy to take my chances."

"I'm sorry, but I can't intervene on your behalf," Thieu told me, explaining that one of the conditions made when Ky agreed to withdraw his presidential candidacy and run as number two on the ticket was that Ky would be allowed to "organize" the elections. "I can't violate that agreement," he added. "There are many things to settle with Ky after the election, and I don't want to upset him now by interfering in a matter that would disturb that understanding."

Returning to Cao, I asked him to do whatever he could, making no bones about the fact that I would not accept a rigged election without fighting back. "If the orders to 'preelect' deputies in Kien Hoa are not withdrawn before the election, I will go public on Sunday [election day] and denounce the fraud to the foreign press and observers."

I returned to Kien Hoa the next day, more determined than ever to win the election. I was still deeply depressed and concerned, however, living with the uncertainty of so many factors. Would voters bypass me because of family loyalty and friendship toward other candidates? Would my threat to "blow the whistle" cause the Ky faction to withdraw orders to local officials that they ensure election of the selected candidates by whatever means necessary?

My fears were allayed the day before the election. A young woman, sister of a captain on the provincial staff, came to me with a tape cassette. "Listen to it," she urged, "but don't tell anyone, much less who it came from, or you will endanger my brother's life.

Recorded on the tape was the provincial governor's directive to his district chief rescinding his previous order to rig the elections, telling them not to interfere in the next day's voting. Obviously he had received his orders from Saigon; since the governor had no way of visiting each of his district chiefs in person, he had contacted them by radio, and the young captain had secretly taped the conversations for me to hear, at great personal risk.

Kien Hoa thus became the sole province to benefit from the sacrifices of the thousands of Vietnamese military and civilians killed since the reopening of the war in 1957, by enjoying the privilege of voting in truly free elections. There were attempts to rig the results in all other provinces and districts. In a few other areas, independent candidates succeeded in overcoming those favored by Ky and his followers, thanks to the support of religious leaders and watchdog activities of the foreign press and observers on hand to help ensure free elections.

A *New York Times* article said, "He [Chau] won a seat in the National Assembly in 1967 in one of the few unrigged contests in the history of the country."

"He won 41.2 percent of the votes, even out of a field of 19. His resounding victory—his runner-up received only 12.6 percent—made Chau the second or third highest vote getter in the Assembly," reported Elizabeth Pond in her later report, *The Chau Trial*.

My friend Thieu had managed successfully to survive political intrigues under Diem, personal rivalries between Vietnamese generals and colonels, and complications created by the Americans, and in the end had defeated "Cowboy" Ky (who had once proclaimed loudly that he "felt like a Texan") to win the presidency.

And Thieu, in my opinion, was by far the best of the Saigon generals. He was intelligent, thoughtful, a moderate Catholic, and above all, very acceptable to the Americans. As I've said, we had been friends for sixteen years, and my wife always spoke of Thieu and his wife as our "brother and sister." I felt that Thieu's assets, background, and experience in navigating his way through the intrigues and rivalries between top army brass and vocal anti-Communist politicians—combined with my background as a Buddhist who was accepted by such Americans as John Paul Vann, Daniel Ellsberg, and others, plus my experience in the grassroots problems of war and pacification—would enable us, working together, to mix practical Western logic with Oriental moral logic and rally Catholics and non-Catholics alike. If we could unite and motivate all factions, legitimizing the war morally and intellectually, we could present a powerful challenge to the Communist ideology and their claims of high purpose for their cause.

On that election night, I felt both honored by and obligated to the 700,000 people of Kien Hoa province as well as the rest of my countrymen who had helped inspire my thoughts and deeds during the previous twenty-five years. I looked to the infinite sky and prayed for cessation of human suffering in Vietnam, making a solemn promise to do my utmost, working with others, to strengthen Thieu's image and help him bring this about. I wanted to bolster Thieu to the point where he would be strong enough to end the war with victory for national independence, human freedom, and social justice.

The generals had all of Diem's faults, with none of his saving graces. As a group they were shortsighted, venal, and concerned with furthering their own interests above all else. They were more than willing to let the United States dictate policy in return for massive infusions of troops, arms, and money. Moreover, members of the military cabal that mounted the coup against Diem in 1963 had consistently shown that they were at least as interested in political infighting and their individual schemes for power as they were in defeating the enemy.

Since the selection of Ky and Thieu as new rulers by other generals in 1965, things had been going well—from the viewpoint of Americans in the Saigon Mission, the Pentagon, and the White House. Dissidents and Buddhists had been bloodily crushed and neutralized. Foreign soldiers had poured into our country. Almost 500,000 Americans and 50,000 Koreans, Australians, New Zealanders, Thais, and Filipinos had joined some 700,000 South Vietnamese troops in the field. Search-and-destroy missions had produced a reported body count of nearly 17,000 enemy dead. A well-coordinated pacification program engineered by the CIA appeared to be progressing smoothly in all controlled areas.

Bowing to the will of the United States (as expressed by President Johnson in the Guam conference) more than to popular demand by their countrymen, the generals had even permitted general elections. Obviously the American leadership hoped this would lessen protests against U.S. involvement in the war at home and abroad: with an elected government in place and inviting assistance, the U.S. role would seem to have a more legal basis. Americans on the scene cared more about the fact that elections were held than whether they were representative and conducted honestly. Many had expressed the opinion that South Vietnam was not ready for real elections. So democracy in South Vietnam was still only a façade. The election process had been largely a sham, orchestrated by Ky, the same Ky who once made the shocking statement that he preferred "the way Hitler had ruled Germany."

Most deputies and senators were former civil servants or officers who left the risks and uncertainty of the military in favor of a more comfortable, prestigious political life. No matter what their religion, ethnic background, social status, or education, all Assembly members were staunch anti-Communists. Candidates were screened and approved before the elections by security, the police, and a special committee created specifically for that purpose. The generals made sure their opposition would be stifled by expanding the definition of "pro-Communist" to include anyone critical of the military regime that had ruled since the Diem coup.

Such critics simply were not allowed even to become candidates in areas under strong military control. There were few exceptions.

Still, I reasoned, there were glimmers of hope. Despite election rigging, my 136 colleagues in the House of Deputies did represent a cross-section of the 15 million South Vietnamese in the forty provinces that constituted the Republic. That was true also of the sixty-member Senate, the upper house of the National Assembly under the bicameral legislative body mandated by our new constitution. A few areas, notably some of the central provinces where Buddhists predominated, defied the generals and elected representatives who were not supporters of the military regime. Several dissident candidates also had been successful in Saigon, where the focus of international attention prevented overly repressive measures by Ky and his minions. About a dozen Assembly members represented political parties, and some twenty deputies represented ethnic minorities: Khmer, Chinese, Cham, and the Highland tribes. Catholics were well represented nationwide, but there were few Buddhist representatives relative to the percentage of Buddhists in the country, due to the church's noncommitment policy, underfinancing, and poor organization. There were doctors, lawyers, pharmacists, and intellectuals as well as two of the country's best-known older revolutionaries, Ho Huu Tuong and Truong Gia Ky Sanh.

I hoped we could become the seeds from which true democracy might flower in South Vietnam. I still believed my old friend Thieu represented the most realistic choice for our country's future. True, he was a figurehead now, with Ky retaining the real power. Prime Minister Nguyen Van Loc, the chiefs of national security and the national police, the chief of the General Staff, and all four military region commanders were all Ky's men. A silent but vigorous war for supremacy was now being waged between Ky and Thieu and their supporters. Thieu had already begun attempts to counterbalance Ky's strength in the military and the administration by establishing a power base in the Assembly. I hoped to help him in that respect.

Although most of the deputies had run in the election as nominal Ky candidates, many of them joined Nguyen Ba Luong in switching sides during the following weeks. Deputy Nguyen Ba Can, a former provincial governor and Thieu supporter, skillfully worked out a coalition of former military officers, civil servants, and businessmen who would back Thieu in the House of Deputies. A similar effort was under way in the Senate.

Thieu's efforts to build support in the National Assembly were increasingly successful. Before the end of 1967 his bloc had grown to include sixty deputies, the largest single group in the House of Deputies. The pro-Ky group had shrunk to fifteen, mostly Catholics from the North. Other blocs included twenty self-proclaimed Socialists, thirty Buddhists, and representatives of political parties from the Central provinces (with which I was affiliated). The remaining dozen or so were independents who refused to join any group. Thieu thus had the largest group of supporters, if not a clear majority. The same thing was true in the Senate, where southerners and Catholics predominated.

Thieu appointed Nguyen Cao Thang as his special assistant for liaison with the legislature, and Thang worked diligently at his job. I had known him for years. He was intelligent and charismatic and had been a successful pharmacist and entrepreneur. Though he was well connected in political circles, having been active during the Diem regime, Thang had always been open about the fact that his primary interest was in the business and financial worlds. "I feel I contribute best by making my own business successful and thus providing a model to benefit the entire nation," was the way he expressed his philosophy. "I will leave political assessments and actions to the president [Thieu] and others in power," he told me in our personal conversations, "because only they, with American support, can handle the Communists. That's why it is important that the National Assembly be united in giving strong support to the president."

Above all else, however, Thang considered himself practical and pragmatic. During his efforts to enlist me in the pro-Thieu bloc, he explained his position in words that went something like this: "I don't necessarily have any great esteem for Thieu, but he is better than Ky—and he now has the support of the Americans." To him, that was the reality of the situation and he accepted it. Although I categorically refused his offer to join the pro-Thieu alliance, Thang knew that I also felt Thieu was the best available choice and remained a close personal friend of the president. He kept making overtures to me to reconsider my position. He even made veiled hints that there might even be more tangible personal rewards than just the satisfaction of better serving the cause of our country.

I thought about the differences between the kind of anti-Communists Thang personified and those I represented. The difference came from moral and intellectual disagreement regarding how to win the war. The Communist leaders persuaded people that the struggle today was simply a continuation of the fight for national independence against oppressors, invaders, and colonialists, now represented by the South Vietnam government and the United States. The American leadership and the Vietnamese who cooperated with them lagged far behind in countering Communist propaganda and indoctrination. They painted a rosy picture of freedom and democracy versus a godless, totalitarian Communist government, which is the lackey of the Chinese and Soviet Communists and would destroy Vietnamese traditions. That might sound logical—but for two reasons it wasn't working.

First, many people accepted the Communist propaganda that told them stern measures were necessary to win the war, but all would be well when the fight was won and a classless society had been established.

Second, they saw no overt signs of Chinese or Soviet Communist involvement, much less control over North Vietnam and NLF leaders. By contrast, they did see widespread and ever-increasing signs of U.S. involvement in the war and control over South Vietnam's government and military leaders. They saw more American troops, and American advisors, generals, and ambassadors dictating policy that their Vietnamese counterparts carried out. They saw search-and-destroy missions on the battlefields, defoliation and destruction in areas not under government control, and elimination of dissent in "pacified" areas.

The anti-Communists I represented saw two equally disastrous results of the war as it was being waged. On one hand, the Communists would impose a totalitarian, atheist regime. On the other, the Americans and the Vietnamese regime they support promised a war that would never end because they could never completely conquer their Communist enemies or subjugate the people who support them.

Meanwhile, the Vietnamese people in both the South and the North had no options other than the ones imposed on them by their respective governments. The Northern leaders had an edge in that they had inherited honor and glory from their war against the French. They used it skillfully to enhance their collective image, playing on the theme that the Americans were simply successors to the French and using the same propaganda and indoctrination techniques that had been successful when France was the enemy.

The cause and ideology of the South, though I regarded both as right and noble in theory, were handicapped by the overwhelming U.S. presence and submissiveness of our military rulers to the Americans. The administration of the country suffered also because, although we supposedly had a constitution and elected officials, they were largely disregarded. To most Vietnamese, the government protected and favored only those who fully supported it and its American backers.

So there were those of us who felt that while South Vietnam needed U.S. support, the presence and influence of the Americans should be reduced to the necessary minimum. U.S. ambassadors, generals, and advisors should, in our view, have been playing much more modest and discreet roles. South Vietnamese leadership should have been accepted by, and responsible to, the grassroots people, either through a genuinely democratic system or some form of consensus arrangement. The situation at the time, with a façade of democracy masking what was essentially the dictatorship of a military junta (engaged in its own internal power struggle), only discredited the noble cause of freedom in the eyes of the people and made a sham of national independence. This played directly into the hands of the Communists and created huge propaganda benefits for them.

The Vietnamese whose views I represented knew that to win the war, we must first win over the people—people in the countryside, in the pacified cities, and in our own army and government. To do this, we had to establish a clear-cut national image and identity, a view of a free and independent future South Vietnam that would promise them a life worth fighting for. Unless the government had the support of a majority of the people, sharing the same views and fighting for the same cause, the war could never be won.

President Diem had realized that, but had thought that his personal example, dedication to national independence, and incorruptible, highly moral leadership would create the necessary unity. He failed because of his own remoteness, inadequate advisors, and obsequious underlings, who lacked his moral fiber. Since Diem's downfall, the Americans, with the self-serving consent of their Vietnamese counterparts, were seen by the public to be the actual rulers of South Vietnam. Now, the new Constitution and recently elected government, despite deficiencies and weaknesses, gave my faction new hope. We wanted to provide the Second Republic of South Vietnam with a more representative government and more responsible leadership. I had vowed personally to work with the rest of the House toward that goal.

Thus, I was pleased that Nguyen Ba Can had been able to gather almost half of the House into a pro-Thieu group. I was now willing to, first, get the Buddhists and Southern Catholics (who I considered the only deputies who truly represented their respective constituencies) together, and then to make an alliance with Can's group. This would create an absolute majority in the House for Thieu. It would be a delicate matter, however. Can's work in assembling his group had been eased because its members, although they owed Ky for their election, also got financial support (through Nguyen Cao Thang) from Thieu. Also, they were not really political activists. By contrast, the deputies I targeted were the most active members of the House, were almost all idealistically motivated, and generally owed nothing to Thieu. They would ally themselves with the pro-Thieu group only if Can, or Thieu himself, would make compromises to bring government policy on the war and working toward peace more in line with their positions.

In a private meeting with Thieu, I told him he needed to broaden his base with popular support from the grassroots level, not just with a few individual members of the National Assembly. As it was, if a member elected by a Buddhist constituency now joined the pro-Thieu group, his credibility with and support from that constituency would disappear—unless Thieu made compromises to accommodate the Buddhist position. Thieu wouldn't buy that approach. He wanted to obtain a numeric majority first, and then add to it by wooing members of opposing groups later. Disappointed at his reaction, I rejected the idea of joining the pro-Thieu group, fearing that I would lose the support of the southern Catholics and the Buddhists.

While all of this political infighting and maneuvering were going on backstage, as it were, more than 1.2 million American, Allied, and South Vietnamese troops, all under the actual leadership of General Westmoreland, had launched a series of operations throughout all four military regions of South Vietnam during 1967.

In I Corps, Operations Prairie II and Prairie IV, continuation of the 1966 Operation Prarie (follow-up to Operation Hastings), Operations Union and Union II; Operation King Kisher; and Operation Swift—all conducted by the U.S. Marine Corps—inflicted significant casualties on NVA formations.

In II Corps, the U.S. First Cavalry conducted Operation Thayer II (continuation of the 1966 Operation Thayer) in northern Binh Dinh province, especially the Kim Son valley; while the Fourth Division and Third Brigade of the Twenty-fifth Division carried out Operation Sam Houston. Two Korean divisions, one headquartered in southern Binh Dinh and the other in Khanh Hoa, were also very active.

U.S. Army and Vietnamese troops mounted Operations Cedar Falls, Junction City, and Gadsen in III Corps north of Saigon. The U.S. Ninth Division planned and conducted Operations Coronado and Coronado V, Enterprise, and Palm Beach in the Mekong Delta provinces of IV Corps.

Additionally, ARVN divisions, sometimes operating with U.S. units, and sometimes conducting independent operations, were also very active especially in I Corps and II Corps.

Finally, the NVA and NLF, especially toward the end of 1967 as they maneuvered into position for their winter/spring offensive (Tet 1968), were not passive. In I Corps, ambitious actions were initiated on the Khe Sanh plateau, around Con Thien, and further south in the Hiep Duc valley area. In II Corps, NVA units were persistently aggressive around Dak To and Duc Co. The Third NVA Division continued attempts to spring from the An Lao valley onto the Bong Son plain. In III Corps, NVA and NLF regiments pressed hard on Loc Ninh and An Loc. Communist casualties, however, were high, and some suggested there was an appearance of desperation.

There was a new air of optimism among Americans and Vietnamese in top levels of the military and government, although the significance of the end-of-year border engagements was not yet understood. Having a constitutional government in place added an appearance of legitimacy and legality to U.S. efforts in Vietnam. These factors encouraged President Johnson to take a step he hoped would hasten an end to the conflict: he authorized bombing of North Vietnam targets previously on the restricted list, hoping this would lead North Vietnam to enter into peace talks. This followed his pledge earlier in the year to persevere in the war despite "more cost, more loss, and more agony." This satisfied such hawks as Senator Barry Goldwater and others who wanted stepped-up military actions. Senator Goldwater returned from a three-day trip to Vietnam and strongly recommended such a course, especially intensive, unrestricted air strikes on the North. These moves did not have the desired result; in fact, they probably were counterproductive. The North Vietnamese refused to open peace talks until the air attacks were halted, and the aerial assaults seemed to harden the resolve of the Communist Party and even the people to continue their fight.

In America itself antiwar sentiment was increasing.[6] Protest rallies attracted 100,000 in New York City, 20,000 in San Francisco, and 50,000 antiwar advocates marched on the Pentagon. Public opinion in the United States by this time was at the point where more people opposed the war than supported it.

About this time, I took a little trip that reminded me forcefully how great a difference there was in the way the war was viewed by the professionals and intellectuals in the cities and the people in the outlying countryside. On the one hand, many of the former were profiting from the war and suffered little because of it. The peasantry and villagers, on the other hand, bore the brunt of the suffering. They were often caught between the Viet Cong and government officials, South Vietnamese soldiers and the U.S military. It was hard sometimes to determine which side caused them greater hardship. I drove on the only highway linking Saigon with the Mekong Delta to visit my Kien Hoa constituency for the first time since the elections. As always during the day, traffic was heavy, split about evenly between military convoys and civilian transport, and it took me almost two hours to cover one thirty-five-kilometer section. Abandoned villages and rice paddies stretched toward the horizon on both sides of the road. This offered a serene, pastoral view that contrasted sharply with the flow of military traffic on the road and the warplanes flying in formations in the sky above. Strong points spotted at intervals along the route—by the Ben Luc Bridge, for example—clashed harshly with their seemingly peaceful surroundings.

I traveled through most of Kien Hoa province during the next three days, visiting many different people: religious leaders, government officials and soldiers, former Viet Cong and Viet Cong family members, ordinary farmers, and villagers. As a result of these meetings and conversations, I came to realize that the shared interests and feelings that had developed between the people of Kien Hoa and me during my two periods as provincial governor had turned into a deeper attachment. It was almost as though I had become part of their extended families. Never in my life had I felt so close to a group of people, in my heart and my mind, as I did to those men and women from the towns, villages, and countryside of Kien Hoa. It was at once an uplifting and humbling experience. It reinforced my feeling that I had done the right thing in resigning from the government and running in the election to become their representative in the National Assembly. It also made me more determined than ever to justify their faith in me by representing them in the best way I knew how.

I returned to the provincial capital and stopped to visit the current governor, who held the rank of colonel in the army. He seemed ill at ease talking to me. He asked me how I felt about the situation in Kien Hoa and seemed very pleased when I told him I had found things to be very peaceful. He immediately launched into an explanation of how active the troops had been, day and night, and how more and more Viet Cong had been killed or captured recently. He personified the professional military officer, trying to implement perfectly the orders that came from above. All his superiors in the government were also professional military men, trained to win the war by killing the enemy.

Unfortunately, this was not a normal war, with a clear-cut line dividing the opposing sides. The Soviets and the Chinese and the philosophy they represented may have been the real enemy—but they were not facing us on the battlefield. Our foes were the Vietnamese Communists, who looked like us and often lived and operated among us, indistinguishable from their fellow countrymen and women. The real battleground was in the countryside, in provinces like Kien Hoa, and only a minority of the enemy wore uniforms and carried weapons openly.

23: REACTION TO THE TET OFFENSIVE (1968)

I was invited to give a series of lectures at the Foreign Service Institute in Washington, DC. I also had appointments in Honolulu, Los Angeles, and New York before returning home through London, Paris, and Rome.

Before departing I had another meeting with President Thieu, and pointed out that he needed to broaden his political base. "The Catholics support you, but you must earn the backing of the Buddhists."

"I know you are closely connected with the Buddhists," he replied. "Can't you do something to get them to support the government?"

"You know I am with you personally, but that doesn't solve the problem," I told him. "The Buddhists won't support you or the government just because I do, or because I ask them to. You must first compromise with them on national policies, give them reason to think backing you will improve things."

Then he parroted the same old refrain so often used by elite Vietnamese who had, consciously or unconsciously, adopted the "blame-Communism-for-everything" attitude of the French first and the Americans currently. He revealed that he *still* did not recognize the real enemies. "How can I compromise with them? Their leaders are at least pro-Communist, if not outright Communists?"

"No, no; you are wrong! They are all anti-Communist, just as much as we are. Communism would put down all religions, including Buddhism, and they know that. It's just that their concept of what needs to be done in our country differs from that of the government and the U.S. leadership. In a word, the Buddhists feel that the Vietnamese government and its leaders must set an example of high personal standards and help foster a sense of national identity and pride. The government must protect and take care of the people; officials and military officers must be more concerned with the welfare of the peasants and workers. Corrupt and unjust officials and officers who use the people as pawns in their struggles to amass power and wealth must be uprooted. Then, by virtue of their deeds, the government and its leaders will have no trouble attracting support from the people. And the real enemies will be at least neutralized, if not converted to the government side."

Thieu listened passively. My words seemed to have little effect on him, and future events showed he neither understood nor heeded what I was trying to explain to him. Before I left, he insisted that I report to him immediately upon my return.

On the first stage of our flight, the 707 hit some turbulence. Suddenly a multicolored skyline seemed to rise out of the ocean and waken me from my reverie. We were approaching Hong Kong. I looked around the plane, noting that most of the passengers were GIs wearing civilian clothes and looking forward to a stretch of R&R. I recognized just two familiar faces: Philip Habib, previously Ambassador Lodge's chief political officer at the embassy, now deputy assistant secretary of state for East Asia; and my old friend Lieutenant General Lu Lan, an RVN officer.

Habib enjoyed a reputation in the American bureaucracy as one of the most knowledgeable Americans on Vietnamese affairs. He was an enthusiastic hawk who had opposed Edward Lansdale's sociopolitical approach and could barely hide his disdain for the Vietnamese generals and politicians, most of whom he considered hopelessly corrupt.

General Lu Lan had been a classmate of mine at the military academy, and we had remained close over the years. Although he was two years younger than I was,[1] I regarded him, and the other younger men, more highly than I did some of the older army officers who held high rank at the time. Lu Lan and others of his age formed the young generation of Vietnamese nationalists in the army. They were too young to have been involved in the start of the French war in 1945. They had not had to choose between the nationalists who fought for a free Vietnam and those who sided with the French. The latter group, which included Thieu and others who now headed the government, hid behind the shield of anti-Communism. The fact was, Communism had not yet fully developed when they had submitted to French domination in 1946 and took arms against their fellow countrymen. Anti-Communism was simply a convenient means for them to justify their actions.

Their submissiveness and resulting inferiority complexes made it easy for American political and military professionals such as Habib, Bunker, and Westmoreland to impose their wills on the French-trained officers. These Vietnamese "leaders" were accustomed to taking orders from foreigners. Most Americans, with a few exceptions, had trouble getting along with men of Lan's generation because the latter had more nationalistic pride and resisted presuming outsiders. This explains why the upper levels of South Vietnam's government and military readily went along with U.S. concepts and domination, which those at lower operational levels, and the population at large, neither understood nor accepted.

The plane landed at Honolulu in midafternoon under light showers. The peaceful, relaxed atmosphere contrasted sharply with that of the Saigon airport that I had left just a half-day earlier. John O'Donnell, former USAID representative in Kien Hoa province and now a staff member at the University of Hawaii, met me and drove me to the university. On the way, we reminisced about our work together in Kien Hoa a few years earlier. He also briefed me on my schedule for the coming few days.

During those days I gave a series of lectures to a group of Americans who were being prepared to go to Vietnam, where most of them would work in the pacification program. I did my best to explain the problems they would face, and what the Vietnamese people really wanted and needed from them. I also had a long discussion with the school's staff at a reception held for me, and covered the same subjects with them. Many questions were asked, and there appeared to be a lot of interest. But I wondered how effective such "Vietnam experts" as Thompson and I could be in making our ideas understood. Others covered the same areas—military operations, psychological warfare, and social and economic development—and I got the impression that the people we spoke to did not see where our approaches differed.

I felt frustrated while undertaking a desperate effort to make them understand the need for radical changes in the conduct of the war and the pacification program. I knew that the most dedicated Americans who served in the field in Vietnam would come to see the need for such changes, but usually only after their year of service was almost completed. And by then, they too would feel frustrated, because they would understand that the changes could only be initiated if they were accepted and put in place by the White House or the embassy and Pentagon East in Saigon.

A few days and several thousand miles later, after the long trip from Saigon, two days of uninterrupted activity in Hawaii, and drastic time zone changes, I spent some long working hours at the RAND Corporation think tank in Santa Monica, California. I felt a sense of unreality. I was sitting in Daniel Ellsberg's Malibu beach house, watching the setting sun and rows of incoming waves that seemed almost to die at my feet. I looked around at the houses stretching along the coast, the cars that ran in a constant stream along the Pacific Coast Highway, and the people jogging on the beach. It seemed so remote from the turbulent atmosphere and conditions in my country on the other side of the Pacific. Vietnam's beaches were at least as beautiful, but not secure from the constant threat of war. Only a few of the fortunate elite could enjoy beaches where they were protected by South Vietnamese or U.S. military units. Ellsberg walked in and interrupted such thoughts. He handed me an ad clipped from the *New York Times*. It contained a letter he and five others had signed, protesting the war in Vietnam and urging that the United States withdraw.

After reading it, I took a long look at my friend. He looked a lot older than the last time I had seen him, a bit less than two years earlier, in Vietnam. He was still the same physically—lean, active, and agile—but his face displayed an air of gravity that had not been there when he was based in Saigon. It was obvious that he didn't enjoy his prestigious position at RAND and the enviable life this lovely beach house represented. It's a cliché, but he seemed to be fighting inner demons or, perhaps more appropriately in this case, an inner dragon.

"Dan, how can you publicly oppose the government policy in Vietnam?" I asked him. "RAND lives on government contracts and subsidies. I am afraid that you, and even RAND itself, will be in trouble because of your public stand against the war."

"I cannot allow myself to be bribed or pressed to silence my conscience to the detriment of my country's moral and intellectual values," Ellsberg replied. "Nor can I agree with a policy that continues to let Americans die in a war we can never win. It is for my personal integrity, and my love for those who have been lied to so they will sacrifice themselves over there, that I have decided to go public with my opposition to the war. And I know I am not alone in this battle." His tone then changed, as though to reassure me. "Besides, Harry Rowen, RAND's director, is a man of high moral integrity himself. He doesn't seem to be concerned about the consequences of my actions."

After working with the RAND people for a week, I agreed with Dan about Rowen and his associates. They were a superb group of people working hard to offer Washington ideas and methods that would help fight, and win, the war. One RAND man, Robert Komer, was recruited in 1967 to serve as a presidential advisor for the "Other War," or pacification effort. Komer was later sent to Vietnam as an ambassador seconded to General Westmoreland to be the civilian head of the pacification program. Komer asked President Johnson to assign William Colby as his deputy. Colby, who took leave from a senior post at CIA headquarters to return once more to Vietnam, said this at the time: "Komer knew that if you put pacification under the military it would be lost, because the military would go out and shoot everybody. But Komer also understood that the military would never accept anything but a unity of command. Therefore, the only way to make it work was to put pacification under the military, in civilian hands. He had the genius to see that. He drove the military crazy, of course—did for years."[2] Like Westmoreland, who built a massive war machine of nearly 2 million American, Allied, and Vietnamese troops and was its true commander, Komer successfully built the biggest pacification machine of the war. All U.S. and Vietnamese nonmilitary pacification forces were under his control.

RAND and Hudson Institute people were just a few of the more visible thinkers among hundreds of scholars and experts from the best universities and foundations who worked with top people from the White House and Department of Defense to formulate strategies and tactics. It was ironic that this formidable array of talent, with their advanced degrees and sophistication, opposed a small group of Asian revolutionaries "educated" in the darkness of penitentiaries and wartime jungles, using the writings of Lenin and Marx as their bibles and instructional manuals. In popular current parlance, the Vietnamese Communists pitted their street smarts against the theories of their more intellectually advanced foes. At times I commented on this, only half-jokingly, to Ellsberg.

In this and later conversations with Ellsberg I observed how drastically he himself had changed. From the warrior marine captain and intellectual hawk who first came to Vietnam, believing implicitly in ultimate victory for the United States and South Vietnam, he became a dedicated fighter for U.S. withdrawal as the only way to save American lives and honor.

Upon my arrival in Washington, Tony Cistaro, a former USAID representative in the Mekong Delta and now at the Foreign Service Institute, met me. He took me to the State Department to show me around and familiarize me with my upcoming schedule, and later delivered me to a nearby hotel. Cistaro, in his late thirties, and I worked together during the following three weeks, becoming good friends in the process.[3]

Things were hectic at the institute, with an uninterrupted stream of trainee recruits arriving and departing for Saigon. They were there for "processing" before being sent to Vietnam to work for USAID, mostly at the provincial level, within the framework of the pacification program. Processing included lectures by people who had served in similar posts previously and old Vietnamese hands from various services. Most of the trainees were young college graduates, some with previous military service.

The series of lectures I had been requested to do covered various aspects of the war and its impact on the Vietnamese people, with emphasis on the do's and don'ts that Americans should remember in their dealings with the population. The trainees appeared very interested in learning about the country, its people, and the enemy. The more I talked to them, the more I wondered how effective they would be in Vietnam. Although the Americans who had worked with me generally had produced a positive effect on the population, that hadn't been true in many other provinces. Results depended on how the Americans worked with their Vietnamese counterparts and government officials and, even more important, how the people reacted to the U.S. representatives. If the workers and farmers regarded the Americans simply as successors to the French, U.S. efforts would have little positive effect, no matter how well meant they were. Vietnamese in the government and the military would be considered figureheads, with the Americans having the true power.

That is how it had been during my time as governor, and that's how it would be when these young Americans arrived in my country. If anything, the situation would be more difficult for them. The image of the United States as the neocolonial power, taking over from France, and the South Vietnamese government as subservient to it had been increasing in parallel with the military buildup. Curiously, the American expansion and emphasis on pacification also was backfiring and adding to this image. In Saigon, Ambassador Bunker and American generals were recognized by everyone, Vietnamese and Americans alike, as the true holders of power. At the provincial level, presence of the Americans side by side with Vietnamese officials was obviously reminiscent of the pre-1954 days when the French were in control. Viet Cong propaganda constantly, and effectively, hammered away at this point.

I tried hard to stress these points and make my audience understand their importance. I realized, however, that it would take time for them to appreciate what I was trying to explain to them and for them to understand that these factors were more critical to the overall war effort than anything on the military side.

I had been hoping that during my time in Washington there might be just one opportunity to convey my views to the highest level of the American government. I had to rely on luck and the help of people who shared my vision. The day when I might have that opportunity with the president finally arrived. My old friend who occasionally worked with me in Vietnam, Frank Scotton, picked me up to escort me to the White House. Scotton was one of the many devoted young Americans who had served in rural Vietnam. Like Ellsberg, Vann, Wisner, Holbrooke, Bumgardner, Sauvageot, Horn, Simko, and many others who come to mind, Scotton quickly learned about the cause and effect of the war because he established personal contact and an operational relationship with Vietnamese at the riceroots level. But unlike Vann who fought with and defied the hierarchy, or Bumgardner who usually found a way to work within the bureaucracy, Scotton seemed to simply ignore organizational lines and boxes. I am not sure what he was doing in Washington that winter—studying Chinese he told me—but he arranged for me to meet and explain my views to some of the most influential people in Washington: members of Congress, Secretary of the Army Stanley Resor, General Johnson, and Senator Ted Kennedy.

This day, however, he shocked me with news of a major Viet Cong offensive launched the previous night in Saigon. "It's still going on, Chau," he told me. "In fact, it seems to be intensifying and spreading to other cities in South Vietnam."

That is how I learned of the Tet Offensive, and that it was following the pattern I had predicted some months earlier. That is, it was not a pitched battle involving armies facing each other in the front lines but one waged in the cities and other areas considered to be under the control of South Vietnam and the Americans. The fact that I had been right did not reduce the dismay and concern I felt on hearing the news. Nor did it bode well for my projected visit with the president.

A high level of activity was obvious everywhere during the half-hour we spent going through guarded gates and the many corridors on our way to the office of Harry MacPherson, special counsel to the president. He was on the telephone. He motioned for me to sit down and went on with his conversation. The tone of his voice as he talked on the phone was tense and impatient. When he hung up, instead of having me brief him on the object of my visit, as originally planned, he launched into a long explanation of the current situation in Vietnam, being interrupted frequently by aides or phone calls. "Furious fighting is still going on in most cities and provincial capitals," he told me, "and it's still too early to assess the outcome."

Then presidential advisor Walt Rostow walked in. No sooner had we been introduced and exchanged handshakes than he was called into the president's office. Again MacPherson's telephone rang, and I stood up to tell him I would rather return at a more appropriate time.

MacPherson apologized for the constant interruptions. "I'm sure you appreciate how difficult things are at the moment," he said. "We had fully expected to have you talk with the president, but I don't think that will possible under the circumstances, as I'm sure you will understand. One other thing: I know you must be concerned about the safety of your family back in Saigon. I'll be happy to arrange for a call to be put through to your wife for you, if you like."

I thanked him for his thoughtfulness, knowing it would be almost impossible to make a personal call through normal channels at a time of such crisis. A call coming from the White House was a different matter, however, and I was soon able to have a short conversation with my wife.

I could hear the crackle of automatic weapons in the background as we talked. "The fighting is still going on," she told me. "The children and I have been confined to the house for the past forty-eight hours, but we are all fine. John Paul Vann sent over a dozen security guards to protect our home and sent us enough food so we won't go hungry even if the twenty-four-hour curfew now in effect is prolonged."

I was relieved to learn that my family was safe and well provided with protection and provisions, but I was bitterly disappointed that the coincidence of events foiled what had become the most cherished and ultimate object of my visit to the United States. Days earlier, immediately after I learned that I would meet with MacPherson, with the expectation that the president might see me afterward, I began planning what I would say. I anticipated that I surely would have no more than thirty minutes, perhaps less, to state my case. I sat down with a blank sheet of paper and a pencil to write out what I wanted to say.

In my first attempt it took only a short time to list so many points I wanted to cover: messy military operations; futile pacification efforts; the Thieu-Ky rivalry; corruption in the government at most levels and in some of the military structure; farcical elections that served only to deceive the Vietnamese and American public; misconceptions held by Americans about the Catholics and Buddhists in Vietnam, and how they affected the war; the importance of the Vietnamese "nationalistic image" and how to foster it; and the need for change so people would be motivated to support the government. I paused then, realizing I could go on and on listing my thoughts and expanding on them.

Finally, at 2 a.m., I threw down the pencil in frustration and went to bed, hoping I would think more clearly after a rest. But I couldn't sleep. My mind kept mulling over the problems that must be solved to change the course of the war. I then switched sides, as it were, trying to look at the situation through the eyes of strategists for our opponents. What would they consider the root of our problems?

Strategists for the other side knew very clearly who their enemies were, but the Americans and those ruling South Vietnam did not. They could not because they were hampered by too many misconceptions. I was startled to realize at last that something which had been clear to me since 1962 had never been really clear to the strategists and leaders of the war on our side.

They thought they knew the answer; to them, our enemies obviously were the Northern Communists, the Viet Cong, and those who had been reported to be pro-Communist or Viet Cong supporters. That made conducting the war very simple. You merely searched for the Viet Cong and Communists in the jungles or on battlefields and destroyed them. Simple indeed. It was only necessary to discover and identify the pro-Communists and VC supporters among the villagers, students, intellectuals, workers, and the general populace, and then arrest or eliminate them. So very simple.

These were the concepts and presumptions followed consistently by the government, police and security/intelligence agencies, and the military in pursuing the war. Consequently, that was the mind-set of those who governed the country, collected intelligence on the enemy, and fought the war. And they were wrong, wrong, wrong.

My background with the Viet Minh and experience in the field, especially in Kien Hoa, caused me to rediscover who the real enemy was. Our enemies really were other Vietnamese, be they Viet Cong or Communists, who did not believe in South Vietnam's U.S.-supported leaders or their policies and were willing to fight to the death to change them. I realized that I could easily have been among them, had circumstances been only slightly different at some point during the previous fifteen years. That led me to a realization that many things had to be changed—politically, socially, and militarily—in our direction of the war, or we would only strengthen the resolve of our enemies, and continually create new ones.

The first and most fundamental change, I decided, had to come from the top down. It had to start with and be supported by top Vietnamese leaders, then be translated down through the ranks to the hearts and minds of the lowest in the government and military hierarchy. This was necessary especially to bring about a change in the attitude and methods of those involved in the gathering and analysis of intelligence on the enemy, particularly the enemy among the rural population, which was the real strategic base of the Viet Cong and the Communists. So far, leaders of those civilian and military operations had all been Vietnamese who had been employed, educated, and trained by the French prior to and during their war against the Viet Minh. Consequently, as I have pointed out earlier, anyone who had fought with or supported the Viet Minh in the past was automatically considered to be Viet Cong or pro–Viet Cong, and was treated as such.

My Census Grievance project had been created to remedy that situation. It allowed us to identify true enemies and assess their commitment and importance to the Viet Cong / Communist cause. All subsequent political, social, and military programs could then follow from that application of a technique designed to portray the true situation in a given area.

Does it seem strange to say that we did not know the enemy (or at least those we thought, rightly or wrongly, to be our enemies), even after years of fighting and killing countless numbers of them, and after we had sacrificed tens of thousands of our own men to kill them? Perhaps, but it is the unfortunate truth. And because we did not accurately define and identify the enemy, we had been fighting a war, however noble its cause, in a way that guaranteed we could never win: the more we killed, the more enemy we created.

I had looked at the potential enemy as aggressors from the North; if they came they would come in the way I and many of my fellow officers had been prepared to deal with at in our training at Fort Benning and Fort Leavenworth. My goal was to prepare myself and military students to win that kind of war so as to preserve the South for the independent and peaceful destiny I envisioned for it.

When I was singled out by President Diem and offered a series of positions that opened up the realities of South Vietnam to me, I learned the social and political facts of life in the countryside, which differed a great deal from the comparative comfort of the cities. While a new class of affluent Vietnamese had been growing up in the military and civilian establishments, rooted in American generosity, Vietnamese in the countryside remained as divided in peace as they had been in war. Those who had fought with the French were still the relatively influential elite and formed the local leadership. Those who had opposed the French had become targets of discrimination, sometimes carried to bloody lengths.

As I witnessed the scene, errors led slowly but steadily to local unease, increasing hostility toward the government, a state of emergency as armed resistance grew, and finally to open warfare—predictably accompanied by infiltration and intervention by the North. I realized only then that I finally knew and understood the enemy, something I had thought that I knew much, much earlier. I also knew that both the South Vietnamese and American leadership were fighting a misperceived enemy rather than the true enemy.

What caused such an enormous mistake and allowed it to endure for so long? When the French departed in 1954 and the country was divided into South and North Vietnam, Washington—in its obsession with the domino theory and to contain communism in Southeast Asia—perceived North Vietnam as the threat. That is where the enemy was and would come from if war occurred. Meanwhile, in the South, Vietnamese who had cooperated with the French or spoke against communism were regarded as true patriots. Unfortunately, not many Americans took the time and trouble to learn about the background of their allies, be they politicians or military counterparts. The pro-American and anti-Communist rhetoric such Vietnamese spouted seemed more important.

The United States thus had built up the South Vietnamese government and military systems to fight a conventional war waged from the North, and staffed both government and military with leaders who had worked with and been trained by the French.

From the day I volunteered for the Vietnamese National Army through the end of the war with the French in 1954, although I chose to be in the front lines most of the time, I was confused about the enemy I killed and worried about my true feelings. Was I hiding moral or intellectual cowardice beneath physical bravery? My conscience tortured me because of the better, more comfortable life I enjoyed in comparison with the one I had led with my former comrades in the Viet Minh when we fought the French. In those years we lived and fought without pay, shared the same hard life of guerrilla troops in the field, took solace from the people around us, and were never concerned about interference by Russians, Chinese, or other foreigners besides the few Japanese and Europeans of the French Foreign Legion who had left their old units to join our ranks.

The Vietnamese chief of state, Emperor Bao Dai, and the central government were very remote figures. Province, district, and village chiefs who made up local governments were all holdovers from the French colonial regime. Like other officers of my rank, I was provided with aides and a chauffeur, and my wife and child received monthly allowances. That treatment contrasted sharply with the hardship of my service in the Viet Minh, conditions my old comrades now on the opposite side still had to bear. I had long ago been convinced that we could regain national independence and make changes to benefit the lower classes without adopting communism, which I considered alien to the culture of Vietnam and wholly incompatible to my own religious beliefs and those of nearly all other Vietnamese, be they Catholic, Buddhist, Cao Dai, or small minority sects.

I knew from experience that there had been only a very few true Communists among the Viet Minh cadres when I joined them in the 1940s. Probably even fewer of us who joined to fight for Vietnamese independence knew anything about communism. I have long been convinced that most of my former comrades-in-arms who turned Communist in the late 1940s and 1950s (and later formed the infrastructure of the North Vietnamese Communist Party) did so mainly because it seemed to be the best possibility to rid their country of foreign domination. Even after France granted Vietnam semiautonomy with Bao Dai as chief of state, it was obvious that the French still predominated. The Communists hammered away at this in their very effective propaganda and indoctrination programs.

When the U.S. presence began to grow and as the influence of Americans over our South Vietnamese government and military systems became more evident, Americans simply replaced the French as the repressive ogres in Communist propaganda. It was still true in the 1950s and 1960s that only a small fraction, the top leadership, of the Viet Cong and their sympathizers in the South knew or cared much about Communist doctrine. The vast majority of the people in the southern countryside were concerned primarily with their own safety and personal interests. The South Vietnamese government, and later, the Americans, created many, many more Viet Cong and pro-Communists than did the attraction of Marxist-Leninist dialectics.

After the 1954 Geneva Peace Accords and the establishment of the Ngo Dinh Diem government, those who had been in or supported the fight against the French were hounded, humiliated, discriminated against, jailed, and even executed by the South Vietnamese administration and police. Those people who suffered this treatment, mostly poor peasants and workers, were driven directly into the arms of the enemy. With a base of these disaffected people in the South, plus the roughly 100,000 Southerners who moved north after the Geneva Accords split the country, North Vietnam built a "bridge" into the South. That was the root of this war, politically and strategically, and provided the resources that nurtured the Viet Cong and invaders from the North.

So our current enemy was composed of the Communist government in the North, made up mostly of former Viet Minh comrades, a northern-based regular army, and the new Viet Cong and their supporters in the South. All, basically, were indistinguishable in appearance from those fighting for and supporting our government. As I came to know and understand this, I realized that South Vietnamese and American leaders did not recognize the enemy they were trying to defeat. Even worse, they did not know how our enemies were created, and why their ranks were growing. This was true despite the efforts that scholars and researchers, such as those in the RAND organization, had made to define and profile the enemy. To be more accurate, the element of knowing the enemy, which every junior officer had to learn from Sun Tzu, was never truly taken into consideration by the strategy makers.

The Americans from the beginning failed to recognize that the more predominant they became, the more determined the enemy became. Diem ignored this to a great degree in accepting U.S. support, though he attempted to restrict outright and obvious American control. Ironically, the coup that removed him also removed the only South Vietnamese leader who did try to stand up to the United States. Those who followed him were obviously subservient to the Americans. So the United States kept pouring in men and resources in a wasteful, self-defeating strategy. The result was a great deal of death and destruction that created a fertile source of recruits and strategic options for the other side.

Conversely I had demonstrated that being able to identify and separate the enemy from his look-alike neighbors through the Census Grievance process produced four important benefits. First, it won the support of the general populace, when they saw they were being fairly treated and protected (through the anonymity built into the process), and they could reject the Viet Cong and rally to the government's side. Second, it neutralized the Viet Cong and their sympathizers, and made it possible to convert all but the most committed enemy. Third, it eliminated active enemy and hostile operations from the territory, which meant that, fourth, the people and resources in the area were denied to enemy infiltrators from the North.

Accepting my pacification formula, including the key Census Grievance element, would mean changing the overall strategy drastically. Since the enemy could no longer swim like fish in the water of the rural population, there would be no need for search-and-destroy missions to kill the enemy in the jungle. Instead, our troops could just wait for the foe to come out into the open and then eliminate them. Our military forces would be used, mainly in battalion and brigade strength, to provide security for areas undergoing pacification. As the Census Grievance and other facets of the program began to take effect, the troops would move to eliminate the enemy infrastructure and build up a defense system among the local people that would enable them to protect themselves. Gradually they would become capable of resisting enemy efforts at recruitment, confiscating supplies, gathering intelligence, and using the area for staging purposes or as part of a supply route.

I proved that formula by implementing it in Kien Hoa province, then spelled it out in my book, significantly titled *From War to Peace: Restoration of the Countryside*. For a few years I thought I had succeeded in selling my ideas to the Americans, and certainly some of them understood them and backed me. I finally came to the conclusion that I had failed: the war was being fought, and would continue to be fought, in the same self-defeating fashion. I had worked for change as a member of the South Vietnam military and administration. When that failed, I tried as an elected representative, feeling that I could be more effective in ways and at levels that had not been possible when I was a military man and government servant. But I was not successful. I had worked hard to convince my countrymen in the military and in the administration that changes were necessary, but I had come to realize that was hopeless. The entire Vietnamese leadership, military and administration, deferred totally to the American generals and ambassadors. There was no way our leaders would stand up to or disagree with the U.S. representatives. I realized that if there were to be any change, it would have to be initiated by the United States.

With all that in mind, I longed for an occasion to talk to President Johnson, the one man who could change things. If I could only convince him, as I was able to convince some Americans who understood the problem and its solution—men like General Timmes, Lansdale, the CIA's Colby, Vann, Ellsberg, and many others—victory was still possible. None of us had been able to muster the top-level support needed to implement the necessary policies and programs. That would not be a problem for the president!

So, on that afternoon when MacPherson told me that the president could not see me because of the Tet Offensive, I left the White House and returned to my hotel in utter dejection. When I arrived, I found that television sets in the hotel lobby and restaurant all displayed the bloody results of that offensive. The war in Vietnam was being brought home to Americans in vivid color. People watched in horror and astonishment as houses burned, people died, and injured soldiers and civilians were carried away. I went to my room and watched the war on the screen for hours before I fell asleep.

It is inconceivable that the American public will continue to support the war after watching scenes like this, I told myself. *Surely antiwar sentiment will now be intensified more than ever.* In the days that followed, I toured the city, going from place to place for my lectures, visits, and discussions. I could see how much anxiety there was about the war's outcome, and how many people distrusted the way American generals were handling the war. Television and other media brought scenes of shooting and destruction from Saigon and dozens of other cities 10,000 miles away into the living rooms of American families in a way they could not ignore or forget. The war entered their hearts and minds.

On a short trip to Fort Bragg, North Carolina, officers in the audience questioned me repeatedly on my assessment of the war's progress and the outlook for the Communists. I did my best to be honest, not telling them that everything was going well and that victory was inevitable, but I tried to avoid being overly critical or pessimistic. At a reception that evening, I learned that President Johnson had decided to send additional troops, from the Eighty-Second Airborne, to Vietnam as an installment of the increase requested by General Westmoreland.[4]

Back in Washington I attended a dinner given by South Vietnamese Ambassador Bui Diem. Several members of Congress and a number of Vietnamese old hands, Rufus Phillips among them, attended. The long conversations during and after the meal again centered on the war, with the growing antiwar movement mentioned frequently and at length.

The same subject, and another one rising from an appalling photo taken in

Saigon, came up in a meeting I had later with Leonard Marks, director of the U.S. Information Agency. "I am a personal friend of President Johnson, and I do believe that the president is right in the pursuit of the war," he said, "because it is a noble and just cause. For that reason I have accepted this position, to uphold our image and make our position clear to the public here and around the world: we are trying to help a small, struggling nation remain independent and free of Communist control. My purpose is to counter the distortions and defamation of those who oppose the war." He continued in grave, somber tones.

"But just when I thought I had begun to achieve some results, your men undermined our efforts, to say nothing of ruining the image of my country and yours!" He then took a photograph from his desk and showed it to me. It was the infamous picture of General Nguyen Ngoc Loan shooting a captured Viet Cong in the head— while the captured prisoner had his hands tied behind his back.

"A soldier or general in the field might commit such an act; he would then be court-martialed and punished, but at least people would understand that he acted in the heat of battle. But when the top law enforcement official of a country, the national chief of police, which is this man's title, shoots a captured prisoner who is bound and helpless, there can be no excuse," he went on, becoming angrier by the moment. "When he does it right in the center of the capital, before members of the press, he seems to be defying all civilized conventions.

"How can people of this country and the free world believe that we are fighting for a noble cause that your government is a good one, worthy of the sacrifices being made to preserve it?"

I interrupted his emotional outburst, agreeing with him in my inner heart but trying to temper his anger to some degree. "I am sorry for what happened, but you must remember that the Communists were guilty of equally heinous killings and atrocities, and against civilians, when they brought the war into the densely populated cities."

Leonard Marks would have none of it, however, and his temper rose even higher. "Exactly! Here we are fighting the Communist bad guys to protect what are supposed to be the good guys, the South Vietnamese, and this is a flagrant case that paints your side as being just as bad as the enemy! How can people believe this is a 'good war' if they think that the action of your national police chief is characteristic of your system of government?"

His point was valid, of course, and Loan's callous execution of the helpless prisoner was the kind of outrageous act I deplored among the Saigon generals. Yet I put the blame on the system that put Loan in the position he held more than on Loan himself. He was what he was, and he had shown his cruelty and lack of compassion or mercy in the past. His big performance, the one that earned him his general's star, was the unnecessarily bloody and merciless crushing of the Buddhist uprising in Central Vietnam in 1966. He somewhat reflected the personality of his military academy classmate Ky, who as prime minister had installed Loan in his position as chief of the national police.

Although Thieu had now been established as the elected president for more than six months, he was too cautious to replace Loan for fear of antagonizing the Ky "clan," which was built up in the military. So the entire system had to pay for the wrongdoing of Loan. In a meeting a week later with the Council on Foreign Affairs in New York, in response to a question about the remarks of Senator Robert Kennedy attacking the Loan action and corruption and inefficiency of the South Vietnamese government, I pointed out that the United States must share blame for the situation. "It was the Americans who generated the system and leadership now in place in South Vietnam, and they must accept some of the responsibility for the results, as well as an obligation to the survival of South Vietnam."

Robert Kennedy was a strong advocate for American withdrawal, and his public statement coincided with President Johnson's decision to not send more troops to Vietnam. These were straws in the wind indicating a major change in U.S. policy.

Much more was evident during the following two weeks. I spent the remaining time in the United States traveling to Los Angeles, San Francisco, and New York, visiting and talking to RAND members, Daniel Ellsberg, Mayor Sam Yorty, Senator Ted Kennedy (again), my former military advisor and friend Lieutenant Colonel Simko, and numerous others. The many contacts I had inside and outside of the American establishment brought me to the conclusion that the war had definitely reached the ultimate point of rejection in the United States. Despite General Westmoreland's assessment, both the American public and now the establishment would welcome a negotiated settlement that would allow U.S. withdrawal in a face-saving manner. Suddenly I was terrified at the prospect of the South Vietnamese fighting the Communists alone. I felt confused about whether I was fearful as much because of concern for myself and my family as I was for all of Vietnam.

I finally realized that now there was no hope of an audience with the president; there was no more time to talk to the Americans about changes in the Vietnamese government and military systems, or in military or pacification operations. There now was only time enough to do something that would help South Vietnam to survive as a free country without the United States, and anything that could be done along those lines had to be accomplished before the Americans disengaged themselves from the war.

I said good-bye to Frances Fitzgerald, who had been my gracious hostess on my short stopover in New York, and flew to London on my way home. Frances was a well-known author who had written several articles on Vietnam for major publications: the *New York Times*, the *New Yorker* magazine, and the *Atlantic*. She was of that new breed of intellectuals who wanted to complement their scholarly research in the comfort of libraries with personal knowledge gained in the field.[5]

My short stays in London, Paris, and Rome during the following two weeks corroborated my feeling that the days of the United States having troops involved in the Vietnam War were ending. Long after I heard the remarks of the USIA director in Washington, that picture of General Loan was still being reprinted in major papers in London. Vo Nguyen Giap was featured on the cover of an Italian magazine as "the Napoleon of the 20th century."

In Paris, my most emotional moment came during a meeting with an old friend from the Viet Minh days. Hoang also had joined the Viet Minh in 1945, fought bravely and brilliantly, but then had abandoned the Viet Minh in 1947 and escaped to France. He had returned to school, become an attorney, and established a successful career. He was married to a beautiful Frenchwoman, also an attorney, and had a charming little daughter. He told me his personal story in tears, confessing that he had been living like a moral "lache," a coward, that he felt morally and intellectually ashamed because he had turned his back on his country. "The reason," he said, "is that although I continue to reject communism, I still respect the people who are fighting on the side of the Viet Cong and the North. Yet, while I believe in the idea of democracy and independence for the South, I despise its leaders. So I can't cope with either side."

Hoang also felt guilty about enjoying his current, comfortable lifestyle while his country was going through such desperate times. I was surprised to learn of his state of mind, exceptionally rare for a Vietnamese intellectual. Most did not share his feeling of guilt. In Saigon, I used to see and hear most intellectuals, some turned politicians, who kept haranguing about "the noble cause" while draft dodging or sending their draft-age children abroad or hiding them in safe places thanks to their connections in the government or the military. Other intellectuals felt no compunction about enjoying their pleasant, prosperous lifestyles made possible by American largesse.

During a private tête-à-tête dinner with Ambassador Nguyen Van Hieu, Thieu's older brother, the ambassador complained that he was rarely consulted by his brother or any other member of the South Vietnamese government. In fact, as I talked to Hieu about the many problems that concerned me, he suggested that I would have more influence with his brother than he would, and that I should take up the problems directly with Thieu. Hieu had known me since 1951 and was aware of my close relationship with his brother. Neither he nor I had any idea at the time how soon that relationship would be ruptured, and the consequences I would endure as a result.

24: AFTER THE TET DELUGE, MY PEACE
NEGOTIATION PROPOSAL (1968)

Because of a last-minute change in my flight schedule, I was not able to notify my family of my arrival time. So my wife and the children were happily surprised when they found me standing at the front gate, but no happier than I was to see that they were all safe. My wife quickly reassured me that our other relatives also escaped harm during the fighting. She lost contact with her parents, who lived about eight kilometers away, during the first three days of the offensive but learned later that they survived without injury.

"It was very frightening," she told me. I could see fear and horror in her eyes as she remembered. "The shooting and artillery shelling went on all day and increased during the night. Helicopters flew overhead constantly, circling at times to fire their machine guns and rockets at enemy targets in the city. The noise was horrible! Fires and the flash of explosions lit up the sky. I was grateful that Colonel Thanh[1] and John Vann sent a squad of security guards to protect us and our home. They also delivered food regularly so we didn't go hungry."

I expressed my appreciation to Vann when he came to see me that evening. He waved my thanks aside casually. "Glad I could help," he said, and then, as usual, came straight to the point of his visit. "We beat them badly, very badly. They did surprise us, but they must have gotten a big surprise themselves. We were surprised because, although we had been alerted that there would be some kind of Communist attacks in some cities, we did not believe they would be so widespread, or that they could hit with as much force as they did in the cities we believed we controlled fully.

"They must have been surprised, too, when the Vietnamese people did not rise up and join them in what they used to refer to as the third and final phase of their revolutionary war. And they were equally surprised by our being more prepared to fight back than they anticipated. The Vietnamese troops, and the American and allied forces, did an excellent job of counterattacking."

"How heavy were the enemy losses?" I asked him quietly, "and how many casualties did we suffer?"

"Communist losses were very heavy, some 40,000 reported killed or captured out of an estimated 100,000 enemy committed to the battle," Vann said. "But as you know, those figures were reported by subordinate units throughout the country and could be exaggerated, as they usually are. Still, it was a major blow to the Communists, and I doubt that they will try anything like it in the future.

"I'm not sure about our casualties yet, but I have been informed that American losses were about 1,000 killed and the same number wounded. Losses among the Vietnamese troops, who were the focus of the attack in many areas and fought back fiercely, must have been heavier."

He was very upset with the media for the way they had covered the battle, making the U.S. and South Vietnamese forces appear to be vulnerable and downplaying the heavy enemy losses. I added fuel to his anger when I told him about the heavy coverage in American and European media of the Tet Offensive and especially of General Loan executing the bound prisoner. Vann's face got bright red and he shouted, as if to the skies, "Those bastards! The TV and press photographers and reporters are the ones who distorted the truth for the sake of creating a sensation." I was taken aback, realizing that Vann, who had been so successful in using the media against the establishment in the past, now found the shoe on the other foot. He wasn't comfortable wearing it.

The next day I called Colonel Tran Van Cam, President Thieu's chief of cabinet, and asked him to inform the president that I was back from my trip and wanted to see him, to deliver the detailed report he had requested before I left for the United States. A day passed and I called again.

"I gave your message to President Thieu," Cam told me, "but he merely accepted it and said nothing about setting up a meeting with you." I was surprised and upset because Thieu had seemed so insistent on hearing from me as soon as I returned. Then I decided not to call any more, and flew to Hué to see my father. I hadn't visited him for some time and wanted to know how he and other friends and relatives in and around Hué had survived the Tet Offensive. Fighting was particularly heavy there, and the Communists had occupied the city for twenty-six days.

As always, my father studied me quietly as I bowed to him respectfully.

"How are you, Father?" I asked. "I am happy to be back and to find you in good health. Did the Communists come by here during their occupation of Hué?"

He didn't answer my questions immediately but instead wanted to know how my family had fared in Saigon during my absence. He also inquired about my wife's parents, who were old friends. I reassured him that all were well and had come through the fighting around them unscathed. "I am pleased to learn that," he said. "Now go and refresh yourself after your trip. We will talk after dinner."

After bathing and saying a prayer at the ancestral shrine, I rejoined Father for dinner. We were preoccupied and silent as we ate. Only after the maid cleared the table and left us did he begin to talk, asking me several questions. "What did you do in the United States? Who did you see? Did you learn anything?"

I gave him a condensed version of my trip, the people I had seen, how strange it had been to watch the war on television from thousands of miles away, and the various reactions I had observed to developments here in Vietnam. He then went to the point that obviously was the cause of his concern and preoccupation.

"Do you think the war will continue for a long time?"

"Father, how can I know?" I replied. "The one thing I am sure of, however, is that the United States is going to withdraw from this war in one way or another."

"If what you say is true, how can the South can stand against the North?" he asked me in dismay.

"Frankly, the prospect scares me," I replied. "The way things are now, I can only predict more death and destruction unless President Thieu makes drastic changes to gain more support, both at home and abroad."

"I don't want to go into problems or give advice about things that you know more about that I do," he said. "I only suggest that, since you have been a longtime friend of Thieu, you should talk to the president and other responsible Vietnamese and Americans. Try to impress upon them the need to end the war for the sake of the country and the people. If it continues on and on, we will lose even if we win! For years we were told only the successes and that victory would be ours, especially since the Americans began landing in Danang four or five years ago. Now we have seen the war come right to the heart of Hué, something that never happened before, even during the worst of the French wars. The North came here with tanks, artillery, and thousands of cadres. They overran the area for almost a month, until the Americans came to help retake the city. The Citadel is now in ruins, as are many houses and buildings in the city and its outskirts.[2] Thousands of military and civilians were killed during the fighting. Thousands more were killed before the Communists withdrew, probably because they refused to cooperate with the invaders.[3] The husband of our cousin Huong and their twelve-year-old son were among those slain."

Father paused for a long time, and I could see tears forming in his eyes.

"Father," I told him earnestly, "I did my best with President Diem and now President Thieu to improve things, to help win the war, but I play only a very minor role in this whole system. I don't know what more I can do. I am determined, however, to continue my efforts to help end this war, to bring justice and peace to our country."

My aging parent considered my words and nodded, seeming to indicate both that he understood my frustration and that he fully expected me to go on working in any way I could to end the war. He rose, preparing to go to bed, but first pointed to the front yard.

"A Communist armored unit camped out there for nearly two weeks during the battle," he said. "One day, a North Vietnam officer entered the house and shouted at me, 'The people have denounced you, saying that you have two sons serving in the puppet South Vietnam regime, and that one of them is a high-ranking officer! Is that true?' 'It is very true,' I answered him. 'But I also have three others, two sons and a daughter, plus her husband, my son-in-law, serving on your side. And two of them are also in high positions! Don't you want their names, too?' The officer changed his tone and addressed me more politely after that," said Father, showing a sort of grim humor for the first time in our conversation.

The next day I visited the century-old Bao Quoc pagoda-school where I had received my initial education during the 1930s. Set on a small hill northwest of Hué, it overlooked the entire city and both sides of the Perfume River. It was a bright, sunny day, much too cheerful for the scenes of destruction inside and outside the Citadel that were all too evident from this height. The damage seemed extensive but not as complete as I had been led to expect. Thankfully, the pagoda did not appear to have been damaged. The superior was not there so I talked to some of the monks. They told me that neither side had attacked the compound or the high ground it occupied.

"We escaped the shelling and fighting that destroyed so much of the city," one of the monks explained. "But the Communists did try to rally us to their cause." Several of the monks then said that a number of former students from Hué (though not from the pagoda school) who had joined Ho Chi Minh's forces a long time ago returned with the North Vietnamese troops.

"They exhorted everyone, Buddhists and non-Buddhists alike, to support and welcome the 'liberators' from the North. They gave out flags and banners for the people to wave for that purpose," said one young bonze. "But nearly everyone refused to go along with them. We wonder if that was the reason why hundreds, perhaps thousands, of people were murdered, captured, or simply disappeared in and around Hué before the Communists withdrew."

The sinister news about the murders, kidnappings, and disappearances was confirmed by still another source, a staff officer of the First ARVN Division. The division, though surrounded, stood firmly and successfully for three weeks against multiple attacks by the Communists. He and his fellow officers were frank in saying that though the ARVN fought well, the U.S. troops were the ones who retook the city from the Communists.

I flew to Ben Tre in a helicopter with Robert Coates, a friend I had made during my recent visit to the United States when I stayed in his San Francisco home. He and his charming wife had been most gracious hosts. Coates was a government consultant for agricultural affairs. We toured the city, and I showed him the damage from the Tet campaign. The Viet Cong had been active in the whole area but were not able to capture the province chief's residence, MACV compound, or Civil Guard headquarters. Those sites were defended by Vietnamese provincial units, which held firm until American Ninth Infantry Division troops came to the rescue. Rocket fire was widely used to attack areas where Viet Cong had been reported. As a result, Truc Giang was liberated in a manner that one officer who took part in the battle described, in a statement that became famous, "The city had to be destroyed to be saved." Media correspondents quoted that statement frequently to describe the escalation in Vietnam.

I flew back to Saigon with Coates the same day, but returned to Kien Hoa the next day to visit hamlets and districts. I was surprised to see that much of the province had not fared as badly as I anticipated from watching TV in the States. The Viet Cong, without any North Vietnamese involved, had only deployed their provincial and district units in attacks, while small guerrilla groups intensified their harassment of the many government outposts throughout the province. They either made no real effort or were not capable of penetrating defenses because they failed to overrun any significant government position. They were repulsed by Provincial Civil Guard and Self-Defense forces, except in and around Truc Giang, for two to three days, when they were chased away with the help of American reinforcements.

Although enemy losses were officially reported as very high, I heard a different story from local Buddhist, Catholic, and Cao Dai leaders, men I always trusted for their knowledge of and concern for anything affecting their communities. District and village chiefs confirmed what the religious leaders told me: casualties on both sides had been low, even lower than in some previous critical periods. Curiously also, the entire province had been quiet, with Viet Cong activities greatly reduced, since the Tet Offensive. I could travel easily through many hamlets that formerly had been very insecure. I was sure in my mind that the Viet Cong were now on their usual long individual and unit self-critique sessions, learning from the successes and failures of the operation before planning their next moves.

The House of Deputies was in session, and the defense minister was on hand to answer questions and criticisms about the new general mobilization draft law. It would require all men between seventeen and forty-five years of age to serve in military or defense-related organizations. The government sponsored the bill, and its position was clear and indisputable: if American young men were drafted to protect South Vietnam, there was no reason that South Vietnamese should not do the same. Those opposed to the bill agreed with the need for general mobilization. They argued, however, that Vietnamese leaders had to set an example by encouraging their sons and relatives to volunteer or be drafted into the military and share the dangers in battle, not to hide in cushy headquarters jobs or be assigned as "bodyguards" or "aides" for colonels and generals, as was usually the case for many who did not evade service completely by "study" abroad. Congressman Ngo Cong Duc was from a wealthy family that owned land in the Mekong Delta. Early the previous year, in anticipation of being drafted into the army, Duc volunteered for the local Self-Defense Force. Subsequently, he was elected as a deputy from his province, Vinh Long. Prime Minister Ky's underlings did not subvert his election only because Duc's family enjoyed a good reputation and was prominent in the area. Preventing Duc's election would have created a troublesome protest.

After his election Duc was criticized by the military as a draft dodger. Duc arrogantly threw the gauntlet back at them, pointing out that there were tens, if not hundreds, or thousands of government officials, military officers, and well-connected businessmen who shielded their sons and nephews from the war. He disclosed that he had a long list of people who had paid bribes to ensure that their drafted sons did not have to serve in combat units, and another list of those who moved their sons out of the country to avoid military service altogether. Duc's assertions provoked the government but were nothing new to the general public. When he went further, specifically explaining how the sons of both the minister of defense and chairman of the Joint Chiefs of Staff had been exempted from military service and were enjoying the good life as rich students in Paris, it made sensational news that spread quickly. It was another example of how those in power were taking advantage of their positions.

Deputy Duc began to emerge as a hero among soldiers, young officers in the field, and the public at large, but he became a target for those at the top in Saigon. He enjoyed the sympathy and support of many deputies in the Assembly, but pro-government members began to say they thought he was pro–Viet Cong. Probably his close association with the number-one Catholic in Vietnam, Archbishop Nguyen Van Binh, Duc's uncle, caused repressive elements to hesitate at eliminating the fiery young deputy.

During our first months in the House, I too resented Duc and several other deputies I regarded as draft dodgers. Gradually I realized that they formed the most active group of Southerners opposed to the government's abuses of power. I began to see that their refusal to join the army was a protest against a system that made promotions on favoritism rather than merit, producing senior officers who for the most part were corrupt and incompetent. These dissidents argued that such leadership in government as well as the military made it easy for the Communists to spread their message and gain converts, negating the enormous American effort to support a democratic South Vietnam. This group of Southern deputies chose the National Assembly as their platform to fight for reform. They also established the only real opposition newspaper, *Tin Sang*. Their goal: A better government and military system that would at least neutralize, if not defeat, Communism.

Duc's group was the first in South Vietnam to generate support from intellectuals and students in the cities. It soon expanded its appeal to the population at large.

Most government officials and senior military officers were angered by this, naturally, but because the opposition deputies enjoyed parliamentary immunity and most were Catholics, Thieu's government and the press he largely controlled hesitated to charge Duc and the others with being pro-Communist or Viet Cong members, the usual label they pinned on oppositionists.

Others joined Duc in denouncing corruption and abuse in the army. Minister of Defense Nguyen Van Vy lost his temper and demanded an apology, declaring that he was a representative of the army and the statements made had dishonored the army. "You are only a government appointee, not an elected official," answered Deputy Phan Thiep, a hardcore anti-Communist. "So you represent no one, including the army. But we are the people's elected representatives." Pro-government deputies, in the majority, hastily asked to terminate the session to prevent further embarrassing charges and countercharges.[4]

At this time Thieu was still working to consolidate his power. He was struggling to replace Ky's appointees in key positions, especially chief of police, and attempting to gain a majority in the Senate and House. Most of those who had been "elected" with the support of the Ky faction had already defected from the crumbling Ky bloc and now were in Thieu's camp. Several others had adroitly formed an independent bloc, which raised the price of the bribes they could extract in return for their votes to support measures Thieu wanted passed. Thieu's expeditor, Nguyen Cao Thang, paid a base price to avowed Thieu supporters, a higher price to the independents, and offered the highest price to opposition members for their votes on any given bill.

Deputy Nguyen Ba Can, a former deputy province chief, was the mastermind in building Thieu's base of support. He not only succeeded in building a majority in the House but he also enlisted labor organization leaders and other supposed oppositionists. Senator Tran Van Don (formerly a general) heading the National Salvation Front, a coalition of several political groups, cooperated skillfully with Can.

In fact, the power elite in Saigon and a few other cities still consisted mainly of the same handful of familiar faces who were previously part of Ngo Dinh Nhu's Can Lao party. There was a rumor that most of the groups received financial support from the CIA. In the sixty-member Senate, those elected by a well-organized Catholic constituency formed the majority, and they were ready to support Thieu. Some of the other senators who represented non-Catholic constituencies were willing to go along with the Catholic bloc in the interests of sharing power. Thieu also had a slim majority in the Supreme Court (elected by the National Assembly), the eleven-member Special Court (which had the power to indict high-ranking officials, including the president and of which I was a member), and the Executive.

Chief Supreme Court Justice Nguyen Van Linh (also president of the Special Court) called Thieu "the father of the Second Republic of South Vietnam" in an inaugural address and was supported by Senator Tran Van Don. I was furious. I maintained that such a statement was false in view of the election procedure, and was an insult to the intelligence of the people. I pointed out that the Buddhist Church refused to recognize the validity of the elections due to the way they were manipulated by the military and was still fighting for a rightfully and impartially elected government. I didn't say it publicly because of the antagonism it would have created, but my private feeling was that if anyone was the father of the Second Republic, it was Thich Tri Quang or President Johnson.

Despite all the efforts of Thieu and his cronies to build a majority base and fully control the country, a significant number of deputies and senators, intellectuals and students were genuine oppositionists. Their collective goal was the same as mine: to make South Vietnam a true democracy, eliminating the partisan, ineffective leadership and corruption that alienated the people and created conditions that encouraged the growth of Communism.

I was stimulated by the knowledge that others felt as I did, even though they were still in the minority. I resolved to work more actively for a broad alliance of Vietnamese who were patriotic and non-Communist but were opposed to the past and current leaders of South Vietnam. Such an alliance would appeal to Buddhists, Southern Catholics, intellectuals, and students—to a majority of South Vietnamese. I was encouraged by the fact that, even with the generals' heavy-handed manipulations during the elections, the Thieu-Ky ticket got only 1.6 million votes from an electorate of 5 million. I was convinced that with broader and genuine national support, instead of the current narrow base built largely through chicanery, Thieu would be able to challenge the influence that Ky had built in the army, police, and other sectors in and out of the government. He would also be in a better position to deal with the American pressure.

Meanwhile, like Thieu, I had my own problem. My brother Hien paid me another surprise visit. He appeared to be in high spirits, but I thought I could detect an underlying anxiety, as if he hoped to find out something from me but didn't want me to realize it. My dismay and concern over the appalling aftermath of the Tet Offensive welled up in me and, with only minimal greetings, I said to Hien, "I have been touring the country and I have seen the destruction of cities and homes and learned of the deaths of thousands of civilians caused by the recent attacks by the Viet Cong and the North. Why such enormous atrocities for something you can't achieve?"

"Have you posed the same question to the Americans?" Hien asked in reply. "How about the atrocities the Americans inflicted by their bombing raids and other attacks on cities and villages in both the North and South? We hit the enemy wherever we could; it is war!"

"So it is war and you attack the enemy, but that does not explain the killing of thousands of civilians at Hué, civilians like the husband of our cousin Huong and their twelve-year-old son. They had nothing to do with the government and the Americans. And there were thousands like them."

Hien said that he did not know the details of the killings in Hué so he could not give me a detailed answer, only that he believed if the "revolution" decided someone must die, it would be a sound judgment reached only after a thorough investigation.

I felt it futile to pursue the matter further with one so dedicated to his cause that he accepted such things without question. I thought back to summary justice and quick executions in Dalat and Quang Ngai two decades earlier. There was little investigation or apparent justifiable cause then, and the same seemed true of the recent massacre in Hué.

Hien now came to what seemed the point of his visit: talking at length about the prospect of a peace settlement with the Americans. He cited President Johnson's decision to halt the bombing, to ask for negotiations, and not to run for reelection as indicators that the United States realized it could not win the war and were seeking a way to end it. It seemed to me that underlying Hien's comments were subtle hints that supported my own impression of the situation: that the North and the Viet Cong had also suffered greatly in the Tet Offensive and would be more amenable than ever before to a negotiated peace. "The Americans are repeating the same errors that the French made, both in fighting the war and in ending it, backing Thieu as a figurehead to help them end the war as the French did with Bao Dai. The only difference is that the French treated Bao Dai with more respect than the Americans treated Diem and the South Vietnamese generals."

I was both angry and wounded by Hien's comparison, more so because I knew he was at least partially right. But I had to defend Diem. "Call Diem your most hated enemy or anything else you will, but he was not a Bao Dai or an opportunist like Nguyen Van Thieu! He was a true nationalist."

Hien looked directly into my eyes, as though willing me to listen to him carefully. "If what you say is true, then that is the reason why the Americans let the others survive and murdered Diem." Before I could answer, he went on quickly. "Brother Chau, the Americans did not come here to die just to serve the cause of Vietnamese nationalism. They came here, as they said, to fight communism, to preserve South Vietnam for their neocolonial purposes. They don't need or want Vietnamese nationalists; they need the kind of Vietnamese they can manipulate for their own purposes, puppets like those now in power. Members of the Front sincerely want you to join them. You can choose to serve in any position you desire. They are the true nationalists and non-Communists."

I rejected his suggestion immediately. "Brother Hien, I can't be an opportunist, joining one group or another because of emotional drive or temporary personal gain, nor can I allow myself to be manipulated. I am a believer in principles and I am guided by my principles, doing what they tell me is right. So far, I know that what I believe in are the same things that the majority of Vietnamese believe. The only difference between me and them is that I have been given the position and opportunity to speak out and act in their name while their right of expression and ability to act are suppressed by money, force, or both. I have a moral obligation to be loyal to them. Although I have no consideration for those opportunists at the top who have waged this war more for personal profit than for ideologies, I do feel compassion for the young generation of military officers and professionals who will emerge as the true nationalists and public servants. They will be the dynamic force to lead our children's generation to a modern and better Vietnam."

Then, to counter his optimism about a Communist victory, I warned him not to rely overmuch on the antiwar movement in the United States and other places around the world. "Such activities and criticisms are normal in democratic countries; they won't necessarily sway the U.S. government from the policy of continuing to fight to protect South Vietnam."

In saying this, of course, I was more or less repeating what most vocal anti-Communists in government and Thieu-Ky supporters kept saying year after year. Deep down, I did not necessarily agree. Hien seemed to understand that, and he changed the subject, possibly to avoid further confrontation on the issue. "You are known to have influential connections with the Buddhists, Southern Catholics, and high-ranking officials in both civilian and military circles," he said. "Why don't you do something to settle the war, something involving the varied Vietnamese factions, rather than leaving it all up to the Americans, as the administration seems content to do?"

I looked at my brother for a moment, feeling that this was the key point of his visit and that it was based on an assessment of my long-standing and well-known advocacy of direct negotiations between South and North Vietnam, with the United States taking a subordinate place. "If there is anything I or the people with whom I am allied want to do, it is to talk directly with the North about ending this war."

"We in the North will never recognize or treat directly with the South Vietnamese government," Hien stated. "You must deal with the NLF, and we in the North will negotiate with the Americans!" He then launched into another tirade about the "puppet Vietnamese administration," American neocolonialism, and other familiar Communist propaganda themes.

Shortly after Hien's visit, a deputy with deep Buddhist roots, Duong Van Thuy, talked me into meeting with Nguyen Ngoc Loan, national police chief, at Loan's headquarters. Loan wanted to meet with the group of opposition deputies, especially the Buddhists. After arriving, we sat for an embarrassingly long time in a waiting room, ignored by Loan. We had just decided to leave, humiliated by rushing to answer the police chief's summons only to be made to wait for so long, when Loan finally appeared.

"Hey, you guys don't be upset," he said half-seriously and half-jokingly. "We have serious things to discuss." Then, without looking directly at us, Loan said, "You know that the situation is serious. The Communists are on the verge of overrunning the entire nation because the government is weak and incompetent. General Ky wants to take over the prime minister post to cope with the situation and save the country. But this requires that the Constitution be changed to allow the vice president [which Ky was at the time] to also take the title and function as prime minister. We have almost enough votes for such an amendment, but we still need a few more. And you are the ones who hold those votes. I want you to promise that you will provide them." Loan looked around after this shocking pronouncement, finding no response from the group.

I was astonished at such a blatant attempt to subvert the Constitution and mount another coup. I left the meeting more with anxiety than shame: anxiety for Thieu's vulnerability and shame that such a form of heavy-handed, indecent, Mafia-type manipulation would be used on an elected body such as we represented.

Another day, two other deputies were present when I told Thieu that we must face reality: we must either let the Americans and the North make the decision for us, or arrange a settlement ourselves, that included the NLF, before it was too late. Thieu reacted as if taken off guard. "Would the North agree to such a settlement?" he asked.

"That is a possibility," I told him, "if the Americans will let us take the leading role in the negotiations. Then we could proceed in such a way that all sides could find it possible to make concessions and compromises."

The next day I went to see Information Minister Ton That Thien and discussed with him what South Vietnam needed to do to make such negations successful. I told the minister that, in the best interests of both America and Vietnam, the United States should stay behind the scenes and vigorously support direct talks between South Vietnam, North Vietnam, and the NLF. Thien coolly replied that this would be impossible, because the United States should rightfully take the leading role.

Disappointed, I still fought to sell my ideas. I wrote a series of articles that detailed why South Vietnam should take the lead in initiating and carrying on peace negotiations, arguing that this would enhance the cause of both America and Vietnam. I asked publicly for a meeting between the North Vietnamese and a South Vietnam parliamentary delegation. My activities drew a violent reaction.

The Thieu-controlled press attacked and ridiculed my position. The growing number of people who supported me, especially students and intellectuals, were also castigated. Articles depicted me as either a Communist agent, working for the Communist cause, or as a CIA agent trying to provide a convenient way for the United States to abandon Vietnam to the Communists.

What Thieu's supporters were primarily concerned with was not South Vietnam's role in negotiations but negotiations themselves. At first, they did not want peace talks in any form. When the United States halted bombing raids and it became obvious that the Americans were considering negotiations on their own, the Thieu faction panicked. They feared being on the sidelines if that happened and attacked anyone who advocated any form of negotiations. The situation became so chaotic that U.S. Ambassador Bunker assured the public that the United States would not impose a coalition government on South Vietnam, nor would it recognize the NLF.

I then announced my intention to campaign for the office of secretary general of the House, the position second only to the president of that National Assembly body. I would need an absolute majority of votes from the deputies. A major reason for my decision to run was to check the reaction of my colleagues to suggestions that we pursue peace talks and that South Vietnam, not the United States, take the lead. I publicized these ideas in newspapers, speeches, and a book of nearly 200 pages.

I was elected, thanks to secret balloting that allowed even some of Thieu's supporters to cast their votes in my favor. A voice vote or show of hands might have produced very different results, because many of the deputies would have been afraid to back me publicly.

Very quickly I moved to consolidate my position, working closely not only with the oppositionist minority in the Assembly but also with prominent personalities outside the government. My aim was not to compromise with Assembly majority members; I knew they had no real support from their constituencies. Instead, I wanted to build a strong alliance of people outside the government power structure who would support Thieu if he would make compromises to accommodate both his own minority and agenda *and* the desires of the vast majority of the populace. That would enable him to stand up against the other generals and even to the United States. He could lead the nation in the right direction and not be merely an American puppet.

As I began to gather increasing popular support, I decided to form a political party with a nationwide grassroots infrastructure. Until then, political parties had consisted of only a few thousand adherents. Some of the parties sprang from religious roots, but they were small, representing only a tiny percentage of people in specific sectors. For example, Northern Catholics were mostly in the Saigon and Hué areas, the Caodaists mainly in Tay Ninh province, and the Hoa Hao in other provinces in the Delta. The Dai Viet and Quoc Dan Dang drew their followings mainly from the military and the civil service. None of the parties had been able to unite, to mobilize a majority of the Buddhists and Southern Catholics. The latter remained passive and not motivated to support the government, even when they were in the army or government positions.

I knew that my intent to build the first Vietnamese grassroots party on a nationalistic foundation oriented toward a Western type of democracy would require a vigorous struggle. My effort would be opposed by both the North Vietnamese Communists and the American- supported South Vietnamese military dictatorship, because those two opposing sides actually nurtured each other, despite being bitter enemies. I knew that I had to reassure the Americans that the new party was not pro-Communist, because that is how it would be portrayed by the Vietnamese government. The government's standard practice was to condemn as Communists, or at least as Communist sympathizers, anyone who opposed its policies or was critical of the American establishment.

I discussed my idea briefly with a CIA friend and asked whether he could help. A short time later, another CIA officer, Bill Kohlman, came to my house and, after much discussion, said he would provide financial help provided that I supply a channel through which the money could be supplied. The channel would have to be a person wealthy enough so it would appear that the money came from him, concealing its real source. The CIA representative also wanted a list of my principal collaborators and sponsors. I subsequently told him to assign someone of his own choosing as channel, to ensure that he would have total control of the funds. As to the list he had requested, I gave him only the names of those who were known supporters of my efforts to establish the new party; I did not reveal the full roster of religious leaders and other prominent persons who had offered sub rosa backing or of sympathizers I expected to support me.

About two weeks later Bill Kohlman came back to me and said, "My organization would be glad to help you develop such a plan, but only if you support President Thieu and his current policies; this is a prerequisite to maintain accord with American policy."

I sighed inwardly, thinking that once again the CIA failed to understand the situation. The Agency did not realize the folly of continuing to pursue policies that simply wouldn't work, and ultimately would defeat the worthy goals the United States was trying to attain. I said to Bill, "There are more than enough political parties, national fronts, and labor and professional organizations that will support President Thieu or anyone else in his position, for a consideration. Their major concern is how they benefit, materially or ideologically, from the government. It already has been proved that they can never rally the majority of the population to support the president and the government as it has been constituted to date. What I propose is a new kind of political party, one I am convinced would be able to get President Thieu, or anyone in his office, to work with it to develop a new national agenda and policies that could win the support of most of the people. Only such a party can help achieve goals that would ultimately be of the most benefit to the United States. That is the only way to build a strong, democratic South Vietnam that could withstand both the NLF and the North."

"But we can only assist parties that guarantee to support President Thieu and to conform with U.S. policy," he replied.

We never met again.

The general situation developed as I had anticipated. I believed that the Tet Offensive, misrepresented as a military victory for the North and NLF, instead had really struck a psychological blow that strengthened sentiment in the United States for an end to involvement in Vietnam.[5] The antiwar movement was growing, despite the Nixon administration's best efforts to suppress it. Even hard-line hawks must have been growing restive over the appalling casualty lists and mounting cost of the war.

The United States began to implement a policy of "Vietnamization" of the war: increasing bombing, but gradually disengaging from ground operations so as to reduce American casualties. This policy, directed by President Nixon and National Security Advisor Kissinger, was intended to fulfill the president's campaign pledge to end the war with honor, a theme essential to defeating Hubert Humphrey in the 1968 election. Humphrey had seemed to favor some sort of coalition between the Republic of Vietnam and the NLF as a means to extricate the United States. This was portrayed as "less honorable" than candidate Nixon's proposal to shift all of the ground fighting to the South Vietnamese Army while continuing to support the increasingly repressive government of President Thieu.

President Thieu himself actually expected to benefit from the election of President Nixon because he believed his refusal to fully cooperate in the Paris peace negotiations just prior to the 1968 American elections helped assure a Nixon victory. Furthermore, President Thieu looked upon Hubert Humphrey as an "implacable enemy" because a year earlier when then vice president Humphrey had attended the inauguration of President Thieu and Vice President Ky in Saigon, Humphrey had warned Thieu that there would have to be changes in South Vietnam if American support was to continue. Thieu concluded, "A Humphrey victory would mean a coalition government in six months." Thieu believed there was a better chance of continuing support from the United States with Nixon in the White House. But, "Thieu got a feel for Nixon's well-known duplicity shortly after the election, when the new president leaned on him to take part in the peace negotiations."[6]

On the face of it, the premise for Vietnamization appeared plausible: strengthen

South Vietnam with arms and economic assistance, help the South to recruit and build up its army and air force in order to take over the brunt of the fighting with a minimum of direct involvement by U.S. forces. Continue to employ air power for attack and support missions, avoiding long American casualty lists. Indeed, this approach was sufficient for President Nixon and his meretricious advisor Kissinger, but it was a veritable death sentence for the Republic of Vietnam. Some of us recognized that the South could not survive with the present regime in place unless President Thieu fundamentally changed his policies.

I believed the Nixon administration's primary interest would be to contain the Vietnam military and political situation long enough (the "decent interval") to withdraw without an appearance of having been defeated. The short-term stability that this would require, based primarily on President Thieu and his appointees in the government and military, and without broad public support, would be sufficient for U.S. short-term interest; in the long run, however, the result would be Communists taking over the South. My position was that President Thieu should reach out for support from non-Communist nationalists, perhaps beginning by appointing a "council of notables" from the entire non-Communist spectrum as an advisory body.

I think that at this point President Thieu began to suspect my motives. Knowing that I was friendly with many Americans in Vietnam who also wanted him to broaden his base of support, he seemed to feel that I was being used to test his reactions. His suspicions, and he was always distrustful of others, seemed to increase when I discussed my peace settlement proposal with him. It is ironic that President Thieu suspected me of being a sounding board, or even some sort of operative, for Americans at the very time that I was moving further from U.S. official policy. In truth, the United States was only looking for short-term strengthening of President Thieu's administration as one part of a program to appease public opinion in America. I was seeking long-term political strength that could only be provided by bringing together all the non-Communist political elements in South Vietnam. I suspected that the United States would—for its own "decent interval," short-term interest—support President Thieu no matter what he would do, and that is what occurred. Thieu feared that by reaching out to non-Communist nationalists he would risk losing the support of hardcore militants.[7] He was able to maneuver the United States into continuing to support him because the Americans accepted him as the anchor of the temporary stability that was sole concern of the Nixon administration.[8]

Revelation that U.S. policy would be undergoing a dramatic shift right at the start of President Nixon's first term came in the form of Henry Kissinger's article in the January 1969 issue of *Foreign Affairs*. Kissinger revealed his conviction that victory in Vietnam was impossible, so negotiation would be the last resort for ending the war. (Interesting that on this one point Kissinger and I were in agreement, despite being far apart in every other respect.) The article suggested that the United States was prepared to talk with all parties, including North Vietnam and the NLF, in order to end the war. Kissinger proposed that the peace talks proceed on two tracks, with the United States and North Vietnam arranging a mutual withdrawal, while the NLF and South Vietnam work toward a political settlement in separate talks.

My own proposal, as I developed it, was similar to Kissinger's in some respects. I also believed that we should at least admit the existence of the NLF and provide it with representation in the peace-seeking process.[9] On one critical point, however, my thinking was completely different from that of Henry Kissinger. I was strongly against the United States initiating and taking the lead in negotiations that would determine the future of South Vietnam. I proposed that America play an advisory role, with South Vietnam responsible for the negotiations with both North Vietnam and the NLF.

My position, expressed in a long and widely publicized statement in the National Assembly, was that a delegation from our assembly be sent abroad to advocate the United States yield the authority to conduct direct negotiations with North Vietnam as a matter of political and moral principle. I believed that this was fundamental because I knew that the North was arrogant toward the South and preferred to portray the South in a subservient position by only dealing directly with the United States. This made the South appear to be simply a client or puppet state to America, the same position forced upon the South by France at the 1954 Geneva Conference. This image was beneficial for the North and devastating to the South.

By allowing South Vietnam to play the primary role vis-à-vis the North, the United States could present itself as a real ally, strongly supporting South Vietnam without appearing to control the South's destiny. This would have enhanced the American image as being an understanding ally rather than neo-imperialist, and would have promoted South Vietnam's cause and prestige.

My three-step proposal was as follows:

1. The NLF would be invited to "designate" representatives to take part in the current National Assembly, with Communist Party members excluded.
2. NLF members would be allowed to participate in general elections for both chambers of the National Assembly so long as they would conform with constitutional requirements.
3. The Saigon and Hanoi governments would come together to discuss other issues including problems of reunification.

I was opposed to NLF members moving directly into a government role beyond the National Assembly, and frankly I doubted that they could muster the necessary votes to do even that, especially if government reforms broadened the South Vietnam political base. I believed it made common sense, however, to accommodate them at lower levels—hamlet or village, for example—in areas where the NLF already dominated.

While keeping his distance from me, Thieu at first appeared flexible along these lines. But as soon as he realized that my proposal was at some variance with the U.S. position, he recanted. Although he was still opposed to playing the supporting, secondary role to the United States in peace negotiations, he was too dependent on American support to risk adopting any policy that did not coincide with emanations from Washington.

It was ironic, but perhaps to be expected, that strongly anti-Communist Richard Nixon shared the same viewpoint with Communist North Vietnam: that the United States would take the lead and deal directly with the North, relegating the South to an inferior position.

My proposal led to confusion and some speculation in the semicontrolled South Vietnam press. Opponents condemned me as pro-Communist while others speculated that I was proxy for some CIA scheme. Two such diametrically opposed labels would have been laughable, except that it indicated President Thieu was beginning to regard me as a major problem. The president knew that I was certainly not a Communist, and was aware that I had broken a previous connection with the CIA. The confusion of attacks on my proposal and me personally demonstrated the chaotic state of affairs in the country during early 1969. Even the pro-government media could not agree on a party line.

More discouraging for me was that, in some American circles, my proposal, supporters, and I were becoming an embarrassment. Increasingly, I was depicted as "anti-American" by some senior American officials and members of the resident American media who were insulated from the realities of the situation. Nothing could have been further from my intention and the truth. I was advocating a course that would be best for both South Vietnam and the United States in the long term.

President Thieu's power increased through mid-1969, and not just because of the material support brought forward by Vietnamization. Internally, he had been able to diminish the influence of political opponents. During the May–June 1968 Communist offensive, an errant American helicopter rocket killed several effective officers who were determined supporters of Vice President Ky.[10] National Police Director Nguyen Ngoc Loan was severely wounded in fighting around the National Radio Building, and had to take medical retirement. President Thieu thus had an opportunity to dramatically erode the political power of Vice President Ky. He eased out Prime Minister Nguyen Van Loc, an important member of the Ky clique. Thieu replaced the ousted Loc with Tran Van Huong, who was broadly acceptable, but proved too independent. General Tran Thien Khiem, in a masterful, if sleazy, series of behind-the-scenes maneuvers, later replaced Huong. This was part of a complete overhaul of the cabinet ministers that Elizabeth Pond reported in this way: Thieu "maneuvered Ky into such a clearly subordinate role that left the Vice President plenty of evenings free for mah jongg. Gone were most of the Ky appointed officials from powerful police, military and cabinet posts. Thieu continued to build support in the Parliament and Supreme Court in his usual fashion, by handing out favors and bribes."[11]

The result was hardly what some idealistic Americans would have preferred: that is, President Thieu truly working to broaden his political base and achieving some degree of public popularity.[12] Tran Van Huong's value to Thieu as a sort of balance to Ky came to be outweighed by annoyance at Huong's independence and stubbornness. True to form, however, Thieu avoided a frontal showdown with Huong, but deftly worked surreptitiously to persuade the old gentleman to resign.

President Thieu masterfully orchestrated his campaign to get rid of Huong. The campaign began in early July when ninety-two members of the Chamber of Deputies called for Tran Van Huong's resignation over a tax matter. Chamber members charged that taxes had been raised by executive order, usurping the tax-raising function of the legislature. The charges were broadened to include inaction on inflation, inaction on corruption, responsibility for suspension of publications, and arrest of innocent civilians caught up in the Phoenix Program, the infamous perversion of a portion of the Census Grievance pacification program I had instituted in Kien Hoa province. The Phoenix Program was aimed at kidnapping or eliminating enemy leaders, not true pacification—as I envisioned it (see Chapter 20). It became obvious that President Thieu was behind the ouster movement (despite Huong having been appointed by Thieu) because there was a conspicuous lack of support from the president and many pro-Thieu deputies were involved. Some of the dirty tricks that were applied (like petitions with bogus signatures) were the work of Nguyen Cao Thang, acknowledged bribe master and hatchet man for the president.[13]

During July 1968 a military court completed its processing of a case against former presidential candidate Truong Dinh Du (second to President Thieu in the 1967 balloting), and sentenced him to five years at hard labor for "having reduced the spirit of anti-communism of the people and the army." This was probably, painfully, predictable because of Du's second-place finish and potential to develop into a strong rival. During the campaign Du had advocated entering discussions with the NLF, which marked him as a man to be swept aside in the future.

While all these events and machinations were occurring, my brother Hien and I had further meetings. He came to see me a few weeks after the U.S. election. Hien personally, and his controllers in the North, wanted my assessment of how changes in U.S. administrations might impact the war and political developments in Vietnam. I had grave reservations concerning President-elect Nixon's future course and the effect on South Vietnam. However I concealed those doubts, putting on an optimistic front for Hien when he asked about Thieu's position and what support the South could now realistically expect from the United States. Hien again insisted that South Vietnam should negotiate with the NLF. We both continued trying to convert the other to our respective viewpoints, but I realized Hien was such a dedicated Communist that no argument could sway him. He was also recognizing that I would never embrace communism.

So the meetings with Hien, which later were the substance of the charges against me, came to a futile ending in late 1968. Not only were they of no value to our opposing causes, they ultimately sent both of us to prison.

25: LOYALTY AND HONOR (1969)

Hien's arrest came as a shock.

As I left my house for the National Assembly building one day in April 1969, I had no idea that it marked the beginning of what would become an international cause célèbre and the most disastrous eight years in my life. I enjoyed the early-morning drive through Saigon's quiet streets, planning in my mind the work I wanted to accomplish before other Assembly members and staff arrived. My first clue that this would not be a typical morning came when I saw several dozen people milling about in the Assembly square, which was usually almost deserted this early in the morning. As I drew closer, I realized they were all reporters or photographers.

The official story was that Hien had been arrested in a routine road check, during which an alert security officer spotted Hien's fake identity card. I suspected that the CIA actually triggered the arrest, knowing that the Agency had been aware of my brother's intelligence work since I informed them about our first meeting in 1965. I learned later, while in prison, that this was all too true. The CIA in fact had "turned" Hien's liaison officer contact for North Vietnamese intelligence, and he reported all of Hien's activities to the Americans. When I learned this, it dispelled much of the guilt I had felt because I thought I was responsible for my brother's capture.

Hien's arrest created a furor, both for me personally and in South Vietnam. It led to the arrest and trial of two dozen South Vietnamese officials, some of them quite prominent, who had been meeting with Hien and discussing issues over the years. Among them were Nguyen Lau, publisher of the English-language *Saigon Daily News* (later closed by the government), and Vo Dinh Cuong, a cousin of Hien's and head of the Buddhist Layman's Association (aligned with the An Quang pagoda). A few military officers and policemen also arrested at the time were either acquitted or not brought to trial at all.[1]

The storm centered on me. The fact that we were brothers and that we had a series of meetings, which I admitted publicly before Hien's trial in July, created suspicion in some quarters that I, too, was a Communist sympathizer, if not an intelligence agent serving the North. Some hard-core Catholic anti-Communists who had sided with the French in the 1940s and 1950s had long been suspicious about my true reasons for defecting from the Viet Minh and joining the South. Many of them also regarded all Buddhists as Communist sympathizers, which was false. True, South Vietnamese Buddhists advocated government reform, but they were aware that their fate would worsen under a Communist government.[2]

Others, particularly my political opponents, took advantage of the situation to weaken my support by casting doubt on my true allegiance, though privately almost all of them knew full well that I was not a Communist agent, or even a sympathizer.

My failure to formally notify South Vietnamese officials about my initial and subsequent meetings with Hien was illegal under the letter of the law. One must consider the context of the times, as Elizabeth Pond explained accurately and succinctly:[3] "Chau's decision not to tell Vietnamese authorities anything formally was natural enough, given the inept and ephemeral nature of the post-coup governments. A certain economy of information is advisable when someone new may be in power in a few months and anyone with access to the files could turn information against one. [In this period and later many Vietnamese had contacts with 'the other side' and didn't report them. This situation was considered normal.] And after Thieu came to power Chau probably thought that the private understandings, whatever they were, would cover him." Furthermore, I did believe that my discussions with John Vann and his reports to the U.S. embassy provided evidence of my good faith and loyalty.

I was not too concerned at first. The government did refuse permission for me to travel abroad, but Thieu did not immediately move against me after Hien's trial in July.[4] But true friends were already deeply concerned about what they assessed as my precarious position. My good friend Captain Sauvageot (a colonel when he retired) told me that a few weeks earlier he had been ordered to cut off relationship and communication with me. John Vann told me that the same instructions had been passed to him. They feared for my personal safety, but were in a quandary as to what could be done given the orders that they had received from Ambassadors Bunker and Colby. John's solution was to send a message to Frank Scotton in Taiwan, and ask him to come to Vietnam as soon as possible. Frank arrived a few days later by C-130 out of Taichung. His travel to Saigon was undocumented, and with no record of his arrival, there was no application of the "no contact" orders to him. John Vann briefed Frank and asked whether a safe departure from Vietnam could be arranged for me without implicating himself or Captain Sauvageot.

Frank previously worked with special units in several areas of Vietnam, and had assisted me in Washington during my 1968 visit. He agreed to make arrangements and speak with me on behalf of John and other concerned friends. One night in early July he arrived at my house with another American who was traveling with him.[5] We had not seen each other in a year and a half. Frank said that he came to see me at the urgent and special request of John Vann. He explained that he had already arranged for availability of a helicopter with a Special Forces NCO as escort and security. The plan would be movement by helicopter into a secure area in Cambodia, onward to

Phnom Penh under the protection of his friend Cambodian Major Thach Reng, then to Bangkok, and finally to the United States.[6]

Our discussion was long and intense, and for me very emotional. I told Frank that I felt as though the Americans were selling me out. He responded that he had no defense for the official position, but simply by coming to my house that night he was proving that some American friends believed in me, trusted me, and wanted to save me from an unjust arrest and imprisonment. After more than an hour of discussion, I told Frank that however cruel an arrest and sentence might be, I would not flee my country. Taking that step would mean betrayal of my deepest personal convictions and provide the government with pretext to further slander. We parted with his promise that in the future he would do what he could for me, although that might be at some distance. I could not imagine how many years would pass before we would meet again.[7]

President Thieu, meanwhile, was beset with problems that ultimately made his attack on me politically expedient. The inevitability of American disengagement from the war and South Vietnam would affect the political picture significantly, eroding his position, which was based so heavily on American support. Hardline personalities, particularly within the military, were critical of the president when the CIA uncovered a Communist spy ring that reached right into the presidential palace, further increasing President Thieu's characteristic paranoia.

Generals Duong Van Minh and Tran Van Don, "heroes" of the 1963 Diem coup, had begun to present themselves as an alternative to Thieu, calling for a popular referendum in November 1969. Thieu wanted to squelch this development before it gained any momentum, but it would have been difficult to move against them directly—and confrontation was not normally the president's style anyway.

Thieu did not really have a cohesive organization loyal to him, partially because he was too suspicious to place power in the hands of subordinates that would enable them to help build such an organization. Without a solid base he felt that the way to maintain power was to break up any opposition before it could grow big enough to challenge him. He took action against ethnic Cambodians, students, and Buddhists. One popular composer/singer, Trinh Cong Son, drew a five-year jail sentence in late 1969 for antiwar songs he had composed two years earlier.[8] The Buddhist newspaper and several others were closed. Many lower-level leaders with dissident views were stifled. Thieu used these strategies to solidify his base of right-wing anti-Communists who opposed any individuals or groups that they felt were, in the popular American expression, soft on communism.

During this late summer period I also learned that President Thieu had agents searching for evidence of wrongdoing on my part in every position that I had held, going back as far as my earliest military posts. He may have believed that if proof of dereliction of duty or misuse of funds could be found, that would strengthen any case against me, or perhaps even allow for prosecution solely on those charges while dropping the phony allegation of me being a Communist sympathizer. This effort amused me. I knew that President Thieu's agents would not find anything incriminating in my past. The only interesting point they uncovered was a "technical diversion of funds" during my first assignment as province chief in Kien Hoa. The diversion referred to my cutting regulatory red tape to allow purchase of coffins for poor farmers and out-of-province soldiers killed while on duty in Kien Hoa.[9]

I was angered rather than intimidated. I increased my criticism of President Thieu's administration, the turn from democracy to autocracy, intimidation of citizens, and corruption of the National Assembly by bribes through Nguyen Cao Thang. There were no bridges left to burn. Friends in the police and other personal sources warned me that Vice President Nguyen Cao Ky and the Viet Cong were both plotting to assassinate me. I was skeptical, but it was explained that both sides would try and do it in a manner to incriminate President Thieu. If successful, it would presumably cause political turmoil, further isolate the president, make him more vulnerable to criticism, and thereby accrue benefit either to the NLF or the vice president. I recalled the previous assassination of two other members of the Assembly, and attempts on the lives of other national figures. As a precaution, and to deflect potential harm from my family, I basically left my home and installed myself in the National Assembly building. This gave me some sense of security by day, but was no guarantee for the night. Police were present, but no one could be sure whether they would be responsive to me, Thieu, Ky, or the NLF.

During October, November, and December, the government excited public opinion against me. President Thieu gave a speech at the training center in Vung Tau, attacking me and two other deputies in the strongest terms. Rallies were held in Catholic communities to demand my expulsion from the National Assembly. A mob was actually allowed to ransack the National Assembly building on December 20. Nguyen Cao Thang—at President Thieu's bidding, of course—was working his usual monetary magic to try and have me either expelled from the National Assembly or divested of parliamentary immunity.

I felt that I should not compromise Vietnamese or American friends serving in a government or military position. I finally asked John Vann to be my representative in making arrangements for me to stay temporarily with Keyes Beech. I thought that as a media correspondent he was a free agent and not under direct official control. Keyes immediately agreed. The next evening, as arranged in advance, another friend and his wife (known to be strong supporters of President Thieu) picked me up and brought me to the most notorious nightclub in Saigon. During the show another friend took me out the back door and drove me to Keyes's home, right in front of the presidential palace. I had first met Keyes during one of his frequent trips from Saigon into the countryside, touching base with troops in combat areas, or entering villages to get stories for his reports to the *Los Angeles Times*, reports that were often syndicated to other major U.S. and international publications.[10]

The National Assembly was being pressured to remove my parliamentary immunity. I needed some time, and a place, to think clearly as to what my next step should be. I did not want the pressure of circumstances or my enemies to rush me toward an unprincipled decision. I had already declined Frank Scotton's escape option, and now I needed to consider what alternatives might remain. Keyes Beech provided the temporary sanctuary that I needed.

When Keyes first visited Kien Hoa many years earlier, I was pleasantly surprised by his background knowledge. I was more impressed when he showed specific interest in Kien Hoa, even asking to accompany me in attending a meeting at a village recently "taken back" after having been controlled by the Viet Cong. I agreed, and he joined our group of some ten Vietnamese officials and three American advisors. It was a dark, moonless night, and we trudged along a muddy path beneath a dense canopy of coconut trees to reach the distant village. It could not be reached even by four-wheel-drive vehicle. Dozens of torches greeted us. We visited new facilities: school, nursery, health clinic, and community activities building. Keyes paid little attention until he focused on the fifty or so men and women taking positions on the perimeter. They were armed with a variety of weapons, including some semiautomatic rifles. The American advisors explained that all were volunteers from the village serving without pay.

Keyes wanted to know about enemy activity, how the volunteer defenders were trained and organized, and in what other ways the government planned to provide better living conditions. While still engaged in lively conversation, we all gathered around campfires to eat and exchange ideas about the future. We ignored the occasional staccato bursts of rifles and automatic weapons in the distance. It was early morning when we returned to province headquarters. Keyes caught a nap in the guest quarters at the residence until about 9:00 a.m. As the two of us took breakfast, he told me that the trip and our discussions in the field and hamlets provided him with a new perspective.

That was the beginning of our friendship.[11] Thereafter we had met frequently to exchange information and ideas about events and personalities in Vietnam. Now I was hiding in his guest quarters. We had long conversations about how recent developments had derailed my plans to build a true riceroots political party from hamlets upward, a party that could establish its own national agenda, and be a strong player in a peace settlement process. We talked about the three factors that had impacted that dream: the American change of policy to one of disengagement, President Thieu's sharp turn to repression, and the arrest of my brother Hien.

I summarized the situation, beginning with the first meeting that was reported to the CIA and, through John Vann, to Ambassador Lodge. I had arranged further meetings with Hien at the suggestion of Ambassador Lodge, as relayed by John. The ambassador first said that he would meet with Hien if I could make the arrangements. I had no idea how to directly contact Hien, so I got in touch with another brother and asked him to let Hien know that I wanted to see him again. When Hien next visited, he agreed to meet with Ambassador Lodge. Lodge reneged, however, probably deciding that such a meeting would be too dangerous politically. He suggested instead that John Vann and Hien meet to explore possibilities for an eventual peace settlement, and establish a back channel for future talks. Hien refused, saying that he would only meet with a senior official, like the ambassador, who had real authority. So our initial meetings proved futile, and then ultimately disastrous.

Staying with Keyes provided respite, time to collect thoughts, but I needed to make a decision for the long term. I asked Keyes to contact John Vann and ask for his advice. A day later he told me that John thought I should leave Saigon temporarily, that John would make the arrangements, and that I should be prepared to move on a moment's notice.

Frank Scotton by this time was on distant assignment and not available for the kind of mission that he performed in July. Consequently, even though under orders to the contrary, John Vann and Ev Bumgardner placed their own careers and reputations at risk in order to help me. I can never forget what these two men were willing to do for me. They were placing their loyalty to our shared values above instructions issued by the U.S. Mission.

Ev Bumgardner picked me up. He drove me to Newport, the military port facility on the Saigon River near the Bien Hoa highway. Once inside the gates, we drove straight to the helicopter pads near the trash dump. John Vann met us there in his helicopter and flew me straight to Can Tho. Another friend, Dr. Merill "Bud" Shutt, John Vann's public health officer, put me up in his apartment on one of the American compounds.[12] During the several days that I spent in Can Tho, John and I had discussions and even some arguments as to what I should do. John told me that I would be a fool to stay. "With the U.S. behind him, Thieu will stay in power for a long time," he asserted, "and that means you could rot in jail for years." John had learned to fly his own helicopter. He planned to fly me toward a Cambodian village on the Gulf of Siam, hover offshore, and drop a rubber boat, so that I could board it and paddle to shore. "From there you can make your way to France or the United States, where you will be safe," John insisted. John was determined, and as all who knew him can testify, he could be very persuasive. At one point I concurred as much from weariness as logic. John got the raft (air force issue, instantly inflatable) and rehearsed the "smugglers" flight by taking the helicopter out for a practice run on his anticipated flight path.

Finally, though, I could not accept the notion of running away. John was actually very angry when I told him that I definitely decided not to escape. I stayed with him in IV Corps for a few more days, steeling myself for the confrontation that I knew waited for me in Saigon.[13]

My reappearance put an end to rumors and wild speculation that had spread through the capital and the country during my absence. Reports circulated to the effect that I was really fleeing Vietnam or would remain in hiding to escape any punishment determined by the Mobile Military Field Court, which was trying me in absentia just a few blocks away from the National Assembly. After weeks of near-solitude and agonizing over what my future course should be, I believed even more strongly that abandoning my country would be an implicit admission that Thieu's accusations were true, that I was in fact a Communist sympathizer, if not a full-blown Communist. Those who had been suspicious of me for years because of my time with the Viet Minh would be too easily convinced that was true. Some writers and historians have suggested that one of my motivations for not escaping Vietnam when I had the opportunity was that I would become a martyr and retain a chance at a political future in the country if I stayed, denied the charge, and went to jail. That is false. I simply recognized that fleeing would be letting down my friends and supporters. It could be especially damaging to Buddhists, I felt, and a severe blow to my personal sense of honor.

Now, whatever my fate, my honor would remain intact. I had done nothing wrong; I knew that, and so did Thieu and his cohorts. Their persecution of me was motivated solely by political expediency. If I had fled or remained in hiding, it would have been a tacit admission of guilt, and Thieu could have treated it as vindication of his actions against me. I issued a statement that read, in part, "Consequently, the question the United States should ponder is whether or not the 40,000 American lives lost up to this point have been justified, given the undemocratic, repressive nature of the current South Vietnamese regime."

Almost simultaneously, the Mobile Military Field Court trying me in absentia, without the presence of my lawyers, took less than an hour to find me guilty. The tribunal sentenced me to twenty years of hard labor and confiscation of all my properties.[14] As soon as the sentence was pronounced, reporters rushed to the National Assembly building, anxious to learn how other National Assembly members would react to the judgment and how I would respond.

"What will you do?" they asked. "Will you turn yourself in voluntarily and abide by the sentence?"

"No. I will not be an accomplice with the government in an act that nullifies our laws, and even the Constitution of South Vietnam," I stated firmly, reiterating what I had said earlier. "I came here at the will of the people. I was legally elected by the people to represent them, and will not give up that responsibility by recognizing the illegal efforts of the government to prevent me from doing so. The government will have to take me out of the National Assembly by force, with bayonets and other weapons."

Despite police harassment, nearly two dozen reporters also managed to get to my office and kept vigil through the night with me. Our wide-ranging discussion covered the prospects for peace and how it might be achieved, as well as what the future might hold, both for me and for South Vietnam. My expression of personal thoughts and concepts remained consistent.

The cause for which the United States and South Vietnam were fighting was a just and noble one, but the strategy employed had been and continued to be wrong. Therefore, continuing to prolong the war following the same flawed policies would only benefit a minority of opportunists, while working against the best interests and desires of most of the people. Even with the huge assistance in arms, manpower, and funds that the United States provided for many years, we had been unable to defeat the North. Without that American support, how could we hope to win? My solution was for a tri-party government with international supervision. Thieu's corrupt government, with the legislative and judicial branches serving as little more than window dressing, was creating more and more resentment among the South Vietnamese people, which made them more vulnerable to propaganda and promises from the Viet Cong and the North.

"It's time now for a peace settlement," I stated, summing up my thoughts. "This can only be achieved if we face the reality that almost twenty-five years of war has decimated Vietnam both physically and morally, and that the war is stalemated. Continuing the way we have been will only lead to more tragedy and, ultimately, disaster for our country."

The next morning, learning that the government had definitely decided to delay no further in arresting me, the Most Venerables Thich Tri Thue and Thich Thien Minh—then chairman and vice chairman, respectively, of the Vietnamese Unified Buddhist Church—came to the National Assembly to warn me. In front of the assembled media, Thien Minh gave me a token of benediction. It was the only time the Buddhist Church gave such a blessing to a church member in a dangerous position vis-à-vis the government. It was therefore a definite challenge to Thieu and his regime. Shortly after the Buddhist leaders left, as if to put to rest a long-standing rumor about my relationship with the CIA, an American reporter burst into the room. He handed me a telegram from Senator Fulbright in which the senator confirmed that he had never called me an "agent of the CIA." Instead, the telegram went on, he referred to me as a Vietnamese official working, on order of the South Vietnamese government, with the CIA in the pacification program.

Then came the moment of truth: A uniformed police officer entered the room and informed me that he had been ordered to implement the order of the tribunal to take me to Chi Hoa penitentiary. He asked me if I would accompany him voluntarily.

I said I would not, that I would refuse orders from any government branch other than the National Assembly, as was my right under the Constitution. I added that so far the National Assembly had not removed my parliamentary immunity, despite requests from President Thieu. The officer then withdrew for a long moment. Suddenly a group of plainclothes policemen erupted into the room, pushing out the reporters, who screamed and shouted in protest. I stood alone for a few seconds, watching and listening to the commotion. Then a very large plainclothesman, about half again my size, stormed into the room and jumped me. Before I could do or even think about anything, I lost consciousness.

It was quite some time before I came to my senses, lying on my back and feeling fresh air. I also felt pinned down by something heavy—which turned out to be two policemen, one sitting on my abdomen, the other on my knees. Shortly after I opened my eyes and became fully conscious, another officer looked at me and immediately ordered the two policemen to get off me and let me have some air. I breathed deeply and slowly regained my senses. I was in a Jeep-like vehicle, possibly a Land Rover, about ten or fifteen kilometers outside Saigon. (I learned later that the police had driven there to evade reporters, and waited until after dark to deliver me to prison for the same reason.) We sat until the night approached and started back into the city. It was fully dark when we approached Chi Hoa, the national penitentiary.

All three gates were open; they were expecting us. A deputy warden met us, representing the prison director or head warden, who was an army colonel. (He was an old friend who sent his deputy to admit me because he was embarrassed to face me himself.) Very politely the deputy warden asked me to give him my belt. He also exchanged my shoes for a pair of slippers. Next, the deputy and a couple of guards escorted me through a large hall where several hundred prisoners and guards were gathered. They talked among themselves, looking and pointing at me. Then we came to a large room with about forty inmates in it. As I entered, the inmates stood up and applauded. It appeared that everyone in the prison knew about my arrest and had been awaiting my arrival.

The deputy warden conferred briefly with members of the room committee.[15] Then he and the guards left. I was given a space in the corner of the room, very clean and distant from the toilet. Another inmate later confided that normally the room committee allotted newcomers spaces nearest the toilet, the least desirable location in the room. They made an exception to the rule for me, a tacit indication that they were familiar with my situation and felt I was an innocent victim of government persecution.

Many of my fellow prisoners gathered around me. Several examined my cuts and bruises, then cleaned and bandaged them. They also gave me a suit of black pajamas to wear, because the clothing I had been wearing was torn and dirty.

I did not remain in that large room for long, however. Prison officials apparently noted the sympathetic reception I received from the other inmates and soon transferred me to a small cell of my own. It was about eight by ten feet in size, with no window, just a barred opening in the door.

After a few days I was taken to be interrogated by the military tribunal.

Then I was returned to my cell to await retrial by the military court, which our laws required when a defendant had been tried and sentenced in absentia. The date was February 26, 1970.

26: TRIAL AND TRIBULATION (1970)

hree days later I learned, in Chi Hoa prison,[1] that my retrial (intended to vali-
date the decision of the tribunal) would take place the next day. My fellow inmates treated me kindly, bringing me food and tea. I wore the black cotton garb
issued to convicts and was ready when the deputy warden came for me the following
morning. We drove to the court in a convoy of four or five military vehicles. Each
vehicle had its sirens blaring and its lights flashing, and was filled with armed military policemen. When we arrived, armed guards immediately hustled me to a waiting room, and the door was closed to reporters so I could meet in private with my
lawyers.

My defense staff, unpaid volunteers all, included the following: law professor and
Senator Vu Van Mau, who had served as minister of foreign affairs under President
Diem before resigning in protest over the administration's oppression of Buddhists
in 1963; Senator and Vice President of the Senate Nguyen Phuoc Dai, a well-known
lawyer in France before returning to practice law in Saigon; Tran Van Tuyen, a veteran lawyer well-known for his pro-Thieu and anti-Communist sentiments and who
had held several ministerial positions; and Vu Van Huyen, another widely respected
attorney known as an ardent defender in many antigovernment cases. The defense
team represented a cross-section of well-respected attorneys who represented widely
varying political factions. To prevent confusion, the legal team and I agreed that
only three of the seven or eight attorneys assembled to support me would actually
address the court in my behalf: Mr. Tuyen, Mr. Huyen, and Ms. Dai. The others
would follow the course of the trial and be available for backup and consultation.

The III Corps Mobile Military Field Court was a misnomer. It was located in the
navy yard near the Saigon River, not in the III Corps Tactical Zone. Nor was it mobile, or even solely a military court. First established during the Diem regime, it was
a venue for military cases (e.g., desertion and insubordination) but frequently trials
took place that were also of a political nature, and always in the name of "national
security."

As I entered the room under guard, it looked like nothing more than a one-way
street to prison. The only question was how severe my sentence would be. Still, my
lawyers and I were determined to put up the best defense possible. As I sat at the
defendant's table I glanced around, spotting many familiar faces: friends from the
National Assembly and the press corps, young people from the Students Association,
and several lawyers from the Bar Association (probably there to expand their knowl-

edge of such proceedings as much as to support me). Security was heavy. I also saw agents from the secret police and various intelligence organizations.

Frank Snepp provides a rather blunt description about the conspiracy that brought me to this charade of a trial:

> When Tran Ngoc Chau . . . became a political threat to Thieu in 1970, Shackley and Colby cooperated with the South Vietnamese police to paint him as a subversive and a Communist agent. Since Chau's brother [Hien] was in fact a Communist, and since Chau himself had once contacted him on behalf of the Station, it was relatively easy to build a case against him simply by dressing up certain parts of his police dossier and by de-emphasizing others. Shackley did not actually design the frame-up—it was the brainchild of the CIA confidant General Quang—but he did nothing to avert it, even though he knew the truth. And when the South Vietnamese government surfaced its allegations against Chau in the local press, both Shackley and Ambassador Bunker supported them.[2]

Thoughts about the frame-up, the treachery of the Thieu administration and its American supporters, and my decision not to follow Vann's plan and flee the country flashed through my mind as I sat and awaited my fate, which I knew already would be dismal at best. I thought about those who had been tried in this courtroom before me: dissident students, the Buddhist leader Thich Thien Minh, spies from the North, and others who had indeed really committed crimes.

The court ran through the rituals—identification and swearing in of principals—in short order. Judge Huyen signaled for my lead attorney, Vu Van Huyen, to begin. My attorney stated the following:

> On February 4, 1970 I asked for five witnesses connected with Deputy Tran Ngoc Chau to be present at this trial: John Vann, American civilian chief in the delta, a long-time resident of Vietnam and a long-time friend of Chau's; William Colby, US Deputy Ambassador for Pacification; Eugene Locke, former Deputy Ambassador to Vietnam; Ambassador Ellsworth Bunker; and General Frederick Weyand, commander of all U.S. troops in III Corps surrounding Saigon at the time of the Tet Offensive and currently in the U.S. delegation for peace talks in Paris.[3]

The presence of Vann as a witness on my behalf was especially important. He could testify that my first meeting with Hien had been reported to senior U.S. officials in Saigon, and that further meetings were carried out with the full knowledge and approval of the embassy and CIA Saigon Station. Vann did, in fact, testify to this effect to the U.S. Senate Foreign Relations Committee. Vann had also reported in Foreign

Relations Committee hearings that I was not a Communist, but a dedicated nationalist.

Prosecutor Truong Thanh Kieu prevailed upon the court to deny our request. "Deputy Chau's case concerns national security and not informing Vietnamese government authorities [of contact with brother Hien], so his relations with Americans have no value."

A heated exchange followed, in which my lawyer raised the question of my constitutional rights being violated. The prosecutor replied that this was a special court with special procedures not specified by the Constitution. "This court has nothing to do with the Constitution!" the prosecutor concluded.

So much for the facade of democracy! I thought to myself.[4]

There were further sharp exchanges between my legal team, the prosecutor, and judge concerning whether Attorney Dai would be allowed to actively represent me rather than be limited to providing counsel to other attorneys. Finally it was agreed that she could do so, and court recessed briefly to allow her to review the dossier prepared by the prosecutor.

When the court reconvened at 4 p.m., I asked to speak. First, I objected to being stripped of my National Order Medal after I had been beaten. Second, I protested the legality of my arrest and my previous in absentia trial. As an elected deputy to the Lower House of the National Assembly and recipient of the National Order Medal (to whom "the nation is grateful," read the citation), how could my immunity be ignored by the government? "As of now," I pointed out, "the petition to strip off my immunity failed to obtain the necessary number of valid signatures of deputies as required by the Constitution, despite all the money, pressure, and effort expended by the government."

The prosecutor's response was that with the authorization of the president of the Lower House, I could be arrested.[5] He himself, he said, had talked to the president of the Lower House; second, I had been caught in flagrante delicto[6] in liaison with the enemy, to I could be tried by the court.

I asked that if I was arrested in flagrante delicto, why did Thieu send a letter to the Lower House asking for permission to prosecute me? If it was decided now that I was in flagrante delicto and my appeal for a new trial was accepted, then the previous sentence of the court on February 25, 1970, and the order to arrest me should be canceled. Why was I already treated as a criminal when I had immunity under the Constitution?

The prosecutor argued that I could not plead the Constitution because I had refused to answer three summons to appear before the court and instead tried to hide. I replied that I refused the summons because this court acted in violation of the Constitution, and as a member of the National Assembly it was my duty to defend the Constitution. The judge seemingly disregarded my reply. "Now we ask you, and you must answer. Why didn't you come to the court when you were summoned?"

Lawyer Huyen intervened, bringing up a key point in our defense. "My client did not attempt to hide himself when he was summoned by the prosecutor. The accused could not appear because the lawyer for the accused did not see the resolution of the Lower House under Article 37, Paragraph 2,[7] of the Constitution authorizing the executive to prosecute Deputy Chau. So until the resolution of the House was produced, there was no reason for Chau to appear as ordered by the prosecutor."

There followed a heated discussion about the legitimacy of my arrest and previous trial, with my attorneys pointing out breaches of the Constitution in the process and the prosecutor parrying their challenges. He brushed aside the issue of the legality of my arrest because the process by which my immunity as a deputy was stripped from me was in itself unconstitutional. The prosecutor essentially ignored our argument on this point, by stating that "this court is empowered to prosecute Deputy Chau as authorized on the basis of flagrante delicto."

Attorney Huyen recapped the efforts made by the Thieu administration to have the House of Deputies remove my immunity so the Executive Branch could prosecute me. He did not mention the bribes distributed to many deputies by Nguyen Cao Thang to obtain signatures. He did point out that the document as presented to the House was on two pages clipped together, with the Thieu petition on one page and a list of signatures on the second page. "Who can guarantee that all signatures were for the petition in question?" he asked, adding that in fact many deputies denied signing it. Huyen continued:

"When Deputy Thuong Gia Ky Sanh complained that he had never signed this petition, then 102 signatures became 101. Two other deputies sent letters withdrawing their names because they had thought they were signing a petition only to debate the case of Deputy Chau on the basis of Article 37/2, not to authorize prosecution. Thus the number of alleged deputy signatures came down to 99. This is not even a three-fourths majority. How then could the Executive be authorized by the President of the Lower House to prosecute Deputy Chau?

"When the President and the executive could not obtain authorization to prosecute from the House, they then shifted at will to another argument and arrested Deputy Chau under Article 41 of the Criminal Code dealing with flagrante delicto."

He went on to list the definitions of flagrante delicto in the Code of Criminal Instruction:[8]

> The criminal is caught red-handed on the spot,
> He is caught immediately after committing a crime,

He is followed by public clamor (not rumor), or

He is caught with objects on his person that lead to the presumption that he
has committed a crime.

"Now in the case of Deputy Chau, was he caught red-handed? Was any document found on him or in his house? No. The charge is therefore not valid," Huyen stated emphatically. "He is charged with being in liaison with persons harmful to the national defense from January 1965, so the liaison happened years ago when he was chief of province. Yet in 1967, government security approved Chau as a candidate in the National Assembly elections. That shows that at the time of the meetings the government was not thinking in terms of flagrante delicto."

Here, Lawyer Huyen added a sotto voce comment, a throwaway line that caused the judge to react angrily.

"You do not have respect for this court," snapped the judge.

Huyen was not cowed. "I have respect for you as a judge of this court, but we are talking about the law and you are in an unconstitutional position now!" And he went on to make his outrage clear in no uncertain terms. "Even a little child can understand the meaning of flagrante delicto. If a little boy takes candy and his mother catches him, that is flagrante delicto. But if, three days later, the boy tells his mother he took the candy, that is not flagrante delicto. Chau was not caught flagrante delicto up to the time that Tran Ngoc Hien was arrested—and it was Hien who revealed the meetings between Chau and Hien. Therefore, the executive action was illegal in either case. First, it did not have the authorization [of the National Assembly] according to the procedures of Article 37/2 of the Constitution.[9] Second, neither was Chau caught in flagrante delicto. The action of the executive [branch] was unconstitutional."

The prosecutor, after citing flagrante delicto earlier, now seemed to recant that argument and referred to the "resolution," actually a petition, circulated by Thieu's henchmen. "The resolution signed by 102 deputies was sufficient to agree with the executive to prosecute Deputy Chau."

When the prosecutor cited 102 signatures on the petition, I sat back in disgust. Anyone in the courtroom who previously had any doubts about this trial having a foregone conclusion must now have been convinced that I would be found guilty regardless of the facts, the truth of the charges against me, or the legal basis for my prosecution. It was common knowledge that many deputies had signed the petition under false pretenses, not realizing they were agreeing for me to be arrested and tried. Others signed and took the bribe money offered by Nguyen Cao Thang so that they could later reveal and denounce the corrupt methods Thieu used in his attempts to destroy me. The final tally of legitimate signatures was ninety, far less than the law required.

Following continued sharp argumentation, the judge abruptly declared a recess, saying the tribunal would deliberate whether this matter "was in its jurisdiction."

The recess was short, and the judge surprised no one with his opening statement. "After deliberation, we have decided to reject the argument made by Lawyer Huyen on article 37/2; to reject the appeal of Lawyer Huyen to refer the prosecution to the Supreme Court; to reject the view of Lawyer Huyen that this court is unconstitutional."

He then, finally, pinned down the basis for my prosecution, flying in the face of reason, logic, or the constitutional definition of "flagrante delicto" as he did so. "We consider the case of Chau to involve flagrante delicto, so approval to prosecute by a three-fourths majority of the Lower House is not necessary."

Lawyer Dai immediately asked for an appeal to the Supreme Court; Huyen backed her up, requesting that the trial be suspended to allow Supreme Court consideration.

"We ask the judge not to grant the appeal of Lawyers Huyen and Dai," responded the prosecutor quickly. He stated that the statute (Law 11/62 establishing field courts) did not allow appeals. "The Supreme Court deals with the Constitution and appeals from other courts, not from this court."

In other words, the field court that would decide my fate was above and not answerable to either the Constitution or the Supreme Court.

First Huyen, then Ms. Dai, attempted to argue further for referring the case to the Supreme Court, but Judge Huynh interrupted summarily. "This court has nothing to do with the Constitution. It is a special court under decree law."

I should explain here that the old constitution was done away with after the 1963 coup in which President Diem was assassinated. Existing decree laws, not actually a part of the Constitution, were retained supposedly on an interim basis. Thereafter, decree law became something akin to a U.S. president's ability to issue executive orders, except that decree laws were much more powerful and not so easily overturned or withdrawn. It was under one of these decree laws (11/62) that the field tribunal had been established, and this was the basis for the prosecutor's and judge's arguments that the court was above the Constitution and that the document's structures had no effect in the proceedings of the tribunal.

Finally, late in the day, I was ordered to stand as the clerk began to read the indictment. Specifically, I was charged with being in "liaison with a person carrying out activities detrimental to the national defense."

The first paragraph of description of the charge is translated roughly as follows:[10]

> Toward the end of March, 1969, the security agency discovered the strategic
> cell No. A-68 and at the same time arrested a number of Communists involved,

for investigation. Among them were Tran Ngoc Hien, head of the strategic intelligence network No. A-68, and Tran Chau Khang, liaison cadre. The investigation revealed that there was liaison between these concerned and Tran Ngoc Chau, with the mission of winning Chau over to their side, to re-establish liaison with Tran Ngoc Chau to organize a network aimed at understanding the political and military activities of the Republic of Vietnam and the U.S. in South Vietnam.

Of course those were Hien's goals. He admitted that, and so did I. Hien also told his interrogators that he was unsuccessful. As reported in the *Los Angeles Times*, January 4, 1970, Hien spoke with interrogators after his arrest in April 1969.[11]

Hien said that the mission behind his meetings with me was to persevere in winning me over to the Communist side, apparently because they believed I could be a potent ally.[12] He also told his captors that he made his overture to me in this fashion: "Your interests and mine are identical. They are the interests of the people. No theory or doctrine transcends these fundamental interests. You believe you are a nationalist and a patriot. You should not use any pretext, even anticommunism, to calmly allow the Americans to murder our compatriots and devastate our country.

"Chau argued with me about these ideas, but I avoided an argument with him on principle. He [Chau] then said categorically: 'My stand clearly is to oppose communism but not to hate Communists as individuals.'" Hien added that he reported to his superiors after our first meeting in November 1965, "His ideas and political stand are not favorable; his opposition is still strong and shows signs of becoming stronger." He further stated that at our second meeting (May 1966) he determined that "Chau's ideas had not undergone any change."[13]

The indictment went on for some eight pages, listing each of my meetings with Hien and putting the government spin on them. The conclusion of the indictment was that I was charged with the crime of "liaison with a person who is carrying out activities detrimental to national defense."[14]

At this juncture, Ms. Dai again addressed the court. "I find that my entire defense was fruitless, so I request that the judge ask Deputy Chau whether he needs lawyers or not."

"If the accused refuses to have lawyers hired by him," the judge replied, "we will ask the court to designate a government-hired lawyer."

I interposed. "I ask the court to allow me to consult with my lawyers on this issue."

The judge granted a ten-minute recess. During the recess I told Lawyers Dai and Tuyen that we had achieved our objective. "We have made the tribunal appear to the public as exactly what it is: a tool of repression in the hands of a military regime attempting to masquerade as a democracy. We have shown how the court and the Thieu regime regard the Constitution as mere window dressing, something they totally ignore when it suits them. It is obvious that the tribunal's only purpose is to silence me, by fair means or foul, as it has suppressed other non-Communist nationalists who oppose the regime. You have tried to present social legal arguments and cited legal, constitutional questions on my behalf. The tribunal has ignored or dismissed them out of hand. The prosecutor has been made to look more than a little ridiculous at times, as in the matter of whether or not my case qualifies as a flagrante delicto. He has been reduced to parroting references to Decree Law 11/62 so many times that the audience, if not the judges, must be tired of hearing it.

"It is now time for me to stand defenseless, to let the public know that no matter how many lawyers I have or how brilliantly they present my case, I will be found guilty. I prefer to emphasize the futility of offering any defense by offering none whatsoever from this point forward."

I then thanked the two for their efforts and asked them to withdraw from the case. After a short discussion, they agreed. We returned to face the tribunal and announced our decision. "My lawyers have exhausted all arguments," I said to the judge after the short recess, "but Your Honor has not accepted my defense. I don't think it would be useful to continue in this fashion. I agree to let my lawyers go."

A stunned silence followed. Everyone in the courtroom, from the tribunal judges, prosecutor, clerks, and security detail to reporters and the entire audience seemed to be caught completely by surprise. Only my lawyers and I remained calm. A round of applause from my supporters shattered the quiet. Judge Huynh began pounding his gavel, but it took several minutes to restore order.

"Of course you can resign," Judge Huynh said to lawyers Dai and Tuyen, "but we cannot carry on a trial without a defense."

That was just comically an effort to give the proceedings some semblance of fairness and legality. I again emphasized my point that trying to present any defense would be futile. "I am a knowledgeable citizen, not a dunce. I know in advance that I will be found guilty and sentenced whether I have a lawyer or not. This is the desire of the Thieu regime, as evidenced by months of harangues and threats against me, of money spent bribing deputies to support a vote removing my immunity, of extralegal measures taken to arrest and try me, and of the regime's defiance of public opinion at home and abroad."

Judge Huynh rebuked me, saying in effect that my statement was out of order, that the only point under discussion was whether my original lawyers could resign.

"I came here not so much to defend my case as to defend my dignity," I replied. I pointed out "that I have served my country with distinction for at least twenty-three years, if not more, more faithfully and honorably than any of my accusers." I concluded by saying that I wanted the public to judge the trial and its outcome. In effect, I wanted the court of public opinion to decide the fairness and legality of my treatment, and whether I was truly a threat to national security or simply a political opponent the regime is determined to suppress.

"We see our presence here is no longer necessary," said lawyer Tuyen. "Therefore, we plan to withdraw."

The court then adjourned until the next day.

What followed would have been a comedy of errors had it not been so serious. The next two days were spent in wrangling over who would act in my defense and how long the new defenders would have to review the case and prepare to defend me. I kept saying that I wanted no more lawyers because my case had been pre-judged. Judge Huynh kept insisting that I must be defended as a matter of legality, a laughable stance in view of the irregularities in my prosecution to date.

At one point the tribunal, or Judge Huynh at least, appeared to be wavering on the issue of extension of time for a new defender to review documents, interview me, and prepare his case. As Elizabeth Pond reported, however, President Thieu angrily rejected that idea behind the scenes and ordered that the trial continue immediately and be concluded as quickly as possible. It appeared that he had wanted the trial to be completed in a single day and was irate over how much time had already elapsed. It was clear that he was unhappy about the matter becoming a cause célèbre both domestically and abroad.

I had always known, of course, that I would be convicted and sentenced to a long jail term. But the drama and excitement of events over recent days and weeks had kept that realization largely at bay. Yes, my case would be appealed to the Supreme Court and circumstances might change in some unforeseen way, but I now needed to face the fact that the trial had ended predictably and prison could be my home for the next decade.

My escort brought me to the prison, where guards led me to the same room in the infirmary area that I occupied during the trial. Guards and inmates alike watched sympathetically as I was marched to my jail quarters, some offering quiet condolences as I passed them. I did not know it at the time, but that room was to be my home for the next two years. Normally, anyone sentenced to more than five years served the sentence on the prison island of Con Son.[15] I expected to be sent there but was spared that fate, fortunately, for reasons I still do not know for certain. In hindsight, I believe that Thieu (and some U.S. officials) wanted to muzzle my opposition to his administration and policies, but that Thieu held no personal animosity toward me, having been a close friend for most of two decades, and did not want me to suffer the severe punishment many political prisoners underwent on the island.

I was in solitary confinement, in that I was the sole occupant of a room isolated from the other inmates. However, the room was not a narrow, claustrophobic cell. It measured approximately four meters by four meters (about 169 square feet). It included a washbasin that I curtained off for privacy, a bed, and a small desk. There was a toilet nearby, which I was allowed to use as needed. My room door, as during the trial, was guarded twenty-four hours a day, seven days a week. But now there was a different guard on the eight-hour day shift. He greeted me politely, even kindly, as I entered my room. Exhausted by events of the day, I showered, ate a light meal, meditated and prayed briefly, and went to bed by 10 p.m.

Wake-up time for the general prison population was 5 a.m. Although I was isolated from other prisoners and not allowed to mingle with them, I arose at the same time, partially because of the noise and activity, and partially because I was a habitual early riser. There was a brief respite from lonely isolation after lunch. My room had a barred window that looked out on a yard within the outer prison wall where inmates gathered during their free time, especially those who were on "sick call," waiting for examination or treatment by the medical staff. After finishing my midday meal, I stood for a while looking at the sky through the bars of one of the room's windows, saddened by the thought that this was likely to be as close to the outside world as I would get for a long time.

I spent most of my first full day in Chi Hoa carefully reviewing my situation. I was in prison for an indefinite period, perhaps as long as ten years. How could I cope? I realized something important: I now had time to do things that were impossible during my busy life of the past twenty-five years. In some ways, I could actually benefit from this term of incarceration. But I also knew that I must discipline myself as strictly as I ever had during my time at the Buddhist monastery or during my military and government service. Otherwise, this time would truly be wasted, and my body and mind would deteriorate. I needed to set objectives to achieve, plus a program and daily working schedule that would help me attain those goals.

I spent the next few days in a review process very similar to the self-critique sessions that we used so effectively during my Viet Minh days in the 1940s. I looked back over the twenty-five years of my life since 1945, searching especially for mistakes I made and areas in which I needed more knowledge, more education. It struck me during this self-examination that, for the most part over the years, I reacted to events, and had not been the master of them. To change that pattern, I needed to be able to anticipate rather than merely react.

Gradually I developed a strict daily program that would help me achieve my goals. It included four key elements, which I set down in detail on paper provided for me.

1. Physical and mental health: I would do one and one-half hours of physical exercise every morning, including fifteen minutes running in place and Hatha yoga, and adopt a totally vegetarian diet. Studies and meditation (one hour each day) would keep my mind active and alert. I would continue my lifelong custom of prayer and meditation before bedtime.

2. Self-education: I planned to pursue a structured study of economics and social subjects, especially as they related to Vietnam. I also set for myself the formidable task of learning the Chinese language. (Little did I realize at the time that this decision would be vital to my final escape from Vietnam some eight years later!)

3. Keeping informed: I knew that I needed to stay abreast of current conditions in the prison, in Vietnam, and in the world. This would help keep my mind active and also contribute to my self-education efforts.

4. Meditation and prayer: These had been part of my daily ritual when I was very young and since 1959 when I began government service under President Diem. It was even more vital now than ever that prayer and meditation be part of my daily regimen.

Once I established these goals and guidelines firmly in my mind, I felt less like a captive and freer in my soul. I felt confident that I could cope with my incarceration, that I could make it work *for* me and not shrivel my body, mind, or sentient essence. I began taking steps to implement my program.

First, I arranged for my family to furnish my food twice a week so that I could replace prison fare with a strict vegetarian diet. I developed a routine of exercises that I could perform in the limited space available. I was free to leave my room after the other inmates were confined for the night at 5 p.m., but I was not allowed to go very far, so I walked and ran in place every day in my room.[16]

The guard posted outside my room every day proved to be kind and sympathetic. We talked regularly and soon became more friends than jailer and inmate. He even offered to do what he could to make confinement more bearable. I immediately asked if he could stop by my home and bring my small TV. He did, and also brought me a radio. Normally inmates could not have such "windows on the outside world" in their possession. Nobody seemed concerned about me having these items in my room, however, and I certainly did not bring up the subject. My accommodating guard also agreed to buy newspapers and, later, books for me on his way to work each morning. He often stopped at my home on his way to or from work to pick up items my family wanted to send me or to relay messages to my wife and children. He was my room guard for about two years. I am grateful for his kindnesses during a most difficult part of my life.

Visits by my wife and children quickly became the highlight of each week. I looked forward to seeing them, and to hearing news about family, friends, and the outside world in general. My wife also brought me food for my simple vegetarian meals of noodles, vegetables, and fruit, which I ate just twice a day. The friendly guard brought me my midweek supply of food. On her first visit, my wife reported that the Supreme Court had agreed to hear my case, despite opposition from the Thieu administration. Newspapers kept running front-page stories on the case, however, so there was pressure on the government to let my case be reviewed by the Court. This heartened me to an extent, but I did not feel especially optimistic about the outcome. The chief justice was an honest, reputable man, but some other members of the Court generally supported Thieu and the status quo. Whatever the Court decided, Thieu would have the final say.

For the general population of inmates, each day began at 5 a.m. After they performed morning chores and ate breakfast, guards unlocked doors to the prisoners' quarters so the men were free to walk the prison corridors and mingle with others. (I should explain here that Chi Hoa did not have individual cells like U.S. prisons. Instead, inmates occupied large rooms capable of holding about forty men. Each room had an open communal toilet and simple washbasins.) Part of the daily routine also included constant agitation by the several hundred Viet Cong prisoners who were segregated in rooms that occupied about one-quarter of the prison. They were a constant source of disruption, shouting pro-VC and antigovernment slogans, yelling and making other noises. They rotated their activity by groups, so they were able to keep up the din all day and night, making it difficult for the rest of us to sleep. They also refused to join in a South Vietnam flag ceremony held every morning. They rejected the flag as a symbol because they did not consider South Vietnam a legal separate state. As punishment, guards turned high-pressure hoses on them and singled out some of the most vocal VC for special treatment. They shackled these prisoners and placed ten each of them in totally dark rooms.

In addition to Viet Cong and political prisoners like me, penitentiary inmates included a variety of criminals convicted of everything from robbery to murder. Even some juveniles were present. All except the VC were intermixed as part of the general prison population.

I did not allow any disturbances to affect my own daily schedule. Typically, after getting up at 5 a.m., I meditated, exercised for an hour, made my morning ablutions, and then began working on my self-education. I knew I was weak on economics, for example, so that was one of the subjects that I concentrated on at first. I also studied more deeply about how Vietnam, the country and its society, had developed over the past century. I was raised on stories of our country and its proud, if turbulent, history, going back hundreds of years. There were, however, gaps in the depth of my knowledge of events during the late nineteenth and early twentieth centuries. I wanted to correct that deficiency. I also read current newspapers and magazines extensively to keep abreast of what was happening in the world outside the walls that enclosed me. It was exhilarating, in a way, to find that though my body was imprisoned, my mind was free to explore anytime and anywhere. This was a luxury I never enjoyed before, and it made my captivity far less onerous than it might have been.

I decided to study Chinese (the Mandarin version) because Vietnam and China had a long, complicated, intertwined history, as to be expected between two neighboring countries. Given that proximity, it was inevitable that there would be a continuing important relationship in the future. Educated Vietnamese all knew French at least as well as their native language—better in many cases. With the advent of the Americans, more and more Vietnamese had learned, or were learning, English. Few of my countrymen, except for ethnic Chinese citizens, could speak, let alone read or write, the very complex Chinese language. I felt that having this capability could be an asset when I left prison. My initial bouts with Chinese quickly revealed what a formidable task I had set for myself. Traditional written Chinese has many thousands of words, represented in writing or print by characters composed of up to a dozen, or even more, strokes. Very soon, however, someone else's political difficulty became my good fortune.

It happened after police attacked student activists during an antigovernment demonstration and arrested many of the student leaders. Some, beaten so severely that they required hospitalization, were brought to the Chi Hoa infirmary and locked up in a room near mine. I knew several of them from meetings and demonstrations before my arrest. One, Phong, was from an ethnic Chinese family[17] and knew the Mandarin Chinese language well. He volunteered to help me in my study of Chinese. His tutoring proved invaluable. Prison officials placed the student activists on the same isolation regime as me. Guards unlocked our doors after 5 p.m. and we were free to meet, talk, and walk the corridors. Phong quickly advised me to learn the simplified version of written Chinese introduced by the Mao government shortly after the Communists defeated Chang Kai-shek and the Nationalist Party. Simplified characters reduce the number of strokes required for word-characters. Furthermore, the new Communist government in China identified the 5,000 of those most commonly used as a basis for promoting literacy. This became the common written language of the people, and in this form it was taught in elementary and high schools and used in newspapers and magazines.[18]

My young tutor set me to reading Chinese periodicals and doing writing exercises. Although our time together was somewhat limited, he also began teaching me to speak Mandarin. Thanks to his help and advice, my progress improved far more rapidly than during my self-education attempt with the traditional written language.

In late 1970 my friendly guard came in early one morning and called me to the door of my room, acting very excited. "The Supreme Court has nullified your sentence!" he exclaimed eagerly, and then he thrust the day's newspaper at me. "Look at the headline. Now they will have to let you go, probably in just a few days."

I glanced at the paper, and indeed the story was all over the front page. I felt a surge of elation as I sat down to read. I had been wondering for eight months if this day would come. Even as I read, however, a voice inside me cautioned that I should not let myself get too optimistic. "Believe you are free only when you leave this prison without an armed escort!" it warned. The Supreme Court decision was heartening, but Thieu ultimately would decide my fate. I knew I must not get my hopes up too much until he commented on the Court's ruling, which surprised me more than a little.

Chief Justice Tran Minh Tiet was a Southern Catholic and a distinguished person known for his honesty and independence. He did not know me, but his wife was from Kien Hoa province. She told the judge of my efforts there and how much support and sympathy there was for me in the province. He began to investigate my case and decided I was falsely accused and wrongfully convicted. The other justices were a mixed lot, some pro-government and some not. I had not expected them to go against the president in this case, however. My hope for release was pinned more on the political than the legal side. I thought it likely that I would be freed more because of internal and external pressure on Thieu, especially by the United States, rather than by the Court.

Word of the decision spread quickly through the prison. Inmates smiled at me and made encouraging gestures as they passed by my windows. Shouts of joy and congratulation erupted from the student activists in their nearby room when they heard the news.

One of my lawyers, Tran Van Tuyen, came that afternoon to inform me officially of the court's verdict. "All legal aspects of your case have now been decided by the Supreme Court," he told me. "All that is required now for you to be set free is for the president to accept and abide by the Court's decision." My wife also visited, elated for me, but sobered by bad news she had to report. "My mother is terminally ill of blood cancer," she told me. "We do not expect her to live much longer."

This devastated me, wiping out for the moment any thoughts about the Supreme Court decision. My mother-in-law always treated me as a son, and I cared for her as much as if she were my birth mother. In fact, I had spent more time with her as an adult than I had with my real mother, who died in 1952, almost two decades earlier. She was always a tower of strength for me and my family, and was one of the kindest persons I have ever known.

I wrote a letter to General Khiem, then prime minister, asking for permission to visit my mother-in-law one last time before she died. Unfortunately, she died first, so the petition was amended to allow me to attend her funeral. Officials granted the request, but then withdrew permission just a few hours before I was to leave for the funeral. The excuse was that my appearance in public "might create a disturbance," meaning that my supporters and other antiwar, antigovernment groups might use the occasion to mount a protest demonstration calling for my freedom. In view of the Supreme Court ruling in my case, the administration would find that very embarrassing. An exact replay of events occurred when my father died shortly after that, in 1972. Officials first granted me permission to attend his funeral, escorted by armed guards, of course, then withdrew permission at the last moment.

Nothing changed in my situation for a week or ten days. I remained in prison despite the court's nullification of my conviction. Finally, my lawyer visited the prison. When I saw his somber expression, I knew he bore bad news. Silently he handed me a newspaper with a story reporting that Thieu refused to set me free, splashed in bold letters across the front page. A reporter had asked the president why he would not honor the high court decision. Thieu replied, "It is true that the Supreme Court represents the law, but there is a higher, unwritten law. It requires us to think first about the security of our country, to put the nation's best interest above all else. If Mr. Chau is released, it would be harmful to the country. His views and political stance could encourage the enemy and pose a threat to our national security." And that was that.[19] Our Constitution was exposed as an empty piece of paper, and the Supreme Court shown to be an irrelevant, meaningless fixture of South Vietnam's democratic facade.

I remembered at this point my last meeting with my wife and two older daughters before my arrest. I told them that they must sever all connections with Thieu and Khiem and their families. "And never accept anything—nothing!—from them," I impressed on them. My admonition probably was unnecessary because they understood the situation. At any rate, they followed my instruction to the letter. Thieu did make very indirect attempts to offer the family help, but they were rebuffed.

A break in my solitary existence occurred when I learned that a colonel whom I knew had been brought to Chi Hoa Prison's Death Row to await execution after being found guilty in a major corruption case. This officer at one time was my assistant in Kien Hoa. He was later assigned to the Second Military Region and appointed province chief in Binh Dinh on the coast of the country's central region. I spoke to the prison warden about him, asking that Lieutenant Colonel Tran Dinh Vong be allowed to share my quarters. The warden agreed, so I gained a roommate.[20] Subsequently, he told me details of his transgression.

During 1966 the Americans began to construct an airbase in Phu Cat district of Binh Dinh. Many area residents, hundreds of them, were evicted for relocation as a result. After the completion of the project, the United States provided a compensation fund for the affected families. The total amount was based on a list of qualified recipients provided by the province chief's staff and was to be distributed to families by that staff. Lieutenant Colonel Vong and several members of his staff conspired to inflate the list significantly, showing two or three times as many families as actually displaced by the airport enlargement. Then they gave each family only a portion of what they deserved, keeping large sums for themselves. The colonel's deputy was an honest officer (I knew him personally), and he blew the whistle on the swindle.[21] Nguyen Cao Ky was prime minister at the time, and he made an example of the conspirators to prove he was a good leader fighting corruption. Ky hesitated to go through with an execution, however, because Colonel Vong's cousin was the wife of General Vinh Loc commanding the Second Military Region—and Ky needed army support to maintain his power. The death sentence was never carried out, but Colonel Vong remained in Chi Hoa until the North Vietnamese took over. Later he was sent to a Communist reeducation camp.

I suffered a devastating emotional blow, but not a completely unexpected one, in June 1972. Usually I slept well but this night I could not, so I lay awake listening to my radio. Suddenly there was a report that John Paul Vann had died in a helicopter crash, shot down by enemy fire. The news was sudden, but all his friends could have anticipated it. In a way, I was surprised that Vann had lasted as long as he did. He took great risks from the time I first met him more than a decade earlier, and I often chided him about it.

His death saddened me immensely. He was one of my oldest American friends and, with Daniel Ellsberg, one of the closest. John Vann risked his career to offer me escape from arrest and prison. His death left me with a deep sense of loss. Vann was, at the time, the director of the Second Regional Assistance Group in Military Region II in central South Vietnam. Being former military, he was buried at Arlington National Cemetery with full military honors, which he richly deserved.

Things were not going well in the war during this period, late 1971 and into 1972. The Chi Hoa staff seemed to relax their control somewhat, giving us more freedom of movement within the prison. Many of us political prisoners were then able to meet in the halls and converse occasionally. Some of my fellow inmates included Truong Dinh Dzu, who finished second to Thieu in the 1967 presidential race, during which he advocated reconciliation with the National Liberation Front. After the election he was arrested and imprisoned. Others were Doan An, a dentist and longtime VC supporter; Nguyen Lau, who published English periodicals and was openly pro-VC; and Nguyen Tan Doi, a deputy caught in a financial fraud.

In early 1972 I was moved from my solitary room in the infirmary area to a much larger room—designed to hold forty or so inmates. I shared it with four other prisoners. One was my brother Hien, whose arrest in 1969 ultimately led to my downfall. The others were Nguyen Long, a lawyer and president of the antiwar Student Association; Huynh Van Trong, who infiltrated from the North and rose to be a Thieu advisor but was revealed to be a Viet Cong spy by the CIA; and Huynh Tan Mam, chairman of the Student Association and a vocal critic of Thieu and the United States.

We were together for about a year and had some lively discussions. Both Mam and Long were nationalists who sympathized with the NLF because they believed southern leadership was corrupt and cooperated with Americans in order to personally benefit. Huynh Van Trong was a confirmed Communist. Of course, my brother Hien was also a true Communist. We all had sometimes heated exchanges. Hien and I, as always, disagreed but continued to respect each other. I was a nationalist and anti-Communist who wanted an end to war, felt a coalition government was possible and practical, and hoped for eventual reunification of North and South Vietnam as a true democracy.

I could not understand why the authorities had moved me in with the segregated group of Communists and Communist sympathizers. We talked about the matter. The other four agreed that it was another government attempt to pressure me into accepting a deal from Thieu in return for my freedom. The other four also expected to be sent to the North in a future prisoner exchange, and they suggested that I, too, would be included in the exchange, based on the fact that I had been portrayed as a Communist sympathizer, if not an agent, during my trial.

We discussed our disparate views endlessly, without rancor—but without changing anyone's core beliefs. It was an interesting exchange of ideas, however, and contributed to the education of each one of us, I'm sure. I certainly learned much from those discussions.

I pursued my daily routine of meditation, exercise, vegetarian diet, and study during the period. My family continued to send food twice a week, and now they also brought food for my brother Hien. He had nobody else in South Vietnam, and prison fare was edible but not appealing. In fact, since he did not adopt my vegetarian ways, he enjoyed more varied and tasty meals than I.

U.S. leaders, from Ambassador Bunker to President Nixon and Henry Kissinger, desperately wanted to keep President Thieu in power during the early 1970s. They regarded him as the only real stabilizing force capable of holding the government together until America could complete Vietnamization of the war and withdraw as gracefully as possible from the increasingly unpopular conflict.[22] In 1972, peace negotiators in Paris succeeded in agreeing on an exchange of prisoners between the North and South.

One interesting development during this period involved me alone. A reporter asked a high-ranking North Vietnam official what he thought about reports that I was to be included in the prisoner exchange. The officer, General Hoang Anh Tuan, head of the North's prisoner exchange delegation, replied that "Mr. Chau is not one of us but we will welcome him if he wishes to join us. We respect him and will accept him in the exchange if that is his desire. If he does decide to come North, he will be treated honorably and fairly and will be free to go wherever he wishes. He can remain with us, or we will see that his gets to France, the U.S., or anywhere else he wants." The general's name originally was Ha Xuan Anh, which is how I knew him when were both company commanders in Inter-Regiment 803 during my days with the Viet Minh. He was wounded, losing an eye, and I had no further knowledge of him from 1949 until the prisoner exchange.[23]

Then came the day in early 1973 that all five of us roommates expected. Armed guards took us out of Chi Hoa and escorted us to Tam Hiep in Bien Hoa province, staging area for prisoners held by South Vietnam. From there, prisoners were flown in helicopters to VC-controlled Loc Ninh where the exchanges were made. A contingent of international monitors from Canada, Czechoslovakia, India, and Poland was stationed there to monitor the exchanges. Groups of prisoners released by the Communists came back to the South, and others left to rejoin their Communist comrades in the North, but nobody from our quintet was included in the movement. Finally, after all the other prisoners had been exchanged, we were returned to Chi Hoa.

We did not remain as a group long after returning to the prison. One by one, my companions were removed for exchange with the Communists. Up to the moment that he was taken away, my brother Hien continued to try and persuade me to rally to the NLF. Hien reasoned that the South was abandoned by the Americans and would soon be defeated. He told me that because both the South Vietnam and American governments betrayed me, I really ought to rejoin those who had consistently struggled for Vietnam's future. He personally guaranteed my safety and dignity. I responded firmly that I chose to remain with the South even if defeat could not be avoided, and that I always fought for the best interests of the Vietnamese people against the wrongs of Thieu's government. So I would feel regret, but no shame, in defeat of the South. Hien departed. Our lives to this point were interwoven with the history of our country and our personal, but different senses of duty. Now we parted and could not know whether we would meet again.[24] Soon, as the others were repatriated, I was the only one left in that large room.

Shortly after my last roommate left the prison under guard, I was visited in my room by a Special Branch officer, General Nguyen Van Tay, and his assistant.[25] "The president does not want to send you to the North," the General Tay said, "nor does he want to keep you in prison any longer. For the interest of the country, however, he does not want you to make any trouble for his administration. If you promise that you will not create problems, he will set you free. We don't need to sign papers or make tapes. Just make that promise before both of us as witnesses. We know you are a man of your word."

I told him I would consider the matter overnight and have an answer in the morning. And I did think about it long and hard. I realized that Thieu was at his limit in making this offer. I could not push him much further. Finally, I decided that the government's requirements did not mean I would have to repudiate my principles and policies in any way, just that I would not be able to air them in public for a prescribed time. It did not seem that accepting my liberty would bring dishonor or humiliation to me or those who supported me. In the end, I decided to agree to the stated conditions, but with one condition of my own. "I will agree with your conditions and promise not to make public appearances, give interviews, or issue any statements that would create problems for the administration—but only for three months. That is the only concession I can make."

The two officers went back and forth between headquarters and the prison for nearly a week. We discussed the matter every day, but I remained firm in my promise not to create problems for three months. Then I would decide my future course, I told them. Finally, they came back and told me that they would accept my promise and set me free. "We will release you, but for your own protection and to ensure that nobody harasses you into breaking your agreement, we want to lodge you in a safe, secure place."

So that night, the Special Branch chief, driving an unmarked car himself, picked me up at the prison and took me to a comfortable villa in Saigon. There was a squad of police guarding the villa, and vegetarian meals were brought to me every day. The police allowed my wife and family to come and see me, but not all at once. After a month, seeing that I did nothing to break my promise, they let me move to the home of my father-in-law, where my family lived during my incarceration. The police guard squad moved with me, renting space in a house across the street. (Oddly, the house the police squad occupied belonged to a pro-VC family. A son of the family who was actively VC was in the house when the police squad arrived to begin their vigil. The son had to hide in a tunnel under the house, where the family had to feed him for days until the police left.) I was under what amounted to house arrest, and the police allowed only family members to enter and leave the house.

During the remainder of 1974 I kept busy reading the papers, listening to the radio, and discussing the current state of affairs with my father-in-law, who went out and about daily and was "my eyes on the street," as it were. BBC radio was also an especially valuable source of reliable, objective information, because domestic radio news content was the reverse. It soon became obvious to me that the situation was deteriorating rapidly.

Both the North and the South were violating the Paris Accords agreement to maintain the positions they held at when the accords were signed. The South planted its flags and claimed territory over which it had no real control. The North disputed such claims and kept advancing into these areas—and into others that really were South Vietnam–controlled territory. Fighting went on, ranging from sporadic in some areas to fierce in others. Finally in early 1975 the Communists took two large provinces, one in the Highlands northwest of Saigon and another about 100 or 110 kilometers to the north. By this time, of course, the Americans under President Ford had withdrawn completely from combat operations. It seemed to me that it was only a matter of time before Saigon fell.

We considered leaving Saigon for Vung Tau, a resort town in the province of Dong Nai 125 kilometers from Saigon. I discarded that idea upon learning that the road to the town was being shelled regularly and that passing vehicles often were attacked or blown up by mines planted in the road. Suddenly one day during this tense time, Keyes Beech called. I still don't know how he found where I was and got my father-in-law's phone number, but he was always an enterprising reporter and had many excellent contacts, with the CIA and U.S. embassy in particular. "Can you come to see me at the Caravelle Hotel?" he asked. By this time my police "protectors" seemed to have lost interest in me, so I said I would visit him. I left the house.

"I'm concerned for your safety," Keyes said when I arrived at the Caravelle without interference by the police. "If you want to leave the country, I will make the arrangements for you and your family." Beech then called in an officer at the U.S. embassy, introduced as Mr. Thompson, to brief me on current conditions. The assessment was bleak indeed. Communist forces encircled Saigon, and the fall of the city was inevitable. I finally agreed that leaving would be the wise choice, especially since my family's future under the Communists was uncertain. Would I face prison or even execution because of my anti-Communist efforts or for leaving the Viet Minh to join the South? General Ha Xuan Anh's comments during the prisoner exchange notwithstanding, there were people in the North who almost certainly regarded me as an enemy.

"Here is my home address," Thompson then told me. "Make a list of family members you want to have evacuated with you and bring it to me there. I will make the necessary arrangements." I presumed by this that he would have us flown to a U.S. warship lying off the coast, as was being done with other evacuees. I prepared the list and brought it to his home. After not hearing from him for hours, I went back to his house. A maid let me in but told me Mr. Thompson was not there. I looked around and spotted the list I had given him lying on his desk.

"Where is Mr. Thompson?" I inquired.

"He left last night and hasn't come back," she told me. When I asked if she expected him to return, she nodded rapidly and said, "Oh yes, for sure!" I doubted that seriously, but was uncertain about what to do next.

Then I remembered that General Timmes, the former MAAG chief, had retired and was now a senior civilian official attached to the Saigon embassy. He knew me and had supported my work, so I telephoned him and explained the situation. "Come to see me at my home tomorrow; bring your family, and I will take care of you," Timmes told me. I went to his home the next day but did not take my family because things had worsened overnight. It was April 27, 1975, and enemy forces were tightening the noose around Saigon. About 30,000 South Vietnamese soldiers were crowded inside the city but were leaderless. NVA fire rockets rained into downtown civilian areas as the city erupted into bedlam and widespread looting.

I finally succeeded in getting to Timmes's home through the mobs and chaos that spread throughout the city, only to find he was at the embassy and wanted me to telephone him there. I tried calling the embassy repeatedly but all lines were busy. Frustrated, I called my old friend, General Lu Lan, now the inspector general of the Armed Forces. By this time, Saigon was under curfew so a civilian car could not go anywhere, but one marked as a three-star general's car might get through the pandemonium.

"I need your car to evacuate my family," I told him. "Can you send it to our house immediately?" He agreed to send his car and driver. When the car arrived, I loaded my family into it, and we headed for the port. It proved impossible; chaos had become pandemonium, bedlam, and complete anarchy. Huge mobs were pushing and shoving in all different directions as police stopped cars, arrested people, and generally added to the confusion. Soon our progress was completely blocked. The car couldn't move in any direction.

Fortunately, this happened in front of a pharmacy owned by a good friend, so we left the car and took refuge inside the store. The owner and his family had already evacuated so the place was completely empty, not yet attacked by looters. We spent the night there. The next day, my pregnant daughter experienced problems. We were afraid she would lose her child if we tried to battle the crowds and get to the port, the embassy, or anyplace else that people were desperate to reach. We decided it would be safer to head away from the crowds and return to my father-in-law's home.

Well, the war is finally over, I thought to myself. I headed for home and gathered my entire family around me.

"After thirty years of fighting and suffering, the war is over," I told them. "Millions have died and there has been much destruction. I no longer care who won or who lost. Personally, I did my best but to no avail. Now, I am just happy that that it is over. It is better for the country, for the people in general. We are the losers and must accept that. I don't know what our fate will be, but we must remember that others have suffered much more than us. I know that I will be punished in some way for opposing the victors.

"You, my family, will suffer in some ways, too, but not like other families who paid with their blood and lived under more miserable conditions than we have ever faced. We must be thankful that we have survived to this point. There is no safe way that we can leave the country now, so we will stay here and resign ourselves to whatever we, as losers of the war, must face in the future."

27: RESISTING REEDUCATION (1975–1978)

I sat bolt upright in bed as barking dogs woke me in the middle of an early summer night in 1975. It took a few seconds for me to realize that I was in a private home, not the prison I left just several weeks earlier. Then I was filled with foreboding as I heard men forcing entry into the house. My heart sank as a voice boomed out of a loudspeaker. "Tran Ngoc Chau, Tran Ngoc Chau! Are you there?" I threw on a robe over my pajamas and ran downstairs. Three Viet Cong, wearing their usual black pajamalike uniforms, stood in the living room, with rifles pointing at me. They pushed my wife and the children back to their rooms.

When I said that I was Tran Ngoc Chau, one of them handcuffed me and showed me out of the house without a word. Only the barking dogs disturbed the menacing silence that had fallen over the residential quarter. Streets were deserted, but I knew neighbors must be watching from behind their curtained windows. My captors led me through the neighborhood to a house abandoned by the family of a colonel who had earlier fled the country. The police now used it as a sort of substation to interrogate people like me: former South Vietnam (SVN) officials or people they suspected of being former officials. Some twenty other men were already there: handcuffed, sitting on the floor, and waiting to be interrogated by three policemen seated behind a desk. I was the last of the group to be questioned.

"Why did you not present yourself for enrollment to go to a reeducation center?" I replied that I had been out of the army since 1967, and in prison since 1970.

"According to the newly established government announcement, I understood that Vietnamese who had quit the SVN government or army before 1972 were not obligated to report for reeducation."

My questioner stopped the interrogation to go to another room and make a phone call. He talked at length, then come back and ordered that I be sent home. He told me, however, that I must report the next day to one of the several regroupment[1] centers in town to receive further instructions on my status.

The next day I reported to Gia Long High School, a former all-girls school, now where those waiting to be sent to a reeducation camp were held temporarily. I was directed to a classroom with some forty other unfortunates. Anxiety showed on every face. Most of those detained appeared to be between forty and sixty years of age.

They kept us there for three days, under close watch by armed guards. Finally our captors ordered us to collect our belongings (they allowed each of us one very small bag), loaded us into a convoy of several military trucks, and off we went. The trucks rumbled through the city's deserted streets in the rainy darkness. The weather that night was a match for the bleakness in our hearts and minds.

We arrived at the Long Thanh Reeducation Center, thirty-some kilometers north of Saigon. The complex included about sixty small barracks and five big ones. It covered hundreds of acres of bare land unfit for farming. Constructed during the war for a Thailand military brigade, South Vietnam acquired the camp after the Thais departed and used it for a time as an orphanage for children evacuated from areas overrun by Communist forces. It had since sat abandoned, but now was put to a new use. It was essentially a brainwashing campus.

The new government converted the neglected installation into a vast half-prison and half-indoctrination camp for their defeated enemies. We moved into bare barracks that had nothing but sheet-iron roofs, corrugated metal walls, and cement floors. The temperature ranged from 80 to 120 degrees, night and day. Doors and windows were permanently open, so when it rained the water splashed through the barracks, soaking the interiors but also cooling them. Nearly a full battalion of North Vietnamese infantry provided camp security. High rows of concertina wire surrounded the compound. At night, large floodlights lit up this camp, which stood out spectacularly in the middle of an otherwise deserted area. We began our new life by providing labor for the construction of a high electrified fence around the camp perimeter, the first of many tasks we did to rebuild the camp during our first three months there.

Republic of Vietnam anti-Communists left behind after the American evacuation were assembled here. Among the internees in this camp were Chief Justice of the Supreme Court Tran Minh Tiet and hundreds of other senior judges, cabinet members, senators, congressmen, provincial governors, district chiefs, heads of various administrative and technical departments, and political party leaders. Some 2,000 police officers and 200 female inmates, housed separately from the men, completed the population of detainees.

Now that we were completely isolated, we were allowed to write to our families. It took two to three months for members of our families, many of whom lived just thirty kilometers away, to receive the correspondence—giving the Communists plenty of time to censor it. We were allowed no visitors during the first fourteen months. I lost forty pounds in a year and became such a ghost of my former self that it took a while for my wife and the children to recognize me in their first visit; a second visit would not be allowed until another year later. Our activities consisted of a six-and-a-half-day workweek, and ran from 5 a.m. to 10 p.m. every day—including approximately two hours of meal and break time.

Our captors divided us into squads, platoons, and companies. Each company was housed in one barrack. Our captors forbade us to talk with "trainees" of different companies. Our warden-teachers were all North Vietnamese between forty and fifty-five years of age, some of them known to be senior army officers. They always looked cautious, and we rarely saw them smile. After the three months we spent building our own reeducation and prison camp, our training began. In the opening session, the camp's political commissar lectured us about the curriculum. It was designed, he explained, to accomplish several objectives.

"We must first rid you of the American, Western, and reactionary cultural education and indoctrination you have received, and help you understand and accept the Vietnamese revolutionary and Communist ideology and methods. This will enable you to recognize the crimes you committed against the people and the revolution while collaborating with the Americans and the Saigon regime. This will prepare you to contribute to the building of a new Vietnam under the Communist leadership." The political commissar then ended his opening statement by requiring that students must discuss thoroughly every lecture given in class, at the squad, platoon, and company levels under the guidance of assistant teachers. We must write reports for each one of these discussions, mentioning what we agreed with and what we disagreed with or wanted to know more about.

Weeks later, reacting to almost exclusively negative feedback, the same political commissar required that, from then on, everyone had to express his own individual ideas about the subject discussed. So for the next six months, we spent all day long listening to and discussing:

> The Communist version of the history of the Vietnamese revolution.
> The ideology and performance of the Vietnamese Communists.
> The roles of Ho Chi Minh and the Communist leadership throughout the
>   French and American wars (with the South Vietnamese being considered
>   as American puppets during the latter).
> How the intellectual and moral superiority of those Communist leaders offset
>   the American's material superiority.
> The crimes committed by Americans, their Allies, and South Vietnamese
>   during the war.
> The promising prospects for a future Vietnam under the Communist system.
> The contributions expected from us, and "the opportunity to remedy our
>   mischief and crimes."

The impact of the lectures on the prisoners/students varied with the individual. Most of us weren't interested, although we tried to abide by the Communist rules. But there were some who wanted to learn and know more about communism in general and the Vietnamese Communists, about whom they knew little, in particular. In this environment we, the intellectual products of the capitalist-colonialist systems, as our captors asserted, were to interface with a different kind of Vietnamese: products of the Communist ideology. They gave us all kinds of Communist publications to read. Although I knew many who were, or had become, Communists while fighting against the French back in the 1940s and later during the nearly five years I spent in the Saigon prison, I still didn't understand them well enough. I wanted to know what made the Communist leadership believe that they were fighting for the just cause and that we, in the South, were just American puppets who deserved to be exterminated. With that in mind, I read all the materials they gave us and listened intently to their lectures and explanations.

I soon realized that each lecturer believed firmly in his teachings even on matters about which he obviously knew little. They had been living in a closed society, and had been educated, indoctrinated, and trained to believe whatever their superiors told them. Very few trainees paid much attention to the Communists' lectures; most regarded the lectures and related discussions as part of the punishment they must undergo.

The one subject that attracted almost every student was "the crimes committed by Americans and their puppets against the revolution and the people." Each of us was anxious to know what type of criminal we might be considered. The first three or four sessions covered crimes committed by the military, policemen, and judges. Later, one of my roommates, Dr. Bui Xuan Bao, a Ph.D. from the University of Sorbonne, told me with relief that it was fortunate he had never held any positions that could be considered criminal. In fact, during the thirty years of war, he studied in France and taught philosophy and literature there for many years before he returned to Vietnam to teach at the University of Saigon. The only government position he had held, and that for only a very short time, was the post of assistant to the minister of education.

Ironically, the next morning's lecture included the role of teachers during the war. The lecturer stated that the military personnel who shot and killed indiscriminately, policemen who tortured people, and judges who ruled against the oppressed to protect the oppressors did so because of hatred for the revolution. And, he asserted, they learned that hatred from teachers and educators. That night my good friend Bui Xuan Bao didn't seem to sleep well.

We were required to explain the primary reason or motivation that caused each of us to fight or act against the revolution. The Communists instructed us to explain what action we took, how successful we had been, and with what results. They wanted to know about our assets and bank accounts, our family connections and colleagues, and much more. They supplied pens and paper and set us to work. We spent more than a month writing about our lives. After all the prisoners' biographies were collected, we were directed to go back to the classrooms to continue the curriculum. A month later, the analyzers of the biographies began a series of interviews with individual prisoners selected as being either "typically representative" or "interesting." At least two-thirds of us had been requested to rewrite parts of the document.

I was among some twenty detainees who were asked to rewrite their biographies for the fifth time. At one time my interviewer asked me if I had listed all medals and decorations I had won during my military service. After I insisted that I did, he took a piece of paper out of my file and read it to me. In fact, I had neglected to mention one medal received when I was a lieutenant twenty years earlier. The Communists had set up special committees of at least at three levels to read and scrutinize those biographies. The committees were assisted by special groups of investigators whose duties were to collect data and information related to some specific detainees.

Finally, the period of listening to lectures and writing biographies ended in the fourteenth month of our captivity. As a reward, our wardens allowed members of our immediate families to visit us for the first time. Families were notified of the time, location, and formalities some fifteen days in advance. Our orders the day before were that we had to be well dressed, behave properly, and maintain discipline for the occasion. The day of the visit was a big day. We assembled in the large conference hall under the surveillance of men and women in police uniforms. I sat waiting almost half of the day for my turn. For all of the inmates, this first meeting with their families under the circumstances was a new experience, one highly charged with emotion. I watched their faces on their way back from the meeting place. None of them seemed to be happy, despite the large amounts of supplies their families brought to them. Several showed obvious signs of total depression. They walked heavily, tears running down their faces, as policemen pushed from behind. Two of them were carried back, recovering from emotional shock hours later in the barrack.

Although I had experienced the life of a political prisoner for almost five years under the South Vietnamese regime, the situation now looked dramatically different. Under SVN President Nguyen Van Thieu's system, prisoners suffered because of the government's insensitivity to the inhumane conditions the prisoners endured. Under Communist Party rule, the prisoners suffered as much because of the insensitivity and purpose the Communists directed at their enemies: cruel revenge through physical and mental tortures not only on the prisoners but also on their wives and children outside the walls. Family members of their "enemies" were targets of the Communists' revenge, discrimination, humiliation, and degradation.

It took us a while to recognize each other when I walked into the small room to meet my family in the presence of the two policemen. My wife informed me that some twenty-five members of my sister's and brothers' families, who had been with the Communists throughout the two wars, had sent a petition to the Communist hierarchy seeking clemency for me. Sadly, one of my sons who had been admitted earlier to the National School of Music was asked to withdraw from the school. The Communist director explained that, under the socialist system, his father's background disqualified him for education as a prospective artist and public performer.

A few days later, we were all ordered to the conference hall for an important announcement. One after the other, each of us was sentenced to three years in detention. A few hundred escaped penalty. Late that evening, a friend, Tran Van Ai, who was in a different barrack and who thought he would soon be released because he had received no sentence, managed to come through the darkness to give me all his supplies and to say farewell to me. Ai and a hundred others in the same status wound up spending ten more years in other Communist detention camps. Those sentenced to three years detention also endured ten additional years in prison. Communists had a different morality and interpretation in regard to their statements; what they said often bore little relation to what they did. The Communists' basis of morality was "the end justifies the means." Their bright promises were also shining lies, and those were their weapons.

After the "legal" procedure of sentencing, our captors now considered us adequately educated about the good things of the "revolution," the evil ways of the Americans and their puppets, and our own crimes against the revolution and the people. They probably thought that by now we were prepared to accept whatever they intended. Group discussions on political subjects continued, but only from 7:00 to 10:00 each night in dormitories. Now every day except Sundays and holidays, we labored in the fields and around the camp under heavy guard. We had strict orders not to exchange talk with prisoners of other platoons. Some prisoners went insane. Suicides and deaths occurred frequently. Relatives were not notified until months later. Early one morning, I woke up to find the man sleeping next to me, a former senior justice, had died from an overdose of sleeping pills. We were allowed to wrap his corpse in a blanket and bury him a short distance from our barracks. His family was notified of his death about three months later.

Around Christmas of 1977, prisoners were reorganized into new squads, platoons, and companies, and changed barracks. I found myself this time assigned to a barrack of about 150 prisoners. Half were police officers and the rest consisted of prominent members of the judicial and legislative branches and ambassadors or ministers of the former Saigon administration. Then, one dark, rainy night, the 150 prisoners in the newly formed company were awakened, and we were ordered to gather our belongings. I was handcuffed with Tran Minh Tiet, the chief justice of the

Supreme Court, and we were all brought to another prison. We understood that our next destination would be somewhere in North Vietnam. Some Communist guards from the South, more open than their comrades from the North, told us that thousands of prisoners had already been selected and sent from provinces and districts to this prison for shipment to the North. Such prisoners were generals, military officers, civil servants, religious leaders, political party members, and some private citizens.

We were in Thu Duc prison, located about sixteen kilometers from the U.S. embassy in Saigon and a few miles from the military port that had seen much of the military logistics movement during the war. The prison had been used during the war to detain women suspected of pro-Communist activities. The Communists now used the facility as a transit center. Members of the Saigon government selected as the worst criminals from a hundred reeducation centers and prisons throughout South Vietnam were assembled here, processed in groups of 500, and shipped to the North. We were there for several months. More prisoners arrived almost every day. One of the new arrivals was Roman Catholic Bishop Nguyen Van Thuan, nephew of former president Ngo Dinh Diem. A dozen other Catholic and Buddhist priests arrived shortly after him. As we were preparing mentally for a long journey, guards appeared suddenly, handcuffed former chief justice of the Supreme Court Tran Minh Tiet, and led him away. Tiet was a devout Catholic, known for his professional integrity. He was one of the few justices of the Supreme Court who refused to bend to Thieu's buying of votes.[2]

Then in early 1978, at noon on a hot day, with all of the prisoners confined in their rooms, a familiar guard opened the door, called me out, and led me to the prison office. There I was introduced to two men in police uniforms sitting behind a desk. They stared at me with grim faces for a minute. Then suddenly the older man asked me to give my name while the younger one looked in a notebook. After I gave my name, the man proceeded to check my birth date, place of birth, the names of my wife and children, and the address where I had lived before I was arrested. With the last question answered, the old man made a sign to the guard to take me back to my room. There was no explanation of why they needed the answers to questions they certainly knew already. In the days that followed, I kept wondering about the Communists' plans for me.

Thirty years earlier when I was a Viet Minh officer, I was in a regiment stationed in the city of Quang Ngai. There was a big building filled with hundreds of antirevolutionary suspects across the street from my quarters. Almost every night, I heard a truck come and stop for a very short time, with its engine idling. Then came the sound of a door opening, followed by a human voice protesting and shouting. Next, the truck was shifted into gear and vanished in the night. About an hour later, I heard shots fired a few miles from where we were. The same scenario was repeated night after night until the regiment moved to another area.

I came to believe that I would soon play the same role. Sleeping was difficult. I was convinced that if the Communists planned to execute me, then there would be nothing I could do to change their minds. I prepared myself for the eventuality. I would die as a Buddhist, with the consolation that at least I had survived imminent death a dozen times before. Then every night, I prayed for my soul, my family, and the good of everybody.

Guards didn't come to get me in the middle of the night as I expected. Instead, they came to take me away from the prison in daytime. The same Communist cadre who had come to check my identity several weeks earlier came back this time with two policemen. They handcuffed me and pushed me into a small car. The car sped away with me seated between two armed guards. We drove toward Saigon. I was surprised that they didn't blindfold me. Just as I began to think they were driving me back to Ben Tre, where I was the province governor for three years, the car turned in mid-city and entered the former headquarters of the South Vietnamese national police. Guards led me out of the car into a small room where I was body-searched by two other policemen already there. Then they took me to the third floor of a big building, pushed me into a dark cell, and locked it. During the hour and a half it took to get here from Thu Duc, nobody said a word to me.

Almost an hour passed before I could see where I was. The cell measured about three feet by eight feet and was almost completely dark. The only "facilities" consisted of a hole in the floor with a water tap nearby. The iron door had a small opening, closed from the outside. The floor was rude, bare, and dirty. Now I definitely felt I was waiting for my final hour, but I still thought that the shooting would occur in Ben Tre in the presence of the people there. Why were they keeping me here in the meantime? I could only guess.

As had become part of my daily routine since a few months after I was first incarcerated in early 1970 under Thieu, I did an hour of Yoga exercises in the early morning and another hour of meditation at night. In Thieu's prison, I was treated with special consideration, not necessarily by Thieu's order but probably because of the sympathetic attitude of the prison personnel. None of them ever interfered with my exercise, meditation, or other activities. I did, however, wake up long before the scheduled time for other prisoners and do all my exercises in my tiny cell while listening to the guard walking in the hall outside the cellblock. The meditation in the evening was relatively easy to keep out of the guards' attention. I sat in a lotus position for an hour, relaxing and reenergizing myself before I went on thinking about the activities of the day.

I was convinced that they planned to kill me. I visualized a drama in which they would come to take me before a crowd in Ben Tre, read a sentence, blindfold me, and place me before a firing squad. It wasn't difficult because I had personally witnessed that spectacle on three different occasions while fighting with the Viet Minh. I spent the following days and nights preparing mentally to face the ordeal. I prayed for life after my death and divine protection for my family. I kept repeating to myself that, as there was no way to escape death, I should face it with dignity.

Time passed. It was hard to tell the difference between day and night since I was kept confined in the dark. Even the guard who threw me the food once a day seemed not to care whether I was still alive. Very often during the night I heard the doors of other cells open, an incomprehensible murmur of a human voice, and footsteps along the corridor outside. I waited to hear them return, but they didn't always come back. Curiously, I came to realize that this compound, and this building in particular, with its well-guarded, isolated cells, was built during the war for almost the same purpose. Only then it was the Communists and opponents of the U.S.-sponsored regimes who were the prisoners. With the situation reversed, I'm sure my feelings now were much like those of the Communists and political opponents of Diem and Thieu previously imprisoned here in the same conditions as mine.

Then suddenly one night, two armed guards ordered me to dress and follow them. I thought that the final scene that I anticipated was beginning. They marched me through an open field into another building and then along a long corridor, and finally pushed me into an office. Two Communist cadres between fifty and sixty years of age sat comfortably in their chairs. They looked at me impassively for a few minutes, and then directed me to the remaining chair facing them. While one was lecturing me and asking me questions, the other silently listened and took notes. It was two o'clock in the morning of my twenty-first night there. The older Communist asked me what I thought of my situation. I said I was extremely exhausted, that I had ceased to think many days ago. My words surprised even me, but I was truthful.

The interrogator stared at me for a time, then began his lecture. "You should have recognized by now how guilty you are of all the crimes you committed while serving the American aggressors. Have you ever smelled the blood pouring out of the bodies of people whom men under your command killed in your many years serving the Americans? If other lackeys committed crimes against the revolution and people, they did so out of political ignorance and for the benefit of the U.S. dollars. You personally committed crimes with conviction. Your cooperation with the Americans and the CIA led to the killing of tens of thousands of people throughout the country. Then, as the Americans were about to lose the war, you donned the mask of a man of peace to deceive and divert peace-loving people. Would you answer my questions?"

As I remained speechless, the man suddenly rose up and shouted at me, "I want to hear your comments. Talk to me."

I calmly told him that as a defeated and captive enemy, I would accept whatever condemnations he and the revolution decided. I also said that if I had to pay for whatever crime they saw fit to charge me with, I would do so. I just wanted them to spare me spurious challenges. "I am defeated, I admit. Ascribe to me whatever crimes you want," I told him. He continued his harangue and I continued to reply the same way for another hour. He finally calmed down, ordered me to rewrite my biography, and finish it in twenty days. I told him conditions in the cell made it impossible for anyone to see anything—let alone to do any writing. I was led back to my cell, feeling weak, hungry, and hollow to my core. I soon collapsed into a sound sleep.

I woke at the call of the guard standing at the open cell door. He showed me to a room, on the same floor but about three times the size of my cell. It had a light, a desk, and a chair. Nearly an hour later, a man of about fifty knocked at the door, opened it, and walked in. He placed a thick pad of paper and several pencils on the desk. Then he said that he would come by every day to check on my writing progress. Right after he left, a guard came in with a tray full of food. After meals that would make a dog cry during the last twenty days, I was now served food comparable to that of a good Saigon restaurant. It turned out that the head of that exclusive jail was one of the Communists who served time with me in Thieu's prison. He managed to talk to me discreetly, explaining that he had been ordered to get me into a condition so I could do the assigned writing task. After that, I was given two meals every day and two hours of limited freedom. I could take a walk along the corridor, which was lighted and locked at both ends.

I then realized that there were four other prisoners who had been treated the same way as I was. They numbered six a few months earlier, but their leader, Luong Trong, had been so ill that he was sent home to die. Another, Phan Pa Cam, was transferred to the Central Prison. One of the four who remained was Le Quang Liem, a former deputy in the South Vietnamese National Assembly, a man I knew quite well. All four were notables of the Hoa Hao, a Buddhist-oriented religion rooted in the Delta. The Hoa Hao had been known as staunchly anti-Communist.

Instead of the twenty days he had scheduled, the cadre in charge let me take exactly fifty-eight days to write my biography. I worked ten to fifteen hours a day to complete the 800-page document. The writing was easy for me this time because I had already written a similar biography twice during the first two years of captivity under the Communists. In it, I covered all "the crimes I had committed against the people and the revolution" in a manner that I knew would satisfy my captors. The Communist who interviewed me came by regularly every three or four days to check my progress, but he never made a comment.

Fifteen days after I submitted my writings, I was led to a meeting with the same two Communist cadres. The older man asked me to sit down, gave me a pen and a notebook, and told me to write down his instructions. To begin with, he made a long commentary about my biography. He said he had the impression that I had surrendered in defeat, as I had maintained time after time. He made a point of saying that he wanted me to answer three questions very specifically. Then he referred to his notebook and read the questions he wanted me to answer:

1. What was my personal reason for fighting against the Communist
   Party, the revolution, and the people?
2. What was the motivation behind my attachment to the Americans?
3. Who instigated and supported my peace proposal in 1968?

He stopped then and warned me once again that he would not accept the same explanations I had written in my biography. He told me bluntly that he wanted something different, something more precise.

"I want to be able to better understand the kind of antirevolutionary and enemy of the people you represent," he stated with some heat. "We of the revolution need that kind of understanding to help us bring other antirevolutionaries like you back to the right direction. You will provide this information!"

Back in my room, I took time to think about what exactly this man wanted to learn through these questions. I was sure that he had heard and read answers to the questions hundreds of times and from hundreds of other detainees. I realized then that it was not me as an individual that interested him so much. He was interested in knowing the people who either guided my thinking or shared my conviction. Instinctively, I understood that the Communists were now targeting Buddhist leaders and other nationalists, like the Hoa Hao, whose anticommunism was rooted in ideology and philosophy. I finally composed my response to the three questions.

In my early years as a young student, I was taught that communism has no religion, no country, and no family loyalty. That impression was revived in my mind during 1949 when I left the resistance. Between 1945 and 1949 I had not debated the merits of communism because all my hours were occupied with my responsibilities as a unit commander or responsible staff officer. However, I gradually came to believe that Vietnam could become an independent and democratic nation, and that a Communist government would be detrimental to traditional Vietnamese values. I frankly admit that after leaving the Communist-led resistance I made up my mind to live a life based on my personal convictions. Therefore, I joined the cause of South Vietnam and acted with the same sense of compassion and devotion as I had previously done while with the resistance. I often asked myself whether I was performing my duty because of higher position, salary, and other benefits. I concluded that my motivation for resisting the Communist Party was simply that I had found another path for serving the people.

My answer to the second question was that I thought American assistance would enable the South to win the war, and be the basis for developing an independent and democratic nation that could incorporate traditional Vietnamese social values.

Finally, I wrote that those who supported me during my trial were the same ones who had supported my 1968 peace proposal. Lawyers, Buddhist leaders, prominent Catholic personalities, journalists and intellectuals, and the great, intimidated, silent majority of Vietnamese were all those who were seeking a path to peace and eventual reconciliation.

Only after I had gone over these questions and answers for the third time did the cadres appear to be satisfied with my sincerity. Then I was asked to write about my connections with Americans, from the beginning to the end, covering twenty years. Back and forth, they kept asking me about certain Americans with whom I had contact both in Vietnam and during my 1968 trip to the United States. This broad subject alone—with their follow-up questions, and my writing and rewriting—took almost a month.

I care so much for my family, and to that point I had struggled through eight years of detention in order to eventually be with my wife and children again. But I was still thinking that all of the confessional exercise and questioning was prelude to a mock trial and execution. Thinking that death might be inevitable, I continued to obliquely challenge the Communist cadres during our discussions. This had nothing to do with courage. I was still protecting my sense of honor because if I were to be executed, my personal honor would be all that would remain in the hearts and minds of those who had known me. But I was completely mistaken. The new rulers had other plans for me.

For the first time, guards took me out of my room during the day rather than in the middle of the night. They brought me to meet with a senior cadre from the North (I guessed, by accent). He appeared friendly. I was wary. After an hour or so reviewing their questions and my answers, he suddenly changed the subject. He told me that my responses proved that I was among a small number of Vietnamese who cooperated with Americans because of a misconception that we could be nationalists, anti-Communist, and get along with Americans. "Now is the time for you and others to look back on the past and realize the difference between right and wrong, to differentiate between truth and American falsehood. Because you are among the few who fought against the revolution based on misconception rather than pursuit of material benefit, we want to give you an opportunity to revive your devotion to serve the people."

He paused for one or two minutes, staring intently at me, before stunning me by saying, "The revolution has decided to set you free." He asked me if I would write a letter of appreciation to the government.

My head was buzzing. I felt faint. It took me a few moments to reply. I told him that I was so moved by the revolution's understanding and decision that I needed some time to think about what I ought to do. I spent the next few days wandering in my mind between the reality of prison and the imagination of either execution or actual release. Finally I wrote them a letter in expected form, thanking them for release and promising to do my best to serve the country. I was still suspicious.

On the day of my individual liberation, a cadre, not a guard, came to my room early in the morning. He returned my original, and cleaned, clothes. After I dressed he led me to a reception area. The Communists who handled my case during the last two months were there. My wife and my eldest daughter were also present. We were invited to sit in comfortable armchairs, and we were served tea, cakes, and fruit. After about twenty minutes of polite conversation, the senior Communist present turned to my wife and said, "The revolution has decided to return your husband back to you and the family. Therefore you are all responsible for his happiness and safety." I understood very well that was a not-too-subtle warning against escape. The whole family would be accountable.

For the first three weeks after my release, I enclosed myself within our family home. I avoided any visitors except family members, including those brothers and sisters who were with the Communists throughout the war, and who now returned from the North. Then one day, the senior Communist who interviewed me before my release came to see me. He inquired about my health and expressed his hope to see me living in a normal way with a positive attitude. He said that he wanted me to go out and renew relationships, especially with former political colleagues and religious leaders. I would be an object lesson of the revolution's humanitarian reconciliation.

Although for ideological reasons the Communists had never openly admitted continuing anti-Communist feelings, they had to know that critical people did exist and that they remained influential among the populace. Openly, the Communists accused all anti-Communists of being motivated only by desire for power, privilege, money, and other material benefits generated by U.S. assistance. Party leaders felt that they had little to fear from those kinds of people, but the specter of other true Vietnamese nationalists still hung over the Party even after victory. The Communists were especially interested in me because I was the only prominent South Vietnamese elected representative who had openly advocated and actively worked for a peaceful settlement.

A few weeks after that visit to my home, I was "invited" by the Central Secretariat of the Communist Party to join the Social Sciences Institute. It was (because my wife was already planning our escape) impossible to decline. During my very first session at the institute I learned that a special committee had been organized to study "The Lessons of the War against the U.S. Imperialists in Vietnam." The result of the study would be submitted first to the Central Committee for review before delivery to the Politburo. The final version, I was told, would be forwarded to a special committee in Moscow. The purpose of the study was for the Vietnam Communist Party to "carry out international duty" by providing lessons for the leaders of "oppressed people" around the world in the struggle against the "common enemy"—meaning, the United States of America.

Within the context of that large study on the lessons derived from Vietnam, I was assigned to analyze "The Formation of the South Vietnam Leadership, Motivation and Impact on Society and Conduct of the War." For research purposes I was allowed access to their so-called special library and to discuss my work with other institute members. Most of them were long-standing Communist Party members. There were also other former South Vietnamese personalities who, like me, had been "invited" to participate in this study project.

My six months working at the institute, while my wife secretly planned our family escape, allowed me to reconnect with some of my former Viet Minh friends with whom I had fought for almost five years against the French. Among them now were senior military officers and party members. Although not every one of them expressed the truth of recent history as they understood it, some were open and candid during our discussions. I doubt that they learned much from me, given that they operated extensive intelligence nets in the South during the war, and they now collected "biographies" submitted by detained South Vietnam military officers, administrators, politicians, economists, and religious leaders.

My brother Tran Ngoc Hien came to see me. We did not have much to say, knowing each other so well after so many years of contention. Strangely, Hien seemed sad and somewhat cautious. It was almost as though he doubted that his party's victory had been worth the struggle. Much later my niece's husband, a senior party officer, told me that Hien had been placed on probation after he was released by the South and returned North in the 1973 prisoner exchange. When he returned to the South in 1975 he had already been stripped of party membership and his army rank (colonel) for having failed to recruit me during his final mission. Finally Hien understood: Despite never having betrayed the party or its goals, any member could be betrayed by the party.[3]

My sister Hong Lien and her husband Le Van Kinh also visited with our family. They returned from the North with all their children. We had not been together for more than twenty-five years. In a moment of family intimacy and affection I asked my sister and her husband what had made them feel so comfortable with the

Communists and how had they been able to endure thirty years of poverty and hardship. They told me that it was because they admired their leaders and believed in the national struggle against the Americans as much as they had against the French. They recited the popular, and not entirely inaccurate, mythology of Ho Chi Minh, Pham Van Dong, Vo Nguyen Giap, and others less well known to me. When I mentioned the corrupt behavior of Communist cadres in the South after "liberation," they responded that the social and economic environment in South Vietnam that was the residue of departed Americans and decimated "puppets" had unfortunately infected the minds of otherwise good Communists.

The few months that I spent at the Social Sciences Institute allowed me to observe the dramatic, abrupt, and even cruel changes that the Communist Party imposed on South Vietnam. Hundreds of thousands of people who had connection with the former Southern government or the Americans were placed in jail or re-education camps. Families were forced to relocate to spartan "new economic zones." Owners of small businesses were liable to be displaced elsewhere with appropriation of their property. The Communists called anything that seemed attractive in the South "fictive prosperity." Hundreds of thousands of South Vietnamese abandoned everything to flee. Communist leader Pham Van Dong called the escapees, among them even some who were poor workers, "the residue of the old society." At that point, cognizant that my wife's plans for family escape were becoming feasible, I decided that I would rather be "residue" outside of Vietnam than within. Our family would leave.

28: COMING TO AMERICA (1979)

We planned our departure carefully. Constant surveillance complicated matters, but our awareness of scrutiny allowed us to make some deceptive moves. We purchased a small piece of land in Gia Dinh for raising pigs and told friends that we might settle there. To further confuse matters I made some clumsy and futile inquiries about leaving the country. I wanted observers to be aware and then satisfied that I was discouraged and had finally accepted my fate. Meanwhile, we actually concentrated on a plan that had the greatest chance of success for the whole family.

The new national government organized an "unofficial" programmed expulsion of ethnic Chinese from Vietnam. Most were families who had lived in Vietnam for three or more generations.[1] Many had intermarried with Vietnamese. They were forced out for two reasons. First, Vietnam entered Cambodia in late 1978 to overturn the Khmer Rouge government, which was supported by China and which had been raiding across the border into Vietnam. China responded by making preparations to invade Northern Vietnam. Second, tension with China and the possibility that ethnic Chinese in Vietnam might aid an invasion provided the new Vietnam government with a convenient rationale for seizing property and other forms of wealth. A disgraceful policy, but we were able to take advantage of it by inserting ourselves into a large group of Chinese who were semiofficially leaving. We made our arrangements while still following our daily family routine.

The escape was orchestrated by a woman authorized by the Song Be (formerly Bien Hoa) province police to buy a boat and arrange for the peaceful departure of Chinese. A team of volunteers, screened and approved by the police, worked for two months to prepare the boat. We were told to be ready to move immediately when told that the boat would depart.

At last, a message arrived at our home from the organizers that we should rendezvous the next morning at nine o'clock. We arranged for my wife and each of the children to proceed to the meeting place by different routes. It would be more difficult for me due to surveillance. I enlisted the help of our second-oldest daughter, Tam Phuong, a physician. She and her husband, also a physician, would remain in Vietnam, because it would have been unwise to risk the entire family on a dangerous expedition. Moreover, we were sure that the shortage of medical professionals in the socialist republic would afford them a degree of protection.

Tam Phuong picked me up on her moped very early in the morning, and we went to the crowded outdoor central market. After parking the moped, we went in separate directions into the market maze. I moved swiftly through the crowded market, with enough twists and turns so that I was confident that surveillance was broken. When I exited at a predetermined point, Tan Phuong's husband was waiting there on his own moped. We sped quickly away, and he delivered me to the rendezvous.[2]

The small boat carrying me, my wife Bich Nhan, and five of our children motored slowly down the Dong Nai River, helped by the current flowing to the sea. This river, also known as the Saigon River, is the only waterway linking the ocean to the inland port of Saigon. For thirty years during the war, ships sailing to and from Saigon were escorted by patrol boat because both sides of the river, particularly the Rung Sat area,[3] were infested with Viet Cong guerrillas.

Our craft was a converted wooden boat powered by a small fifteen-horsepower engine. Originally designed for fishing along the coast, it was about fifty or fifty-five feet in length and normally carried a crew of no more than twenty, plus the catch from several days of fishing, perhaps 2,000 pounds in all. Now, converted by a team of volunteers, it was holding more than 400 escapees. When we lay down to sleep, or tried to, we were packed together as tightly as sardines in a can. A smaller boat following us, loaded with 200 passengers, was equally crowded. We talked in hushed tones, as though our enemies lurked in the dense vegetation that lined the banks of the narrow river. Our pilot-navigator was a former schoolteacher whose knowledge of navigation was derived only from reading manuals and studying the steering and guidance mechanism while the boat was being converted. He had a map and compass—no sextant, radio, direction finder, or other instrument.

About 300 of our fellow passengers were families of Chinese descent. The remaining 100 or so were pure Vietnamese, posing as ethnic Chinese to escape the country. Chinese had to pay the equivalent of $2,500 in gold for each family member and sign a waiver stating that they were "happy to leave [my] property to the Vietnamese government." Nobody leaving the country was allowed to take anything, especially gold. Vietnamese who wanted to escape quickly found that, with proper bribes, low- and mid-level officials were willing to help them become "Chinese" overnight by supplying papers and arranging for them to be included on a boat leaving Vietnam with official approval.

It was more expensive for Vietnamese like us than it was for true ethnic Chinese. Besides the $2,500 each, we had to pay an additional $1,000 to get papers identifying us as ethnic Chinese and to be incorporated into a real Chinese family.[4] Then we had to pay an extra $7,000 to the boat owner for her services. (A friend helped us with a loan of $25,000, which we repaid some twelve years later.)

As we neared the halfway point to the coast—still about fifty-five kilometers away—we were gradually shaking off the tension of our hasty, covert flight from

Saigon. I fell into a deep sleep finally, after making myself as comfortable as possible on the crowded deck, only to be jolted awake by gunshots and screams about 5 p.m. It was a patrol boat. And after firing shots into the air, the police officers on board directed us to follow their craft to a tiny port on a small island near the river's mouth. Meanwhile, the other, smaller boat with 200 aboard must have sailed past the patrol boat crew unnoticed. We never saw it again.[5]

This was just the beginning of months of adventure, danger, intrigue, and ultimately, salvation. While our boat was detained, our family was split up and each of us had to maintain our cover story and depend on the support of others. Fortunately I could speak Chinese, thanks to the young student held with me in the Chi Hoa prison, and I was able to deceive the interrogators. But my son Tam was placed in a group suspected of not being ethnic Chinese. My concern for his fate was so great that I felt paralyzed. I could hardly stand up. I passed it off by saying that I had a health problem.

It was past 1 a.m. when the police led us back to our boat. The women and children were still missing. I felt like I was suffocating and sleep was impossible. Of the seven of us who had set out on this boat, I was the only one aboard. I climbed up on the top deck and was struck by the stillness all around. The men down below were as silent as I was, surely feeling the same sense of loss and concern for their families. Looking at the sky, I turned my thoughts to my religion.

Over the years I have made mistakes, including some serious ones, I mused to myself, almost as though I was conversing with Buddha. *But I have tried to live a righteous life, in accordance with Buddhist teachings of moral and intellectual integrity and compassion for human and other natural beings. Why is it now that my family is broken up and separated from me?*

Suddenly a hand touched my shoulder. It was my eldest son, Tien Duc. Having worked on preparing the boat for our journey, he was very familiar with it. When the police ordered us ashore, he had been able to go over the side unnoticed and hid in the water under the boat. He stayed in the water until he saw us return and the police leave, then crept back on board and searched for me. We discussed what we should do until dawn. Then, as the sky turned pink and began to grow light, I saw one of the most welcome sights of my life. The women and children were being returned to the boat, with my wife and our three youngest children among them. As Tien Duc and I rushed to embrace them (daughter Tam Minh, nineteen; son Truc Giang, sixteen; and daughter Tam Huong, fourteen), I mentally thanked Buddha for reuniting us. Our joyous reunion was spoiled when they realized that son and brother Tam was still missing. We all had tears in our eyes with the thought that we might never see Tam again.

We spent the rest of that sad day on the boat. At least we did not have to be hungry; three of us were allowed ashore to buy food at the village market. Later, we were told we would be allowed to leave the island and continue on our journey. A patrol boat would escort us the short distance to where the river entered the South China Sea. The patrol boat carried twenty-seven men singled out as non-Chinese, including Tam and a brother of the boat owner. It would take them to a jail in Song Be. The boat owner had already taken care of the arrangements by bribing the officials for the release of her brother. As the patrol boat pulled alongside for her brother to board our boat, a shout was heard from our boat. "Mr. Chau's son should be released, too!" Other families took up the cry, pleading and demanding for the release of their relatives. Finally, the police allowed three or four of the remaining twenty-six prisoners to rejoin us. To our great delight, Tam was among them. Our family was complete again. My joy was indescribable!

Our tension subsided somewhat when our boat reached international waterways. We held an informal meeting of all passengers to discuss how we should organize ourselves. I was asked to serve as spokesman and coordinator for the group. We formed a committee of heads of families to set up daily schedules, rationing of food and water supplies, living spaces, and the like. I made it a point to consult with this committee and to achieve a consensus whenever possible. At times, however, differences of opinion arose. No matter what decision I finally made, some of the family heads were unhappy with me. Many of these men had held powerful positions in the past. They included successful businessmen, physicians and other professionals, even former government officials and judges. They were accustomed to giving orders, not taking them.

The immensity of the sky and the sea stretching out all around us made us aware of our fragility. We saw large ships occasionally, but they all steamed past us, ignoring our distress signals and calls for help. That was typical of the situation at the time. Immediately after the 1975 Communist victory, almost the entire world community was very generous in aiding refugees from Vietnam. For a time, the international media was filled with articles about the boat people, especially the hundreds of thousands who perished at sea trying to escape. Attitudes changed when the Hanoi government began the "peaceful expulsion" program for ethnic Chinese, resulting in escapees becoming a mixture of Chinese and Vietnamese, like our family, using false papers to leave the country. The previous generosity was replaced by indifference, if not dislike, for a variety of reasons.

First, neighboring countries were mostly third-world nations with limited economic resources themselves. What was at first a relative trickle became a flood when hundreds of thousands of boat people left Vietnam during this peaceful expulsion program. When other countries around the world showed signs of reluctance in granting asylum to more refugees, neighboring countries found that it was increasingly difficult to move the refugees forward to countries where they could settle permanently. Second, most of the refugees were now Chinese who had been expelled by the Vietnamese. Neighboring countries did not want to be manipulated by Vietnam into taking their cast-off citizens, nor did they want to offend the Chinese government. Taiwan admitted a limited number of Chinese-Vietnamese, but mainland China did not accept many of them.

We especially feared encountering Thai fishing boats. The reason was simple. We had all heard reports of what happened when refugee boats were captured by Thai fishermen-turned-pirates. In many cases, the men were slaughtered and young women raped, some subsequently thrown overboard.[6] Others were taken to the mainland and sold into sexual slavery. The pirates seized all the money, jewelry, and other possessions of value that they could find. Their victims totaled in the thousands. On the occasion when we were pursued, we managed to escape in darkness.

But no sooner had we breathed a sigh of relief and begun to discuss our narrow escape than another problem was discovered. We were lost. The pilot/navigator had a map, but our sudden change of course and hasty flight in the dark left him confused about our location. Our boat plodded on over the seemingly endless sea for three days and nights with no sight of any other boats, large or small. Water and food supplies dwindled. We rationed them carefully, but soon everyone aboard was hungry and thirsty. Children cried while their parents prayed for help. Some among us screamed in despair. Most were simply listless, however, too weak to do anything but sit or lie quietly on the deck awaiting their fate. The odor of unwashed bodies and excrement was almost overpowering.

As I crawled along the deck trying to encourage people, to counsel them to keep their hopes up and have patience, I felt like a hypocrite. Inside myself I wondered whether we were in the last hours of our existence. Would we perish at sea as so many thousands like us had already done in similar plights? Looking around and taking in the whole situation, I also felt despair. Had I done the right thing by setting out on this perilous voyage? Was it right to subject my wife and five of our children to these conditions?

Sunrise of our sixth day at sea brought no respite from our difficulties. Water surrounded us as far as the eye could see. We could see not even a single bird, so we knew there was no land anywhere near. We had set out on what was planned as a three-day journey, with supplies and fuel to match. The crew decided to stop the overworked engine. Since we had no idea about which direction to head in, we thought we might as well save fuel and avoid damaging the engine. So the boat drifted freely for a few hours. Then a sharp-eyed crewman spotted a dot far off on the horizon. When studied through binoculars, it appeared to be a large ship, seeming to stand still, almost as though anchored. Our engine was restarted hastily, and we headed for the strange ship. It loomed larger and larger as we approached. We were encouraged when people waved from its decks in a friendly manner. Then, when we got closer, a small boat with three men aboard was lowered over the side and motored over to meet us. Our crew stopped the engine again as they approached.

They appeared to be Caucasian, but not like the French or Americans with whom we were familiar. One of them, a uniformed ship's officer, spoke broken English, enough to ask who we were and what we wanted. As spokesman for the group, I explained our situation: We had almost no food or water, and we were running low on fuel. We invited them to examine the people and conditions aboard our crowded boat.

"Can you help us?" I asked. "Could you possibly take us aboard your ship and drop us at the nearest port?

The answer was a gentle "no." The ship's officer in the small boat told us they were on their way to Saigon (now Ho Chi Minh City, of course). Some of us then looked more closely at the ship lying not too far away and realized that it flew the flag of Soviet Russia. This created new anxieties because we had all heard about Russian ships picking up and returning boat people like us to Vietnam. On the other hand, there had also been reports of some Russian ships assisting refugees they encountered on the open sea.

The Russian officer seemed friendly enough, and he asked us to wait where we were while he returned to his ship. He said he would bring back food and water for us. We decided to take a chance that his offer of help was genuine. We had little choice actually, since we had nowhere else to turn. The Russian was as good as his word. He returned with the promised supplies, three big bags of canned food and bread, then pointed us in the direction of Singapore.

We set off toward Singapore in somewhat better spirits. The first thing we did was dole out rations of food and water from our newly replenished supplies. It was no feast, but at least our hunger pangs and thirst lessened slightly. About three or four hours later we began to see shorebirds in the sky, indicating that we were nearing the coast. The waves now got higher and rougher. Our boat developed leaks and ominous cracks. We struck a sandbar about 300 yards from the beach. Our little boat, already weakened by pounding waves, began to founder. Panic spread through our ranks. Water now washed freely over the deck. Dozens of local fishing boats lay at anchor not far away, but not one moved to help us.

I grabbed several children in my arms and leaped into the water. I immediately realized it was shallow enough so we could evacuate everyone safely to the beach. It would require only a short swim before we could wade ashore. Some people even risked swimming back to the boat during the night, salvaging what belongings they could. A great many of us, however, lost everything but the clothes we wore and what little we had been able to carry ashore with us. After we were all safe on the sandy beach, we began counting noses and checking families to make sure everyone had escaped from the sinking boat. By this time most of the hull of our little craft was underwater.

This beach, which we soon found out was in Malaysia, offered only temporary sanctuary for us. Like other nations in that part of the world, Malaysia had no desire to harbor the Chinese refugees. The country's hospitality and resources were severely strained by this time. In addition, Malaysia had no love for the Chinese. Following World War II, an insurgency, led primarily by the Chinese minority, had nearly devastated the country. Singapore, then a Malaysian state where ethnic Chinese were very powerful, was a hotbed of rebellion at the time. So Malaysians did not welcome more Chinese coming into their country. Consequently, our boat and its passengers would not be allowed to remain. Ordinarily, we would have been forced back out to sea. Since our battered craft was now at least half-submerged, this obviously was impossible.

Next morning, local inhabitants from a nearby village came to sell us food, water, and other items. Somehow, most families had managed to bring jewelry or U.S. dollars with them, and to hold on to these valuables through our trials and adventures. They now were able to trade for the supplies we needed, but at exorbitant prices. We gradually improved our primitive encampment with material obtained from local villagers. Families constructed shelters over their allotted areas, using coconut fronds, plastic, driftwood, and any other material that came to hand. Miraculously, nobody was seriously ill. The Malaysian Red Cross provided us with enough rice and canned food for us to live on, if rather frugally, but getting enough fresh drinking water was a problem. We finally arranged to pay the only landowner nearby to get water from her well. Our area was crowded, but we grew accustomed to the living conditions.

Then one morning after nearly three weeks spent in the beach encampment, a squad of police arrived. They inspected our half-sunken boat for two hours, with a representative from our group permitted to accompany them. The police had a long discussion among themselves, out of the hearing of our representative. Apparently they were talking about the condition of the boat and whether it could be made seaworthy, though it seemed apparent that could not possibly be done. It was so severely damaged that even the experts brought by the Malay police to inspect it agreed that the boat could not be repaired. The answer came a week later. A long line of military vehicles pulled up at the entrance to our beach compound. Orders boomed through loudspeakers, commanding us to gather all our belongings, assemble with our families, and prepare to board the trucks. No destination was mentioned.

Our convoy of more than ten trucks traveled all that day, going through village after village and passing many rubber and cherry plantations. We crossed the entire Malay peninsula, finally arriving at another beach. This one was far different from the isolated one we had left that morning, however. It was a resort, a beach city called Muong Shin. We looked enviously at the beautiful villas, hotels, and shops, and people strolling leisurely on the streets and beachfront promenade. Police ordered us from the trucks and told us to camp for the night, but gave us no information on what would happen next. A uniformed police squad was detailed to keep us under surveillance and ensure that we stayed together as a group in our designated area. Despite their presence, some of us were able to talk covertly and briefly with local vendors, learning that this area was used regularly as an assembly and debarkation point for refugees being transferred from the mainland to island internment camps. There were already several other groups of refugees in the area waiting to be towed back to sea.

The next morning we were ordered to embark on two small boats, taken from previous refugee groups. Our group was assigned to one boat, another group to the second boat. We were fearful about boarding the boats because they were even much smaller that the one in which we had left Saigon. Moreover, they appeared to be in much worse condition, and we doubted their ability to remain afloat should we encounter heavy seas. The police said we would be escorted to an island internment camp. At first we refused to board the frail-looking craft, both tied to a Malaysian Navy ship, but the police forced us. The navy ship weighed anchor about 3 p.m., towing the two boats behind it. The trip went smoothly through the remaining daylight hours. We passed several small islands before nightfall, wondering as we first caught sight of each one whether it was our destination. The navy ship just kept plowing over the vast sea with our boats following behind like puppies on a leash.

When darkness fell we were in a vast void, lit only by the stars, luminescent wave tops and lights on the ship ahead. The waves seemed to grow higher, noisier, and rougher as the night progressed, increasing our dread of the unknown. We had all heard about refugee boats capsizing in these conditions, their towlines being cut and all the passengers being left to drown. So we spent the night in terror and despair, praying that such would not be our fate. We were spared, but passengers in the second boat were not so lucky. Their craft capsized during the night, and all aboard perished. We did not realize what had happened until morning, when the other boat was nowhere to be seen. The darkness hid the tragedy from us, and our boats were far enough apart so that the noise of the wind, waves, and engine of the navy ship drowned out what must have been the horrifying screams of the refugees as they struggled in the surging waves.

For us, however, sunrise brought renewed hope. We survived the night, and our boat rode buoyantly behind our towing vessel. We were now on a broad expanse of ocean, with large freighters and passenger liners steaming in both directions. We tried to attract their attention by displaying distress signals, but they all ignored us. Our journey continued all that day. Then, without warning, the navy ship cut us adrift. The engine in our small boat would not start so we were dead in the water, moving solely at the mercy of the winds and current. The crew on the tow ship ignored us and steamed off without offering directions, advice, or assistance in repairing our engine. We had no idea where we were or where the current might take us. We floated aimlessly in the dark for three or four hours. Then we saw lights ahead, in the direction the current was taking us. We feared the current might be taking us back to the coast of Vietnam, or even worse perhaps, into the hands of Thai pirates.

Imagine our relief as we drew closer and saw that the lights were those of a small fleet of Malaysian fishermen. We had drifted back to the Malay shore. The fishermen greeted us in friendly fashion, and we discussed our situation with them for nearly an hour. Then several of them repaired our engine and gave us some fuel for it. The Chinese-Malaysian captain of one of the fishing boats agreed that he would guide us to a refugee island for $1,000. We followed in the wake of our guide boat throughout that night with a mixture of hope and anxiety, passing island after island. A couple of hours after sunrise the boat ahead throttled back and our guide signaled that the island we were nearing was the authorized refugee center described to us earlier.

But once again, this would only be a temporary stop on our pilgrimage to America.

By mid-afternoon the next day, a Malaysian Navy boat took charge of us. The commanding officer allowed some of us to go ashore and buy supplies at the village, but told us we must soon be ready to leave the little port. His boat would tow our craft out of Malaysian waters. So we were soon back at sea, being towed to we knew not where. At least the ride was smoother than when we were towed earlier. Once again we felt fearful. The only sounds except for the steady beat of the navy boat's engine and lapping of water at our hull were children crying and women sobbing. Again we prayed that we would somehow reach a safe haven.

At sunrise, the navy boat slowed almost to a stop, allowing our boat to draw near. The officer pointed to a flock of birds circling in the sky some distance away. He told us to head in that direction to make landfall, and then they cut the towline. We started our own engine and headed in the direction of the birds. After about an hour, with the sun rising higher and the sky lightening, we saw land straight over the bow—but still some distance away.

We didn't know it then but learned later that we were in the Anambas Islands, about 200 miles northeast of Singapore in a very isolated region of the South China Sea. Although they are part of Indonesia, the Anambas are closer to Vietnam than

Jakarta, the Indonesian capital. After we anchored the boat, one of the men who had signaled us[7] came aboard. He introduced himself as the local authority. When asked where we were, he replied that this was Letung Island. We were informed that they could arrange to take us to a nearby refugee island, Bahala, where we could set up a semipermanent camp. From there, it might be possible for us to seek permanent asylum in a friendly country. It would take $3,000 to make the arrangements, however: $1,000 up front and $2,000 when we landed on the island.

Finally, we gathered together enough money to meet the demands.[8]

True to his word, the man boarded our boat and guided us to a smaller island less than a mile away. The two islands were close enough so one could swim from one to the other, which many of us did later. Our new "home" turned out to be about the size of several football stadiums. By nightfall, we were all safely ashore. We talked briefly with refugees who were already on the island and got some food from them. We ate, then stretched out on the bare sand to get a good night's sleep after our two nights of terror and fear of what lay ahead on the small boat. It was a pleasant, balmy night, with stars twinkling through the canopy of coconut palm fronds overhead.

The government of Indonesia eventually dispatched a squad of police from district headquarters on the island of Tampa, about 1,000 kilometers away, to oversee activities of refugees from Vietnam. They were billeted on Letung and did not bother us a great deal. Two- and three-man teams visited our camp regularly and seemed content with the cleanliness and order we maintained. They were strict about allowing only a few of us at a time to visit the Letung market and shops.

There were no TV, post office, telephone, or radio transmission facilities available. The only means of communication with the mainland was sending messages with the merchant ships that came about once a month to trade supplies, clothing, and other goods for coconuts, copra, and dried fish. Gradually we established routines on our island encampment. Since the earlier group had already established itself on the southern portion of the island, we settled on the northern half. We built rude huts of native materials, mostly fronds from the coconut palms that flourished everywhere and driftwood. We dug pit toilets and laid out cooking areas.

We set up schedules for daily chores: cooking in the morning and afternoon, taking turns to cross to the other island to shop at the market, washing and doing laundry across the bay in the many streams that ran down from the interior mountains. Fishing was also a big part of our life. Fortunately, fish were plentiful in all the surrounding waters and made up an important part of our diet. We also began to receive some canned food and rice from the Indonesian Red Cross. I listened every evening to my shortwave radio, one of the few possessions we had managed to retain. A month went by, although it seemed like a year to us.

Suddenly, our routine was interrupted in a most threatening manner. Two policemen came to our family's hut during the middle of the night, wanting to question me. They told me they had received information that I was a Communist, only posing as a refugee on a mission to infiltrate the refugee community for the Hanoi government. This was a very serious charge because the Indonesians had a long history of dealing harshly with Communists. Just a decade before, they had massacred thousands of people, mostly of Chinese origin, suspected of being pro-Communist. The situation was very dangerous for me. We were all still illegal aliens—in effect, trespassers on their land. I could be detained or even killed with impunity. I had to give pause to their suspicions somehow.[9]

I said quickly that their information was not true. "Would I bring my family with me if I was working for the Communists? How could anyone believe I would put them through the ordeals we have suffered? If I was an agent for Hanoi and in favor with the government, I could simply have left them behind in safety and relative comfort. Please check with the American embassy in Jakarta about my status. I worked with the Americans and am well known to many of them. I think it would be wise for you as well as for me to make sure you have correct information before making any decision about what to do with me."

Even while telling them this, however, I felt tendrils of fear running through my mind. What if Jakarta got in touch with the wrong person or persons at the embassy? Someone who was not familiar with my case and took my conviction as a Communist sympathizer at face value? Or, worse, someone like Ambassador Bunker or the CIA's Ted Shackley, who had at least condoned Thieu's actions and possibly even helped orchestrate the whole affair.

I managed to plant seeds of doubt in the minds of the policemen about the accuracy of their information. They talked in Indonesian (which I could not understand) for a half-hour. Finally they agreed to check with Jakarta about me before taking any action.

We continued our routine as before, although conditions on the island deteriorated as more and more refugees arrived. The population jumped from about 600 when we first landed there to 800 during the next two or three months. Three hundred of them later had to transfer to another small neighboring island. Getting adequate water for drinking and cooking was always a problem. The only sources were streams in the highlands, and the increased demand strained the supply.

I listened to the BBC every evening on my radio. That is how I learned about the Vietnamese invasion of Cambodia, where they replaced the China-backed Khmer Rouge with the Hun Sen regime. I followed events as the Chinese invaded the northern provinces of Vietnam in retaliation, "to teach the Vietnamese a lesson," as one Chinese leader put it. They succeeded at first, destroying several cities, but finally withdrew after suffering heavy losses.

One night I listened to a long report on the overall situation in Southeast Asia. At its conclusion, my old friend Keyes Beech, *Los Angeles Times* correspondent, was credited as author of the report, having filed it from Bangkok. I sat up as an idea occurred to me. Keyes had helped me in the past; perhaps he would be able to do so again.

The next morning I visited the police sergeant in charge of the detachment on Letung. I offered him my Rolex watch, concealed from Vietnamese and Malaysian searches, if he would arrange to send a telegram to Beech via the U.S. embassy in Bangkok. At first the sergeant protested that providing such a service would be illegal. Then the bargaining began. He explained he would have to pay a merchant on a trading ship to Tanjung Penang, a day and a half away by boat. The wire could be sent to Bangkok from a telegraph office there. I convinced him the Rolex would more than cover the costs. Finally he agreed, but cautioned me that the next boat was not due to arrive for about two weeks.

The following days passed peacefully, but with agonizing slowness. I tried to put the message out of my mind. Even if it reached my friend Keyes—which was far from certain, given the circuitous route it must take—what could he do? I tried not to pin too much hope on it, going about my daily routines as usual. The influx of refugees gradually changed the pleasant, peaceful life on Letung for both good and bad. The indigenous population amounted to only about 2,000 people before their area became a haven for refugees. Now the population had increased by 40 or 50 percent. There was no real crime, but the refugees, most of whom had little or no means, helped themselves to coconuts and bananas, which the people of Letung regarded as theirs. Friction and misunderstandings inevitably resulted, but they were minor. For the most part, we all got along well, especially considering the circumstances. No incidents occurred that were serious enough to require police intervention.

Two months went by, and I had almost forgotten about sending the telegram. It was always a long shot that it would reach its destination—and if it did, that it would produce any results. Then one day at noon, a helicopter appeared and circled our encampment. It flew so low for a time that we could clearly see the pilot and several passengers. Then it flew off to the other side of the island. (We learned later it landed at a soccer field on Letung.) Refugees and local residents were both very excited; this was the first helicopter ever seen in this area.

About two hours later, a boat landed at our beach. Four men came ashore, jostled by a crowd of refugees pushing forward to watch and to learn what was happening. One called my name. It took me a minute to recognize the man; it had been some ten years since I had seen him last. Then it dawned on me. It was Tony Cistaro, a friend I had made back in early 1968 while I was in Washington during the Tet Offensive.

He told me Keyes Beech did indeed get my much-traveled message. He immediately went to see the U.S. ambassador in Bangkok and James A. Schill, Singapore-based U.S. refugee coordinator. Cistaro explained that he now headed the International Rescue Agency in Southeast Asia, a nonprofit organization dealing with refugee problems. He heard about my message, learned where I was, and joined the team delegated to come and get firsthand information about refugees in this area—and to see me. He then gave me a letter and $500 from Keyes Beech. We talked for two hours. I gave him a brief account of what had happened to me, and my family, since my last contact with Keyes Beech. He was appalled by the ordeals we had faced since leaving Vietnam, but not really surprised. In working with refugees as he did, he heard similar accounts all too frequently.

In the weeks that followed I had more visitors: reporters who came to interview me. The first were from the Australian ABC and American NBC television networks. They interviewed me at length. Other reporters followed, including one from the *Far Eastern Economic Review* in Hong Kong.[10] Many networks, including the BBC, broadcast accounts of our escape from Vietnam and current plight. It was the first news my daughter in Saigon had heard about us since we left Vietnam seven months earlier. She and the other relatives and friends we had left behind were relieved to learn we were safe.

Keyes Beech himself finally got permission to visit Letung for one day only and came to see me. It was a happy reunion. We filled each other in on our respective adventures since we last saw each other just before the fall of Saigon. He was particularly interested in what went wrong with the evacuation plans he made for me and my family before leaving Saigon himself.[11] He questioned me about how the Hanoi regime had dealt with me, and marveled that I had survived everything that happened to me since we last met.

Another week passed uneventfully; then Tony Cistaro returned by boat with a team of five from the American Refugee office and the International Rescue Committee. They began the arduous task of identifying and processing the refugees for resettlement in a dozen countries (mainly Australia, Canada, France, and the United States) that had agreed to accept certain quotas of them as immigrants. Cistaro and his team worked on Letung by day and returned to their boat at sunset.

About a month later we moved to a new, larger island, called KuKu, where some 2,000 refugees were assembled, waiting final processing and then transportation to new homes in strange lands. Then, one day in September 1979, a group of 400 of us boarded a large ship and sailed for a day and a night to yet another island. It was a pleasant voyage, far different from our earlier experiences on small boats. Food, water, and medicines were plentiful. We had room to move freely on the deck as we passed island after island, waved to fishing boats and watched flying fish and birds cavorting in the sea and sky.

We landed at Tanjung Penang, one of the larger islands in the Indonesian archipelago. My family and I were taken to a refugee camp near the harbor; all the other passengers went to another camp some eighty kilometers away. Our new camp was small, only about as big as a soccer field. It contained only about thirty makeshift homes, surrounded by barbed wire and guarded at all times by two or three policemen. We completed all the necessary papers and procedures for admission to the United States as legal immigrants. Tony Cistaro visited us regularly to report on progress of these efforts and to bolster our spirits.

Then the great day arrived: October 30, 1979. A small boat took our family of seven and about 100 other refugees to Singapore, where we boarded a chartered airplane for the sixteen-hour flight to Los Angeles.

When I first stepped on U.S. soil, I was almost overcome by conflicting emotions. I knew I had definitely given up my homeland and the people I had done my best to serve for thirty years. The decades of physical and mental anguish, accomplishments, defeat, joy, and sorrow flashed through my mind, accompanied by a series of images. I remembered the jungles and battlefields, gracious villas and prisons, working in Danang and Kien Hoa, my triumphant election and inglorious arrest. Always trying to conduct myself in an honorable manner, I was betrayed by men whom I had trusted, and yet redeemed by others who would not abandon me. I know the past can only be recalled, sweetly or painfully, but never revived.

In one way, I felt like a deserter, defeated and humiliated, leaving my ancestral home and heritage behind. On the other hand, I looked at my wife and children, thinking they had suffered enough. Now they faced a far better future in this land of opportunity than they would have faced in Vietnam. Under the Communist regime they would always suffer the stigma of being related to me, a nationalist who had resisted the Communist philosophy for thirty years. I had paid for that, but they had, too, more than their share. The new life we faced would be a far better one.

EPILOGUE

For the long-term benefit of my grand- and great-grandchildren, and fellow Americans with whom they will live together for generations to come, I am writing this epilogue to summarize the most important factor relating to foreign policy—and that which is also exactly what Americans neglected or ignored in Vietnam. This most important factor is awareness other countries' national cultures, the product of their own special histories. Failure to recognize and take into account different national cultures during the exercise of diplomacy and peacekeeping operations, or field operations, is an accelerant for failure.

Americans of some authority and reputation came to Vietnam with the objective of stopping Communist expansion. The objective was clear and noble, and Vietnam appeared to be an appropriate location for a bastion opposing possible Chinese advance into Southeast Asia. That American objective was acceptable for some venal Vietnamese who could separate themselves from waning French presence for better opportunities with Americans. Religious and nationalist traditional idealists—including me—found temporary common cause with those calculating opportunists. But the majority of Vietnamese, in particular the peasantry and revolutionary nationalists, had already determined a different immediate objective: national independence.

After the 1954 French defeat at Dien Bien Phu and the Geneva Accords, with French influence and presence fading, the Americans provided direct economic, military, and technical assistance to President Ngo Dinh Diem, who built a Republic of (South) Vietnam as an authoritarian regime. Despite a brutal and humiliating anti-Communist denunciation campaign down to the riceroots of the nation, the secret police and military that the U.S. financed and helped to organize and operate failed to completely eradicate the Viet Minh precursors to the Viet Cong. The Americans put the blame on Diem and looked for a change. With the 1963 Buddhist crisis providing convenient context, the Americans replaced Diem with a group of generals, all of whom had served with the French during their war with Ho Chi Minh.

From 1963 forward, with those Vietnamese generals in power, the Americans were in almost total control and conducted the war as they wished. U.S. troops reached a level unimaginable during the previous Diem period: over 500,000 compared to fewer than 20,000 during the First Republic; with almost 47,000 Americans killed in action compared to fewer than 300 in Diem's presidency. "Search and destroy," bombing, and body counts competed with "winning hearts and minds." Then, amid claims of military and pacification success, came the 1968 Viet Cong Tet Offensive. The light at the end of the tunnel was, after all, a Viet Cong campfire. America experienced the painful limits of imperial power when confronting a distant and determined smaller nation.

"Que sera sera" seemed to be what the United States said to the Southern Vietnamese generals after the withdrawal of American combat elements in 1973. Without the presence of American military forces, President Thieu and his generals fought on for another two years before collapsing in April 1975. This abbreviated and sad sketch of the American involvement in Vietnam illustrates the consequences and catastrophic effect of ignoring the Vietnam national cultural factor up to and during the Vietnam War. American leaders and policymakers, conscious of their own military supremacy, made decisions about political policy and strategy and imposed them on the Vietnamese, without consideration for or consultation with the real majority of the nation's people. That majority was slowly growing alienated: the rural population became the symbol, roots, and resources for the Viet Cong, and even (in some areas) the launchpad for the final attack by North Vietnamese divisions.

With a monumental superiority complex, American generals on the Vietnamese scene—and their superiors at the White House and Pentagon—skipped applying the essential maxim to "know one's allies and enemy" in the process of developing policy and strategy. Ignorance of Vietnam's history and political culture resulted in the following missteps.

1. Predominant presence of American troops and personnel in South Vietnam created South Vietnamese dependency on the Americans until the South Vietnamese collapsed without them. The enormity of the American establishment in Vietnam helped Communist propaganda boost morale and motivation of their soldiers and sympathizers to fight Americans and their "puppets."

2. The United States deployed inexperienced, uninformed (of Vietnamese culture and history), illiterate (in Vietnamese) "advisors" at almost all levels. Vietnamese allies thus appeared as dependable puppets in the eyes of rural and urban Vietnamese. Most advisors were, at best, fact checkers or reporters for the U.S. Military Assistance Command.

3. Americans supported reactionary Vietnamese personalities (as viewed by peasants) and even consolidated them into authoritarian regimes that would not accept any anti-Communist concept other than extermination. The result was incubation of more and more "neutral" and pro-Communist sympathizers. These people

eventually cooperated with the National Liberation Front, or as refugees moved to the cities as passive opponents to the South Vietnam government.

4. The United States relied on superior military power to search for and destroy the enemy, and to pacify the people, creating more enemy than they killed. The same personnel who were trained by, and served under, the French (in police, security, and intelligence agencies) sought information on the NLF. They shared a preconception that all former supporters of the Viet Minh were now Viet Cong. Because the Viet Cong wore no particular uniform, the Vietnamese government and Americans were incapable of identifying them from the air or during operations on the ground. However, the estimated killed count was subtracted from the enemy order of battle, thus contributing to the illusion of progress or success.

The four major points above illustrate how American leadership failed to develop and apply appropriate strategy and tactics in Vietnam. A few Americans working at the riceroots level did comprehend the actual situation, but they were unable to influence the outcome due to the inertia of the mistaken direction of the war.

To conclude, I will again remind readers that we Americans are still—even now in the emerging multipolar world—a superpower in every field. But in culture there is no objective standard for qualitative comparison. National cultures and histories are not inferior or superior, only different. In our relationship with every foreigner, every foreign nation, we must take their national culture into consideration. We absolutely must understand the people whom we ally ourselves with as well as those whom we oppose.

Only through understanding different national cultures, and acknowledging the importance of that understanding, can we Americans make fewer mistakes than we did in Vietnam. Our grandchildren and great-grandchildren will have a better chance for a harmonious future, with friends and opponents, when we adjust our policies in any region to the reality and vitality of other national cultures.

NOTES

All footnotes ending with [KF] were written by Ken Fermoyle, the writer who worked with Tran Ngoc Chau on *Vietnam Labyrinth* for more than twenty years. All other information, comments, and explanations are those of Tran Ngoc Chau.

CHAPTER 1

1. Last emperor of the Nguyen dynasty, founded in the early nineteenth century.

2. Tran Huy Lieu was a revolutionary, a professor, and a writer with the pen name of Nam Kieu and many others. He was born in Van Cat commune, Vu Ban district, Nam Dinh province on November 5, 1901; he died July 28, 1969.

3. The latest and final alias ("The Enlightened") adopted by the revolutionary leader during World War II.

4. Ellsberg: released the Pentagon Papers; Colby: CIA director; Vann: first "civilian general" to lead U.S. troops in war; Lansdale: supported Magaysay in Philippines and curbed Huk insurgency; Holbrooke: U.S. ambassador to the United Nations; Beech: veteran foreign correspondent. We learn more about each of these men in later pages.

5. Originally named Nguyen Tat Thanh and born in Nghe An province of Central Vietnam.

6. Afraid of the consequences if he refused, Bao Dai consented to reign under the Japanese as he had under the French.

7. *Vinh-loc Dai-phu Hiep ta Dai-hoc-si Thuy Van-Y*, in Vietnamese.

8. Volume 2, *Les Vieux Amis de Hué* (The Old Friends of Hué), 1939.

9. His abdication and agreement to accept the title of supreme counselor to Ho Chi Minh also consolidated Ho's position as the new leader.

10. The Viet Minh later became known as primarily a Communist organization. In 1945, however, Chau estimates that there were only about 5,000 true, dedicated Communists in the entire country at the time. [KF]

11. See Barbara Tuchman, *March of Folly* (New York: Ballantine, 1984), 241–42.

12. Viet Minh intelligence targeted both the Japanese and the French puppet government, concentrating on the French after the Japanese surrendered to the Allies in August 1945.

13. The relation of a son or child to a parent.

14. Leader of the Boy Scout Association at the time was Ta Quang Buu; years later he

became Vo Nguyen Giap's deputy defense minister and served as head of the Communist delegation at the 1954 Geneva Peace Conference.

15. Three of my classmates, Thich Tri Quang, Thich Thien Minh, and Thich Thian Hoa, became leaders in the 1960s and 1970s of the Buddhist Unified Church. The church led mass demonstrations and self-immolations in protest against Diem's discriminatory and repressive treatment of Buddhists, creating the chaotic situation in 1963 that helped a group of Vietnamese generals stage the successful U.S.-supported coup that toppled Diem, a Catholic.

16. Teenage boys like me commonly served in this way; because of our youth we were able to come and go without arousing suspicion among the French and Japanese.

17. *Area Handbook for Vietnam*, Foreign Area Studies of the American University, 1967.

CHAPTER 2

1. This is a rough translation from the original Vietnamese.

2. Even a year later, in late 1946, Ho Chi Minh had an estimated 60.000 soldiers in the field, but only 40,000 rifles to arm them, as reported by George K. Tanham in *Communist Revolutionary Warfare* (Santa Monica, CA: RAND Corporation, 1961).

3. Remember that this was after the official Japanese surrender.

4. My stay there turned out to be the last taste of easy living for some time. In fact, shortly after this I would go for two years without any shoes to wear.

5. Stanley Karnow, *Vietnam: A History* (New York: Viking, 1983), 137.

6. Ibid., 148.

7. Tuchman, *March of Folly*, 241.

8. Karnow, *Vietnam*, 139.

9. Ibid., 151–52.

CHAPTER 3

1. A port town about ninety-five kilometers southeast of Saigon.

2. During the Japanese occupation, the term "fascist" had replaced "imperialist."

3. The French regarded this area around Dalat as their own and gave French names to all towns. Vietnamese names were used officially only after the Revolution began. French names and their Vietnamese equivalents were: Bellevue / Deo Ngoan Muc; Dran / Do Rang; Arbre Broye / Tram Hanh; Entrerays / Cau Dat; Le Bosquet / Trai Mat.

4. Not to be confused with the minister of information of the same name who served in Tran Van Huong's cabinet.

CHAPTER 4

1. Communication was vital; we had to coordinate operations with other areas, exchanging combat and intelligence information. These matters had to be handled on our local level, with no help from higher levels, and we had no existing infrastructure on which to build. Our leaders were successful chiefly due to shortcomings of the French and the cooperation of Vietnamese people inside and outside of French-controlled areas. The pattern set during this difficult time was the basis for the success of the Viet Minh (and later the National Liberation Front, or Viet Cong) in the South.

2. The term "political commissar" has negative connotations for Americans—and may not even be completely accurate. In the Russian Communist definition, a commissar is in charge of political indoctrination and enforcement of party loyalty. Our commissars' responsibilities went far beyond that. It wouldn't be too great an exaggeration to say that success or failure of our struggle for independence rested to a great extent on our political commissars and the quality of their efforts.

CHAPTER 5

1. A very few sergeants and corporals were Vietnamese.

2. This is a lesson that the French, most Americans, and nearly every South Vietnamese government and military official failed to understand. Conversely, it was the cornerstone of my personal philosophy, and I endeavored to put the principle to work later as province chief in Kien Hoa and mayor of Danang.

3. This kind of indoctrination began in 1945 and continued, both for the military and civilians, over the next thirty years of warfare in Vietnam. I am convinced that it was a critical factor in the success of Ho Chi Minh.

CHAPTER 6

1. I estimate that there were perhaps 5,000 dedicated Communists in the whole of Vietnam at the time, based on what I learned at the time and from later research.

2. Again, these were lessons that I used effectively later as a military officer and administrator for South Vietnam.

CHAPTER 7

1. One of my fellow company commanders in that engagement was Ha Xuan Anh, a native of Hué like me, and member of a notable family. Anh lost one eye as a result of

wounds in 1946. He took the alias Hoang Anh Tuan to protect his family from reprisals when he joined the Viet Minh, and some twenty-four years later, still as Hoang Anh Tuan, was a major general commanding the NVA Second Division in the Que Son area of Quang Nam province. In 1973 after the Four-Party Joint Military Commission was succeeded by the Two-Party Joint Military Commission on March 31, he headed the Communist military delegation for the PRG at Camp Davis on the Tan Son Nhut airbase. Colonel Vo Dong Giang was his well-known spokesman. Subsequently General Tuan was ambassador to India, and after returning to Hanoi he was appointed vice minister of foreign affairs.

2. It was standard practice for unarmed volunteers to be mixed in with the armed men in every platoon. Normally they carried ammunition and other equipment, and were prepared to replace troops who were killed or wounded; otherwise, they took charge of captured enemies and weapons.

3. Again, this was a philosophy that the French and later the Americans never seemed to comprehend.

4. Once more I must point out that such depredations were the best recruiting arguments for the Viet Minh.

5. This followed the example set earlier by the Japanese occupation troops.

CHAPTER 8

1. Those selected for the party served six months as provisional or probationary members. If deemed acceptable, they then were accorded full membership.

2. Luong was an enigma. A senior Communist who spent fifteen years in French prisons, he was released when the Japanese threw out the French administration in 1945. No one was sure how he obtained his position, but his power was pervasive. He had final authority to select, promote, or demote all cadre in the Zone.

CHAPTER 9

1. Duties of this organization had included control, taxation, and registration of all manufactured products, including spirits. Under colonial rule, the agency assured that the production and sale of alcoholic beverages remained a monopoly of the French.

2. He also became a good friend, but later caused my imprisonment when I became a political thorn in his side.

3. For example, mandarins Bui Bang Doan and Pham Phu Tiet, Buddhist leader Le Dinh Tham, and Confucian scholar Huynh Thuc Khang. Catholic Bishop Le Huu Tu also joined Ho Chi Minh for a short time and bore the title of "government counselor."

4. Nguyen Ngoc Le had been a sergeant in the French Local Guards before 1945, then

later a lieutenant under the French, and at this point (still with the French) a captain. Subsequently he was a general during the presidency of Ngo Dinh Diem.

5. The Second Bureau, equivalent of the U.S. Army G2, gathered enemy military intelligence and, to some degree, cooperated with the Military Security Service in espionage and counterespionage operations.

6. Like many traditional Buddhist families, we always had a small shrine in our family home.

CHAPTER 10

1. President Auriol did so in a letter written on March 8, 1949, and addressed to former emperor Bo Dai. In it Auriol officially acknowledged negotiations conducted between Bo Dai and Emile Bolleart, French high commissioner for Indochina, including Vietnam, on a French Navy ship in Halong Bay eight months earlier.

2. There were a few Cambodians on the service staff (cooks, janitors, etc.) but no Vietnamese. This apparently was due to the French concerns about security and fears that Viet Minh agents might infiltrate the staff.

3. One difference between St. Cyr and the Vietnamese academy was that the St. Cyr training program extended over two years while our training was to be completed in just one year. However, since the St. Cyr program included time off for vacations and holidays and general education subjects (e.g., history) and ours did not, the actual military training time was roughly equal.

4. A board headed by a French citizen of Vietnamese descent, Lieutenant Colonel Nguyen Van Hinh of the air force, conducted the recruiting/selection process. Although a few Vietnamese were on the board, French officers essentially controlled the process.

5. It was known as the School of Vietnamese Officers and was run by the French.

6. The Viet Minh military command Interzone V.

7. Catholic chaplains were the norm for Vietnamese Army units. Not until the overthrow of the Ngo Dinh Diem regime in 1963 did the Ministry of Defense begin to appoint Buddhist chaplains.

8. One was killed later, but the other, Second Lieutenant Tran Thanh Chieu—later promoted to lieutenant colonel and first given command of the Fourteenth Light Division for a few months and then the Thirteenth Light Division by President Diem—was a fervent Catholic. The Thirteenth was one of the components of the Twenty-first Infantry Division when it was organized in 1959, and Chieu was briefly commanding general.

9. The Catholic bishop of that area, Le Huu Tu, originally supported Ho Chi Minh and was given the title of government advisor. Less than a year later, after the French reconquered Hanoi and a large part of the North, he switched sides and increasingly became known as a leading figure among the anti-Communist Catholic clergy.

10. Major Nhu not only publicly protested my treatment by President Thieu, but later in the United States was instrumental in curbing the hate campaign against me and my family during our first year in America. Friends informed me later that he repeatedly and publicly defended me in this fashion: "I know Tran Ngoc Chau and served with him in the army. He was and is an honest, honorable man. I did not always agree with his politics, but I know he is a patriot, a nationalist, and was never a Communist supporter."

11. The French term was more accurate and preferable. "Advisor," when translated into Vietnamese, had an unfortunate connotation, suggesting a sort of subservience on the part of those being "advised."

12. R&R a decade later was understood as "rest and recreation" for U.S. forces on leave.

13. One man was dead and we couldn't collect his body until the enemy retreated. Another died while we were under siege in the cemetery.

14. We did not learn until several days later that the Viet Minh regulars retreated and only the local units remained.

15. Chapter 7 of Bernard B. Fall's book *Street Without Joy: Insurgency in Indochina, 1946–63*, 3rd rev. ed. (Harrisburg, PA: Stackpole, 1963), gives perhaps the best detailed account available of Operation Camargue.

CHAPTER 11

1. This was my third journey to Hoi An. The first was upon leaving the Viet Minh. Later I was briefly there as an intelligence officer to a provincial unit before joining the Groupe Mobile as described in the previous chapter.

2. The French High Command recommended me for the Legion d'Honnor but then came the fall of Dien Bien Phu and the Geneva Accords. I never followed up to see whether the recommendation had been approved.

3. The major lived in San Jose when this was written originally. Chau saw him occasionally until his death. "He still remembered that incident and brought it up every time we met. He also related again how his wife berated him later, apparently blaming him for my actions." [KF]

4. Chau's genuine concern for the families of Vietnamese soldiers killed in action continued on down the years. He later made special efforts to provide widows with pensions and funded orphanages for Vietnamese children out of his own pocket. [KF]

5. He later became a full general and served as prime minister under Thieu for several years. [KF]

6. There may have been Vietnamese officers commanding subsectors elsewhere, but I was unaware of any others at that time.

7. Le Van Nghiem was subsequently promoted to brigadier general, and later, major general during the Republic of Vietnam period.

8. Nguyen Thanh Sang was also promoted to general during the Republic of Vietnam era.

CHAPTER 12

1. A Major Robert was my immediate predecessor.

2. Fort Mason, an old U.S. Army post, was much later closed, and is now part of San Francisco's Golden Gate Park and Recreation Area.

3. This was a pentangular division designed to fight on the tactical nuclear battlefield envisioned in the 1950s. Each battlegroup would have to be a self-contained task force that could fight dispersed on a sustained basis, thus enhancing its effectiveness and survival during highly and broadly lethal combat conditions.

4. Our first action, against a mixed force of mostly Japanese, supplemented by a few British and French troops, as previously described.

5. The Cholon facility served initially as a headquarters for the Military Advisory and Assistance Group (MAAG) after the 1954 Geneva Agreement. MAAG furnished U.S. logistical and training support to the Army of the Republic of Vietnam (ARVN). The facility had been expanded, however, since I left for America in 1955.

6. The office of governor for Central Vietnam was later abolished as being an unnecessary bureaucratic level of administration. Tanh and Governor Duyen fell out when Tanh refused to go along with the governor over use of provincial funds. Both Duyen and Tanh were colleagues in government earlier, during the French colonial period, but this did not keep Tanh from losing his job.

7. A few younger junior officers, lieutenants mostly, had received some English training but virtually no Vietnamese officers of the rank of captain or higher could speak any English—but some were fluent in French.

8. Can Lao translates roughly into "good workers" in English.

9. Neil Sheehan, *A Bright Shining Lie: John Paul Vann and America in Vietnam* (New York: Vintage Books, 1989).

10. The Fourth Division was the first to be converted from French standard and re-equipped and retrained according to an American table of organization and equipment. It was redesignated the Seventh Division and transferred to My Tho.

11. In hindsight, the U.S. quarters might have been better served by fewer amenities and more security. Several months after I left Bien Hoa and the Seventh Division, a Viet Cong force staged a night raid on the area and inflicted the first American casualties in Vietnam.

12. The same officer to whom I reported in Hué for new assignment following an

argument with a French officer while I was an instructor at the Dalat Military Academy in 1952.

13. It was from Colonel Son that I learned more about Can Lao. I had paid little attention to the organization before I was transferred to the Seventh Division from the military academy at Dalat.

14. It seemed that President Diem's brother Nhu did not fully trust Xuan and did not want him to have a major role in the secret security forces. Moving him to the army and a nonsensitive post like the training center saved face all around.

CHAPTER 13

1. President Diem's office was also his bedroom, and he conducted all of his business there, except meetings with foreign dignitaries. There was a separate reception hall for that. Otherwise, he received visitors and conducted business meetings from a large chair at the foot of this bed. Visitors sat at a table opposite his chair, but did not face him directly.

2. Few farmers, especially in the Mekong Delta, owned their land. They were essentially similar to sharecroppers in the United States.

3. While working in the fields, they chanted songs that told of Vietnam's history and national and local heroes. Every village had its community theater, with local people playing parts in performances about similar subjects, as well as basic morality plays.

4. Over 100,000 Vietnamese voluntarily chose to move to North Vietnam at that time.

5. The Communists had not yet begun serious guerrilla tactics but did work secretly to recruit, indoctrinate, and train new members. They also collected voluntary taxes from followers, and even from others who feared retribution if they did not contribute.

6. He later became a three-star general and was killed in combat.

7. Colonel Clay was later wounded by Viet Cong ground fire on his helicopter.

8. The insurgency began in 1948, largely among the huge ethnic Chinese population in the Federation. The Emergency, as it was called, was declared ended officially in 1960, but terrorist outbreaks continued to occur sporadically.

9. This was our first meeting and the beginning of a friendship that continued over the years. I visited him on a trip to England to participate in a BBC documentary during the early 1990s.

10. On November 28, 1961, Secretary of State Dean Rusk cabled the American embassy in Saigon this terse message: "DO NOT GIVE OTHER THAN ROUTINE COOPERATION TO CORRESPONDENTS ON COVERAGE CURRENT MILITARY ACTIVITIES IN VIETNAM."

CHAPTER 14

1. We have used the terms "province chief" and "provincial governor" almost interchangeably in this and other chapters, although "province chief" was the more common term at the time. It would be misleading to think of province chiefs as the equivalent of state governors in the United States, however. They were, as noted, not elected but appointed by the president. They had much broader powers than U.S. governors, ruling their provinces with little outside control. There were Provincial Councils, but these were primarily advisory boards with little power—definitely not similar to state legislatures in the United States. They mainly rubber-stamped the provincial chiefs' policies and decisions.

2. Throughout the period of President Diem's administration, province chiefs were usually civilians.

3. Ben Tre became temporarily famous in 1968 after Viet Cong forces captured the city during the Tet Offensive. Overwhelming American and South Vietnamese forces, bolstered by massive air strikes, recaptured Ben Tre, but the artillery and air strikes all but destroyed the town. An American major asked by journalist Peter Arnett to justify the indiscriminate use of explosives replied, "It became necessary to destroy the town in order to save it."

4. Insurgent forces had been using Kien Hoa as a gathering place in the Mekong Delta since 1942 when the Viet Minh was born. Its numerous waterways and canals made transportation easy for them. Dense undergrowth along the banks make men and material easy to conceal for ambushes or to escape discovery. With these ideal conditions for guerrillas, Kien Hoa had long been a problem for the government.

5. Various sources, including Elizabeth Pond, *The Chau Trial* (Westminster, CA: Vietbook USA, 2009), and U.S. estimates at the time.

6. One would have to say Chau was very successful. Proof: The people of Kien Hoa welcomed him after the coup and Diem's assassination, later voted overwhelmingly for him to be their representative in the Lower House of the National Assembly. Also, nearly four decades later, in 2004, the Association of Kine Hoa Expatriates held a party to celebrate Chau's eightieth birthday. More than 300 attended. [KF]

7. He lives in Washington state, and he and Chau keep in touch regularly. [KF]

8. Chau had been viewed with similar suspicion at times over the years since leaving the Viet Minh. By this time, however, he had established that, although an outspoken maverick in some respects, he was a staunch nationalist committed to securing and maintaining an independent South Vietnam. President Diem had come to trust him implicitly. [KF]

9. Eventually Colonel Thao's fascination with plotting cost him his life, as he was murdered in 1965 while in hiding in Thu Duc district outside Saigon. After North

Vietnam and South Vietnam were united, the new national Communist government claimed that he was one of their secret agents all along, working to destabilize any separate government in the South. But the Communists take a hagiographic approach to history, and so their posthumous claim on Colonel Thao may be specious.

10. The number of Census Grievance groups grew quite rapidly and ultimately rose to about twenty-five.

11. Unfortunately, in later years, the U.S. CIA concentrated increasingly on counterterrorist operations that led from ICEX to the Phoenix Program.

12. The CIA later estimated that ultimately some 20,000 left the province as a result of the Census Grievance program.

13. Chau apparently made a very favorable and lasting impression on General Lansdale. Years later, when Chau and his family finally arrived in the United States after their harrowing ordeal as boat people, Lansdale wrote an impressive letter of recommendation for Chau. It read in part, "Beyond his managerial and political skills, [Chau] is a person of high morals, honest, very bright and dedicated to the ideals and principles shared by Americans." [KF]

CHAPTER 15

1. The Buddhist flag is a comparatively modern creation; it was jointly designed by J. R. de Silva and Colonel Henry S. Olcott to mark the revival of Buddhism in Ceylon in 1880. It was accepted as the International Buddhist Flag by the 1952 World Buddhist Congress. Colonel Olcott designed a flag from the six colors of the aura that he believed shone around the head of the Buddha after his enlightenment. The first five stripes in the patchwork design of the flag are of five symbolic colors: blue, universal compassion; yellow, the middle path; red, blessings; white, purity and liberation; orange, wisdom. The sixth stripe is a combination of all five of those colors.

2. Diem's family had been among the first Vietnamese converted to Catholicism in the seventeenth century. He favored the Catholics who had left the North, rewarding them with position, power, and status. His younger brother ruled Central Vietnam as his personal domain, while his older brother was the archbishop of Hué.

3. Such a message by the Buddhist leader was a tradition established for many years as part of the Buddha's birthday celebration, just as Catholic leaders delivered messages to their followers to celebrate the birth of Christ during the Christmas season.

4. He meant, of course, Counselor Nhu; Catholic Senior Archbishop Ngo Dinh Thuc, highest-ranking Catholic prelate in South Vietnam; and Ngo Dinh Can, who held no official position but wielded significant influence from his home in Hué.

5. When France ruled the country, the port cities of Danang and Haiphong (in the North) were directly run and totally governed by the French. There was no Vietnamese

infrastructure in these city governments. The standards of feudal service they required had remained in place ever since.

6. The I Corps (First Military Region) commander, General Le Van Nghiem, had reported himself ill at that time, and was at home during the crisis. So Colonel Phat, commanding the Second Division, was effectively in charge in southern I Corps, and Colonel Do Cao Tri, commanding the First Division, played the same role in the northern I Corps, although Archbishop Ngo Dinh Thuc seemed to have ultimate power.

7. I learned later from an officer on the colonel's staff that the withdrawal could have been completed by 11 p.m. Extending the deadline was Colonel Phat's way of saving face, implying that he was able to change the order as he wished.

8. I learned later that the order was Counselor Nhu's doing, with the connivance of his older brother, the archbishop. It was done without President Diem's prior knowledge and presented to him as a fait accompli. What could he do then but go along? To rescind the order would result in severe loss of face for both his brothers and his administration. Rescinding might placate the Buddhists to a degree but would significantly alienate his core group of supporters, particularly the Catholics.

9. When I returned, I asked my aide how soon after I left the priest exited. "Almost immediately," he replied, adding with a wry smile, "His parting words were that 'the mayor is a very arrogant boy!'" I was thirty-seven at the time.

CHAPTER 16

1. There were abortive coup attempts earlier. In one of them during 1960, Khiem had supported the president and helped stop the coup. President Diem promoted him to general afterward.

2. Neil Sheehan, in *A Bright Shining Lie*, reported that John Paul Vann and other U.S. military advisors often criticized Cao for his lack of aggressiveness, if not timidity, in battles with Communist forces. To be fair, however, he was severely reprimanded by President Diem for casualties (about twenty killed, forty wounded, not heavy by military standards for the type of action involved) in a Communist ambush at the Plain of Reeds. After that, he became more reluctant to commit his Seventh Division troops to aggressive actions in which they might sustain more than light casualties (Sheehan, *A Bright Shining Lie: John Paul Vann and America in Vietnam* [New York: Vintage Books, 1989]).

3. Many military and government officials converted to Catholicism during Diem's administration to curry favor with the devoutly Catholic president. This was not the case with Thieu. He converted because he married into a prominent Catholic family.

4. I am aware that this explanation after the fact was self-serving, because if Thieu had stayed loyal to President Diem and brought the Fifth Division to relieve rather than attack, the whole coup may have failed or changed in emphasis.

5. Much later I learned that General Mai Huu Xuan was ordered to proceed to Cholon and take the two brothers in custody. He brought along Captain (later promoted to major) Nguyen Van Nhung on General Minh's staff and Major Duong Hieu Nghia (later promoted to lieutenant colonel), an armor officer and Dai Viet party member, with an armored vehicle. On the way back to Joint General Staff (JGS, South Vietnamese equivalent of the U.S. Joint Chiefs of Staff), the vehicle stopped on Hong Thap Tu Street near the railroad tracks, and the two brothers were murdered there. It is notable that Major Nhung was the sole casualty of the subsequent January 1964 coup, and it was said that he too had committed suicide.

6. The archbishop's tirade about Buddhists when I visited him in Hué shortly after I took office as mayor of Danang (recounted in the previous chapter) showed he had an almost irrational hatred of Buddhists. He regarded them as the major threat to Diem's regime and blamed them for many of the country's problems.

7. I had forgotten this incident until I met Nguyen Van Thanh, a former Vietnamese teacher, in 2000 at a wedding party in California, and he said that he had been at that demonstration. "It was more than thirty-five years ago, but I still remember you standing on that platform and speaking to the largely hostile crowd. I think you earned a great deal of respect from all of us for your courage and forthrightness that night. I know that those were my personal feelings." It turned out that he lived only about 30 kilometers or so from my home in the San Fernando Valley.

8. He was my wife's uncle, but he always addressed me formally and never tried to take advantage of our relationship.

9. He had commanded all Civil Guard units when President Diem appointed me head of CG units in the seven northern Delta provinces.

10. I believe the sole casualty was Major Nhung, who had killed the president and his brother three months earlier.

11. Population of the Saigon metropolitan area totaled about 4 million at the time, with Saigon and Cholon accounting for 2.5 million of that number.

12. I was surprised not only by his visit but by the fact that he was familiar with exactly what I was doing. On reflection, I realized that the CIA may have been monitoring me.

13. Gordon Jorgenson, CIA chief of station in Saigon.

14. Just who engineered my transfer back to the province and why, I am still not certain to this day. I am sure that influential Americans were responsible. There definitely was a group of them who believed in what I had been doing in Kien Hoa earlier and wanted to have my programs, especially the Census Grievance project, reinstated. This was particularly true of the "Lansdale group." Rufe Phillips was originally one of Lansdale's people, of course, and I have always felt that perhaps he had something to do with my return to Kien Hoa as province chief.

CHAPTER 17

1. As explained earlier, Khanh now headed the Military Council and was more or less chief of state.

2. Apparently General Khanh had passed the buck to Khiem.

3. They received notification from Saigon of my appointment and were awaiting my arrival.

4. All province chiefs in the country were replaced after the coup because they were Diem appointees. Most were reassigned to other positions or military commands. Others were discharged from the army, but many were arrested and went to prison. Some of the latter were imprisoned because they had close ties to the Ngo family and the generals now in charge did not trust them. Others were tried on various charges of corruption.

5. Although our program during my previous tour of duty in Kien Hoa had not concentrated on establishing Strategic Hamlets as such—we ranked about thirty-fourth among all provinces in that respect—a fair number had been formed as an outgrowth of Census Grievance operations.

6. Military Assistance Command Vietnam (MACV) was established in February 1962 and began with a focus on plans and logistics with supervisory responsibility for the already existing (since April 1956) Military Assistance and Advisory Group (MAAG). In April 1964 MAAG was folded into MACV and ceased as a separate entity. MACV itself terminated after the 1973 Paris Agreement and was replaced by the Defense Attache Office (DAO).

7. I avoided having Americans accompany me regularly during my first tour as province chief of Kien Hoa. I did not want the people to think that I was a puppet controlled by the United States. I wanted them to know that I was a Vietnamese nationalist, dedicated to freedom and true independence for my country from both the Communist North and from status as an American "colony." People in every village and hamlet had long since been aware of my position, so at this point in my second tour of duty I felt free to have Americans accompany me frequently wherever I traveled in the province.

8. I am sorry to note here that Andrew Simko, later promoted to lieutenant colonel, was killed April 1970 in Binh Dinh province.

9. Actually, the term of address used was "Anh" Tran Luong, "elder brother," employed to connote a sense of almost familial respect.

10. John Paul Vann was the Seventh Division advisor, following Lieutenant Colonel Clay, until the spring of 1963. We developed personal regard for each at that time and resumed our friendship in 1965 when John returned to Vietnam with (USAID) to work in provincial development.

11. Some years later I learned that Hien lied to me about his trip. He had no intention of going to Paris, and he was spending much more time in South Vietnam conducting intelligence operations than he led me to believe.

12. When Vann dutifully reported the visit to the Saigon CIA Station as well as to the ambassador, it alerted CIA officers to the fact that a senior Hanoi intelligence officer infiltrated the area regularly and with impunity. Soon after, they got on his trail, and even "turned" the Communist liaison officer who passed messages back and forth between Hien and Hanoi. So the CIA knew almost every move Hien made during the almost four years before his "surprise arrest." Yet the CIA and the U.S. embassy both denied such knowledge when they conspired with President Thieu to arrest, try, and imprison Chau in 1970. [KF]

13. Chau recalls it as an event to celebrate the addition of another village to the list Chau considered as "pacified," which meant it was ready and able to defend itself against whatever VC remained in the area. Daniel Ellsberg, in May 2003, remembers only that "it must have been some sort of special occasion because Vann and I wore suits and ties. I do remember to this day the strong impression that Chau made on me during that first meeting." [KF]

14. Ellsberg felt the same about Chau. In his best-selling 2002 book *Secrets*, he made these comments: "Vann took me out to meet Chau in Kien Hoa. In his strongly accented but fairly fluent English Chau made a strong impression on me. . . . Chau was a brave soldier as well as an intellectual. . . . Like others who knew him, I found his commitment reassuring, insofar as it confirmed my belief at the time that we were present in Vietnam not merely to promote our own interests but to further the interests of the Vietnamese. Here was obviously a very thoughtful, brave, and dedicated Vietnamese who was happy to see American involvement" (Daniel Ellsberg, *Secrets: A Memoir of Vietnam and the Pentagon Papers* [New York: Viking, 2002], 53).

15. After this first meeting I lost contact with Ellsberg until I was assigned in 1966 to head the National Pacification Cadre Office and moved to Saigon. We became close friends and regularly exchanged ideas.

16. It was not until after the fact, when we learned from survivors of the initial onslaught of the ambush, how the battalion had grown somewhat careless after five or six hours of probing through the dense palm forest without finding any sign of the enemy. And in all fairness, I knew from experience of being on both sides of such ambushes, that the enemy was extremely skilled at concealment, even in terrain with relatively little cover. In the palm forest, with ample time to dig in and set their trap, Viet Cong troops had all the advantages.

17. That friendship continues to this day. Chau and Rufus Phillips have kept in touch and visited each other occasionally over the years. [KF]

18. *Prelude to Tragedy: Vietnam 1960–1965* focuses on the unconventional military tactics and even more important nonmilitary efforts needed to remove root causes of the

insurgency. Sadly, such efforts, even those that showed great promise, were cast aside or perverted by U.S. policy makers and a succession of subservient South Vietnam regimes that took power after the coup and assassination of President Diem. As the book's editors note in the introduction: "During this period, fateful decisions were made that led the United States and South Vietnam down the slippery slope to shameful defeat in 1975. . . . The real tragedy of the Vietnam War is that it didn't have to happen" (Harvey Neese and John O'Donnell, eds., *Prelude to Tragedy: Vietnam 1960–1965* [Annapolis, MD: Naval Institute Press, 2001]).

19. O'Donnell was another member of Rural Affairs with previous background in Southeast Asia. He served in Laos during the late 1950s with a PsyWar unit while an enlisted man in the U.S. Army. He met the famous medical missionary, Tom Dooley, at the time, and the two became good friends. Since Dooley was involved in the evacuation of refugees from North Vietnam to South Vietnam in 1954, perhaps O'Donnell had picked some of his sympathy for, and knowledge of, Vietnam and its people from Dooley.

20. U.S. Military Assistance Advisory Group.

CHAPTER 18

1. The Vietnamese rolls are made with rice paper, and are lighter and crispier than the Chinese ones.

2. USIS was the field operations side of the United States Information Agency (USIA), which was dissolved in 1998 as a consequence of restructuring the American foreign affairs bureaucracy.

3. General Maxwell Taylor said after the war, "First, we didn't know ourselves. We thought we were going into another Korean war, but this was a different country. Second, we didn't know our South Vietnamese allies. We never understood them, and that was another surprise. And we knew even less about North Vietnam. Who was Ho Chi Minh? Nobody really knew. So, until we know the enemy and know our allies and know ourselves, we'd better keep out of this dirty kind of business. It's very dangerous."

4. A "super-minister" in the Vietnam of that time was one to whom the ministers of other cabinet-level departments reported.

5. The concept for the Quang Ngai units originated with Frank Scotton, Bob Kelly, and Phan Manh Luong, and then was further developed as pacification teams by Nguyen Be in Binh Dinh province.

CHAPTER 19

1. "Kien Hoa had been a Viet Minh hotbed from the beginning and continued as a Viet Cong stronghold in the later period. When Lt. Col Chau took over, only 80,000 of a

population of 530,000 could be said to be under government control. Within a year, more-over, in which the general situation was deteriorating elsewhere Chau raised this number to 220,000" (Elizabeth Pond, *The Chau Trial* [Westminster, CA: Vietbook USA, 2009]).

2. John Vann was stationed in Hau Nghia province as advisor when he returned to Vietnam in 1965, but now he was temporarily working in the USAID Saigon office for rural development.

3. Frank Scotton envisioned the teams as promoting political change from hamlets upward and wanted to retain local recruitment and training at the district level. He had some disagreement with the expanded CIA program and was reassigned by USIS to work with MACV and later Special Forces.

4. Neil Sheehan, *A Bright Shining Lie: John Paul Vann and America in Vietnam*, 611.

5. Pond, *The Chau Trial*, 6. Pond wrote this three-part report in March 1970 as an Alicia Patterson Fund Award winner on leave from the *Christian Science Monitor*.

6. Ibid.

7. Sheehan, *A Bright Shining Lie*, 613.

8. The only honest and reliable American in the training center at this point was Captain Jean Sauvageot, who was not CIA, but a Vietnamese-speaking U.S. Army infan-try officer, and in fact another member of an informal but very real Vann-Bumgardner-Scotton team.

9. Like myself, Major Be had a complicated relationship with U.S. advisors who sometimes did not appreciate his unorthodox style. Additionally, he was extremely, and openly, critical of corruption on the part of province chiefs and military region com-manders. Under threat of assassination by corrupt elements, Frank Scotton extracted him from Qui Nhon on a U.S. Army aircraft to Pleiku. General Vinh Loc, the Second Military Region commander, complicit in the chain of corruption, was nonplussed but relieved when I suggested taking Major Be for reassignment with me.

10. General Nguyen Chanh Thi is another of the fascinating characters of this period in Vietnam's history. A former member of the colonial militia, he had been imprisoned in 1945 at Ba To (Quang Ngai) by the Viet Minh. He escaped and, returning to his family home in Hué, found that his mother had been killed by Communists in that confusing period. In 1955 and 1956 as an airborne battalion commander he was an ardent sup-porter of President Diem, but in 1960 he led elements of the Airborne Brigade in a failed coup attempt intended to broaden the government. He went into exile in Cambodia until after President Diem was killed in 1963. He was allowed to return, was given command of the First Division in the far North, and was later promoted to First Military Region commander. He was removed from command by a vote of the other generals on the Military Council because they feared his ambition and were discomfited by his criticism of corruption. Although he was the proximate fuse for the political struggles of 1966 that

led to a new constitution and an elected government, General Thi was exiled to America and never allowed to return. He died in Pennsylvania in 2007.

CHAPTER 20

1. During the 1968 Tet Offensive, Long Binh was attacked and the United States had significant casualties there.

2. It was called the "Secret War" because it was hidden from the U.S. public. During it, American planes flew an average of one bombing mission every eight minutes for a full nine years.

CHAPTER 21

1. Henry Kissinger, *White House Years* (New York: Little, Brown, 1979).

2. A similar request that would have allowed me to run for election to the Constituent Assembly was denied the previous year; but the new constitution drafted by that constituent assembly would allow me to stand for election without having to resign my commission. This point became clear only later.

3. This was the second time Vann had mentioned working with him. Earlier, when he thought he might get a new job working at a high-level post in the U.S. Saigon embassy, he said that if it worked out he would manage to have me appointed as his counterpart.

CHAPTER 22

1. It is ironic that General Thang himself was increasingly frustrated by the lack of sincere and effective support for pacification, and more than a year later in January 1968 (just days before the Tet Offensive) he resigned as minister for pacification.

2. "Tri Quang was flown to Saigon, though we had quite a problem getting this politically minded monk into the aircraft for, as the pilot told me, when Tri Quang heard the plane would be flying over the sea on its way to Saigon, he became convinced he was only being put on board so we could dump him into the water. I had to be careful with Tri Quang since I did not want to create a martyr, so I decided on a compromise, and confined him to house arrest in a hospital" (Nguyen Cao Ky, *Twenty Years and Twenty Days* [New York: Stein and Day, 1976]).

3. Stanley Karnow, *Vietnam: A History* (New York: Viking, 1983).

4. Ellsworth Bunker replaced Lodge as U.S. ambassador in mid-March 1967. Robert Komer arrived at the same time to direct U.S. pacification operations, and in early May

pacification programs on the American side were organized as part of the MACV command structure.

5. Truong Dinh Du (sometimes spelled Truong Dinh Dzu) was subsequently charged with advocating a coalition government and jailed at hard labor. He was originally from Binh Dinh, although at the time he lived and practiced law in Saigon.

6. We note here that actually this was not so much antiwar sentiment as it was an "anti-me in the war" movement. Later President Nixon and National Security Advisor Kissinger realized this and abolished the draft, thereby effectively killing the antiwar demonstrations (although the war persisted for about five more years). Stopping the draft also fundamentally altered American history by moving the army from one that was citizen based in time of need to a professional standing army that a president could commit without much concern for public protest.

CHAPTER 23

1. Because entering the academy lacked appeal when in its early years, the first classes were open to men of twenty to thirty years so those of us who attended it then were not all nearly the same age.

2. Zalin Grant, *Facing the Phoenix* (New York: W. W. Norton, 1991).

3. Tony Cistaro was a Marine Corps veteran before working for USAID in Chau Doc province, where he met Frank Scotton and Phil Werbiski in the summer of 1965 while they were in An Phu district for a Special Forces project. In December 1965 Tony was severely wounded in a Viet Cong ambush of a Special Forces element in the Seven Mountains area near Ba Chuc. Special Forces Major Arnn and Sergeant Torello were killed in that incident.

4. The full request was not provided. One brigade of the Eighty-second was dispatched, and in March President Johnson decided to seek peace through negotiation and not stand for reelection.

5. Her father, Desmond Fitzgerald, had been a senior CIA official and certainly on her first visit to Vietnam that family credential was useful.

CHAPTER 24

1. The same Nguyen Viet Thanh subsequently promoted to general, a true field officer, and was often referred to as one of the few completely honest generals. He was killed in an air collision in May 1970 during an operation in Cambodia. We had worked together in a Civil Guard improvement program years earlier.

2. There were an "estimated 114,000 refugees (out of a population of 140,000)," ac-

cording to Keith William Nolan, *Battle for Hué: Tet, 1968* (Novato, CA: Presidio Press, 1983), 266.

3. There was more to it than that, according to Nolan: "The Viet Cong and North Vietnamese had massacred many of the people of Hué. Over the years, the evidence was collected in bits and pieces: the discovery of mass graves, captured Communist documents, statements by prisoners of war. It was learned that with the typical cold-blooded efficiency of the Communists, the VC had gone into Hué with lists of so-called Enemies of the People. Those marked included government officials, city administrators, intellectuals, teachers, college students, soldiers, foreigners, and their families, all those suspected of being enemies of the Communist cause. There was one other category: all those who could identify the VC infrastructure now that it had surfaced for the Tet Offensive. That could include an innocent bystander" (ibid.).

4. The law for general mobilization was signed by President Thieu on June 19, 1968.

5. "Chau was one of the first to recognize that the Tet offensive would prove to be the last straw for the US and that Washington henceforth would try to disengage from Vietnam as quickly as possible" (Elizabeth Pond, *The Chau Trial* [Westminster, CA: Vietbook USA, 2009]).

6. Zalin Grant, *Facing the Phoenix* (New York: W. W. Norton, 1991), 311–13. Both Grant and Theodore White, the political journalist who specialized in presidential elections, believed that Thieu's blocking of full participation in the Paris peace negotiations was probably decisive in determining the 1968 election.

7. "Thieu was not prepared to risk losing his core of right-wing support in some chancy appeal to an unknown middle ground, whether at America's, Chau's or anyone else's urging" (Pond, *The Chau Trial*, 8).

8. Tragically, President Nixon's "de-Americanization . . . with all deliberate speed" actually prolonged the war and perpetuated U.S. casualties. Nearly 21,000 Americans were killed in Vietnam during the Nixon presidency, and approximately 53,000 more were seriously wounded. Total civilian and military casualties in all of Vietnam (North and South), Laos, and Cambodia were even higher than those registered for Americans

9. "By 1969, Chau, who had once been a strong political associate of Thieu, had become an outspoken advocate of a peace settlement that included political representation for the National Liberation Front" (Claude Pomonti, *Le Monde*, January 17, 1969).

10. One of those killed, Colonel Dam Van Quy, had been an outstanding regimental commander and was highly regarded throughout the army.

11. Elizabeth Pond, "Vietnamese Politics: Short Term," report written for the *Christian Science Monitor* and the Alicia Patterson Fund, September 1968.

12. Minister Phan Quang Dan, a man with an honorable record of service, was dismissed from the cabinet in June for having expressed political views contradictory to the

spirit of the Constitution and policy of the government. Dan had declared that the South Vietnam government had to start talking with the NLF "because it is difficult to kill all of them."

13. I should have paid closer attention to the tactics used to force Huong's ouster, because some of the same tactics were later used against me. I just paid a higher price than Huong, losing not only my position, but also my liberty.

CHAPTER 25

1. Elizabeth Pond, *The Chau Trial* (Westminster, CA: Vietbook USA, 2009), 19.

2. The Communist North Vietnam government did in fact persecute Buddhists after 1975, attempting to break up the Unified Buddhist Church. Hien's reaction in support of the Buddhists was at least one factor in his post-1975 arrests and imprisonment by the Communist regime.

3. Pond, *The Chau Trial*, 20.

4. Ibid.

5. This young foreign service officer was Daryll Johnson, many years later appointed U.S. ambassador to Thailand.

6. Thach Reng was an unconventional Cambodian officer who Frank had befriended in 1961. Eventually promoted to colonel and commander of Cambodian Special Forces, after the collapse of the Lon Nol government he fought on as a KPNLF officer against the Khmer Rouge. A devout Buddhist, he was elected to the National Assembly after the Khmer Rouge defeat. Thach Reng died in Phnom Penh in 2002.

7. More than a year later, and after my arrest and conviction, Frank Scotton returned to Vietnam on assignment as a special assistant to William Colby. He visited General Tran Van Hai, his friend since 1963, and although General Hai had already returned to Rangers, a special branch of the army, and was no longer the national police director, Frank asked Hai, friend to friend, to exert residual influence to assure that I would not be physically mistreated. General Hai, whose final assignment was as Seventh Division commander (where he committed suicide after the surrender of South Vietnam in 1975), was an honorable man true to his word. Frank also visited my family and offered to work with friends to arrange a scholarship for my eldest child to study in America, but my entire family decided to remain in Vietnam until I could be released from prison.

8. Trinh Cong Son was an artist as well as a musician. His popularity transcended politics. In 1975 the new Communist government sentenced him to three years of reeducation camp. He died in 2001 in a hospital in Saigon. Thousands mourned him. His songs, even today, are admired by all Vietnamese. There has been assertion that Son was a Communist, but I am doubtful. Communists often make such claims to bolster appearance of omnipresence and omniscience.

9. Previously described in account of my first term as governor.

10. Keyes Beech traveled in, and wrote about, Asia for most of five decades; first as a U.S. Marine combat correspondent in 1942. He covered the Korean War and arrived in Saigon during the early involvement of Americans in Vietnam. After his death, a colleague noted that Keyes "prided himself on being a battlefield correspondent" who believed that the "real story was out where the troops were and not in a briefing room."

11. The reader will find that Keyes Beech was an important figure for my whole family at a much later time in our lives.

12. Unknown to us at the time, police agents had followed Ev Bumgardner and me to Newport, and then seen Ev depart alone. Knowing my close ties with Bumgardner and Vann, it was not difficult for President Thieu and others to guess what was happening.

13. "Had Chau let Vann go through with the plan, Vann's career in Vietnam would have been terminated. Thieu would have been so angry at being cheated of vengeance that he would have demanded Vann's expulsion" (Neil Sheehan, *A Bright Shining Lie: John Paul Vann and America in Vietnam* [New York: Vintage Books, 1989], 738).

14. My only property consisted of an average house in a middle-class neighborhood that was quite in contrast with the lavish residences accumulated by some business, government, and military families.

15. Each of the large prison rooms had a committee, appointed by the director, to organize and maintain discipline among the inmates quartered there. They were responsible for keeping the room in good order and resolving any disputes that might arise.

CHAPTER 26

1. France built Chi Hoa Prison originally. It was the largest structure built by the French in Saigon, and it had an infamous reputation during their reign and through all of the U.S.-backed South Vietnam regimes. This has not changed under the North Vietnamese Communists, as harsh treatment and torture have been reported regularly by prisoners since 1975.

2. Frank Snepp, *Decent Interval* (New York: Random House, 1977), 15. Theodore Shackley was Saigon CIA Station chief. William Colby, formerly chief of the CIA East Asia Division, headed up Civil Operations and Rural Development (CORDS) in MACV. Frank Scotton, who worked for Colby in CORDS from mid-1970 onward, believes that Colby scrupulously avoided involvement in Station business, and therefore Shackley had principal culpability on the U.S. side.

3. *Vietnam: Policy and Prospects, 1970.* Hearings of the Senate Foreign Relations Committee on Civil Operations and Rural Development Support in Vietnam, February 17–20; March 3, 14, 17, and 19, 1970, 750 pp. Includes testimony of William Colby, John

Paul Vann, and others, on topics including the Phoenix Program and the case of Tran Ngoc Chau.

4. We refer the reader to the articles that Elizabeth Pond wrote for the *Christian Science Monitor* that are also available through support offered by the Alicia Patterson Fund. Pond provides excellent descriptions of the physical setting and the drama of the exchanges between the participants.

5. This is at least highly questionable, if not totally inaccurate.

6. Since the definition of "flagrante delicto" is "in the very act of committing an offense; red-handed," this was another inaccurate statement. My first meting with Hien occurred several years earlier, and second, nobody would have known about it had I not reported it through Vann to the CIA and U.S. embassy in Saigon. This act put the CIA on Hien's trail and led to his eventual arrest.

7. The key paragraphs of the Article read: "2), Removal from office must be proposed by 2/3 of the total number of Representatives or Senators, and 3), The resolution to remove a member from office must be approved by 3/4 of the total number of Representatives or Senators. And only by removal from office may a Representative or Senator lose the immunity from prosecution" in such cases as the one brought against Chau. So the defense argued that Chau's arrest and this trial were unconstitutional. The South Vietnam Supreme Court agreed later, in a decision finding that his arrest, trial, and imprisonment were indeed unconstitutional. [KF]

8. This Code was modeled after the French Criminal Code, which meant it had applied in Vietnam for many decades, and had been the standard since the formation of South Vietnam.

9. Article 37/2 states, "During their entire term of office, Representatives and Senators cannot be prosecuted, pursued, arrested or judged without the approval of three-fourths of the total number of Representatives and Senators, except in the case of flagrante delicto."

10. Quoted from Elizabeth Pond's report.

11. Artur Dommen of the *Times* obtained a full text of Hien's statement, which appeared in abridged form in the January 4, 1970, edition.

12. As Chau learned later, while a Communist prisoner in 1975, the NLF and Hanoi recognized that he was one of their most effective foes. He understood their methods better than South Vietnamese and U.S. leaders and policymakers, and thus was able to mount effective campaigns against them, as his pacification efforts in Kien Hoa proved. [KF]

13. It certainly would seem that this testimony by the Communist agent involved in the meetings which formed the basis for Chau's prosecution was germane to the case. And the fact that it appeared in a publicly available newspaper proved that the information was widely and readily available. Yet nothing of the testimony was admitted by the military tribunal. [KF]

14. Of course this person was my elder brother, whom I had not betrayed, but had instead attempted to persuade him to reconsider a non-Communist path. Tragically, we eventually both served time in Communist as well as South Vietnam prisons. After the Communist victory in 1975 Hien became disillusioned by the repressive policies of the new government, especially efforts to dismantle the Buddhist Church. He was sentenced to prison three times for supporting "revisionist policies" and "antisocialist activities," including from 1981 to 1987 and again in the mid-1990s. He died in Hué in 1998.

15. Con Son Prison in South Vietnam was located in the South China Sea. Under the French, it was used as a prison for opponents of French colonialism. In 1954 the prison was taken over by the South Vietnamese government. It was the largest South Vietnamese prison, designed to hold 9,600 inmates. It had a notorious reputation at the time, with many prisoners being held in the infamous "tiger cages of Con Son." At the time, some called it "worse than France's fearsome Devil's Island penal colony." U.S. Senator Tom Harkin, then an ex-navy lieutenant working as a staff assistant on an ad hoc congressional committee on Vietnam, instigated an investigation (despite strenuous objections from the U.S. embassy in Saigon) that revealed appalling conditions and treatment of prisoners on the island.

16. Chau was still continuing his practicing of walking an hour each day after he turned eighty-six in 2010, though perhaps not as rapidly as he did more than three decades earlier. [KF]

17. Many Chinese-language families had lived in Vietnam for generations at the time. Later, after unification, the Vietnam Communist Party began a campaign to force them out of the country.

18. Traditional written characters are still taught in Taiwan. When speaking of the Chinese language, one has to distinguish between spoken and written language. There are more than one spoken tonal Chinese languages, and so-called Mandarin—referred to in China as the "national" or "commonly spoken" language—is the language (with some regional dialects) of North China and Sichuan. The South China languages, like Cantonese and the Wu Chinese spoken in Shanghai, are completely are completely different from each other as well as the North China / Sichuan spoken language. The written language unifies all, however, because having an ideographic origin it can be applied to different spoken languages.

19. Except that thirty-three years later former president Thieu visited our family and expressed his regret and apology for what he caused to happen. I responded that we had in the end both lost our country and should leave the past behind.

20. My sympathy for Colonel Vong's situation was based on my understanding that he was an instrument of a corrupt system, and at the same time, a clinical symptom of a social illness. The virulence of this illness was such that it could draw even good people into corruption.

21. This was Major Nguyen Be, and the circumstances are described in an earlier chapter.

22. Despite this, rumors persist to this day that Secretary Kissinger deliberately retarded peace talks in 1971 to perpetuate the war and negotiation process so as to maximize prospects for Nixon's reelection.

23. He changed his name when joining the Viet Minh in 1945. Many volunteers changed their name to protect their families.

24. Hien had his own difficulties with the inflexible Communist government of unified Vietnam after 1975. My brother died in 1998. In 2006 I was able to visit his grave during my visit to Viet Nam.

25. Special Branch was the name for the police group that handled political matters.

CHAPTER 27

1. These centers were set up specifically to interview and process people, especially former SVN military and government officials, regarded as candidates for "Reeducation Centers" established by the Communists.

2. Former chief justice Tiet was subsequently released from Thu Duc and allowed to expatriate to France. Eventually the family immigrated to the United States, and he died in 1983 while living in Monterey Park, California.

3. Hien was allowed return to party membership and (retired) military rank in 1979, but continued to have disciplinary difficulty with the party due to disagreement with their policy to repress Buddhist organizations.

CHAPTER 28

1. Before departing Vietnam, I learned from old Viet Minh friends that this policy was directed for the Politburo by Minister of Interior Tran Quoc Hoan. In southern Vietnam, Mai Chi Tho, police director for Ho Chi Minh City, was responsible for implementation.

2. Tam Phuong and her husband did not suffer serious consequences. We learned later that the government began an exhaustive search for us after my disappearance. Tam Phuong, her husband, and their two sons were allowed to depart to America in 1992.

3. Rung Sat can be translated as "assassin forest."

4. Each of the seven of us was "adopted" by a different Chinese family, with ID to match. Trying to leave as a Chinese family group would have lessened our chances to escape without being found out by the police.

5. We heard rumors later that it sank and all 200 passengers were lost. Whether that

happened, or it was captured by pirates or suffered some other disaster, we never knew. At any rate, it disappeared, and to the best of our knowledge no survivors ever surfaced.

6. We learned years later that a daughter of one of my sisters-in-law had suffered this fate.

7. We learned later that he was a member of the local Civil Guard. Since the island was too small to have a police post and formal government offices, the people had set up an informal village committee. It had organized the Civil Guard to keep order when necessary. They were armed only with a few old shotguns. The first man was second in command of the Civil Guard.

8. People in our group were very adept at concealing their cash and other valuables. Despite the searches we had all undergone and the misfortunes—from a sinking boat to our possessions being confiscated at times—many still retained assets. We regularly pooled our funds to buy food and other necessities, or, as in this care, to pay bribes. I was impressed by the way those with means were willing to share them for the common good, to help take care of those who had been unable to escape Vietnam with money and other assets, or those who had lost everything during the journey.

9. I learned later that their information came from a man in the first group that had landed on Bahala. He remembered seeing reports of my arrest, trial, and conviction in the South Vietnam newspapers controlled by the Thieu regime, and evidently believed the slanted accounts reported at the time.

10. In addition to information on our exodus from Vietnam, they were all interested in the fate of South Vietnamese who had worked with the Americans during the war, and the story of our experiences in Communist prisons and reeducation camps. They also wanted my views on Vietnam's invasion of Cambodia and subsequent hostilities with China.

11. As discussed earlier, Beech had arranged for a CIA man named Thompson to take care of evacuating me and my family. I learned years later, from Beech and Frank Snepp in his book *Decent Interval* (New York: Random House, 1977), that Ted Shackley, CIA Chief of Station, Saigon, overruled those evacuation plans.

INDEX

The letter *n* following a page number indicates a note on that page. The number following the *n* indicates the number of the note in the chapter.

Tran Huy Lieu, 3, 399n2
Tran Luong, 95–96, 402n2
Tran Minh Tiet, 357, 367, 372, 422n2
Tran Ngoc Chau, 104
　as aide-de-camp to Nguyen Ngoc Le, 119
　in Anambas Islands, 389
　anti-Communism of, 293–95
　on apparent pacification, 284
　arrest and imprisonment of, xviii
　assassination attempt on, 218–19
　asthma attacks and, 226
　as battalion political commissar, 78–79
　Buddhism and, 8
　building grass-roots political party and,
　　326–27
　Census Grievance approach, 179–83,
　　217, 222, 229, 241, 284
　as chief of staff of the Quang Trung
　　Training Center, 151, 152–55
　in Chi Hoa prison, 353–59
　combat against the French and, 25–30,
　　34–37
　combat against the Japanese and, 21–24
　as commandant of cadets at Dalat, 142,
　　145–49
　as commandant of Eighth Battalion,
　　137–38
　as commandant of Regional Military
　　NCO School (Hué), 139
　as commander of the Civil Guard in
　　seven Mekong provinces, 165–67
　as commander of the Third Company,
　　Twenty-Seventh Battalion, 60–68
　Communist Party membership and,
　　90–92
　as deputy commandant of the
　　Forty-fourth Battalion at Hoi An, 131
　on effectiveness of pacification
　　program, 273–76
　on election to the National Assembly,
　　290–91
　escaping Saigon by boat, 382–83
　explanation to his father re: current
　　politics, 259–64
　exploring possible peace negotiations,
　　321–26
　family of, 4–5, 8, 109, 109–10
　Foreign Service Institute lectures of,
　　303–4
　at Fort Benning, Georgia, 143
　Fort Benning, Georgia, training at, 143
　on his limited view of Vietnamese
　　society, 12
　honors and awards, 129, 134, 135, 136,
　　137, 140
　immunity from prosecution and,
　　420n7, 420n8
　life overview of, xiii–xvi
　malaria and, 18, 43–44, 94
　in Malaysia on the way to America,
　　387–89
　marriage to Bich Nhan, 118
　on Marxism-Leninism, 85–87, 92, 104
　as mayor of Danang, 188–98
　on military-civilian relations, 76, 402n3
　mutinous troops and, 135–36
　in the National Assembly, xviii
　as national director of the Pacification
　　Cadre Program, 227
　National Liberation Front and, 417n9
　NLF and, 330
　at Office of Cadres at Military Zone
　　Headquarters, 95–96
　philosophical doubts and, 79–80
　on President Diem, 203–4
　President Thieu and, 336–37
　prisoner exchange and, 361
　prison regimen, 353–54

ABOUT THE AUTHORS

Tran Ngoc Chau escaped from Vietnam via Indonesia among the masses of boat people seeking refuge in the late 1970s, reestablishing himself and his family in the United States with the encouragement of American friends.

During **Ken Fermoyle**'s sixty-five-year career as a writer, editor, photojournalist and author, he has published thousands of articles in major publications and served as book and magazine editor. He and Tran Ngoc Chau launched a business venture together in 1987 and began work on *Vietnam Labyrinth* a year later.

Texas Tech University Press acknowledges the contributions of

Rufus Phillips, III, Thomas L. Ahern, Jr., Douglas K. Ramsey,

Daniel Ellsberg, Colonel (Ret.) John V. Gibney,

Colonel (Ret.) Andre Sauvageot, Frank Snepp,

an anonymous donor, and the sons and daughters of

Tran Ngoc Chau, whose donations made possible the timely

publication of this important first-person account of the

1945–1975 period of Vietnam history.